ARTIFICIAL HELLS

Participatory Art and the Politics of Spectatorship

CLAIRE BISHOP

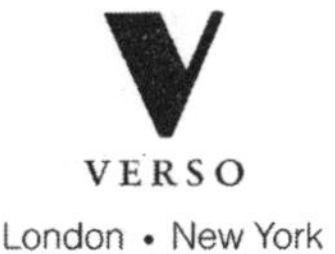

VERSO

London • New York

This edition published by Verso 2022
First published by Verso 2012
© Claire Bishop 2012
Preface © Claire Bishop 2022

1 3 5 7 9 10 8 6 4 2

Verso
UK: 6 Meard Street, London W1F 0EG
US: 388 Atlantic Avenue, Brooklyn, NY 11217
versobooks.com

Verso is the imprint of New Left Books

ISBN-13: 978-1-83976-775-3

British Library Cataloguing in Publication Data
A catalogue record for this book is available from the British Library

The Library of Congress has cataloged the hardcover edition as follows:
Bishop, Claire.
  Artificial hells : participatory art and the politics of spectatorship / by
Claire Bishop. – 1st [edition].
    pages cm
  Includes bibliographical references and index.
  ISBN 978-1-84467-690-3 – ISBN 978-1-84467-796-2 (ebook)
1. Interactive art. I. Title.
N6494.I57B57 2012
709.04'07–dc23
                            2012010607

Typeset in Fournier by Hewer Text UK Ltd, Edinburgh
Printed by CPI Group (UK) Ltd, Croydon CR0 4YY

Contents

Preface to the Tenth Anniversary Re-edition

Artificial Hells first appeared in print ten years ago, but my research and writing on participatory art began a decade before that. Frustrated with contemporary accounts of this work, which conflated ethics with aesthetics and posited participation and collaboration as unquestionably 'good' – i.e., a leftist political end in and of itself – I argued that participation is an artistic strategy with a long, complicated history over the course of the previous century. The book, then, attempted to do four things. First, it sought to map flashpoints in twentieth-century art's engagement with participation, pointing out its changing political valence under different ideological conditions. Second, because participation centers people as a 'medium', the book provides a reading of twentieth-century art through theatre and performance, displacing the ready-made and abstraction. A third goal was to propose a new model of the 'global contemporary', tracing the legacy of the historical avant-garde across the Western Hemisphere. Finally, the book tried to put in motion a Benjaminian theory of history by taking a present-day concern – the neoliberal co-option of participation in Northern Europe – as a springboard for somersaulting back in time, arranging a new constellation of works and places in order to rethink the current moment in a new light.

Returning to *Artificial Hells* after a decade, I find that much of my original argument stands: participation can be employed across a range of work (community art, socially engaged art, social practice, performance), surfacing and declining at specific historical moments. In its purest form, participation involves a rethinking of the relationship between the artist, the work of art, and the audience. Artists who engage with modes of participation often favor an open-ended process, motivated by social amelioration, over the formal closure of a traditional artwork. In other respects, however, my position on participatory art has shifted. My method and approach have taken new directions – not least as a result of relocating from Britain to the United States – and I've become ever more glaringly aware of the book's two largest blind spots: race and technology, about which I'll say more below.

The political context has also altered drastically since publication, causing the book's central aesthetic argument, in favor of antagonism, to change in valence. *Artificial Hells* is very much a product of post–Cold War geopolitics. The transitions of 1989 to 1991 led to a sense of political deadlock that only intensified after 9/11: a centrist neoliberalism that fused a business-friendly center-left and an identity-friendly center-right in hegemonic immobility, which theorists on the left described as 'post-politics'. In the 1990s, it seemed clear that liberal democracy had triumphed, so the question became what *form* democracy should take. The result was a preoccupation with horizontal structures and ethical frameworks, manifested through innocuous actions that can now be itemized as the leitmotifs of social practice (the Meal, the Walk, the Garden, the Screening, the Discussion). The politics were broadly anti-capitalist, informed by a nascent anti-globalisation movement, while the aesthetics were homespun and DIY, rejecting mainstream art-market polish.

In the following decade, the political mood increasingly became one of paralysis, with a loss of faith in protest after the failure of the anti-war demonstrations of 2003. Across the US and Europe, artists depicted, staged or re-enacted protests (e.g., Felix Gmelin, Sharon Hayes, Mark Tribe, Artur Żmijewski), while others lamented the loss of collectivity and asserted the need to 'come together' (e.g., Kateřina Šedá, Johanna Billing, Paweł Althamer). All of these works had a subdued tone of resignation, and participatory art became an oblique substitute for politics. Despite invoking a leftist lineage of inclusion, participatory artists' preference for consensus often ended up replicating the suffocatingly smooth operations of third-way centrism. *Artificial Hells* took shape against this foreclosure of conflict, to which it responded by appealing for disruption and friction.

Since 2012, however, participation – at least as a discourse – has almost completely dropped out of visual art. This might seem a perverse claim. From an institutional perspective, participatory art has gone from strength to strength over the last decade. You can now get an MFA in social practice (as it's called in North America) or an MA in socially engaged art (the preferred term in Europe) in such far-flung locales as Arizona and Bolzano, Geneva and Indianapolis, the Scottish Highlands and Queens, New York.[1] There's a dedicated journal, *FIELD*, and pedagogic guides to teaching socially engaged art.[2] Socially engaged artists have won a slew of notable

---

1 Social Practice Queens (SPQ), led by artists Greg Sholette and Chloë Bass, is the program I have been most involved with since its inception in 2010. Both directors were generous interlocutors as I drafted this preface. I am also indebted to formative conversations with Yates McKee and Dominic Willsdon.

2 *FIELD: A Journal of Socially Engaged Art Criticism* was founded in 2015 by art historian Grant Kester and offers an impressive take on social practice globally. In 2018, Bass and Sholette co-edited *Art as Social Action: An Introduction to the Principles and Practices of Teaching Social Practice Art*, New York: Allworth Press. Also of note is Pablo Helguera's *Education for Socially Engaged Art: A Materials and Techniques Handbook*, New York: Jorge Pinto Books, 2011.

awards: MacArthurs, Guggenheims, Artes Mundi, the Velázquez Award, the Turner Prize.[3] Documenta 15 (2022) not only was organised by an artist collective, ruangrupa, but also featured innumerable artist collectives in the biggest display of social practice to date. Biennials have restaged historical participatory works and exhibited archival documentation.[4] Key figures have received major museum retrospectives and their works have entered permanent collections (e.g., Rasheed Araeen, Suzanne Lacy, David Medalla, Lorraine O'Grady, Mierle Laderman Ukeles). Some of these artists are now even represented by commercial galleries (e.g., Rick Lowe at Gagosian). Institutions have commissioned high-visibility projects, sometimes with blockbuster levels of popularity (and accompanying critical ambivalence) – think of Superflex's *One Two Three Swing!* at Tate Modern in 2017, an installation of large, interconnected group swings weaving through the Turbine Hall.

Yet none of this has been central to contemporary artistic debates in mainstream magazines, museums and biennials. Instead, the preoccupations of the last decade seem to fall into two clear phases. The first was a fascination with the post-digital, speculative realism and the non-anthropocentric (roughly 2011–16), which largely sidelined questions of the social in favour of objecthood, matter and posthuman agency.[5] The second phase, which began to appear in earnest in 2016, was dominated by questions of identity (especially Black, disabled, Indigenous, queer, trans) – assertions of radical subjectivity in autonomous works of art, often in traditional media like painting and photography. It is not coincidental that this second phase grew ascendant in tandem with hate crimes, bathroom bills, police brutality, anti-immigrant xenophobia and the rise of right-wing reactionary politics more generally. As a result, a different set of terms came to the fore, consolidated by the pandemic and the uprisings of summer 2020.

So why did the discourse of participation fall out of favour? I'd like to propose two reasons: Occupy Wall Street (and the subsequent proliferation of activism that followed, especially Black Lives Matter) and social media. Although *Artificial Hells* was published in June 2012, the manuscript

---

3   MacArthur 'genius' grants were given to Rick Lowe in 2014 and Mel Chin in 2019; Sharon Hayes won a Guggenheim Fellowship in 2014; Theaster Gates won Artes Mundi in 2014; Assemble won the Turner Prize in 2015, and all five finalists for the 2021 Turner Prize were socially engaged collectives; Tania Bruguera won the Velázquez Award in 2021.

4   A key year here is 2017, when the Venice Biennale showed works by Rasheed Araeen, Anna Halprin, David Medalla, Antoni Miralda and Bonnie Sherk, placing them next to more recent participatory works by Olafur Eliasson, Dawn Kasper, Lee Mingwei and Ernesto Neto; that year's Documenta 14 offered a similar juxtaposition, placing archival materials and performances by Halprin, Oscar Masotta and Cornelius Cardew alongside contemporary works and an education program called *Parliament of Bodies*.

5   The more progressive strand of non-anthropocentrism centered ecology, as at Documenta 13 (2012). See also T. J. Demos's *Against the Anthropocene: Visual Culture and Environment Today*, Berlin: Sternberg Press, 2017.

was completed just prior to the start of Occupy Wall Street in autumn 2011. Occupy marked the new decade as having a qualitatively different political dynamic from that of the previous twenty years. It heralded a conspicuous shift toward dissent and mobilisation – a movement from the artistic representation of resistance to its actualisation. The makeshift encampment and signage at Zuccotti Park even looked like a work by Thomas Hirschhorn.

By 2016, art historian and activist Yates McKee could argue that Occupy signaled 'the end of socially engaged art', which had now matured into real-world movement building.[6] The decade was characterised by the imperative to show up, be present and protest: Tahrir Square, Occupy, Gezi Park, Euromaidan, Black Lives Matter, Standing Rock, the Women's March, the Umbrella Movement and (more ambiguously) the *gilets jaunes*. Gently ameliorative microtopias flew out the window; embodied protest became mainstream.[7] Galvanised by the new communicative resources of social media, the ubiquity of cameraphones and a roiling sense of indignation, people took to the streets in new formations, often with photogenic visual identities (yellow umbrellas, pink hats, neon vests).

Throughout the 2010s, a constant and prolific thread of art activism took place outside the purview of the art market. The most high-profile examples pointed inwards to the museum, with calls for divestment, decolonisation, boycott and unionisation (e.g., Liberate Tate, Not an Alternative, Gulf Labor, Decolonize This Place, P.A.I.N. [Prescription Addiction Intervention Now], Strike MoMA). Participatory strategies were deployed by some of these groups, such as Not an Alternative's Indigenous pedagogies, or P.A.I.N.'s 'die-in' at the Guggenheim Museum in 2019.[8] But participation was now one of many political tactics, rather than a process for its own sake.

Artists also worked in collaboration with an existing ecology of organisations, such as groups campaigning to end for-profit prisons, gentrification, the refugee crisis and environmental destruction – think of Carolina Caycedo with La Asociación Jaguos por el Territorio, or Cannupa Hansker Luger at Standing Rock.[9] The targeted nature of these campaigns, and their direct

6   Yates McKee, *Strike Art: Contemporary Art and the Post-Occupy Condition*, London: Verso, 2016, and 'Occupy and the End of Socially Engaged Art', *e-flux journal*, 73, April 2016.

7   Fascist activism has also increased in the US and Europe, from the Unite the Right rally in Charlottesville in 2017, to the rise of the Alternative für Deutschland in Germany, to Trump's minions storming the Capitol in January 2021.

8   P.A.I.N. was founded in 2017 by the artist Nan Goldin in response to the opioid crisis in the US. It targets the Sackler family for manufacturing and promoting the drug OxyContin; the Sacklers are also notable philanthropists of the arts. The practice of staging 'die-ins' goes back to ACT UP (AIDS Coalition to Unleash Power) at St Patrick's Cathedral, New York City, in 1990. It was also taken up by Black Lives Matter at Grand Central Station in New York City in 2014 and 2015 and by Extincton Rebellion at the Natural History Museum in London in 2019.

9   Caycedo's *Be Dammed* (2015–), inspired by Indigenous cosmologies in South America, explores the impact of hydroelectric dams in that region; the action *Rios Vivos* (2014) was made with

opposition to corporate behemoths, differs from socially engaged art of the 1990s and 2000s that focused on broader and less-contested notions such as urban regeneration, alternative economies and civic participation.

From 2013 onwards, the rise of Black Lives Matter unleashed a different vocabulary for social relations, one that conspicuously avoided the word *participation*. Take, for example, the most powerful form of collective creativity in 2020, which was the re-semiotisation of monumental statuary through graffiti, projections and social activation, best seen at the statue of General Robert E. Lee in Richmond, Virginia. Participation was in evidence all over the monument and its environs but was never invoked; instead, the rhetoric was one of reclaiming space, collective knowledge and communal healing.

The word that came to epitomise this new attitude was *care*. For example, Simone Leigh's *Free People's Medical Clinic* (2014), and to a lesser extent *The Waiting Room* (2016), both fall squarely in the lineage of social practice but center a Black feminist discourse of care. Located in the Stuyvesant Mansion in Brooklyn, the *Free People's Medical Clinic* referred back to nineteenth-century Black women medical pioneers and nurses who had lived in that area. A month-long working clinic, it offered a number of alternative health services, including classes on 'Afrocentering (Pilates)', 'Well Woman Care', and 'Community Acupuncture'. The emphasis was holistic and intergenerational, while also serving as a critique of the racism endemic to the US healthcare system.[10] The ongoing projects *Nap Ministry* (Tricia Hersey, 2016–) and *Black Power Naps* (Navild Acosta and Fannie Sosa, 2018–) continue this call, asserting the right of people of colour to refuse the grind of capitalism and to practice self-care, presenting 'rest as resistance' and 'rest as reparations'.[11] A notable aspect of *Black Power Naps* has been its insistence on 'aftercare': pushing institutions to provide artists the kind of benefits they give permanent employees.[12] Indigenous performance has taken up a related rhetoric of care, but with an additional emphasis on healing and guardianship of the environment.

Jaguos por el Territorio and Rios Vivos Colombia. Cannupa Hansker Luger's *Mirror Shield Project* (2016) was initiated to support the water protectors at Standing Rock, North Dakota.

10　Part of the *Free People's Medical Clinic* was a space called *The Waiting Room* (which then gave its name to Leigh's New Museum installation of 2016), which honoured the life of Esmin Elizabeth Green, who died in 2008 after waiting twenty-four hours in a Brooklyn emergency room without receiving medical attention.

11　Tricia Hersey, 'Rest as Resistance,' on her blog post 'Rest Is Anything That Connects Your Mind and Body', thenapministry.wordpress.com, 21 February 2022. Janine Francois, "Rest as Reparations," *Black Power Naps Magazine*, 2 (2019), n.p. The radical roots of self-care as survival and the first step to community care go back to Black feminist 'love politics' in the 1970s, and to Audre Lorde's oft-quoted statement 'Caring for myself is not self-indulgence, it is self-preservation, and that is an act of political warfare'. Audre Lorde, *Burst of Light*, New York: Ixia Press, 2017 (first published 1988), p. 130. The discourse of self-care spiked in the wake of BLM activism and burnout.

12　This aspect of *Black Power Naps* is explored in Danielle Drees, 'Napping in Public: Feminist Practices of Care in Sleeping Performance Art', *Frontiers*, 41:3, 2020, pp. 1–28.

There has been a conspicuous revival of ritual as a mode of performance over the last five years, both from European artists interested in Indigenous epistemologies (e.g., Maria Lucia Cruz Correia, Grace Ndiritu) and by First Nations artists in the Americas (as programmed in the series 'Knowledge of Wounds' at Performance Space New York, 2021). Ritual implicitly rejects a Western epistemology of political action and appeals to forces beyond individual agency: land, spirit, transgenerational knowledge. Such practices have honored victims of racist violence and reaffirmed contact with ancestral land. The nonbinary First Nations artist S. J. Norman, for example, created a durational ceremony in which participants each pledged a drop of blood or received a nail tattoo while the artist's back was incised with 147 cuts, each representing the death of a "Blak" person in police custody.[13] In such works, the line between performer and participant is as fluid as that between temporalities, genders and generations. At the same time, the division between Indigenous and non-Indigenous participation remains fraught, sometimes deliberately so. Unlike ritual, which describes a more open series of actions performed for symbolic value, certain aspects of ceremony cannot be revealed to outsiders.[14]

In the above examples by Black and Indigenous artists, the specificity of themes and audiences contrasts with artists of the 1990s and 2000s who positioned themselves as 'repairing the social bond', largely in relation to a public defined site-specifically and only secondarily as working-class or immigrant.[15] The artist thus assumed the role of benefactor to a disenfranchised other—or conversely, flaunted that disparity as part of the work. The most provocative project to continue in the latter vein is Renzo Martens's ambitious long-term plan to create a 'white cube' gallery on a former plantation in the Congo, together with its former employees.[16] By contrast, Black and Indigenous artists have tended to address work to their own communities, and to carefully manage the relationship between

13   S. J. Norman, *Cicatrix 1 (that which is taken/that which remains)*, 2019. In Australia, *Blak* signifies contemporary urban Indigeneity, in contrast to the racialised experiences of non-Indigenous communities of colour.

14   Thanks to Joseph Pierce for a helpful conversation about this aspect of Indigenous performance. For a discussion of art and ceremony, see Crystal Migwans and Anne Spice, 'Art, Ceremony, and Activism: Evading Capture in Visual Representation', in the Vera List Center's anthology *Indigenous New York, Critically Speaking*, 2017, n.p., https://veralistcenter.org/wp-content/uploads/2019/07/Indigenous-New-York-Program.pdf

15   Miwon Kwon's *One Place after Another: Site-Specific Art and Locational Identity*, Cambridge, MA: MIT Press, 2004, offers a critique of community defined site-specifically. In *Artificial Hells*, I discuss examples of participation that foreground class, employment or immigration status (e.g., Jeremy Deller, Santiago Sierra, Christoph Schlingensief), some of which had racial implications, but this was never made explicit by the artists.

16   Martens created the Institute for Human Activities in collaboration with the CATPC (Cercle d'art des travailleurs de plantation congolaise) in 2014. See humanactivities.org/en.

publicity and privacy. Leigh, for example, refers to her work as 'auto-ethnographic' and conceives it explicitly for Black women, tightly controlling her photo-documentation.[17]

One effect of the last decade's turn to care has been to expose the *whiteness* of participation as a discourse – a whiteness reinforced, unfortunately, by *Artificial Hells*. The book features Latin American artists, but they are almost exclusively Euro-descendent, and only one Asian American artist. Because I had wanted to avoid examples from the United States (since to my eyes it already played an outsize role in accounts of public art, site-specificity and art activism), I ended up centering the historical avant-garde and its legacy in white European art, rather than pushing to uncover other genealogies. As a result, artists such as Rick Lowe (*Project Row Houses* in Houston, 1993–) and Theaster Gates (*Dorchester Projects* in Chicago, 2009–), to name just two major figures, were omitted.[18] A revision of the book might include a chapter charting Black social practice in the United States: a trajectory in which participation is inextricable from a politics of regeneration, resistance and support that goes back to the Black Panther Party, whose liberation schools and People's Free Medical Clinics are also an explicit point of reference for Simone Leigh.

Indeed, the biggest shifts in social practice over the last decade can best be seen through the work of Black artists: the invocation of history, an engagement with urban regeneration and infrastructure, and a new attention to design. Previous forms of social practice tended to be insistently presentist, focusing on contemporary urgencies. By contrast, Leigh's projects discussed above, and Dread Scott's *Slave Rebellion Reenactment* (2019), place history into juxtaposition with present-day injustice. Attention to infrastructure is another important development: short-term microtopias, long critiqued for merely 'parachuting' into a community, have given way to longer-term institution building. Gates's Rebuild Foundation is emblematic of a broader turn to creating non-profit organisations that offer residencies, fellowships, apprenticeships, incubators and more. NXTHVN, Denniston Hill, Art + Practice, Guest Artists Space (G.A.S.) Foundation – each of these projects was set up by a commercially successful artist of colour to support the generations that follow.[19]

---

17 Leigh commissioned Madeleine Hunt-Erlich to produce a film about the *Free People's Medical Clinic*, thus ensuring that the fullest documentation of it was by another Black woman: Simone Leigh, 'Free People's Medical Clinic (project documentation by Madeleine Hunt-Erlich)', 2016, vimeo.com.

18 Working some twenty years apart, Lowe and Gates have very different approaches to social practice. See Larne Abse Gogarty, 'Art and Gentrication,' *Art Monthly*, 373, February 2014, pp. 7–10.

19 Among these, Gates stands out for his willingness to collaborate with politicians and businesses. In 2009, he established the Rebuild Foundation to oversee the acquisition and renovation of vacant buildings in Chicago; it currently has seven offshoots, including Dorchester Art + Housing Collaborative (which oversees mixed-income rental units) and Dorchester Industries (2016–),

Rebuild also exemplifies the new emphasis on design: Gates's work has an unmistakable aesthetic, in direct contrast to the anti-aesthetic posturing of the 1990s and 2000s. Social practice artists everywhere now pay far more attention to the branding of their projects and identities – in part because their work must circulate on social media and in digital space, not just on-site and in person. With backgrounds in design or architecture, artists even supplement their practice through graphic design work or renting out affordable studio space (e.g., Futurefarmers, the Black School, Assemble). The shift to material infrastructure, non-profit and for-profit organisation, and graphic/architectural design is a decisive shift away from the previous decades' emphasis on temporary, informal and DIY modes of collective gathering. In line with commercial enterprise, the social has become more designed, more aesthetic – and at times uncomfortably entangled with gentrification.[20]

This brings me to the second blind spot of *Artificial Hells*: participation's relationship to digital technology. Web 2.0 is, of course, a watershed in the history of participation, inadequately confronted in the book. Written only a handful of years into the rise of Twitter and Facebook (2006), the iPhone (2007) and Instagram (2010), *Artificial Hells* fails to develop any relationship between participation and social media. In the conclusion, I dismiss Antony Gormley's mediagenic project *One and Other* (2009) as 'Twitter Art'. As it turned out, this type of artist-organised amateur free-for-all became much less visible in the 2010s, precisely because social media platforms like TikTok (2017) came to offer more effective sites for self-expression. Such platforms have managed to remove the artist as well-meaning intermediary while also producing a repertoire of images that feel more authentic because they are generated by users themselves. The ubiquity of social media, its efficacy in terms of reaching huge audiences, and the hits of dopamine it gratifyingly drip-feeds have been central to the loss of artistic interest in participation over the last decade. Further, apps such as Facebook, Instagram and TikTok have intensified artists' antagonism towards participation by rendering it synonymous with metrics and monetisation.

Superficially, participatory art and social media share an embrace of levelled hierarchies, decentralisation and unpaid labour; in reality, as we know, these platforms are run by transnational corporations in the service of surveillance capitalism. While the same urge for community, communication and feedback mobilises social practice and social media, they differ

---

which trains residents of Chicago's South Side to create furniture and art for industrial production. The latter has just established the Dorchester Industries Experimental Design Lab in collaboration with Prada Group.

20   See for example Shellyne Rodriguez, 'How the Bronx Was Branded,' *The New Inquiry*, 12 December 2018, thenewinquiry.com.

in scale and ambition: social practice is insistently local in its reach, rather than aspiring to a global network, and relationships are consolidated in person rather than virtually. The rising interest in NFTs does little to shift this dynamic. Despite the phenomenon of supposedly participatory NFTs – last spring Adidas and Prada just launched one with artist Zach Lieberman – it is unclear how this is anything other than digital marketing. NFTs return art to reactionary notions of originality and authorship as criteria of economic value.

Museums have assisted in the demise of participatory art through their embrace of digital technology as 'viewer engagement' – from museum apps and social media accounts to the creation of online collections and immersive, interactive experiences.[21] Many a dull article has assessed the uses of Web 2.0 for museum education – trends like participatory tagging or using QR codes that have peaked and waned as engagement strategies.[22] The discourse of 'engagement', sprinkled liberally across institutional mission statements, conveys the idea that access to and participation in culture is an unquestionably democratic, even universal good. Yet engagement is an ideological reframing of participation – away from collective cultural production and towards marketing and audience development. It is also paternalistic and monodirectional: a matter of audiences dutifully consuming content, rather than challenging the ideas on display. Engagement, we might say, is where participation goes to die.

Yet even before the rise of social media and engagement, technology had a role to play in participatory art that I wilfully ignored. My definition of participatory art in *Artificial Hells* was unequivocally *in person*: a group of people doing things together, in a shared place and time. The construction of meaning had to be embodied and located, a visible assembly rather than a dispersed community of anyone, anywhere, connected online. The decision to exclude digital participation from my purview seemed logical at the time: I needed to keep the scope manageable, I had no interest in digital

21   See for example Tate Modern's collaboration with Bloomberg Connects. The Tate app uses geolocation to offer 'a more bespoke, behind-the-scenes and personalized experience than traditional museum audio-guides . . . One Bloomberg Connects Explore space dedicated to performance art will be "aware" of visitors' presence through a network of sonar motion sensors. Visitors will use their own movements to drive a responsive content display related to the history of live art. Another space will invite visitors into artists' studios around the world, using floor-to-ceiling projections, light and sound to explore the relationship between artist and location.' 'New Tate Modern to Redefine Visitor Experience with Expanded Bloomberg Connects Digital Engagement Program', Bloomberg Philanthropies press release, June 2014, bloomberg.org.

22   Shelly Bernstein's 'Clear Choices in Tagging' offers an interesting overview of the Brooklyn Museum's participatory games *Tag, You're It* and *Freeze Tag* (2008–16) and the institution's decision to withdraw them (22 July 2014, brooklynmuseum.org). The Van Abbemuseum in Eindhoven has experimented with non-digital forms of participatory display, such as 'DIY Archive' (2013–17), which allowed visitors to handle works in the collection – only possible in a small museum.

aesthetics, and I wanted to sustain a continuity between contemporary participation and its historical forebears. As a result, I drew a cordon sanitaire between the 'interactive' (into which I lumped everything technological) and the 'participatory' (which centred presence and thus aligned art with theatre). In retrospect, this decision ignored the rich interplay between digital and live, virtual and IRL, public and private, which had long been visible in experimental theatre since the late 1970s (e.g., the Wooster Group), strands of tactical media since the 1990s (e.g., the Yes Men), and most activism since the mid-2000s. This hybridization has only intensified through the vicissitudes of the pandemic.

The prevalence of social media has not just impacted social practice but has decisively driven research- and montage-based art that incorporates vernacular material – procedures that, in previous decades, might have foregrounded this process of gathering *as* participation. Forensic Architecture, for example, regularly draws upon open-source and citizen journalism as part of its research process, but this fact is so internalised that it barely registers in the group's description of its projects. Other artists, like Martine Syms and Arthur Jafa, scour the internet for footage and integrate it into their videos. This is never framed as participation because their sources are not the result of a targeted open call but already 'out there'. Participants no longer need to be interpellated, and the artist no longer needs to generate their own footage of this interpellation (as was the case, for example, with Phil Collins or Artur Żmijewski in the 2000s). Today, the art lies in aggregating pre-existing sources, rather than staging situations.[23]

A brief note is needed about the flourishing of participation over the last decade in theatre, performance and, to a lesser extent, dance. In Europe, numerous performance practitioners have reframed the question of participation in terms of Judith Butler's post-Occupy theory of 'assembly', experimenting with various forms of gatherings, parliaments and debates – see Jonas Staal, Milo Rau, or Rimini Protokoll (tellingly, all white men).[24] The exchange of knowledge has remained a focus, as seen in large-scale events by Hannah Hurtzig (begun in 2004) as well as small-scale temporary tents in public squares by Ivana Müller, Lotte van der Berg or Sarah Vanhee (where the knowledge-exchange model has converged with a post-Occupy aesthetics of encampment). Other artists, primarily women, have hybridized the participatory and the algorithmic, translating technological platforms

23   For a signal account of this method, see David Joselit, 'On Aggregators', *October*, 146, Fall 2013, pp. 3–18.

24   See Florian Malzacher, 'Theatre as Assembly', in Ana Vujanovic and Livia Piazza (eds.), *A Live Gathering: Performance and Politics in Contemporary Europe*, Berlin: b_books, 2019, pp. 178–99. Assembly has more recently come into the horizon of the visual art world: see 16 Beaver's *Testing Assembling* (2020–), the exhibition *Assembly: New Acquisitions by Contemporary Black Artists* (Blanton Museum, 2021), and Rashaad Newsome's *Assembly* (Park Avenue Armory, 2022).

into human presence, albeit with the effect of underscoring the enduring power of liveness (Alexandra Pirici, Annie Dorsen, Nora Chipaumire). The popularity of participation reached a level where it had to be skewered, a job that fell to performance artists like Ivo Dimchev, whose camp and hilarious *P Project* (2012) encouraged and even paid the audience to humiliate themselves onstage, and Michael Portnoy, whose *Relational Stalinism: The Musical* (2016) underscored the coercive side of participation.[25]

In contemporary dance, the most high-profile and controversial instance of participation over the last decade was unquestionably Jérôme Bel's collaboration with Theater HORA, a troupe of developmentally disabled actors (*Disabled Theatre*, 2012), and his work with amateur performers of all abilities in *Gala* (2015). Bel's work is explicitly influenced by philosopher Jacques Rancière's theory of the emancipated spectator, a key reference for *Artificial Hells*. While both of us, following Rancière, emphasise the importance of a structured performance as mediating object, Bel nonetheless believes in the transformative potential of participation. And it is precisely his strong authorial structure that made audiences uneasy and led to the claim that in *Disabled Theatre* he forecloses the performers' agency.

The incursion of contemporary dance into museums, which began to intensify around 2011, traded on the participation-adjacent pleasures of immediacy, engagement and collective presence; it was also a reaction to the aesthetics of de-skilling in participatory art. Choreographers engaged in experiments with the public – who were either trained up for evening performances (Bel, Michael Clark) or taught in parallel workshops (Boris Charmatz, Anne Teresa De Keersmaeker) – dovetailing with museum efforts at engagement.[26] More often, however, participation was consciously ambient, as in Isabel Lewis's *Occasions* (2014–18), which managed to synthesize a relationship between dance, social event and designed environment, harking back to the conviviality of 1990s relational art. Maria Hassabi's decelerated museum choreographies invited the audience to step over or around the dancers, who lay on the floor or staircase; even more participated by taking photographs and then uploading them to Instagram

---

25 Commercial theatre, meanwhile, preferred to accommodate participation as competitive immersivity, as in long-running shows like Punchdrunk's *Sleep No More* (2011–). Adam Alston sees this kind of individualistic risk-taking as synonymous with neoliberal work culture, while fragmenting the collective power of a unified audience. Alston, 'Audience Participation and Neoliberal Value: Risk, Agency and Responsibility in Immersive Theatre,' *Performance Research*, 18:2, 2013, pp. 128–38.

26 Clark trained volunteers for a performance at Tate Modern in 2011, and again at the Whitney Biennial in 2012. Bel has made numerous versions of *Gala*, juxtaposing trained professionals with members of the public. In Charmatz's *Roman Photo*, volunteers from the audience are invited to learn his dance *Flip Book*, based on David Vaughan's 1997 photo-book *Merce Cunningham: Fifty Years*. In parallel with Anne Teresa De Keersmaeker's *Work/Travail/Arbeid* at MoMA in 2017, members of her company gave small workshops teaching the core movement vocabulary to interested museum visitors.

(*PLASTIC*, 2016). A satire of participation took place here, too, by queer artists who relished interpassivity and stage-bombing: in Ryan McNamara's *ME3M: A Story Ballet about the Internet* (2013), the seated audience is individually wheeled to performances in different locations of the theatre, while in Dimchev's *Selfie Concert* (2018), the artist invites the audience to crowd him out and take selfies as he sings. While these participatory experiments in theatre, performance and dance rectify some of the aesthetic issues that I critiqued in *Artificial Hells*, they also generate new problems by turning participation into an object.

The last decade, then, has seen a fragmentation of participation as a discourse into a number of competing terms like *assembly*, *engagement* and *care*.[27] Of these, care seems to be the most pervasive. It suggests an aesthetic associated with slowness, duration and humanism: taking time to nurture, to look after, to take notice, to be alongside (rather than looking at), to attend and to reclaim.[28] Care, then, opposes harm. It also opposes antagonism.

Artificial Hells is underpinned by Ernesto Laclau and Chantal Mouffe's theory of radical democracy as antagonism, but this translates uneasily into an ethics and aesthetics of care. I turned to Lacanian ethics to try to grasp the production of art as an individual psychic necessity, stemming from *desire* rather than from a guilty sense of obligation to society. I set the freedom of the id against the guilty conscience of the superego. This model of the artist, however, resonates uneasily with libertarian individualism. The same daring that enables an artist to corral a group of people into a potentially uncomfortable social situation can also be deployed towards a narcissistic extravaganza of transgressive post-truth appropriation.[29] The artistic subjectivity proposed in *Artificial Hells* and the freedom-at-all-costs attitude of contemporary libertarians play out very differently but share a common root: both deploy and enjoy disruption. The alt-right co-option of transgression thus not only complicates the legacy of the historical avant-garde and the counterculture, but intensifies the drama, played out in the final pages of the book, between the artistic and social critiques of capitalism.

Antagonism in society and politics is quite different from antagonism in art, of course, and far more dangerous. The global rise of far-right

27   A further term to consider is the rethinking of participation as 'access' among disabled artists and activists. Thanks to Jeff Kasper for this point.

28   See Tina Campt, *A Black Gaze: Artists Changing How We See*, Cambridge, MA: MIT Press, 2021, for an example of how care might function both as a mode of attention to art and a way of describing artists' relationships to their subjects. See also the number of books on care published by Verso alone in the last two years: the Care Collective's *The Care Manifesto* (2020), the Boston Review's *The Politics of Care: From COVID-19 to Black Lives Matter* (2020), Emma Dowling's *The Care Crisis* (2022) and Boris Groys's *Philosophy of Care* (2022).

29   Consider how Milo Yiannopolis used these strategies to produce a twisted performance against immigration for the '#DaddyWillSaveUs' exhibition in Brooklyn on 8 October 2016.

nationalism and repressive authoritarianism has stained the last decade, generating atmospheres of nihilism and conflict.[30] As social media upended traditional journalism, it was manipulated by those in power to manufacture social discord, a polarisation that political theorist Jodi Dean has compared to civil war.[31] The resulting climate of hostility to immigration, women's bodies, the environment and gun control was inevitably accompanied, in some countries, by a repression of artistic freedom. This has created a completely different context for participation (in both art and activism) from the neoliberal cultural policies of Northern Europe that were the point of departure for *Artificial Hells*.

A decade ago, it seemed unthinkable that antagonism and disruption might become the political norm. Today, millions are living in artificial hells. In retrospect, my book seems cosseted by a privileged Northern European worldview of the 2000s. I berated the state's instrumentalisation of culture and creativity to create a positive image of social unity, yearning instead for art's freedom. Yet what followed, in many places, was so much worse: the far-right instrumentalisation of social media to sow division and distrust. Outrage, hatred and suspicion became the affects of daily life, prompting new genres of political fatigue and disillusionment – hence the appeal of a retreat to care and self-care.

Just as the terms *participation* and *social engagement* became ways of addressing the individualism and privatisation of the neoliberal '90s, so has *care* become the dominant response to the nationalist, white-supremacist 2010s. The difference between the two is arguably a matter of racial and temporal inflection. Care seeks to repair a damage that is historical and ongoing; in some works, this is manifest as direct historical quotation. Yet the politics of care, like that of participatory art, tends to be defined *via negativa*, in opposition to what is dominant – in this case, individualism, objectification, harm. As we move forward, we should recall that while terminologies may shift and acquire new resonances, the need for critical interrogation remains. Care and engagement are not exempt from co-option by institutions and corporations, and the critique of care (primarily by disability rights advocates) has drawn attention to its limitations.[32] What we are witnessing, then, is not so much the demise of participation as a discourse but its transformation – the latest one of many over its long history – to suit the political needs of today's climate.

---

30   Take, for example, this indicative line-up: Viktor Orbán in Hungary (2010–), Xi Jinping in China and Vladimir Putin in Russia (both 2012–), Recep Tayyip Erdoğan in Turkey (2014–), Law and Justice in Poland (2015–), Trump (2016–20), the Five Star Movement in Italy (2018–21), Bolsonaro in Brazil and Díaz-Canel in Cuba (both 2018–).

31   Jodi Dean, in the podcast *Art of Assembly, III: Assemblism*, March 2021, art-of-assembly .net/podcasts.

32   For disability activists, care is associated with dependency, coercion and paternalistic intervention, rather than positive associations of reciprocity and interdependence. See Jonathan Herring, 'The Disability Critique of Care,' *Elder Law Review*, 8, 2014, pp. 1–14.

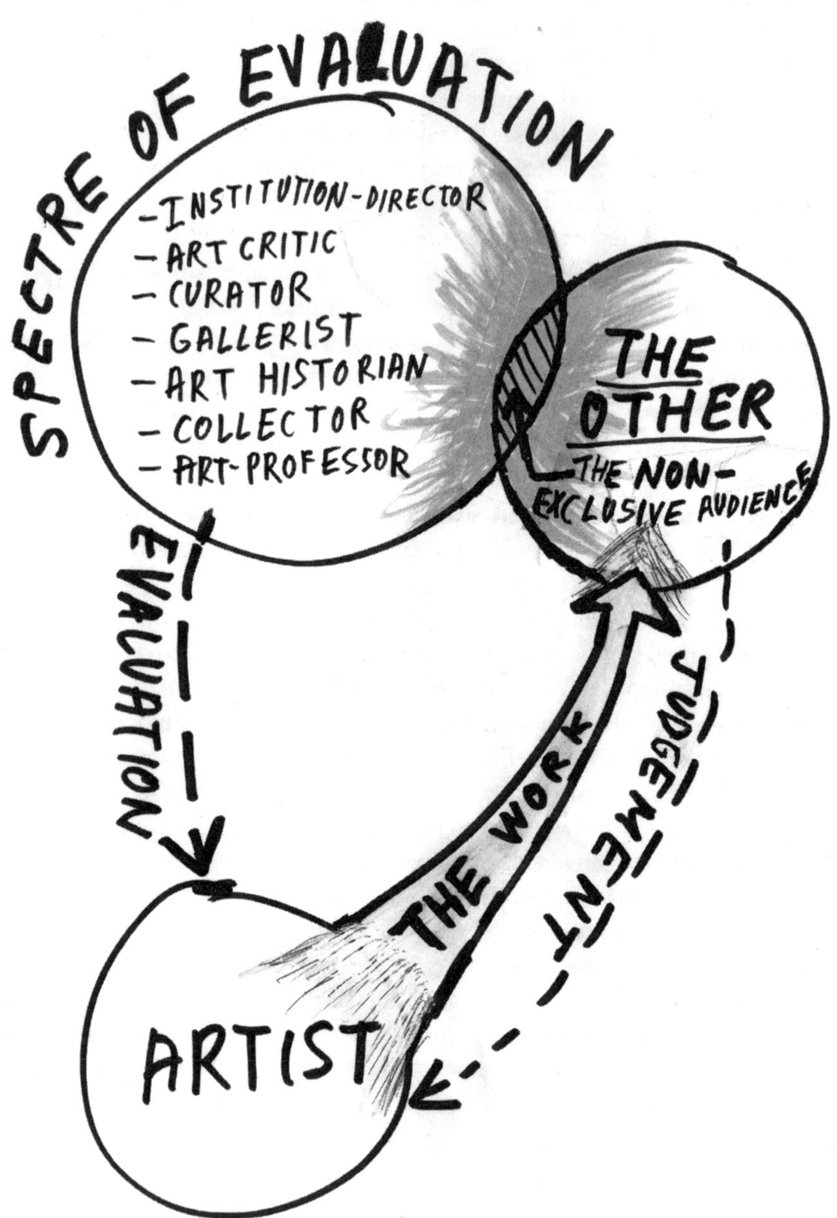

Thomas Hirschhorn, *Spectre of Evaluation*, 2010, ink on paper

Introduction

All artists are alike. They dream of doing something that's more social, more collab-orative, and more real than art.

Dan Graham

Alfredo Jaar hands out disposable cameras to the residents of Catia, Caracas, whose images are shown as the first exhibition in a local museum (*Camera Lucida*, 1996); Lucy Orta leads workshops in Johannesburg to teach unemployed people new fashion skills and discuss collective solidarity (*Nexus Architecture*, 1997–); Superflex start an internet TV station for elderly residents of a Liverpool housing project (*Tenantspin*, 1999); Jeanne van Heeswijk turns a condemned shopping mall into a cultural centre for the residents of Vlaardingen, Rotterdam (*De Strip*, 2001–4); the Long March Foundation produces a census of popular papercutting in remote Chinese provinces (*Papercutting Project*, 2002–); Annika Eriksson invites groups and individuals to communicate their ideas and skills at the Frieze Art Fair (*Do you want an audience?*, 2004); Temporary Services creates an improvised sculpture environment and neighbourhood community in an empty lot in Echo Park, Los Angeles (*Construction Site*, 2005); Vik Muniz sets up an art school for children from the Rio favelas (*Centro Espacial Vik Muniz*, Rio de Janeiro, 2006–).

These projects are just a sample of the surge of artistic interest in participation and collaboration that has taken place since the early 1990s, and in a multitude of global locations. This expanded field of post-studio practices currently goes under a variety of names: socially engaged art, community-based art, experimental communities, dialogic art, littoral art, interventionist art, participatory art, collaborative art, contextual art and (most recently) social practice. I will be referring to this tendency as 'participatory art', since this connotes the involvement of many people (as opposed to the one-to-one relationship of 'interactivity') and avoids the ambiguities of 'social engagement', which might refer to a wide range of work, from *engagé* painting to interventionist actions in mass media; indeed, to the extent that art always responds to its environment (even *via negativa*), what artist *isn't* socially engaged?[1] This book is therefore organised around a definition of participation in which people constitute the central artistic medium and material, in the manner of theatre and performance.

It should be stressed from the outset that the projects discussed in this book have little to do with Nicolas Bourriaud's *Relational Aesthetics* (1998/2002), even though the rhetoric around this work appears, on a theoretical level at least, to be somewhat similar.[2] In truth, however, many of the projects that formed the impetus for this book have emerged in the wake of *Relational Aesthetics* and the debates that it occasioned; the artists I discuss below are less interested in a relational *aesthetic* than in the creative rewards of participation as a politicised working process. One of the achievements of Bourriaud's book was to render discursive and dialogic projects more amenable to museums and galleries; the critical reaction to his theory, however, catalysed a more critically informed discussion around participatory art. Up until the early 1990s, community-based art was confined to the periphery of the art world; today it has become a genre in its own right, with MFA courses on social practice and two dedicated prizes.[3]

This orientation towards social context has since grown exponentially, and, as my first paragraph indicates, is now a near global phenomenon – reaching across the Americas to South East Asia and Russia, but flourishing most intensively in European countries with a strong tradition of public funding for the arts. Although these practices have had, for the most part, a relatively weak profile in the commercial art world – collective projects are more difficult to market than works by individual artists, and less likely to be 'works' than a fragmented array of social events, publications, workshops or performances – they nevertheless occupy a prominent place in the public sector: in public commissions, biennials and politically themed exhibitions. Although I will occasionally refer to contemporary examples from non-Western contexts, the core of this study is the rise of this practice in Europe, and its connection to the changing political imaginary of that region (for reasons that I will explain below). But regardless of geographical location, the hallmark of an artistic orientation towards the social in the 1990s has been a shared set of desires to overturn the traditional relationship between the art object, the artist and the audience. To put it simply: the artist is conceived less as an individual producer of discrete objects than as a collaborator and producer of *situations*; the work of art as a finite, portable, commodifiable product is reconceived as an ongoing or long-term *project* with an unclear beginning and end; while the audience, previously conceived as a 'viewer' or 'beholder', is now repositioned as a co-producer or *participant*. As the chapters that follow will make clear, these shifts are often more powerful as ideals than as actualised realities, but they all aim to place pressure on conventional modes of artistic production and consumption under capitalism. As such, this discussion is framed within a tradition of Marxist and post-Marxist writing on art as a de-alienating endeavour that should not be subject to the division of labour and professional specialisation.

In an article from 2006 I referred to this art as manifesting a 'social turn', but one of the central arguments of this book is that this development should be positioned more accurately as a *return* to the social, part of an ongoing history of attempts to rethink art collectively.[4] Although art of the 1990s and 2000s forms the primary motivation for this research, artists' preoccupation with participation and collaboration is not unprecedented. From a Western European perspective, the social turn in contemporary art can be contextualised by two previous historical moments, both synonymous with political upheaval and movements for social change: the historic avant-garde in Europe circa 1917, and the so-called 'neo' avant-garde leading to 1968. The conspicuous resurgence of participatory art in the 1990s leads me to posit the fall of communism in 1989 as a third point of transformation. Triangulated, these three dates form a narrative of the triumph, heroic last stand and collapse of a collectivist vision of society.[5] Each phase has been accompanied by a utopian rethinking of art's relationship to the social and of its political potential – manifested in a reconsideration of the ways in which art is produced, consumed and debated.

The structure of the book is loosely divided into three parts. The first forms a theoretical introduction laying out the key terms around which participatory art revolves and the motivations for the present publication in a European context. The second section comprises historical case studies: flashpoints in which issues pertinent to contemporary debates around social engagement in art have been particularly precise in their appearance and focus. The third and final section attempts to historicise the post-1989 period and focuses on two contemporary tendencies in participatory art.

Some of the key themes to emerge throughout these chapters are the tensions between quality and equality, singular and collective authorship, and the ongoing struggle to find artistic equivalents for political positions. Theatre and performance are crucial to many of these case studies, since participatory engagement tends to be expressed most forcefully in the live encounter between embodied actors in particular contexts. It is hoped that these chapters might give momentum to rethinking the history of twentieth-century art through the lens of theatre rather than painting (as in the Greenbergian narrative) or the ready-made (as in Krauss, Bois, Buchloh and Foster's *Art Since 1900*, 2005). Further sub-themes include education and therapy: both are process-based experiences that rely on intersubjective exchange, and indeed they converge with theatre and performance at several moments in the chapters that follow.

The first of the historical chapters begins with the invention of a popular mass audience in Italian Futurist *serate* (1910 onwards) and the theatrical innovations that took place in the years following the Bolshevik

Revolution, focusing on the gaps between theory, practice, cultural policy and audience reception. These contested events are contrasted with the Dada Season of 1921, when André Breton and his colleagues 'took to the street' in order to shift the tenor of Dada performance away from one of scandal.[6] The following four chapters examine post-war forms of social participation under four disparate ideological contexts, with a view to showing the divergent political investments that can accompany ostensibly similar artistic expressions. The first of these (Chapter 3) focuses on Paris in the 1960s: it examines the alternatives to visual art devised by the Situationist International, and contrasts their 'constructed situations' to the participatory actions devised by the Groupe Recherche d'Art Visuel (GRAV) on the one hand, and Jean-Jacques Lebel's anarchic and eroticised Happenings on the other. Although the literature on the Situationist International is extensive, it also tends to be partial; my aim has been to provide a critical reading of the group's contribution to art, even though this cuts against its avowed intentions and those of its supporters. If the French scene offers a liberatory repertoire of responses to consumer capitalism in Europe, then participatory actions in South America were formulated in relation to a series of brutal military dictatorships beginning in the mid 1960s; the aggressive and fragmented artistic and theatrical propositions that this gave rise to in Argentina are the subject of Chapter 4. The following chapter turns to Eastern Europe and the Soviet Union, specifically to the proliferation of participatory happenings in former Czechoslovakia in the late 1960s and early 1970s, and to the work of the Collective Actions Group in Moscow from 1976 onwards. These examples from socialist contexts aim to problematise contemporary claims that participation is synonymous with collectivism, and thus inherently opposed to capitalism; rather than reinforcing the collectivist dogma of dominant ideology, these case studies indicate that participatory art under state socialism was often deployed as a means to create a privatised sphere of individual expression. The last of these four 'ideological' chapters focuses on participation in a welfare state social democracy, turning to two artistic innovations that flourished in the UK in the 1970s: the Community Arts Movement and the Artist Placement Group. Little art historical work has been undertaken on either of these phenomena, and it is hoped that this provocative conjunction will trigger further debate.

The third section of the book begins by providing a narrative of the rise of social engagement in contemporary art in Europe after the fall of communism, focusing on the 'project' as a privileged vehicle of utopian experimentation at a time when a leftist project seemed to have vanished from the political imaginary. Chapters 8 and 9 focus on two prevalent modes of participation in contemporary art: 'delegated' performance (in which everyday people are hired to perform on behalf of the artist) and pedagogic projects (in which art converges with the activities and goals of education). Both of these chapters aim to take on board the methodological implications of process-based participatory art, and to propose alternative criteria for considering this work. The book ends with a consideration of the changing identity of the audience across the twentieth century, and suggests that artistic models of democracy have only a tenuous relationship to actual forms of democracy.

The scope of this book is of course far from comprehensive. Many important projects and recent tendencies have been left out. I have not, for example, dealt with transdisciplinary, research-based, activist or interventionist art, in part because these projects do not primarily involve people as the medium or material of the work, and in part because they have their own set of discursive problems that I would like to address as a separate issue in the future. I have been similarly strict about the geographical scope of this book, which is organised around the legacy of the historic avant-garde – hence the decision to include Eastern Europe and South America, but not Asia.[7] Readers may also wonder about the paucity of case studies from North America. When I began this research, I was initially interested in producing a counter-history, since the discussion around social engagement has for too long been dominated by North American critics writing on North American art – based on issues of new genre public art, site specificity, and dialogic practices. My desire to put these debates aside was not intended to undermine their importance; on the contrary, the work of these critic-historians has been central to the emergence of this field and the terms that we have available for its analysis.[8] As the research developed, however, more focused political concerns replaced my naively anti-hegemonic desire to avoid a re-rehearsal of North American art history, despite my eventual inclusion of a few key US examples. One of the motivations behind this book stems from a profound ambivalence about the instrumentalisation of participatory art as it has developed in European cultural policy in tandem with the dismantling of the welfare state. The UK context under New Labour (1997–2010) in particular embraced this type of art as a form of soft social engineering. The US context, with its near total absence of public funding, has a fundamentally different relationship to the question of art's instrumentalisation.

I will conclude this introduction with some methodological points about researching art that engages with people and social processes. One thing is clear: visual analyses fall short when confronted with the documentary material through which we are given to understand many of these practices. To grasp participatory art from images alone is almost impossible: casual photographs of people talking, eating, attending a workshop or screening or seminar tell us very little, almost nothing, about the concept and context of a given project. They rarely provide more than fragmentary evidence, and convey nothing of the affective dynamic that propels artists to make these projects and people to participate in them. To what extent is this a new problem? Some of the best conceptual and perfor-mance art in the 1960s and '70s similarly sought to refute the commodity-object in favour of an elusive experience. Yet visuality always remained important to this task: however 'deskilled' or desubjectivised, conceptual and performance art nevertheless manage to prompt a wide range of affective responses, and their photo-documentation is capable of provoking deadpan amusement, wry embarrassment, iconic reverence or appalled disgust. By contrast, today's participatory art is often at pains to emphasise process over a definitive image, concept or object. It tends to value what is invisible: a group dynamic, a social situation, a change of energy, a raised consciousness. As a result, it is an art dependent on first-hand experience, and preferably over a long duration (days, months or even years). Very few observers are in a position to take such an overview of long-term participatory projects: students and researchers are usually reliant on accounts provided by the artist, the curator, a handful of assis-tants, and if they are lucky, maybe some of the participants. Many of the contemporary case studies in this book were gleaned through hit-and-miss field trips, which led me to understand that all of this work demands more on-site time commitment than I was habitually used to as a critic of instal-lation art, performance and exhibitions. Ideally several site visits were necessary, preferably spread out over time – a luxury not always available to the underpaid critic and tightly scheduled academic. The complexity of each context and the characters involved is one reason why the dominant narratives around participatory art have frequently come to lie in the hands of those curators responsible for each project and who are often the only ones to witness its full unfolding – at times present even more so than the artist.[9] An important motivation for this study was my frustration at the foreclosure of critical distance in these curatorial narratives, although I have come to realise that in staging multiple visits to a given project, this fate increasingly also befalls the critic. The more one becomes involved, the harder it is to be objective – especially when a central component of a project concerns the formation of personal relationships, which inevitably proceed to impact on one's research. The hidden narrative of this book is therefore a journey from sceptical distance to imbrication: as relationships with producers were consolidated, my comfortable outsider status (impo-tent but secure in my critical superiority) had to be recalibrated along more constructive lines.

This trajectory is reflected in this book: readers may note the shift between the polemic in Chapter 1 – first published (in shorter form) in 2006 – and the conclusion from 2011. The book's title, *Artificial Hells*, is intended to serve both as a positive and negative descriptor of participatory art. Taken from André Breton's eponymous post-mortem of the *Grande Saison Dada* in Spring 1921, in which he argues for the exquisite potential of social disruption in the public sphere, the title appeals for more bold, affective and troubling forms of participatory art and criticism. Breton's analysis also suggests that work perceived by its makers to be an experimental failure in its own time (like the Dada Season of 1921) may nevertheless have resonance in the future, under new conditions. This model of delayed reaction has been foundational to my selection of examples, whose inclusion is based on their relevance to the present day, rather than for their significance at the time of their making.

From a disciplinary perspective, any art engaging with society and the people in it demands a methodological reading that is, at least in part, sociological. By this I mean that an analysis of this art must necessarily engage with concepts that have traditionally had more currency within the social sciences than in the humanities: community, society, empowerment, agency. As a result of artists' expanding curiosity in participation, specific vocabularies of social organisation and models of democracy have come to assume a new relevance for the analysis of contemporary art. But since participatory art is not only a social activity but also a symbolic one, both embedded in the world *and* at one remove from it, the positivist social sciences are ultimately less useful in this regard than the abstract reflections of political philosophy. This methodological aspect of the 'social turn' is one of the challenges faced by art historians and critics when dealing with contemporary art's expanded field. Participatory art demands that we find new ways of analysing art that are no longer linked solely to visuality, even though *form* remains a crucial vessel for communicating meaning. In order to analyse the works discussed in this book, theories and terms have been imported from political philosophy, but also from theatre history and performance studies, cultural policy and architecture.[10] This combination differs from other interdisciplinary moments in art history (such as the use of Marxism, psychoanalysis and linguistics in the 1970s). Today, it is no longer a question of employing these methods to rewrite art history from an invested political position – although this certainly plays a role – so much as the acknowledgment that it is impossible adequately to address a socially oriented art *without* turning to these disciplines, and that this interdisciplinarity parallels (and stems from) the ambitions and content of the art itself.[11]

At the same time, it must be emphasised that one of the goals of this book is to show the inadequacy of a positivist sociological approach to participatory art (as proposed, for example, by cultural policy think-tank studies that focus on demonstrable outcomes) and to reinforce the need to keep alive the constitutively undefinitive reflections on quality that characterise the humanities. In the field of participatory art, quality is often a contested word: rejected by many politicised artists and curators as serving the interests of the market and powerful elites, 'quality' has been further marred by its association with connoisseurial art history. More radical options have tended to advocate a confusion of high/low boundaries or to prioritise other terms (in the words of Thomas Hirschhorn, 'Energy yes, quality no!'). This book is predicated on the assumption that value judgements are necessary, not as a means to reinforce elite culture and police the boundaries of art and non-art, but as a way to understand and clarify our shared values at a given historical moment. Some projects are indisputably more rich, dense and inexhaustible than others, due to the artist's talent for conceiving a complex work and its location within a specific time, place and situation. There is an urgent need to restore attention to the modes of conceptual and affective complexity generated by socially oriented art projects, particularly to those that claim to reject aesthetic quality, in order to render them more powerful and grant them a place in history. After all, aesthetic refusals have happened many times before. Just as we have come to recognise Dada cabaret, Situationist *détournement*, or dematerialised conceptual and performance art as having their own aesthetics of production and circulation, so too do the often formless-looking photo-documents of participatory projects have their own experiential regime. The point is not to regard these anti-aesthetic visual phenomena (reading areas, self-published newspapers, parades, demonstrations, ubiquitous plywood platforms, endless photographs of people) as objects of a new formalism, but to analyse how these contribute to and reinforce the social and artistic experience being generated.

A secondary methodological point relates to the pragmatics of my research. I have already mentioned the geographic purview of this book: it is international but does not attempt to be global. To stay local is to risk provincialism; to go global risks dilution. Language has been an ongoing problem: in conducting my case studies, I was confronted with the unavoidable reality that I do not have the language requirements to do original archival work in so many different contexts. For better or worse, English is the lingua franca of the art world, and is the language in which I have undertaken the bulk of this research. And due to the experience-based character of participatory art and its tangential relationship to the canon, the bulk of this research has been discursive: seven years of conversations, interviews and arguments with artists and curators, not to mention the audiences to whom I have lectured, colleagues who were patient interlocutors, and students at numerous institutions.

One of this book's objectives is to generate a more nuanced (and honest) critical vocabulary with which to address the vicissitudes of collaborative authorship and spectatorship. At present, this discourse revolves far too often around the unhelpful binary of 'active' and 'passive' spectatorship, and – more recently – the false polarity of 'bad' singular authorship and 'good' collective authorship. These binaries need to be taken to task, and with them the facile argument – heard at every public debate about this art I have ever attended – that singular authorship serves primarily to glorify the artist's career and fame. This criticism is continually levelled at participatory art despite the fact that since the late 1960s, artists across all media continually engage in dialogue and creative negotiation with other people: technicians, fabricators, curators, public bodies, other artists, intellectuals, participants, and so on. The worlds of music, film, literature, fashion and theatre have a rich vocabulary to describe co-existing authorial positions (director, author, performer, editor, producer, casting agent, sound engineer, stylist, photographer), all of which are regarded as essential to the creative realisation of a given project. The lack of an equivalent terminology in contemporary visual art has led to a reductive critical framework, underpinned by moral indignation.

Academic research is no less subject to these valorising paradoxes of single and collective authorship: single-authored monographic books have more status than edited volumes, while the most reputable scholarship is subjected to the collective monitoring called 'peer review'. I am acutely aware that the form of this research is conventional, resulting in a monographic study – rather than exhibition, DVD, website, archive or more collaborative form of output.[12] On the other hand, while a number of edited anthologies and exhibition catalogues around this subject already exist, few of them make a sustained argument.[13] We should bear in mind that there is no fixed recipe for good art or authorship. As Roland Barthes reminded us in 1968, authorships (of all kinds) are multiple and continually indebted to others. What matters are the ideas, experiences and possibilities that result from these interactions. The central project of this book is to find ways of accounting for participatory art that focus on the meaning of what it produces, rather than attending solely to process. This result – the mediating object, concept, image or story – is the necessary link between the artist and a secondary audience (you and I, and everyone else who didn't participate); the historical fact of our ineradicable presence requires an analysis of the politics of spectatorship, even – and especially – when participatory art wishes to disavow this.

1

The Social Turn: Collaboration and Its Discontents

A recurrent set of theoretical reference points governs the current literature on participatory and collaborative art: Walter Benjamin, Michel de Certeau, the Situationist International, Paulo Freire, Deleuze and Guattari, and Hakim Bey, to name just a few.[1] Among these, the most frequently cited is the French film-maker and writer Guy Debord, for his indictment of the alienating and divisive effects of capitalism in *The Society of the Spectacle* (1967), and for his theorisation of collectively produced 'situations'. For many artists and curators on the left, Debord's critique strikes to the heart of why participation is important as a project: it rehumanises a society rendered numb and fragmented by the repressive instrumentality of capitalist production. Given the market's near total saturation of our image repertoire, so the argument goes, artistic practice can no longer revolve around the construction of objects to be consumed by a passive bystander. Instead, there must be an art of action, interfacing with reality, taking steps – however small – to repair the social bond. The art historian Grant Kester, for example, observes that art is uniquely placed to counter a world in which 'we are reduced to an atomised pseudocommunity of consumers, our sensibilities dulled by spectacle and repetition'.[2] 'One reason why artists are no longer interested in a passive process of presenter-spectator', writes the Dutch artist Jeanne van Heeswijk, is 'the fact that such communication has been entirely appropriated by the commercial world . . . After all, nowadays one could receive an aesthetic experience on every corner.'[3] More recently, the artist/activist Gregory Sholette and art historian Blake Stimson have argued that 'in a world all but totally subjugated by the commodity form and the spectacle it generates, the only remaining theatre of action is direct engagement with the forces of production'.[4] Even the curator Nicolas Bourriaud, describing relational art of the 1990s, turns to spectacle as his central point of reference: 'Today, we are in the further stage of spectacular development: the individual has shifted from a passive and purely repetitive status to the minimum activity dictated to him by market forces . . . Here we are summoned to turn into *extras* of the spectacle.'[5] As the philosopher Jacques Rancière points out, 'the "critique of the spectacle" often remains the alpha and the omega of the "politics of art" '.[6]

Alongside a discourse of spectacle, advanced art of the last decade has seen a renewed affirmation of collectivity and a denigration of the individual, who becomes synonymous with the values of Cold War liberalism and its transformation into neoliberalism, that is, the economic practice of private property rights, free markets and free trade.[7] Much of this discussion has been given impetus by Italian workerist theories of contemporary labour. In this framework, the virtuosic contemporary artist has become the role model for the flexible, mobile, non-specialised labourer who can creatively adapt to multiple situations, and become his/her own brand. What stands against this model is the collective: collaborative practice is perceived to offer an automatic counter-model of social unity, regardless of its actual politics. As Paolo Virno has noted, if the historic avant-garde were inspired by, and connected to, centralised political parties, then 'today's collective practices are connected to the decentred and heterogeneous net that composes post-Fordist social co-operation'.[8] This social network of an incipient 'multitude' has been valorised in exhibitions and events like 'Collective Creativity' (WHW, 2005), 'Taking the Matter into Common Hands' (Maria Lind et al., 2005), and 'Democracy in America' (Nato Thompson, 2008). Along with 'utopia' and 'revolution', collectivity and collaboration have been some of the most persistent themes of advanced art and exhibition-making of the last decade. Countless works have addressed collective desires across numerous lines of identification – from Johanna Billing's plaintive videos in which young people are brought together, often through music (*Project for a Revolution*, 2000; *Magical World*, 2005) to Kateřina Šedá inviting everyone in a small Czech village to follow her mandatory programme of activities for one day (*There's Nothing There*, 2003), from Sharon Hayes' participatory events for LGBT communities (*Revolutionary Love*, 2008) to Tania Bruguera's performance in which blind people dressed in military garb stand on the streets soliciting sex (*Consummated Revolution*, 2008). Even if a work of art is not directly participatory, references to community, collectivity (be this lost or actualised) and revolution are sufficient to indicate a critical distance towards the neoliberal new world order. Individualism, by contrast, is viewed with suspicion, not least because the commercial art system and museum programming continue to revolve around lucrative single figures.

Participatory projects in the social field therefore seem to operate with a twofold gesture of opposition and amelioration. They work against dominant market imperatives by diffusing single authorship into collaborative activities that, in the words of Kester, transcend 'the snares of negation and self-interest'.[9] Instead of supplying the market with commodities, participatory art is perceived to channel art's symbolic capital towards constructive social change. Given these avowed politics, and the commitment that mobilises this work, it is tempting to suggest that this art arguably forms what avant-garde we have today: artists devising social situations as a dematerialised, anti-market, politically engaged project to carry on the avant-garde call to make art a more vital part of life. But the urgency of this *social* task has led to a situation in which socially collaborative practices are all perceived to be equally important *artistic* gestures of resistance: there can be no failed, unsuccessful, unresolved, or boring works of participatory art, because all are equally essential to the task of repairing the social bond. While sympathetic to the latter ambition, I would argue that it is also crucial to discuss, analyse and compare this work critically *as art*, since this is the institutional field in which it is endorsed and disseminated, even while the category of art remains a persistent exclusion in debates about such projects.

I. Creativity and Cultural Policy

This task is particularly pressing in Europe. In the UK, New Labour (1997–2010) deployed a rhetoric almost identical to that of the practitioners of socially engaged art in order to justify public spending on the arts. Anxious for accountability, the question it asked on entering office in 1997 was: what can the arts do for society? The answers included increasing employability, minimising crime, fostering aspiration – anything but artistic experimentation and research as values in and of themselves. The production and reception of the arts was therefore reshaped within a political logic in which audience figures and marketing statistics became essential to securing public funding.[10] The key phrase deployed by New Labour was 'social exclusion': if people become disconnected from schooling and education, and subsequently the labour market, they are more likely to pose problems for welfare systems and society as a whole. New Labour therefore encouraged the arts to be socially *inclusive*. Despite the benign ring to this agenda, it has been subject to critiques from the left, primarily because it seeks to conceal social inequality, rendering it cosmetic rather than structural.[11] It represents the primary division in society as one between an *included majority* and an *excluded minority* (formerly known as the 'working class'). The solution implied by the discourse of social exclusion is simply the goal of transition across the boundary from excluded to included, to allow people to access the holy grail of self-sufficient consumerism and be independent of any need for welfare. Furthermore, social exclusion is rarely perceived to be a corollary of neoliberal policies, but of any number of peripheral (and individual) developments, such as drug-taking, crime, family breakdown and teenage pregnancy.[12] Participation became an important buzzword in the social inclusion discourse, but unlike its function in contemporary art (where it denotes self-realisation and collective action), for New Labour it effectively referred to the elimination of disruptive individuals. To be included and participate in society means to conform to full employment, have a disposable income, and be self-sufficient.

Incorporated into New Labour's cultural policy, the social inclusion discourse leaned heavily upon a report by François Matarasso proving the positive impact of social participation in the arts.[13] Matarasso lays out fifty benefits of socially engaged practice, offering 'proof' that it reduces isolation by helping people to make friends, develops community networks and sociability, helps offenders and victims address issues of crime, contributes to people's employability, encourages people to accept risk positively, and helps transform the image of public bodies. The last of these, perhaps, is the most insidious: social participation is viewed positively because it creates submissive citizens who respect authority and accept the 'risk' and responsibility of looking after themselves in the face of diminished public services. As the cultural theorist Paola Merli has pointed out, none of these outcomes will change or even raise consciousness of the structural conditions of people's daily existence, it will only help people to accept them.[14]

The social inclusion agenda is therefore less about repairing the social bond than a mission to enable all members of society to be self-administering, fully functioning consumers who do not rely on the welfare state and who can cope with a deregulated, privatised world. As such, the neoliberal idea of community doesn't seek to build social relations, but rather to erode them; as the sociologist Ulrich Beck has noted, social problems are experienced as individual rather than collective, and we feel compelled to seek 'biographic solutions to systemic contradictions'.[15] In this logic, participation in society is merely participation in the task of being individually responsible for what, in the past, was the collective concern of the state. Since the Conservative-Liberal Democrat coalition came to power in May 2010 this devolution of responsibility has accelerated: David Cameron's 'Big Society', ostensibly a form of people power in which the public can challenge how services such as libraries, schools, police and transport are being run, in fact denotes a laissez-faire model of government dressed up as an appeal to foster 'a new culture of voluntarism, philanthropy, social action'.[16] It's a thinly opportunist mask: asking wageless volunteers to pick up where the government cuts back, all the while privatising those services that ensure equality of access to education, welfare and culture.

The UK is not alone in this tendency. Northern Europe has experienced a transformation of the 1960s discourse of participation, creativity and community; these terms no longer occupy a subversive, anti-authoritarian force, but have become a cornerstone of post-industrial economic policy. From the 1990s to the crash in 2008, 'creativity' was one of the major buzz words in the 'new economy' that came to replace heavy industry and commodity production. In 2005, a policy document *Our Creative Capacity*

(Ons Creatieve Vermogen) was presented to the Dutch right-wing coalition government by the Ministry of Education, Culture and Science and the Ministry of Economic Affairs. The paper's aim was to 'intensify the economic potential of culture and creativity by boosting the creative powers of Dutch trade and industry' by operating on two fronts: firstly, to give the business community more insight into the possibilities offered by the creative sector, 'generating a wealth of ideas for the development and utilisation of new technologies and products', and secondly, to encourage the cultural sector to have a greater awareness of its market potential.[17] In the same document, we find that the authors of this paper acknowledge no difference between 'creative industry', the 'culture industry', 'art' and 'entertainment'. What results from this elision is not a productive blurring and complication of both terms (as we might find in certain cross-disciplinary artistic practices) but rather the reduction of everything to a matter of finance: 'the fact that some people attribute greater artistic merit to certain sectors is completely irrelevant when looked at from a perspective of economic utilisation'.[18] One year later, in 2006, the Dutch government inaugurated a €15 million 'Culture and Economy' programme, capitalising upon creativity as a specifically Dutch export, as if taking the logic of De Stijl to its unwitting expansion as an entrepreneurial opportunity. At the same time, Amsterdam City Council began an aggressive rebranding of the Dutch capital as a 'Creative City': 'Creativity will be the central focus point', it claimed, since 'creativity is the motor that gives the city its magnetism and dynamism'.[19]

One of the models for the Dutch initiative was New Labour, who placed an emphasis on the role of creativity and culture in commerce and the growth of the 'knowledge economy'.[20] This included museums as a source of regeneration, but also investment in the 'creative industries' as alternatives to traditional manufacturing.[21] New Labour built upon the Conservative government's openly instrumental approach to cultural policy: a 2001 Green Paper opens with the words 'Everyone is creative', presenting the government's mission as one that aims to 'free the creative potential of individuals'.[22] This aim of unleashing creativity, however, was not designed to foster greater social happiness, the realisation of authentic human potential, or the imagination of utopian alternatives, but to produce, in the words of sociologist Angela McRobbie, 'a future generation of socially diverse creative workers who are brimming with ideas and whose skills need not only be channelled into the fields of art and culture but will also be good for business'.[23]

In short, the emergence of a creative and mobile sector serves two purposes: it minimises reliance on the welfare state while also relieving corporations of the burden of responsibilities for a permanent workforce. As such, New Labour considered it important to develop creativity in schools – not because everyone must be an artist (as Joseph Beuys declared), but because the population is increasingly required to assume the individu-alisation associated with creativity: to be entrepreneurial, embrace risk, look after their own self-interest, perform their own brands, and be willing to self-exploit. To cite McRobbie once more: 'the answer to so many prob-lems across a wide spectrum of the population – e.g. mothers at home and not quite ready to go back to work full time – on the part of New Labour is "self employment", set up your own business, be free to do your own thing. Live and work like an artist'.[24] Sociologist Andrew Ross makes a similar point when he argues that the artist has become the role model for what he calls the 'No Collar' workforce: artists provide a useful model for precari-ous labour since they have a work mentality based on flexibility (working project by project, rather than nine to five) and honed by the idea of sacri-ficial labour (i.e. being predisposed to accept less money in return for relative freedom).[25]

What emerges here is a problematic blurring of art and creativity: two overlapping terms that not only have different demographic connotations but also distinct discourses concerning their complexity, instrumentalisa-tion and accessibility.[26] Through the discourse of creativity, the elitist activity of art is democratised, although today this leads to business rather than to Beuys. The dehierarchising rhetoric of artists whose projects seek to facilitate creativity ends up sounding identical to government cultural policy geared towards the twin mantras of social inclusion and creative cities. Yet artistic practice has an element of critical negation and an ability to sustain contradiction that cannot be reconciled with the quantifiable imperatives of positivist economics. Artists and works of art can operate in a space of antagonism or negation vis-à-vis society, a tension that the ideological discourse of creativity reduces to a unified context and instru-mentalises for more efficacious profiteering.

The conflation between the discourses of art and creativity can be seen in the writing of numerous artists and curators on participatory art, where the criteria for the work's assessment in both cases is essentially sociologi-cal and driven by demonstrable outcomes. Take for example the curator Charles Esche, writing on the project *Tenantspin*, an internet-based TV station for the elderly residents of a run-down tower block in Liverpool (2000–), by the Danish collective Superflex. Esche intersperses his article with long quotes from governmental reports about the state of British council housing, indicating the primacy of a sociological context for under-standing the artists' project. But his central judgement about *Tenantspin* concerns its effectiveness as a 'tool' that can 'change the image of both the tower block itself and the residents'; in his view, the major achievement of this project is that it has forged a 'stronger sense of community in the build-ing'.[27] Esche is one of Europe's most articulate defenders of politicised artistic practice, and one of its most radical museum directors, but his essay is symptomatic of the critical tendency I am drawing attention to. His

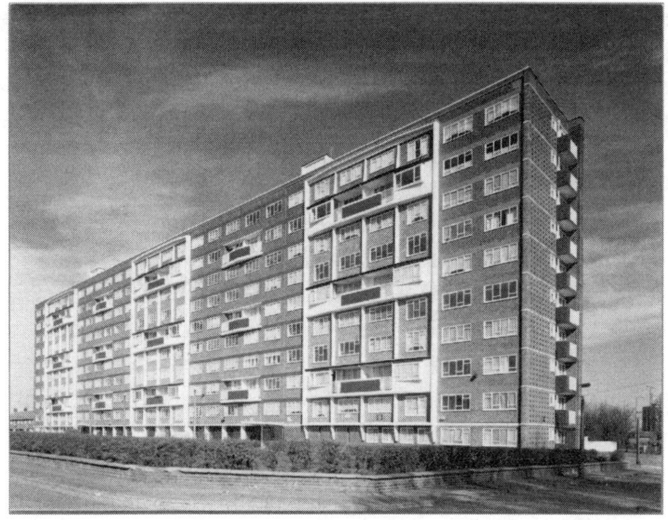

Superflex, *Tenantspin* (2000) view of Coronation Court, Liverpool

decision not to address what it means for Superflex to be doing this project *as art* ultimately renders these value judgements indistinguishable from government arts policy with its emphasis on verifiable outcomes.

And so we slide into a sociological discourse – what happened to aesthetics? This word has been highly contentious for several decades now, since its status – at least in the Anglophone world – has been rendered untouchable through the academy's embrace of social history and identity politics, which have repeatedly drawn attention to the way in which the aesthetic masks inequalities, oppressions and exclusions (of race, gender, class, and so on). This has tended to promote an equation between aesthetics and the

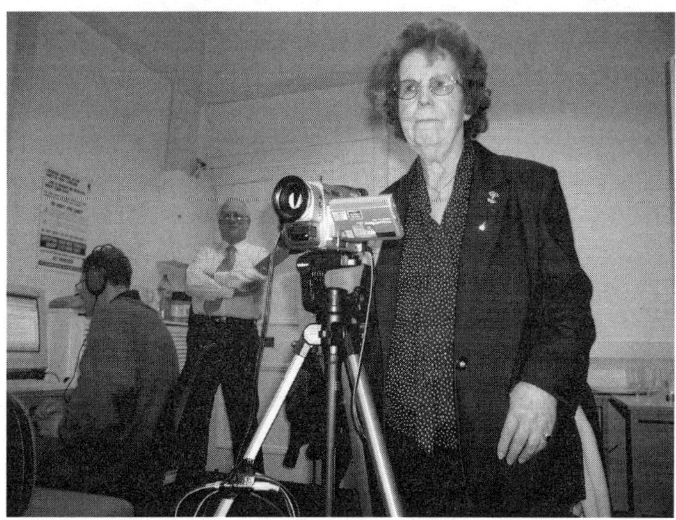

Superflex, *Tenantspin* (2000), Kath operating film equipment

triple enemy of formalism, decontextualisation and depoliticisation; the result is that aesthetics became synonymous with the market and conservative cultural hierarchy. While these arguments were necessary to dismantle the deeply entrenched authority of the white male elites in the 1970s, today they have hardened into critical orthodoxy.

It was not until the new millennium that this paradigm was put under pressure, largely through the writing of Jacques Rancière, who has rehabilitated the idea of aesthetics and connected it to politics as an integrally related domain. Before the popularisation of his writings, few artists seeking to engage with socio-political issues in their work would have willingly framed their practice as 'aesthetic'. Although Rancière's arguments are philosophical rather than art critical, he has undertaken important work in debunking some of the binaries upon which the discourse of politicised art has relied: individual/collective, author/spectator, active/passive, real life/art. In so doing, he has opened the way towards the development of a new artistic terminology by which to discuss and analyse spectatorship, until that point somewhat schizophrenically governed by the critical untouchability of Walter Benjamin ('The Work of Art . . .' and 'The Author as Producer') and a hostility to consumer spectacle (as theorised by Debord).[28] When I began researching this project, there seemed to be a huge gulf between market-driven painting and sculpture on the one hand, and long-term socially engaged projects on the other. At the conclusion of this research, participatory work has a significant presence within art schools, museums and commercial galleries, even if this accommodation is accompanied by a degree of mainstream confusion as to how it should be read *as art*. Without finding a more nuanced language to address the artistic status of this work, we risk discussing these practices solely in positivist terms, that is, by focusing on demonstrable impact. One of the aims of this book, then, is to emphasise the aesthetic in the sense of *aisthesis*: an autonomous regime of experience that is not reducible to logic, reason or morality. To begin this task, we first need to examine the criteria by which socially engaged projects are currently articulated.

II. The Ethical Turn

It is often remarked that socially engaged practices are extremely difficult to discuss within the conventional frameworks of art criticism. Take, for example, Liisa Roberts' *What's the Time in Vyborg?* (2000–), a long-term project in the city of Vyborg on the Russian-Finnish border, undertaken with the assistance of six teenage girls, and comprising a series of workshops, exhibitions, performances, films and events carried out around the still-ongoing restoration of the city library that Alvar Aalto designed and built in 1935. The critic Reinaldo Laddaga has commented in relation to this project that

What's the Time in Vyborg? is difficult – perhaps even impossible – to assess as an 'art' project in as much as the criteria of its success for those involved could not be described as artistic. The objective of Roberts and the core group of *What's the Time in Vyborg?* wasn't simply to offer an aesthetic or intellectual experience to an outside public but to facilitate the creation of a temporary community engaged in the process of solving a series of practical problems. The project aspired to have a real efficacy in the site in which it came to happen. Accordingly, any valuation of it should be at the same time artistic and ethical, practical and political.[29]

This brief quotation throws up a number of important tropes: the division between first-hand participants and secondary audience ('temporary community' versus 'outside public'), and the division between artistic goals and problem solving/concrete outcomes. Inasmuch as Laddaga calls for a more integrated mode of addressing such work ('artistic and ethical, practical and political'), his writing also points to a tacit hierarchy between these terms: aesthetic experience is 'simply' offered, compared to the implicitly more worthwhile task of 'real efficacy'. This uneven inclination towards the social component of this project suggests that contemporary art's 'social turn' not only designates an orientation towards concrete goals in art, but also the critical perception that these are more substantial, 'real' and important than artistic experiences. At the same time, these perceived social achievements are never compared with actual (and innovative) social projects taking place *outside* the realm of art; they remain on the level of an emblematic ideal, and derive their critical value in opposition to more traditional, expressive and object-based modes of artistic practice. In short, the point of comparison and reference for participatory projects always returns to contemporary art, despite the fact that they are perceived to be worthwhile precisely because they are non-artistic. The aspiration is always to move beyond art, but never to the point of comparison with comparable projects in the social domain.[30]

All of this is not to denigrate participatory art and its supporters, but to draw attention to a series of critical operations in which the difficulty of describing the artistic value of participatory projects is resolved by resorting to ethical criteria. In other words, instead of turning to appropriately social practices as points of comparison, the tendency is always to compare artists' projects with other artists on the basis of ethical one-upmanship – the degree to which artists supply a good or bad model of collaboration – and to criticise them for any hint of potential exploitation that fails to 'fully' represent their subjects (as if such a thing were possible). This emphasis on process over product – or, perhaps more accurately, on process *as* product – is justified on the straightforward basis of inverting capitalism's predilection for the contrary. Consensual collaboration is

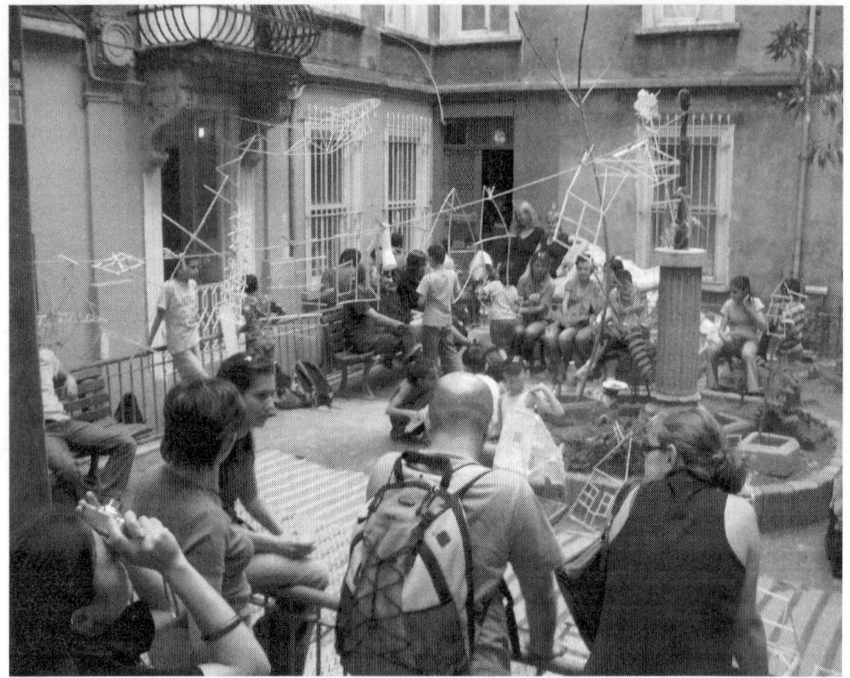

Oda Projesi, *FAIL # BETTER* project by Lina Faller, Thomas Stussi, Marcel Mieth and Marian Burchardt, 2004. Two-week workshop about building structures in the city, in the Oda Projesi courtyard.

valued over artistic mastery and individualism, regardless of what the project sets out to do or actually achieves.

The writing around the Turkish artists' collective Oda Projesi provides a clear example of this tendency. Oda Projesi is a group of three artists who, between 1997 and 2005, based their activities around a three-room apartment in the Galata district of Istanbul (*oda projesi* is Turkish for 'room project'). The apartment provided a platform for projects generated by the group in co-operation with their neighbours, such as a children's workshop with the Turkish painter Komet, a community picnic with the sculptor Erik Göngrich, and a parade for children organised by the Tem Yapin theatre group. Oda Projesi argue that they wish to open up a context for the possibility of exchange and dialogue, motivated by a desire to integrate with their surroundings. They insist that they are not setting out to improve or heal a situation – one of their project leaflets contains the slogan 'exchange not change' – though they evidently see their work as oppositional. By working directly with their neighbours to organise workshops and events, they evidently wished to produce a more creative and participatory social fabric. The group talks of creating 'blank spaces' and 'holes' in the face of an over-organised and bureaucratic society, and of being 'mediators' between groups of people who normally don't have contact with each other.[31]

Because much of Oda Projesi's work exists on the level of art education and neighbourhood events, immediate reaction to it tends to include praise for their being dynamic members of the community bringing art to a wider audience. It is important that they are opening up the space for non-object-based practice in Turkey, a country whose art academies and art market are still largely oriented towards painting and sculpture. The fact that it is three women who have undertaken this task in a still largely patriarchal culture is not insignificant. But their conceptual gesture of reducing authorship to the role of facilitation ultimately leaves little to separate their work from arts and museum educators worldwide, or indeed the community arts tradition (discussed in Chapter 6). Even when transposed to Sweden, Germany, South Korea and the other countries where Oda Projesi have exhibited, it is difficult to distinguish their approach from a slew of community-based practices that revolve around the predictable formula of children's workshops, discussions, meals, film screenings and walks. When I interviewed the group and asked by what criteria they judge their own work, they replied that dynamic and sustained relationships provide their markers of success, rather than aesthetic considerations. Indeed, because their practice is based on collaboration, Oda Projesi consider the aesthetic to be 'a dangerous word' that should not be brought into the discussion.[32]

Where artists lead, curators follow. Oda Projesi's approach is reiterated by the Swedish curator Maria Lind in an essay on their work. Lind is an ardent supporter of political and relational practices, and she undertakes her curatorial work with a trenchant commitment to criticality. In her essay on Oda Projesi, she notes that the group is not interested in showing or exhibiting art but in 'using art as a means for creating and recreating new relations between people'.[33] She goes on to discuss a project she produced with Oda Projesi in Riem, near Munich, in which the group collaborated with a local Turkish community to organise a tea party, hairdressing and Tupperware parties, guided tours led by the residents, and the installation of a long roll of paper that people wrote and drew on to stimulate conversations. Lind compares this endeavour to Thomas Hirschhorn's *Bataille Monument* (2002), his well-known collaboration with a mainly Turkish community in Kassel for Documenta 11. In this work, as in many of his social projects, Hirschhorn pays people to work with him on realising an elaborate installation dedicated to a philosopher, which often includes an exhibition display area, a library and a bar.[34] In making this comparison, Lind implies that Oda Projesi, contrary to Thomas Hirschhorn, are the better artists because of the equal status they give to their collaborators: '[Hirschhorn's] aim is to create art. For the *Bataille Monument* he had already prepared, and in part also executed, a plan on which he needed help to implement. His participants were paid for their work and their role was that of the "executor" and not "co-creator".'[35] Lind goes on to argue that Hirschhorn's work was rightly criticised for '"exhibiting" and making

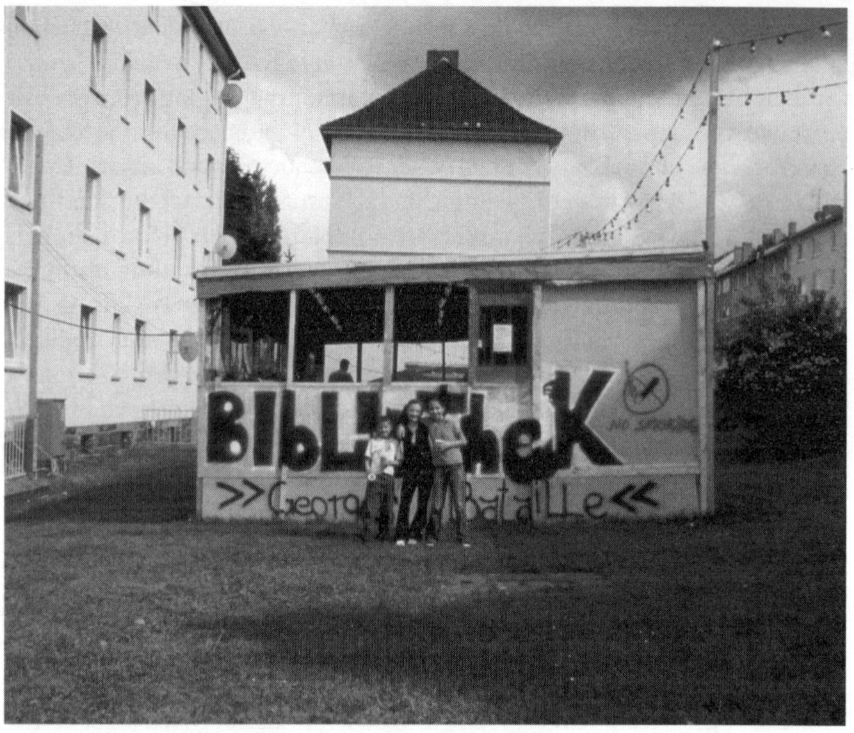

Thomas Hirschhorn, *Bataille Monument*, 2002. Installation view showing library.

exotic marginalized groups and thereby contributing to a form of a social pornography'. By contrast, she writes, Oda Projesi 'work with groups of people in their immediate environments and allow them to wield great influence on the project'.

It's worth looking closely at Lind's criteria here. Her comparison is based on an ethics of authorial renunciation: the work of Oda Projesi is better than that of Thomas Hirschhorn because it exemplifies a superior model of collaborative practice, one in which individual authorship is suppressed in favour of facilitating the creativity of others. The visual, conceptual and experiential accomplishments of the respective projects are sidelined in favour of a judgement on the artists' relationship with their collaborators. Hirschhorn's (purportedly) exploitative relationship is compared negatively to Oda Projesi's inclusive generosity. In other words, Lind downplays what might be interesting in Oda Projesi's work *as art* – the achievement of making social dialogue a medium, the significance of dematerialising a work of art into social process, or the specific affective intensity of social exchange triggered by these neighbourhood experiences. Instead her criticism is dominated by *ethical* judgements on working procedures and intentionality. Art and the aesthetic are denigrated as merely visual, superfluous, academic – less important than concrete outcomes, or the proposition of a 'model' or prototype for social relations. At the same time, Oda Projesi are constantly compared to other artists, rather than to similar (but non-art) projects in the social sphere.

This value system is particularly marked in curatorial writing, but theorists have also reinforced the disposition towards the ethical. The front cover of Suzanne Lacy's *Mapping the Terrain* (1995) reads: 'To search for the good and make it matter', while the essays inside support a redefinition of art 'not primarily as a product but as a process of value-finding, a set of philosophies, an ethical action'.[36] The curator and critic Lucy Lippard concludes her book *The Lure of the Local* (1997) – a discussion of site-specific art from an ecological and post-colonial perspective – with an eight-point 'ethic of place' for artists who work with communities.[37] Grant Kester's key text on collaborative art, *Conversation Pieces* (2004), while lucidly articulating many of the problems associated with socially engaged practices, nevertheless advocates an art of concrete interventions in which the artist does not occupy 'a position of pedagogical or creative mastery'.[38] The Dutch critic Erik Hagoort, in his book *Good Intentions: Judging the Art of Encounter* (2005), argues that we must not shy away from making moral judgements on this art: viewers should weigh up the benefits of each artist's aims and objectives.[39] In each of these examples, the status of the artist's intentionality (e.g. their humble lack of authorship) is privileged over a discussion of the work's artistic identity. Ironically, this leads to a situation in which not only collectives but individual artists are praised for their conscious authorial renunciation.[40] This line of thinking has led to an ethically charged climate in which participatory and socially engaged art has become largely exempt from art criticism: emphasis is continually shifted away from the disruptive *specificity* of a given practice and onto a *generalised* set of ethical precepts. Accordingly, a common trope in this discourse is to evaluate each project as a 'model', echoing Benjamin's claim in 'The Author as Producer' that a work of art is better the more participants it brings into contact with the processes of production.[41] Through this language of the ideal system, the model apparatus and the 'tool' (to use Superflex's terminology), art enters a realm of useful, ameliorative and ultimately modest gestures, rather than the creation of singular acts that leave behind them a troubling wake.

If ethical criteria have become the norm for judging this art, then we also need to question what ethics are being advocated. In *Conversation Pieces*, Grant Kester argues that consultative and 'dialogic' art necessitates a shift in our understanding of what art is – away from the visual and sensory (which are individual experiences) and towards 'discursive exchange and negotiation'.[42] He compares two projects undertaken in East London in the early 1990s: Rachel Whiteread's concrete sculpture *House* (1993), cast from the inside of a demolished terrace, and Loraine Leeson's billboard project *West Meets East* (1992), a collaboration with local Bengali schoolgirls. He argues that neither is the better work of art; they simply make different

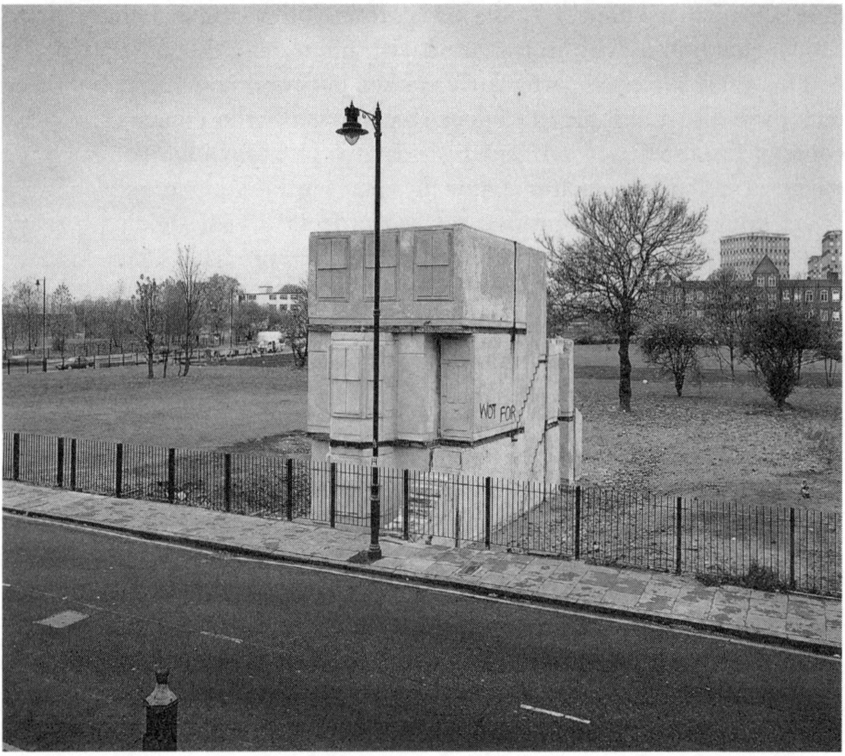

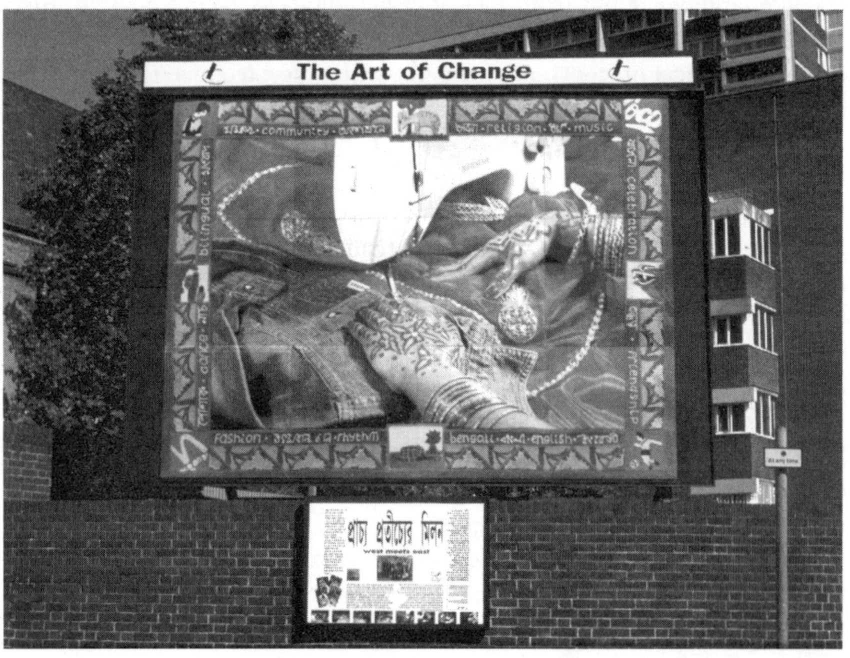

Rachel Whiteread, *House*, 1993

Loraine Leeson, *West Meets East*, 1992

demands upon the viewer. However, his tone clearly contains a judgement: *House* emerged from a studio practice that has little to do with the specific conditions of Bow, while Leeson and her partner Peter Dunn (working under the name The Art of Change) 'attempt to learn as much as possible about the cultural and political histories of the people with whom they work, as well as their particular needs and skills. Their artistic identity is based in part upon their capacity to listen, openly and actively.'[43] In this type of project, empathetic identification is highly valued, since only this can facilitate 'a reciprocal exchange that allows us to think outside our own lived experience and establish a more compassionate relationship with others'.[44] Here I should be clear: my aim is not to denigrate Leeson's work, but to point out Kester's aversion to dealing with the *forms* of both works and the *affective* responses they elicit as equally crucial to the work's meaning – be this the jarring conjunction of traditional decorative patterns and garish colour photography in the montage aesthetic of *West Meets East*, or the bleak, haunted, cancerous white husk of Whiteread's *House*.

Kester's emphasis on compassionate identification with the other is typical of the discourse around participatory art, in which an ethics of interpersonal interaction comes to prevail over a politics of social justice. It represents a familiar summary of the intellectual trends inaugurated by identity politics and consolidated in 1990s theory: respect for the other, recognition of difference, protection of fundamental liberties, and a concern for human rights. The philosopher Peter Dews has described this development as an 'ethical turn', in which 'Questions of conscience and obligation, of recognition and respect, of justice and law, which not so long ago would have been dismissed as the residue of an outdated humanism, have returned to occupy, if not centre stage, then something pretty close to it.'[45] At the centre of opposition to this trend have been the philosophers Alain Badiou, Jacques Rancière and Slavoj Žižek who, in different ways, remain sceptical of the jargon of human rights and identitarian politics.[46] It might seem extreme to bring these philosophical indictments of the ethical turn to bear upon the well-meaning advocates of socially collaborative art, but these thinkers provide a poignant lens through which to view the humanism that pervades this art critical discourse. In insisting upon consensual dialogue, sensitivity to difference risks becoming a new kind of repressive norm – one in which artistic strategies of disruption, intervention or over-identification are immediately ruled out as 'unethical' because all forms of authorship are equated with authority and indicted as totalising. Such a denigration of authorship allows simplistic oppositions to remain in place: active versus passive viewer, egotistical versus collaborative artist, privileged versus needy community, aesthetic complexity versus simple expression, cold autonomy versus convivial community.[47]

A resistance to rupturing these categories is found in Kester's rejection of any art that might offend or trouble its audience – most notably the historical avant-garde, within whose lineage he nevertheless wishes to situate social participation as a radical practice. Kester criticises Dada and Surrealism for seeking to 'shock' viewers into being more sensitive and receptive to the world – because for him, this position turns the artist into a privileged bearer of insights, patronisingly informing audiences as to 'how things really are'. He also attacks post-structuralism for promulgating the idea that it is sufficient for art to *reveal* social conditions, rather than to change them; Kester argues that this actually reinforces a class division whereby the educated elite speak down to the less privileged. (It is striking that this argument seems to present the participants of collaborative art as dumb and fragile creatures, constantly at risk of being misunderstood or exploited.) My concern here is less the morality of who speaks to whom and how, but Kester's aversion to disruption, since it self-censors on the basis of second-guessing how others will think and respond. The upshot is that idiosyncratic or controversial ideas are subdued and normalised in favour of a consensual behaviour upon whose irreproachable sensitivity we can all rationally agree. By contrast, I would argue that unease, discomfort or frustration – along with fear, contradiction, exhilaration and absurdity – can be crucial to any work's artistic impact. This is not to say that ethics are unimportant in a work of art, nor irrelevant to politics, only that they do not always have to be announced and performed in such a direct and saintly fashion (I will return to this idea below). An over-solicitousness that judges in advance what people are capable of coping with can be just as insidious as intending to offend them. As my case studies in the chapters that follow bear out, participants are more than capable of dealing with artists who reject Aristotelian moderation in favour of providing a more complicated access to social truth, however eccentric, extreme or irrational this might be. If there is an ethical framework underpinning this book, then, it concerns a Lacanian fidelity to the singularity of each project, paying attention to its symbolic ruptures, and the ideas and affects it generates for the participants and viewers, rather than deferring to the social pressure of a pre-agreed tribunal in which a cautious, self-censoring pragmatism will always hold sway.

III. The Aesthetic Regime

As I have already indicated, one of the biggest problems in the discussion around socially engaged art is its disavowed relationship to the aesthetic. By this I do not mean that the work does not fit established notions of the attractive or the beautiful, even though this is often the case; many social projects photograph very badly, and these images convey very little of the contextual information so crucial to understanding the work. More significant is the tendency for advocates of socially collaborative art to view the aesthetic as (at best) merely visual and (at worst) an elitist realm of unbridled seduction complicit with spectacle. At the same time, these advocates also argue that art is an independent zone, free from the pressures of accountability, institutional bureaucracy and the rigours of specialisation.[48] The upshot is that art is perceived both as *too removed* from the real world *and yet* as the only space from which it is possible to experiment: art must paradoxically remain autonomous *in order to* initiate or achieve a model for social change.

This antinomy has been clearly articulated by Jacques Rancière, whose work since the late 1990s has developed a highly influential account of the relation between aesthetics and politics. Rancière argues that the system of art as we have understood it since the Enlightenment – a system he calls 'the aesthetic regime of art' – is predicated precisely on a tension and confusion between *autonomy* (the desire for art to be at one remove from means–ends relationships) and heteronomy (that is, the blurring of art and life). For Rancière, the primal scene of this new regime is the moment when, in Schiller's fifteenth letter *On the Aesthetic Education of Man* (1794), he describes a Greek statue known as the Juno Ludovisi as a specimen of 'free appearance'. Following Kant, Schiller does not judge the work as an accurate depiction of the goddess, nor as an idol to be worshipped. Rather, he views it as self-contained, dwelling in itself without purpose or volition, and potentially available to all. As such, the sculpture stands as an example of – and promises – a new community, one that suspends reason and power in a state of equality. The aesthetic regime of art, as inaugurated by Schiller and the Romantics, is therefore premised on the paradox that 'art is art to the extent that it is something else than art': that it is a sphere *both* at one remove from politics *and* yet always already political because it contains the promise of a better world.[49]

What is significant in Rancière's reworking of the term 'aesthetic' is that it concerns *aisthesis*, a mode of sensible perception proper to artistic products. Rather than considering the *work of art* to be autonomous, he draws attention to the autonomy of our *experience* in relation to art. In this, Rancière reprises Kant's argument that an aesthetic judgement suspends the domination of the faculties by reason (in morality) and understanding (in knowledge). As taken up by Schiller – and Rancière – this freedom suggests the possibility of politics (understood here as dissensus), because the undecidability of aesthetic experience implies a questioning of how the world is organised, and therefore the possibility of changing or redistributing that same world.[50] Aesthetics and politics therefore overlap in their concern for the distribution and sharing out of ideas, abilities and experiences to certain subjects – what Rancière calls *le partage du sensible*. In this framework, it is not possible to conceive of an aesthetic judgement that is not at the same time a political judgement – a comment on the 'distribution of the places and of the capacities or incapacities attached to those places'.[51] While brilliantly theorising the relationship of aesthetics to politics, one of the drawbacks of this theory is that it opens the door for all art to be political, since the *sensible* can be *partagé* both in progressive and reactionary ways; the door is wide open for both.

In *Malaise dans l'esthétique*, Rancière is nevertheless outspokenly critical, attacking what he calls the 'ethical turn' in contemporary thought, whereby 'politics and art today are increasingly submitted to moral judgement bearing on the validity of their principles and the consequences of their practices'.[52] It is important to note that his targets are not the kind of art that forms the subject of this book, but Jean-François Lyotard's arguments concerning the unrepresentability of the sublime (vis-à-vis representations of the Holocaust in art and film), together with relational art as theorised by Nicolas Bourriaud. For Rancière, the ethical turn does not, strictly speaking, denote the submission of art and politics to moral judgements, but rather the collapse of artistic and political dissensus in new forms of consensual order. His political target is even more important to bear in mind: the Bush administration's 'war on terror', in which 'infinite evil' was subjected to an 'infinite justice' undertaken in the name of human rights. As in politics, Rancière argues, so too in art: 'Just as politics effaces itself in the coupling of consensus and infinite justice, these tend to be redistributed between a vision of art dedicated to the service of the social bond and another dedicated to the interminable witnessing of the catastrophe.'[53] Moreover, these two developments are linked: an art of proximity (restoring the social bond) is simultaneously an art seeking to witness what is structurally excluded from society. The exemplary ethical gesture in art is therefore a strategic obfuscation of the political and the aesthetic:

> by replacing matters of class conflict by matters of inclusion and exclusion, [contemporary art] puts worries about the 'loss of the social bond', concerns with 'bare humanity' or tasks of empowering threatened identities in the place of political concerns. Art is summoned thus to put its political potentials at work in reframing a sense of community, mending the social bond, etc. Once more, politics and aesthetics vanish together in Ethics.[54]

Although we should be sceptical of Rancière's reading of relational art (which derives from Bourriaud's text rather than artists' works), his arguments are worth rehearsing here in order to make the point that, in his critique of the ethical turn, he is not opposed to ethics, only to its instrumentalisation as a strategic zone in which political and aesthetic dissensus collapses. That said, ethics stands as a territory that (for Rancière) has little to do with aesthetics proper, since it belongs to a previous model of understanding art. In his system, the aesthetic regime of art is preceded by two other regimes, the first of which is an 'ethical regime of images' governed by the twofold question of the truth-content of images and the uses to which they are put – in other words, their effects and ends. Central to this regime is Plato's denigration of mimesis. The second is the 'representative regime of the arts', a regime of visibility by which the fine arts are classified according to a logic of what can be done and made in each art, a logic that corresponds to the overall hierarchy of social and political occupations. This regime is essentially Aristotelian, but stretches to the academy system of the fine arts and its hierarchy of the genres. The aesthetic regime of art, ushered in with the Enlightenment, continues today. It permits everything to be a potential subject or material for art, everyone to be a potential viewer of this art, and denotes the aesthetic as an autonomous form of life.

One of Rancière's key contributions to contemporary debates around art and politics is therefore to reinvent the term 'aesthetic' so that it denotes a specific mode of experience, including the very linguistic and theoretical domain in which thought about art takes place. In this logic, all claims to be 'anti-aesthetic' or reject art *still function within the aesthetic regime*. The aesthetic for Rancière therefore signals an ability to think contradiction: the productive contradiction of art's relationship to social change, which is characterised by the paradox of belief in art's autonomy *and* in it being inextricably bound to the promise of a better world to come. While this antinomy is apparent in many avant-garde practices of the last century, it seems particularly pertinent to analysing participatory art and the legiti-mating narratives it has attracted. In short, the aesthetic doesn't need to be sacrificed at the altar of social change, because it always already contains this ameliorative promise.

Because of this structural openness, Rancière's theory of the politics of aesthetics has been co-opted for the defence of wildly differing artistic practices (including a conservative return to beauty), even though his ideas do not easily translate into critical judgements. He argues, for example, against 'critical art' that intends to raise our consciousness by inviting us to 'see the signs of Capital behind everyday objects', since such didacticism effectively removes the perverse strangeness that bears testimony to the rationalised world and its oppressive intolerability.[55] Yet his preferences incline towards works that nevertheless offer a clear (one might say didactic) resistance to a topical issue – such as Martha Rosler's anti-Vietnam collages *Bringing the War Home* (1967–72), or Chris Burden's *The Other Vietnam Memorial* (1991). Despite Rancière's claim that topical or political content is not essential to political art, it is telling that the 'distribution of the sensible' is never demonstrated through abstract forms unrelated to a political theme. In the chapters that follow, Rancière has therefore informed my thinking in two ways: firstly, in his attention to the affective capabilities of art that avoids the pitfalls of a didactic critical position in favour of rupture and ambiguity.[56] Good art, implies Rancière, must negotiate the tension that (on the one hand) pushes art towards 'life' and that (on the other) separates aesthetic sensoriality from other forms of sensible experience. This friction ideally produces the formation of elements 'capable of speaking twice: from their readability and from their unreadability'.[57] Secondly, I have adopted Rancière's idea of art as an autonomous realm of experience in which there is no privileged medium. The meaning of artistic forms shifts in relation to the uses also made of these forms by society at large, and as such they have no intrinsic or fixed political affiliation. The history traced in this book aims to reinforce this point by situating participation as a constantly moving target. Audience participation techniques pioneered in the 1960s by the Happenings, and by companies like The Living Theatre and Théâtre du Soleil, have become commonplace conventions in the theatrical mainstream.[58] Today we see a further devaluation of participation in the form of reality television, where ordinary people can participate both as would-be celebrities and as the voters who decide their fate. Today, participation also includes social networking sites and any number of communication technologies relying on user-generated content. Any discussion of participation in contemporary art needs to take on board these broader cultural connotations, and their implementation by cultural policy, in order to ascertain its meaning.

IV. Directed Reality: The Battle of Orgreave

Despite Rancière's argument that the politics of aesthetics is a *meta*politics (rather than a party politics), his theory tends to sidestep the question of how we might more specifically address the ideological affiliations of any given work. This problem comes to the fore when we look at a work that has arguably become the epitome of participatory art: *The Battle of Orgreave* (2001) by the British artist Jeremy Deller. Since the mid 1990s, Deller's work has frequently forged unexpected encounters between diverse constituencies, and displays a strong interest in class, subculture and self-organisation – interests that have taken the form both of performances (*Acid Brass*, 1996) and temporary exhibitions (*Unconvention*, 1999; *Folk Archive*, 2000–; *From One Revolution to Another*, 2008). *The Battle of Orgreave* is perhaps his best-known work, a performance re-enacting a violent clash between miners and mounted policeman in 1984. Nearly 8,000 riot police clashed with around 5,000 striking miners in the Yorkshire village of Orgreave; this was one of several violent confrontations prompted by Margaret Thatcher's assault on the mining industry and signalled a turning point in UK industrial relations, weakening the trade union movement and enabling the Conservative government to consolidate a programme of free trade. Deller's reconstruction of this event brought former miners and local residents together with a number of historical re-enactment societies who rehearsed and then restaged the conflict for the public, on the site of the original hostilities in Orgreave. At

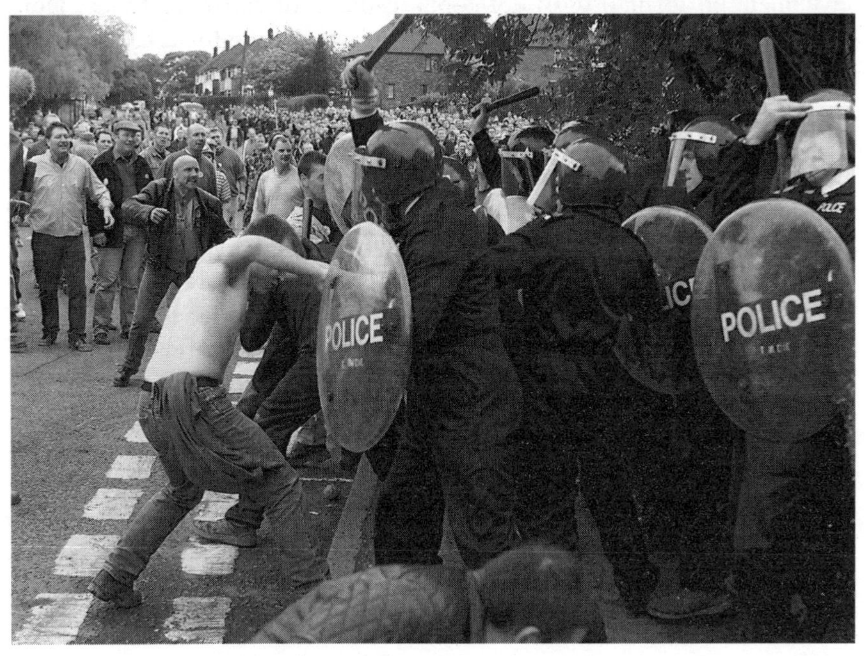

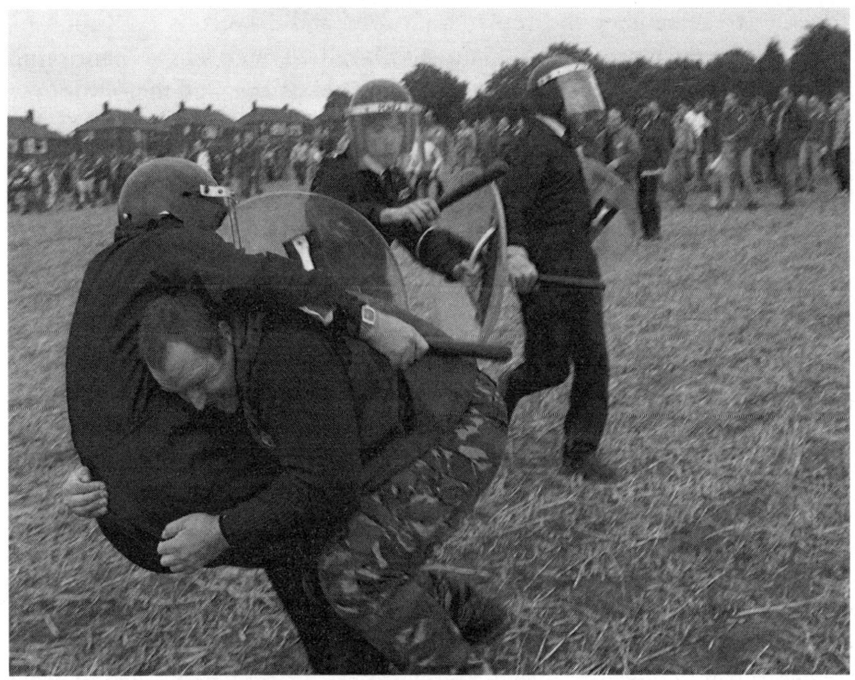

Jeremy Deller, *The Battle of Orgreave*, 2001

the same time, Deller's work has a multiple ontology: not just the live re-enactment on 17 June 2001, but also a feature-length film by Mike Figgis, who explicitly uses the event as a vehicle for his indictment of the Thatcher government (*The Battle of Orgreave*, 2001), a publication of oral history (*The English Civil War Part II: Personal Accounts of the 1984–85 Miners' Strike*, 2002), and an archive (*The Battle of Orgreave Archive [An Injury to One is an Injury to All]*, 2004).[59]

At first glance *The Battle of Orgreave* appears to be therapeutic: letting former miners re-live the traumatic events of the 1980s, and inviting some of them to switch roles and play policemen. But the work didn't seem to heal a wound so much as reopen it, as evidenced in the video documentation and publication, which includes a CD of recorded testimonies by the protagonists.[60] Figgis's film shows emotional interviews with former miners, a clear testimony to ongoing class antagonism, belying Thatcher's claim that 'there is no such thing as society'.[61] The ex-miners' anger at their treatment by the Conservative government is still raw, and emerges in casual footage of rehearsals the day before, where several participants are choked with bitterness. Importantly, however, while the book and film are partisan in their approach to the miners' strike, the performance itself is more ambiguous. Figgis's video footage of the latter takes the form of short sequences inserted between his interviews with former miners, and the clash of tone is disconcerting. Although Deller's event gathered people together to remember and replay a charged and disastrous event, it took place in circumstances more akin to a village fête, with a brass band, children running around, and local stalls selling plants and pies; there was even an interval between the two 'acts' when mid-1980s chart hits were played (as one critic noted, in this context '"Two Tribes" and "I Want to Break Free" acquired an unexpected political urgency').[62] As the film footage testifies, *The Battle of Orgreave* hovers uneasily between menacing violence and family entertainment. In other words, it is hard to reduce *The Battle of Orgreave* to a simple message or social function (be this therapy or counter-propaganda), because the visual and dramatic character of the event was constitutively contradictory. For David Gilbert, Figgis's film is most successful when it captures this convergence of emotions, showing 'how the re-enactment provoked memories of pain, camaraderie, defeat and indeed the excitement of conflict'.[63]

In his introduction to the publication *The English Civil War Part II*, Deller observes that 'As an artist, I was interested in how far an idea could be taken, especially one that is on the face of it a contradiction in terms, "a recreation of something that was essentially chaos." '[64] This problem of attempting to perform chaos carried a double risk: either deadening a re-staged riot into over-organised choreography, or conversely, losing order so entirely that the event becomes illegible turmoil. These poles were managed through the imposition of a structure that had a tight conceptual kernel – a re-enactment of the strike by former miners and battle re-enactment societies – but allowed for formal laxity and improvisation, even while the 'conditions of participation' issued to the performers were fairly strict.[65] It is precisely here that one sees the grey *artistic* work of participatory art – deciding how much or how little scripting to enforce – rather than in the *ethical* black-and-white of 'good' or 'bad' collaboration. The artist Paweł Althamer has referred to this strategy as 'directed reality', and this evocative phrase is a useful way to describe the combination of clear conceptual premise and partially unpredictable realisation that characterises some of the best examples of contemporary participation (including Althamer's own).[66] At one point in Figgis's film, Deller is interviewed crossing the field where the action is about to happen, noting with trepidation that the project has developed a life of its own. When asked by the interviewer 'How's it going?', he replies uneasily: 'It's going interesting . . . This is the first time we've actually got these two groups together, and it's difficult to say what's going to happen. Look at it . . . I'm not in charge any more, really. As you would be in a real situation like this, you'd be a bit excited and a bit worried as well.'

The point I am making is that this anxious thrill is inseparable from the work's overall meaning, since every one of Deller's choices had both a social and artistic resonance. The decision to restage one of the last major working-class industrial disputes in the UK by involving over twenty battle re-enactment societies (including the Sealed Knot, the Wars of the Roses Federation and the Southern Skirmish Association) impacted on both the process and outcome of the project, as well as its broader cultural resonance. In terms of process, it brought the middle-class battle re-enactors into direct contact with working-class miners. Deller noted that 'A lot of the members of historical re-enactment societies were terrified of the miners. During the 80s they had obviously believed what they had read in the press and had the idea that the men that they would be working with on the re-enactment were going to be outright hooligans or revolutionaries.'[67] This had the effect of dismantling (and indeed seemed to critique) any nostalgia for sentimental class unity. On the level of production, meanwhile, the battle re-enactment societies were essential to accomplishing the dramatic and technical success of the re-performance, but also to shifting *The Battle of Orgreave* away from a journalistic register. Since battle re-enactors usually perform scenes from English history at a sufficiently safe remove from contemporary politics, such as Roman invasions or the Civil War, the inclusion of these societies symbolically elevated the relatively recent events at Orgreave to the status of English history (as Deller makes explicit in the title of his publication, *The English Civil War Part II*). But this also forced an uneasy convergence between those for whom the repetition of events was traumatic, and those for whom it was a stylised and sentimental invocation. Re-educating the battle re-enactors to be more politically self-conscious about their activities emerged as an important subtheme of the event.

The Battle of Orgreave therefore manages to dialogue simultaneously with social history and art history, a point reinforced by the work's reception in the mainstream media, journals of oral history and art magazines. In 1984, the press presented the riot as having been started by unruly miners, rather than by the decision to send mounted cavalry into the frontline of strikers – an impression achieved by reverse editing the sequence of events on the television news. Deller has described his counter-narrative as 'history painting from below', evoking a genre of historical writing referred to as 'people's history' or 'history from below'.[68] The work also invites us to make a comparison between two tendencies conventionally considered to be at opposite ends of the cultural spectrum: the eccentric leisure activity of re-enactment (in which bloody battles are enthusiastically replicated as group entertainment) and performance art (then at the outset of a trend for re-enactment). However, Deller's work forms part of a longer history of popular theatre comprising gestures of political re-enactment, including the Paterson Strike Pageant of 1913 and the Storming of the Winter Palace in 1920 (discussed in Chapter 2). Deller does not shy away from these connections, and has referred to *The Battle of Orgreave* both as a contemporary history painting through the medium of performance and as a work of 'community theatre'.[69] In 2004 *The Battle of Orgreave* was given a further

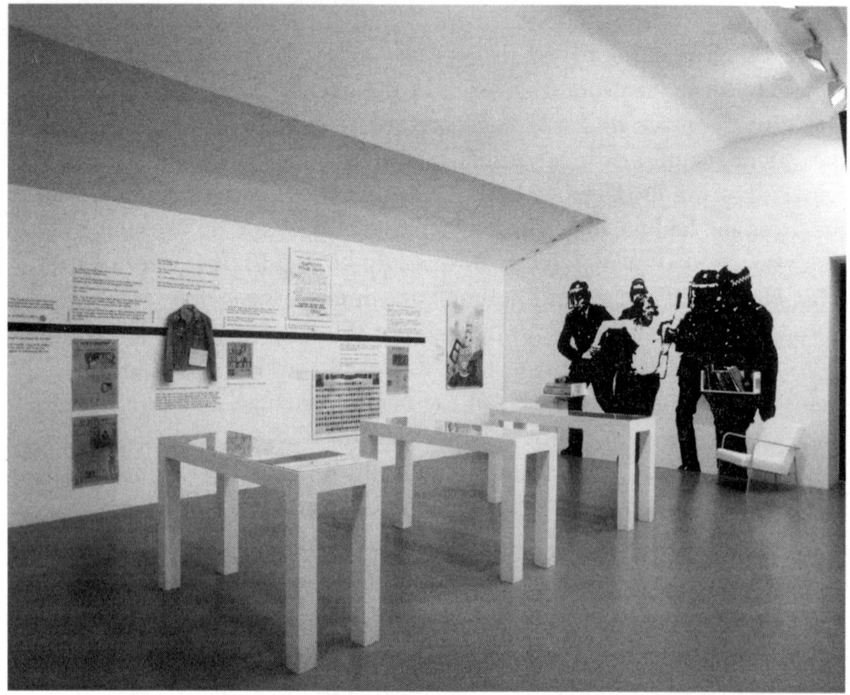

Jeremy Deller, *The Battle of Orgreave Archive (An Injury to One Is an Injury to All)*, 2004

mode of dissemination in the form of the installation *The Battle of Orgreave Archive (An Injury to One Is an Injury to All)*, which comprises a timeline of events leading up to and after the riot at Orgreave, displayed on the gallery walls alongside objects (badges, posters, a jacket, a riot shield, and a painting entitled *I am a Miner's Son* made in a Young Offenders Institution in 2004); a number of vitrines presenting archival information about the National Union of Mineworkers and copies of letters sent to Deller's participants; a small collection of books on the strike available for viewing; a collection of accounts of the strike on CD (with headphones); and two videos on monitors (one of police riot training and one of a re-enactment society 'Festival of History'). *The Battle of Orgreave Archive* is therefore a double archive: a record of the riot in 1984 and the strike leading up to it, but also of the artist's reinterpretation of these events in a performance seventeen years later.

The reason why Deller's *The Battle of Orgreave* has become such a *locus classicus* of recent participatory art therefore seems to be because it is ethically commendable (the artist worked closely in collaboration with former miners) as well as irrefutably political: using a participatory performance and mass media to bring back into popular consciousness 'an unfinished messy history' of the state crushing the working class and turning it against itself.[70] And yet I would like to suggest that *The Battle of Orgreave* also problematises what we mean today when we refer to a work of art as 'political'. It is noticeable that a number of reviewers perceived the event to be politically *non*-committal, particularly when compared to the overt partiality of Figgis's documentary and Deller's collection of oral histories, which privilege the picket position.[71] Others, such as Alice Correia, maintain that the event was biased: 'the casting of the striking miners as "right" and the anti-strike policemen as "wrong" in *Orgreave* avoids some of the complexity of how to position non-striking miners'.[72] The Marxist critic Dave Beech argues that although Deller's aims were 'political' (to rewrite history from below), the involvement of re-enactment societies compromised this intention: *The Battle of Orgreave* became a 'picturing' of politics, rather than political art, and despite Deller's good intentions, the use of battle re-enactment societies meant that the work ultimately took sides 'with the police, the state and Thatcher's government'.[73] For other critics, it was the very performativity of *Orgreave* that allowed it to be more than just a work 'about' the miners' strike, since performance was a way to sustain awareness of history by re-living it as experience.[74] For the artists Cummings and Lewandowska, it was 'a rich, profound, and provocative contemporary art work that uses the legacy of a Marxist cultural critique to bring one strand of this ideological text explosively into the present'.[75] For the artist, *Orgreave* 'is a political work without a doubt', even though it had to be pitched in a neutral way to secure the collaboration of the battle re-enactment societies.[76] Because *Orgreave* commemorates one of the last gasps of class struggle in the UK, we could also add that the re-enactment reflects upon the changed aesthetic lexicon of social protest movements between the 1980s and today, when organised class resistance has morphed into a more sprawling, acephalous anti-globalisation struggle, with its 'multitude' of alignments and positions, no longer aligned around class.[77]

In this brief survey of responses to *The Battle of Orgreave*, the 'political' has myriad connotations: it denotes the theme of a strike, a conflict between the people and the government, the adoption of a working-class perspective, the artist's failure to withstand state co-option, his updating of key Marxist tenets, performance as a critical mode of historical representation, and the nostalgic use of the insignia of working-class demonstrations. The only way to account for the 'political' here is through Rancière's concept of *meta*politics, the destabilising action that produces dissensus about what is sayable and thinkable in the world. At the same time, this conclusion seems inadequate for describing the specific party political interests at play in *The Battle of Orgreave* (in this case, the history of a working-class strike and its suppression by a right-wing government). To argue that *Orgreave* is metapolitical does little to help us articulate the evident – but far from univocal – ideological position of Deller's work: it is neither a straightforward re-enactment of the type produced by the Sealed Knot, nor an agit-prop, activist theatre promoting a political cause.[78] It is tempting to suggest, then, that *Orgreave* has become such a celebrated instance of participatory art not just because it was one of the earliest and highest profile examples of the 2000s, but because Deller's aesthetic decisions also reorganised the traditional expression of leftist politics in art. Rather than celebrating the workers as an unproblematically heroic entity, Deller juxtaposed them with the middle class in order to write a *universal* history of oppression, therefore disrupting not only the traditional tropes of leftist figuration but also the identificatory patterns and tonal character by which these are habitually represented.

The fact that so many views can be thrust at *The Battle of Orgreave*, and that it still emerges intact, is evidence of the work's artistic plenitude: it can accommodate multiple critical judgements, even contradictory ones. *Orgreave* also shows the paucity of the tendency to assess social art projects in terms of good or bad models of collaboration. Rather than being undertaken as a corrective to social fragmentation ('repairing the social bond'), *Orgreave* engages a more complex layering of social and art history. It summons the experiential potency of collective presence and political demonstrations to correct a historical memory, but (as the title of the *Orgreave* archive indicates) it also aspires to extend beyond the miners' strike in 1984–85 and stand symbolically for all breaches of justice and acts of police oppression. In contrast to the dominant discourse of socially engaged art, Deller does not adopt the role of self-suppressing artist-facilitator, and has had to counter criticisms that he exploits his various collaborators.[79] Instead he is a directorial instigator, working in collaboration with a production agency (Artangel), a film director (Figgis), a battle re-enactment specialist (Howard Giles), and hundreds of participants. His authorial role is a trigger for (rather than the final word on) an event that would otherwise have no existence, since its conceptualisation is too idiosyncratic and controversial ever to be initiated by socially responsible institutions. In short, *The Battle of Orgreave*'s potency derives from its singularity, rather than from its exemplarity as a replicable model.

V. Emancipated Spectators

It should be stressed that such an extended discussion of *Orgreave* is only possible because the work takes into account the apparatus of mediation in relation to a live performance. *The Battle of Orgreave*'s multiple identity allows it to reach different circuits of audience: first-hand participants of the event in 2001, and those watching them from the field (primarily Yorkshire locals); those who saw the television broadcast of Figgis's film of this work (Channel 4, 20 October 2002) or who bought the DVD; those who read the book and listen to the CD of interviews; and those who view the archive/installation in the Tate's collection. In these diverse forms, *The Battle of Orgreave* multiplies and redistributes the art historical categories of history painting, performance, documentary and archive, putting them into dialogue with community theatre and historical re-enactment.[80]

Of course, at this point there is usually the objection that artists who end up exhibiting their work in galleries and museums compromise their projects' social and political aspirations; the purer position is not to engage in the commercial field at all, even if this means losing audiences.[81] Not only is the gallery thought to invite a passive mode of reception (compared to the active co-production of collaborative art), but it also reinforces the hierarchies of elite culture. Even if art engages with 'real people', this art is ultimately produced for, and consumed by, a middle-class gallery audience and wealthy collectors. This argument can be challenged in several ways. Firstly, the idea that performance documentation (video, archive, photography) is a betrayal of the authentic, unmediated event has been questioned by numerous theorists in the wake of Peggy Phelan's polemic *Unmarked: The Politics of Performance* (1993).[82] Secondly, the binary of active versus passive hovers over any discussion of participatory art and theatre, to the point where participation becomes an end in itself: as Rancière so pithily observes, 'Even when the dramaturge or the performer does not know what he wants the spectator to do, he knows at least that the spectator has to do something: switch from passivity to activity.'[83] This injunction to activate is pitched both as a counter to false consciousness and as a realisation of the essence of art and theatre as real life. But the binary of active/

passive always ends up in deadlock: either a disparagement of the spectator because he does nothing, while the performers on stage do something – or the converse claim that those who act are inferior to those who are able to look, contemplate ideas, and have critical distance on the world. The two positions can be switched but the structure remains the same. As Rancière argues, both divide a population into those with capacity on one side, and those with incapacity on the other. The binary of active/passive is reductive and unproductive, because it serves only as an allegory of inequality.

This insight can be extended to the argument that high culture, as found in art galleries, is produced for and on behalf of the ruling classes; by contrast, 'the people' (the marginalised, the excluded) can only be emancipated by direct inclusion in the production of a work. This argument – which also underlies arts funding agendas influenced by policies of social inclusion – assumes that the poor can only engage physically, while the middle classes have the leisure to think and critically reflect. The effect of this argument is to reinstate the prejudice by which working-class activity is restricted to manual labour.[84] It is comparable to sociological critiques of art, in which the aesthetic is found to be the preserve of the elite, while the 'real people' are found to prefer the popular, the realist, the hands-on. As Rancière argues, in a scathing response to Pierre Bourdieu's *Distinction* (1979), the sociologist-interviewer announces the results in advance, and finds out what his questions already presuppose: that things are in their place.[85] To argue, in the manner of funding bodies and the advocates of collaborative art alike, that social participation is particularly suited to the task of social inclusion risks not only assuming that participants are already in a position of impotence, it even reinforces this arrangement. Crucially for our argument, Rancière points out that Bourdieu preserves the status quo by never confronting 'the aesthetic thing' directly. The grey area of *aisthesis* is excluded:

> Questions about music without music, fictitious questions of aesthetics about photographs when they are not perceived as aesthetic, all these produce inevitably what is required by the sociologist: the suppression of intermediaries, of points of meeting and exchange between the people of reproduction and the elite of distinction.[86]

Rancière's point is important for drawing attention to the work of art as an intermediary object, a 'third term' to which both the artist and viewer can relate. Discussions of participatory art and its documentation tend to proceed with similar exclusions: without engaging with the 'aesthetic thing', the work of art in all its singularity, everything remains contained and in its place – subordinated to a stark statistical affirmation of use-values, direct effects and a preoccupation with moral exemplarity. Without the possibility of rupturing these categories, there is merely a Platonic assignment of bodies to their good 'communal' place – an ethical regime of images, rather than an aesthetic regime of art.

Yet in any art that uses people as a medium, ethics will never retreat entirely. The task is to relate this concern more closely to *aesthesis*. Some key terms that emerge here are *enjoyment* and *disruption*, and the way these converge in psychoanalytic accounts of making and viewing art. It has become unfashionable to import psychoanalysis into readings of art and artists, but the discipline provides a useful vocabulary for diagnosing the heightened ethical scrutiny that so much participatory art engenders. In his seventh Seminar, on the ethics of psychoanalysis, Jacques Lacan connects the latter to aesthetics via a discussion of sublimation, proposing an ethics founded on a Sadeian reading of Kant.[87] Setting individual *jouissance* against the application of a universal maxim, Lacan argues that it is more ethical for the subject to act in accordance with his or her (unconscious) desire than to modify his or her behaviour for the eyes of the Big Other (society, family, law, expected norms). Such a focus on individual needs does not denote a foreclosure of the social; on the contrary, individual analysis always takes place against the backdrop of society's norms and pressures. Lacan links this ethical position to the 'beautiful' in his discussion of Antigone who, when her brother dies, breaks the law to sit with his body outside the city walls. Antigone is an instance of a subject who does not relinquish her desire: she persists in what she has to do, however uncomfortable or difficult this task may be (the key phrase here is from Beckett's *The Unnameable*: 'I can't go on, I'll go on'). Lacan connects this ethical position to an art that causes disruption by suspending and disarming desire (as opposed to extinguishing and tempering it). In his schema, art that gives full rein to desire provides access to subjective 'good'.

One could extend Lacan's argument to suggest that the most urgent forms of artistic practice today stem from a necessity to rethink the connections between the individual and collective along these lines of painful pleasure – rather than conforming to a self-suppressing sense of social obligation. Instead of obeying a super-egoic injunction to make ameliorative art, the most striking, moving and memorable forms of participation are produced when artists act upon a gnawing social curiosity without the incapacitating restrictions of guilt. This fidelity to singularised desire – rather than to social consensus – enables this work to join a tradition of highly authored situations that fuse reality with carefully calculated artifice (some of which will be discussed in the chapters that follow). In these projects, intersubjective relations are not an end in themselves, but serve to explore and disentangle a more complex knot of social concerns about political engagement, affect, inequality, narcissism, class, and behavioural protocols.

At present, the discursive criteria of participatory and socially engaged art is drawn from a tacit analogy between anti-capitalism and the Christian 'good soul'; it is an ethical reasoning that fails to accommodate the aesthetic or to understand it as an autonomous realm of experience. In this perspective, there is no space for perversity, paradox and negation, operations as crucial to *aesthesis* as dissensus is to the political. Reframing the ethical imperatives of participatory art through a Lacanian lens might allow us to expand our repertoire of ways to attend to participatory art and its negotiation of the social. Instead of extracting art from the 'useless' domain of the aesthetic to relocate it in praxis, the better examples of participatory art occupy an ambiguous territory between 'art becoming mere life or art becoming mere art'.[88] This has implications for the politics of spectatorship: that Rancière's 'metapolitics' of art is not a party politics is both a gift and a limitation, leaving us with the urgency of examining each artistic practice within its own singular historical context and the political valencies of its era. The next chapter, which traces the origins of participatory art back to the historic avant-garde, offers precisely this challenge to contemporary equations between participation and democracy, since it begins with Italian Fascism.

2

Artificial Hells:
The Historic Avant-garde

This chapter will focus on three key moments from the historic avant-garde that anticipate the emergence of participatory art. Each shows a different position towards audience inclusion, and all three have a fraught relationship to political context. The first concerns Italian Futurism's break with conventional modes of spectatorship, its inauguration of performance as an artistic mode, addressing a mass audience for art, and its use of provocational gestures (both onstage and in the streets) to increasingly overt political ends. The second case study, which highlights the theoretical problems most central to this chapter and to the book as a whole, concerns developments in Russian culture after 1917. My focus here will not be on the well-trodden ground of visual art but on the formulation of two distinct modes of performance as theorised and implemented by the state: Proletkult theatre and mass spectacle. Neither of these phenomena are conventionally included within histories of art, but the themes they embody are crucial to contemporary socially engaged practices: ideas of collective authorship, of specifically working-class (popular) modes of expression, and the (in)compatibility of these imperatives with issues of quality. My final case study concerns Paris Dada: under the influence of André Breton, the group shifted its relationship to audiences away from combative cabarets and towards more participatory events in the public sphere. Although strictly deserving a chapter apiece, these three case studies together function as a microcosm of subsequent chapters in this book by representing three modes of participatory practice in relation to three ideological positions (emergent Fascism in Italy, Bolshevism in Russia, and in France, a post-war rejection of nationalist sentiment); collectively they suggest that the pre-history of recent developments in contemporary art lies in the domain of theatre and performance rather than in histories of painting or the ready-made.

I. Provocation, Press and Participation

In the light of subsequent innovations in twentieth-century theatre, it is commonplace to think of Futurism's approach to performance as conventional, based as it is on a proscenium division between performers and audience, with roles clearly allocated between the two. However, it is important to remember that what was being presented in this context were not traditional plays but brief actions in a variety of media that anticipate what we now call performance art: these *serate* (Italian for 'evening party' or *soirée*) usually included recitations of political statements and artistic manifestos, musical compositions, poetry and painting.[1] The first *serata* took place on 12 January 1910 at Politeama Rossetti in Trieste, but it was not until the third *serata* (on 8 March 1910, at the Chiarella in Turin) that visual artists were involved: Umberto Boccioni, Carlo Carrà and Luigi Russolo appeared onstage during this event, having met the poet Filippo Tommaso Marinetti (1876–1944) less than a month before. It is telling that the literature on Futurist *serate* pays less attention to the individual performances than to their overall effect on the audience: verbal descriptions convey the impression of complete chaos, as do visual records – such as Boccioni's *Caricature of a Futurist Serata* (1910) and Gerardo Dottori's *Futurist Serata in Perugia* (1914), in which paintings are shown on stage amid a flurry of projectiles from the audience. However, the evenings were not without structure. The *Grande Serata Futurista*, held at the Teatro Costanzi in Rome on 9 March 1913, was divided into three clear sections:

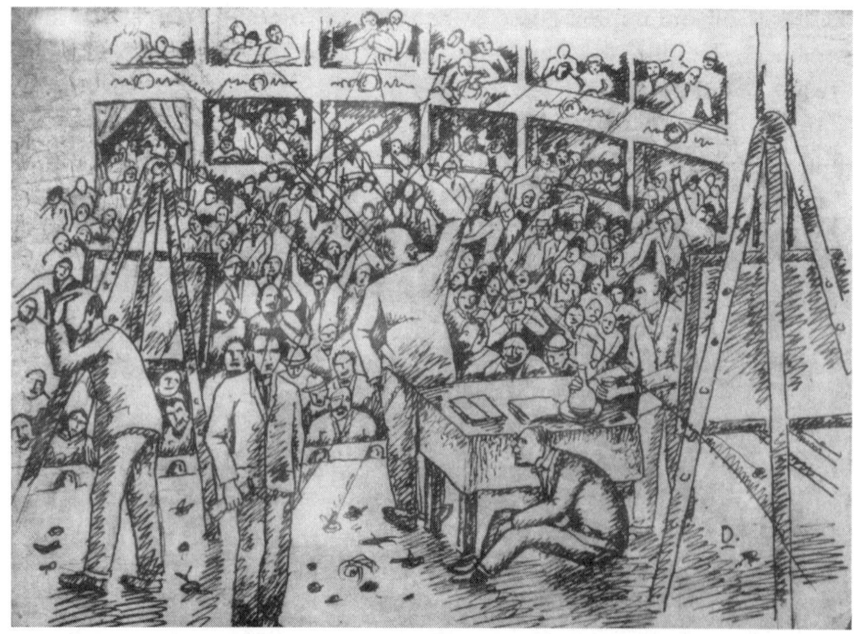

Gerardo Dottori, *Futurist Serata in Perugia*, 1914. Ink on paper.

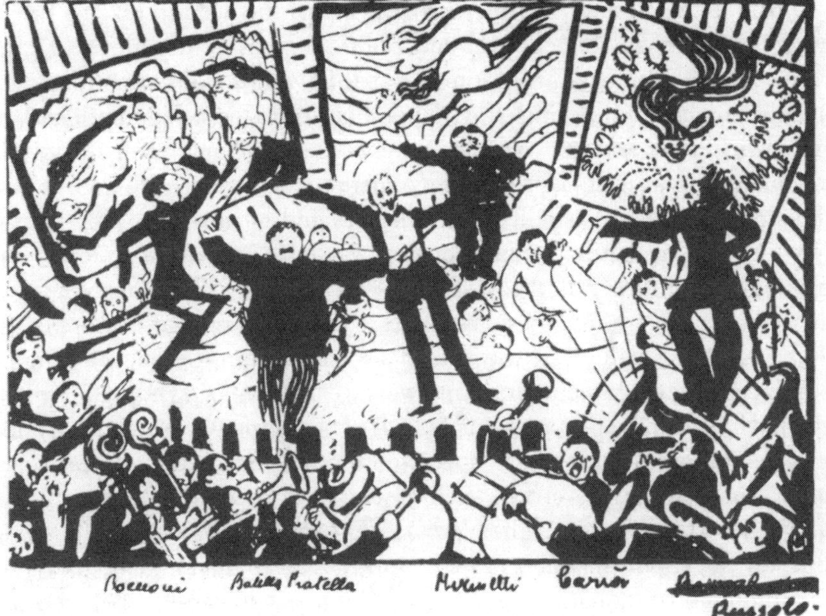

Umberto Boccioni, *Caricature of the Futurist Serata Held in Treviso, 2 June 1911*. Ink on paper.

a Futurist symphony, a reading of Futurist poetry, and a presentation of Futurist painting and sculpture. Part of theatre's attraction to Futurist artists therefore seemed to lie in its offering an alternative space of exhibition: artists were in direct control of a display format in which audiences could be confronted directly, rather than through the meditation of an exhibition or book.

Viewing the *serate* as a new form of exhibition display, we can begin to understand how abrupt and innovative the Futurist engagement with spectatorship really was. Until that point, modern art had for the most part been restricted to the display of two- and three-dimensional work indoors: in salons, commercial galleries, and in the newly emergent form of the biennial (1895 onwards). What art was shown outdoors was sculptural, and tended to take the form of either monumental statuary or architectural decoration; in both cases its role tended to be affirmative in relation to official culture.[2] By contrast, Futurist activities were performance-based, held in theatres but also in the streets, assertively itinerant (touring cities throughout Italy), and supported by a comprehensive assault on public consciousness via printed matter. Events were preceded by manifestos and flysheet actions in the city to stir up attention; after performances, press releases were written up and sent to national and foreign newspapers.[3] To describe Futurist experimentation as performance art, however, does not adequately convey the conflation of press, promotionalism and politics devised by its leading spokesman, Marinetti.

From the beginning, Marinetti was aware of the need to reach a broad audience to realise his cultural and political goals of overthrowing the ruling bourgeoisie and promoting a patriotic, industrialised nationalism. To this end he aligned himself with populist strategies of communication. According to Marinetti, 'Articles, poems and polemics were no longer adequate. It was necessary to change methods completely, to go out into the street, to launch assaults from theatres and to introduce the fisticuff into the artistic battle.'[4] The fact that the first Futurist manifesto was printed in its entirety on the front page of *Le Figaro* (20 February 1909) – as well as in several Italian newspapers – is a staggering feat of publicity. The manifesto eulogised the crowd as an aspect of modernity to be embraced alongside technology and warfare: 'We will sing of great crowds excited by work, by pleasure, and by riot . . .'.[5] Christine Poggi has argued that the Futurist conception of spectatorship was indebted to contemporaneous theorists of the crowd such as Gustave Le Bon's *Psychologie des foules* (1895) and Scipio Sighele's *L'intelligenza della folla* (1903).[6] Le Bon had written about the importance of images rather than logical discourse for communicating with crowds – and this precisely paralleled the Futurist adoption of visual performance as the primary vehicle with which to connect with large audiences. It was also a medium ripe for reinvention, as the collaboratively authored 'Futurist Synthetic Theatre Manifesto' (1915) makes clear:

> For Italy to learn to make up its mind with lightning speed, to hurl itself into battle, to sustain every undertaking and every possible calamity, books and reviews are unnecessary. They interest and concern only a minority, are more or less tedious, obstructive, and relaxing. They cannot help chilling enthusiasm, aborting impulses, and poisoning with doubt a people at war. War – Futurism intensified – obliges us to march, and not to rot in libraries and reading rooms. THEREFORE WE THINK THAT THE ONLY WAY TO INSPIRE ITALY WITH THE WARLIKE SPIRIT TODAY IS THROUGH THE THEATRE. In fact ninety percent of Italians go to the theatre, whereas only ten percent read books and reviews. But what is needed is a FUTURIST THEATRE, completely opposed to the passéist theatre that drags its monotonous, depressing processions around the sleepy Italian stages.[7]

Here, then, we see the beginning of the active/passive binary that holds such sway over the discourse of participation throughout the twentieth century: conventional theatre is derided as producing passivity, while Futurist performance allegedly prompts a more dynamic, active spectatorship. In this regard, it is important that the ideal model of the Futurist *serate* was not theatre based on traditional conventions of plot, character, lighting, costumes, etc., and produced by and for middle-class audiences; rather, the model was variety theatre, which had lower-class connotations, and tended to comprise a non-sequential appearance of spectacle, gymnastics, slapstick, singing, anatomical monstrosities, and so forth.[8] Variety theatre asserted the Futurists' allegiance to popular culture; moreover, it had its own spectatorial conventions, aiming to place the audience at the centre of an experience, which was already the aim of Futurist painting: the artists proclaimed that, using techniques such as simultaneity and force-lines, the spectator *'must in future be placed in the centre of the picture.* He shall not be present at, but participate in the action'.[9] Marinetti's 1913 manifesto on variety theatre – first published in London's *Daily Mail* and subsequently in Paris, Rome and Milan – explained the appeal of this dynamic spectatorial relationship:

> The Variety Theatre is alone in seeking the audience's collaboration. It doesn't remain static like a stupid voyeur, but joins noisily in the action, in the singing, accompanying the orchestra, communicating with the actors in surprising actions and bizarre dialogues. And the actors bicker clownishly with the musicians.
>
> The Variety Theatre uses the smoke of cigars and cigarettes to join the atmosphere of the theatre to that of the stage. And because the audience cooperates in this way with the actors' fantasy, the action develops simultaneously on the stage, in the boxes, and in the orchestra. It continues to the end of the performance, among the battalions of fans, the honeyed dandies who crowd the stage door to fight over the star; double final victory; chic dinner and bed.[10]

As a lower-class form of popular entertainment, variety theatre provided ample opportunities for heckling and improvisation on both sides. In its Futurist iteration, this participation became directly antagonistic, with performers and audience making direct attacks on one another, frequently culminating in riot. Some of the techniques suggested to provoke conflict can be found in the variety theatre manifesto: spreading 'a powerful glue on some of the seats, so that the male or female spectator will stay glued down and make everyone laugh', selling 'the same ticket to ten people: traffic jam, bickering and wrangling', offering 'free tickets to gentlemen or ladies who are notoriously unbalanced, irritable, or eccentric and likely to provoke uproars with obscene gestures, pinching women, or other freakishness', and sprinkling 'the seats with dust to make people itch and sneeze'.[11] However infantile these gestures appear, they seem minor compared with the insults hurled back at the artists, including a member of the audience at the Teatro Verdi, Florence, on 12 December 1913, who gave Marinetti a pistol and invited him to commit suicide on stage.[12]

Rather than viewing these gestures as displaying an anti-audience attitude (as Michael Kirby and many others have suggested), we should perhaps regard them as spectator*philic*: Futurist performances were not designed to negate the presence of the audience, but to exaggerate it, to make it visible to itself, to stir it up, halt complacency, and cultivate confidence rather than docile respect.[13] To this end, Futurist performers reversed the conventional criteria of audience engagement: they were willing to undergo 'the scorn of the public', especially on the opening night, and developed a 'horror of immediate success'.[14] However, the extent to which spectators needed this retraining was debatable. With audiences (of all classes) attending in their thousands, there was clearly a pre-existing desire on the part of the public to participate in such events: to be harangued and provoked, and to have the opportunity to heckle and assault in return. Moreover, this desire for self-assertion on the part of the audience was already manifest in art galleries elsewhere in Europe. Kandinsky recalled that during an exhibition in Munich in 1910, 'the owner of the gallery complained that after the exhibition closed each day he had to wipe clean the canvases upon which the public had spat . . . but they did not cut up the canvases, as happened to me once in another city during my exhibition'.[15] A year later Albert Gleizes, writing on the Cubist section of the Salon d'Automne in Paris, noted that the room became 'a mob like the one at the *Indépendants*':

> People struggle at the doors to get in, they discuss and argue in front of the pictures; they are either for or against, they take sides, they say what they think at the tops of their voices, they interrupt one another, protest, lose their tempers, provoke contradictions; unbridled abuse comes up against equally intemperate expressions of admiration; it is a tumult of cries, shouts, bursts of laughter, protests.[16]

In this context, Futurism's innovation was not so much about empowering the audience as harnessing and redirecting its energy and attention: Futurism created the conditions for a symbiosis between an artistic embrace of violence and audiences who wanted to be part of a work of art and feel legitimated to participate in its violence. Importantly, this applied not only to working-class members of the audience at Futurist *serate* but also to the upper and middle classes who threw vegetables and eggs, and brought along car horns, cow bells, whistles, pipes, rattles and banners. The aim was to produce a space of participation as one of total destruction, in which expressions of hostility were available to all classes as a brutal form of entertainment.

Theatrically framed provocation was not the only means deployed by Futurists to stir up public opinion. It was supported by other public activities: meetings, riots, speeches, poetic tournaments, picket lines, rallies and boycotts. In 1910, for example, Marinetti and friends climbed the campanile in St Mark's Square, Venice, to shower 80,000 copies of their tract *Contra Venezia Passatista* ('Against Past-Loving Venice') over the piazza, before improvising a 'Speech to the Venetians' that ended in a brawl. Other events specifically targeted the working class: in summer 1910, Marinetti lectured on 'The Necessity and Beauty of Violence' at the Labour Exchange in Naples, the Chamber of Unionised Labour in Parma, and the Revolutionary Hall in Milan.[17] It is worth remembering that these social disruptions did not take place to *épater le bourgeois*, but rather to convert the widest possible range of Italians to a nationalist, militaristic, techno-futurist cause that aimed to motivate colonial expansion and rouse enthusiasm for war. Participation in Futurist theatre was explicitly viewed as a way to train and prepare the spectator for participation in this new age: using the metaphor of sports practice, the Futurist Synthetic Theatre manifesto optimistically proclaimed that '*Futurist Theatre* will be a gymnasium to train our race's spirit'.[18] It didn't matter if audiences claimed to hate Futurism; their ongoing presence and violent reactions created a small-scale war that proved the validity of the artists' programme. As long as audiences continued to pay attention and be provoked, then Futurism was achieving its goal of a political project geared towards affirming Italy's entry into the modern world through war, technology and destruction. Failure could only have been marked by audience neutrality: its remaining unaffected, in a traditional spectatorial mode of benign and detached contemplation.[19]

For Marinetti, participation was therefore understood as the end of traditional spectatorship, and as total commitment to a cause. Experiencing new aesthetic modes such as Futurism meant abandoning one's traditional expectations and operating instead on the basis of total openness: 'it is necessary to forget entirely one's intellectual culture, not in order to *assimilate* the work of art, but to *deliver one's self up* to it heart and soul'.[20] If this abandonment evokes Romantic rapture ('to disturb the peace of the audience's mind, to let it be overwhelmed by powerful emotions, albeit negative ones'), then it was also accompanied by unquestionably regressive aspects too: a reduction to mob mentality, and the abandonment of critical distance and reasoned logic to a mindless anticipation of the future through nationalist violence.[21] When reading accounts of the *serate*, it is hard not to conclude that what was provoked above all was the lowest common denominator:

> When the curtain went up, a howling tribe of cannibals raised their thousands of arms and greeted our apparition with a volley of objects from the animal, vegetable and mineral world . . . No one thought of taking the first word. We were totally overwhelmed by this reception. We looked at our audience and began to read the banners that were displayed from the dress circle: 'Perverts! Pederasts! Pimps! Charlatans! Buffoons!'[22]

On the other hand, this cataclysm of insults and attacks can also be read as the sign of a desire on the part of the audience to participate – a demand that is increasingly gratified as the twentieth century progresses.

After 1918, when Marinetti returned from service at the front, Futurist performances became more spectacular and overtly political. Up until 1914, the Futurist *serate* had no regular structure, and could consist of poetry readings, political declamations, plays, lectures, art displays and brawls. Typical early *serate* presented politically provocative speeches alongside recitals of the key ideas of Futurism (as declared in their manifestos), and demonstrated how the latter could be translated into a performative language. Paintings were brought on stage, music was played and free-verse poetry recited, but the evenings could also include juggling, dancing and competitions. At this point, Futurist aesthetics were in harmony with political goals but not entirely subservient to them. Gradually, political ambitions grew more prominent, with more clearly defined claims for anti-traditionalism and militant nationalism, leading to a consolidation of formal developments. After 1914, a scenographic component was introduced and the style of production was less casually improvised. Performances were more scripted, and engaged with the conventions of theatre: Marinetti's *Le Basi* (Feet, 1915), for example, was a series of seven scenes with minimal dialogue, in which the public saw only the actors' legs beneath a partially raised curtain.[23] New technology was embraced in the form of electric reflectors, coloured panes of glass, beams of coloured light, neon and ultraviolet tubes, all theorised by Enrico Prampolini.[24] Audiences were far larger (as many as 5,000) and Marinetti's close friendship with Mussolini meant that the group now had the means to build an experimental theatre in the baths of Septimius Severus in Rome, leading to ambitious experiments in total theatre, such as Anton Guilio Bragaglia's *Il Teatro Sperimentale degli Indipendenti* (1923–36).

In Futurism, then, performance became the privileged paradigm for artistic and political operations in the public sphere. More than painting, sculpture or literature, performance constituted a space of shared collective presence and self-representation. The Futurist desire for dynamism, activation and emotional arousal is repeated in innumerable avant-garde calls of subsequent decades, when performance was perceived as able to rouse emotion more vividly than the perusal of static objects. But if the Futurist approach to participation was *via negativa* – as a form of total emotional response in which one could not occupy the position of a distanced observer but was incited to take part in an orgy of destruction – then the 1960s model would be conducted in a more optimistic light, as an artistic metaphor for emancipation, self-awareness and a heightened experience of the everyday. Paradoxically, the creative options available to audiences seem less determined in Futurist performances than in the scored participation of the Happenings and other experiments of the

1960s, suggesting that destructive modes of participation might be more inclusive than those that purport to be democratically open.[25] This is an uncomfortable conclusion to support: as is well known, Futurism's embrace of nation and war came to establish the ideological foundations of Italian Fascism, and as Walter Benjamin pointed out, Fascism is precisely the political formation that allows people to participate in, and enjoy, the spectacle of their own destruction.[26] In 1924, Leon Trotsky asked:

> did not Italian Fascism come into power by 'revolutionary' methods, by bringing into action the masses, the mobs and the millions, and by tempering and arming them? It is not an accident, it is not a misunderstanding, that Italian Futurism has merged into the torrent of Fascism; it is entirely in accord with the law of cause and effect.[27]

Trotsky goes on to point out the similarity of means between Italian Fascism and the Russian Revolution. The difference between the two, he explains, is that 'We stepped into the Revolution while the Futurists fell into it.'[28] In other words, if Italian Futurism blindly harnessed participatory destruction, then collective cultural production in post-revolutionary Russia was based on strategic affirmations of social change.

II. Theatricalising Life

In the years immediately following the 1917 Revolution, the triad of author, work of art and audience underwent an ideological reprogramming that spanned art, theatre and music. In general terms, the aim was to bring cultural practice into line with the Bolshevik Revolution, although what exactly this comprised was a fraught question: to reduce the aristocracy's grip on culture, or to promote cultural production by the working class? To abandon traditional media and embrace new technology, or to destroy bourgeois culture altogether? To reflect social reality, or to produce it? The best-known examples of the post-revolutionary avant-garde – defined initially as Futurist, then Constructivist, and after 1921 as Productivist – dealt with these questions by rejecting bourgeois, individually produced forms of art (such as painting), founded in taste and produced for a patron market, in favour of practices integrated into industrial production and designed for collective reception. Artists such as Tatlin, Rodchenko, Popova and Stepanova sought a social and practical application for their work, designing clothing, ceramics, posters and furniture for mass production and consumption. In the discussion that follows I will not be focusing on this elision of the fine and applied arts, but rather on theatre and performance as privileged vehicles for collective participation. Although film is frequently regarded as the advanced art form *par excellence* of the Soviet Revolution, it is the immediacy, economy and proliferation of theatrical productions, and the debates they occasioned, that provide the most informative parallel with today's participatory art.[29]

This discussion, however, needs to be prefaced by the acknowledgement that one of the main problems in summarising Russian artistic developments of this period is the difficulty of isolating them from the complexities of a political context in which internecine disagreements led to appointments, conflicts and resignations almost on a monthly basis. Even within avant-garde groups there were internal disagreements that make it hard to generalise, and even harder to produce an intelligible chronology of the period. The situation is exacerbated by the paucity of images in relation to this material, and a lack of first-hand accounts to illuminate what images we have. In what follows I shall focus on the themes of new versus old culture, collective versus individual authorship, and equality versus quality. These will be used as the steering ideas through a discussion of the main theoretical positions immediately following the Revolution, and contrasting accounts of the invention and spread of mass spectacle. I will conclude with some reflections on the Soviet attempt to recalibrate music along participatory lines.

The question of whether or not the Revolution should occasion an entirely new form of culture produced by and for the proletariat, or should retain its ties to cultural heritage despite its ideological flaws was a key point of conflict between theorists immediately following 1917. The Proletkult (an acronym for 'proletarian cultural-educational organisations') was formed as a coalition of working-class interest groups shortly before the Revolution, but by 1918 had become a national organisation dedicated to defining new forms of proletarian culture in keeping with collectivist doctrine. Its founding theorist, Aleksandr Bogdanov (1873–1928), was an economist, philosopher, physician, sci-fi writer and activist, who identified an important gap in Marxist thinking between the proletariat as revolutionary force and as builder of a new society. For Bogdanov, this hiatus had to be filled through education and training in a new political culture, producing a workers' intelligentsia in place of a party intelligentsia. As such, he was the most outspoken advocate of suppressing bourgeois culture of the past in favour of a new proletarian culture that made no reference to cultural heritage. As Zenovia Sochor has argued, the Proletkult sought to revolutionise culture on three fronts: in labour (by merging the artist and the worker), in lifestyle (at home and at work), and in feeling and sentiment (creating a revolutionary consciousness).[30] All of these had radical consequences for culture, which Bogdanov viewed as 'the most powerful weapon for organising collective forces in a class society – class forces'.[31] Art, literature, theatre and music were all subject to a reorganisation that aimed to bring cultural production in line with collectivist ideals.

Bogdanov's emphasis on the independence of working-class culture at arm's length from the Communist Party and the Soviet state meant that he came into conflict with Lenin's idea of revolutionary change, although this difference was as much political as it was artistic. Lenin, to the extent that he was even concerned with art and culture, wished them to proceed on the basis of existing bourgeois standards, rather than wiping the slate clean for the Proletkult vision of workers' culture. This was motivated not solely by an attachment to traditional art, but by a political scepticism concerning the naive utopianism of Bogdanov's schematic plans for a 'new proletarian culture' when over 150 million Russians were not even literate and the country needed basic modernisation; this, in his view, was the 'real dirty work' to be achieved by the party.[32] Lenin's objection to the Proletkult was also based on a long-standing rivalry with Bogdanov, who for many years had been second to Lenin in his influence on the Bolsheviks. These differences led to Lenin writing a resolution against the Proletkult in 1920, in which he argued that Marxism was historically significant precisely because it did *not* reject the cultural achievements of preceding ages, but instead 'assimilated and refashioned everything of value in the more than 2000 years of the development of human thought and culture'.[33] The Proletkult was henceforth turned into a subsection of the Commissariat of Enlightenment (Narkompros), with severely reduced funds and correspondingly decreased influence. In 1921 Bogdanov was removed from the Central Committee of the Proletkult altogether.

One of the main arguments for the rejection of previous culture was the fact that it was produced and consumed by individuals, rather than exemplifying the new model of collective authorship. For Bogdanov, cultural production should be rationalised as if it were an industry, leading to a redefinition of authorship in which originality was no longer understood to be an independent expression of the artistic subject, but rather 'the expression of his own active participation in the creation and development of the collective's life'.[34] Creativity was detached from its Romantic heritage of individual seclusion and 'indeterminate and unconscious methods ("inspiration", etc.)', and redirected towards rationally organised production.[35] Bogdanov's refusal of art's autonomy led him to maintain the position that 'there is not and cannot be a strict delineation between creation and ordinary labour': art can and should be re-imagined as an organised, industrialised process like any other, since '(artistic) creation is the highest, most complex form of labour' and 'its methods derive from the methods of labour'.[36] From now on, to be creative meant to surmount contradictions, to combine materials in new ways, and to generate systemic new solutions (such as the collective authorship of newspapers). Art as a category was to be subordinated to the instrumental ends of 'socially directed artistic work', as Alexei Gan, author of *Constructivism* (1922), argued:

A time of social expediency has begun. An object of only utilitarian significance will be introduced in a form acceptable to all . . . Let us tear ourselves away from our speculative activity [i.e. art] and find the way to real work, applying our knowledge and skills to real, live and expedient work . . . Not to reflect, not to represent and not to interpret reality, but to really build and express the systematic tasks of the new class, the proletariat.[37]

Here, then, we see the beginnings of the idea that art should be useful and effect concrete changes in society. Against bourgeois individualism, it was argued, the Proletkult should foster '*comradely*, i.e. consciously collective, relationships'.[38] Putting aside the overt emphasis on industrialisation, many of these instrumentalising sentiments chime with today's discussions around interventionist, activist and socially engaged art. And these discussions repeat the same paradoxes that were present in the 1920s: despite Bogdanov's enthusiastic belief in the rational organisation of proletarian culture, there was a clear contradiction between his humanist desire to end alienation and his intolerance for those who strayed from the recommended path of collectivism. The proletariat were expected to participate of their own free will, but only in a manner appropriate to their class position. With creativity rewritten as a social (rather than individual) enterprise, the status of interiority and individual emotion became problematic. Art, for Bogdanov, was a tool to mobilise sentiment, but of a strictly political variety: 'Art can organise feelings in exactly the same way as ideological propaganda [organises] thought; feelings determine will with no less force than ideas.'[39]

This conscription of affect was one of the main objections raised by Trotsky to the work of the Proletkult. An infinitely more subtle thinker of culture than Bogdanov, Trotsky found the privileging of collective over individual psychology to be one of the Proletkult's central stumbling blocks:

> What does it mean to 'deny experiences', that is, deny individual psychology in literature and on the stage? . . . In what way, on what grounds, and in the name of what, can art turn its back to the inner life of present-day man who is building a new external world, and thereby rebuilding himself? If art will not help this new man to educate himself, to strengthen and refine himself, then what it is for? And how can it organise the inner life, if it does not penetrate and reproduce it?[40]

Trotsky's vision of culture advocated creative freedom as self-education, instead of injunctions to produce ideologically driven art: in his view, there was no point making demands on what should be the content of art for the masses, since this had to evolve of its own accord, as a collective psychological movement. Instead of homogenising the masses to a singular entity, he pointed out that class speaks *through* individuals.[41]

I dwell on Trotsky here because his position is an important one to bring to bear on the contemporary discourse of socially engaged art, which is frequently characterised by an aversion to interiority and affect: it can often seem that the choice is between the social *or* the solipsistic, the collective *or* the individual, with no room for manoeuvre between the two. It is perhaps telling that Bogdanov, the most fundamentalist of the Proletkult theorists, was trained not in art but in medicine; it is tempting to ascribe his willingness to jettison past culture, and his plodding directives for proletarian art, to an innate lack of sympathy for the arts. (Indeed, he returned to medicine after he left the Proletkult in 1921, and died following an unsuccessful blood-transfusion experiment in 1928.)

But how did the results of these theoretical debates play out in the works produced under the Proletkult's guidance? In insisting upon the collectivism of theatre 'as the art closest and most comprehensible to the working class', the Proletkult built upon innovations in anti-hierarchical participation that had already begun in theatre prior to the Revolution.[42] Vsevolod Meyerhold, for example, had been experimenting with such theatrical forms since 1910: removing the proscenium, introducing different stage levels, attempting to create a unity of action between actors and audience. His production *The Dawn* (1920) featured free admission, news bulletins, the walls hung with placards, an audience showered with political leaflets, and a harsh white light to dispel illusionism, all of which served to augment the content (a Symbolist verse drama about proletarian uprising by the Belgian poet Emile Verhaeren). In order to deal with the stage direction requiring a crowd, Meyerhold suggested involving the audience itself, which he presented as an educational mission, a way of training the populace to be actors. Even more successful than *The Dawn* was Meyerhold's collaboration with Vladimir Mayakovsky, *Mystery-Bouffe*, first performed in 1918 and rewritten in 1921 to increase its relevance to events since the Revolution. The play concerns a universal flood and the subsequent joyful triumph of the 'unclean' (the proletariat) over the 'clean' (the bourgeoisie), and combined folk drama and avant-garde experimentation in the service of a revolutionary message. Once again, Meyerhold dismantled the proscenium to reveal the scenery mechanisms; the stage was taken up by platforms on different levels, interconnected by steps, and a big ramp sloped down to the first row of seats. Throughout the performance, the audience were allowed to come and go as they liked, and to respond to the acting with interjections; in the last act, the performance spread into boxes in the auditorium and the audience were invited to mingle with actors on stage.[43]

Although these theatrical experiments attempted to erode the distinction between performers and audience, by contemporary standards their respective roles always remained fairly clear. It was Proletkult theoreticians such as Platon Mikhailovich Kerzhentsev (1881–1940) who were instrumental in developing a more total form of collective theatre for revolutionary ends.

Kerzhentsev advocated the end of bourgeois repertoires and even bourgeois actors, and instead promoted drama that took as its subject matter the crises of class struggle (strikes, upheavals, insurrections, revolts) and which was performed by the proletariat as part of 'a permanent workshop . . . where stars and extras are unknown'.[44] Some Proletkult theatre groups therefore took the form of a collective institution in which every member of the theatre, from the stage-hand to the actor, participated in all aspects of the production – from the sewing of costumes, to the making of props, to the directing of scenes, to the choice of plays. This was perceived as a way to express collective consciousness; as such, the Proletkult's aims were both social and technical: 'On the one hand, to establish a centre of collective self-expression for the workers; on the other, to break down specialisation in the theatre.'[45] For Kerzhentsev, it was important that this new theatre follow the 'principle of amateurism', in which actors avoided professionalisation in order to keep their proximity to the masses; he hoped that audiences of the future would not say 'I am going to see something' but 'I am going to participate in something.'[46] Unlike the sets of Mayakovsky and Meyerhold, those of Proletkult theatre are never photographed as environments in their own right and are strikingly meagre – planks, ladders, simple risers and painted back-cloths, as in the numerous examples reproduced in Huntly Carter's *The New Theatre and Cinema of Soviet Russia* (1924).

Despite economic hardships, amateur theatre proliferated across the country after 1917; the formalist critic Viktor Shklovsky noted that 'Drama circles were multiplying more rapidly than protozoa. Not the lack of fuel, nor the lack of food, nor the Entente – no, nothing can stop their growth.'[47] Carter reported that 'In Kostroma alone there are 600 village dramatic circles. In the Nishni-Novgorod district there are about 900.'[48] Workers

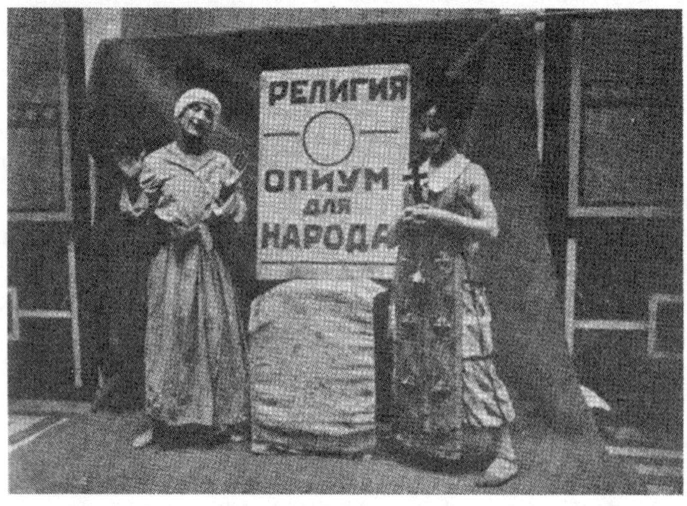

Proletkult theatre: Eisenstein's production of Aleksandr Ostrovsky's *Enough Stupidity in Every Wise Man*, 1923. The sign reads 'Religion is the opiate of the people'.

wrote plays collectively, the most successful of which passed into the Proletkult repertory for others to perform.[49] However, the extent to which these plays matched the innovations of pre-revolutionary theatre is debatable. Scripts tended to be burdened by ideological affirmation, such as *The Bricklayer* (1918), by the Proletkult activist Pavel Bessalko. As Katerina Clark wryly observes: 'Written in praise of the new age of technology and proletarian hegemony, it concerns the wife of an architect who, predictably, becomes disaffected with her bourgeois husband and runs off with a bricklayer to join the revolutionary movement – to her greater fulfilment, no doubt, but not to the satisfaction of critics, who found the plot poorly motivated and the play terribly dull.'[50]

Such an emphasis on social content over artistic form was a problem for professional theatre too. Anatoly Lunacharsky, Lenin's key cultural advisor, believed in preserving classical culture (such as the Bolshoi Ballet and Mariinsky Theatre) since the proletariat were uninspired by contemporary political performances:

> And imagine, comrade Kerzhentsev, I have not only seen how bored the proletariat was at the production of a few 'revolutionary' plays, but have even read the statement of sailors and workers asking that these revolutionary spectacles be discontinued and replaced by performances of Gogol and Ostrovsky![51]

In turn, Kerzhentsev reports on a competition for a new repertoire of socialist plays, but the quality of entries was so poor that the jury struggled to find works, even from Europe, with a sufficiently correct ideological bias. Predictably, Kerzhentsev did not feel this to be a problem, just symptomatic of a period of transition: 'a large part of them [i.e. theatrical works] are not of a sufficiently high level in the artistic sense. That is understandable: proletarian culture is only now being born. Proletarian theatre has not had the chance to express itself; there were no conditions for its existence in historical reality.'[52]

However, the backlash against these political requirements was already visible in the early 1930s. In 1931, the author Evgeny Zamyatin noted that 'the repertory is now the weakest spot in Russian theatre. It seems that something quite inconceivable has taken place: it was much easier to move the tremendous weight of economics and industry than a seemingly light and ethereal substance – such as dramatics.'[53] For Zamyatin, the state demand for drama dealing with contemporary issues had fuelled an epidemic of bad plays; he notes that, of the longest running productions in Moscow during 1930, 'only one treated current problems such as industrialisation, the kolkhozes, etc.'[54] It is telling that one of the great novels of this period, Andréy Platonov's *The Foundation Pit* (1930), addresses precisely these themes, but as a finely judged satire of Stalin's forced programme of collectivisation.

It is unsurprising, then, that only a handful of Proletkult plays retain a place within theatre history. One of them is Sergei Eisenstein's production of Sergei Tretyakov's *Gas Masks* (1923), performed on four nights in March and April 1924. The play recounts the heroic struggle of Soviet workers to fix a gas leak without the assistance of protective garments or masks, and was staged inside the Moscow Gas Works on the outskirts of the city. Despite the vivid and highly innovative use of site specificity – the audience was seated on wooden benches in a cleared area of the factory surrounded by turbines, steel tanks, catwalks, revolving machinery and the smell of gas – the play had numerous problems. Tretyakov's plot was predictable (a radical journalist leads the gas workers to fix the leak and save the factory), and it proved difficult to draw an audience to the outskirts of the city, while the gas factory's own staff considered the performance to be a nuisance.[55] Even so, Jay Leyda reports that although the play was crude and the acting untutored and rhetorical, when the men facing death went down the shaft to save the factory, 'the minutes were tense with an actuality that

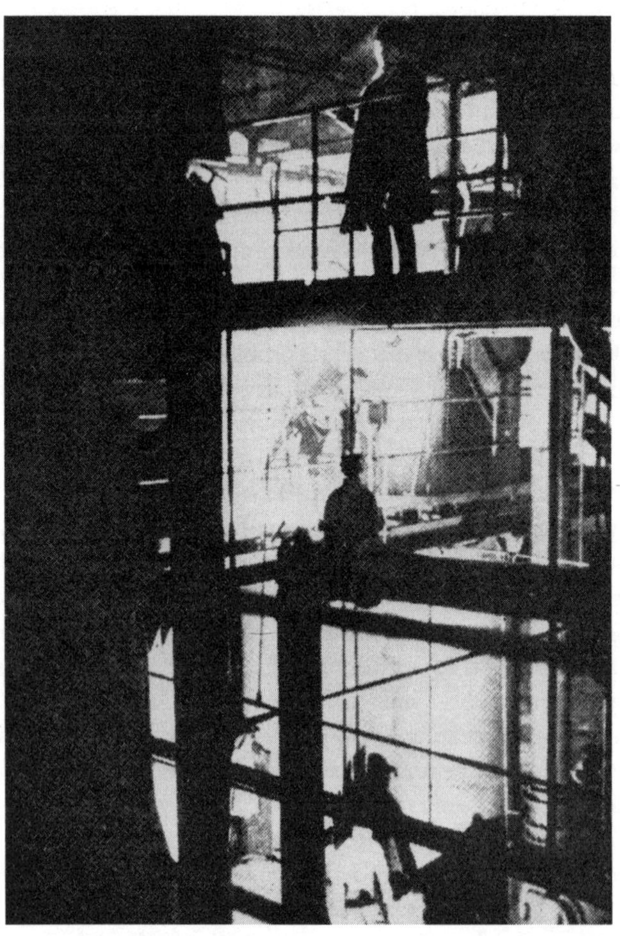

Sergei Tretyakov's *Gas Masks*, produced by Sergei Eisenstein, Moscow Gas Works, 1924

no stage performance, with trained actors and modern lighting, could touch the fringe of'.[56] This immediacy is detectable in what images of the production exist: the silhouette of a man standing on a walkway above an industrial chasm of pulleys, bars and pipes, backlit by an industrial glow. Eisenstein's example immediately stands out from the vast body of Proletkult theatre productions, whose formulaic character leads one to imagine each production as being more or less the same play with minor variations in personnel and plot. In *Gas Masks*, the chasm between quality (of production) and equality (in both its message and accessibility) seems to have been far less gaping than usual.

Amateur theatre groups also gave rise to related organisations such as the Living Newspaper (1919) – a theatrical 'feuilleton' or dramatised montage, based partly on political events and partly on local themes emerging from everyday life – and the agitpop collective Blue Blouse (1923 onwards).[57] By 1927 there were over 5,000 Blue Blouse troupes and 7,000 Living Newspaper groups in clubs, collectives and factories, as well as hundreds of peasant amateur theatre companies in each province. This enthusiasm for theatre extended to pageants and demonstrations; the Austrian writer René Fülöp-Miller offers an amusing account of these events, which included allegorical scenes about labour and industry, public trials to enlighten the people (about health, illiteracy, the murderers of Rosa Luxemburg, and so on), and a very creative pageant involving diagrams of factory output, and a funeral and cremation of old farm machinery, with participants dressed up as turnips and cucumbers.[58] Characteristically, Fülöp-Miller also dismisses the message of these events as politically simplistic and naive – but it was only a short step from these parades and pageants to the open-air mass spectacle, a craze that reached its peak in St Petersburg in 1920.

Before discussing mass spectacle, we should note that art history and theatre history offer distinct genealogical narratives for this phenomenon. For art history, the precursor took place in 1918, when Russian Futurist artists produced a dynamic scenographic reworking of the Winter Palace and the square in front. In this setting,

> Altman, Puni, Bogoslavskaya and their friends decided to stage a mass re-enactment of the storming of the Winter Palace . . . The realism was provided by a whole borrowed battalion and their equipment, and thousands of good Petrograd citizens, the whole dramatised by giant arc-lights . . . Small wonder that when the authorities heard about it later – no permission had been thought necessary for a theatrical pageant – there was a severe reprimand for the commander of the battalion who had known nothing about it. It might have been real![59]

Theatre historians, by contrast, present mass spectacle as emerging from a set of theoretical and ideological commitments that had been brewing since the early 1900s, and never mention the event in 1918. Once again the key figure is Kerzhentsev, an influential advocate of collective non-professional theatre. His book *The Creative Theatre* (1918) was informed by his experiences of viewing folk and traditional pageants in the US and the UK, and by Romain Rolland's *The People's Theatre* (1903), an account of French theatre 'by and for the people', covering the period from 1789 to the turn of the twentieth century.[60] Kerzhentsev saw these as examples of alternatives to professional theatre and an opportunity for culture to evolve from the people themselves. He encouraged pageant and mass spectacle as particularly effective forms of theatre, since both encouraged the use of public space: 'Why confine theatre to the proscenium arch when it can have the freedom of the public square?'[61] Monumental outdoor spectacles encouraged mass participation, sublating individualism into visually overpowering displays of collective presence. These were particularly popular in St Petersburg, where a series of mass festivals took place over 1919–20. The first of these was held for the May Day celebration in 1919, entitled *The Third International* ('a staging of slogans about revolution, the end of tyrants, the burial of martyrs, and a world of peace') and was followed by four no less ideologically driven spectacles during 1920.[62]

The first spectacles of the 1920 cycle, *The Mystery of Freed Labour* (on May Day) and *The Blockade of Russia* (on 20 June), involved thousands of participants. Both were directed from within the action, and attracted audiences of over 35,000 people in the square. *The Mystery of Freed Labour* represented a historical schema that would become the standard feature of revolutionary festivals, in which the Bolsheviks were heir to a long tradition of rebellion against illegitimate authority. It was also typical in presenting a paean to the October Revolution as a way of staking the Bolshevik claim to leadership of international communism; in other words, despite its ostensibly internationalist diegesis, mass spectacle also functioned as a way to assert Russian primacy over other national socialist groups. The third spectacle of this series, *Toward a World Commune*, was held on 19 July 1920 and also adopted a historical structure (the first, second and third internationals) and vast numbers of performers (4,000 participants playing to a crowd of 45,000). It featured re-enactments of the French Revolution, the 1914 war and the triumph of the Red Army. In the words of Fülöp-Miller, it was an attempt 'to pass directly from the illusion of dramatic action to reality: a great part of the town was used as the stage of the events; real troops appeared, and the "representation of the whole world" was so far "real" in that it actually consisted of representations of the international communist party organisations'.[63]

James von Geldern usefully highlights some of the artistic problems that arose in the production of mass spectacles, all of which revolved around a conflict between artistic and ideological requirements. The principle of using amateurs meant that the acting was weak, the desire for spontaneity in fact led to chaotic action, and the use of thousands of bodies – after rehearsals involving mere hundreds – led to slow performances: 'the unexpected need to stagger exits and entrances created long periods of dead air, to the point that the performance lasted a full six hours'.[64] Moreover, the repetitive nature of the plots – endless uprisings and rebellions – needed more variation to succeed artistically, but this could not be done without jeopardising historical accuracy and a consistent ideological message. As von Geldern notes, 'each revolt was a swirling mass of bodies – no leader could stand out in their midst; and each revolt was equally unorganised as it stormed the staircase'.[65]

The culmination of the 1920 spectacles, and arguably the most successful artistically, was *The Storming of the Winter Palace*, held on 7 November to celebrate the third anniversary of the Revolution. Directed by Nikolai Evreinov, the re-enactment involved over 8,000 participants and over 100,000 spectators who were assembled into two groups in the centre of Uritzky Square. It focused on a single event – the Bolshevik-led Red Guards leading an assault on the Winter Palace – and therefore lacked the Leninist historicism of the preceding spectacles; from a theatrical point of view, this also meant that it was more concise and negotiable (the event lasted an hour and a quarter). The proceedings began at 10 p.m. and the action took place over three areas in front of the Winter Palace, which were floodlit at different key moments in the action. According to the theatre historian František Deák, the direction was very effective and much better organised than the actual storming of the Winter Palace, which had been full of confusion.[66] Three stages appeared simultaneously – two conventional ones (representing the 'red' and 'white' armies respectively), and a 'real, historical stage' (the Winter Palace itself) – but only one was lit at any given time, to focus viewers' attention.[67] Richard Stites has observed how the organisational model of these colossal events was wholly military, with performers grouped into units of ten and receiving instructions through a chain of directorial command: 'actors were divided into platoons whose leaders were rehearsed by directors according to a detailed score or battle plan and deployed by the use of military signals and field telephones'.[68] As such, the re-enactment was highly directed and seemed to aim at producing a screen memory, improving the original events and allowing a secondary incident in the Revolution to play a leading part in the collective imaginary, even for those who had participated in the original events. Evreinov reportedly

> went as far as to look for the actual participants in the event and used them in the performance. This was very much in agreement with his theories of the theatricality of life and of a theatre of memory in which the past (the mental spectacle) is changed into the present – the spectacle of live action – by a full re-creation of the circumstances pertaining to the actual event as it took place in reality.[69]

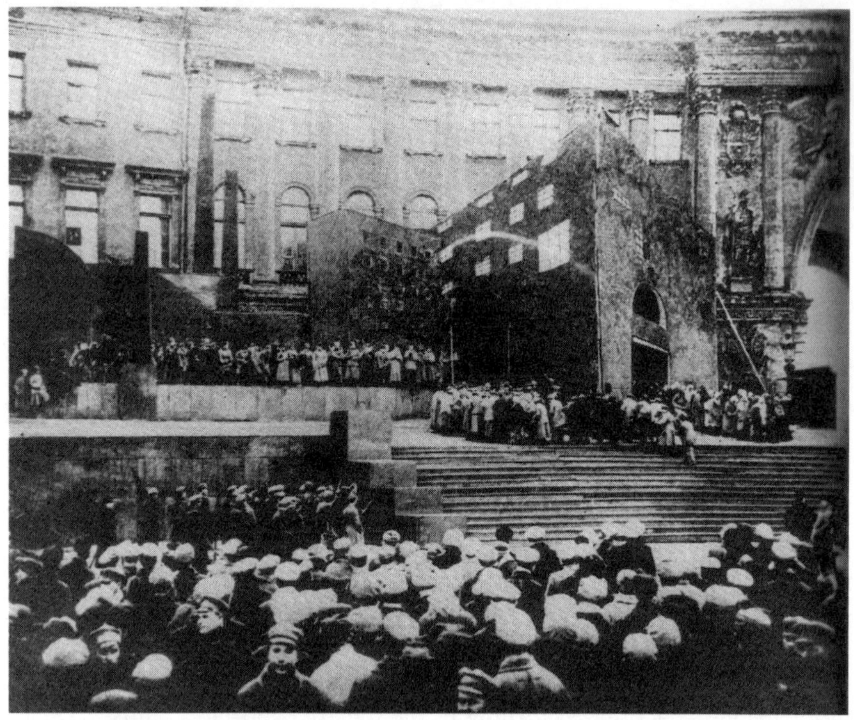

Re-enactment of the Storming of the Winter Palace, 1920. View of the 'Reds'.

At the same time, as Susan Buck-Morss notes, mass theatre not only staged revolution, it staged the *staging* of revolution: the performance was potentially politically precarious, since it recreated the conditions for revolutionary overthrow.[70]

Although Evreinov was something of a classicist, not known for his experimental approach to productions, he had published several books on theatre, including the three-volume *Theatre for Oneself* (1915–17), in which he called for the end of theatre on stage and its realisation in everyday life. Under the slogan 'Let every minute of our life be theatre', he encouraged people to become the actors and playwrights of their own lives.[71] This chimed with the Bolshevik ambition to 'theatricalise life', in other words, to evolve with scenic means a form of environmental propaganda that exceeded what might be attainable within proscenium theatre. Through the size and scale of the re-enactment, a performance could become greater than reality. One of its goals was to work on popular memory: mass spectacle's 'theatricalisation of life' sought to turn historic events of the recent past into 'lived memory', continually re-activated, in order to maintain the euphoria of revolutionary promise while consolidating an origin myth in which the masses make their own history and announce solidarity with the world proletariat. Taken as a whole, the four mass spectacles in St Petersburg formed a genealogy of the Russian Revolution through a two-line family tree:

a Russian line of peasant rebellion, intellectual radicalism, Populism, the first storm of 1905, War, and the revolutionary year 1917 . . . and a European line of slave revolts, the French Revolution, the Paris Commune, and three generations of the socialist family – the grandparents (the utopian socialists), the parents (Marx and Engels), and the children (the Bolsheviks).[72]

The displays of participatory *presence* in mass spectacle, then, stand as the aesthetic and ideological counterpoint to Proletkult theatre's emphasis on participatory *production*: in the former, a hierarchical apparatus of state propaganda used theatre to mobilise public consciousness through the overwhelming *image* of collectivity; in the latter, the state gave support to a grass-roots amateur culture that encouraged the workers to participate in a de-hierarchised creative *process*. The question of how success was to be measured in each instance continues to be vexed. Fülöp-Miller's horror of Bolshevik collectivism is manifest in the very first illustration in his book: a black-and-white photograph of a grimly downtrodden crowd, tersely captioned 'the masses'. He argues against the Bolshevik commitment to 'theatricalised life', drawing attention to its waste of resources and function of distraction, scathingly noting that mass spectacle was done primarily to raise morale, but had nothing to say on the actual problems of the day (the rationing of food, the requisitioning of houses, the electrification of Russia, or the need for new agricultural equipment in the countryside).[73] This distance between theatrical representation and social reality is corroborated by the Lithuanian anarchist Emma Goldman, who describes appalling levels of poverty and education, poor factory conditions, labour camps, breakdowns of the train system, and the continuation of high living standards for the bourgeoisie while the masses remained exactly where they were prior to the Revolution.[74] For both writers, the artistic impact of mass spectacle was undermined by a calamitous economic context and a colossal waste of resources, and for Fülöp-Miller, by rendering the proletariat the subject of a representation that was crassly symbolic and superficial.[75] Mass spectacle, he argued, was hypocritical both in its structural organisation and artistic values:

These 'compositions' are not, however, the work of proletarians; they originate entirely with the intelligentsia, and merely betray what a poor opinion Bolshevik leaders have of the level of this 'mass man', to whom, in the same breath, they assign the sole right to artistic production. All these symbols, all the laboriously thought-out effects of these mass festive performances unmistakably bear the stamp of the artistic, and thus, it may be unconsciously, betray that their authors are not proletarian poets, but in the highest degree Bolshevik aesthetes. Perhaps the 'mass man' has the capacity for new artistic creation in him; but, in order to develop it, he must be free of himself to create, without regard to the political desires of the Government.[76]

It goes without saying that Kerzhentsev's record of the audience reaction to mass spectacles was unproblematically positive. He noted that during *Toward a World Commune*, which finished at 4 a.m. with fireworks and sirens, 'the spectators remained almost motionless and followed the individual scenes with enthusiasm'; by contrast, *The Mystery of Freed Labour* had a livelier impact: when the enormous choir of workers started singing 'The Internationale', 'the electrified masses trampled down the fences surrounding the scene of action, stormed the door of the Stock Exchange and joined the actors in the powerful final chorus'.[77] Huntly Carter was equally swept away, offering the following gushing evidence of mass spectacle's seductive force:

> No-one who sees a mass spectacle of the kind can fail to be impressed by its magnitude, and the almost ecstatic spirit of the multitude . . . As for that rarity, the man of the theatre possessing social ideals, to him it can appear only as a revelation, pregnant with suggestion towards that theatre of the future which shall fully answer the need of spiritual social service.[78]

Once again, Emma Goldman offers a more complex, troubled view. Observing the May Day celebrations in St Petersburg, she notes that the visual decoration of Uritzky Square was impressive – a mass of red flags – but the crowd 'seemed peculiarly quiet, oppressively silent. There was no joy in their singing, no mirth in their laughter. Mechanically they marched, automatically they responded to the claqueurs on the reviewing stand shouting "hurrah" as the columns passed.'[79] Goldman wonders how to explain this silence and the fact that only 'faint applause' could be heard from 'the great throng'. She asked a Bolshevik friend and was told that since people had actually lived through the October Revolution, 'the performance necessarily fell flat by comparison with the reality of 1917'. Unsatisfied with this answer, she asked her neighbour for an opinion: '"The people had suffered so many disappointments since October, 1917", she said, "that the Revolution has lost all meaning to them. The play had the effect of making their disappointment more poignant." '[80] Any interpretation of these events means reading between the lines, as Goldman deftly demonstrates. Her conflicting accounts bear close resemblance to accounts of French revolutionary festivals after 1789, presented alternately as interminably dull ceremonies or orgiastic masquerades, depending on whether writers were favourable or unfavourable to the political aims of the Revolution.[81]

Looking back at these debates, it is perhaps inevitable that attention comes to focus on questions of authentic engagement, since descriptions of the action in mass spectacle are overwhelmingly tedious to read, and do not convey the clash of styles in which they were acted, from unpolished realism to clowning and grotesque buffoonery. What stands out from these accounts are the impressive statistics rather than the plodding historical plotlines and their delivery. The predictability of each spectacle's message has the effect of rendering them increasingly indistinguishable, to the point where – like Proletkult theatre – we seem to be dealing with only one play, performed over and again with minor variations. Participation was more important than watchability, dramatic impact or technical skill. For Kerzhentsev, speaking on behalf of the Proletkult, this was also true of neighbourhood theatre: artistic talent was not in itself considered essential because 'in the revolutionary epoch, it is not the centre of our concerns. A correct theoretical line, precise slogans, and burning enthusiasm are just as important.'[82] It was more pressing for a play to express collective consciousness than to attain the old bourgeois goals of quality and posterity. Here, then, we see the beginning of a clash of criteria that persists today: an art of formal innovation that has relevance beyond its immediate historical moment, capable of speaking to both local and future audiences, versus a dynamic culture that involves as many workers as possible and in so doing provides an ethically and politically correct social model. The same dilemma is posed by the substantial overhaul of music that took place during the post-revolutionary period, and I will conclude this section with two striking examples whose forms reiterate this tension between quality and equality, artistic and social goals.

Despite the popularity of collective theatre and amateur photography in the 1920s, the attempt to eliminate hierarchy and individualism in Soviet culture can be seen most vividly in two forms of musical innovation. The first was the conductorless orchestra movement, which demonstrated its commitment to collectivism in musical performance by renouncing the tyranny of a single privileged conductor, but also by organising rehearsals and performances in a way designed to ensure maximum participation and equal voice. Musicians bore responsibility for the correct technical execution of their individual parts, but also for tempo, nuance and interpretation; the orchestra sat in a circle, facing each other for maximum eye contact, even if this meant that some of them had their backs to the audience.[83] The best known of these orchestras, Persimfans (1922–32), performed in the main concert halls in Moscow, but also in factories, working-class neighbourhoods and army garrisons. Concerts were introduced by short oral presentations on the social background of the composer, and pieces were often played twice to help them stay in the mind of the listener. Stites has argued that Persimfans 'was an example of continued belief in unalienated labour, equality, anti-authoritarianism . . . a utopia in miniature, a tiny republic and model workshop for the communist future'.[84] However, the project was also plagued by technical issues: without a conductor to unify the group, the orchestra had problems with timing – and since there were no great revolutionary composers, they were obliged to keep performing the old bourgeois classics.[85] As with theatre, the principle of collective composition was ideologically desirable but artistically premature.

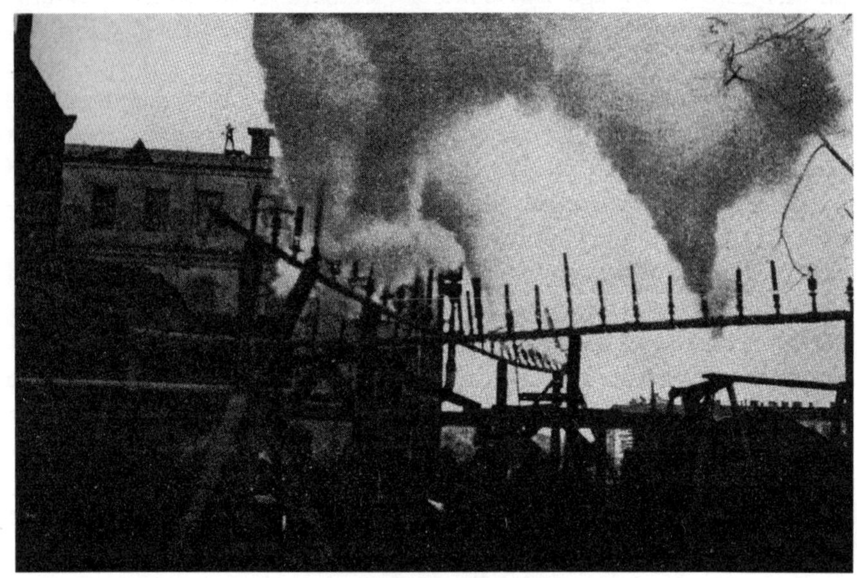

Hooter Symphony, c.1920

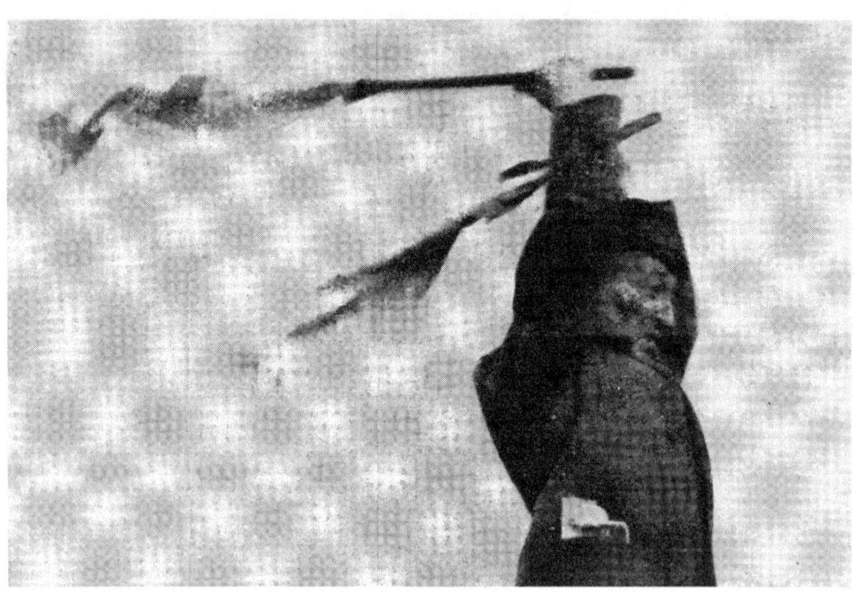

Conductor of a Hooter Symphony, c.1920

My second example, the 'Hooter Symphonies', is one of the most mind-boggling cultural gestures of the post-revolutionary period. Not only did this musical endeavour seek to facilitate mass participation, it also reinvented the entire concept of instrumentation by harnessing the sirens and industrial noise of the modern city into a new understanding of what constituted an orchestra. Conceived as a new and truly proletarian music, the Hooter Symphonies aimed to turn the whole city into an auditorium for an orchestra of new industrial noise, conducted from a rooftop by a man carrying large flags; they embraced 'all the noises of the mechanical age, the rhythm of the machine, the din of the great city and the factory, the whirring of the driving belts, the clattering of motors, and the shrill notes of motor horns'.[86] The Hooter Symphonies were initiated by the music theorist Arsenii Avraamov (1886–1944), a reformist who in 1920 had asked the Commissariat of Enlightenment to confiscate and demolish all pianos as a necessary first step in destroying bourgeois music and the twelve-tone scale. After experiments with factory whistle symphonies in St Petersburg (1918) and Nizhnyi Novgorod (1919), Avraamov oversaw a spectacular noise symphony to celebrate the anniversary of the Revolution in the Baku harbour on 7 November 1922. The event used sirens and whistles from navy ships and steamers, as well as dockside shunting engines, a 'choir' of bus and car horns, and a machine-gun battery. The aim was to evoke the struggle and victory of 1917, and involved versions of 'The Internationale' and 'The Marseillaise' with a 200-piece band and choir, and a large portable organ of steam-controlled whistles on the deck of a torpedo boat. With characteristic scepticism, Fülöp-Miller notes that the results of such experiments were unhappy, to say the least:

> on the one hand, the capacity of modulation in the instruments used was not very great, and, on the other hand, the 'compositions' performed were much too complicated. Although the 'conductors', posted on high towers, regulated by waving flags the intervention of the various sirens and steam-whistles, which were at considerable distances from each other, it proved impossible to attain a uniform, acoustic impression. The distortions were so great that the public could not even recognise the well-known and familiar 'Internationale'.[87]

The (un)recognisability of a tune seems to be a minor quibble in the face of the searing impression that remains of these efforts today, both visually and conceptually: a barely visible man forlornly stands on a factory roof, a tiny speck in the face of an invisible (but one imagines overwhelming) industrial cacophony swirling around him. The futility of this proposition and his impotent centrality stands as the poignant inverse of the conductorless orchestra. Here, the lack of a new repertoire really doesn't matter, because the proposition and its outcome exceed all existing categories: Avraamov's Hooter Symphonies are perhaps more visionary than any other Russian cultural experiments of this period, since they rethink not only *who* makes music, but its instrumentation, audience and site of reception. Persimfans, however pleasingly eccentric in its ideological rejection of the conductor, remains wedded to existing conventions of classical musical performance: modulating a convention but falling short of overhauling the idealist category of music.

III. Excursions and Trials

It is telling that the avant-garde examples from this period of Russian history tend to be attached to single names rather than collectively co-authored productions; even mass spectacles such as *The Storming of the Winter Palace* are attributed to a singular director. While this can be attributed to history's preference for the monographic, it also, perhaps, indicates the artistic weaknesses of collectively authored Proletkult theatre in this period, or at least its inability to transcend local topics and concerns. In a different way, the Dada Season or *Grande Saison Dada*, held in spring 1921, also serves as proof that collective production survives only with difficulty within the canon, further sidelined by being performance- rather than object-based.[88] Using techniques of media provocation and publicity honed by the Futurists, Paris Dada built on the innovations of Zurich Dada's Cabaret Voltaire (1915–17) and organised mixed bills of performance, music and poetry in concert halls such as the Salle Gaveau. By spring 1921, for reasons that I will elaborate below, the group decided to take performance out of a cabaret context and into extra-institutional public space. The experimental events of the Dada Season form a poignant contrast to the Russian experiments at this time. Both sought to involve the public, and to use public space, but to entirely different ends; if Russian mass spectacle was overtly ideological and affirmative, the Dada group was (at least in its early phase) all-negating, anti-ideological and anarchist.

The focus of the *Grande Saison Dada* was a series of manifestations in April and May 1921 that sought to involve the Parisian public: 'Visits – Dada Salon – Conferences – Commemorations – Operas – Plebiscites – Summons – Accusation Orders and Judgements'.[89] Louis Aragon mentions a series of meetings and discussions, designed to give 'all possible pomp and grandeur to this new offensive', but the most salient events of the season were an excursion to the church of Saint Julien-le-Pauvre and the *Barrès Trial*.[90] In a radio interview broadcast in 1952, André Breton identified three phases of Dada activity as it developed in Paris: a phase of lively agitation initiated by the arrival of Tristan Tzara in the city (January–August 1920); a 'more groping phase' that tended towards the same goals but through 'radically renewed means', under the impulse of Aragon and himself (January–August 1921); and a 'phase of *malaise*' where the attempt to return to the initial form of manifestations caused more divisions until August 1922 when the group dissolved.[91] The Dada Season belongs to the second of these three phases, and denotes a period of fracture within the group; specifically, it testifies to increased tension between Breton, Tzara and Francis Picabia. In the light of contemporary debates around collectivity, it is worth noting that Dada saw itself as a collection of individuals united by opposition to the same causes (war, nationalism, etc.) but little else. As Breton explained,

> Everyone insists on using words like group, leader of a group, discipline. Some people even say that, under the pretence of stressing individuality, Dada is really a danger to individuality. They do not understand for a moment that it is our differences that unite us. Our common resistance to artistic and moral laws gives us only momentary satisfaction. We are very well aware that, beyond and above it, the individual imagination retains its total liberty – and that this, even more than the movement itself, is Dada.[92]

In this ongoing attachment to the 'individual imagination', Dada also betrayed its Romantic roots, even while it attempted – without huge success – to reach out to the working class. For example, in February 1920 the group held discussions at the Club au Faubourg, where Dada was explained to more than 3,000 workers and intellectuals, and at the Université Populaire du Faubourg de Saint-Antoine, where they had been invited to give a public presentation of their activities.[93] Hans Richter reports that

> this event took place in a markedly civilised atmosphere. Tzara's Dada style may have been a little cramped by his respect for the working class; provocations were avoided at the outset. Here, as in Berlin, Dada showed itself to be an anti-bourgeois movement which had a certain feeling of solidarity with the anti-bourgeois working class.[94]

Even so, he adds, 'the Dadaists failed to convince the workers', since the latter found it hard to stomach the way in which the artists 'consigned Napoleon, Kant, Cézanne, Marx and Lenin to the same scrap-heap'.[95]

The Dada Season therefore tried to take a different tack. The first part of the Season involved 'Excursions and Visits', projecting Dada events into a new type of public realm beyond that of the music halls. The first of these excursions was scheduled for 14 April 1921 at 3 p.m., meeting in the churchyard of Saint Julien-le-Pauvre: 'a deserted, almost unknown church in totally uninteresting, positively doleful surroundings'.[96] The Surrealist writer Georges Hugnet described the excursion as an 'absurd rendez-vous, mimicking instructive walks, *guide à la clé*'.[97] The fliers advertising the event, which were also published in several newspapers, stated that the artists wished 'to set right the incompetence of suspicious guides' and lead a series of 'excursions and visits' to places that have 'no reason to exist'.

ExcuRsIons & visiTES DADA

UN CULTE NOUVEAU : LEÇONS DE COUPE

LA PROPRETÉ EST LE LUXE DU PAUVRE SOYEZ SALE

DISTRIBUTION DE BAS DE SOIE A 3,85

DADA

1ÈRE *L'Église* VISITE :

Saint Julien le Pauvre

PROCHAINES VISITES :
Musée du Louvre
Buttes Chaumont
Gare Saint-Lazare
Mont du Petit Cadenas
Canal de l'Ourcq
etc.

JEUDI 14 AVRIL A 3 h.

RENDEZ-VOUS DANS LE JARDIN DE L'ÉGLISE

Rue Saint Julien le Pauvre — (Métro Saint-Michel et Cité)

COURSES PÉDESTRES DANS LE JARDIN

ON DOIT COUPER SON NEZ COMME SES CHEVEUX

Les dadaïstes de passage à Paris voulant remédier à l'incompétence de guides et de cicerones suspects, ont décidé d'entreprendre une série de visites à des endroits choisis, en particulier à ceux qui n'ont vraiment pas de raison d'exister. — C'est à tort qu'on insiste sur le pittoresque (Lycée Janson de Sailly), l'intérêt historique (Mont Blanc) et la valeur sentimentale (la Morgue). — La partie n'est pas perdue mais il faut agir vite. — Prendre part à cette première visite c'est se rendre compte du progrès humain, des destructions possibles et de la nécessité de poursuivre notre action que vous tiendrez à encourager par tous les moyens.

LAVEZ VOS SEINS COMME VOS GANTS

★ EN BAS LE HAUT ▬ EN HAUT LE BAS

MERCI POUR LE FUSIL

Sous la conduite de : Gabrielle BUFFET, Louis ARAGON, ARP, André BRETON, Paul ELUARD, Th. FRAENKEL, J. HUSSAR, Benjamin PÉRET, Francis PICABIA, Georges RIBEMONT-DESSAIGNES, Jacques RIGAUT, Philippe SOUPAULT, Tristan TZARA.

et encore une fois BONJOUR

(Le piano a été mis très gentiment à notre disposition par la maison Gavault.)

Excursions and Visits, flyer for the Dada Season, 1921

Instead of drawing attention to picturesque sites, or places of historical interest or sentimental value, the aim was to make a nonsense of the social form of the guided tour. The flier also listed a number of proposed future visits – which in fact would never be carried out – to destinations including the Louvre, the park at Buttes Chaumont and the Gare Saint-Lazare. The fliers were festooned with slogans laid out in typical Dada typography: 'You should cut your nose like your hair', 'Wash your breasts like your gloves', 'Property is the luxury of the poor, be dirty', 'Thanks for the rifle'.[98]

The audience figures for this event are disputed: Richter reports that 'it rained and no-one came. The idea of further similar enterprises was abandoned.'[99] Breton, meanwhile, states that they attracted 'one or two hundred onlookers'.[100] Photographs testify to a figure somewhere in between, a modest-sized group in smart dress, standing around in evidently dismal weather conditions. The group had acquired a popular following, in part thanks to Tzara's canny manipulation of the press (for example, for the Dada event on 5 February 1920, Tzara advertised the presence of Charlie Chaplin lecturing on the Dada movement in order to draw crowds and press coverage).[101] Breton read a manifesto out loud, while Georges Ribemont-Dessaignes played the part of guide, holding a large Larousse dictionary in his hands; in front of particular sculptures or monuments, he read definitions from the book, chosen at random; 'the most sparkling ones', he recalled, 'were those without a value judgement'.[102] A downpour of rain drew the tour to an early close after about an hour and a half, and prevented an 'auction of abstractions' from taking place.[103] The audience

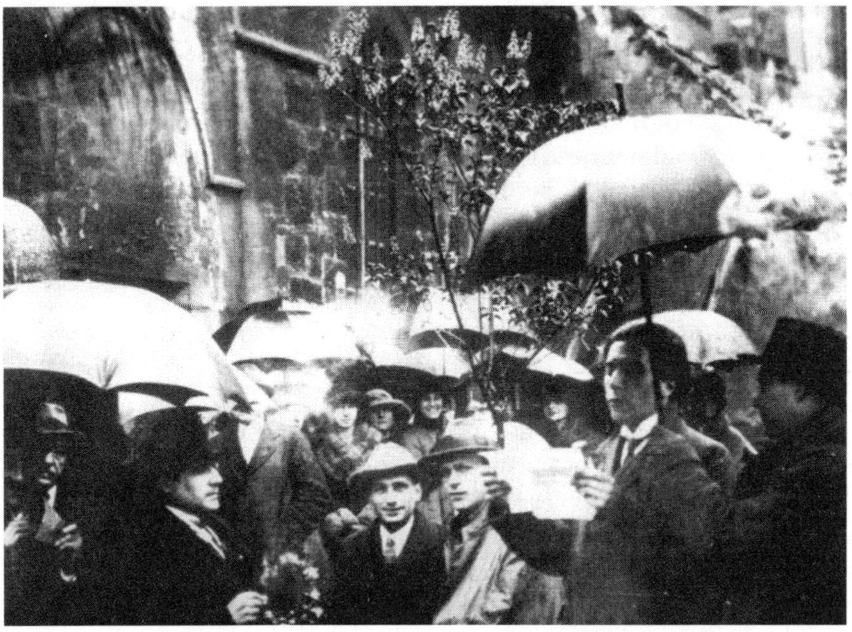

Excursion to Saint Julien-le-Pauvre, 14 April 1921

started to scatter and as a parting token they were offered surprise envelopes containing phrases, portraits, visiting cards, bits of fabric, landscapes, obscene drawings, even five franc notes defaced with erotic symbols. The Dada group then decamped to a nearby café to appraise the event. According to Michel Sanouillet, at this point collective depression set in: Breton had wanted the event to be threatening and subversive, but it had fallen into a rut – through a lack of preparation, because certain people hadn't turned up (notably a porcelain repairer called Joliboit and a peanut seller who were supposed to comprise an 'orchestra'), and in part because the public 'never ceased to play the Dada game'.[104]

The latter point is crucial, along with Breton's numerous observations in 'Artificial Hells', his post-mortem of the event written on 20 May (one month after the excursion), that the public had 'acquired a taste for our performances' and that 'a successful man, or simply one who is no longer attacked, is a dead man'.[105] Breton seems to imply that the group's search for a new relationship between performer and audience was difficult to attain due to the latter's entrenched expectation of (and desire for) provocation. As Richter reported, 'it was obvious that the public was now ready to accept "a thousand repeat performances" of the evening at the Salle Gaveau . . . At all costs, they must be prevented from accepting shock as a work of art.'[106] The extent to which audience enthusiasm for Dada performance had become ossified can be seen in Tzara's recollection of the Salle Gaveau on 26 May 1920: 'For the first time in our experience we were assaulted, not only with eggs, cabbages and pennies, but even with beef steaks. It was a very great success. The public was extremely Dadaist. We had already said that the true Dadaists are against Dada.'[107] He goes on to note that at another event at Théâtre de l'Oeuvre the same month, 'enthusiastic members of the audience had brought musical instruments to interrupt us'. For Breton, by contrast, this mode of event had exhausted its potential and did not need to keep being repeated; the tactic of audience provocation was rapidly becoming 'stereotyped' and 'fossilised'.[108] The Parisian public, Breton noted, had 'made itself increasingly our accomplice', goading them into more scandal, to the point where 'we ended up gauging our appeal by the cries made against us'.[109]

Henceforth, Breton became more interested in rethinking Dada events as less driven towards the production of scandal:

Dada events certainly involve a desire other than to scandalize. Scandal, for all its force (one may easily trace it from Baudelaire to the present), would be insufficient to elicit the delight that one might expect from an artificial hell. One should also keep in mind the odd pleasure obtained in 'taking to the street' or 'keeping one's footing,' so to speak . . . By conjoining thought with gesture, Dada has left the realm of shadows to venture onto solid grounds.[110]

For Breton it was crucial that Dada should enter the public realm, breaking out of cabaret and theatre conventions to create situations where the public would be confronted with a new type of artistic action and spectatorship: 'We imagined guiding our public to places in which we could hold their attention better than in a theatre, because the *very fact of going there entails a certain goodwill on their part*. The visits, of which Saint-Julien-le-Pauvre was the first in the series, had absolutely no other pretext.'[111] This desire for the audience's attention implies a serious shift in Dada's mode of audience relations to that point, which had been predicated on an antagonistic one-upmanship akin to the Futurist *serate*. Rather than operating within the proscenium frame, with all the connotations of escapism that this connoted, Breton implied that viewers should find a continuity between the work of art and their lives: 'taking to the streets' would thus be a way to forge a closer connection between art and life. As such, Breton seemed keen to develop more subtle areas of social investigation, and to refute the chaotic anarchism that had been the hallmark of Dada to date. The new direction leaned instead towards more refined and meaningful forms of participatory experience.

Not that this new direction was unilaterally welcomed by the group. It was a source of anxiety for Picabia, who considered Dada to have nothing to do with beliefs of any kind; the use of a churchyard, for example, seemed to him to announce a 'political clerical or non-clerical character'.[112] The event's press release had nevertheless emphasised a lack of targeted critique: 'It's not about a demonstration of anti-clericalism as one would be tempted to believe, rather a new interpretation of nature applied this time not to art, but to life.'[113] This sentiment indicates the degree to which Breton was moving towards a Surrealist stance: conventional tourism was taken as

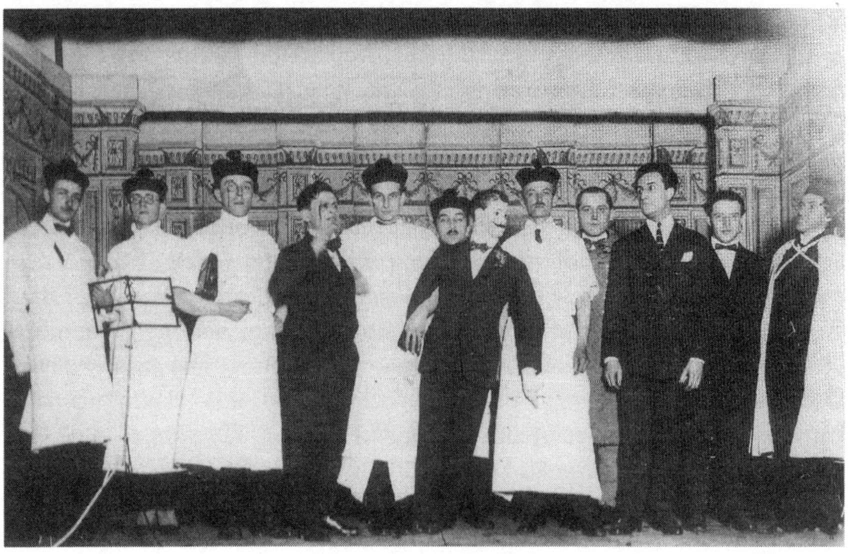

The Maurice Barrès Trial, 1921

a point of quasi-anthropological investigation, appropriating a social form and subverting its conventional associations. (This principle was repeated three years later in the *Bureau of Surrealist Research* [1924] – an office for meetings, discussions, interviews and the collection of information about dreams from the public – and in the Surrealist group's nocturnal strolls around the city.) In 'Artificial Hells', Breton defended his position against Picabia, and stated a reorientation of Dada towards moral and political goals. What he meant by this reorientation was made more evident in the second major event of the Dada Season, the *Barrès Trial*.

Held on Friday 13 May 1921, the *Barrès Trial* was advertised as a hearing of the author Maurice Barrès (1862–1923), whose book *Un Homme Libre* (1889), had been a great influence on Breton and Aragon in their youth. Barrès had advocated anarchism, freedom and total individualism, but more recently had changed his colours and turned right-wing, nationalist and bourgeois. The aim of the trial was, in Breton's words, 'to determine the extent to which a man could be held accountable if his will to power led him to champion conformist values that diametrically opposed the ideas of his youth'.[114] Like the excursion to Saint Julien-le-Pauvre, the event annexed and *détourned* a social form (the trial), and involved the participation of the public, now with a more active role, since the fliers advertising the event invited twelve people to apply to sit on the jury.[115]

The tribunal took place in the Salle des Sociétés Savantes, with the Dada group dressed up in the ceremonial outfits of the Palais de Justice (white robes with clerical caps – red for the defence and black for the prosecution). Each member of the group had a specific role – defence, public prosecution, president, a stream of witnesses, and so on. Barrès himself was invited to attend, but declined, claiming that he had a prior engagement; the group produced a surrogate of him in the form of a tailor's dummy. The photograph documenting the event doesn't record the twelve jurors (who apparently sentenced Barrès to twenty years of hard labour), nor does it give any impression of the space and the audience. Even so, the event's appropriation of the social form of a trial and its non-confrontational collaboration with the public point to a distinct break with cabaret-based performances such as the Salle Gaveau. The transcription of the proceedings indicates a degree of self-searching on Breton's part: he seems to be attempting to understand Dada's own position, politically and aesthetically, through the case of Barrès, the radical young thinker turned President of the League of Patriots. The resulting discussion was notably less absurdist than Dada performances to that point, including the visit to Saint Julien-le-Pauvre. As is made clear by the first line of the *Acte d'accusation du Procès Barrès*, the time had come for Dada to adopt values other than that of nihilism, which had characterised Zurich Dada's embrace of nonsense as a refusal of the nationalist rhetoric of the First World War: 'Dada, deciding that it's time to give its spirit of negation an executive power, and determined above all to exercise this against those who try and prevent its dictatorship, from today onwards takes measures to quash their resistance.'[116] Aragon described these events as 'a sort of intrusion of the moral domain into the people's private lives', while Breton, in 'Artificial Hells', repeatedly refers to the events of the Dada Season as a 'discussion on moral grounds', and hints that Paris Dada is coming to an end and that it would not be surprising to find the group 'in art, philosophy or politics'.[117]

The *Barrès Trial* marks a turning point in Dada performance and a step towards Surrealism, with the ascendency of Breton's intellectualised approach over the anarchic provocations of Picabia and Tzara. Picabia left the hall theatrically before the end of the trial, while Tzara did his best to spread disorder: during the event he claimed to have no interest in Barrès whatsoever, and referred to him as 'the biggest pig of the century' – like Breton, Fraenkel, Aragon and the rest of his colleagues.[118] For Hugnet, the most significant shift in this regard was the fact that Dada now presumed to *judge* rather than simply to *negate*; in other words, it attempted to find a position rather than offering an a priori rejection of *all* positions.[119]

Ribemont-Dessaignes similarly observed that 'Dada itself was no longer on the scene. Dada could be a criminal, or coward, a destroyer or a thief, but not a judge. The first indictment left us morose, with an unpleasant taste in our mouths.'[120] Rather than a space of nonsensical chaos, then, the *Barrès Trial* presented a conflicted parody of the courtroom as a formal space for debate, ultimately revolving less around political than *moral* criteria: the betrayal of switching allegiance, which applied not only to Barrès but perhaps also to Breton himself, in shifting Dada's focus away from anarchic negation to more clearly articulated judgements of denunciation. As Richter notes, after the Barrès trial, 'Not much remained of . . . the *anti*, which had been Dada's original moral credo.'[121] In short, morality was making inroads, informed by Breton's nascent allegiance to Marx and Freud, both of whom offered their own accounts of freedom.

IV. Cohesion and Disruption

These 'artificial hells' across the political spectrum begin to expose some of the contradictions between intention and reception, agency and manipulation, that will become central problems in the contemporary discourse of participation. It is telling that a full spectrum of ideological positions are already represented in its diverse points of origin. Futurism (and later, Dada cabaret) created situations in which the audience were mobilised to participate in an orgy of hostility towards Futurist artists and poets engaged in a political mission of pro-war militaristic nationalism. Perversely, such an attack on the performers stood not as a failure but as a mark of success, an indicator of the public's active readiness towards accepting the artists' goals. That audiences were not only ready for but *demanding* an active role can be seen by the lengths to which they went to buy food to hurl on stage, or bring musical instruments along to the theatre. Breton struggled to negotiate this transition away from consuming violence and towards an intelligible stance of moral consistency through the creation of small-scale collectively realised social actions, in which the audience position was more prescribed, but which were perceived at the time to be failures. By contrast, the mobilisation of mass audiences and performers in St Petersburg abandoned any pretence to spontaneity; as Lunacharsky stipulated, 'by means of General Military Instruction, we create rhythmically moving masses embracing thousands of and tens of thousands of people – and not just a crowd, but a strictly regulated, collective, peaceful army sincerely possessed by one definite idea'.[122] Paris and St Petersburg thus stand as polar opposites in the imagination of an unframed art in public space. In Paris Dada, an authored and subversive lineage attempts to provoke audience-participants into a self-reflexive examination of their norms and mores; in Russian mass spectacle, the state imposes the aesthetic potency of collective presence to provide a focus for national achievement masked as a celebration of transnational proletarian identity. If the former is disruptive or interventionist, presenting small-scale instances of dissensus in the face of dominant moral and aesthetic norms, the latter is constructive and affirmative, presenting public space as the locus of an artificial mass cohesion.

In all three instances, which tentatively mark out a new territory for audience inclusion in the twentieth century, the issue of participation becomes increasingly inextricable from the question of political commitment. For Futurism, participation ushered in an active embrace of right-wing nationalism. In post-revolutionary Russia, participation denoted an affirmation of revolutionary ideals. Only Dada, in its negation of all political and moral positions, provided a compelling alternative to ideologically motivated participation, even while its Parisian iteration moved towards a position of moral analysis and judgement.[123] As such it is popular today to claim that such art is 'implicitly political', as if this term had any identifiable meaning; if this phrase tells us anything, it is less about Dada's (anti-) artistic achievements than the pervasiveness of our present-day determination to find a 'political' character for art in the face of liberal democratic consensus. The relationship between artistic form and political commitment becomes increasingly fraught as these early case studies transform in the following decades: Dada and Surrealist excursions become the Situationist *dérive*, while the most immediate heir to Russian mass spectacle is found in the grotesque displays of military prowess and mass conformity at the Nuremberg rallies (which deployed the slogan 'No spectators, only actors' to describe its liturgical form of mass participation).[124] The memory of these totalitarian regimes weighed heavily on the post-war generation, for whom mass organisation became anathema. Instead, as we shall see in the following chapter, participation was directed away from the imposition of social equality and onto the question of freedom: a celebration of the everyday worker was replaced by a re-evaluation of everyday objects and experiences as a point of opposition to cultural hierarchy.

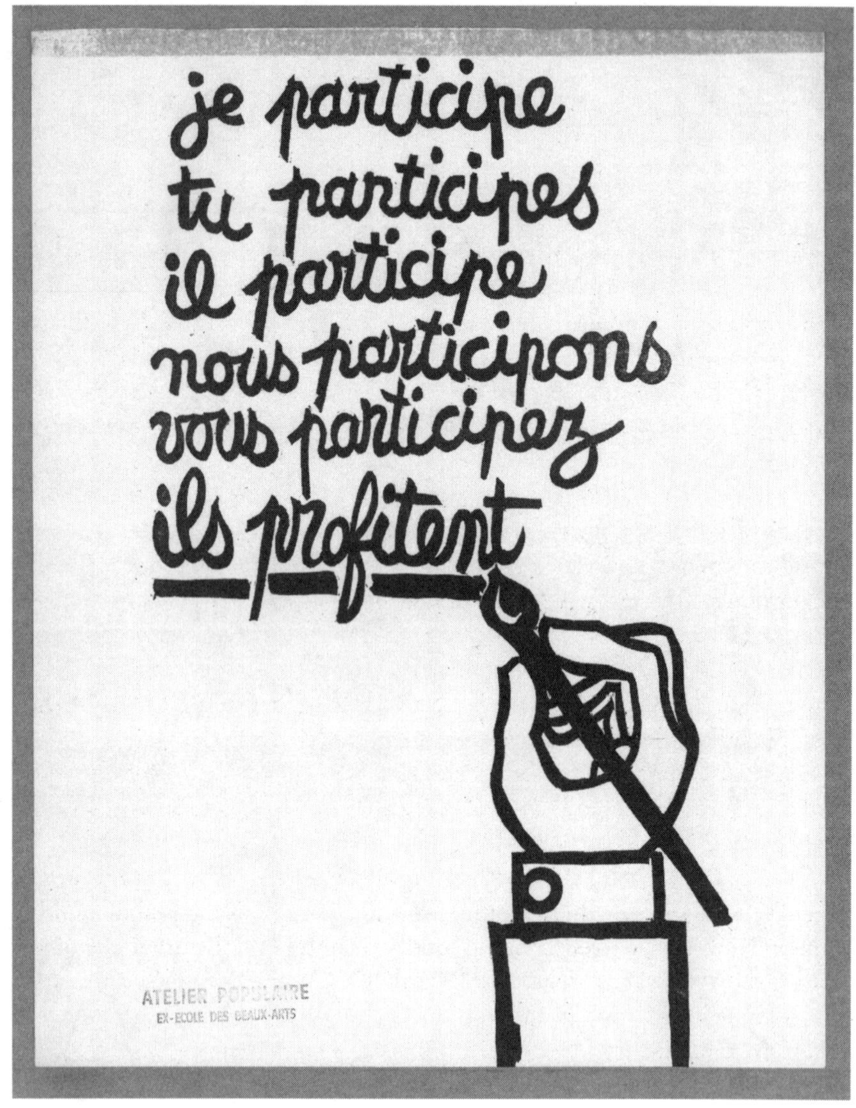

Atelier Populaire, *Je participe, tu participes, il participe…*, 1968. Poster screenprint on paper.

3

Je participe, tu participes, il participe . . .

With its roots in Dada excursions and Surrealist nocturnal strolls, the *dérive*, or goal-less 'drifting', was employed by artists and writers associated with the Situationist International (SI) from the early 1950s to the late '60s as a form of behavioural disorientation. Best undertaken during daylight hours, and in groups of two or three like-minded people, the *dérive* was a crucial research tool in the Situationist para-discipline of 'psychogeography', the study of the effects of a given environment on the emotions and behaviour of individuals. As a mode of increasing one's awareness of (specifically urban) surroundings, the *dérive* differed from Surrealist wandering in that it placed less emphasis on automatism and the individual unconscious. Rather than being an end in itself, the *dérive* was a form of data-gathering for Situationist 'unitary urbanism', an attempt to undo and move beyond what they saw as the disciplining, homogenising and ultimately dehumanising effect of modernist forms of urban high-rise living, exemplified by the modular architecture of Le Corbusier.[1]

From an art historical perspective, the *dérive* offers very little for visual analysis. Written accounts, which Debord described as 'passwords to this great game', tend to be variable in their usefulness.[2] An early report from 1953 describes Debord undertaking an 'extended *dérive*' with Gilles Ivain and Gaetan Langlais; this amounts to little more than hanging around in bars on New Year's Eve, speaking loudly to aggravate the other customers until Debord becomes 'dead drunk'; after this, Ivain 'continues alone for a few hours with a similarly marked success'.[3] New Year's Day carries on in much the same fashion, but in a Jewish bar. The report of 6 March 1956 is more in keeping with what one might hope to find in a *dérive*: Debord and Gil Wolman drift north from the rue des Jardins-Paul and find an abandoned rotunda by Claude-Nicolas Ledoux.[4] They continue to drift around the district of Aubervilliers, taking in a bar, and end the *dérive* when it gets dark. Although this particular *dérive* is described as being 'of little interest of such', it is strikingly flaneurial, in contrast to the overtly critical and political tenor of other Situationist texts.[5] Other psychogeographical reports are more analytical, if less vividly narrative, such as Abdelhafid

77

Khatib's 'Attempt at a Psychogeographical Description of Les Halles' (1958). The essay pays attention to the area's diurnal and nocturnal ambience, the main routes of access and the use of particular areas, and makes constructive suggestions for rethinking this central area of Paris as a space for 'manifestations of liberated collective life'; in the meantime, Khatib suggests, it would do well to serve as 'an attraction park for the ludic education of the workers'.[6]

I begin with this discussion of the *dérive* because, in Guy Debord's contribution to the SI's seventh conference in 1966, he observed that the group's strategies of the *dérive* and unitary urbanism had to be understood in terms of their 'struggle' with utopian architecture, the Venice Biennale, the Happenings, and the Groupe Recherche d'Art Visuel (GRAV).[7] In keeping with his suggestion, this chapter will examine three forms of open-ended participatory art in Paris during the 1960s, contrasting the theory and practice of the Situationist International to the 'situations' of GRAV and to the eroticised and transgressive Happenings of Jean-Jacques Lebel. It should immediately be acknowledged that, art historically, none of these figures are canonical: in an Anglophone context, there is little literature on GRAV, while Lebel has only recently become the focus of attention (most notably in the work of Alyce Mahon). The SI cannot be considered straightforwardly as artists, and especially not as producers of participatory art, even if today's proliferation of neo-Situationist activities, which frequently denigrate art and the aesthetic, all demand a re-visitation of the SI's activities from an art historical perspective; in this case, it is one that places their claims for participation alongside a laboratory model of artistic experimentation and an eroticised theatrical counterculture.[8] Despite the mountain of literature on the SI produced within Cultural Studies, there have been very few attempts to contextualise the group within artistic tendencies of the period.[9] More usually, writers defer to the SI's self-proclaimed exceptionalism and distance from mainstream artistic activities, particularly following the controversies occasioned by their first museum show in 1989.[10]

This chapter picks up a number of themes outlined in previous chapters: the tension between collective and individual authorship, the cultivation of multiple audiences, and the conflicting demands of individual agency and directorial control. Once again, theatrical metaphors are prevalent: Lebel was influenced by Antonin Artaud's Theatre of Cruelty (from *The Theatre and Its Double*, 1938), while an early tract by the French section of the SI is titled 'Nouveau théâtre d'opérations dans la culture' (1958). Each of the groups presents a different solution to the problem of visualising ephemeral participatory experiences: GRAV leave us with sculptures and (more rarely) installations; Lebel and his contemporaries offer partially drafted scores and photographs to be re-interpreted; while the SI hand down films, discursive tracts and architectural models, which serve primarily as suggestions or tools with which to continue the spirit of their project. Finally, it should be noted that all three claimed a central role in the events of May 1968, despite occupying distinct political positions: a left-of-centre technophilic populism (GRAV), a sexually liberated anarchism (Lebel), and a dogmatic, anti-visual Marxism (the SI).

The political context for these artistic activities is important to grasp. The Cuban Revolution took place in 1959, providing renewed hope to the left. Domestically, the late 1950s saw the collapse of the Fourth Republic and the election in June 1958 of Charles de Gaulle, who rewrote the constitution and inaugurated the Fifth Republic. He gradually withdrew French troops from Algeria (granting it independence in 1962), which led to a huge influx of immigrants populating appallingly basic *bidonvilles* (shanty towns) in Lyon, Marseille and Nanterre – within sight of the overcrowded university campus where the events of May 1968 began. Despite mass rural migration to the cities and a rising consumer culture (whose imagery was analysed by Roland Barthes in *Mythologies*, 1957), social mobility did not become correspondingly flexible. De Gaulle's presidency has since been characterised as having two themes, 'marrying the century one is living in' and 'dependent participation', the latter phrase taken from the left-wing sociologist Alain Touraine.[11] Touraine coined this phrase as a critical descriptor of consumer society, but for de Gaulle it denoted a society based on willing consent, and was to be celebrated. It is worth keeping in mind these various resonances of participation. Some artists enthusiastically made participation a foundational principle of their artistic practice, while others vocally rejected it as a mode of artistic coercion equivalent to social structures.[12] During May 1968, one could find graffiti proclaiming 'To be free in 1968 means to participate', while at the same time the Atelier Populaire produced posters showing a hand and pen, conjugating the verb to more sceptical ends: '*Je participe, tu participes, il participe, nous participons, vous participez, ils profitent.*'

In artistic circles, participation was primarily understood in terms of interactive and kinetic art, and hailed as a popular new democratic mode. Michel Ragon's *Vingt-cinq ans d'art vivant* (1969) concludes with a chapter on the 'democratisation of art': his signs of art's new mass accessibility include GRAV's experiments with the game and labyrinth (discussed below), which synthesise sculpture and spectacle.[13] His other indicators of 'democratic art' include collaborations with industry, such as GRAV's Nicolas Schöffer working with Philips; artists making unlimited multiples; department stores organising exhibitions; and architectural projects synthesising the arts in murals, mosaics and light projections. Frank Popper's *Art – Action, Participation* (1975) also makes an explicit connection between participation and social equality; for him, the work of kinetic artists 'helped to lay the foundation of a new art, a truly DEMOCRATIC ART'.[14] Informed by cybernetics and alluding to a wide range of European case studies (many of which have sunk without art historical trace), Popper rightly points to the difficulty of establishing a hard and fast distinction between physical activation and the incitement to mental activity. The final page of his book features a flow chart in which three genealogies of art (Post-Dada/Pop/Conceptualism, Political Art/Socialist Realism, and Post-Bauhaus/Constructivist Kinetic Art) all come together via spectator participation to form 'Democratic Art', defined as one in which 'the power of aesthetic decision lies in the hands of all'; its consequences – 'the disappearance of the work and the diminished responsibility of the artist' – are, he argues, only 'superficially negative phenomena' when seen in light of the resulting social and artistic gains.[15]

These writers' equation between democracy and participatory art, as a radical new tendency with social implications, needs in turn to be contextualised by French art in the 1950s, which was dominated by the abstraction of *art informel* on the one hand (Jean Dubuffet, Henri Michaux, Jean Fautrier) and the figurative realism of *art engagé* on the other (socialist realist painters such as André Fougeron). Surrealism continued to be a lingering cultural presence into the 1960s, albeit in a decadent mode: the commitment to Marx and Freud that had characterised Surrealist activities of the 1920s had transformed into an embrace of mysticism and the occult, as witnessed in the group's elaborate *Eros* exhibition at Galerie Daniel Cordier in 1959. For a younger generation of artists, the unconscious was overrated as a revolutionary principle, while the group's Oedipal organisation around Breton as paternal leader was explicitly to be rejected.[16] Dada rather than Surrealism became the primary point of reference, not only for the SI but for Lebel and the Nouveaux Réalistes, formed in 1960.[17] In 1959, the first Paris Biennial, for artists under the age of thirty-five, encouraged popular interest in visual art, bolstered by the convergence between art and high fashion (such as Yves Saint Laurent's 'Mondrian' dress, 1965) and the popularisation of art and multiples (the department store Prisunic produced artist editions in 1967, leading Martial Raysse to declare that 'Prisunic stores are the museums of modern art').[18] In short, the artistic backdrop to participatory art in Paris of the 1960s was an idea of democracy as the levelling equality of consumer capitalism. Everyday culture, accessible to all, was at the core of this understanding of democracy; while this stood in some degree of opposition to elitist cultural hierarchies, and to figurative modes of leftist art in the 1950s, it rarely delved into questions of class difference and social inequality.

I. The SI: Surpassing Art

As has often been stated, the SI emerged from a number of post-war artistic and literary groups including Lettrisme (1946–52), the Lettriste International (c.1952–7), the International Movement for an Imaginist Bauhaus

(1953–7) and CoBrA (1948–51). The core of the group (Guy Debord and Gil Wolman) had in the early 1950s clustered around the Romanian poet Isidore Isou, attracted by his ambition to destroy literary language – a tradition that Isou saw passing from Victor Hugo via Mallarmé and Tristan Tzara to himself. In 1952 Debord and Wolman split from Isou, perceiving his ideals to be too aesthetic; they formed the Lettriste International, whose aim was nothing less than the transformation of everyday life.[19] For this group (whose average age in 1952 was 23), the purpose of art was not to produce objects but to critique the commodification of existence. In 1957, members of the Lettriste International joined with Danish and Italian artists to create the Situationist International. Their main activities were spread across Paris, Amsterdam and Copenhagen, with branches in Germany, Italy and the UK, and took the form of films, collages, discussions and vast amounts of writing compiled into the twelve issues of their metallic-covered journal *Internationale Situationniste* (*I.S.*), 1958–72. The *I.S.* contains images and essays, many of them anonymous or collaboratively authored, on topics as varied as racism, the political situation in Algeria, Spain and the Middle East, reports on SI conferences, analyses of the first stirrings of youth revolt, and attacks on Jean-Luc Godard, the media and spectacle. There is very little writing on art, although there are articles on cultural revolution, and brief dissections of the group's two attempts to overturn exhibition formats via the 'labyrinth' ('Die Welt als Labyrinthe', Stedelijk Museum, Amsterdam, 1960) and the 'manifestation' (RSG-6, at Galleri Exi, Odense, 1963).

The immediate context for the emergence of the SI is therefore characterised primarily by an interest in literature and current affairs rather than visual art, even if the first issue of the *I.S.* is preoccupied with statements about Surrealism: the first article is titled 'The Bitter Victory of Surrealism' and argues that capitalism has co-opted the surrealist interest in a revolutionary unconscious (for example in business 'brainstorming' sessions).[20] In the same issue, the group stated that its desire was to 'appropriate, with greater effectiveness, the freedom of spirit and the concrete freedom of mores claimed by Surrealism'.[21] However, the movement rapidly diminished in importance as a point of reference and was replaced by Dada. Michèle Bernstein observed, 'There was the father we hated, Surrealism. And there was the father we loved, Dada. We were the children of both.'[22] At the same time, the SI's relationship to visual art was paradoxical and fraught with contradictions. In principle, the group advocated that art should be suppressed in order to be realised as life. In reality, the situation was more complicated, and histories of the SI tend to be divided over the extent to which the group can be considered to have had an early and a late phase, on the basis of its relationship to visual art.

The first phase (1957–62) is commonly agreed to be a period when the group was most sympathetic to art: this period saw commercial gallery exhibitions in Paris by Asger Jorn (*Modifications* [*Peinture détournée*] at Galerie Rive Gauche) and Giuseppe Pinot-Gallizio (*Cavern of Anti-Matter* at the Galerie René Drouin), both in 1959. Both shows sought to complicate traditional ideas of single authorship: Jorn by painting over existing paintings purchased in flea markets, and Pinot-Gallizio by producing abstract painting on rolls to be purchased by the metre, which he referred to as 'industrial paintings'. In the same year, the experimental architect Constant Nieuwenhuys exhibited his model precinct maquettes at the Stedelijk Museum, Amsterdam. In 1960, however, the balance between artistic and literary interests began to shift: Pinot-Gallizio was excommunicated from the SI, and Constant resigned at the same time; both exits were the result of disagreements and denunciations stemming from contacts made in the art world. A year later Asger Jorn resigned, and after 1962 – in part triggered by Jorn's brother Jørgen Nash setting up a rival 'Second Situationist International', and in part by Debord's increased politicisation following his dialogue with the Marxist sociologist Henri Lefebvre – the group became increasingly opposed to art as an activity separated from revolutionary praxis.[23] Membership tightened to the extent that artists were excluded for activities and attitudes that did not synchronise with Debord's demand that art be radical not solely in its subject matter, but also its form.[24] Although some critics have disputed this division of the movement into an early aesthetic position that evolved into a late political vanguardism, it is conspicuous that by 1961, most of the artists had left the organisation, either voluntarily or by expulsion.[25] Further evidence of this rupture is the fact that art was no longer included on the programme of the SI's fifth conference in summer 1961.

Peter Wollen was one of the first to advocate this theory of an artistic split in the SI in an early essay on their work: 'The denial by Debord and his supporters of any separation between artistic and political activity . . . led in effect not to a new unity within Situationist practice but to a total elimination of art except in propagandist and agitational forms . . . Theory displaced art as the vanguard activity.'[26] Critics still invested in the SI, such as T. J. Clark and Donald Nicholson-Smith (both of whom were excommunicated in 1967), argue otherwise: for them, it is precisely the continual intersection of art and politics that makes the SI so distinctive.[27] However, they do not offer any concrete examples of how that intersection was made manifest – in situations, images or text. (It is in fact Wollen who provides the most compelling evidence of this conjunction when he describes Debord's writing as a combination of Western Marxism and Bretonian Surrealism, and pays equal attention to the poetic aspect of the group's writing and their political ambitions.) Tom McDonough, by contrast, emphasises that the theory of a rupture circa 1962 is too simplistic: the SI were not against art and culture, he argues, but against the production of commodifiable objects. He makes the point that collections of SI writings (in particular Ken Knabb's 1981 anthology) create a misleading impression by obscuring the group's cultural analyses in favour of political ones, thereby de-emphasising the SI's abiding interest in issues of visual and literary culture. As a consequence, he argues, what makes the SI (and Debord in particular) distinctive tends to disappear: 'its paradoxical blend of the concreteness of the political manifesto with a poetic elusiveness'.[28]

My own position on the SI is one of ambivalent bystander, exhausted by the SI's elitism, *ad hominem* attacks and vitriolic superiority, but invigorated by their theorisations of *détournement,* the *dérive* and 'constructed situations'.[29] For Debord, there had been no revolutionary movements in politics *or* modern art since the end of the 1930s, and the task of the SI was therefore not to subordinate art to politics, but to revive both modern art and revolutionary politics by surpassing them both – that is, by realising what was the most revolutionary demand of the historic avant-garde, the integration of art and life. This Hegelian sublation implied a tabula rasa: art and poetry should be suppressed in order to be realised as a fuller, more enriching life.[30] Herein lies the central paradox of the SI's nihilist romanticism: art is to be renounced, but for the sake of making everyday life as rich and thrilling as art, in order to overcome the crushing mediocrity of alienation. This is why their writings are anti-visual, but not necessarily a rejection of the aesthetic *per se*: art and poetry remain the perpetual benchmarks for passionate, intense, experimental, non-alienated experience. The SI therefore had no reservations about calling itself an artistic avant-garde, but this was just one aspect of a triple identity, the others being 'an experimental investigation of the free construction of daily life', and 'a contribution to the theoretical and practical articulation of a new revolutionary contestation'.[31]

Even so, there could be no Situationist works of art, wrote Debord, only Situationist *uses* of works of art. In an article from 1963, he provides some examples of art's revolutionary function, including the example of a group of students in Caracas who made an armed attack on an exhibition of French art and carried off five paintings which they subsequently offered to return in exchange for the release of political prisoners. 'This is clearly an exemplary way to treat the art of the past, to bring it back into play for what really matters in life', remarks Debord, observing that Gauguin and Van Gogh had probably never received such an appropriate homage.[32] Another important example was the UK activist group Spies for Peace, who viewed the British government's use of the threat of nuclear war as a way to control a docile populace. The group broke into a high-security military compound near Reading (RSG-6, the 'Regional Seat of Government') and copied information concerning the UK government's emergency-shelter plans for politicians and civil service personnel. This information was published in 4,000 pamphlets (*Danger! Official Secret RSG-6*) and widely distributed, prompting a media scandal.[33] Spies for Peace also overloaded forty telephone lines belonging to British security centres through the continuous dialling of numbers that had been discovered during the raid. Debord enthusiastically describes these examples, and follows them with a discussion of '*cultural* activity that one could call Situationist', implying that he did not view the examples given above in those terms. For Debord, a critical *cultural* practice would not create new forms, but rather use 'the existing means of cultural expression' through the Situationist technique of *détournement*, the subversive appropriation of existing images to undermine their existing meaning.

Michèle Bernstein exemplified this strategy of *détournement* when she assembled a book out of two pre-existing popular fictions, *Tous les chevaux du roi* (1960) and *La Nuit* (1961), to form a parody of Laclos's *Les Liaisons dangereuses*. Like other forms of Situationist *détournement*, Bernstein's text combines contemporary pop cultural clichés and the SI's language of capitalist critique ('"What is it that you really do? I don't understand", says Carole . . . "Reification", says Gilles.').[34] *Détournement* was regarded as the more successful the less it approached a rational reply. A series of erotic postcards, for example, were *détourned* by the addition of handwritten captions, so that nude pin-ups addressed the viewer in speech bubbles: 'The emancipation of the workers will be their own work!', or 'There's nothing better than sleeping with an Asturian miner. Now there you have real men!'[35] For the SI, a good *détournement* reversed the ideological function of the effluvia of spectacle culture, but without adopting the form of a simple inversion of the original, since this would keep the latter's identity securely in its place (Debord gives the example of a black mass: it inverts the Catholic service but sustains its metaphysical structure). This theory of *détournement* clearly builds upon Dada photomontage and Surrealist assemblage that sought to unravel meaning, be this through gender subversion (Duchamp's moustachioed Mona Lisa, *L.H.O.O.Q.*, 1919) or biting political critique (John Heartfield's numerous anti-Hitler photomontages of the early 1930s). A good *détournement* seems to harness both types of strategy, combining subversive irrationality and caustic political topicality.

Debord was adamant that critique of any kind should not take the form of rational argument: he was hostile to structuralist interpretations of culture, and to all critical languages that assert their mastery over preceding methodologies. At the same time, Debord's own writing frequently fell into this trap: *The Society of the Spectacle* (1967) alternates brilliant and incisive aphorisms with turgid, embittered orthodoxies. The SI's other alternatives to visual art, the *dérive* and the constructed situation, also avoided rational critique and emphasised the importance of playfulness and games. Because these experiential activities are rarely documented, they are difficult to analyse, but numerous maps and sketches produced by the group provide an important visual analogue. Debord's

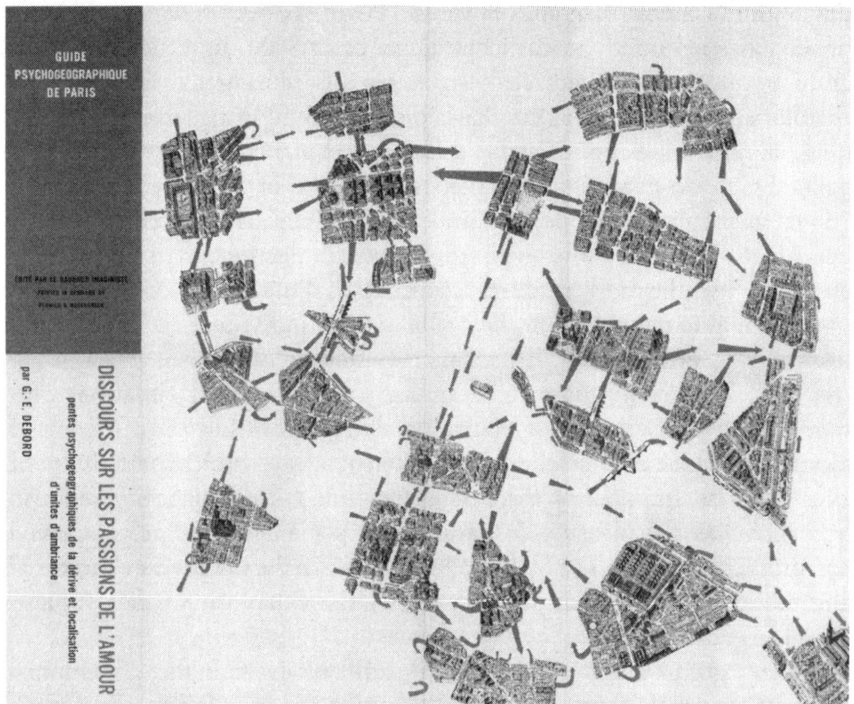

Guy Debord, *Psychogeographical Guide to Paris*, 1957, fold-out map

Psychogeographical Guide to Paris (1957), a fold-out map subtitled 'Discourse on the passions of love: psychogeographic descents of drifting and localisation of ambient unities', is highly suggestive for considering the instructional character of SI activities. The city is shown as fragmented, joined by blank areas indicated only by the flow of red arrows. It is not a record or report of a state of affairs, nor does it have a function: the map is unquestionably hopeless as a guide to Paris, but also as a guide to understanding Debord's own subjective responses to the city. (In this, it differs from the Surrealist group's *Map of the World*, 1929, in which certain countries are vastly enlarged while others vanish altogether, corresponding to their status in the Surrealist imaginary.) Like Debord's map of Parisian 'unités d'ambiance' dated January 1957, in which particular districts are circled and shaded, his *Psychogeographical Guide to Paris* shows a form of notation that is significant less as a record than as a trigger for us to ponder our own sensitivities to the urban environment. It suggests a method or tool, or – following Ivan Chtcheglov's psychoanalytic reading – a technique.[36]

When the Lettriste International was superseded by the Situationist International in 1957, a third term came to prevail: the 'constructed situation'. This was defined in the first issue of *I.S.* as 'a moment of life, concretely and deliberately constructed by the collective organisation of a unitary ambiance and a game of events'.[37] One of the key characteristics of the constructed situation was its participatory structure, devised in deliberate opposition to spectacle's principle of 'nonintervention' and its corollary, alienation. This emphasis on collectivity was, from the beginning, conceived as politicised: as Debord explains, the very idea of a collective avant-garde involves the transposition of organisational methods from revolutionary politics into art; inevitably, the latter activity 'is henceforth inconceivable without some connection with a political critique'.[38] Collectively realised 'constructed situations' were figured as oppositional to capitalism in their sublation of individual authorship, but primarily in their refusal of bureaucracy and consumerism through the free activity of the game. The notion of constructed situations was indebted to the writings of Henri Lefebvre, specifically his 'theory of moments': perishable instants that intensify 'the vital productivity of everydayness, its capacity for communication, for information, and also and above all for pleasure in natural and social life'.[39] The SI viewed constructed situations as a halfway point between the Lefebvrian 'moment' and the everyday 'instant', more particularised than the former yet also less clearly demarcated.

As the group admitted, one of the difficulties with the 'Situationist moment' was identifying its precise beginning and end. In this it had much in common with other forms of post-Brechtian theatre, such as Happenings. Tellingly, it is hard to find informative examples of constructed situations in the *I.S.*; emphasis is continually placed on the structure and rationale for a situation, rather than reporting specific examples. This aversion to documentation presumably stands as a deliberate ploy to avoid imitation, as well as reification as a work of art. The emphasis was on instaneity and rupture (in comparison to the purportedly eternal beauty of traditional art), immediacy (directly organising sensation rather than just reporting on it) and self-determination ('producing ourselves, and not things that enslave us').[40] Most importantly, it ascribed importance to finding spaces of play in the urban environment, understanding play as non-alienating human activity available to all.[41] Ultimately, life could be conceived as a series of constructed situations.

It is telling that the constructed situation had a specific relationship to hierarchy: each situation required the temporary leadership of an individual who would play the role of director. In an anonymous essay from 1958, entitled 'Preliminary Problems in Constructing a Situation', the example is given of a research team seeking to arrange 'an *emotionally moving gathering* for a few people for an evening'.[42] Within the group, certain roles would be parcelled out: a director or producer who coordinated the basic elements necessary for the décor and certain interventions in the event; '*direct agents living the situation*', who collaborated on devising its ambiance; and 'a few passive spectators who have not participated in the constructive work, who should be reduced to action'.[43] In other words, rather than attempting to embody a de-hierarchised collective consensus, the constructed situation necessitated a clear structure, headed by a temporary but clearly defined leader, who would organise the situation's *viveurs* (those who live it). While today single authorship is perceived negatively, as hierarchical, the SI largely avoided such criticism through their lack of interest in working with a general audience. The group seemed to focus only on producing situations with other members – an exclusiveness that matched Debord's increasingly hard-line membership policy.

The SI's only notable attempt to construct a series of situations for a broader public seems to have been the unrealised exhibition 'Die Welt als Labyrinth' planned for the Stedelijk Museum, Amsterdam, in May 1960.[44] This project would have combined a three-day *dérive* within the centre of Amsterdam with a micro-*dérive* (between 200m and 3km in length) within two galleries of the museum, essentially an installation comprising a system of artificial fog, rain and wind, sound interventions and a tunnel of Pinot-Gallizio's industrial painting. The outdoor *dérive* was to have involved two groups, each comprising three Situationists, linked by walkie-talkie, wandering the city and occasionally following instructions to particular places prepared by the *dérive*'s director, Constant. Significantly, the *I.S.* journal makes no mention of including the public in the Amsterdam *dérive* – only of its desire to damage the institution's budget by demanding a daily salary of fifty florins a day for the Situationists undertaking it. However, the group also note that the *dérive* would have 'a certain theatrical aspect by its effect on the public'; this presumably alludes to the visual spectacle of the group moving around the city, but the point is not elaborated. Even so, it suggests a fruitful comparison to the visual theatre of the Dada Season thirty-nine years earlier (discussed in Chapter 2), in which Breton and others had appropriated the social form of the guided tour to produce a 'social sculpture' with the general public in the churchyard of Saint Julien-le-Pauvre.

II. GRAV: Perceptual Re-Education

Today there is such widespread desire and expectation that artists will engage with a general audience that the SI's apparent reluctance to do so seems surprising, but it is also consistent with the group's dismissal of open-ended modernist art forms that sought to integrate the viewer – be this in film (Alain Robbe-Grillet), music (Karlheinz Stockhausen), literature (Marc Saporta) or biennials ('the Himalayas of integration').[45] The Groupe de Recherche d'art Visuel (GRAV), which made consistent attempts to reach as wide a public as possible, came in for particular attack. Founded in Paris in 1960, GRAV's members included a number of international artists working with kinetic and Op-art; their main theorist, Julio Le Parc was Argentinian and had studied with Lucio Fontana in Buenos Aires during the 1940s.[46] Although most of GRAV's work was undertaken in Paris, the group also showed internationally: in Europe (Documenta 3), the United States, South America, and in Japan. The emphasis was on polysensorial environments and kinetic sculpture as a means to affect the viewer's perception, on rethinking the 'work–eye' (*oeuvre–oeil*) relationship to transform conventional experiences of time, and on establishing 'new means of public contact with the works produced'.[47] In a manifesto from 1967, GRAV asserted that they aimed

> through provocation, through the modification of the conditions of environment, by visual aggression, by a direct appeal to active participation, by playing a game, or by creating an unexpected situation, to exert a direct influence on the public's behaviour and to replace the work of art or the theatrical performance with a situation in evolution inviting the spectator's participation.[48]

Accompanying this, but of secondary importance, was an attack on the 'mystification' of the individual artist, the cult of personality and the art market. This position was explicitly anti-elitist, with a commitment to 'rehabilitating a certain concept of the public, belittled by obscurantist art criticism'.[49] GRAV's output comprised two- and three-dimensional optical and kinetic installations exploring psychological and physiological responses to movement, colour and light, but it also included works directly involving the general public and random passers-by: visitor surveys (*Public Investigation*, 1962; *Public Investigation in the Streets*, 1966) and organised games (*A Day in the Street*, 1966, discussed below).

The group's name reflects the way in which they felt this activity to constitute a supra-individual project of quasi-scientific visual research; until they disbanded in 1968, GRAV basically functioned as a communal studio. On the whole, critics responded to this and understood their work to be about generating open-ended propositions, even while there was the continual risk that the emphasis on play and perception risked appearing somewhat slight.[50] Later the group came to recognise the limitations of their approach, but throughout the '60s they did not hesitate to give their activity-based art an emancipatory and didactic gloss: expanding the viewer's perception was perceived as the first step to their disalienation and increased autonomy.

GRAV's *Labyrinth* (1963), for example, produced for the third Paris Biennial, comprised a series of twenty environmental experiences, from wall-based reliefs to light installations and mobile bridges. It was designed to trigger nine different categories of spectatorship: from 'perception as it is today' and 'contemplation', to 'visual activation' (in front of works both static and kinetic), 'active involuntary participation', 'voluntary participation', and 'active spectatorship'.[51] Like most participatory art in the 1960s, the ideal viewer of GRAV's installation was conceived in universalist terms, as a classless (male) subject capable of returning to perception with an 'innocent eye'. This use of new materials and technologies to access a primitive untainted perception resulted in kinetic environments with a certain emotional uniformity, despite the strong emphasis on play. The installation was accompanied by a short manifesto entitled 'Assez des Mystifications' (Enough Mystifications), whose anti-romantic sentiments were a fitting counterpart to the group's scientistic approach:

> If there is a social preoccupation in today's art, then it must take into account this very social reality: the viewer.
> To the best of our abilities we want to free the viewer from his apathetic dependence that makes him passively accept, not only what one imposes on him as art, but a whole system of life . . .
> We want to interest the viewer, to reduce his inhibitions, to relax him.
> We want *to make him participate*.
> We want to place him in a situation that he triggers and transforms.
> We want him to be conscious of his participation.
> We want him to aim towards an interaction with other viewers.
> We want to develop in the viewer a strength of perception and action.
> A viewer conscious of his power of action, and tired of so many abuses and mystifications, will be able to make his own 'revolution in art'.[52]

The conflicting messages of this manifesto are undeniable: the very idea of 'making' someone participate undermines the claim to defeating apathy, and almost incapacitates the viewer from the beginning; all he or she can do is fulfil the artists' requirements to complete the work appropriately. Despite the group's rhetoric of openness, the viewer's experience in *Labyrinth* revolved around a limited range of prescribed responses that go hand in hand with an insistence on 'perceptual re-education', as Schechner described the Happenings in 1965.[53] Equally striking is the group's emphasis on a 'revolution in art' rather than in society. If the SI wished to transform the world by starting with their own life experience in non-alienated 'moments' and 'situations', GRAV were more modest in aiming to shift the institutional art world's valorisation of individuality (by working in a group) and to expand the perception of viewers who participated in their visual research.

Despite their claims for the centrality of the audience, the experiences produced by GRAV's installations are primarily individual rather than social, and today we would more correctly describe them as interactive rather than participatory. Even so, the group came to believe that these experiences had social implications. Initially, GRAV's frequent and outspoken disparagement of single authorship and the market implied only a critique of art as commodity; if the group ascribed any political agency to art, it was to be found within perception, and specifically in empowering the viewer to rely on his or her own sensory faculties and interpretation. However, as the '60s progressed, the emphasis on perception was increasingly perceived as only the first step towards increased agency:

> The second [step] might be, for example, to produce, no longer only the works, but ensembles which would play the part of *social incitement*, at the same time as liberating the spectator from the obsession with possession. These 'multipliable' ensembles could take the form of centres of activation, games rooms, which would be set up and used according to the place and the character of the spectators. From then on, *participation would become collective and temporary*. The public could express its needs otherwise than through possession and individual enjoyment.[54]

As if sensing the momentum towards 1968, GRAV were at pains to stress that their work was political in its implications, emphasising social and collective participation as an antidote to individualism. Yet this line of thinking was never attached to an overt political project, despite Le Parc's participation in the occupations of May '68. It is telling, for example, that

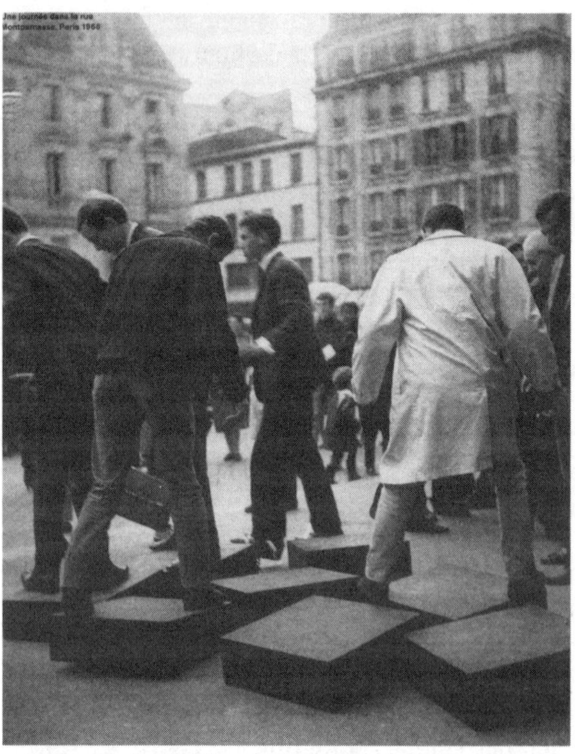

Groupe Recherche d'Art Visuel, *A Day in the Street*, 1966.
Participants in Montparnasse.

the SI did not regard individualism to be a central problem; if anything, it was the route to more enriching and less alienated forms of intensely lived experience.[55]

The most idiosyncratic of GRAV's efforts towards social cohesion was *A Day in the Street*, an itinerary of public actions around Paris, held on Tuesday, 19 April 1966. Running from 8 a.m. to midnight, the itinerary began with the entrance to the metro at Châtelet, with the group handing out small gifts to passengers; at 10 a.m. on the Champs Elysées, changeable structures would be assembled and disassembled; at midday, by the Opéra, habitable kinetic objects were available for passers-by to manipulate; at 2 p.m. in the Jardin des Tuileries, a giant kaleidoscope was offered for the curiosity of children and adults, while large balloons floated in the fountain; at 6 p.m. in Montparnasse, the public were invited to walk on movable paving slabs; the day culminated with a promenade along the Seine with flashing electronic lights. Photo-documentation of the project shows a Parisian audience of all ages laughing and smiling as they engage with various objects (boxes, springs, blocks, balloons) in public space, under a variety of weather conditions.[56] A drawing of the day's itinerary shows a strictly timetabled event, with quirky diagrams anticipating appropriate participation from the public. GRAV's justification for *A Day in the Street* is not dissimilar to the premise of Situationist unitary urbanism: 'The city, the street are crisscrossed with a network of habits and actions repeated daily. We think that the sum total of these routine gestures can lead to total passivity, and create a general need for reaction.'[57] However, the two groups' responses to this state of affairs is programmatically different. GRAV's 'series of deliberately orchestrated interruptions' is modest in ambition: the group openly confess that they are not able to 'smash the routine of a weekday in Paris', but hope that they can bring about 'a simple shift in situation', and 'bypass the traditional relationship between the work of art and the public'.[58] *A Day in the Street* was carnivalesque: a single, exceptional day of ludic events designed to enliven social interaction and create a more physically engaged relationship to public space. If the Futurists turned to variety theatre as a model for their activities, it is telling that GRAV looked to the amusement park, which they perceived to be a place where time is in motion, rather than accumulated (as in museums).

The SI viewed these developments with predictable disdain. Le Parc's desire to turn the 'passive spectator' into a 'stimulated spectator' or even 'spectator-interpreter' through the manipulation of elements in kinetic work was, in their eyes, a question of requiring the viewer to fulfil a pre-existing set of options devised by the artist.[59] As such, this merely replicated the systematised control exercised over citizens in the society of the spectacle, which organises 'participation in something where it's impossible to participate' (in other words, the enforced division of time into work and private leisure). An unsigned article in the *I.S.* noted that GRAV's audience

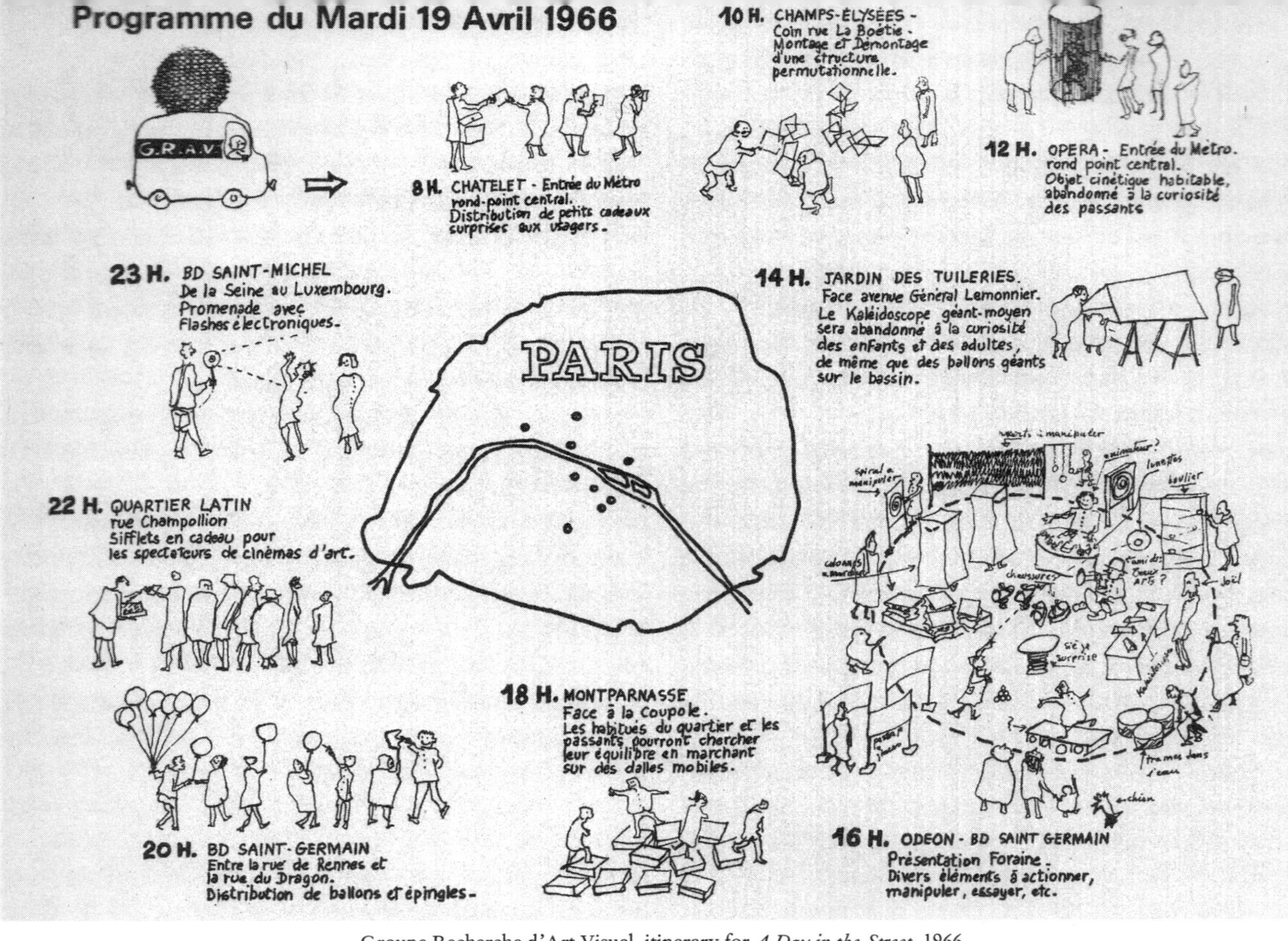

Groupe Recherche d'Art Visuel, itinerary for *A Day in the Street*, 1966

is 'the "solitary crowd" of the society of the spectacle, and here Le Parc is not so advanced that he believes in reality; in the organisation of this alienation, there is certainly no spectator free to stay purely passive, even their passivity is organised, and the "stimulated spectators" of Le Parc are already everywhere'.[60] In other words, the participants of GRAV's perceptual experimentation were insufficiently distinct from the passive spectators of mass consumer capitalism; without a choice *not* to participate, it replicated this structure wholesale. It was more important, felt the SI, to entirely abandon the present-day function of art and art criticism under capitalism; to repress both in the name of a revolutionary critique. To be fair, GRAV's Joël Stein later acknowledged this problem:

> At the start, this interaction between the spectator and the work tends to establish a direct contact and provoke a spontaneous reaction, independent of a given culture or pre-established aesthetic considerations. But it can become a sort of entertainment, a spectacle in which the public is one of the elements in the work. The public can become subject to taking ideological sides; it can also be a new way to condition the public, even numb them.[61]

In sum, although GRAV deployed a terminology of 'situations' and superficially shared a great deal of the SI's political rhetoric, their attempt to encourage viewer participation was experientially somewhat pedestrian. At the same time, we should be wary of siding too rapidly with the SI's hectoring dismissals: it is symptomatic of the forcefulness of a Marxist critique of art that GRAV's modest shifts in perception seem minor and inconsequential in comparison with the total (and utopian) overhaul of both society and sensibility that the SI were claiming as their goal. It should be recognised that, for all their prosaic output, GRAV's artistic propositions aimed to engage with the general public in a far more generous fashion than the SI's cliquish events, which were underpinned by competitive and dogmatic pronouncements against those who co-operated with the existing institutions of art. At the same time, the banality and earnest didacticism of GRAV's work foreground an ongoing paradox with participation as an artistic device: from opening up a work to manipulation and alteration by the viewer, it rapidly becomes a highly ideologised convention in its own right, one by which the viewer in turn is manipulated in order to complete the work 'correctly'.

III. Lebel: Collective Exorcism

It was not just Le Parc and GRAV that came under attack from the SI for pseudo-participation. Happenings, in their 'naïve search to "make something happen" ' and 'desire to liven up a little the impoverished range of human relations', were also the subject of scathing rejection.[62] The first

Happenings in Europe took place during Jean-Jacques Lebel's 'Anti-Procès' festivals (1960 onwards), a travelling exhibition-cum-protest against the Algerian War, in which a number of artists hung work, played music and read sound poems in an ephemeral multi-media event. The first single-authored European Happening was created during the second 'Anti-Procès' festival in Venice (July 1960), which ended with Lebel's *L'Enterrement de la chose de Tinguely* (Burial of the Thing of Tinguely), a complicated quasi-ritualistic performance that made references to the Marquis de Sade, J. K. Huysmans, and Lebel's recently murdered friend Nina Thoeren.[63] Lebel (b.1936) maintains that he arrived at this mixed-media format independently of the New York avant-garde, taking his lead from Dada, Surrealism and Artaud rather than from John Cage and Jackson Pollock (the two touchstones for US Happenings).[64] Lebel was nevertheless based in Paris and New York in the early 1960s and participated in Claes Oldenburg's *Ray Gun Theater* (1961) as well as in several works by Allan Kaprow, with whom he remained close friends until the latter's death. For Lebel, both European and US Happenings shared a concern to 'give back to artistic activity what has been torn away from it: the intensification of feeling, the play of instinct, a sense of festivity, social agitation'.[65] However, there were important differences between US-style Happenings and those that Lebel promoted in France.

The former, as theorised by Allan Kaprow (1927–2006), were indebted to the compositional innovations of John Cage, and developed in response to the action painting of Jackson Pollock. The first work to adopt the name 'Happening' was Kaprow's own *Eighteen Happenings in Six Parts*, which took place over several evenings in Autumn 1959 at the Reuben Gallery in New York. In his early writings, Kaprow positions Happenings against conventional theatre: they deliberately rejected plot, character, narrative structure and the audience/performer division in favour of lightly scored events that injected the everyday with risk, excitement and fear. The audience rarely had a fixed point of observation and, by the mid-1960s, tended to be involved directly as participants in the work's realisation.[66] Initially performed in lofts and galleries, Happenings later took place in outdoor areas such as farms and university campuses (working directly in the city streets was far rarer).[67] Lebel, however, drew on painting and especially jazz as an improvisational structuring device for collaborative events with a changing entourage of artist colleagues and colourful hangers-on. Unlike Kaprow, Lebel's events were not scored, but unfolded in an ad hoc fashion around a cluster of scenes or episodes, arrived at through group discussion.[68]

However, it was the references to contemporary political events that represented the strongest dividing line between European and North American Happenings. As Günter Berghaus argues, the European work (Lebel, Wolf Vostell, Robert Filliou, the Viennese Actionists) contained a conscious socio-political critique of affluent consumer society; the North Americans, by contrast, 'regarded their activity as an apolitical means of changing people's attitudes toward life. In some cases, this may have implied a sociocritical attitude. But more often it was restricted to altering the process of perception'. He continues:

> Life as experienced in a [European] Happening was no longer a mere reproduction or symbolic interpretation of our existential reality. It was rather a confrontation with our alienated existence in late-capitalist society, a discourse on the conflict between our real self and its alienated state. Through the performance the audience was encouraged to experience the authenticity of their existence in opposition to 'life unlived.' . . . Alienating through artistic means an alienating existence (reality) approximates the Hegelian triad of negation of negation. Dialectics as 'the mother of progress' lies at the basis of many Happenings in Europe.[69]

In the work of Lebel, this 'negation of negation' was evidenced in numerous references to current affairs, and in a libertarian emphasis on free expression ('the advent of sexuality'), myth and hallucinatory experience.[70] His 1962 Happening *Pour conjurer l'esprit de catastrophe* (To Exorcise the Spirit of Catastrophe) was held in the context of a group show Lebel had organised at Galerie Raymond Cordier, and featured many of his regular collaborators, including the artists Erró and Tetsumi Kudo. The poster for the event was typical in reproducing a lengthy manifesto by Lebel, which in this instance denounced

> Blackmail, the war of nerves, of the sexes, of the eye and the stomach, the coercion of nuclear Santa Claus, tricolour terror, moral misery and its political exploitation, physical misery and its political exploitation, modern art on its knees before Wall Street, the Paris Commune forgotten in favour of a stupid school of the same name. Enough of this. We have to engage in a collective exorcism . . .[71]

The event comprised a stream of actions accompanied by a five-piece jazz band whose improvised music was directly analogous to the loose compositional structure of the events that took place around the audience. Erró projected images of erotica and works of art onto the naked stomach of Johanna Lawrenson (wearing a mask in the style of a Gustave Moreau painting); Lebel wore a cardboard-box TV set on his head and spoke about permanent revolution and conscientious objectors; Tetsumi Kudo brandished one of his huge 'phallus' sculptures and gave a lecture in Japanese on 'The impotence of philosophy'; Jacques Gabriel and François Dufrêne conversed in an invented language; various performers wore a de Gaulle mask (including Dufrêne and Lebel); dressed as an old lady, Lebel pushed a pram draped in the French flag weeping 'Baby, my baby!' before impersonating a robotic Nazi; an unknown woman got undressed and climbed into a hammock; three others (including Erró) began frenetically dancing; the climax was Lebel and several others removing their clothes and making an 'action painting' in which Lebel leapt across the canvas and out of the gallery shouting 'Heil art! Heil sex!' Lebel later described this Happening as

> reactive, but dialectically: reversing the very terms of anxiety, a bit like a voodoo rite . . . I took consumer society and returned it, like a bag with all its crap: nuclear technology, war (1962, it was the end of the Algerian war), exploitation, misery, racism, pop fans, advertising, porno, cars, sport, the serious threat of a generalised nuclear conflict (the Cuban Missile Crisis and Soviet missiles).[72]

With its overt references to consumer society, and to sexual and political taboos, Lebel's work could not be more different from the average Happening by US artists at this time; it was much closer to the Artaudian sensibilities of The Living Theatre, then touring Europe in self-imposed exile from New York.[73] In both Lebel's events and those

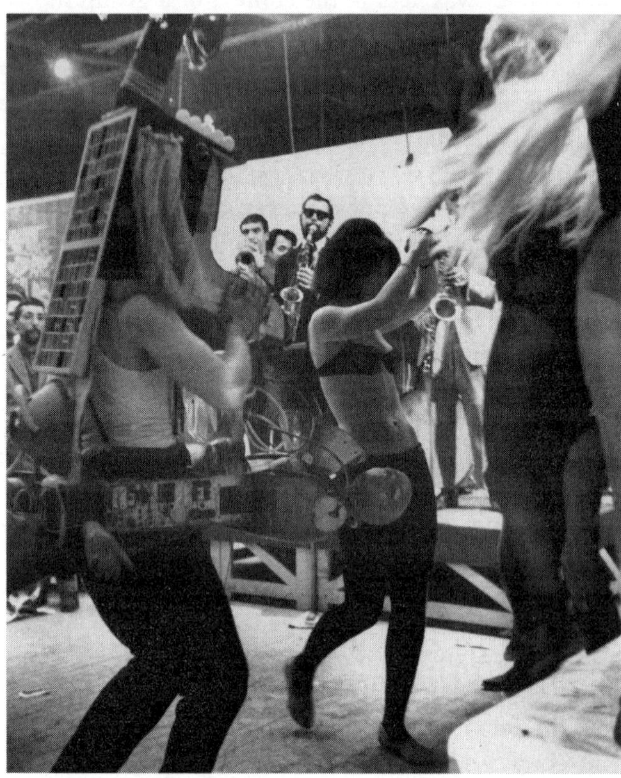

Jean-Jacques Lebel, *To Exorcise the Spirit of Catastrophe*, 1962

The Living Theatre, nudity was a vehicle for sexual liberation and political consciousness, but if The Living Theatre's events could be toured and repeated, Lebel's tended to be more unstructured, improvisatory and subject to change, because they were one-off performances.[74] *Pour conjurer l'esprit de catastrophe* is an exception in this regard, since it was remade in a film studio in February 1963 for two Italian film-makers who wished to make a documentary about Happenings.[75] Taking place over several hours, and using many of the same performers, the second version contained similar references to current affairs: the most striking image was of two nude female performers in a bathtub of blood wearing Khrushchev and Kennedy masks, a clear allusion to the recent Cuban Missile Crisis.

It is important to recognise the extent to which Lebel's work presents a specific understanding of viewer participation and the role of the artist. In his tract *Le Happening* (1966), Lebel draws on a wide range of theorists, including Freud, Bataille, Marcuse, Sade, Lévi-Strauss, Artaud and Mauss.[76] As this selection might indicate, Lebel understood the artist's role in society to be one of moral transgressor, giving image and voice to what is conventionally repressed. The artist is not so much a leader or educator as a conduit for collective hopes and desires, which Lebel has compared to a group mind or 'egregore'. For this reason, his approach to participation differs significantly from that of GRAV, for whom the artist's role was a simple question of organisation: producing situations

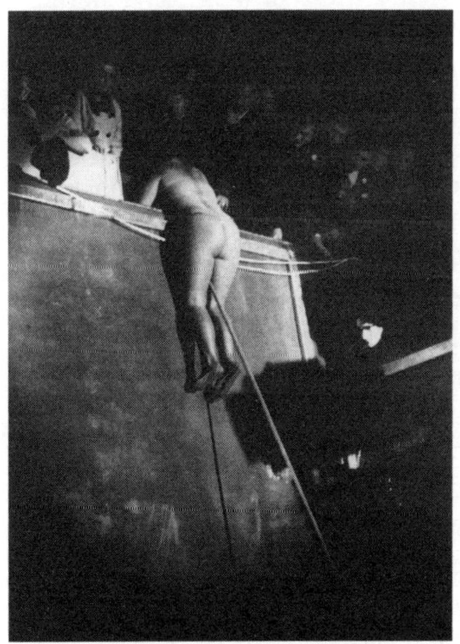

Jean-Jacques Lebel, *120 Minutes Dedicated to the Divine Marquis*, 1965. Shirley Goldfarb descending from the balcony.

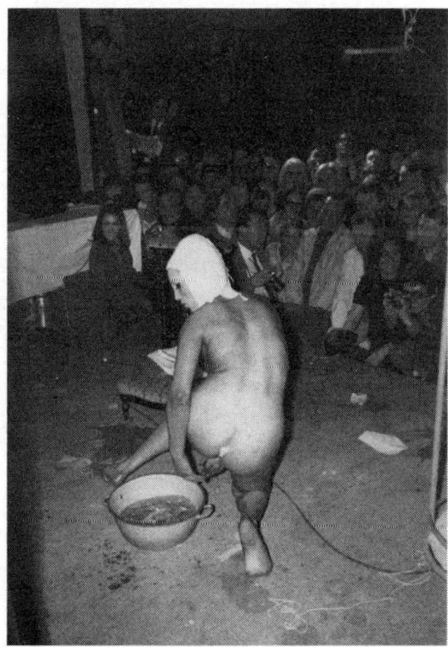

Jean-Jacques Lebel, *120 Minutes Dedicated to the Divine Marquis*, 1965. Cynthia washing herself.

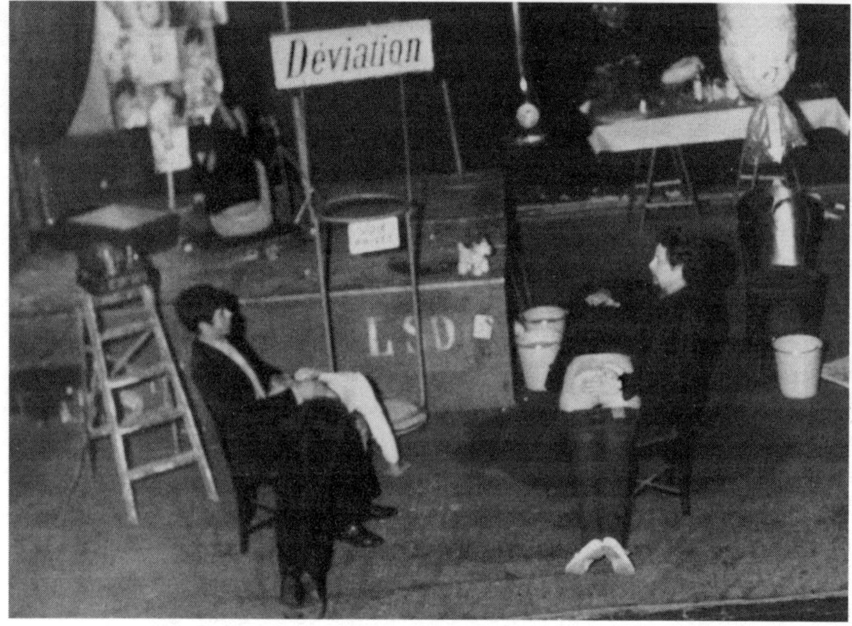

Jean-Jacques Lebel, *120 Minutes Dedicated to the Divine Marquis*, 1965.
The spanked rendition of 'La Marseillaise'.

to physically activate the viewing subject and expand their perception. Lebel, by contrast, refuses to recognise the performer/audience distinction:

> I never envisaged a separation between artist and audience. I never accepted some of the main divisions that the dominant culture has driven into our brains with sledgehammers. I don't believe those divisions exist. For instance, the division between politics and art, between revolution and creation (the creation of artworks, not creation in a religious sense), and the object and the subject . . . There is no frontier between art and life.[77]

As such, Lebel maintains that everyone present at a Happening, be they on stage or in the audience, was a participant in a collectively produced mythic experience. The artist is a *dispositif* through which people's 'desires and hopes and languages and impulses merge into one collective voice', and Lebel draws a direct analogy between this and what Félix Guattari referred to an *'agencement collectif d'énonciation'*.[78] Lebel places this radical blurring in direct contrast to a 'capitalistic' organisation of ideas in society, where 'everything is organised like a department store'; to undo this rational organisation and expedient control he turned to sexual abandonment and hallucinogenic drugs to break down the barrier between subject and object, creating a space of *'both/and'* and *'neither/nor'*.[79]

The most extreme instance of this approach was the Happening *120 minutes dédiées au divin marquis* (120 Minutes Dedicated to the Divine

Marquis), performed on 4 April 1966, and which advanced territory already broached in Lebel's scandalous *Déchirex* at the American Center in 1965.[80] *120 minutes dédiées au divin marquis* took place in the Théâtre de la Chimère, located at 42 rue Fontaine – the building in which André Breton lived – and seemed a conscious provocation to the Surrealist writer (who had ejected Lebel from the Surrealist group in 1960). The event took its lead from the recent censorship of the film *La Religieuse* (dir. Jacques Rivette, 1966) and of the publication of the Marquis de Sade's *Oeuvres Complètes*. Around 400 people entered the building via the stage door (the same entrance that Breton used to enter his apartment), a wry reference to Sade's delight in the 'back passage'; they were welcomed by nude women acting as customs officers who took their fingerprints before allowing them to pass through a narrow corridor hung with bloody fresh meat ('a return to the maternal belly'). Potentially smeared in blood, viewers entered the theatre directly onto the stage, where the action was taking place, but could also descend into the auditorium, from which all seats had been removed.[81] Twelve sequences were staged, which served as the point of departure for improvisations. These included a naked soprano, Shirley Goldfarb, descending from the rafters, singing excerpts from Sade's *120 Days of Sodom* and urinating on the audience in the orchestra pit. Lebel himself wore a blue wig and a priest's chasuble smeared in shit to officiate over Goldfarb (still naked, now on a ceremonial table), covering her in whipped cream and inviting the audience to lick it from her body; when finished, she stood up and wore a mask of de Gaulle. In another section, Lebel and the artist Bob Benamou 'spanked' a rendition of 'La Marseillaise' on two half-naked girls, before reversing these roles to be spanked in turn. The most notorious part of the evening featured a transsexual prostitute called Cynthia, dressed in a nun's habit, who stripped, washed her genitals, and then auto-sodomised herself with carrots and leeks. (When she turned around to reveal her breasts and penis to the crowd, the writer Lucien Goldmann had a heart attack.)[82] As might be imagined, the event caused a huge scandal: the police were alerted, and attended the second night's performance in plain clothes, but the performers self-censored. Lebel was arrested for 'offence to the head of State and insult to moral conduct', prompting a public letter of support in defence of the artist, signed by a slew of luminaries including Breton, Duchamp, Sartre, de Beauvoir and Rivette.[83]

In her 1962 essay on Happenings, Susan Sontag argues that their 'dramatic spine' is an 'abusive' treatment of the audience; reading this 'art of radical juxtaposition' through Surrealism and Artaud, she makes a strong case for the centrality of its aggression towards the viewer.[84] Although Sontag's essay was written in response to US Happenings, it actually applies to very few of them; most New York artists from that period argue that US Happenings were never directly antagonistic towards the audience, and functioned much more like traditional theatre, albeit one in the round.[85] Lebel is a much more fitting recipient of Sontag's description, as reinforced by Sartre's observation in 1967:

> Most of the time, in effect, the Happening is a skillful exploitation of the cruelty of which Artaud spoke. In France, Lebel exercises a certain sadism towards the public: the latter is stunned by flashing lights, unbearable noises, sprayed with diverse objects that are usually filthy, you have to go to these Happenings in old clothes . . . [86]

Among US Happenings, only Carolee Schneemann's *Meat Joy* (1964) contains anything close to Lebel's level of physical transgression, and it is telling that Lebel not only encouraged her to develop this work but was the first to show it in Europe, at the First Festival of Free Expression in Paris, 1964. A Dionysian response to Abstract Expressionist painting, Schneemann's *Meat Joy* involved performers writhing half naked to pop music while smearing each other with paint and raw fish and chickens. Audience participation was not a formal component of the work, but Schneemann recalls that when the work was performed in Paris,

> the public started to get undressed, to crawl across the room and tie themselves in knots, mixing with the actors on stage, it was very puzzling and we had to send them back to the other side of the footlights. The following evening, something even stranger happened. A man came onto the stage and started to strangle me and bang my head against the wall before I had time to scream or even make a move. The most terrifying thing was that the public, even if it realised something was going on, was unsure and told themselves that it was part of the performance. Finally, two men understood the situation . . . [87]

When reading the SI's denunciations of the Happenings, no reference is made to such extremities of behaviour; it is unclear whether their condemnation is directed at the local, French iteration of this genre, or at the US variant, which was also known in Paris. (In 1963, Kaprow performed on three consecutive evenings at the Bon Marché department store.[88]) Lebel, for his part, maintains that Debord never attended his events, and that his knowledge of them was, ironically, attained entirely through the media.[89] Artistically, however, they had much in common: both were influenced by (and came to reject) Surrealism; both railed against the museum as mausoleum; both were highly suspicious of mediation and commercialisation; both sought an authentic lived experience to heighten and liberate the everyday through play. But while Debord viewed this heightened experience in Marxist terms – as resistance to spectacle, defeating alienation, and auguring revolution (in which recognised forms of artistic practice would be surpassed) – Lebel found an anarchist model for this heightened experience in hallucinogenic drugs and sexual liberation.[90] On several occasions Lebel cited the Situationist Alexander Trocchi on the need for artists to seize control of the social fabric, but invariably retreated to note that however determinant the political ambition of the Happenings, their psychical intent as 'interior communication' would remain primary.[91]

Finally, if Happenings artists sought to bring the everyday *into* the work of art ('We were presenting a piece of daily reality that is itself a spectacle'), then Debord and the SI, by contrast, found it necessary to question the very category of art altogether, sublating art into a more intensely lived everyday life.[92] Their activities therefore proceeded in two opposite directions – one preserving the category of art, but expanding it to include transgressive activities; the other dissolving this category to make life itself more artistically fulfilling. As Raoul Vaneigem argued, personal self-realisation within the collective was the most revolutionary form of art, and this went much further than giving the audience things to do: the Happenings, he argued, 'supposedly provoke spontaneous participation on the part of the spectators' but effectively force the audience – 'passive agents *par excellence*' – to participate only in a cultural and ideological vacuum.[93] This complaint seems more artistic than political, as if the SI could not bear to see the trivialisation of (what they perceived to be) their own ideas by the producers of Happenings who gained media attention:

> When these people [use our concepts] in order to finally speak of some new problem (after having suppressed it as long as they could), they inevitably banalise it, eradicating its violence and its connection with the general subversion, therefore defusing it and subjecting it to academic dissection or worse.[94]

In other words, the group resented the lack of *poetic* intensity in activities they viewed as derivative of their own. This much seems a fair enough accusation to level at Kaprow and GRAV, but if the group had actually attended Lebel's Happenings they would have had to reckon with a wholly different poetics of transgression and an appeal to a new intensity of group experience; these events were less about 'giving people things to do' than entering into a space of collective transformation where categories of individual and social, conscious and unconscious, active and passive, would purportedly disintegrate in a '*défoulement*' or unleashing of pent-up tensions.[95]

IV. A Theatrical Uprising

Each of the group activities discussed in this chapter aimed to impact directly upon the viewer's consciousness and liberate them in different ways. If the SI provided blueprints for creative and conceptual games within an over-rationalised city and the excess of consumer culture, then this also required the rejection of recognised art forms, their institutions, and the concept of a mass audience. The paradox of this position is that the SI rejected art but continually invoked it as the benchmark for non-alienated life: art is at once a privileged zone of non-alienated activity and an alibi for the continued alienation of life in all other activities. The contradictory logic of this position is nevertheless generative, and easily surpasses the technophilic interactivity of GRAV, whose insistence on first-hand physical and sensorial experiences suffers from a certain oversimplification of the work of art's agency. Lebel, by contrast, created quasi-therapeutic collective rites where societal taboos and inhibitions could be expressed and challenged. His work sought to surpass the established binaries that structured the thinking around participation, such as the distinction between artist and audience, and between active and passive spectatorship – although arguably this idea was more vivid as a goal than as a reality. All three tendencies should be viewed as contributions paving the way for the largest social (and theatrical) refusal of the 1960s, May '68.[96]

The extent to which May '68 could be seen as the culmination of these multifarious experiments in art and theatre was the focus of an article by Lebel in 1969. In it, he connected the radicalism of Paris Dada and Happenings to the recent effusion of politicised street theatre both during and after May '68, and presented its events as a form of Happening:

> The May uprising was theatrical in that it was a gigantic fiesta, a revelatory and sensuous explosion outside the 'normal' pattern of politics . . .
>
> The results of this individual as well as social change were immediate: human relations were freer and much more open; taboos, self-censorship, and authoritarian hangups disappeared; roles were permutated; new social combinations were tried out. Desire was no longer negated but openly expressed in its wildest and most radical forms. Slavery was abolished in its greatest stronghold: people's heads. Self-management and self-government were in the air and, in some instances, actually worked out. The subconscious needs of the people began to break through the ever present network of repressive institutions which is the backbone of capitalism. Everywhere people danced and trembled. Everywhere people wrote on the walls of the city or communicated freely with total strangers. There were no longer any strangers, but brothers, very alive, very present. I saw people fucking in the streets and on the roof of the occupied Odeon Theatre and others run around naked on the Nanterre campus, overflowing with joy. The first things revolutions do away with are sadness and boredom and the alienation of the body.[97]

It is telling that after May '68 Lebel ceased to make Happenings, considering them to have been achieved in the occupations, barricades and protests; the avant-gardist dream of turning art into life via a collective creative experience had (for him) finally been realised.

Constant had anticipated something akin to this state of affairs when he wrote that in the proposed city of New Babylon, 'the whole of life will become a Happening, making Happenings redundant'.[98] The SI, for their part, equally claimed May 1968 as the realisation of their ideas, but gave them a slightly less glorious status: 'The occupations movement was the rough sketch of a "situationist" revolution, but it was no more than a rough sketch both as practice of revolution and as situationist consciousness of history. It was at that moment intellectually that a generation began to be situationist.'[99] After that point the SI's activities became increasingly strained: Debord attempted to devolve power with a new editorial board, but acknowledged that 'if "boredom is counter-revolutionary" then the SI was very quickly succumbing to the same fate'.[100] Mustapha Khayati resigned in 1969, Vaneigem in 1970, and Viénet the year after. GRAV, meanwhile, disbanded in November 1968, but this derived from internal differences rather than from a crisis prompted by political commitments.[101]

In the light of contemporary artistic practice, these experiments with participation leading to 1968 give rise to several important points about audience. It is telling that none of the collective efforts described above pay particular attention to who their participants might be; one could even claim a total absence of class consciousness among the artists in this regard. Despite their frequent attacks on 'bourgeois' art and its institutions, Debord and Lebel came from well-to-do families and did not countenance the possibility of targeting activities towards an audience outside their community of artists and bohemian intelligentsia; these events consolidated (rather than created) group identity. GRAV, by contrast, explicitly sought a general audience, locating *A Day in the Street* in a series of public spaces, but understood the viewer to be a generic passer-by, a universal 'everyman'. The SI were content to function as a club, continually seeking membership but subjecting potential applicants to rigorous enforcements of purity.[102] The desire of today's artists to reach disenfranchised or marginal constituencies is a more recent development that reflects the influence of community arts in the 1970s (discussed in Chapter 6) and the fragmentation of class politics into myriad identitarian concerns in the 1980s.

With hindsight, however, these artistic differences dissolve into a shared narrative: on a political level, the artists were united against colonialism and racism, French intervention in Algeria, and consumer society's valorisation of the individual. From this perspective, artistic differences can and should be reframed as variations on a common theme of opposing imperialist capitalism in favour of generating a collectively produced cultural alternative; together with other intellectual and social pressures, these eventually contributed to permanent changes of attitude and reform.

Although the SI cannot be reduced to participatory art, many of the ideas they proposed, together with those of GRAV and Lebel, nevertheless consolidate the 1960s discourse around participatory art as founded on a binary of active and passive spectatorship, linked in turn to the desirability of working outside the gallery system. Today, both of these tropes have become somewhat entrenched into black and white positions that tend to lack the dialectical subtlety accompanying the most radical iterations of the SI's aim to surpass art in order to realise it as life, as well as of Lebel's 'negation of negation'. The latter idea, together with an apparatus of semiotic theory and psychoanalysis, was imported to Argentina in the mid 1960s, where the valorising concept behind all of the examples discussed in this chapter – unmediated first-hand experience – was questioned, reversed and transformed into an interrogation of mass mediation. In both contexts, participation became a means to deal with anxieties about reality, representation and political oppositionality, but if the French examples discussed here addressed this through situations of collective unity, the Argentinians more characteristically approached participation through experiments in social division.

4

Social Sadism Made Explicit

Western interest in Argentinian art of the 1960s has only begun to be felt in the last decade: the country's leading figures, such as León Ferrari, are still not as established in Europe and North America as they should be, and individual artists are less well known than the names of the collective projects they participated in, such as *Tucumán Arde* (Tucumán is Burning) (1968). My focus in this chapter will be on the specifically conceptual forms of participatory art that were developed in Buenos Aires in the mid 1960s under the influence of Oscar Masotta, and on the Rosario Group's Ciclo de Arte Experimental (Cycle of Experimental Art, 1968). As a second bridge between artistic actions and left politics, I will discuss the theatrical innovations of the Brazilian director Augusto Boal (1931–2009), who developed an influential mode of theatrical therapy geared towards social change while in exile in Argentina in the 1970s.[1] Although these two bodies of work were not known to each other at the time, they share common artistic strategies: taking reality and its inhabitants as a material, and the desire to politicise those who encountered this work. However, the artists did not abandon an attachment to the value of artistic experience – each practitioner felt him/herself to be working politically, but *within* art – while Boal's priority was the revolution itself. In this he was more akin to the Situationist International, who rejected art as an institutionally framed category of bourgeois experience in favour of social change; the premise of Boal's innovations, however, was to devise new modes of public education and to build the confidence of those in participating in this process.

These participatory actions produced in Argentina stand in sharp contrast to the better known and more canonical artistic experiments produced in Brazil during this period, in which the cool constructive forms of European abstraction are redirected towards a liberatory experience of colour, texture and intermediary objects. If the master narrative of Brazilian art was (and to a large extent remains) the sensuous, then Argentinian work is more cerebral and self-reflexive; its performances are less visually oriented, and more willing to tarry with nihilistic consequences of producing coercive situations. The '60s scene in Argentina also differs from Brazil in that it tends to be a history of isolated gestures by artists without a consistent oeuvre, trained in diverse backgrounds.[2] It is complicated further by the interruptive character of increasingly coercive dictatorships (the Revolución Argentina of General Onganía 1966–70, General Levingston 1970–71, and General Lanusse 1971–73, and the 'Dirty War' of 1976–83), each of which imposed new forms of censorship and inhuman repression on its citizens.[3] Despite these discontinuities, Argentina's early reception of European semiotics and communications theory gave rise to a consistent line of thinking among its artists. If the best examples of Brazilian art during this period invite viewers to *sense* and to *feel*, their Argentinian counterparts seem to demand that viewers *think* and *analyse*. This specifically analytic approach – combined with a willingness to subject participants to situations that have a distinctly brutal tenor – ensures that this body of work offers a significant counterpart to participatory art in North America and Western Europe. In the latter, the immediacy of first-hand relationships amongst viewers is staked as a challenge to the atomised social body of consumer capitalism, united only in its isolation; in Argentina, this model – synonymous with the Happenings – was challenged almost immediately and subjected to critical analysis via structuralism and media theory.

I. Social Sadism Made Explicit

In some respects it is perverse to begin a case study on participation in Argentinian art by discussing Oscar Masotta (1930–79), a writer and intellectual best known for introducing Lacanian psychoanalysis into Argentina. He made only three works of art during his lifetime, and these are generally overlooked as idiosyncratic experiments that stand as an exception to his overall intellectual output.[4] And yet Masotta's involvement with artistic production in the early 1960s was extensive and influential: he was closely engaged with contemporary art (writing key texts on Pop and coining the term 'dematerialisation'[5]) and organised a reading group for young artists, while also teaching at the Instituto Torcuato Di Tella, the epicentre of Argentinian avant-garde production in the 1960s.[6] Masotta's theoretical work was formative for the development of media art in Argentina and for defining the country's reception of the latest artistic imports from North America. However, his intellectual formation was marked by an orientation towards Europe, particularly France: after studying philosophy at the University of Buenos Aires, he engaged with Marxism and existentialism in the 1950s, reading Sartre and Merleau-Ponty in *Les Temps modernes*, and writing for the leftist journal *Contorno*.[7] In the 1960s he turned to structural linguistics and visual art, and his 1965 lecture 'Pop Art and Semantics' (Arte Pop y Semántica) is one of the earliest attempts to use linguistic analysis in the interpretation of works of art.

In 1966, Masotta led a reading group that met almost daily – at Di Tella, in bars, at the Álvarez publishing house – and whose members included the artists Roberto Jacoby, Eduardo Costa, Raúl Escari, Juan Risuleo and the sociologist Eliseo Verón. The group read and applied structural linguistics and communications theory to works of art, visual imagery and their lived context; the texts tackled included Marshall McLuhan, Roland Barthes, Umberto Eco, Susan Sontag, Claude Lévi-Strauss, Gregory Bateson and Roman Jakobson.[8] The reading group took place alongside the formation of El Grupo de los Artes de los Medios Masivos (Group of Mass Media Art, 1966–68), whose best-known production was an 'anti-Happening' in July 1966, known variously as *Primera obra de arte de los medios* (The First Work of Media Art), *Happening para un jabalí difunto* (Happening for a Dead Boar) or *Participación Total* (Total Participation). Authored by Jacoby, Escari and Costa with the participation of nine other artists (including Marta Minujín and Masotta), the work directly responded to the way in which the term 'Happening' had become a buzzword in the media.[9] The three artists issued a press release announcing the Happening, together

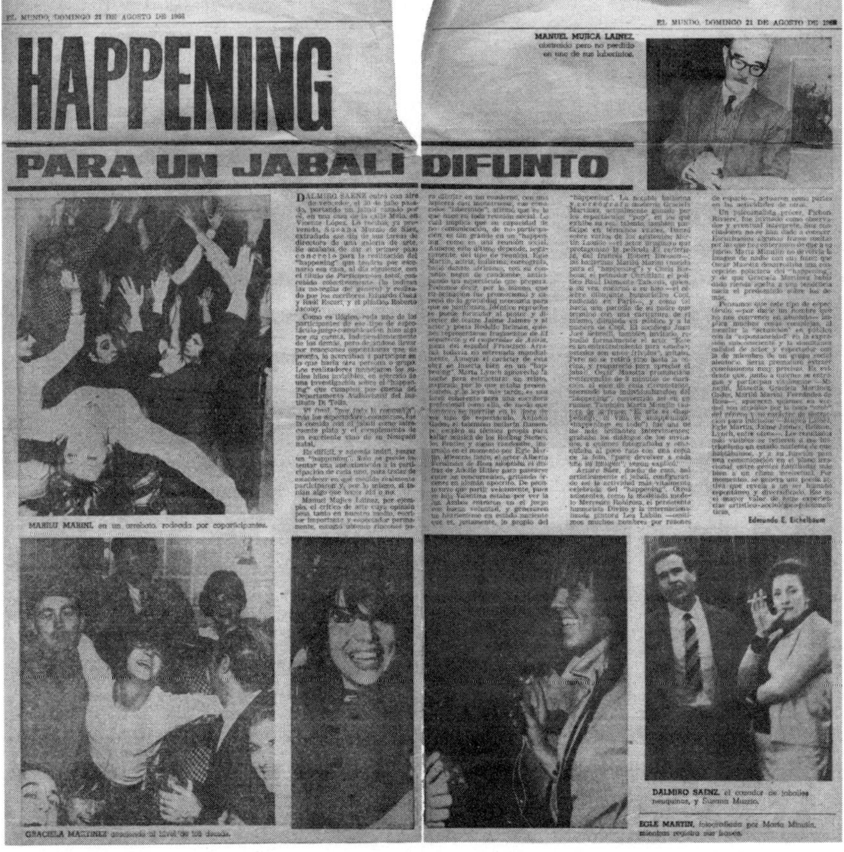

El Grupo de los Artes de los Medios Masivos, *Total Participation*, 1966, newspaper intervention

with photographs of the event (which resemble an exuberant party); reports appeared in *El Mundo* and a number of magazines. But in fact, the Happening never actually took place: it comprised only photographs staged for media dissemination. The second press release revealed this construction, seeking to expose the way in which the media operated, and served to generate yet further press coverage.[10] Unlike Happenings in Europe and North America during this period, which emphasised the existential thrill of unmediated presence, the *Happening for a Dead Boar* existed purely as information, a dematerialised circulation of facts. As such, it obliterated the problematic dividing line between (first-hand) participant and (secondary) viewer, since there was no 'original' event to have attended in the first place. The media itself became the medium of the work, and its primary content.

Earlier that year, between January and March 1966, Masotta had visited New York, where he experienced a number of Happenings first hand. He was there to accompany Marta Minujín, whose environment *Un Batacazo* (The Long Shot) was opening at Bianchini Gallery in February 1966, and through her was introduced to many of the artists associated with Pop and Happenings that he went on to discuss in *El 'Pop' Art*.[11] In the summer following this trip, Masotta and the reading group, now joined by Oscar Bony, Leopoldo Maler and Miguel Angel Telechea, produced *Sobre Happenings* (About Happenings), a Happening composed of Happenings by other artists: two works by Claes Oldenburg (including *Autobodys*, 1963), Carolee Schneemann's *Meat Joy* (1964) and an untitled work by Michael Kirby were re-performed as one new synthetic Happening.[12] Importantly, the actions were based not on first-hand experience of these works, but on their descriptions in magazines – in other words, they were already mediated. As with *Total Participation*, the idea was to undermine Happenings' insistence on immediacy and presence, to challenge their exaggerated media status and prod fun at the people who attended these events expecting to be entertained. A live event was underpinned by complex layers of mediation and analysis. Jacoby described *Total Participation* as addressing the paradox between 'the characteristics of the Happening (the lack of mediation, direct communication with objects and persons, short distance between the viewer and the viewed) and a great deal of mediation between objects and events, the nonparticipation of the receptor'.[13] In line with their reading of Barthes' *Mythologies* (1957), myth was invoked and put to work in order to destroy myth.

It was in this highly intellectualised, analytical context that Masotta produced his first Happening in November 1966, *Para inducir al espíritu de la imagen* (To Induce the Spirit of the Image). The work is distinctive in terms of its aggressive attitude towards participants – although it was not without precedents, as I will discuss below. Masotta's unflinching defence and post-mortem of this action, 'I Committed a Happening' (1967), provides an invaluable resource not only for understanding the event but also for approaching contemporary controversies around the display of people in art (discussed in Chapter 8). The basics of the event were as follows: twenty elderly people were paid to stand in a storage room, in front of an audience, and be subjected to fire-extinguishers, a high-pitched deafening sound and blinding white light. At the beginning of the event, Masotta lectured the audience on the subject of control, even though the exact opposite seemed to be taking place: he recalled that as the audience filed in, 'I felt as though something had slipped loose without my consent, a mechanism had gone into motion.'[14] In this introduction, Masotta also made reference to the economic circuit in which his work was imbricated, reminding the audience that they had each paid 200 pesos to watch the event, while the participants had been paid 600 pesos each to perform.

Masotta's text repeatedly brings up the question of guilt, along with a number of other psychoanalytically inflected terms. The guilt implied by the title ('I Committed a Happening') is an ironic confession directed at the Marxist intellectual Gregorio Klimovsky, whose reactions typified the dominant leftist response to contemporary art at that time, and Happenings in particular, disparaging them as a frivolous waste of resources. Having been criticised by Klimovsky for 'concocting' a Happening when the correct leftist attitude would be to 'abstain' from Happenings altogether and address real problems (such as hunger), Masotta recounts that he felt queasy – but was determined to refute the false option 'either Happenings or Left politics'.[15] The rest of the text serves as a justification for his artistic experiment – not as an ideal social model (one of the hallmarks of the utopian avant-garde) but as a lens through which to engage more directly with the contradictions of the existing social and political context. This context was tumultuous: the Revolución Argentina took place on 29 June 1966 – the coup d'état by which General Onganía seized power from Arturo Illia, the democratically elected president, and suspended the constitution.[16] Masotta had been planning his work for a festival of Happenings during that summer, but had put the plan on hold since many felt it was inappropriate to be making Happenings at a time of such political upheaval. Finally realising the project in November 1966, Masotta changed some details of the work from his initial proposal: rather than hiring thirty or forty performers recruited from the 'downtrodden proletariat: shoeshine boys or beggars, handicapped people, a psychotic from the hospice, an impressive-looking beggar woman who frequently walks down Florida Street', he chose to hire twenty elderly, lower-middle class men and women.[17] He encouraged them to dress as the class beneath them, since this process of acting would enable them to be more than merely passive subjects.[18] Despite this apparent concession, Masotta revoked his earlier decision to provide little flags so that the performers could indicate if they wanted to leave, since it had the effect of 'softening the situation'. The effect he wanted was a 'spare, naked, hard' experience, in direct contrast to the frivolous media image of the Happenings. An aesthetic decision, then, came at the cost of his participants' comfort, and yet Masotta persisted with his vision. For example, he noted that the participants paid him much more attention after he increased their fee from 400 pesos to 600 pesos: 'I felt a bit cynical', he wrote, 'but neither did I wish to have too many illusions. I didn't want to demonise myself for this social act of manipulation which in real society happens every day.'[19]

In *To Induce the Spirit of the Image*, this manipulation was figured through an act of overt reification: turning glaring spotlights onto the elderly participants to subject them to the audience's gaze, emphasising the economic and psychological distance between viewer and performer – in direct contrast to the Happenings' tendency to collapse this distinction. Masotta observed:

> Against the white wall, their spirit shamed and flattened out by the white light, next to each other in a line, the old people were rigid, *ready to let themselves be looked at for an hour*. The electronic sound lent greater immobility to the scene. I looked toward the audience: they too, in stillness, looked at the old people.[20]

The conclusion to Masotta's text is revealing. The Happening clearly perturbed his friends on the left, who wished to know what it meant. His

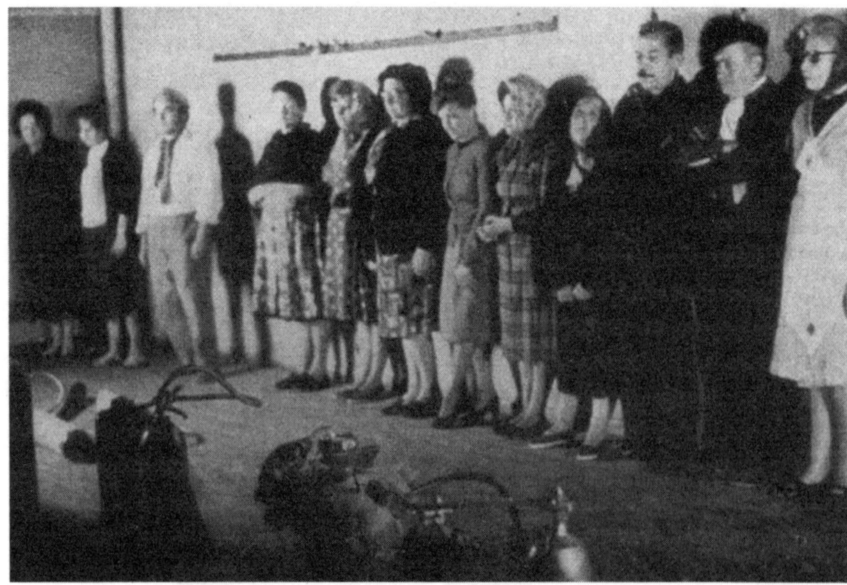

Oscar Masotta, *To Induce the Spirit of the Image*, 1966

answer was concise: 'an act of social sadism made explicit' (*un acto de sadismo social explicitado*).[21] This allusion to the psychic mechanism of sadism has both visual and economic overtones, and makes Masotta's subsequent interest in Lacanian psychoanalysis entirely fitting.[22] In his seventh Seminar, *The Ethics of Psychoanalysis* (1959–60), Lacan draws upon Sade as an alternative model to Kant, encouraging analysands not to compromise on their unconscious desire in the face of social and familial pressure (the 'big Other').[23] In both the Happening and his post-mortem of it, Masotta seems to establish a different ethical framework for leftist performance art, one whose territory is informed more by the anti-human-ism of Lacanian ethics – in which 'the only thing one can be guilty of is of having given ground relative to one's desire' – than with a normative ethics in the tradition of Aristotelian modesty and temperance.[24]

Masotta's title, *To Induce the Spirit of the Image*, was a direct reference to Jean-Jacques Lebel's Happening, *To Exorcise the Spirit of Catastrophe* (1962), discussed in Chapter 3, although the works could not be further apart in character; if anything, Masotta seemed only to desire an interna-tional reference point for his work. Lebel's event referred to Cold War politics and sought collective emancipation through nudity and sexual expression, which Masotta emphatically rejected.[25] A more pertinent inter-national reference point was an event by LaMonte Young that Masotta had experienced in New York earlier in 1966, which had also used a continuous, unaltered sound at high volume; Masotta reported that the work produced 'an exasperating electronic endlessness' that 'penetrated one's bones and pummelled one's temples' to the point where it became a commentary 'on the continuous as continuous, and thereby induced a certain rise in consciousness with respect to its opposite'.[26] This aggressivity towards the audience in US Happenings, despite their prevailing lightness and good-humoured unpredictability, was central to Susan Sontag's reading in *Against Interpretation* (1966), with which Masotta's reading group were familiar.[27]

However, there were other, more local, points of reference for Masotta's aesthetic of social aggression. The novelist Roberto Arlt (1900–42), on whom Masotta had published a book in 1965, was a fiction author whose edgy, unromantic stories frequently focused on the lives of criminals, outsiders and the poor.[28] Another point of influence was Alberto Greco (1915–65), whose series of photo works *Vivo-Ditos* (Living Finger) (1962–64), involved the artist encircling passers-by with chalk and signing them as 'living sculptures'. Without exception, Greco always encircled the poor and down at heel. Greco had also employed people to be present within one of his gallery installations: *Mi Madrid querido* (My Beloved Madrid), held at the Galería Bonino in Buenos Aires in December 1964, included two shoeshine boys hired to sit in front of canvases with shoe polishes, inks and brushes. Another artistic precedent was Minujín's *Suceso Plástico* (25 July

1965), an ambitious Happening in Montevideo that revealed her own interest in audience aggression.[29] Held in a working-class neighbourhood, the event involved participants being herded into the Peñarol stadium at 3 p.m., to the accompaniment of Bach's 'Mass in B Minor', where they were encircled by motorbikes blaring sirens. Women and children were lifted up by body builders; men were kissed by twenty female variety singers; fifteen fat ladies rolled around on the floor; twenty embracing couples were fastened together with adhesive tape.[30] A helicopter appeared overhead and dropped flour, lettuce and 500 live chickens on top of the audience, moving up and down so that wind from the propeller sent the hens and lettuce leaves flying around. Throughout this short but intense event, the audience could not escape the stadium: hemmed in by the motorcycles, the stadium door was also closed off until, after eight minutes, Minujín signalled the end.[31] Together with the work of Greco and Arlt, *Suceso Plástico* provided an important precedent for the development of a type of performance in which participants were centred as object and material of the work.

To Induce the Spirit of the Image was Masotta's third Happening; the two others that preceded it – *El helicóptero* (The Helicopter) and *El mensaje fantasma* (The Ghost Message) are less pertinent to the history I am tracing.[32] However, what all three have in common is an interest in dividing audiences to forge two irreconcilable bodies of experience. In *To Induce the Spirit of the Image*, the audience and performers were divided, with both subjected to an excruciating noise, but one group paid to view the other's discomfort. In *The Helicopter* (2 July 1966) the audience was divided into two groups of forty, who were taken by buses to two different venues: to the basement of the Americana Gallery at Theatrón, in the

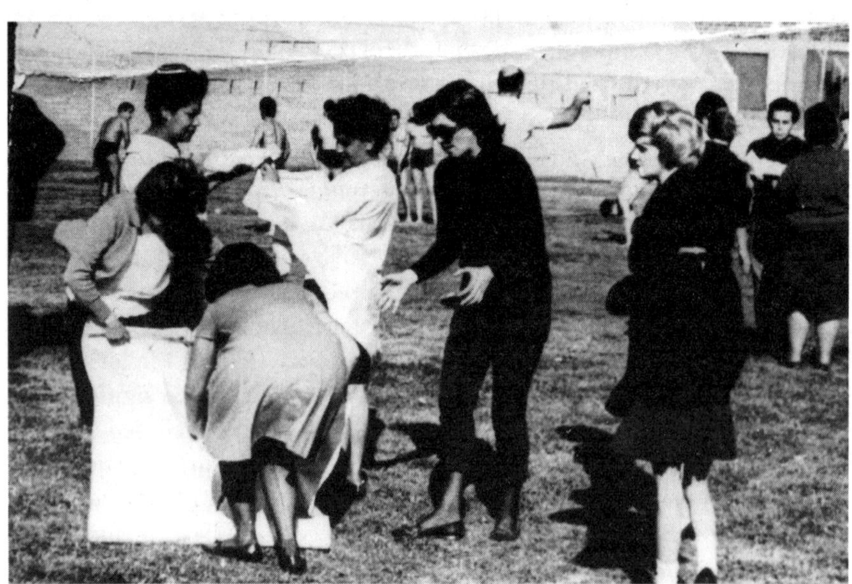

Marta Minujín, *Suceso Plástico*, 1965

centre of the city, and to a little known, abandoned railway station at Anchorena, on the outskirts of Buenos Aires. The first group were treated to an event with live music and film screenings (more akin to expanded cinema), after which the bus took them to Anchorena; their journey was timed to arrive just too late to see a helicopter overhead, purportedly carrying the film star Beatriz Matar. The second group, meanwhile, *had* seen the helicopter, and described this event to the group from Theatrón. In other words, Masotta staged a missed encounter, dividing the audience into those who did and didn't see the helicopter.[33] Participation, in this instance, is divisive and negative, based around an *absence* of participation: missing an event and needing to recover this information through dialogue. The point was a fragmentation and a lack of unified experience, a discontinuity that interrupted the communicational flow.[34] To this extent, *The Helicopter* fulfils Masotta's claim, made a year later in 'After Pop, We Dematerialise', that 'there was something within the Happening that allowed us to glimpse the possibility of its own negation'.[35]

II. Artist as Torturer

Masotta's *To Induce the Spirit of the Image* received no press coverage at the time, since it took place in a small rehearsal space at Di Tella, rather than as part of the official programme. However, Oscar Bony's response to this work the following year attracted a great deal of media controversy. We could view Bony's *La Familia Obrera* (The Worker's Family, 1968) as a condensation of Masotta's happening and Greco's *Vivo-Ditos*. At the same time, it stands as an isolated example within Bony's overall work. First shown in the controversial exhibition 'Experiencias 68' at the Instituto Di Tella, the performance comprises a working-class family – an Argentinian man, woman and child – sitting on a platform for eight hours a day.[36] The family responded to a job advertisement in the local paper and were paid to sit on a plinth throughout the opening hours of the exhibition, accompanied by a recording of everyday sounds made in the home of the same family. The label accompanying the piece, written by Bony, explained that 'Luis Ricardo Rodríguez, a professional die-caster, is earning twice his usual wages for just staying on show with his wife and son.' In photographic documentation of the project, the Rodríguez family are shown self-absorbed, reading books to pass the time of day while visitors examine them. In reality, their gestures were less contained: they were constantly shifting position in the middle of the exhibition hall – eating, smoking, reading and talking amid the audience's largely adverse and horrified response; the child in particular found it hard to stay put on the plinth and often ran around the exhibition.[37] Although reviewers framed the work within contemporary discussions around Pop Art, *The Worker's Family* clearly plays on the conventions of figurative art in a socialist realist

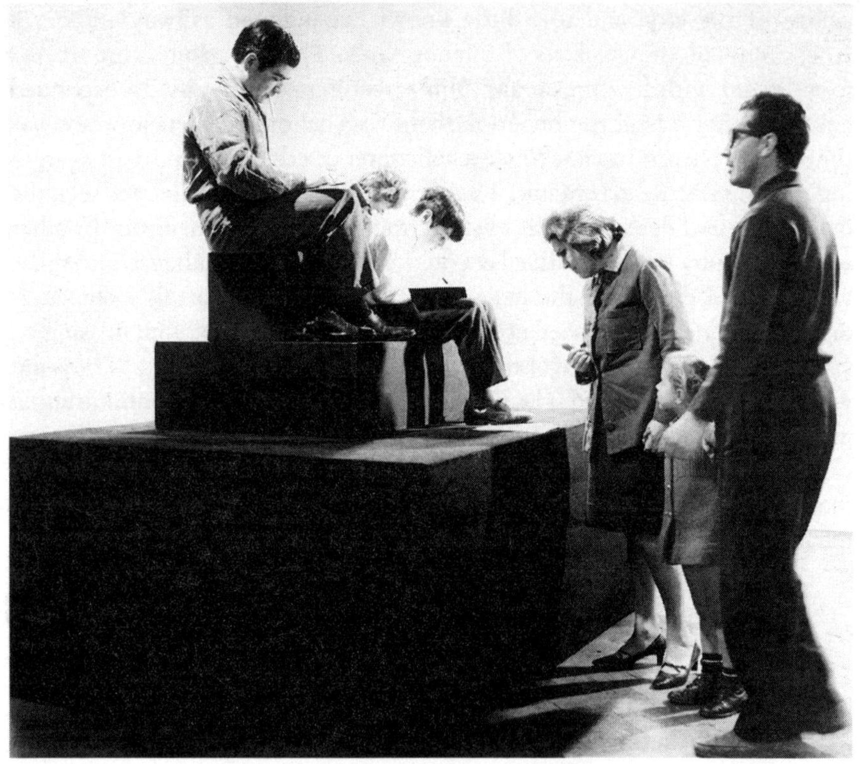

Oscar Bony, *The Worker's Family*, 1968 with viewers

tradition: elevating an everyday family to the dignity of exemplary representation or ideal.[38] Nevertheless, the use of a 'real' family as models for this task complicates such a reading: although the family are literally and symbolically elevated, they are also subject to the scrutiny of a primarily middle-class audience who came to view them, as installation shots make clear: a well-to-do family of three inspect the shorter, less well-dressed family, who avert their gaze.

This double presentation of the family – on display both symbolically (as representatives of the working class) and literally (as the singular Rodríguez family) – was conceptually reinforced in the father's double pay.[39] But the family also functioned as a third type of representation – as an avant-garde 'experience' or 'experiment', in line with the exhibition's title. Indeed, the critic and curator Jorge Romero Brest, director of the art centre at the Instituto Di Tella, considered Bony's work to be among the 'most authentic' of the experiences he presented at the show, along with that of Roberto Plate.[40] Plate had contributed a simulacrum of public conveniences, into which the public entered to find no toilets, only an empty space – which they duly began to deface with graffiti. Counter to Masotta's interest in mediation and semiotics, Brest viewed many of the

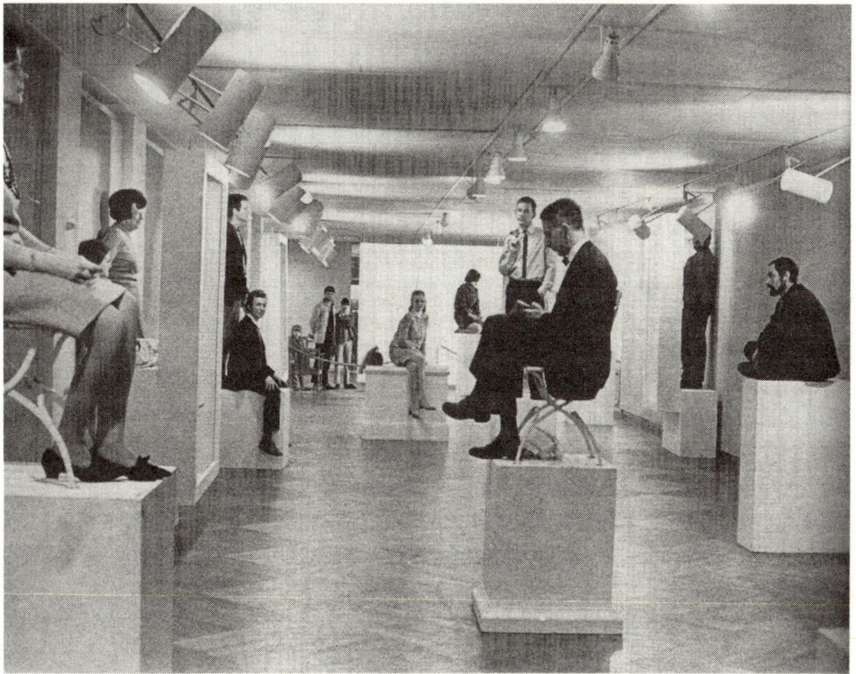

Pi Lind, *Living Sculptures*, 1968

works in 'Experiencias 68' as concerned with overcoming the space between artist and viewer, traditionally occupied by the representational work of art. Many of the artists in the exhibition, however, sought a more complex approach to the dialectic of live/mediated, as in Roberto Jacoby's telex machine that fed constant live reports from Agence France Presse on the May '68 demonstrations in Paris. Eventually, many of the artists destroyed their own works when the police censored Plate's installation: on May 23, seven days after the opening of the exhibition, the rest of the artists withdrew their pieces, hurling them out of the window into Florida Street in protest at the censorship of Plate's installation and the participation it had generated.

Critics brought other complaints against the show, including the accusation that Bony's *The Worker's Family* would have been more effective if shown within a labour union; for one critic, exhibiting the work in a gallery showed a refusal to communicate with a non-specialist public.[41] But instead of taking art to the workers, Bony brought a fragment of the workers into the exhibition – a gesture comparable to Robert Smithson's contemporaneous 'non-sites' in which a fragment of an unbounded outdoor location is removed and relocated to the gallery. Bony's other concern was dematerialisation, the predominant theme of 'Experiencias 68' as a whole following Masotta's lecture on this subject at the Instituto Di Tella in 1967. It is worth recalling that in Argentina, dematerialisation referred less to the ephemerality of works of art (as per Lippard's classic reading of US conceptualism, in which dematerialisation denotes an 'escape' from the market system), than to the diffusion and circulation of art in the mass media. At the same time, we should be mindful of the different ways in which dematerialisation was manifested in Argentinian art: works that existed solely in the media (such as the *Happening for a Dead Boar*) are significantly different to Bony's *The Worker's Family*, which attracted media attention but primarily takes the form of a live material presence (the human body) and exists today as a large-scale, framed black and white photograph, prominently displayed in the collection of the Museo de Arte Latinoamericano de Buenos Aries (MALBA).

Bony's work, however radical in its use of people as a medium, could also be said to restrict itself to rather conservative means: exchanging the fixed contours of traditional figurative sculpture for the live human being. The work is similar to a number of other delegated performances that attempted to stage this exchange in the late 1960s, such as *Living Sculptures* by the Swedish theatre director and writer Pi Lind, who in 1967 placed around twenty people on plinths in the Moderna Museet in Stockholm, for nine hours a day for five days. The event was conceived as a series of portraits, each of which was accompanied by a text panel indicating specific information about each person: their name, age, sex, profession, education, economic background, family history, pets, religion, and so on. A wide variety of Swedish citizens were on display, including a teacher, a photographer, a housewife, a Vietnam activist, a father-to-be, and a girl with a St Bernard dog. In an interview with the press, Pi Lind described the whole thing as a 'sociological exhibition' or a wild mix between a 'beauty fair and social realism'.[42] Images and press cuttings of the exhibition indicate a relatively seamless continuity between the performers and audience, arguably reflecting the social equilibrium of Scandinavian social democracy. By contrast, the specificity of Bony's provocation lies in its emphatic pointing to a particular social demographic and their payment: the working-class family were paid to work a full eight-hour day, in front of a gallery audience. Work – as activity and payment – is the subject of the piece as much as the representation of an 'ideal' or exemplary family unit.

The apparent 'normality' of Bony's family could also be contrasted to the display of Paolo Rosa, a man with Down's Syndrome, at the 1972 Venice Biennale as part of a live installation by the Italian artist Gino De Dominicis.[43] Entitled *The Second Solution of Immortality (The Universe is Motionless)* (1972), the installation comprises a person affected by Down's Syndrome seated on a chair, gazing at a beach ball and a rock placed on the ground before him/her. Each of these components have their own extremely long titles: the beach ball is *Rubber ball (fallen from a height of two meters) at the instant immediately prior to its rebound*, while the rock is titled *Waiting for a general random molecular movement in a single direction to generate spontaneous movement of the material.* In addition to these objects, an *Invisible Cube* is placed in front of the seated performer. Since De Dominicis once observed that a person with Down's Syndrome 'was to be interpreted as a different state of being', the whole installation adds up to a situation of non-communication.[44] The work stages two irreconcilable types of vision and consciousness: the gaze of the performer with Down's Syndrome, and the gaze of those who look at him. This reading is reinforced by the one official photograph of this performance, in which we see a viewer in the middle of putting on her spectacles; the image seems to emphasise the disjunction between two different experiences of looking and thinking (three, in fact, if we count ourselves).[45]

Each of these examples, like Bony's *The Worker's Family*, are isolated precedents for a tendency that has become familiar in contemporary art since the early 1990s. But it is telling that Bony, when interviewed in 1998 at the time of its restaging, confessed that he still didn't know how to describe this piece, since it existed as both a conceptual operation and concrete materiality: he referred to it as a 'conceptual proposition' since 'a group of people can't be the material of the work': 'it wasn't a performance, because it hasn't got a script, it isn't body art, there's no clear category for this work, and I like that very much, the fact that not even I can find a precise categorisation. I find extremely important the fact that there is a certain feeling of being on the limit.'[46] Bony's uncertainty about how to define his piece, as well as his feeling of liminality, continues in the critical queasiness that accompanies the exhibition of people in works of art today. In Bony's case, the viewer's self-consciousness in front of the family is not simply the heightened awareness of a phenomenological encounter – as one ideally experiences in relation to minimalist objects – but a shared embarrassment: it imposes upon us, as one critic wrote in a review of Bony's work, 'the shared humiliation of looking at these people who have been paid in order to let themselves be seen'.[47] This complicated dynamic seems to have been in Bony's mind as he referred to himself as a 'torturer' – for him, *The Worker's Family* was based less on politics than on the production of moral unease: 'it is obvious', he said, 'that the work was based on ethics, for exposing them to ridicule made me feel uncomfortable'.[48]

The Worker's Family is an exception within Bony's oeuvre: until that date his work had spanned figurative painting, 16mm films, realist sculpture, minimalist structures and installations with projection; his subsequent output, like most artists under the dictatorship in the 1970s, underwent enormous adaptation in order to survive.[49] But when placed alongside the early work of Minujín and Masotta, *The Worker's Family* consolidates a narrative of performance-based work in '60s Argentina as one of adopting particularly aggressive strategies of reification, frequently played out in relation to class. Although the best-known works of this period have a more light-hearted pop sensibility (such as Marta Minujín and Rubén Santantonín's elaborate installation *La Menesunda*, 1965), Minujín's solo work has an aggressivity belied by her colourful persona and fashionable media presence, in structure if not always in realisation. One of her later works makes a direct link between aggressive forms of participation and the political context of Argentina itself: in *Kidnappenings*, held over three evenings at MoMA in 1973, ninety participants volunteered to be kidnapped, blindfolded and subjected to a range of experiences devised by assorted art-world volunteers, their faces painted in the style of Picasso's paintings, in reference to his recent death.[50] This combination of glitzy pop chic and allusions to a political framework of repression is somewhat uneasy, and arguably tells us more about Minujín's self-exploitation for a US audience than it does about the specific tenor of participatory art produced in Argentina. In that country during the 1960s, the combined pressures of military dictatorship and an imported European intellectual heritage gave rise to a singular mode of participatory art in that country, which transformed the celebratory immediacy of the Happenings into an intellectual framework of mediated constraint, manipulation and negation.

III. The Closed Gallery, the Scuffle, the Prison

This coercive new approach to participation is played out most vividly in the *Ciclo de Arte Experimental* (Cycle of Experimental Art), organised by the Grupo de Artistas de Vanguardia (Group of Avant-Garde Artists) in the city of Rosario between May and October 1968. The group initially formed out of a desire for autonomy: to have their own space to exhibit, to organise their own shows, and to write about their own work – in short, to be their own curators and critics, rather than being dependent on institutional infrastructures. Although the Cycle was developed by the artists working individually, the group was in daily discussion, and their increasingly ambitious actions reflect the group's politicisation as the year went on, given impetus by their opposition to the Braque Prize (June 1968), the assault on Romero Brest's lecture (July 1968), and the National Encounter of Avant-Garde Art (in August 1968), which led to *Tucumán Arde* (discussed below).[51] Like artists in Buenos Aires, the group were voracious consumers of literature and theory, and Brecht was a particular obsession, along with Barthes, McLuhan, Lévi-Strauss, Marcuse, Marx (who they read in the original), and Eco's *The Open Work*.[52]

The Cycle took the form of a series of ten actions, one every fifteen days, many of which appropriated social forms, behaviours and relations. As Ana Longoni has argued, most of the events were based on a common idea: withdrawing from institutional spaces, finding new audiences, and merging art with the praxis of life by 'working on the audience as the privileged material of artistic action'.[53] The first event in the Cycle, by Norberto

Julio Puzzolo, involved filling the space of the gallery with chairs facing towards the shop window onto the street. At the opening, visitors sat on the chairs waiting for something to happen. The artist defined the piece as a 'reversible spectacle': spectators observed the street while being turned into a performance for passers-by.[54] For the third event, Fernández Bonina left the space completely empty, apart from the presence of notes forbidding viewers to speak, smoke, or bring objects of any kind into the space. Bonina explained that 'the experience occurs as long as each spectator accepts the prohibitions'; the aim was to make the audience more aware of the restraints imposed upon them in other spheres of life.[55]

Near the end of the Cycle, the artists began to move out of the gallery. The eighth action, by Eduardo Favario (9–21 September), invited the audience make a direct connection between gallery conventions and mechanisms of social control: he left the exhibition space as if in a state of abandon, with tape across the door to indicate its closure, and put up a notice instructing visitors that the work could be found in a bookshop in another part of the city. As Favario explained, 'the spectator will have to "track down" the work, abandoning his more or less static position. He will be forced to participate actively, which will turn him into the executor of an action which, in turn, has been posed as a work of art.'[56] Such work stood (for Favario) as a proposition for social change: 'a theoretical proposal that affirms the possibilities of some action with the purpose of changing our reality'.[57] The ninth event in the Cycle was an unframed participatory situation in the street, produced by Rodolfo Elizalde and Emilio Ghilioni (23–28 September). It involved the two artists simulating a street fight outside the premises of the gallery. Beginning verbally, the confrontation soon became physical. Passers-by started approaching the two men and tried to stop the fight by physically separating them. The work was intended to provoke a direct response from the public, who were unaware that the fight was staged – until flyers explaining the work's proposal were thrown in the air, communicating the artistic nature of the event. The artists stated that their intention was to create '*un arte social*': to break the 'narrow scope of the institutionalised art market' by invalidating 'the traditional exhibition space', to use a 'clear, effective artistic language in order to obtain the audience's involvement', to install 'the real piece of work in daily reality' and to incite a questioning 'of ideas and attitudes that are accepted without objections out of the mere fact that they resort to authority'.[58]

The most striking of these events, planned to take place at the end of the Cycle on 7 October, was devised by Graciela Carnevale. Unlike the previous event in the Cycle, Carnevale allowed her action to unfurl without dénouement of intentions. Her action has received considerable attention since 2000, and was a central component of Documenta 12 in 2007. The artist describes her intervention as follows:

The work consists of first preparing a totally empty room, with totally empty walls; one of the walls, which was made of glass, had to be covered in order to achieve a suitably neutral space for the work to take place. In this room the participating audience, which has come together by chance for the opening, has been locked in. I have taken prisoners. The point is to allow people to enter and to prevent them from leaving . . . There is no possibility of escape, in fact the spectators have no choice; they are obliged, violently, to participate. Their positive or negative reaction is always a form of participation. The end of the work, as unpredictable for the viewer as it is for me, is nevertheless intentioned: will the spectator tolerate the situation passively? Will an unexpected event – help from the outside – rescue him from being locked in? Or will he proceed violently to break the glass?[59]

After an hour, the visitors trapped inside the gallery removed the posters that had been placed on the windows to prevent communication with those outside. Excitement – and the sense that this was all a joke – inevitably turned to frustration but, contrary to Carnevale's hopes, no one inside the gallery took action. Eventually it was a person on the street who smashed

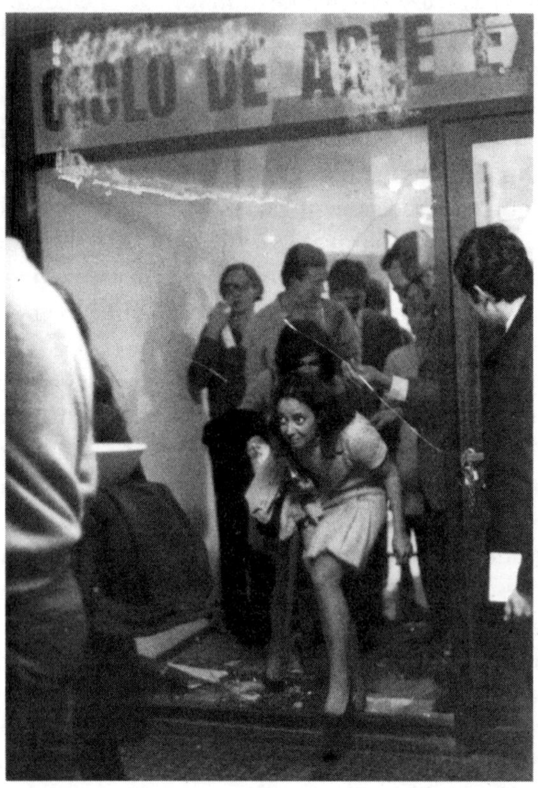

Graciela Carnevale action for the *Cycle of Experimental Art*, 1968

one of the windows open, and the private view-goers emerged to freedom through the ragged glass orifice. Some of the people present nevertheless believed that the rescuer had ruined the work and began hitting him over the head with an umbrella. The police arrived and – making a connection between the event and the first anniversary of Che Guevara's arrest – closed down the event and with it the rest of the *Ciclo de Arte Experimental.*

The Rosario Cycle presents a number of important issues for the genealogy of participatory art I am tracing: not simply the move out of gallery into public space, and a rethinking of the exhibition as a series of collaborative yet highly authored events, but as signalling a change in the use of people as a material in Argentinian art. Rather than hiring people to perform themselves as a social sculpture to be observed by others (as in Masotta's *To Induce the Spirit of the Image* and Bony's *The Worker's Family*), Carnevale proposes the work of art as a situation collapsing performer and viewer into a fractured social body. The provocation of this entity, and the unpredictability of its response, constitute the core of the work's artistic and political resonance. Unlike Masotta, who presents the work of art as a critical experiment, Carnevale's event is both metaphorical and phenomenological: to make the audience aware of, and to feel in their own bodies, the violence they were living in ('we couldn't stay neutral, we needed to make an action to get out of this imprisonment').[60]

During the following year, many of the artists involved in the Cycle collaborated with sociologists, journalists and artists from Buenos Aires to redirect their activities away from the production of visual art and towards an exhibition of counter-propaganda in defence of exploited sugar workers in the northern province of Tucumán. The interdisciplinary group who undertook the project *Tucumán Arde* conceived it as a denunciation of a corrupt government and as a call to revolt. It did not reinforce an already-existing aesthetic programme, but embodied an activist, partisan approach to a social and political crisis; the aim was to expose the viewer to the reality of social injustice, and to generate press that would reveal the truth of the situation.[61] The floor of the exhibition's entrance was covered with banners bearing the names of the sugar-plant owners of Tucumán and indicating their connections to figures of power within the ruling class. The walls were plastered with a collage of newspaper reports on Tucumán and the refineries, gathered and arranged by León Ferrari. In the central room, banners with slogans and statistics were positioned alongside massive blown-up photographs and projected slides of Tucumán inhabitants, their living conditions, and protests. Other components included interviews recorded in Tucumán played on loud speakers, while the floor was obstructed with heaps of food donated to be sent to Tucumán. A blackout threw the building into darkness every two minutes as a reminder that a Tucumán child was dying at these intervals. On the opening day, sugarless coffee was served as an allusion to the sugar shortage brought about by refinery owners hoarding the sugar. *Tucumán Arde* has subsequently become a locus classicus of political exhibition-making, but it is telling that in order to communicate forcefully an unequivocal message, participation as an artistic strategy had to be sacrificed for a return to a more conventional mode of spectatorship, albeit one informed by an aesthetic of multi-sensory installation.

IV. Invisible Theatre

It was precisely the limitations of didactically motivated political art in the face of an increasingly repressive dictatorship that formed the starting point for the Brazilian director Augusto Boal (1931–2009), whose innovative strategies for public theatre in South America seem at first glance to have much in common with the final events of the *Ciclo de Arte Experimental*, even though the two groups were unaware of each other at the time.[62] These innovations grew out of developments in the late 1960s in Brazil, and were honed during the director's exile in Argentina (1971–76) and travel to Peru (1973), and are documented in his book *Theatre of the Oppressed* (1974; English 1979) – an explicit reference to Paulo Freire's *Pedagogy of the Oppressed* (1968; English 1970) – which he wrote while living in Buenos Aires. Boal had been a catalysing figure in São Paulo's Arena Theatre in the mid to late '60s, whose productions initially nationalised foreign classics (such as Gogol and Molière) before shifting to Brechtian-influenced musicals such as *Arena Conta Zumbi* (1965), co-authored by Boal and Gianfrancesco Guarnieri. Boal's close reading of Brecht led him to break not only with identification as a key theatrical device, but to reconfigure entirely the audience/actor relationship in new forms of participatory performance for raising consciousness and empowering the working class.[63] One of Boal's key arguments is that spectators should be eliminated and reconceptualised as 'spect-actors'. However, this is not done in the name of symbolically realising a community to come (the utopian mode invoked so often in European participatory art), but more forcefully as a practical training in social antagonism, or what Boal vividly describes as a 'rehearsal of revolution'.[64]

Of the many innovations in social theatre that Boal devised, the most relevant to contemporary art is Invisible Theatre, developed in Buenos Aires as an unframed mode of public and participatory action designed to avoid detection by police authorities. Boal wrote that in Invisible Theatre, 'spectators would see the show, without seeing it as a show'.[65] The form was developed in collaboration with a group of actors who wanted to promote a humanitarian law whereby those without money could eat at restaurants (dessert and wine excepted) on showing a particular identity card. The result was less a play than a loosely constructed situation in a restaurant, in which some of the cast were actors, while the roles of manager and waiter were unwittingly played by the real manager and waiter – who said, 'almost word for word, what we had scripted'.[66] Moreover, being set in a busy restaurant at lunchtime, this form of theatre was guaranteed always to have a full house. In *Theatre of the Oppressed*, Boal recounts one particular example unfolding as follows: a number of actors are seated at different tables in a restaurant; the protagonist loudly announces that he wants to eat *à la carte*, since the rest of the food available is too bad. The waiter tells him it will cost 70 *soles*, which the actor says is no problem. At the end of the meal he receives the bill, and announces that he's unable to pay for it. (Boal notes that the diners nearby are of course closely following this dialogue, and far more attentively than if they were witnessing it as a scene on stage.) The actor offers to pay with his own labour power – perhaps taking out the rubbish, or doing the washing up. He asks the waiter how much he would get paid for taking out the rubbish. The waiter avoids answering, but a second actor, at another table, pipes up that he's friends with the rubbish collector and knows that he earns 7 *soles* per hour – so he would have to work ten hours for a meal that took ten minutes to eat. The first actor says he would perhaps rather do the gardening for them – how much do they pay the gardener? A third actor pipes up: he's friends with the gardener, and knows that he gets 10 *soles* per hour. By this point the head waiter is in despair. He tries to divert the attention of the customers, but the restaurant is already becoming a public forum. Eventually one of the actors starts collecting money to pay the bill – which offends some people, and causes more disturbance, but they manage to amass 100 *soles*.[67]

It is tempting to compare this level of integration between artifice and reality to the last two events of the *Ciclo de Arte Experimental*. Both operate by stealth, unannounced to the public as works of art. Both turn the audience into active agents and rely on their intervention for the work to unfold. But whereas the actions of the *Ciclo* operate on a metaphoric level with an art audience, activating spectatorship as a transitive passage to political action, Boal's work takes theatre to an audience who don't even recognise themselves as an audience, and stages with them a discussion about specific issues of labour. For Boal, a political agenda requires precise aesthetic solutions. It is crucial, for example, that the actors do not reveal themselves to be actors: 'On this rests the invisible nature of this form of theatre. And it is precisely this invisible quality that will make the spectator act freely and fully, as if he were living in a real situation – and, after all, it is a real situation!'[68] Needless to say, the invisibility of this theatre was politically necessary given the extreme violence of the dictatorship at this point.[69] Boal's Invisible Theatre can be seen as an explicitly Marxist iteration of the *Ciclo*'s metaphorical events (the closed gallery, the scuffle, the prison). If the artists in Rosario produced coercive situations that function as poetic analogues for political repression (inflicting restriction on the viewer as a wake-up call to his/her oppression by the Onganía dictatorship), Boal connected this oppression more explicitly to the economics of class inequality. His Invisible Theatre was aimed at training the public to be more conscious of class difference and to provide them with a forum for articulating dissent. The didacticism of this approach cannot be denied, but the artistic means devised to achieve it – an eruption of semi-staged conflict in public space, combining scripted acting and unwitting real time dialogue – is a precedent for much contemporary art that seeks to go unannounced in public space.

Boal is less known today for Invisible Theatre than for his internationally acclaimed technique of Forum Theatre, developed in Peru in 1973 following a sobering experience in north-east Brazil when he came to understand 'the falsity of the "messenger" form of political theatre'.[70] If Invisible Theatre requires a great deal of rehearsal (in order to anticipate every possible outcome from the public), and maintains a division (albeit invisible) between the actors who attempt to steer the situation and audience who respond to it, Forum Theatre is more spontaneous, improvised, and takes place within a protected, educational framework; indeed, Boal has described it as 'transitive pedagogy'.[71] Forum Theatre begins with a situation presented by actors to the audience, who then take the part of the protagonists to devise alternative courses of action to the events initially depicted; this can involve the performance of current situations (such as a factory dispute) or classic works (such as Brecht's *The Jewish Wife*), where the spect-actors are asked, 'would you do the same thing in her position?' The aim of Forum Theatre, writes Boal, 'is not to win, but to learn and to train. The spect-actors, by acting out their ideas, train for "real life" action; and actors and audience alike, by playing, learn the possible consequences of their actions. They learn the arsenal of the oppressors and the possible tactics and strategies of the oppressed.'[72] Boal's aim was to have a constructive impact on the audience, rather than eliciting emotional responses to the representation of difficult social reality. According to this thinking, the play as a medium could be used for other purposes, namely, to brainstorm ways in which reality can be changed. In this way, alienation could be channelled to directly useful ends as the audience itself assumes the function of protagonist. Inevitably, this redirects theatre towards education rather than entertainment, but not in the traditional sense of political theatre; rather, it is informed by Freire's rejection of the 'banking' model of education in favour of shared knowledge: 'it is not the old didactic theatre. It is pedagogical in the sense that we all learn together, actors and audience'.[73]

As a critique of traditional theatre and its conventional fate as compensatory entertainment or catharsis, the Theatre of the Oppressed is presented by Boal as the culmination of previous spectatorial paradigms, including Aristotle, Machiavelli and Brecht. In Aristotelian tragedy, catharsis purifies the audience of their antisocial characteristics (through their identification with the protagonist's *hamartia*). The function of this is to maintain social stability and ultimately, for Boal, this type of Greek tragedy serves as an instrument of repression ('what is purified is the desire to change society – not, as they say in many books, pity and fear . . . I don't want the people to use the theatre as a way of not doing in real life').[74] Instead, he sought to trigger in the viewer a desire to practise in reality the act that he/she had rehearsed in the theatre, and Boal is meticulous in considering the *affective* impact of this technique: 'the practice of these theatrical forms creates a sort of uneasy sense of incompleteness that seeks fulfilment through real action'.[75] In the context of contemporary art, it is telling that we do not have images of these experiences: the force of Boal's thinking is best communicated verbally. His most compelling innovations parallel those of Eisenstein in the 1920s: using reality as a set, and real people as performers, to produce a heightened consciousness of social injustice.

Before concluding, it is worth considering the relocation of Boal's techniques from the context in which they were devised: rural illiteracy and oppression under the conditions of military dictatorship, in which anything less than a positive reference to society would be censored. Working in Sicily, Stockholm, Paris and other European cities in the later 1970s and 1980s, Boal found himself creating Invisible Theatre based on issues of racism, ageism, sexism and homelessness, rather than class inequality; he gives examples of Invisible Theatre performed on the Paris Metro and on passenger ferries in Stockholm.[76] Despite his hostility towards the West as the source of Latin America's problems, he noted that the same extremes of wealth and poverty existed there too, together with new forms of oppression that Boal referred to as 'the cop in the head' – solitude, incommunicability, emptiness. Rather than an external armed threat, the West suffered from an internalised oppression, an anomie leading a greater occurrence of depression and suicide.[77] Theatre scholar Mady Schutzman had argued that the Theatre of the Oppressed was devalued by such a relocation: it is 'reduced to a technique for coping rather than changing – adapting oneself to the so-called "demands" an affluent and privileged society makes upon a consumption-minded, capitalist individuality'.[78] What were 'rehearsals for revolution' in Latin America became 'rehearsals for healing' in the West.

For Boal, the Theatre of the Oppressed has different goals in different contexts: it could be political (events and demonstrations), therapeutic (Boal collaborated with his wife Cecilia, a psychoanalyst), pedagogic (in schools), and legislative (in cities). The latter is perhaps the most relevant from today's perspective: on returning to Brazil in 1986, Boal was invited by a Rio TV station to make a twenty-minute programme of Invisible Theatre every Sunday. One episode involved a dark-skinned man selling himself as a slave in the market because he found out that he earned less than a slave did in the nineteenth century. Another concerned nuclear power: a group of actors dressed in black went to the beach at Ipanema and started digging graves, and when asked what they were doing, replied, 'If the nuclear power plant explodes we'll need 5 million graves so we'd better start digging graves now.'[79] Invisible Theatre here seems to anticipate reality television and candid camera documentaries; the important difference is that Boal used theatrical techniques such as Legislative Theatre towards implementing social reform, and was elected to the city council of Rio de Janeiro from 1992 to 1996.

Boal's Invisible Theatre seems to be the hidden precursor of innumerable performance-based artistic experiments in public space that operate unannounced and unframed by a gallery apparatus. Invariably these are geared less towards consciousness-raising and more towards our heightened anxiety about the collapse between live and mediated, actual and fiction. Works like Roman Ondak's *Good Feelings in Good Times* (2003), Paweł Althamer's *Real Time Movie* (2000) or Dora García's *The Beggar's Opera* (2007), all insert themselves unannounced into the everyday flow of street life, preferring to risk being overlooked entirely than to announce themselves to an audience whose responses might be predetermined by this knowledge. Comparing this recent art to Boal's Invisible Theatre, Catherine Wood notes that the former does not 'imply an enabling sense of agency for the participating spectator but instead registers the fear that any instance of personal encounter might be being manipulated invisibly'. She continues:

> [They propose] a paranoid cityscape laced with a pervasive mistrust of perception, and, therefore, of many of the assumptions upon which one's social and economic navigation of the city – and of the institutional spaces of art – depend . . . In different ways, these artworks register the uncomfortable nature of this environment, pointing to the hysterical eruptions of theatre in every facet of interaction – from the casual encounter in the street, to a view of the passing crowd, to the figure of authority.[80]

In this context, Argentine media art – such as the *Happening for a Dead Boar* – seems astonishingly prescient: a work that exists solely as mediation and operates by rumour becoming a meta-commentary on mediation and its capacity to fictionalise.

V. Art as a Terrorist Act

Participatory actions in Argentina therefore emerge in response to a far harsher set of contextual co-ordinates than does participatory art in Europe, and have very different aesthetic consequences. If European and North American participatory art is figured as a critique of spectacle in consumer capitalism and seeks to promote collective activity over individual passivity, then Argentinian artists responded to and questioned this valorisation of first-hand immediacy, and combined this with opposition to the US-backed dictatorships, in which peaceful political protest was abolished, and social trust shattered in a climate of constant suspicion. This led to the production of situations that deploy two contradictory impulses: to bring art and life closer (mapping the two onto each other by using people as a medium) while at the same time incorporating distanciation from both (be this through a Brechtian *Verfremdungseffekt* or the critical reader exemplified by Barthes' *Mythologies*). The result of these contradictory impulses leads, on the one hand, to a reification of the human body in live installation (Masotta, Bony) and on the other to the production of alienating events in which the viewer plays a role within an unannounced but predetermined situation (*Ciclo de Arte Experimental*, Boal). Although the Argentinian work shares with its Western counterparts an emphasis on active spectatorship, this is overtly steered towards coercion: people are used as an artistic material, and this stands as a consciousness-raising weapon against an even greater brutality (the dictatorship). It is not unimportant that this work is informed by an early reception of French theory (far sooner, for example, than in an Anglophone context), since this creates a distinctly existential and psychological tenor, compared to the pragmatic rationalism of North American art of this period.[81]

One could therefore argue that these Argentinian examples are both non-Western (in their response to the specific historical conditions of the dictatorship) and ultra-Western (in their use of European theory). They set an important precedent for the present-day uses of participation while also questioning the assumption that participation is synonymous with democracy. At the same time, these artists also developed a directly confrontational approach to public space and an increasingly precarious relationship with art institutions. This position was articulated most clearly at the National Encounter of Avant-Garde Art, held in Rosario in August 1968, where several of the conference papers – particularly those by Nicolás Rosa and León Ferrari – asserted that political commitment alone was not enough; an effective artistic revolution was essential to supplement their cause. At the point of reception, they argued, a work of art should have a similar effect to a political action: 'If the contents are to be expressed in a revolutionary manner, if the work is to make an effective impact on the recipients' consciousness, it is essential to deal with the material in a shocking, disquieting, even violent way.'[82] The artist León Ferrari took this sentiment the furthest: 'Art will be neither beauty nor novelty; art will be efficacy and disturbance. An accomplished work of art will be that which, in the artist's environment, can make an impact similar to the one caused by a terrorist act in a country struggling for its freedom.'[83] Importantly, this 'terrorist' approach did not involve a suppression of art – as we find in the Situationist model – but maintained the inextricability of a political and aesthetic programme, since it was pointless for artists to suppress their area of expertise ('Otherwise, we run the risk of becoming ambiguous and, as a consequence, of losing efficacy').[84] For the SI, by contrast, artistic competence had no role in advancing the Revolution (which at any rate, was messianically distant and had to 'bide its time'); they conceived their alternatives to art as anticipating the *consequences* of revolutionary upheaval, rather than *paving* the way towards it.[85] For the artists in Rosario, artistic expertise was their most powerful weapon, not something to be rejected or surpassed. The interdisciplinary research project *Tucumán Arde*, the main outcome of the National Encounter of Avant-garde Art, was the final attempt by Argentinian artists to redirect art towards political ends; but *Tucumán Arde*, for all its political clarity, left only one option for the viewer: the Marxist re-education of his or her perspective on society. The other artistic examples I have discussed in this chapter present more open-ended models for reimagining art's relationship to a leftist political imaginary. After this moment, the dictatorship grew increasingly surreal and deadly and many artists either sought exile or took other jobs.[86] In the 1970s, such experimentation was forcibly halted, and replaced by public demonstrations by women's movements, most famously the Madres de Plaza de Mayo (1977–), whose collective grief found vivid ways to visualise protest at the seemingly interminable state kidnappings and torture.

5

The Social Under Socialism

This chapter turns to what is perhaps the most complicated episode in the history of participatory art, namely the impulses motivating collaborative practice when collectivism is an ideological requirement and state-imposed norm. Unlike the dominant discourse of participatory art in Western Europe and North America, where it is positioned as a constructive and oppositional response to spectacle's atomisation of social relations, the participatory art of Eastern Europe and Russia from the mid 1960s to late 1980s is frequently marked by the desire for an increasingly subjective and privatised aesthetic experience. At first glance, this seems to be an inversion of the Western model (despite Guy Debord's observation that bureaucratic communism is no less spectacular than its capitalist variant: it is simply 'concentrated' as opposed to 'diffuse').[1] However, and crucially, the individual experiences that were the target of participatory art under communism were framed as *shared* privatised experiences: the construction of a collective artistic space amongst mutually trusting colleagues. Rather than frame this work as 'implicitly political', as is the habit with current Western approaches to Eastern bloc art history, this essay will argue that work produced under state socialism during these decades should rather be viewed in more complex terms. Given the saturation of everyday life with ideology, artists did not regard their work as political but rather as existential and *a*political, committed to ideas of freedom and the individual imagination. At the same time, they sought an expanded – one might say democratised – horizon of artistic production, in contrast to the highly regulated and hierarchical system of the official Union of Soviet Artists.[2]

This chapter must also begin with the proviso that it is difficult to generalise about participatory art under post-war communism. Artistic responses to the regime vary strongly between different Eastern European countries, in line with each region's specific relationship to Moscow and their distinct negotiations of its policies. Certain countries managed to keep Soviet power at arm's length during the 1945–89 period, although the outcomes of this distance varied hugely, from the crippling dictatorship of Nicolae Ceauşescu in Romania (1948–89) to the more liberalising tendencies of non-aligned former Yugoslavia under Josip Broz Tito (1943–80), where internationalism was embraced, along with greater ease of travel to and communication with the West. These geographical variations must in turn be cross-referenced with a chronology of cultural policy changes in Moscow itself: Nikita Khrushchev's partial de-Stalinisation (1953–64) was followed by the hardline conservative backlash of Leonid Brezhnev (1964–82), although policy oscillated even within these respective regimes. A final point to note is that there are no easily drawn lines of artistic communication between East and West, since these depended on individual relationships between specific critics and artists rather than on general international alignments. However, one can cautiously claim that the most influential artistic communication took place between individual artists and specific centres in Western Europe (especially Paris and Cologne) rather than between neighbouring countries in the Eastern bloc; the relative isolation of these parallel histories is, among other things, revealed in IRWIN's *East Art Map* (2007).[3]

In the present chapter, I want to focus on two moments of socially oriented, performance-based actions in the 1960s and 1970s: the first in former Czechoslovakia (with two distinct scenes in Bratislava and Prague), and the second in Moscow from the mid 1970s to mid 1980s, focusing on the Collective Actions Group. Participatory art is rare in the Soviet bloc, and these two contexts form an important exception. Unlike some of the Latin American artists discussed in the previous chapter, for whom social participation in art denotes the inclusion of the working class, or at least everyday non-professionals (rather than the artists' friends and colleagues), the political context of the examples in this chapter rendered such distinctions redundant. The contemporary impulse to collaborate with disenfranchised communities was an alien concept: under Cold War socialism, every citizen was (at least nominally) equal, a co-producer of the communist state. Class difference did not exist.[4] Finding participants for one's art was therefore a question of selecting reliable colleagues who would not inform on one's activities. In an atmosphere of near constant surveillance and insecurity, participation was an artistic and social strategy to be deployed only amongst the most trusted groups of friends. Most of the case studies that follow therefore break with this book's criterion for inclusion, since they are concerned almost solely with participation as a device to mobilise subjective experience in fellow artists and writers, rather than with the general public.

The restrictions of life under Cold War communism do more than simply affect who participates in art, they also govern the appearance of these works: materially frugal and temporally brief, many of these actions and events were located in the countryside, far away from networks of surveillance. The fact that many of these actions do not look like art is less an indication of the artists' commitment to blurring 'art and life' than a deliberate strategy of self-protection, as well as a reaction to the state's own military displays and socialist festivals (mass spectacle) as visual points of reference, which dissuaded artists from contrived displays of collective unity even if they had had the resources to emulate them.[5]

I. Prague: From Actions to Ceremonies

Czechoslovakia came under Soviet control in February 1948. Only months after this change of regime, the eminent art critic Jindřich Chalupecký described the immediate impact of the upheaval in an article expressing his confusion and anger that a leftist project (with which he and many of his contemporaries had identified in the 1930s) turned out to be a repressive force that prevented individual expression and dissent. 'In place of a diverse and sophisticated culture', he wrote, 'we were presented with something so incredibly barren, monotonous and base as to defy reason.'[6] He goes on to describe the crushing effect of these enforced changes that effectively eroded any space for private thought: time became organised, with compulsory membership of organisations demonstrating loyalty to the regime, to say nothing of 'the diabolical invention of collective "organised leisure", which makes sure that people are unable to devote themselves to their own private concerns even during their vacations'.[7] The ownership of private property was systematically eliminated, along with privacy and individuality as an emotional and psychological refuge.

As a satellite state of the USSR, Czechoslovakia's fortunes in the post-war period were closely linked to changes in the Russian regime. After the death of Stalin in 1953, Khrushchev came to power and openly denounced Stalin's arbitrary rule and political purges. After 1964 the conservative reformist Brezhnev reversed the positive changes that Khrushchev had begun to introduce. In Czechoslovakia, by contrast, liberalisation continued through the 1960s: growing economic difficulties led to the gradual increase of reformist ideas, opposing the persistence of Stalinism and holding it responsible for Czechoslovakia's political and economic ills. During this period, artists were in contact with international colleagues and could travel to exhibitions in Paris and Germany. The Prague Spring of 1968 – Alexander Dubček's 'socialism with a human face' – loosened restrictions on the media, speech and travel.[8] This window was all too brief. The Soviet invasion of 21 August 1968 led to the imposition of 'normalisation', that is, the absolute restoration of centralised control, in which a local system was recalibrated to match the Soviet model. In Czechoslovakia this process was particularly harsh, with the reintroduction of media censorship, a restriction on private travel, and an increasingly vigilant secret police.[9] The 1970s in Czechoslovakia were therefore an extremely dark period, with changes only coming slowly after Charter 1977, a manifesto criticising the government signed by 243 citizens (including some artists) and published in West German newspapers on 6 January

1977. Although the government retaliated predictably and violently by imprisoning several of the signatories, Charter 77 gave momentum to organised opposition in the 1980s and played an instrumental role in the Velvet Revolution of 1989.

With this political background in mind, it is possible to observe the changing idea of public space as manifested in participatory art from the 1960s (when actions in public were possible) to the 1970s (when public gatherings were banned), and the different ways in which artists dealt with this in Prague and Bratislava. The first figure to be considered is Milan Knížák (b.1940), an idiosyncratic character based in Prague, associated with Fluxus, and organiser of the first Happenings in Czechoslovakia. Through the critic Jindřich Chalupecký, Knížák was in contact with Allan Kaprow and Jean-Jacques Lebel, and in 1965 was nominated as 'Director of Fluxus East' by George Brecht. Yet Knížák rejected both Fluxus and the Happenings: Fluxus for the contrived slightness of its events (which remained tied to the format of conventional stage performance) and the Happenings for their excessive theatricality.[10] He felt that his own work was more 'natural', and closer to the reality of human life. As such, he preferred the term 'actions', and sought to set his work at one remove from Western trends. Significantly, the key factor for him was the status of the participants:

> the majority of actions – happenings – in the United States and of those created by other Western authors, and almost all actions of the Fluxus group, as far as I was able to ascertain from recent publications, are quite easily realised without the input of the participants. This is because they rely more on spectators than on participants. What they really create are *tableaux vivants* which intend to impress by virtue of their uniqueness and their drastic impact. Thus, they fall readily into the traditional framework . . .[11]

An additional difference, for Knížák, was the question of urgency. In the mid '60s he frequently claimed that action art was not a matter of art at all, but of necessity, a fundamental concern to man. Western art, by contrast, seemed to him a 'titillation, a delicacy, a topic of conversation'; his activities, he wrote, 'are not experimental art, but *necessary activity*'.[12] It is important to understand that this necessity was not construed as political urgency: Knížák sought a fusion of art and life (in the most utopian and naive manner) that has no direct equivalents in the West. His approach is less politically motivated than those of Guy Debord and Jean-Jacques Lebel, and more poetic and provocational than Kaprow's, even while he shared with all of these figures the desire for a more intensely lived social experience.

Most of Knížák's actions took place outdoors, on the street and in backyards. In order to minimise interruption by police authorities, they were undertaken swiftly and lasted no longer than twenty minutes. One of his most celebrated actions was *A Walk Around Nový Svět* (1964).[13] Knížák prepared a walk for his friends through one of the more picturesque streets of Prague, moving past different assemblages, environments and attractions, located both in the street and within people's homes. In order to maintain a low profile, the action was advertised solely by word of mouth; once present, the audience was invited to perform simple tasks – akin to the semi-scored participation of Kaprow's early Happenings but with a slightly surreal and absurdist edge.[14] The actions were designed to enhance each of the senses (in keeping with the work's alternative title, *A Demonstration for All the Senses*): participants were given an object to carry for the duration of the walk; they were led past an open window where a man sat at a laid table and began to eat; they were locked for five minutes in a small room, where perfume had been spilt on the floor (as 'preparation, a disturbance of their normal state of mind'); they were led past a man lying in the street playing a double bass; then herded into a small area where they were encircled by the organisers on motorcycles and in cars; they were asked to arrange a number of objects in a row, and to rebuild this row 20 cm further on; they watched a man glaze a window then break it; they were presented with a book, from which each one tore a page; finally, participants returned the objects they had been carrying since the beginning. At the end of this sequence (which Knížák referred to as the 'active part of the

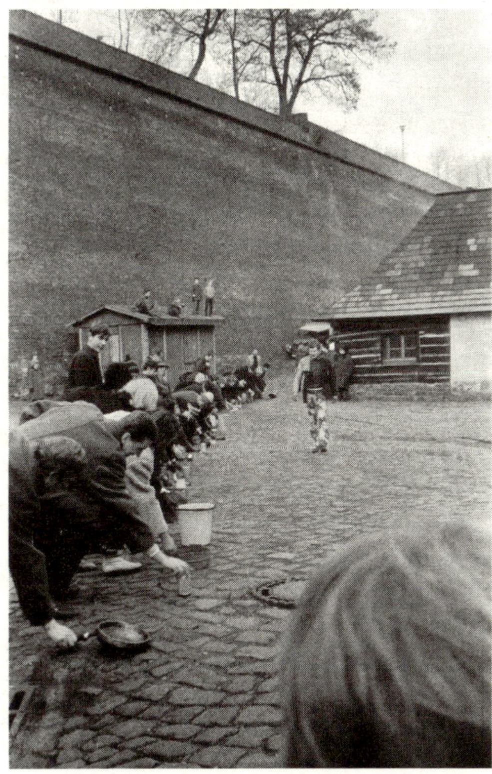

Milan Knížák, *A Demonstration for All the Senses*, 1964

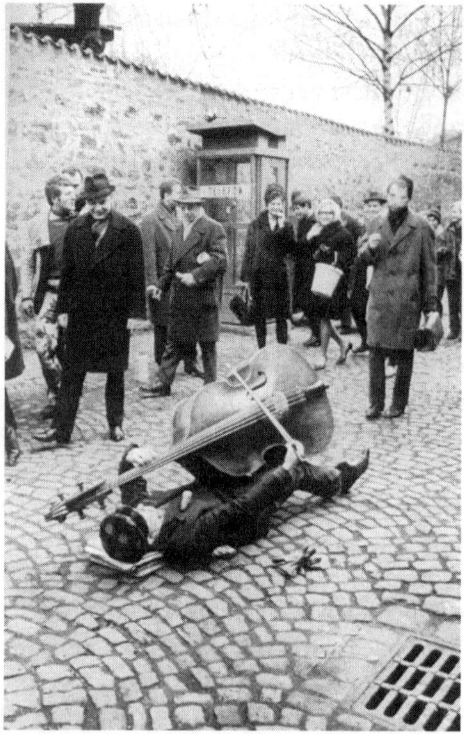

Milan Knížák, *A Demonstration for All the Senses*, 1964

demonstration'), the participants were instructed to go back to their homes. Knížák designated as the 'second demonstration' everything that took place in the subsequent fortnight, as if to draw attention, almost pedagogically, to the continuous resonance of these actions in the weeks that followed. For Knížák, the emphasis was on playfulness, shared experience, and blurring the line between everyday actions and events. It aimed to create a different mindset in the participants, disrupting their usual behaviour, producing a non-conformist attitude that broke with everyday routine. However, we should resist the temptation to make leftist political claims for this non-conformity: the work sprang from an existential impulse, seeking to generate a territory of free expression, a celebration of idiosyncrasy rather than social equality.[15]

To these ends, Knížák also sought to provoke the anonymous public by distributing large quantities of public letters. In *Letter to the Population* (1965), he incites the public to disruptive but life-affirming actions:

> Scribble obscene inscriptions on every street corner in the vicinity of your apartment!
> Give your salary to the first nice person whom you meet!
> Masturbate incessantly for 8 hours!
> Burn every book on your bookshelf! . . .

Drink 2 quarts of rum every day for 7 days!
Do not drink at all for 3 days!
Ask your wife (husband) to demolish your radio, television set, record-player, refrigerator!
Say hello to every person who passes you!
Commit suicide!
Live![16]

Such an injunction to disruptive, nonsensical, non-conformist behaviour can be seen in many of Knížák's works from the mid '60s, which sought to engage participants as unwitting artistic accomplices. In 1965, he theorised the difference between two types of audience participation – 'enforced action' and 'spontaneous reaction'. The former produced disorientation, but was less productive than the latter, which indicated the full commitment of the participant. Knížák felt that two types of participation needed to be defined, because there are two types of participant, the passive and the active.[17] Ideally, he felt, artists should deploy a combination of both modes, an idea that he exemplified in *An Event for the Post Office, the Police, and the Occupants of no.26 Vaclavkova Street, Prague 6, and for all Their Neighbours, Relatives and Friends* (1966), realised in collaboration with Jan Maria Mach.

As the unwieldy title indicates, the somewhat arbitrary recipients of the project were the residents of a randomly selected building and all their acquaintances. The inhabitants were subjected to three types of intervention: firstly, being sent packages containing various objects (such as lumps of bread, or a leaflet advising them to 'get a cat'). Secondly, objects were spread around the halls of the building: books and goldfish on the floor, coats on hooks, calendars and paper gliders, unmade beds, chairs, and so on. Finally, the inhabitants of the house were sent free cinema tickets to a movie, so that they might (ideally) all be sitting together in reserved seats in the same theatre. Using Knížák's typology of two types of participation, the first phase corresponds to the idea of enforcement: 'the participant is imposed upon, restricted; in some way, he is insulted, hurt. His effort to regain his normal (previous) status constitutes the activation'. The second – going to the cinema – is the spontaneous component: 'the participant voluntarily joins in both physically and mentally'.[18] The artist sought an experience of individualised yet collective disruption as a way to open people's minds, bringing objects into their immediate domestic environment, while also hoping to displace these same people from one building (26 Vaclavkova Street) into another (the cinema) in the form of a large-scale, unannounced social sculpture.

We might also see *An Event for the Post Office* . . . having a sly social goal in the creation of a situation that encouraged conversation and debate amongst neighbours; in effect, however, the work seemed only to exacerbate the distrust that already existed under the regime. The police investigated *An Event for the Post Office* . . . for two months and Knížák recorded an account of their meeting with the residents in a *samizdat* newspaper of that year.[19] While offering an amusing and vivid description of the discussion, Knížák provides no photographs, and offers no analysis of his intervention, only a testimony to the diverse responses it solicited. He reports that about half of the people are 'not too much against us, and the rest are totally against us'; infighting between the different factions in the building (an army major, a mouthy blonde, a teacher, and so on) seems to predominate.[20] His tone is rather distant and brusque, as if poking fun at the protagonists. It is clear that the residents failed to understand the artistic aim of his intervention, focusing on questions of time and money, the anxiety caused by the packages (they could be bombs), and so on. The text shows Knížák's commitment to documenting participant feedback, but it prompts more questions than it answers. What were his criteria of success for such a piece? Since none of the participants actually went to the cinema, did he consider this work to be a failure? Was the conceptual proposition more important than its actual realisation and consequences? Bereft of photographic documentation, the work nevertheless stands as an idiosyncratic combination of aggression, generosity, absurdity, didactics and provocation. It's worth recalling that at the time of this performance, Knížák was still only twenty-six years old.

Alongside these provocations of the anonymous public, Knížák founded a social organisation in Prague between 1963 and 1971 called the A-Community, which also had a branch in West Bohemia. 'A' stood for 'Aktual', reiterating his Fluxus attachment to the everyday. Under Knížák's charismatic leadership, the group explored music, performances, mail art and other 'necessary activities' not always framed as art, and which demanded a maximum level of personal engagement from the participants. Knížák later described the A-Community as a group of self-elected people who desired to be different, and that this was the sole criterion for joining: its basic aspiration was to find a more vivid, all-encompassing experience of everyday life. (Knížák reports that 'drunkenness, drug abuse and sex became burning elements of a wild asceticism aiming towards the unveiling of the quintessence of experience'.[21]) Photographs of the A-Community are typical of countercultural gatherings anywhere in the mid to late 1960s: long hair, flowing clothes, beaming smiles and musical instruments. The heightened consciousness sought by the A-Community was not tied to political awakening but to the formation of an alternative parallel community. Unlike Argentinian actions of the late 1960s (discussed in Chapter 4), which intended to create a transitive link between awareness of one's situation and the desire to change it, Knížák's primary concerns were aesthetic rather than political: to change one's life into art, rather than changing the system under which you live. From his perspective, capitalism or communism were irrelevant categories; what mattered was one's freedom of perception and experience of the world.

Despite this somewhat escapist framework, in which Knížák effectively became leader of his own social group, the character of his actions nevertheless changed substantially after travelling to the West. During the Prague Spring, Knížák obtained a visa to visit the US, at the invitation of Fluxus artist George Maciunas. He lectured there and produced two new actions in 1969. However, in comparison to his extrovert provocations of the mid '60s, the works made in the US are notable for their emphasis on solitude and meditative silence. *Lying-Down Ceremony* (Douglas University, New Jersey, 1967–68) invited participants to lie down on the floor of a room, wearing blindfolds; *Difficult Ceremony* (1966–69), performed at Greene Street, New York City on 18 January 1969, was a twenty-four-hour event in which participants were instructed to spend time together without 'eating, drinking, smoking, sleeping, getting high, talking, or communicating in any other way (for example, by writing, sign language, etc.). 24 hours later, the company parts in silence.'[22] If Knížák's earlier works sought to provoke the public in outdoor settings, his events in the US are characterised by refusal, interiority, austerity, and the privileging of subjective experience. With students as his participants, *Lying-Down Ceremony* in particular seems to invite parallels to Lygia Clark's experiments at the Sorbonne during these years; but Knížák's event is austere in comparison with the sensory blurring of interior and exterior that takes place in Clark's 'collective body'.[23] The introverted character of these works can be ascribed in part to the period Knížák spent in jail in Vienna en route to New York (for not having the correct papers), during which time he wrote *Action for My Mind* – an interrogative mantra in the

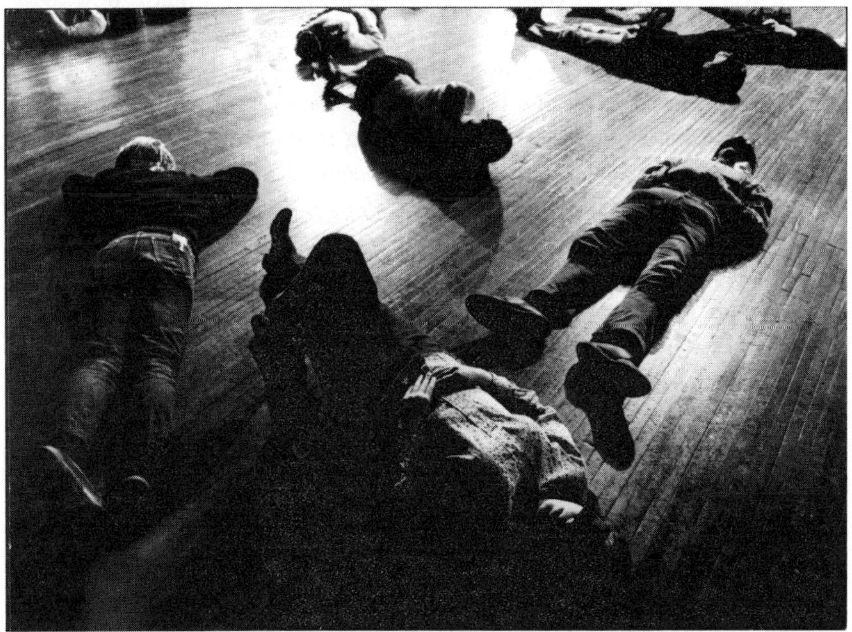

Milan Knížák, *Lying-Down Ceremony*, 1967–68

form of a stream of questions.[24] The two works produced after this experience seem to place participants in a similar condition of introspection, and it is telling that two accounts of this work both emphasise how the participants felt gently 'manipulated' by the artist.[25] Knížák's use of the word 'ceremony' to describe these events nevertheless maintains an allusion to collective action, and looks ahead to his work of the 1970s, in which participation becomes increasingly silent and ritualistic.

It seems revealing that Knížák found his experience in the US to be frustrating, and returned to Prague long before the expiry of his visa. The critic Pierre Restany reports that he could not express himself through American reality, suggesting that ideological differences continued to be crippling for artists from the East ('the new generation in eastern Europe has been grown in an absolutely non-competitive structure, the perfect antinomy of the occident').[26] Restany's summary is correct if somewhat idealised: after being a minor celebrity in Prague, it was hard for Knížák to adjust to being one of hundreds of artists in New York City, all of whom seemed to have a similar approach to blurring art and life. Knížák's difficulty in making an impact there is reinforced by his diaristic travelogue of this period, *Cestopisy* (Travel Book), where he laments that the only people who pay attention to art are other artists and their friends (unlike, one assumes, the general public addressed by works like *A Walk Around Nový Svět*). In Prague, Knížák was alone in proclaiming the radical fusion of art and life; he was dumbfounded to find this a commonplace idea in the US:

> I've discovered a huge paradox here. Certainly all of you know how the entry of simple things into art, the rapprochement of art and reality, that modest and noble celebration of the simplest acts, has become glorified and exaggerated. Now it's reached the point where many artists who sweep the stairs claim that they are doing their piece . . . Any kind of activity whatever, even the most insignificant, is almost instantaneously stamped with the hallmark of art.[27]

Knížák describes running up and down escalators in several department stores, and how, after the intensity of this experience, 'all these artistic programmes tasted like distilled water to me'.[28] His identification with Fluxus rapidly dwindled, although he engaged in productive dialogue with Allan Kaprow.[29] Finally, the need for money to survive in the US meant that paradoxically he felt *less* free than in Czechoslovakia. Not only was the cost of living in Prague very low, since the state provided housing, but this same state gratifyingly responded when he provoked its authority. In the US he lacked an Oedipal father to antagonise and thereby receive affirmation through its acknowledgment; at the end of *Travel Book* he speaks of being hugely content to be back in Prague where he had organised seven concerts that were banned.

In the 1970s, however, normalisation conspired to make such tauntings of the state more difficult. The introverted direction of Knížák's work, which had begun with *Actions for the Mind* and the 'ceremonies' in New York, was now necessitated by a repressive political situation in which gatherings in public space were forbidden. Accordingly, the work of younger Czech artists of the 1970s – such as Petr Štembera, Jan Mlčoch and Karel Miler – turned inwards, to body-art rituals in interior spaces, performed for a handful of close friends.[30] In tune with this sober mood, Knížák's practice became more ritualistic, with collective actions such as *Stone Ceremony* (1971) in which participants create a small circle of stones and stand silently inside it; the photographs of this ritual show a bleak pattern of isolated figures in a remote landscape. One of the participants in *A March* (1973) – an action in which a crowd of around forty people were tied together with a rope before marching silently through the landscape of the Prokopské Valley – noted that they were unsure how many people would show up as 'word was out that the cops would show up'.[31] These works stand in sharp contrast to the exuberant merriment of *A Walk Around Nový Svět*, which was observed by the police but never halted, and to *Demonstration for J.M.* (1965), in which the artist co-opted police instructions to clear up the props for his action into part of the action itself.[32] In this action, as Tomáš Pospiszyl points out, the police constituted a new type of participant: 'The police was an active third party – besides artists and their audience – that had control over the whole action. Here we have an example of secondary audience of a special kind: a state apparatus that can interpret every strange activity as a threat to its security.'[33]

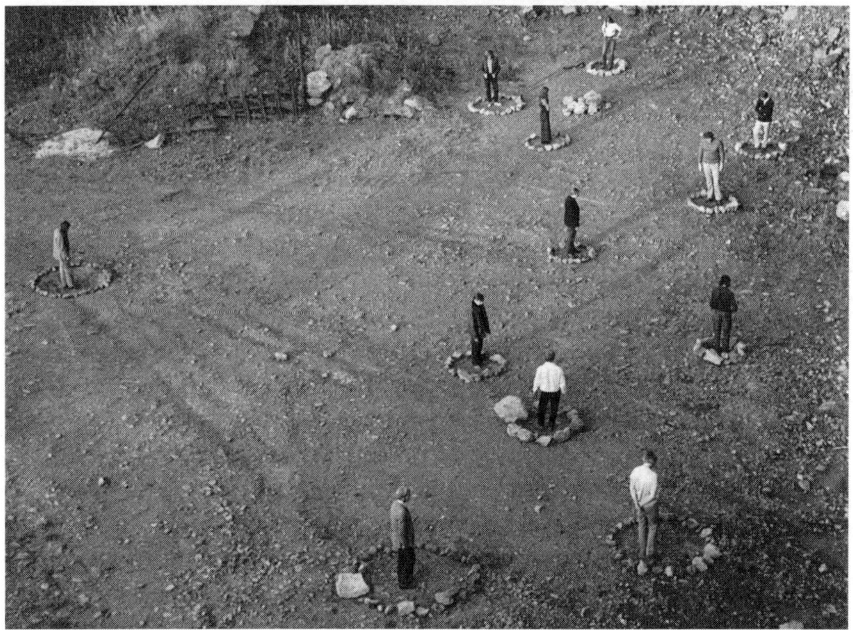

Milan Knížák, *Stone Ceremony*, 1971

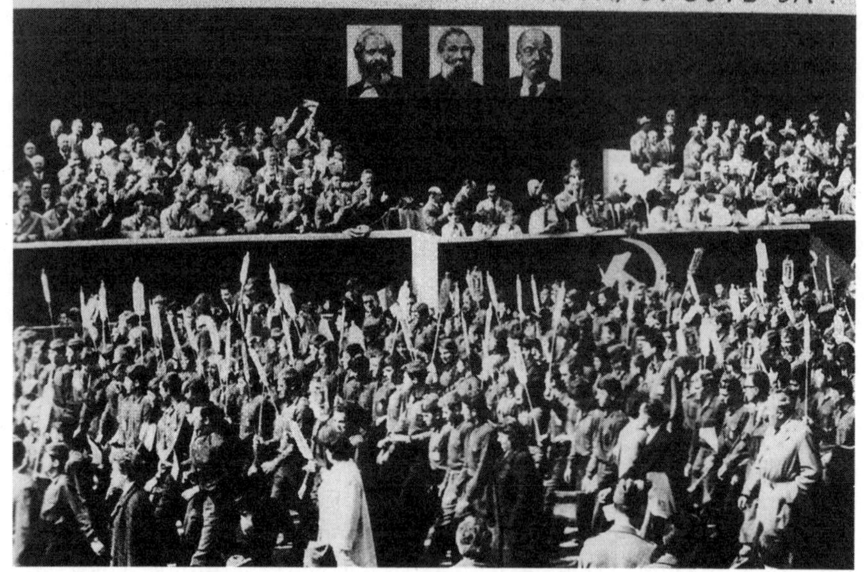

Stano Filko, Alex Mlynárčik, *Happsoc I*, 1965, Bratislava, 1 May 1965

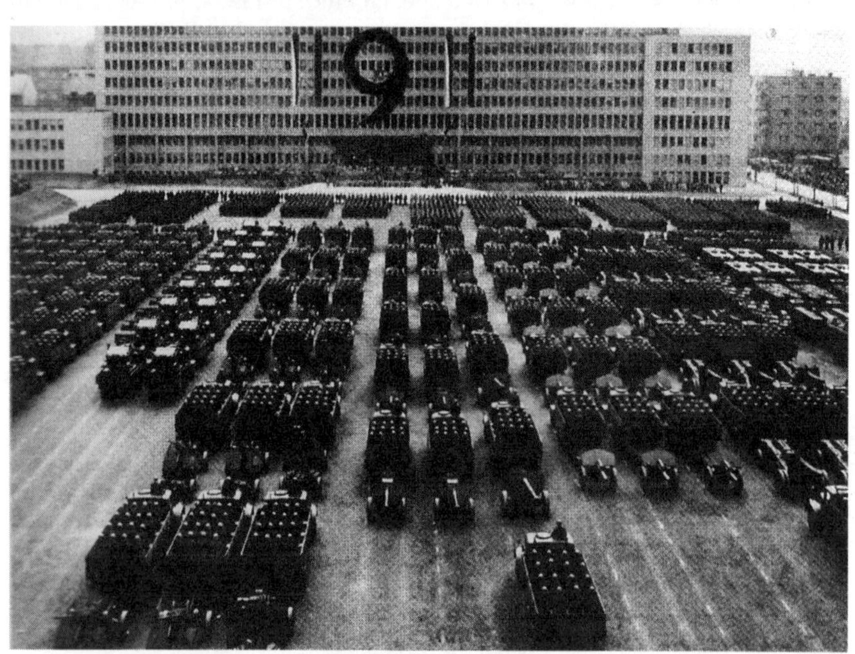

Stano Filko, Alex Mlynárčik, *Happsoc I*, 1965, Bratislava, 9 May 1965

II. Slovakia: Permanent Manifestations

The provocative forms of witting and unwitting participation initiated by Knížák in Prague can be contrasted with artistic events in Bratislava during the same period. If Knížák's early work was resolutely avant-garde, seeking disruption as a means to higher consciousness of everyday experience, then the Slovakian artist Alex Mlynárčik was more interested in consensual, optimistic and vernacular forms of collective activity that had their roots in rural tradition.[34] The documentation of his works bear a striking resemblance to recent socially engaged art, although today Mlynárčik is something of a controversial figure (as is Knížák, but for different reasons).[35] He is also overlooked historically, as a younger generation of Slovakian artists have found a greater affinity with his contemporaries Stano Filko (b.1937) and Július Koller (1939–2007).[36]

Mlynárčik began working in the early '60s, making unremarkable mixed-media compositions on wood. On first visiting Paris in 1964 he found an immediate affinity with Nouveau Réalisme (César, Arman, Saint Phalle, Christo), the impact of which can be seen in the development of his 'permanent manifestations' (1965 onwards), three-dimensional assemblages overlaid with public graffiti as a kind of consumer palimpsest.[37] It can also be seen in *Happsoc I* (a neologism of 'happenings', 'happy', 'society' and 'socialism') by Mlynárčik, Stano Filko and the theorist Zita Kostrová. The trio announced a series of 'realities' to take place in Bratislava during the week of 2–9 May 1965. On 1 May, the three members wrote a manifesto explaining their planned artistic action and idea of art, which was founded upon the then current vogue for nominalism, that is, excising an experience or event from the flow of everyday life and declaring it to be a work of art.[38] In this particular instance, it was the whole city of Bratislava and its society that was announced as an exhibition. However, the manifesto also went beyond the reductiveness of neo-Duchampian nominalism by including a parody of a national census that had taken place the previous month, listing twenty-three types of object and their number to be found in Bratislava: one castle, one Danube, 142,090 lampposts, 128,729 television aerials, six cemeteries, 138,936 females, 128,727 males, 49,991 dogs, and so on. The manifesto and data were sent to 400 people in the form of a printed invitation to *Happsoc I*, which designated the city of Bratislava during the week of 1–9 May as a work of art. This period was framed by two public holidays: Workers' Day, a key event in the socialist calendar, and 9 May, which commemorated the liberation of Slovakia by the Soviet Army in 1945.[39] It seems evident that this framing sought to draw attention to two types of participation: official parades, on the one hand, and the artists' creation of an invisible, involuntary and imaginary participation, on the other.

Interpretations of *Happsoc I* somewhat depend upon one's translation of 'happsoc': 'happy society' or 'happy socialism' implies a position of ironic distance towards these compulsory celebrations; 'sociological happening' produces a more ethnographic reading in which state spectacle is recoded as a form of avant-garde event.[40] The artists did not lean towards either of these, but rather chose to emphasise their lack of intervention, which they viewed as the primary difference between *Happsoc* and Happenings: the former was 'non-stylised reality, free from all direct intervention . . . it's a process in which we use what objectively exists *to induce subjective points of view*, which make it appear with a superior reality'.[41] The approach of *Happsoc* (in keeping with much of the Nouveau Réaliste attitude) was also a question of claiming temporary possession as a means to expand the horizon of what could be considered artistic work, on the one hand, and authorship, on the other. Significantly, the only documentation of *Happsoc I* is the printed manifesto and two images of the official parades, and they have a bureaucratic air that reflects the totalitarian aspirations of the work itself: it was impossible for the residents of Bratislava *not* to be part of *Happsoc I*, and presumably, any photograph taken between 2–9 May 1965 could conceivably form part of its documentation. It is tempting to see the structure of *Happsoc I* as rather Cagean – the artists defined the duration of an event but not the action within it or the ways in which it was interpreted – but there is no direct evidence for this influence, even if Cage had visited Prague in 1965. The point of reference is neo-Dada, with a view to producing art not destined for the gallery space but to be integrated back into daily life. Ironically, this task was easier in the East than in the West due to a complete absence of commercial galleries and institutional support for avant-garde practice.

Presenting Bratislava as an *objet trouvé*, *Happsoc I* invited a select group of 400 participants (those who had received the announcement) to experience the city 'doubly' – as reality, and as work of art – with a view to questioning their paradigms of seeing, experiencing and perceiving reality.[42] The emphasis was therefore on *mental* rather than physical participation: 'to see Bratislava as a ready-made'.[43] The drawback of this radically de-authored re-perception is the loss of art's signifying character that inevitably accompanies the complete dispersal of the work of art into everyday life (a drawback that also plagues many of Kaprow's later works). The *Happsoc* manifesto called upon people to participate in events and see reality through the lens of art, which certainly dispersed authorship into collective imagination, but it also eliminated any kind of concentrated artistic experience; in the artists' own rather oblique words: 'It is a synthetic manifestation of social existence as such and therefore, by necessity, a shared property of all.'[44] The next *Happsoc* experiment was more ambitious: *Happsoc II: The Seven Days of Creation* took place later that year, also between two significant holidays (Christmas and the New Year); it comprised an invitation in the form of a semi-scored series of instructions for participants.[45] *Happsoc III: The Altar of Contemporaneity*, by Stano Filko, went on to posit the appropriation of the entire territory of Czechoslovakia as the artist's own work in June 1966, and the gesture is typical of his fervently megalomaniac cosmic conceptualism.

As tightly scored conceptual experiments with the social, *Happsoc* stands in sharp contrast to Mlynárčik's subsequent participatory works in the later 1960s, which were more emphatically physical, visual and collective. These events alluded to vernacular tradition (such as weddings and village festivals) and to art history (restaging nineteenth-century masterpieces as live events), and often involved the participation of people who had no idea they were forming part of a work of art. Many of these took place in the countryside or in Mlynárčik's home town of Žilina in the north of Slovakia. In part this rural relocation was a necessary consequence of 'normalisation': action art had to take place illegally, and expelled itself to the margins of the city or more frequently into the countryside (such as the Tatra mountains) to avoid surveillance; the landscape stands as a symbolic escape from contemporary social reality organised by bureaucratic directives, and perhaps also as an assertion of Slovak national identity (mountains cover 40 percent of the country).[46]

Mlynárčik referred to these events as 'permanent manifestations of joining art and life', a category that he had proposed and defined in Autumn 1965, and which he used to refer to the *Happsoc I* and *II*, but also to his photographs of graffiti in Paris and Czechoslovakia during May '68. One of his most striking works of this period is the collaboratively authored *First Snow Festival* (1970), with the artist Miloš Urbásek and the experimental musicians Milan Adamčiak and Robert Cyprich, which was organised as an unofficial parallel to the world skiing championships in the High Tatras. The leitmotif of the *First Snow Festival* was the recreation of works of art from the Renaissance to the present day; the main material was snow, which the artists used in various ways, interpreting works that seem to have no apparent or direct link to snow or skiing, but which usefully indicate the degree of international contact between artists at this time. Urbásek, for example, painted a series of snowmen in a *Homage to Niki de Saint Phalle*, while Robert Cyprich's *Cross-Country Homage to Walter de Maria* comprised two parallel ski tracks in the snow for fifty kilometres. Milan Adamčiak paid homage to Otto Piene of the Zero Group with a work comprising a burning circle in the snow. Other artists referenced included figures from US Pop (Lichtenstein, Wesselmann, Oldenburg, Segal), European contemporaries (Arman, Christo, Kounellis, Miralda, Uecker) and historical figures such as Brueghel, da Vinci, Malevich and Magritte. The emphasis was on transient material, and playful reappropriation of works of art, amounting to a temporary improvised biennial in the snow.[47]

Other works by Mlynárčik took the form of festivals restaging historic

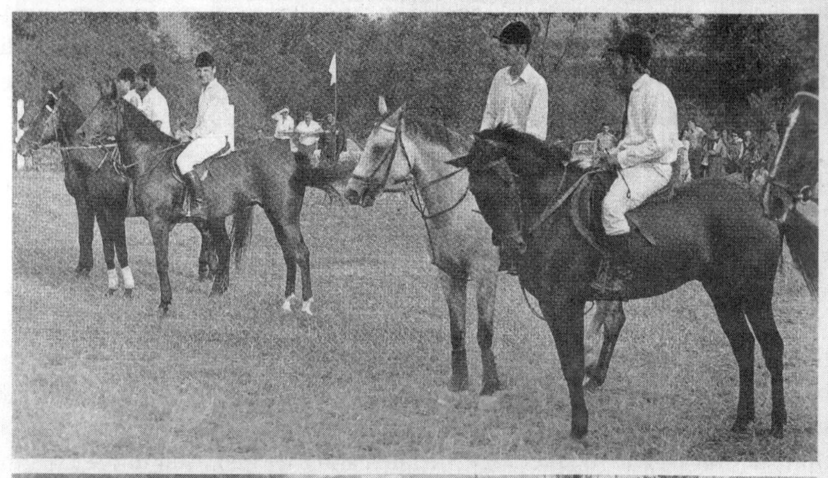

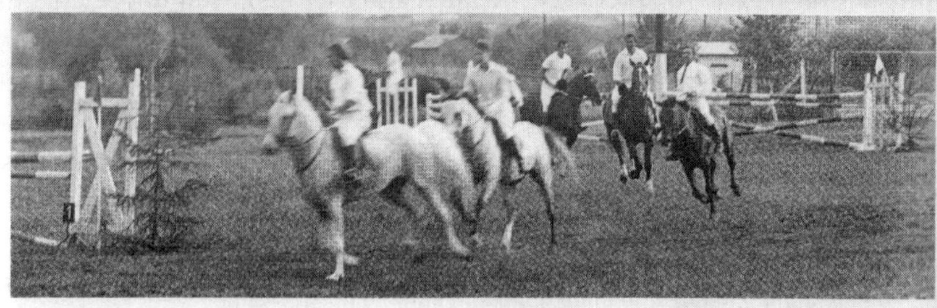

Alex Mlynárčik, *Edgar Degas' Memorial*, 1971

works of art, such as Renoir (*Moulin de la Galette [Juniones]*, Piešťany, 1970) and an equestrian painting by Degas (*Edgar Degas' Memorial*, Bratislava, 1971), restaged in the form of a horse race, complete with competitions and prizes. *Eva's Wedding* (Žilina, 1972) was also based on a work of art: the painting *Village Wedding* (*Dedinská svatba*) (1946) by the Slovak artist L'udovít Fulla (1902–80), whose seventieth anniversary was being celebrated that year. After lengthy research, Mlynárčik found a young couple in Žilina who were planning to marry and offered to organise the entire ceremony as a theatrical event. Eva Albertová and Tichomir Pišta agreed to perform as the leading actors in their own wedding, organised over two acts and eight scenes with a prologue and epilogue; the locations were the town hall, the church and a restaurant. The fact that the bride's name evoked Eve was seen as particularly symbolic, as was the time of year (23

September, near the equinox), considered by Slovak peasants as an auspicious time for weddings. As such, the work was deeply rooted in folkloric celebrations, while continuing the theme of 'theatricalised life' so important to early Soviet spectacle (discussed in Chapter 2).

Mlynárčik embellished this ready-made event at his own expense, transforming the wedding into a grand celebration.[48] Outside the town hall, a helicopter dropped leaflets of congratulation over the town square, while the newly wed couple sat in a yellow carriage accompanied by a violinist (as in Fulla's painting). Mlynárčik sought out amateurs in local folklore societies who advised on ancient Slovak customs such as the distribution of *mrváne* (traditional round cakes in the shape of doughnuts), the honey ceremony, and the *pánca*, a huge phallus-shaped vodka barrel; the latter was transformed into a red sculpture over two metres high, packaged by Christo and installed on a wagon. The French critic Pierre Restany, with whom Mlynárčik had been in close dialogue since 1966, was invited as master of ceremonies. Restany presided over the celebratory dinner and gave a speech before distributing presents to the couple: works of art from seventeen artist friends from eleven countries, including César, Niki de Saint Phalle and Raymond Hains.[49] The gift from Russian artist Lev Nusberg was a firework display, with which the day concluded. As with *Happsoc I*, Mlynárčik piggybacked an event to give it a double ontological status: both a wedding *and* a happening, reality *and* a play, a wedding dress *and* theatrical costume, wedding photos *and* art documentation.

Mlynárčik framed the work as 'a celebration of life and joy, hope and love. At the same time, it becomes a manifestation of the international

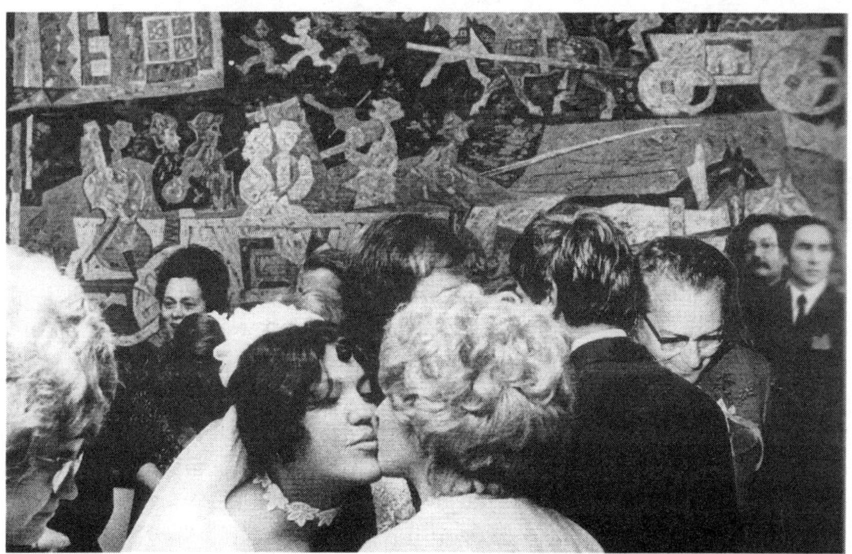

Alex Mlynárčik, *Eva's Wedding*, 1972

nature of artistic creation and cooperation.'[50] However, this 'sociological happening' was not without conflict and tension: the painter Fulla issued an official statement the following day denying his agreement to the event; a scandal burst out, Mlynárčik's work was called 'an insult to Slovakian culture' and he was dismissed from the Union of Soviet Artists (membership of which was necessary to exhibit one's work).[51] These incidents reveal the gap between Mlynárčik's optimistic rhetoric and the dominant conditions of normalisation: the celebratory tone of his 'permanent manifestations' such as *Eva's Wedding* seem strikingly in disaccord with political reality, especially when we consider the introverted character of art produced in Prague during this period.

There are various ways of explaining this disjuncture. On the one hand, we can point to the particular reception of socialism in Slovakia: in general, the conditions there were more liberal than in the Czech land, while the advent of state socialism had substantially modernised this rural and primarily agricultural country (hence the possibility of a non-ironic reading of *Happsoc* as 'happy socialism').[52] Slovaks tend to assert that their national character is one of quiet co-operation rather than heroic resistance (there is, for example, no tradition of masochistic body art as one finds in Austria and the Czech Republic), and this argument sheds light on the affirmative mood of Mlynárčik's participatory art. Traditional events such as weddings offered an opportunity for festivities and a perfect guise for unusual activities; the underground rock band Plastic People of the Universe, for example, often camouflaged their concerts as wedding celebrations. For Mlynárčik, a wedding with folkloric elements would seem to provide a legitimate cover for an extravagant art event. But however we account for the tenor of Mlynárčik's work, events like *Eva's Wedding* are unquestionably compensatory: a utopian fantasy geared towards the co-creation of a more tolerable experience of the everyday, an escape through festivity and *hommage* anchored in vernacular tradition rather than sombre ritual. This is not to undermine the work by subjecting it to contemporary criteria; rather, it is to point up the extent to which Mlynárčik – like Knížák – is always more interested in individual liberation than in social justice or solidarity.[53]

Rather like Knížák setting up the A-Community, Mlynárčik seems less interested in the formation of a counter-public sphere than in the creation of a sovereign domain of which he is the sole organiser (of artists and non-artists alike). This interpretation is borne out by a subsequent project, the imaginary land of Argíllia that he founded in 1974. Although a local peasant called Ondrej Krištofík was proclaimed King of Argíllia, everything to do with the formation of Argíllia's protocols and representation was the preserve of Mlynárčik and his colleagues in the art world. Galerie Vincy in Paris was renamed the head of Agence Argíllia-Presse, while friends and critics were given elaborate titles (Chalupecký, for example, was 'Dean of the Royal Counsel and Keeper of Seals'). Various photomontages produced an amusing false history for the activities of Restany as 'President of the National Assembly' (meeting Stalin, Brezhnev, Roosevelt, etc.). It is instructive to compare this imaginary realm with Marcel Broodthaers' fictional institution brought to a conclusion shortly before Argíllia was formulated, the *Musée d'art Moderne* (1968–72). Both use the trappings of an institution (headed paper, fictional directors, badges, stamps, etc.) and make reference to the nineteenth century, but Mlynárčik's project has none of the elliptical poetics of Broodthaers' pseudo-museum (which was geared towards an oblique demystification of museum institutions and their imperial foundations). Rather, Argíllia is inspired by Saint-Exupéry's novel *The Little Prince* (1943), the story of a boy who visits other planets, including earth, all of them inhabited by flawed adults. Like Mlynárčik's earlier festivals, Argíllia is above all escapist. In an interview undertaken in 1981, Mlynárčik reflected on this tendency in his work:

> Since 1970 our world has been so greatly permeated with ideology that should you even decide to plant a flower somewhere it is perceived as a political gesture. Especially if your name is Mlynárčik . . . Should ideology be the problem of my life, or some politician currently in power, or some regime? I would like to live in transcendence, somewhere else, and be devoted to different values . . . There are much higher gains to consider which do not overlap with superficial worldly planes.[54]

Artists like Mlynárčik present something of a problem for Western critics keen to find heroic gestures of dissident opposition to totalitarian regimes. Participation and collaboration were for him a way to manageably live with the world, to create a 'total expression' of art as life (for which he unexpectedly references Mayakovsky and LEF as precursors): in short, 'to fuse organically with life in the name of the totality of life, the totality of reality!'[55]

What matters art historically is that Mlynárčik's brand of collective happening is not an isolated example in Slovakia: other actions by artists during this period are equally festivalist and escapist, with an interest in even more ancient forms of nature ritual. Jana Želibská's *Betrothal of Spring* (1970), for example, invited friends of the artist to a remote country location (in this case a field close to a wood).[56] Her work, like that of Mlynárčik, exemplifies some of the typical characteristics of art of this period in Slovakia: while adopting an avant-garde position vis-à-vis collective production, participation and appropriation, it remains attached to folkloric tradition and mythology as vestiges of a national culture that had been erased by the Soviet presence.

III. Problematics of Public Space

Mlynárčik and Żelibska represent the extrovert and social side of Slovak art in the 1970s, whereas the art produced in Prague at this time is conspicuously more introvert, as we have already observed in the development of Knížák's ritualistic ceremonies of the everyday. The self-immolation of Jan Palach in Wenceslas Square, January 1969, as a protest against the regime, signalled a decisive change of tone. The congress of the Union of Soviet Artists passed a resolution on 2 November 1972 denouncing the experimental activities of the 1960s; some artists found their work excluded from acquisition for public collections, were forbidden from producing publications on their work, and from participating in exhibitions in Czechoslovakia or abroad. This congress also re-endorsed Socialist Realism and a uniform cultural policy for the Soviet bloc countries, in which Marxist-Leninist theory became a binding criterion in judging art.[57] The effect upon alternative art was immediately to force it into further privacy: actions were performed only for a close circle of trusted friends. As Jaroslav Anděl observed in 1979, 'the art of the 60s pretended to be international and had collectivist aspirations not without an optimistic flavour; in the 70s it has turned out to look international but, ironically enough, it has lost its collectivist and optimistic undertones'.[58] What came to replace it was the psychically charged expression of solitary individuals: an emphasis on the body in space, performed with the minimum of materials.

The artists associated with this period of Czech art, such as Jan Mlčoch (b.1953, active 1974–80) and Jiří Kovanda (b.1953) do not make participatory art with the general public, but excruciatingly pared-down works that testify to the restricted nature of public space and social interaction during this period. Mlčoch's early work involves physical endurance, with an emphasis on the body as a material extension of the spiritual.[59] Some actions were performed alone, others for groups of eight to ten people who took it in turns to do a performance, one of whom would photograph the event. The description accompanying Mlčoch's *Washing* (1974), for example, is devastatingly spare, as is the intimate photograph accompanying it: 'In the presence of a few friends, I washed my whole body and hair.'[60] His later works of the '70s tend to involve aggressive actions against other people. The text accompanying *Night* (1977) is typically terse:

> A strange office in a strange building. A girl was brought to this office who didn't know what was going to happen. I waited for her there with a tape recorder, camera and a strong lamp. After an hour of questioning I let her go. She left the building with the other people who were waiting outside.[61]

We can see a reference here to secret-police interrogations, although it is important to note that Mlčoch, like Peter Štembera, protested against the inclusion of their work in the 'Dissident Art' exhibition in Venice (1977) – not because they were afraid of the reaction of the authorities at home, but because they didn't agree with such a reading of their work. These artists continue to assert their disinterest in being considered as 'political', even though it seems hard not to read their actions as operating in critical relationship to the social reality of its time, especially actions such as Mlčoch's *Classic Escape* (1977): 'I threw out everyone present from an empty room of a borrowed flat into the corridor and nailed the door down from the inside. With the help of a rope, I climbed down to the courtyard and left.'[62] This action could be regarded as the inverse of Graciela Carnevale's proposition for the *Cycle of Experimental Art* (discussed in Chapter 4): if the Argentinian artist used a locked room in order to catalyse a collective reaction from the public, Mlčoch used similar artistic means to find a space not for a shared political project but for personal deviance and non-compliancy.

Mlčoch's work took place in domestic interiors or on the outskirts of the city; Jiří Kovanda, by contrast, used Prague and its public as the backdrop to his subtle social actions. His quietly abbreviated documentation – black and white photographs with accompanying text, often replete with ellipses – amount to a form of invisible theatre, albeit one aimed at a secondary audience of viewers, rather than the primary audience who witnessed and collaborated in the work's production (Kovanda has stated that these 'friends are not observers, they're fellow participants').[63] Kovanda frequently staged these actions in Wenceslas Square, where he was photographed by his friend Pavel Tuč, producing images which resemble the furtive quality of secret police photos of that era.[64] In his final action, *Untitled (I arranged to meet a few friends . . . we were standing in a small group on the square, talking . . . suddenly, I started running; I raced across the square and disappeared into Melantrich Street . . .)*, *23 January 1978*, Kovanda's escape is, like that of Mlčoch a year earlier, painfully lyrical, and Tuč's photograph captures the artist as a blur as he hurtles away from a startled group. Strained social pathos is a hallmark of many of Kovanda's actions in public spaces, such as *Attempted Acquaintance (I invited a group of friends to watch me making friends with a girl, 19 October 1977)*, or the micro non-conformity of *Untitled (On an escalator . . . turning around, I look into the eyes of the person standing behind me . . . , 3 September 1977)*.

These attempts at intimacy seem to testify to the strain of living in a society where privacy was all but eliminated. Following a trip to Czechoslovakia in 1981, Ilya Kabakov described the psychological and topographical condition of a people born in 'the void' (state socialism), and which penetrated every aspect of their life, referring to home as a

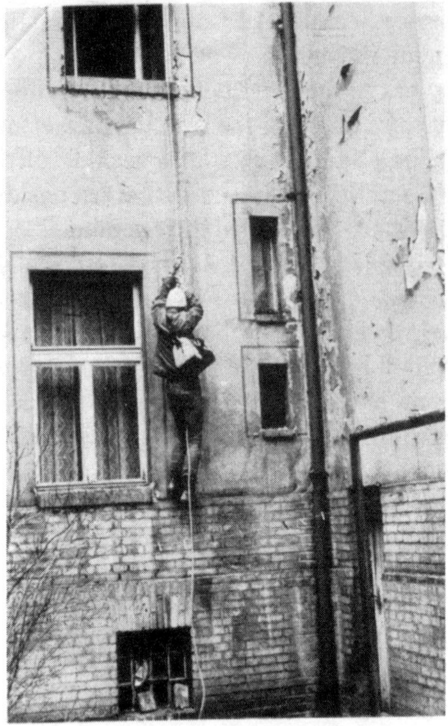

Jan Mlčoch, *Classic Escape*, 1977

'burrow' and everything outside as a threat that needed to be traversed as quickly as possible.[65] It would be wrong, however, to read Kovanda's works as metaphors for alienation in the 'void' or as gestures of resistance. Czech artists sought a far more modest form of expression: 'to act against the manifest ossification of society in the late 1970s, to transcend it and to find traces of an expression of individuality'.[66] Kovanda, like Mlčoch and Štembera, even today refuses to frame his work as political, since communist society was so heavily politicised that he did not want his art to participate in anything approximating the same mechanisms. By contrast, he has always insisted on a personal reading of the work, putting himself through experiences that test his notorious shyness.[67] Social space, for all of these Czech artists, is an arena in which to experience subjectivity all the more strongly, as Kovanda recently stated: 'You just moved about within the limits that were given to you. I didn't experience that as something that I had to fight against . . . there was definitely no political subtext. I worked within the framework of a particular set of possibilities and I didn't feel like I was rebelling against anything.'[68] Mlčoch reinforces this assertion of individual survival when asked about the fundamental idea behind his creative efforts in the 1970s: 'It was all individualism. In those days we all strived for the integrity of our personality, as a reaction to the

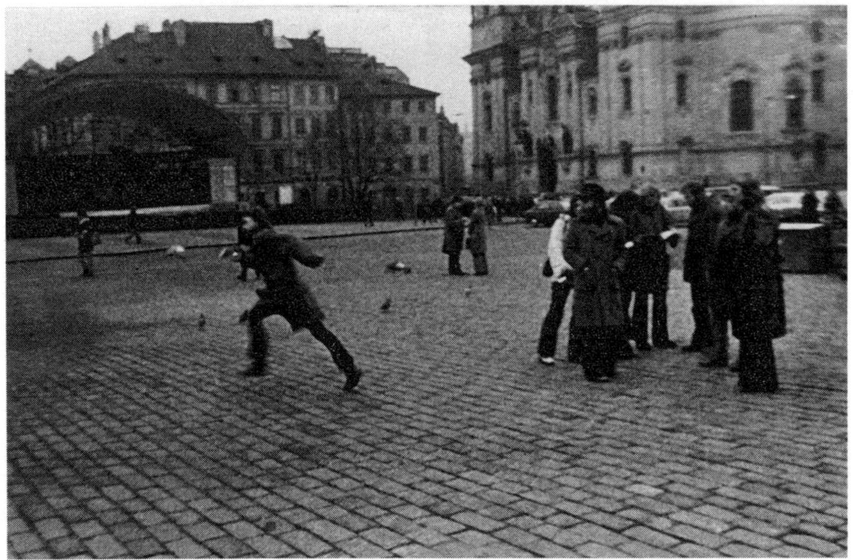

Jiří Kovanda, *Untitled (I arranged to meet a few friends ... we were standing in a small group on the square, talking ... suddenly, I started running; I raced across the square and disappeared into Melantrich Street...), 23 January 1978.*

prevailing political stagnation. The next generation no longer put so much emphasis, if any, on individuality.'[69]

The most telling break with this generational orientation towards subjective experience is the work of Ján Budaj in Bratislava. Not trained as an artist, and working as a coal heating engineer, Budaj undertook gestures in public space with particularly vivid means. He is unique amongst artists in Czechoslovakia at this time in consciously addressing his work to the public as a random sector of the population rather than to a trusted group of friends. *The Lunch* (1978), for example, involved relocating his kitchen table, chairs and a meal to a prominent spot in the parking lot of the Dubravka housing estate, and framing the composition with white tape to increase its visibility to people living in the upper storeys.[70] Budaj invited friends to eat a meal with him, and amplified their discussion with microphones and speakers. The action seemed to reinforce (one might even say overidentify with) the absence of privacy under state socialism, offering a domestic scene in exaggerated exposure to surveillance; at the same time, it also sought to invent an idea of public space and to occupy it with eccentric non-conformity. Unlike Kovanda, Budaj's photo documentation is clearly secondary; the live experience is the event, and spectatorship is no longer privatised. And not unlike Knížák's early assaults on the general public, Budaj also sought to provoke, but through gently assertive parody: his organisation, the Temporary Society of Intense Experiencing, produced a *Week of Fictive Culture* (January–February 1979). The group placed posters around the city announcing events that would never happen, but which tapped into the unspoken desires of audiences who thronged to the advertised venues: to see concerts by Bob Dylan and Abba, an Ingmar Bergman film subtitled *Homosexuality in Modern Times*, an exhibition of Dalí and Magritte at the National Gallery, and a play by Ionesco in a new theatre that didn't exist.[71] Budaj's urban interventions, along with those of L'ubomir Durček, break with the melancholic introspection of Czech body art in the 1970s, but also with Slovakian artists' retreat to the countryside.[72] They begin to imagine what public space might be – a collective culture founded on shared desires rather than ideology. Just as the numerous participatory experiments in Paris contributed in their own way to the events of May '68, so too did these events in late '70s and early '80s Bratislava serve to continually test and pressure a system that finally crumbled in 1989. Budaj went on to play a pivotal role in the Velvet Revolution as leader of Public Against Violence and, after 1989, as deputy leader of the Slovak National Assembly.

IV. Moscow: Zones of Indistinguishability

Artists in Moscow, meanwhile, found different solutions to the problem of individual experience and public space. 'Unofficial art' had begun in Moscow in 1964, after Khrushchev visited the thirtieth anniversary show of the Moscow Union of Artists at the Manezh Gallery, which had included a display of non-figurative, abstract paintings; Khrushchev declared these to be (among other things) 'private psycho-pathological distortions of the public conscience'.[73] The extent of his reaction led to the ever increasing domestic isolation of independent artists and their being denied the right to show their works to the public in any place or form. And yet, despite being severely criticised and censured, unofficial art continued into the mid 1970s, when the first legalised exhibitions took place and a shadow union for unofficial artists was set up (the Graphics Moscow City Committee). After the controversial 'Bulldozer' exhibition of September 1974 (in which an exhibition of unofficial art was destroyed by bulldozer), cultural authorities decided to regulate and legalise their relationships with 'underground' art via the State Committee for Security (KGB). Most unofficial art took place inside apartments, forcing a convergence of art and life that surpassed what the majority of twentieth-century avant-gardists had ever intended by this term. The phenomenon of 'Apt-Art' (apartment art), initiated by Nikita Alekseev in the 1980s, loosely matches the Czech work of the early 1970s that I have described above – exhibitions and performances taking place in private homes, for small networks of trusted friends.

It was in this context that the most celebrated of Moscow

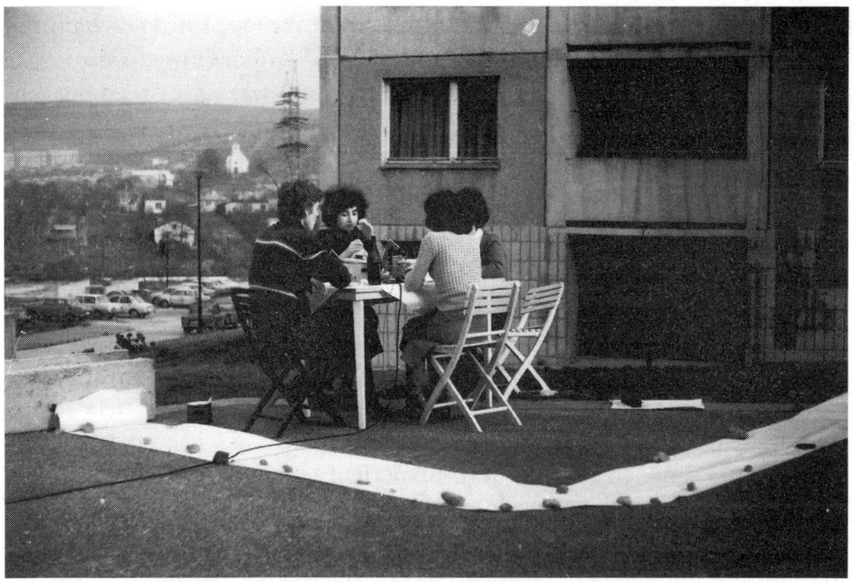

Ján Budaj, *The Lunch (I)*, 1978

Conceptualists, Ilya Kabakov (b.1933), developed his personal work alongside his official job as a children's book illustrator. Kabakov's *Albums* (1972–75) are illustrated narratives, each revolving around one fictional character, most of whom are isolated, lonely, idiosyncratic figures on the margins of society, cocooned in a private dream world. The first, *Sitting in the Closet Primakov*, is typical in that it describes the life of a boy who sits in a dark closet and refuses to come out; when he does, he sees the world in terms of modernist abstract paintings. Each *Album* was accompanied by drawings, and general comments on the character spoken by other fictional commentators. These *Albums* were not read as books but were performed by the artist for small groups of friends. Boris Groys recalls that one would make an appointment with Kabakov (rather like organising a studio visit) and go to his home, where the artist would place the book on a music stand and read the entire text in a neutral and unexpressive tone of voice. The experience was extremely monotonous, but had a ritualistic quality in which the turning of the pages became central. Most readings took an hour, although Groys recalls once undergoing a five-hour performance.[74] One of the key points to emerge here is the use of a neutral, descriptive, analytical language, focusing on the inconspicuous, the banal and the marginal; another is that the stories are geared more towards invented forms of survival and endurance than of criticism; and another is the repeated motif of isolated individuals negotiating the endless and uncomfortable scrutiny of neighbours in the communal apartment.[75] All of these points provide an important contextual precursor for the work discussed in the remainder of this chapter.

It is in this literary context, with a strong reverence for textual expression, that the Collective Actions Group (CAG) (*Kollektivnye Deistvia*, or *K/D*) was formed in 1976; at its inception there were four members; by 1979 there were seven.[76] The group took its lead from the first generation of Moscow Conceptualists, especially Kabakov; their central theorist, Andrei Monastyrsky (b.1949), has recalled that their earliest pieces were perceived as a form of poetry reading.[77] Most of their actions typically followed a standard format: a group of fifteen to twenty participants were invited by telephone (at a time when, of course, phone lines were tapped) to take a train to a designated station outside Moscow; they would walk from the station to a remote field; the group would wait around (not knowing what would happen), before witnessing a minimal, perhaps mysterious, and often visually unremarkable event. On returning to Moscow, participants would write an account of the experience and offer interpretations of its meaning; these subsequently became the focus of discussion and debate amongst the artists and their circle.[78]

It should immediately be apparent that the intellectualism of this structure is a considerable development of the 1960s model, in which it was regarded as sufficient simply for things to 'happen', and through which the participating subject would attain a more vivid, authentic level of reality (as seen for example in the work of Knížák and Kaprow). Monastyrsky complicates this paradigm by aiming to produce situations in which participants had no idea what was going to happen, to the point where they sometimes found it difficult to know whether or not they had in fact experienced an action; when participants' engagement finally occurred, it was

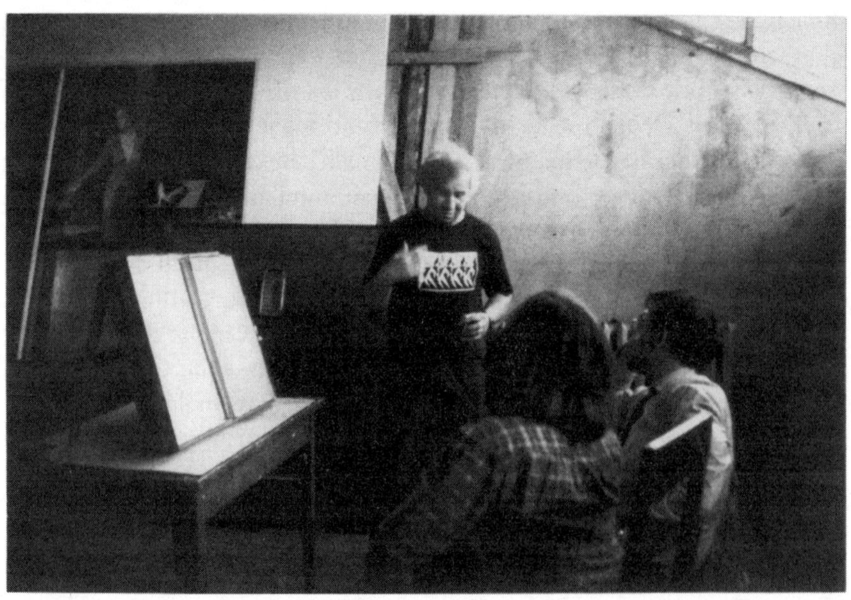

Ilya Kabakov in his studio, reciting one of his *Albums*, c. 1976

never in the place where they were expecting it.[79] CAG stretched the temporality of event-based art away from pure presence and into a relationship of distance between 'then' (I thought I experienced . . .) and 'now' (I understand it to be otherwise . . .). It is also of central importance that this production of distance was not only temporal but social, prising open a space for communicational ambiguity otherwise absent in the rigid and monolithic ideology of Soviet collectivism. Each event is effectively an 'empty action', designed to preclude interpretation from taking place during the performance, and thereby serving to prompt as wide a range as possible of responses, which were undertaken individually but shared within the group.

The first key action that crystallised this form of working was *Appearance* (13 March 1976). Devised by Monastyrsky, Lev Rubinstein, Nikita Alekseev and Georgii Kizevalter, it involved around thirty audience members as participants. On arriving in a remote field at Izmaylovskoe, the group was asked to wait and watch for something to appear in the distance. Eventually a couple of the organisers became visible on the horizon, in what Monastyrsky refers to as the 'zone of indistinguishability': the moment when one can tell that something is happening but the figures are too far away for one to clarify who they are and what exactly is taking place. The figures approached the group and gave them certification of having attended the event (CAG refer to this as 'factography'). Monastyrsky later explained that what had happened in the field was not that they (the organisers) had appeared for the participants, but rather, that the participants had appeared *for them*. This inversion of what one might expect of an artistic action – an unfurling of events for the *organisers* rather than for an audience – was matched by the group's preference for the banality of waiting rather than the production of a vivid and visually memorable event: Monastyrsky described the participants' eventual appearance in the work as a 'pause', thereby reconceptualising the waiting not as a prelude to some more specific action, but as the main event.[80] Typically, CAG's primary focus is never on the ostensible action taking place in the snowy landscape, but the deferral and displacement of this action both physically (events happen where one was not prepared to see them) and semantically. The phenomenological experience of events was subordinated to the conceptual and linguistic activity that subsequently took place in the participants' minds: in Monastyrsky's words, the mythological or symbolic content of the action is 'used only as an instrument to create that "inner" level of perception' in the viewer.[81]

This technique can be seen in other early works such as *Pictures* (11 February 1979), which divided the participants into two groups, one of which undertook an action in the snow, watched by the other group. Twelve sets of twelve coloured envelopes (in gradually larger sizes) were distributed to twelve of the thirty participants. Inside each envelope was a description of the key components of the event: from schedule, setting and weather to audience reaction, meaning and interpretation. After they had read the description, the participants were instructed to fold and paste each set of envelopes on top of each other, to form a concentric pattern of colour; these were later signed as certification of the participants' attendance. While all this was going on, three of the organisers crossed the field and wandered into the woods on the other side. Once again, the 'zone of indistinguishability' was put into play: the participants' preoccupation with making the pictures was a distraction from the action on the margin, namely the organisers' disappearance into the woods. The ostensible action (finding and assembling the coloured envelopes) was undermined by the sly subtraction of the organisers' presence, indicating that – contra US and European models of the Happening – works by CAG are not founded on a shared experience of authentic presence and immediacy.

In his article 'Seven Photographs' (1980), Monastyrsky presents seven near identical photographs of a snowy field, each of which relates to a different action by CAG, including *Appearance* and *Pictures*. The bleak similarity of the images is amusing, but drives home his point that secondary material such as photographs, instructions, descriptions and participant recollections have a completely separate aesthetic reality to the action itself. (At best, he writes, 'a familiarity with the photographs and texts can bring about a sensation of positive indeterminacy'.[82]) Influenced by semiotics and making frequent reference to Heidegger, Monastyrsky argues that the group's actions result for the participants in a real experience, but not in an *image* of that experience. The event's existential presence takes place in the viewer's consciousness (as a state of

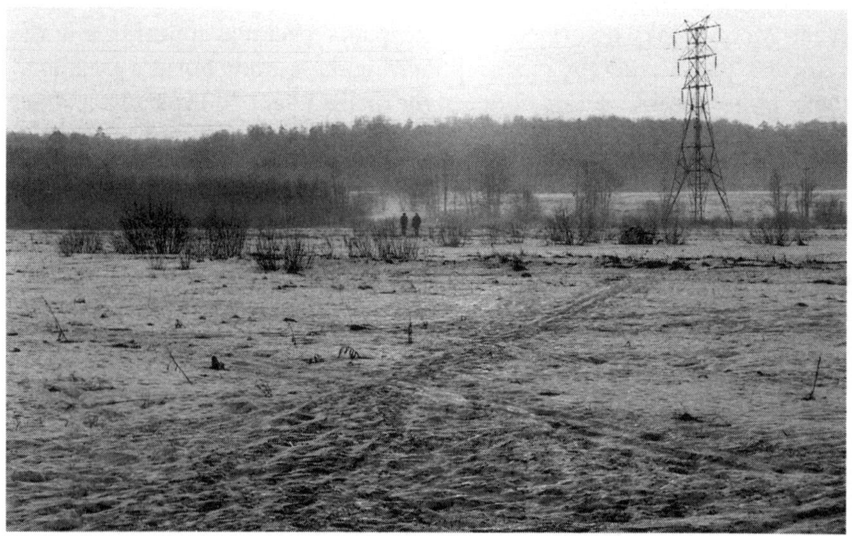

Collective Actions Group, *Appearance*, 1976

'completed anticipation') and thus cannot be represented: 'The only thing that can be represented is the thing that accompanies this internal process, the thing that takes place on the field of action at the time.'[83] The enigmatic precision of this idea, in which documentation is conceived as a representation of what *accompanied* an artistic experience, explains the repetitive quality of CAG's photographs of (apparently) nothing taking place, since they record only what seems to be a withdrawal of action. Each photograph is to be considered, Monastyrsky writes, as 'a sign of a higher order, a sign of an "unarbitrary emptiness" with the following meaning: "nothing is represented on it not because nothing happened at that given moment, but because the thing that happened is essentially unrepresentable" '.[84] The highly theorised, quasi-mystical flavour of this position gives CAG a unique status within a history of performance documentation, while also being highly suggestive of a documentary approach ripe for re-exploration today.

Monastyrsky's article was written before *Ten Appearances* (1981), and seems to pave the way for the centrality of photography in this work. The participants were notified that everyone attending would have to be a participant; those who were not willing were advised not to come. The action took place in a snowy field, and was organised around a flat board with dozens of nails with bobbins, each wound with 200–300 metres of white thread. The assignment was for the ten participants to walk away from the board in different directions towards the forest that surrounded the field, while holding onto the end of the thread that had been given to

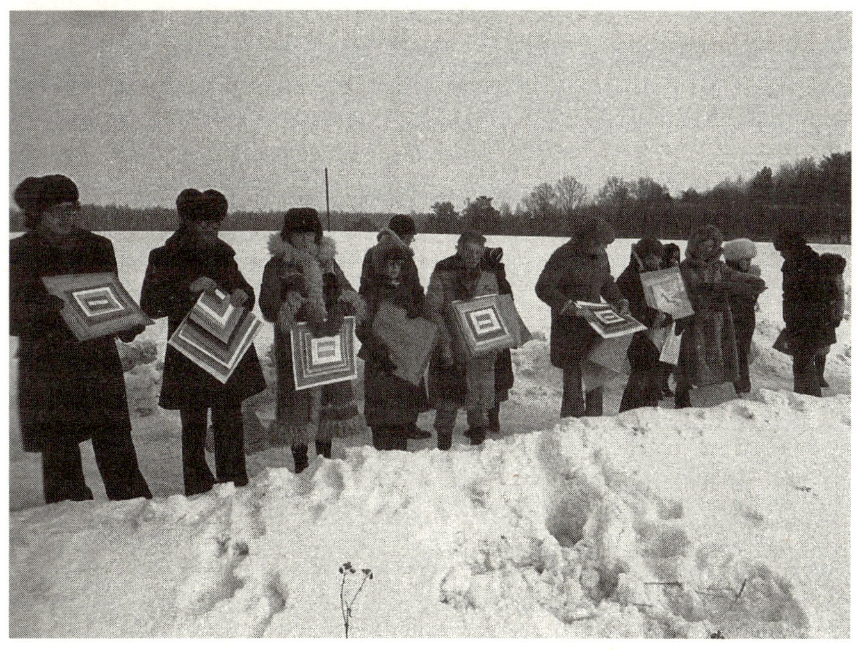

Collective Actions Group, *Pictures*, 1979

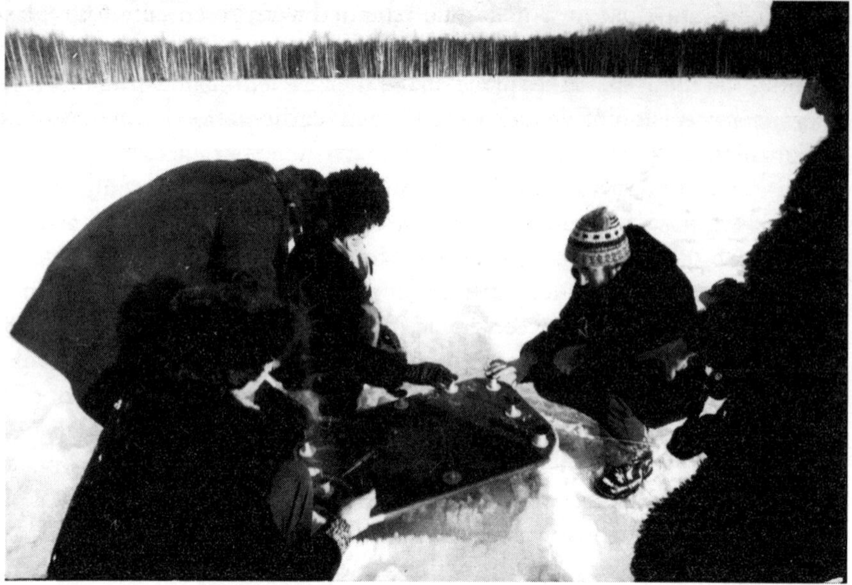

Collective Actions Group, *Ten Appearances*, 1981

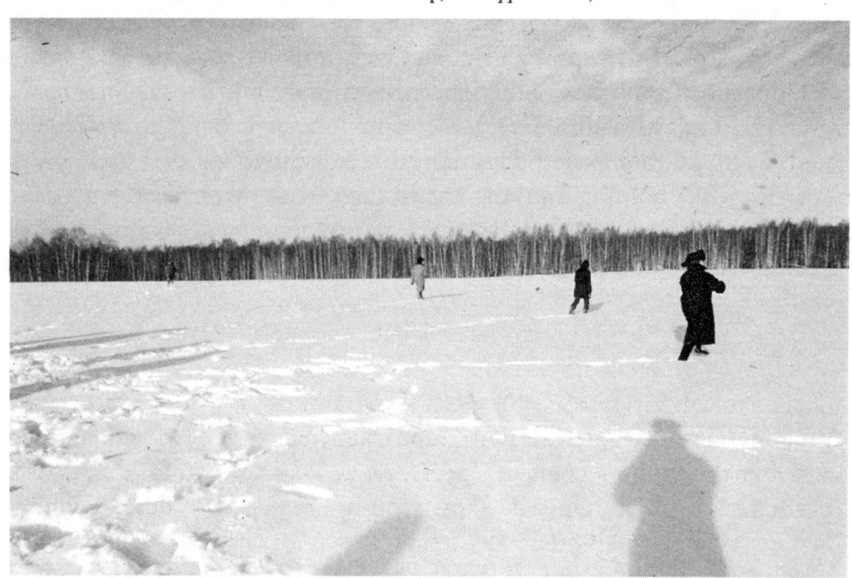

Collective Actions Group, *Ten Appearances*, 1981

each of them. Kabakov describes in detail the emotional rollercoaster that ensued: from anxiety (about how long he would be standing in the cold) to fear (suspecting the organisers of sadism) to sheer joy and 'mystic melancholy' on finally reaching the end of the thread, to which was affixed a piece of paper bearing the 'factographic text' (the name of the organisers, time, date and place of the action).[85] At this point it was up to the participants to decide what happened next. Eight of them walked back out of the forest to rejoin the organisers; two did not return and got a train back to Moscow. Those who returned were given a photograph of themselves emerging from the forest, captioned 'The appearance of [name] on the first of February, 1981.' This simulated photographic documentation had been taken a few weeks earlier but was not differentiable from the actual appearance of the participants as they emerged from the forest. Monastyrsky also uses the phrase 'empty action' to refer to these photographs: a mere sign of the elapsed time between the end of the first phase of the action for the participants (receiving the factographic text) and their reappearance in the field ('the signified and culminating event in the structure of the action').[86] Both the act and the image are empty signifiers; the meaning is formulated subsequently by reflection on the totality of the events experienced.

Of course, the poignant fact that two participants, Nekrasov and Zhigalov, didn't return to the group did not mean that the work was a failure. Rather, Monastyrsky asserted, it showed that the participants had emerged from a 'non-artistic, non-artificially-constructed space' – in other words, an everyday reality in which they were capable of acting of their own free will.[87] This, Monastyrsky reasoned, was why the same people kept coming back to their events over the course of fifteen years: the 'pretextual' nature of the group's experiences ensured that participants were continually intrigued, as well as continually motivated to write descriptions and analyses. Since it was near impossible to scrutinise the events as they were happening, these hermeneutical efforts had a compensatory aspect, endlessly chasing a meaning that remained elusive, precisely because the generation of different interpretative positions *was* the meaning.[88] The surfeit of texts that resulted from these actions were collected into books every three to five years, and are published in Russian and German under the title *Trips to the Countryside*; the group is currently at work on an eleventh volume.[89] Volume two, from 1983, for example, has a typical structure: a theoretical preface by Monastyrsky; descriptions of the events with photographs; an appendix of documentation, which includes the schema of *Ten Appearances* and a list of slides; texts by participants (including Kabakov); photographs and descriptions of actions by individual artists that relate to CAG's actions, such as Monastyrsky's *Flat Cap* (1983); commentaries and photographs. Later volumes also include interviews and a list of videos, produced after Sabine Hänsgen joined the group from Germany.

Boris Groys has observed how CAG's performances were 'meticulously, almost bureaucratically, documented, commented on, and archived'.[90] This textual production is one of the dominant characteristics of their practice, and positions it as the inverse of the impulse to make participatory art in Western cultures – which is invariably opposed to the atomisation of social relations under consumer spectacle. Groys has argued that Soviet society, by contrast, was a society of production without consumption. There was no spectator and there was no consumer. Everyone was involved in a productive process. So the role of Collective Actions and some other artists of the time was to create the possibility of consumption, the possibility of an external position from which one could enjoy communism.[91]

What CAG's works gave rise to, then, was not unified collective presence and immediacy but its opposite: difference, dissensus and debate; a space of privatised experience, liberal democratic indecision, and a plurality of hermeneutical speculation at a time when the dominant discourse and spectatorial regime was marshalled towards a rigidly schematised apparatus of meaning.[92] This is borne out by Monastyrsky's observation that

> in the Stalin or Brezhnev era, contemplation of an artwork involved a certain compulsion, a kind of tunnel vision. There was nothing peripheral. But when one comes to a field – when one comes there, moreover, with no sense of obligation but for private reasons of one's own – a vast flexible space is created, in which one can look at whatever one likes. One's under no obligation to look at what's being presented – that freedom, in fact, is the whole idea.[93]

The use of a field as the backdrop to so many of CAG's works is therefore doubly salient.[94] It did not designate a specific rejection of the city or a conscious embrace of nature; as Sergei Sitar notes, the field is not chosen for its independent aesthetic merits, 'but simply as "the lesser evil" – as a space that is the least occupied, the least appropriated by the dominant cultural discourse'.[95] For Monastyrsky, it is a space 'free from any affiliation': 'the countryside, for us, isn't the countryside tilled by peasants but that of the thinking classes' vacation retreats'.[96] The fields are less about framing (in the way that Prague's Wenceslas Square frames Kovanda's actions) than *un*framing; the countryside's multiple perspectives corresponded to the group's open-ended, neutral actions that were contrived to leave room for the greatest number of hermeneutic possibilities. The result was a privatised liberal space that existed in covert parallel to official social structures. As Kabakov recalls:

> From the moment I got on the train . . . my goals, the questions and affairs that constantly preoccupied me, my fears of myself and others, were all, as it were, taken away from me. The most remarkable thing, however, was that those who led us had no goals either! And, of course, there is something else: for the first time in my life, I was among 'my own'; we had our own world, parallel to the real one, and this world had been created and compressed by the C.A. Group until it had achieved complete materiality, or, one might say, tangibility – if this notion is at all applicable to something absolutely ethereal and elusive.[97]

Between Monastyrsky's highly theoretical musings on semiotics and orientalism, and the more accessible narratives of those who participated in the works, it was this emphasis on freedom – the self-selecting construction of a self-determining social group – that formed the social core of CAG's practice.[98] Participation here denoted the possibility of producing individual affect and singular experience, relayed through a meditative relationship to language that in turn presupposed collective reception and debate.

V. Against Dissidence

Participatory art under state socialism in the 1960s and 1970s provides an important counter-model to contemporaneous examples from Europe and North America. Rather than aspiring to create a participatory public sphere as the counterpoint to a privatised world of individual affect and consumption, artists seeking to work collaboratively under socialism sought to provide a space for nurturing individualism (of behaviour, actions, interpretations) against an oppressively monolithic cultural sphere in which artistic judgements were reduced to a question of their position within Marxist-Leninist dogma. This led to a situation in which most artists wanted nothing to do with politics – and indeed even rejected the dissident position – by choosing to operate, instead, on an existential plane: making assertions of individual freedom, even in the slightest or most silent of forms.[99] We can contrast this approach with that of artists in Argentina (discussed in Chapter 4), where participation was used as a means to provoke audiences into heightened self-awareness of their social conditions and thereby (it was hoped) to impel them to take action in the social sphere. For artists living under communism, participation had no such agitationary goals. It was, rather, a means of experiencing a more authentic (because individual and self-organised) mode of collective experience than the one prescribed by the state in official parades and mass spectacles; as such it frequently takes escapist or celebratory forms. Today these terms elicit criticism in contemporary art writing, signifying a wilful refusal of artists to engage in their political reality and express a critical stance towards it. But this judgement also signifies the paucity of our ability to defend the intrinsic value of artistic experiences today. If the examples of the 1960s and 1970s avant-garde under socialism are 'political', then it is only in Rancière's sense of the 'metapolitical': a redistribution of the sensible world, rather than in an identifiable (and activist) political position. In a society where equality is repressively enforced, artistic expressions of individual liberty come to the fore.[100] The work discussed in this chapter reminds us that there is an unimaginably large gap between managing such contextual awareness and heroic acts of dissidence (the latter being, for the most part, a

Western fantasy). The reality of daily life under these regimes necessitates a more sober understanding of the artistic gestures achieved there, and appreciation of the consummate subtlety with which so many of them were undertaken.

6

Incidental People:
APG and Community Arts

The post-'68 period in Britain saw the formation of two attempts to rethink the artist's role in society. The first was set in motion in 1966, and its politics were contested within years of its inception: the Artist Placement Group (APG), founded by the artist John Latham and his then-partner Barbara Steveni, and which continued until 1989 when it was renamed O+I.[1] The second is the community arts movement, whose emergence in the UK forms part of an international push across Europe and North America to democratise and facilitate lay creativity, and to increase accessibility to the arts for less privileged audiences. These developments represent two distinct poles of rethinking the artist's place in society in the late 1960s and 1970s: one in which the artist undertakes a placement with a company or government body, and one in which the individual artist assumes the role of facilitating creativity among 'everyday' people. It should be noted that the academic literature on both of these movements is scanty: the bulk of publications on community arts tend to comprise reports and evaluations of specific projects rather than a synthesised narrative; the APG have only recently begun to be the focus of historical re-evaluation in the UK, in part due to the death of John Latham in 2006 and the deposit of APG's archive at Tate in 2004 (at the time of writing still uncatalogued), but also due to the interest of a younger generation of artists and curators who see parallels between their own intervention-based activities and those of APG.[2]

I. The Formation of APG

APG is usually credited as the brainchild of John Latham (1921–2006), a mixed-media artist peripherally involved with Assemblage and Fluxus during the 1960s.[3] He began making reliefs and assemblages from 1954 onwards, using the then new technology of spray paint; he also made films, actions, and participated in the Destruction in Art Symposium at the

163

London ICA in 1966. Latham's interests bridged art, philosophy and science, and can be seen in his use of books as a sculptural material from 1958 on: publications are turned into monuments, burnt, incorporated into assemblages, or even submerged in a tank of piranhas. He is probably best known for his 1966 performance *Still and Chew*, in which he and some of his students masticated a copy of Clement Greenberg's *Art and Culture* borrowed from the library of St Martins School of Art. When the library requested that he return the book, Latham did so – but as a vial of chewed-up pages. (The performance caused Latham to be fired from his job at St Martin's, but its remains – *Art and Culture* [1966–69] – were acquired by MoMA in 1970.) In the same year, 1966, Latham established APG with his partner Barbara Steveni, also trained as an artist.[4] The organisation was premised on the idea that art has a useful contribution to make to the world, and that artists can serve society – not by making works of art, but through their verbal interactions in the context of institutions and organisations. To this end, Steveni and Latham organised placements or residencies for British artists in a range of private corporations and public bodies.

Steveni recounts that the original idea for such an organisation was her initiative. She was in contact with Fluxus artists in the early '60s, and recalls how the idea of APG came to her one night in 1965 while collecting detritus for Daniel Spoerri and Robert Filliou on the Slough Trading Estate on the outskirts of West London. She realised that it might be more socially useful for artists to work *inside* these factories rather than to use the materials abandoned outside them. The idea was given further momentum when Steveni was invited by Frank Martin to give a lecture at St Martins on the role of the artist in society, and to do a weekly questionnaire on this topic with the students. Martin encouraged her to meet Sir Robert Adeane, an influential chairman of several companies (including Esso and ICI). Adeane was enthused by Steveni's proposal and offered to be on APG's board; Steveni hastily assembled one and in 1966 APG became an organisation ready to negotiate placements between artists and business.[5]

How the artists' placements were organised was not simply a matter of pragmatics, but provides an insight into the ideological orientation of APG. To state the procedure at its baldest: Barbara Steveni would write to a selection of host organisations outlining the goals of APG; these organisations were invited to pay a fee to the artist, who would undertake a residency on site; in return, companies were advised not to anticipate the production of a work of art, but rather to think of themselves having the benefit of a creative outsider in their midst (an 'Incidental Person', in APG's terminology). Steveni frames APG's purpose as a new form of patronage bringing together two disparate domains, industry and the arts:

APG exist to create mutually beneficial association between artists and organisations in industry, commerce and the public service. Their intention is not that of the traditional relationship of patronage. Rather, they seek to have an artist involved in the day-to-day work of an organisation. The latter may be expected to benefit in a variety of ways. These may vary from contributions to the creation of some concrete object to new ideas about work methods . . . APG's aim is an attempt to bridge the gap between artists and people at work so that each may gain from the other's perspectives and approaches to an activity.[6]

Of course, the procedure was more complex than this summary indicates. The host was expected to pay around £2,000 to £3,000 per artist depending on their age and experience – a generous fee, even by today's standards, especially when we consider that there was no contractual commitment on the part of the artist to produce a work of art. The project would ideally proceed in three phases. Firstly, a feasibility study, which would last around a month: the company would pay a fee to APG, who would put forward the names and CVs of three artists, who in turn would visit the organisation and report on the possibilities for their placement. Phase two comprised an agreement between APG and the organisation regarding practical and legal questions: the artist's brief, the length of contract, the artist's fee, the amount of commission received by APG, the ownership of any works produced, and so on. The third phase was an exhibition, although this was not viewed as necessary or essential to the placement.

APG's status as an art historical object is therefore extremely complex, since it requires that we confront multiple authorships in specific contexts: first, the theoretical frame of Latham and Steveni; second, the practice and inclinations of the artists they placed; and third, the character of the businesses and organisations in which these placements were held – each one a constellation of specific individuals more or less open to collaboration.

By 1969 the first placements were underway. Many of the artists involved are well known within the British context of the 1960s and '70s, but only a few have reputations with international reach today. The video artist David Hall was placed at British European Airways and Scottish Television; the performance artist Stuart Brisley at the Hille Furniture Company; Lois Price at the Milton Keynes Development Corporation; John Latham at the National Coal Board, and the hospital of Clare Hall, Cambridge; the sculptor Garth Evans at the British Steel Corporation.[7] Subsequent placements included Ian Breakwell (who worked in film, drawing and diary-writing) at British Rail and the Department of Health; artist and musician Andrew Dipper at Esso; artist and musician David Toop at London Zoo; and the sculptor Barry Flanagan at a plastics producer (Scott Bader). From this list it can immediately be seen that the choice of organisation tends towards heavy industry and nationalised companies, and that the artists are all male, yet the driving force behind the placements was Barbara Steveni, whose persistence in chasing organisations cannot be underestimated.[8] Many more letters were sent out than replies received; by the time of the Hayward show in 1971, only six placements had been established after over 100 letters of approach.[9]

APG's slogan was 'the context is half the work', an idea in tune with the post-studio tendencies of art in the later 1960s, and indebted to earlier works such as Robert Rauschenberg's *White Paintings* of 1951 (a series of glossy monochrome canvases that reflect shadows and light in the gallery) and to John Cage's *4'33"* (1952, a 'silent' performance in which peripheral sound becomes the composition's content). However, instead of pulling the audience *into* the work, as Rauschenberg and Cage had done, APG operated on the inverse principle of pushing the artist *out* into society. The idea of artists working with business and industry was a familiar tendency during the late '60s. Early APG documents reference examples in Europe as comparative models: in France, the Groupe Recherche d'Art Visuel (GRAV, discussed in Chapter 3), who were sponsored by industrialists interested in the exploitation of techniques and visual phenomena; in Holland, the Philips electricity company worked directly with an artist to make robot art; in Italy, competitions were sponsored by Esso and Pirelli; while in Britain, various sculptors were working in new materials that demanded close collaboration with steelworks (Eduardo Paolozzi), nickel laboratories (John Hosking) and glass fibre manufacturers (Phillip King). In the US, Experiments in Art and Technology (EAT), set up in 1966 by the Bell Labs scientist Billy Klüver in collaboration with Robert Rauschenberg, aimed to bring science to the service of artistic innovation, while on the West coast in the same year, curator Maurice Tuchman established the Art and Technology programme at LACMA.[10] APG differed from all of these models in its heavily theorised underpinnings, and in not basing the placements around sponsorship or using collaboration as a way to gain access to new technology. Science and industry were not at the service of art, but rather, the two domains were to confront each other ideologically. From today's perspective, it is tempting to suggest that the tacit agenda for each placement was for art to have a positive, humanising effect upon industry through the inherent creativity of artists and their relative ignorance of business conventions, but Steveni maintains that this was not the case. Outcomes were not determined in advance, and entirely depended on the individual artist in a given context; this was what APG called the 'open brief'.[11] Nevertheless, some artists were clearly more politicised than others, and this was reflected in their decisions to work either on the shop floor or in the management of a given company. Latham himself claimed to be beyond party politics, which he derided as a 'form of sectional interest civil war'.[12]

First-hand immersion in an industrial workplace could nevertheless have the effect of strengthening artists' existing political commitments. Stuart Brisley, who chose to work on the shop floor of Hille Furniture factory, proceeded with his placement in a manner that will sound familiar to any artist working site-responsively today: the main task was social (earning trust) rather than realising a sculptural object. Going to the factory three to four days a week while also holding down a teaching job, Brisley chose to focus on the department with the most onerous work, the metal-polishing room. Workers were initially suspicious of an artist foisted upon them by the management, and it took time to gain their confidence. Brisley initially began by asking questions about how the production line could be improved. Unsurprisingly, the answer was a sceptical 'why?', since the workers habitually felt that no one was interested in or listened to them, even though they had many questions and criticisms, which Brisley in turn began to relay to the management. As an outsider this left him feeling empowered, since he could begin to initiate change. One of his contributions was painting the polishing machinery in the colours of football teams chosen by the workers; another was to introduce large mobile noticeboards which could be pushed around the factory floor, so that workers could exchange information and communicate with each other.[13] He also made a sculpture using 212 Robin Day chairs, which when stacked formed a complete circle, 'a syndromic sign of the factory line itself'.

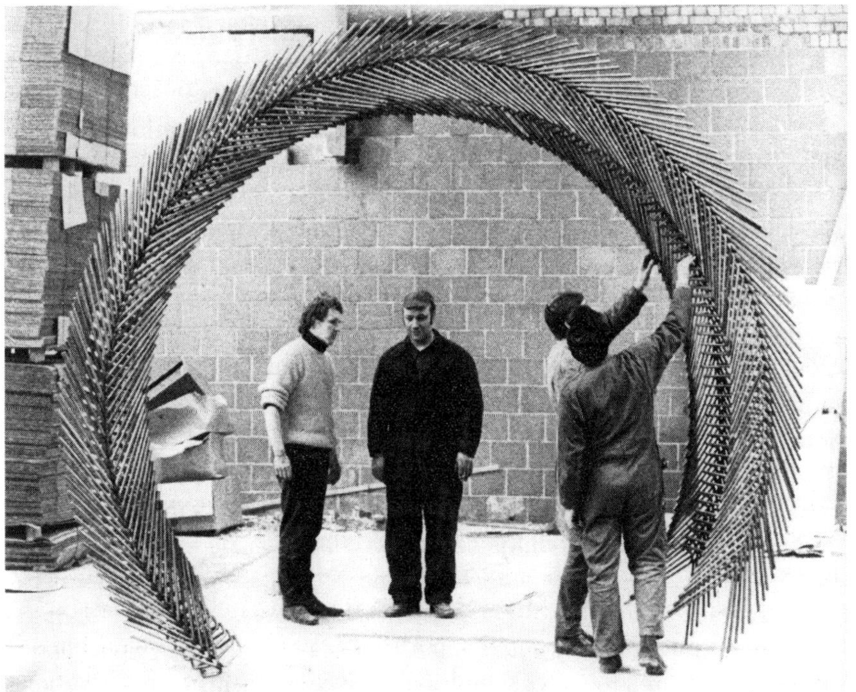

Stuart Brisley speaking to workers at Hille Furniture Company constructing his sculpture of stacked Robin Day chairs, Haverhill, Suffolk, UK, 1970

Brisley felt that the machinery painting project had begun to confuse his identity as an artist, since 'one was actually moving away from art more into a kind of potentially collective situation', while the information board incident led him to feel caught in a 'permanent conflict' between 'factory and management'.[14] Despite the modesty of these interventions, Brisley argues that the placement at Hille went on to inform his work in setting up an Artists' Union (1972 onwards), and impacted upon his protest-based performances of the 1970s. It also had the effect of distancing Brisley politically from APG's efforts, which he felt to be too enamoured with management (rather than workers), and whose structure he perceived to be 'a tightly knit, highly autocratic family business, with a poor record of human relations'.[15]

II. Exhibiting Process: 'Inno 70'

Such long-term, process-based placements do not lend themselves easily to exhibition display. It is a testimony to APG's ambition and faith in future outcomes that Steveni managed to secure funding for an APG exhibition at the Hayward Gallery in 1968, a year before the first placements had even taken place. The exhibition, titled 'Inno70', but also known as 'Art and Economics', was held 2–23 December 1971 and intended to show the achievements of the preceding two years, regardless of the point at which the placements had arrived.[16] According to institutional lore, it was the worst attended exhibition in the Hayward's history.

The contents of 'Inno70' were decided by the artists in collaboration with the organisations hosting them. The Hayward's exterior windows contained posters for the show with the prominent slogan 'FOR SALE Hayward Gallery, South Bank, London SE1'.[17] Inside the gallery entrance were copies of Latham's 'Report and Offer for Sale', a parodic business report about APG, available for consultation on a table. Inside, three types of exhibition space could be discerned: displays reporting on placement activities, single-room installations, and an interactive discussion zone called 'The Sculpture'. Several galleries were filled with blown-up photographs showing various stages of the associations to date, alongside videotaped interviews and discussions between artists and representatives of industry, business, government and education, relayed on monitors scattered throughout the Hayward. Alongside these were a handful of works produced by the artists: a film by Andrew Dipper, made while on board a ship during his placement with Esso, and a fibre sculpture by Leonard Hessing, made during his placement with ICI Fibres.[18] Only the sculptor Garth Evans presented his placement as an installation occupying an entire gallery: he gathered together samples of steel components from every steel mill in the UK (which looked not unlike sculptures by Anthony Caro), and invited other artists to rearrange these objects over the course of the

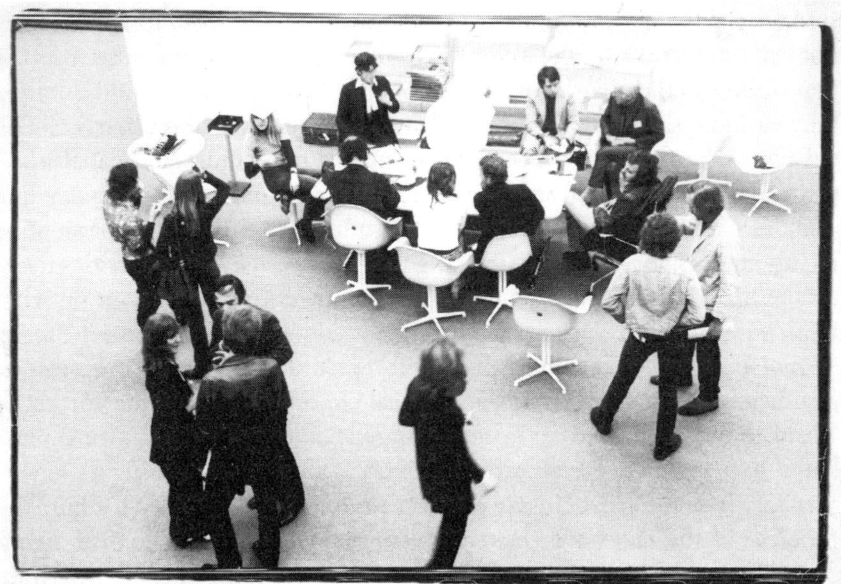

Artists Placement Group, 'Inno70', 1971. View of 'The Sculpture'.

exhibition, to the sound of an eight-hour steel-making process from Ebbw Vale in Wales.[19] Reviewers complained that the noise of this exhibit was too deafening to endure for any length of time.

The third type of space in 'Inno70', 'the Sculpture', was the most prescient in terms of contemporary exhibition models: a boardroom hosting daily meetings between APG and members of invited organisations. A large area demarcated by a long white wall (like an art-fair booth) contained shelving units, an information desk manned full-time by Steveni, a large table and chairs. The meetings throughout the exhibition were recorded and archived although, contentiously, the public were not allowed to participate; indeed, they were separated from the boardroom by a clear plastic curtain.[20] The catalogue for the show also harbingers the self-reflexivity of contemporary curatorial projects: beginning in 1970, seven inserts were placed in the magazine *Studio International*, imitating the format of the *Times Business News* with fake news items, photographs and collages.[21] With such a cryptic and temporal unveiling, the 'catalogue' served more as a long-term trailer advertising the show than as a coherent summary of what was exhibited within it.[22]

The exhibition aimed to be polemical and accomplished this, prompting harsh reactions from a number of critics and artists, including some who had participated in the placements. The main focus of complaint was the exhibition's dry impenetrability and corporate appearance. 'Andrew Dipper's photographs taken on board an Esso tanker may have some pattern behind them, but on the visual evidence look no different from company publicity', wrote Caroline Tisdall in the *Guardian*.[23] 'One is immediately struck by the atmosphere that has been created here. It is the atmosphere of the boardroom, of "top-level" managerial meetings', opined Guy Brett in *The Times*.[24] For Nigel Gosling, writing in the *Observer*, 'The gallery displays various subjects held up for non-commercial analysis – town-planning, hospital treatment, mining, shipping, etc. – besides live samples of boardroom discussion which must strike fear rather than hope in any innocent breast.'[25] It is striking that all three newspaper critics focus on the exhibition's bureaucratic atmosphere, a corporate variant on what Benjamin Buchloh subsequently termed conceptual art's 'aesthetic of administration'.[26] This atmosphere prompted anxiety because it seemed insufficiently distanced from the political conservatism that the corporate world connoted; indeed, it seemed to signal collaboration with – or capitulation to – the managerial, rather than critical distance towards it. This is certainly how the artist Gustav Metzger responded to 'Inno70': for him, the problem of the Hayward show was less aesthetic than ideological, being symptomatic of APG's operation in shamelessly attempting 'to penetrate the richest powers in the land – the giant industrial corporations'.[27] He was repelled by the exhibition for trying to steer two mutually opposed groups together into dialogue (young artists and powerful corporations) and taking what he called 'The Middle Way', since 'The history of the twentieth century has shown that this always leads to the Right.'[28]

The most searing (and politically informed) critique of APG's show was by the Marxist critic Peter Fuller. His arguments are useful to rehearse here since they recur in contemporary debates about APG and its relation to the corporate world.[29] Fuller, on the one hand, noted that the premise of APG's placements should be recognised as impressive: getting companies to agree to sponsor artists who were there explicitly to work against the profit motive was no small achievement, and he admitted that this agreement alone must surely 'make some impact on the conventional criteria by which decisions are made in large firms'.[30] On the other hand, he felt that APG were naive to place an artist in an organisation and declare him automatically to be a free agent.[31] For Fuller, the system of collaboration proposed between APG and corporations was flawed from the start since power relations were stacked against the artist. He cites the experience of Brisley, who argued against APG's management-level approach and their contractual promise not to harm the host companies, which removed the artist's right to find fault.[32] Fuller takes glee in relaying the following dialogue: 'Latham admits to having no knowledge of Marx – "I've never read him", he says. His wife, Barbara, is even more illuminating on this point: "I am very interested in all that Russian thing . . . my father was a Russian. Trotsky, did you say. No, I don't know him; who is Trotsky anyway?" '[33] Fuller's point is not that artists should have a working knowledge of Marx and Trotsky, but that Latham and Steveni were too ready to dismiss the usual ways of looking at society and verbalising political ideas despite having no real knowledge of what these involve ('one would have thought that for anyone intent on transforming capitalism, and imposing an alternative value structure not based on the commercial premise, or the "profit motive", at least a minimal knowledge of Marxist theory would have been obligatory').[34]

Fuller has a point, but completely misunderstands Latham's idiosyncratic artistic thinking, which was akin to a total cosmology. For Latham, the artist as Incidental Person transcends party politics and 'takes the stand of a third ideological position which is off the plane of their obvious collision areas'.[35] Latham's thinking was informed by two scientists he had met in the mid 1950s, Clive Gregory and Anita Kohsen, who invited him to be a founding member of their project, the Institute for the Study of Mental Images; in parallel with them he developed his own complex, rather long-winded system for understanding the world. Like Gregory and Kohsen, Latham believed that human conflicts arose through an absence of an overarching theory of mankind, which they set about producing by identifying common features across multiple disciplines; one of the central ideas to emerge from this was a theory of 'event-structure', in which the 'least event' is the minimum unit of existence. Another key idea for Latham was the 'Delta unit' (Δ), a new way to measure human development, and moreover to determine the value of a work of art, by measuring its importance not in monetary terms but through the degree of awareness it produces (from unconsciousness to the most heightened state) over a sustained period.[36] This idea was key to APG, since the organisation as a whole was committed to the long-term effects of artistic intervention in society, rather than seeking short-term demonstrable goals.[37] For Latham, the mysterious dynamism of the Delta unit could surpass in a new great social force both capitalism and socialism, which he derided as 'mere stratified habits of thought that have little to do with change'.[38] In order to convey these inversions of conventional thinking, Latham devised a specific vocabulary: 'books' became 'skoob', 'noit' reversed the suffix normally used to denote abstractions ('-tion'), while the word 'artist' was replaced by the unromantic and contingent category of 'Incidental Person'. As a new cultural term, Steveni later explained, the Incidental Person 'applies particularly to those in whom specific formulative abilities are apparent. It indicates a broader area of practice (e.g. "multimedia") and a specific concern with "art in context" rather than with "painting", "sculpture", and so on.'[39] As such, the Incidental Person seems to presage the job description of many contemporary artists who undertake projects in the social sphere and are required to deploy a broad range of social skills that go beyond the production of objects for visual consumption. The replacement of heavy industry by a service economy has also allowed APG to seem a forerunner of recent attempts to remodel the flexible worker along artistic lines (as discussed in Chapter 1).

III. Placements in the 1970s and After

After 'Inno70', Steveni sought to avoid accusations of collaborating with business by redirecting her attention towards securing placements in government departments, placing artists alongside civil servants. The best known of these is Ian Breakwell's residency at the Department of Health and Social Security in 1976, during which time he focused on the high-security hospitals Broadmoor and Rampton, and worked with a team of specialists to initiate minor reforms within the healthcare system. Prior to working at the DHSS, Breakwell's work had revolved around the representation of so-called 'normal' life in his *Continuous Diary* (1965 onwards); in the eyes of APG this made him eminently suitable to comment on the 'abnormal' within the healthcare system.[40] The first phase of Breakwell's research was based at the DHSS Mental Health Group (Architects Division) at Euston Tower, from which he visited different types of hostels and hospitals. For the next phase he proposed working at Broadmoor Special Hospital, where he collaborated with an interdisciplinary team who had been asked to prepare a report on how to improve conditions there; Breakwell was recruited as a professional observer, the team making use of his 'Diary' to introduce a consultative approach in which patients were asked for their views. The results angered the Broadmoor administration, who felt that the team had stepped 'outside their brief as architects' and 'embarrassed the higher level of the DHSS hierarchy'; as such, the research was restricted by the Official Secrets Act.[41] However, the Architects Division saw the outcome positively:

> Ian has succeeded in giving us a real and lasting image, from his point of view, of the insanity surrounding insanity. This work should be reproduced and distributed to all our contacts, especially those who deceive themselves that all is right in the Mental Health world. We should also keep it on hand and read it ourselves periodically 'lest we forget'.[42]

Breakwell thus concluded that on the first host level (the DHSS) the placement had been successful, while on the second host level (Broadmoor), 'the end result was "failure" '.[43]

In terms of concrete outcomes, Breakwell's placement yielded slides of the squalid conditions at Rampton which were used in a Yorkshire Television documentary on high-security hospitals ('The Secret Hospital', 1979); in turn, this led to media coverage, public outcry, and a government enquiry. Artistically, the placement resulted in a notebook of his time there, and a film called *The Institution* (1978), made in collaboration with the recording artist and former nurse Kevin Coyne. The connecting thread between all aspects of the project was Breakwell's ongoing interest in the environmental nature of institutions. As Katherine Dodd points out,

Breakwell's experience – being part of an interdisciplinary research team – is exceptional in the panorama of APG placements, where the artist is more usually a lone individual.[44] It also differed from other placements in having a mandate to directly improve the object of research. Although the hospitals in question were unhappy with his APG placement, Breakwell went on to a second phase of collaboration with the DHSS, devising the Reminiscence Aids Project, which was eventually implemented with the help of the charity Age Concern in 1981.[45]

Another well-known placement from the later 1970s, which anticipates the last decade's infatuation with archival art, is Stuart Brisley's *History Within Living Memory* for Peterlee New Town, one of eight 'new towns' planned after the Second World War to deal with housing shortages in impoverished areas.[46] Despite his political disagreements with APG, Brisley leapt at the opportunity to work in a northern mining community.[47] When he arrived there in 1976–77, new housing had been allocated to people from the surrounding villages, but Peterlee itself was a town without history. Faced with a dearth of culture and community, Brisley set about producing an archive of photographs and interviews with the local populace, constructing a history for the town from 1900 to the date of his arrival, 1976, which he defined as the period of 'living memory'.[48] Significantly, one of the models for this project came from community arts: the Hackney Writers Workshop, in East London, in which non-professional writers produced their own history through individual life stories.[49]

Brisley worked with a retired and disabled former stone mason (Mr Parker) to mediate his idea to the immediate community; he secured for him a paid position within Peterlee's Social Development department, together with five women who were trained to use recording equipment and undertake the interviews that would form the basis of the archive. This constituted the first phase of the project; the second was to commission the Sociology Department of Durham University to write a history of Peterlee Development Corporation (PDC); and the third phase was to organise a series of community workshops, by which the local populace could place questions directly to the PDC.[50] The latter two phases were abandoned in 1978 when Peterlee's administration was handed over to Easington District Council; what remained was a heritage centre rather than a living archive, albeit one with over 2,000 photos and over 100 interviews. Unlike the 'archival impulse' of much contemporary art, in which an accumulation of oral histories, documents and photographs are amassed into an aestheti-cised display for the general public, Brisley's project was conceived for a specific constituency as an expression of their heritage.

Significantly, Brisley today is adamant that what he produced in Peterlee is an archive, and not a work of art – even though he exhibited it at the Northern Arts Gallery, Newcastle upon Tyne, during Autumn

1976. Rather, the artist considers himself to have been testing out techniques from performance in a social context, 'to be a model for others to use in different situations if it proved to have some virtue'.[51] He nevertheless always includes the Peterlee placement in his exhibition catalogues, listed as a 'project', rather than as a work of art; in other words, it remains authored, but has an ambiguous status, because for Brisley, the Peterlee archive has a social function, rather than an aesthetic one.[52] As I will elaborate in the next chapter, the word 'project' has subsequently come to replace 'work of art' as a descriptor for long-term artistic undertakings in the social sphere. Brisley keeps apart two domains that in subsequent decades many artists have attempted to map onto each other, and the distinction he upholds (that nominalism is inadequate: art is only art if it's recognised beyond the frame of the artist) is not a position shared by the more radical practitioners of participatory art today.

APG's activities go straight to the heart of contemporary debates about the functionality of art, the desirability (or not) of it having social goals, and the possibility of multiple modes of evaluation. It seems indisputable that APG sought to give the artist more power within society, rather than empowering workers on the lower rungs of the organisations where placements were held. To this extent, its goals seem more perceptual rather than social: to change the *awareness* of those working within organisations, but not actually to galvanise insurrection. This much is self-evident. However, it is arguably more productive to focus on APG's contribution to one of the largest problems concerning socially engaged practice: the question of evaluation, and over what period of time such judgements should be made.

Latham frequently asserted that the world needs to develop a new mode of accountancy for art – hence the Delta unit, which relocated value away from finance and onto 'units of attention' over time. And yet, in APG's later writings, we find the group resorting to a monetary overestimation of the artists' contributions to society, such as valuing Ian Breakwell's contribution during his first year at the DHSS to be £3.5 million. It seems telling that this *financial* calculation becomes the criterion of success, rather than a conceptual or artistic value (even if artists like Brisley did not consider their projects to be art). In 1977, Latham mischievously sent invoices for 'services rendered' to the British government – one for a million pounds on behalf of APG and one for half a million pounds for his own services in 'creating a successful C20th art movement' – and proceeded to stop paying taxes from that year on. Although the invoice was clearly a provocation, his translation of artistic practice into monetary value seems hard to square with APG's determination to rethink conventional modes of accounting. This tendency to focus on demonstrable outcomes persisted in APG's supporters as late as 1992, when *The Journal of Art and Art Education* ran an article by Graham Stevens that also argued for the importance of APG's activities by listing the new museum in Peterlee as a direct result of Stuart Brisley's placement, the conservation of monumental industrial sites in Scotland (by John Latham at the Scottish Office), and two local resident associations in Birmingham (developed by the filmmaker Roger Coward in a Department of the Environment placement at Small Heath).[53] In short, although APG rightly sought to redirect the value of art away from financial outcomes and concrete indicators, it ended up resorting to these in order to justify public investment in the organisation. The latter was a sore point: as a direct result of the exhibition 'Inno70', the Arts Council of Great Britain withdrew its funding for APG on the basis that it was 'more concerned with social engineering than with straight art'.[54] To the chagrin of Latham and Steveni, the Arts Council then took over the role of artist's placements, claiming in 1973 the sole governmental right to be funding artists.[55]

It is ironic that the UK government between 1997 and 2010 rendered the Arts Council explicitly beholden to social engineering, using culture to reinforce policies of social inclusion (see Chapter 1). APG's argument that artists can have long-term effects on society has been realised and acknowledged, but perhaps not quite in ways that they imagined. The Delta unit prefigured New Labour's preferred method of assessing cultural value through a statistical analysis (audience demographics, marketing, visitor figures, etc.) rather than the more difficult terrain of debating artistic quality. APG could be said to have pre-empted the use of artists by management consultancies, and to have ushered in the growth of the 'creative industries' as a dialogue between art and business in the wake of heavy industry, not to mention the centrality of artist residency schemes to the regeneration of inner cities.[56]

The challenge, then, is to identify the specifically artistic achievements of APG. Despite the highly administrative character of its practice, and the quasi-corporate greyness in which all documentation surrounding the project seems to be saturated, its achievements were primarily discursive and theoretical. For example, it defined a new model of patronage organised around the 'open brief', even if the power balance of this relationship remained open to question. It contributed to a broader post-war effort to demystify the creative process – replacing the term 'artist' with 'Incidental Person' – even if this mystification returned via the back door in the elusive Delta unit to measure artistic efficacy. It provided windows for open-minded organisations to rethink their hierarchy and basic assumptions, and in so doing was more provocative and adventurous than the 'artist in residence' schemes subsequently offered by the Arts Council. Curatorially, its contribution is central: the inclusion of a discussion space within 'Inno70', and APG's subsequent decision not to use an exhibition format but to present its projects through panel discussions throughout the 1970s, anticipate the 'discursive platform' as a contemporary exhibition strategy, and the symposium as a viable way to present non-object- and process-based art.[57] Even if APG's intention to confront business with another system of thinking was idealistic (and perhaps ultimately rather toothless), its work with government departments was more successful; in both instances, the artists could provoke conflict within each context if so desired; indeed, the best placements produced, in the words of Ian Breakwell, 'abrasive mutual debate'.[58]

In sum, what needs to be appreciated today is APG's determination to provide a new post-studio framework for artistic production, for providing opportunities for long-term, in-depth interdisciplinary research, for rethinking the function of the exhibition from show-room to locus of debate, for its desire to put two different ideological value systems into constant tension, and for its aspiration to set in motion a long-term evaluative framework for both art and research. More than any other artists' project of the 1970s, APG asks whether it is better for art to be engaged with society even if this means compromise, or to maintain ideological purity at the expense of social isolation and powerlessness. These questions are more intellectual than affective – it's unlikely that they will prompt many pulses to accelerate – but they harbinger broader changes in art and the economy since the 1970s. The political naiveties of APG are therefore inextricable from its achievements as an artistic provocation. It is only because APG lacked an identifiable (party) political

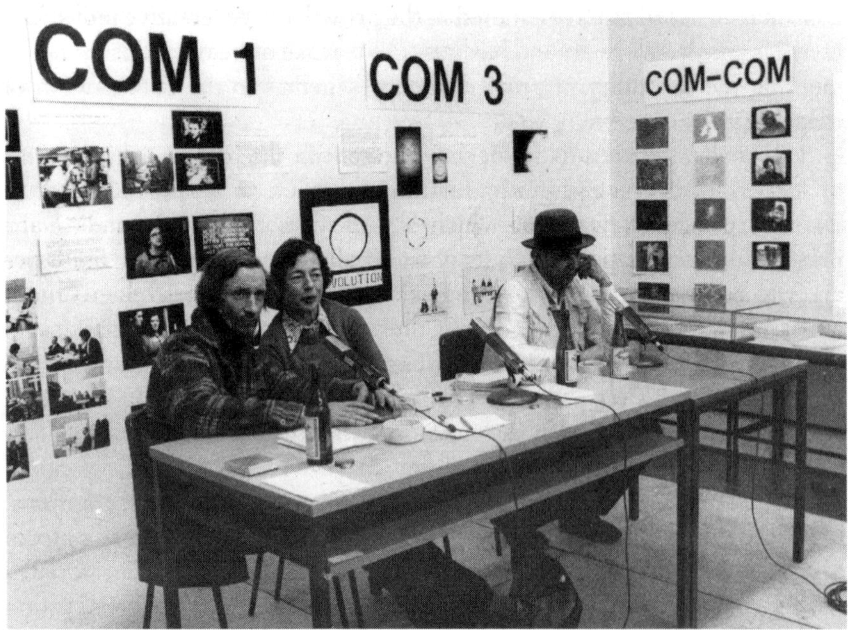

John Latham and Joseph Beuys at the conference 'Streitgesprache: Pragmatismus gegen Idealismus' (Discussion: Pragmatism Versus Idealism), Kunstverein Bonn, 1978

position that it could make such manoeuvres towards power, in all its ambiguous openness – and this is precisely the organisation's limitation (a joyless bureaucratic aesthetic) and its strength (believing that art can cause both business *and* art to re-evaluate their priorities).

IV. The Community Arts Movement

The countercultural foil to APG in the 1970s is without question the UK community arts movement. Both attempted to establish a new role for the artist in relationship to society, and as Steveni observes, both share the same components: 'people and time'.[59] Moreover, both have histories in which their fortunes are closely intertwined with public funding for the arts. Yet if APG positioned artists at the nerve centre of decision-making bodies, the community arts movement operated in less glamorous contexts, at a grass-roots level of community activism. John Walker describes how APG found it necessary to combat the idea that it was a 'community art' organisation, an agency for 'artists in residence' schemes, or that its aim was 'help for the artist'.[60] Rather, APG's concern was always to impact upon the thinking of corporations and government organisations, rather than directly empowering those people who work within them. By contrast, the ideological motivations of community arts revolved around precisely this attention to the marginalised, whom they sought to empower through participatory creative practice, and through an opposition to elitist cultural hierarchies. (It is worth remembering that in the 1970s the Arts Council of Great Britain was still headed by the aristocracy and upper middle classes.) Despite the pitfalls of generalisation when defining community arts – its multiple organisations had quite distinct aims and methods – the recurrent characteristics of the movement can be summarised as follows: it was positioned against the hierarchies of the international art world and its criteria of success founded upon quality, skill, virtuosity, etc., since these conceal class interests; it advocated participation and co-authorship of works of art; it aimed to give shape to the creativity of all sectors of society, but especially to people living in areas of social, cultural and financial deprivation; for some, it was also a powerful medium for social and political change, providing the blueprint for a participatory democracy.[61]

Although there is a large literature produced by community arts organisations, very little of this is historical or scholarly, and even less is critical.[62] The analysis of community-based visual arts tends to take the form of reports on specific projects in local contexts, by people invested in supporting these initiatives, without any overarching history or meta-theoretical discourse beyond a loosely Marxist opposition to cultural elites and the occasional mention of Benjamin's 'The Author as Producer'. Important exceptions are Owen Kelly's critical history of the community arts movement, *Community, Art and the State* (1984), and Charles Landry's *What a*

Way to Run a Railroad (1985), a critique of post-'68 radical movements in the UK.[63] Neither book emphasises the extent to which the concerns of community arts were closely related to those of contemporary art, in contrast to today's tendency to keep the two at arm's length (as can be seen in the ongoing separation between curatorial work and education/community outreach).[64]

In the UK, the first community arts groups were formed in the late 1960s: professional artists took equal roles alongside members of the community in the collaborative production of a politicised artistic project: murals, street theatre, festivals, film and video collectives, etc.[65] For many organisations, the collectivist ethos extended into squatting, communes and a self-sufficient lifestyle; it was part of an outpouring of radical activity at this time that included recreational drug taking, free festivals, new contraception, a desire to return 'power to the people', university occupations (most notably at Hornsey School of Art in 1968) and the Grosvenor Square riots (in opposition to US involvement in Vietnam). Organisers were unwaged but able to survive either from parental handouts or unemployment benefit from the welfare state.[66] In a visual art context, the community arts movement was in dialogue with a number of alternative initiatives, including Pavilions in the Parks (1967–71), which showed art in lightweight portable structures in public spaces; the Poster Workshop on Camden Road, which printed posters for strikers, tenant groups and anti-war protests; Cornelius Cardew's radically egalitarian *Scratch Orchestra* (1968–72), in which a group of thirty to forty players would each develop a theme for a composition and be responsible for their individual contributions; and David Medalla's 'participation-production-propulsion' events (1968 onwards, discussed below). In each of these initiatives, questions of audience, accessibility and elitism were strongly contested; participation was a central strategy and ethos for democratic cultural production.[67]

Finding a definition for these new activities was recognised to be a problem early on. By the early 1970s, the Arts Council's Experimental Projects Committee was deluged with applications for funding, and in 1974 set up a working committee to define the new tendency, coming to the following conclusions:

> 'Community artists' are distinguishable not by the techniques they use, although some (e.g. video, inflatables) are specially suited to their purposes, but by their *attitude* towards the place of their activities in the life of society. Their primary concern is their *impact on a community* and their relationship with it: by assisting those with whom they make contact to become more aware of their situation and of their own creative powers, and by providing them with the facilities they need to make use of their abilities, they hope to widen and deepen the sensibilities of the

community in which they work and so to enrich its existence. To a varying degree they see this *as a means of change, whether psychological, social
or political*, within the community. They seek to bring about this increased
awareness and creativity by involving the community in the activities
they promote . . . They therefore differ from practisers of the more
established arts in that *they are chiefly concerned with a process rather than
a finished product*; a many-sided process including craft, sport, etc., in
which the 'artistic' element is variable and often not clearly distinguish-
able from the rest.[68]

As can be seen from this description – which comes very close to the working definition of much socially engaged art today – emphasis is placed on
social process rather than outcomes, and on attitude rather than achievement. Yet the thorny question of how to evaluate this new category
remained unclear. The only suggestion offered by the 1974 committee was
a recognition of the importance of site specificity: projects could 'be evaluated only by enquiry and observation on the spot', hence 'visits to the
localities concerned should be paid wherever possible'.[69] The committee
also observed that the activities of community artists overlapped with those
of other public bodies (education, social welfare, sport, leisure, etc.) – yet
it stopped short of proposing to bring experts from those fields into the
process of evaluation. Despite acknowledging that community arts aimed
to impact upon the community, it did not develop a method for establishing
how this was to be measured.

V. The Blackie and Inter-Action

Two of the longest-running community arts projects in the UK were established in 1968, and exist in some rivalry with each other.[70] The Blackie
(founded by choreographer Bill Harpe and his wife Wendy) continues to
be based in St George's Church in the Chinatown area of Liverpool. Its
original aim was to establish 'the facilities of a Community Centre and the
best the Contemporary Arts could offer under one roof, the Blackie roof'.[71]
From its inception it had a commitment to showing 'high' art alongside
everyday productions of local people; early visitors included choreographer Meredith Monk and the jazz musician Jon Hendricks, while many of
its workshops and social games have taken their initiative from avant-garde
culture (John Cage, Merce Cunningham, Samuel Beckett, Liliane Lijn,
John Latham). In the early 1970s, performances of work by Cage and
Morton Feldman took place alongside participatory activities such as mothers' bingo and children's playgroup, assorted workshops (typing, puppetry,
woodwork, cookery, photography), a small press (for producing publicity
and publications), and a radio station (Radio Blackie, set up in 1973). Still
occupying the enormous former church it took over in 1968, The Blackie

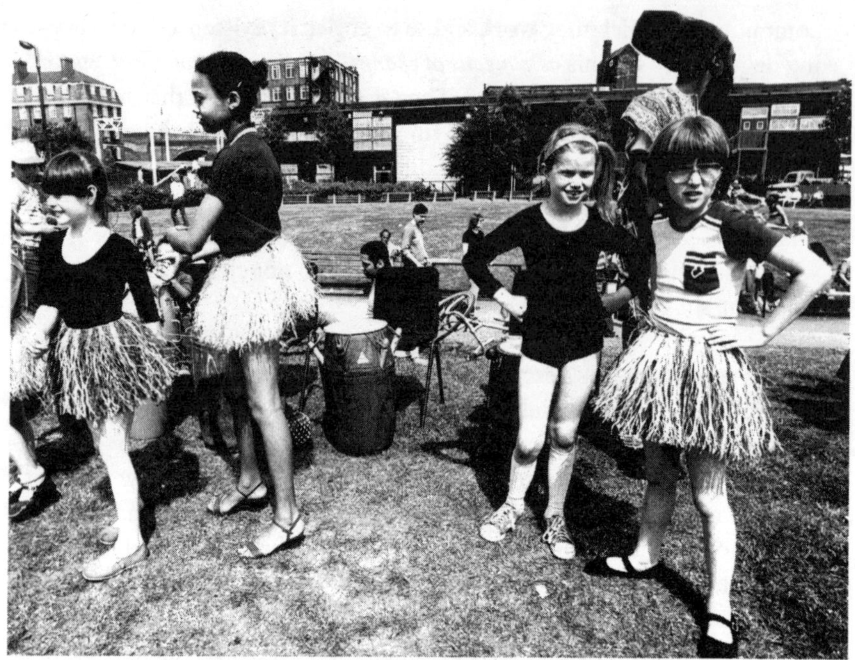

Children outside the Inter-Action Centre, Kentish Town, London, after 1976

today houses several rehearsal rooms, studio production facilities, and an exhibition space.[72] Participation was key to all aspects of the project, including infrastructure, although this was not without a degree of realism as to how far power could actually be devolved and shared equally.[73] Staff and volunteers were expected to undertake a mix of creative and uncreative activities; in the early years this led to secretaries resigning, unable to feel sufficiently 'creative'.[74]

My second example, Inter-Action, was founded by the US theatre director Ed Berman in London in 1968, and views itself as a pioneer in the community arts field. For many years it also occupied the UK's first dedicated community arts centre, designed by the experimental architect Cedric Price in 1976 as the small-scale realisation of his unbuilt Fun Palace.[75] (Inter-Action's campaign against Camden Council to secure this site is the subject of the film *The Amazing Story of Talacre*, 1974.) In the 1970s, Inter-Action served as an umbrella organisation for a number of experimental theatre companies dedicated to broadening audiences, under the banner 'art where it's least expected'. These included the Dogg's Troupe (a children's street theatre group), the Ambiance Theatre Club (a free lunchtime theatre in the basement of the Ambiance restaurant in Queensway), the Fun Art Bus (a converted double-decker whose passengers were variously entertained with poetry, theatre and song, and which also included sound and video recording equipment), and the Almost Free Theatre (in which people could pay what they wanted, in direct contrast to the high ticket prices of West End theatre). The

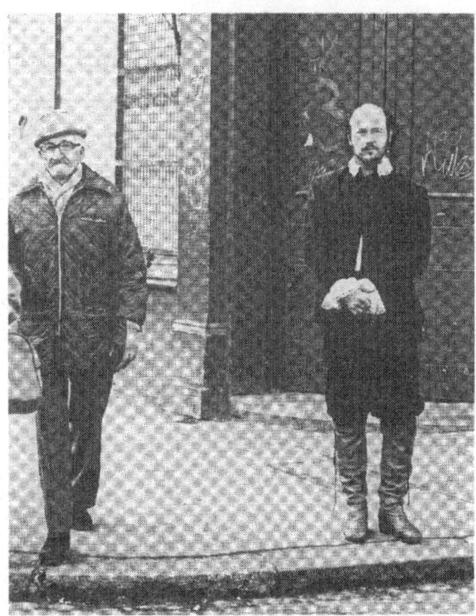

Community Cameos, 1970s, William Shakespeare performed by Phil Ryder

organisation supported new forms of identitarian theatre, such as the Gay Sweatshop and Women's Theatre, and held one of the UK's first seasons of Black Theatre. Inter-Action also set up the city farm in Kentish Town, the Weekend Arts College (a free education centre for children, mostly from ethnic minorities), and pioneered 'social enterprise' – getting management consultancies to fund self-organised, not-for-profit community groups.[76] Berman refers to himself as the organisation's 'artistic director', with total control over the plays produced; this ensured ongoing Arts Council support, since his policy was always to have one well-known actor or director involved (from the playwright Tom Stoppard to actors such as Prunella Scales and Corin Redgrave). Berman asserts that he was committed to professional standards; it was important to ensure quality, since community theatre was part of the same market of actors and directors.

Inter-Action's multiple and energetic wings aimed to be both educational and artistic, as can be seen in the long-term performance project *Community Cameos*. Three actors were each trained to live and speak as one of three historical figures – William Shakespeare, Captain Cook and Edward Lear – before being disseminated around London (and eventually around the UK and as far as Los Angeles) as a walking repository of information about each historic character.[77] Each actor, having intensively researched his role, and wearing period costume, would behave as a time traveller not only in public situations (schools, community centres, etc.), but also when taking the bus or taxi to and from jobs, or when checking into hotels. John Perry (who played Lear) also operated from a Victorian parlour in the Cedric Price building, which children could visit, travelling back in time to the nineteenth century as Lear travelled forwards to meet them in the twentieth. A large educational load was carried by the cameos, but at the same time this aimed to be 'a joyous and creative' mode of inter-active performance.[78] For the actors, the continuous embodiment of a historical figure over two to three years placed a new spin on the idea of durational performance.

Aside from a striking investment in the co-existence of 'high' and 'low' artistic forms, one of the most distinctive aspects of both The Blackie and Inter-Action's identity is a commitment to games that are co-operative rather than competitive. Each week at The Blackie, the regular staff continue to engage in games, all of which are seen as 'a means to an end rather than an end in itself'.[79] Games are understood as metaphors for social relations and thus demonstrate the possibility of producing change. In a recent promotional DVD about The Blackie, Bill Harpe speaks of his non-competitive reworking of the children's game 'Musical Chairs', which uses decreasing numbers of carpet tiles rather than chairs. When the music stops, participants leap towards one of the tiles, even if there are already people standing on it. The point is co-operation – a balancing act – rather than elimination. As Harpe wryly observes,

> The conventional musical chairs game is a very good preparation for unemployment, because most of the players discover that they aren't needed once the game gets going, they sit it out and watch. It's an image of a world in which a lot of people do sit out and watch, and are unem-ployed or redundant. In the upside down game everyone's involved in the game right up to the end, everybody's making a contribution, every-one's doing something. That's an image of a different sort of society.[80]

Harpe has collected over forty of these games in a publication *Games for the New Years* (2001).[81] The games are given titles that spell out what is achieved through them – almost all of which promote social harmony: 'the accom-plishment game in which expectation promotes unity', 'the unison game in which democracy is tested to its limits', 'the rescue game in which becom-ing breathless may also become a friendly habit'.

Ed Berman talks proudly of the Inter-Action Creative Games Method, a training 'for people who are interested in their own or group creativity, or in a profession that works with people', although this remains unpub-lished.[82] Berman offers the following example of a game where participants have to get from one side of a room to another, not first but last; by discon-necting the goal (the other side of the room) from the means of advancement (speed), competition becomes co-operative, and more creative. Despite the similarity of this example to Harpe's upside-down musical chairs, Berman's approach is more analytic and less overtly value-laden, informed by his training in Educational Psychology and an understanding of community arts as 'action research'.[83]

Games were also a structuring principle for The Blackie's theatrical experiments in the late 1960s and early '70s. Unlike the work of Augusto Boal (whom Bill Harpe met twice), participatory performances at The Blackie tended less towards 'a rehearsal for revolution' than towards a melancholic exposé of how society really operated.[84] These extended social games, often based on government statistics, included *The To-Hell-With-Human-Rights Show* (December 1968) and *Educational Darts* (March 1971). In *Sanctuary* (November 1969), performed at Quarry Bank High School, the participating audience were assigned different types of housing on the basis of filling in a form, which included questions about their income and number of dependents. The housing ranged from 'Breck Moor' (a large detached house) to 'Box Street' (slum dwellings), each of which was provided with appropriate entertainment: at the former, sherry and chess; at the latter, brown ale (but no bottle opener). The action unfolded from this point, with four improvised performances emerging simultaneously from these scenarios. Some participants would obey the law (which moved very slowly and bureaucratically, in order to mirror real life), while others broke it and were arrested, imprisoned, and so on.[85] Half structured, half improvised, such productions positioned themselves against the education programmes of theatre companies (in that they allowed the audience to produce the work themselves, rather than learning about somebody else's performance) but they also worked against theatrical productions in which the audience members all experience the same thing simultaneously; in *Sanctuary* there were at least four possible types of audience experience.

Berman, by contrast, found it more difficult to introduce participatory theatre to Inter-Action's repertoire, since there were so few good playwrights interested in exploring this genre. He ended up producing his own plays, based on a formula defining the amount of changes that an audience could make in the work, from pantomime (where only one answer is possible within the script) to theatrical situations where the outcome is entirely unplanned. His play *The Nudist Campers Grow and Grow* (1968) began with actors playing Adam and Eve, dressed in synthetic fig leaves, entering the theatre from Hyde Park, and performing from behind two bushes. Their dialogue concerned a debate about whether or not they could be seen nude, eventually inviting the audience to take off their clothes and join them behind the bushes onstage – which people did. The more usual format for Inter-Action projects, however, was one-act theatre (as compiled in Berman's *Ten of The Best*, 1979) or the popular interactive entertainment of the Fun Art Bus.

The pre-eminence of performance as the community arts medium *par excellence* was facilitated by two events: the Theatre Act of 1968 (in which the Lord Chamberlain ceased to be the censor of what theatre could be shown in public) and the launch of *Time Out* magazine in 1969 (which listed all cultural productions in London indiscriminately of status or

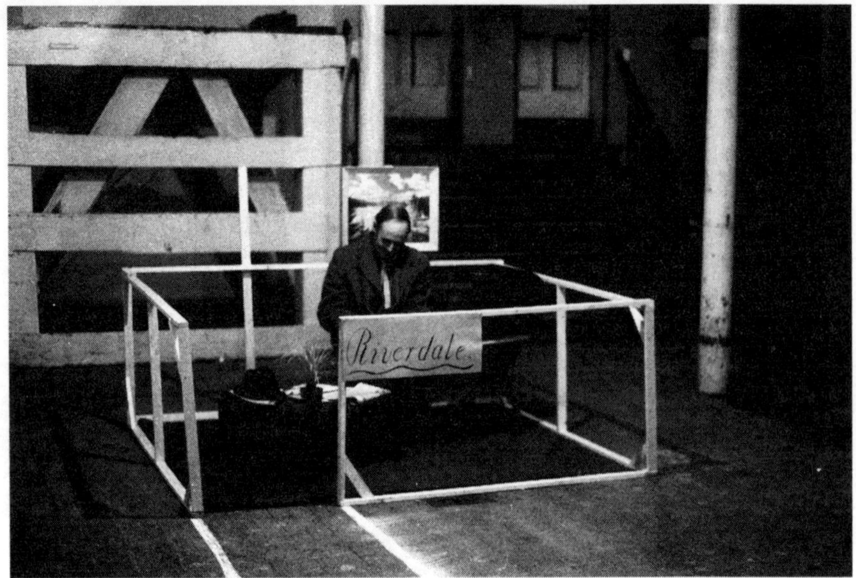

The Blackie, *Sanctuary*, 1969. Middle-class housing 'Riverdale' with occupant.

quality). Both had a huge impact on the promotion of a popular culture committed to broadening audience participation, rather than the consumption of high art as part of a profit-making system. Moreover, collective authorship in theatre did not require a radical overhaul of its traditional *modus operandi*, which has always been collaborative.

Visual art, by contrast, was more fraught as a participatory activity.

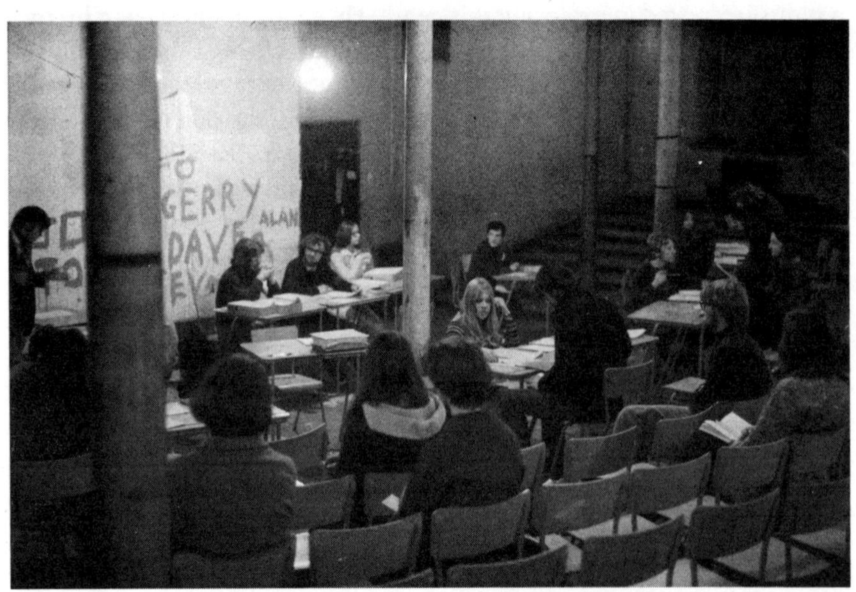

The Blackie, *Sanctuary*, 1969. The housing department.

Historically dominated by singular expression and clearly defined author-ship, both of which are indexed to financial value, visual art was more difficult to reconcile with the community arts agenda. Mural painting as a popular mode of collective expression seemed somewhat dated by the 1970s, so Inter-Action's Liz Leyh took a different approach, making concrete sculptures at the new development of Milton Keynes, the maquettes of which were created in collaboration with local residents. The Blackie also tried to experiment with participatory visual art in the exhibition project 'Towards a Common Language', held in the Educa-tion Room of Liverpool's Walker Art Gallery, 22–28 October 1973. The show comprised blank canvases, boards and paper attached to the gallery walls, ready to be painted by visitors, who had the choice of looking at the completed works or creating one of their own. In one week over 3,475 visitors came to the museum; 301 works were completed by adults and 642 by children. Visitors could take their painting away, or leave it in the gallery, where it would be put on display in poster racks. 'The exhibition will consist of the blank "pieces" and/or people at work/play', wrote Harpe in his notes for show, and 'there will be no "opening" or private view'.[86]

Despite the overlapping ambitions of community arts and contempo-rary art in the 1970s, it is conspicuous that the gestures undertaken by the former remained localised in impact and have fallen out of historical memory; when similar projects were undertaken by a single artist, such as David Medalla, a critical debate was formed, established and defended.[87] Medalla, a London-based Filipino artist associated with Signals Gallery, connected his installations to emancipatory politics and Asian ideas of community. His outdoor work *Down with the Slave Trade!* (1968–71) involved the installation of a selection of chairs, coloured flags and a mesh of colourful plastic tubing in a given city square.[88] People were invited to interact and become entangled with the work, which seemed to serve as a metaphor for oppression, but also as an opportunity for individuals to be linked (at least visually) in collective solidarity. *A Stitch in Time* (also 1968, subsequently shown in Docu-menta 5, 1972) comprised a large swathe of fabric suspended across the gallery, onto which the public were invited to embroider designs and slogans. It is tempting to put Medalla's work into direct comparison with The Blackie's 'Towards a Common Language': both are collectively produced projects whose process is as important as the final result. But in the case of Medalla, substantial photographic documentation allows us to connect these images and ideas to an authored corpus of ongoing interests and visual experiments. The artist produces an object or instal-lation as container for the participatory process, and moves away from traditional modes of drawing and sculpture to the slower activity of embroidery (with its associations of women's work), whose durational

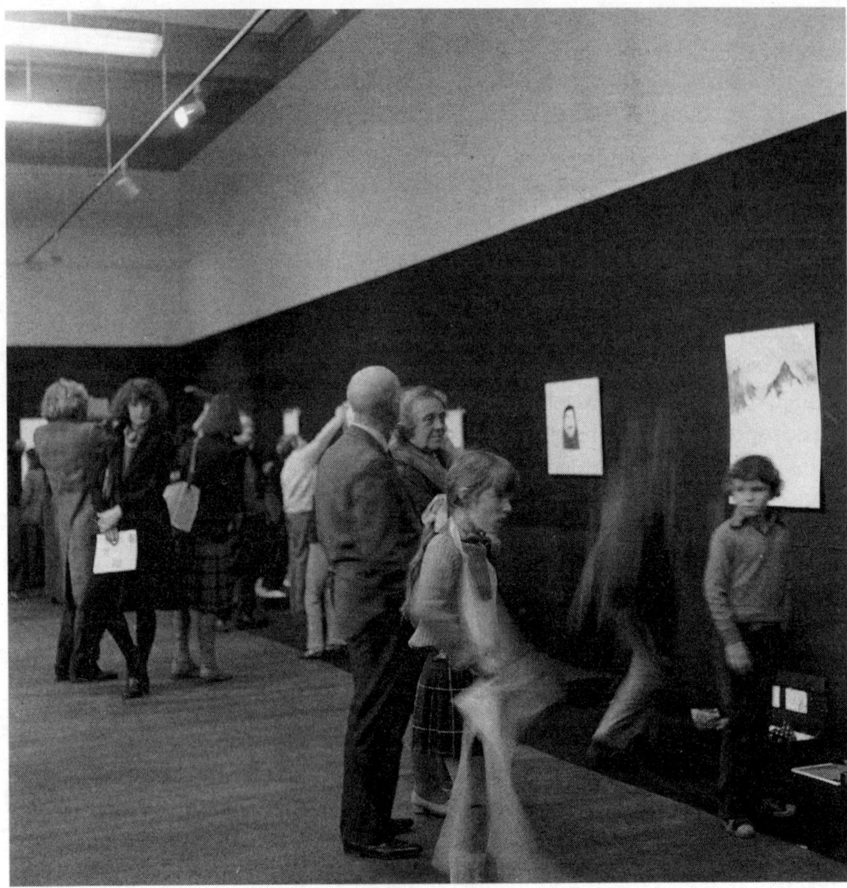

The Blackie, 'Towards a Common Language', 1973

character would also offer a window for social interaction. Even if the specific contents of *A Stitch in Time* amount to a laborious form of graffiti, the totality has a surprisingly consistent, dense and layered appearance, and a not unimpressive sculptural presence. 'Towards a Common Language', by contrast, presents blank canvases in the museum for the public to fill in, but these do not remain on display in the museum to trouble its hierarchies; despite encouraging popular partici-pation, the use of canvases remains conservatively tied to traditional art and single authorship, as does the attachment to a museum as venue. It is therefore not just the presence of a steering authorship (in this case, Medalla) that is decisive for the difference between contemporary and community art, but the entire conceptualisation of his event in terms of authorship, materials (the non-canonical medium of embroidery or plastic tubing), location (a city square) and final result (an installation or performance).

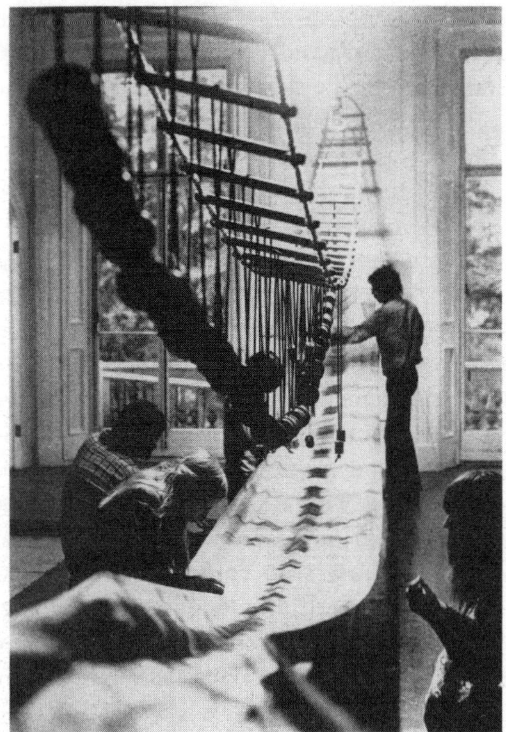

David Medalla, *A Stitch in Time*, 1972

VI. Decline

The Blackie and Inter-Action are in certain respects atypical of the community arts movement, since the majority of organisations founded in the late 1960s and 1970s are no longer in existence. They are both rarities in having survived the funding upheavals of the 1980s, in no small part due to the strong identity of their leadership and inventive ethos.[89] However, it is also important to note that Berman's collaborations with business ensured financial stability for Inter-Action, together with a decidedly apolitical stance ('I didn't think it was appropriate for charities to be politicised').[90] The more common tale is one of gradually eroded funding under Margaret Thatcher's Conservative government (1979–92) leading to the near total disempowerment of the movement by the mid 1980s. Increasing controls were placed upon community arts, and by 1982, the Arts Council had almost entirely ceased funding community arts directly.[91] When we add to this the internal problems of collective work as an ideological mission – summarised by Charles Landry as 'voluntary disorganisation', the deadlock of allocating individual responsibility (since this creates inequality and hierarchy), and the belief that skills are 'bourgeois' – the sustainability of community arts became extremely fragile.[92] Owen Kelly has argued that, by the 1980s, community arts had moved away from its countercultural origins and faced major problems that needed to be resolved if it were to have any critical purchase and avoid its impending fate as a harmless branch of the welfare state ('the kindly folk who do good without ever causing trouble').[93]

The original impulse for community arts – in Kelly's words, 'a liberating self-determination through which groups of people could gain, or regain, some degree of control over their lives' – became a situation of grant-dependency, in which community artists were increasingly positioned 'not as activists, but as quasi-employees of one or another dominant state agency. We were, in effect, inviting people to let one branch of the state send in a group of people to clear up the mess left by another branch of the state, while at the same time denying that we were working for the state.'[94] Mopping up the shortfalls of a dwindling welfare infrastructure, community artists became professionalised, subject to managerial control, and radical politics were no longer necessary or even helpful to their identity and activities. An egalitarian mission was replaced by the conservative politics of those who controlled the purse-strings.[95] For Kelly, this was as much the fault of community arts as the government: the movement was rendered impotent as a result of having no clear understanding of its history and no consistent set of definitions for its activities, only an ethical sense of what it was 'good' to be doing. As we have seen in the Arts Council's 1974 report on community arts, written in close collaboration with its leading figures, the definition of community art is obscure, focusing more on *how* it operated rather than *what* it did: we know that community artists work with children, but we don't know *what* they do with children.[96] What came to define community arts was less an artistic agenda than a behavioural attitude or moral position ('What matters most is not an organisational form, nor bricks and mortar, but the commitment and dedication of the individuals involved').[97] Its criteria were more ethical than artistic, with a politics deliberately left inexplicit so as not to jeopardise funding.

Given this understandable cautiousness – it is a difficult task to be countercultural while asking for state approval and support – it is not hard to see how, in the following year's annual report for the Arts Council, the chairman Lord Gibson could twist the meaning of community arts: from subversive dehierarchisation to a conduit for appreciating the canon of received and established culture. In other words, community arts was no longer about democratising cultural production, but a means to introduce people to elite art, by letting them find out (through first-hand participation in a creative project) what they had been missing by not attending operas and museums. In short, community arts was rebranded as an educational programme, a civilising path leading people towards high culture. For the community arts movement, this had always been a possible side-effect of their activities, but never its main goal, which was more accurately

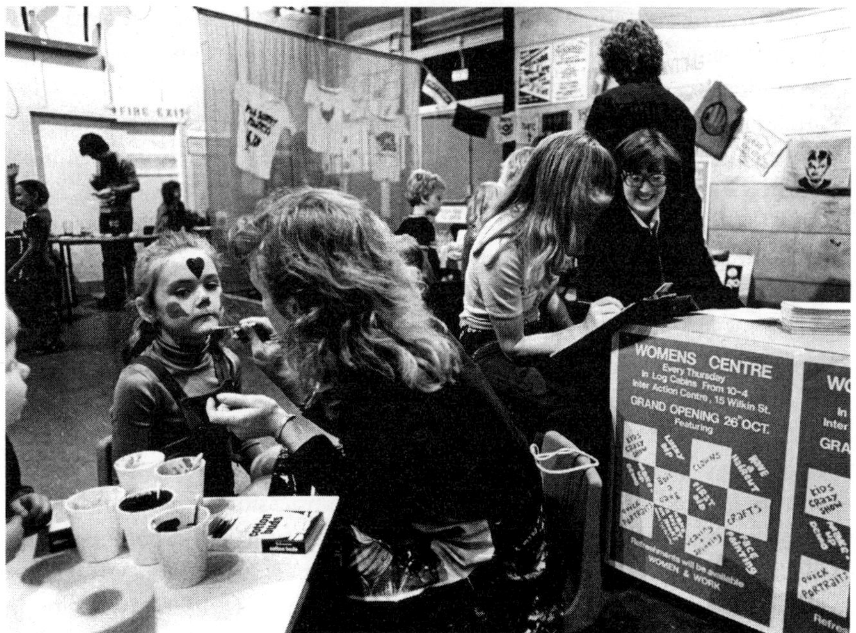

Main hall of the Cedric Price building in Kentish Town, London, undated

premised on *undoing* such cultural hierarchies. This situation finds an uncomfortable parallel in the relationship of participatory and socially engaged art to New Labour cultural funding policy in England (1997–2010), discussed in Chapter 1.

In short, the 1974 report seemed to backfire since its vagueness gave the Arts Council the tools to redevelop community arts for its own ends, i.e. as 'social provision' (face painting for deprived children, getting teenagers to paint the walls of community centres) rather than community empowerment fomenting and supporting campaigns for social justice. One could argue that the original impetus of community arts – as a dehierarchised, participatory mode of art making – found its popular legacy in the 1980s in an emergent rave culture, through groups such as the Survival Research Lab and the Mutoid Waste Company making large-scale temporary installations from recycled materials at outdoor festivals.[98] Its 'high art' legacy is the softly-softly approach of present-day socially engaged art, where situations of negation, disruption and antagonism (the hallmarks of the historic avant-garde) are no longer perceived as viable methods. Sean Cubitt has articulated this convention as follows:

> The problem with art undertaken in the public sphere, with its faint aura of social therapy and social work, is that though it may develop expressive powers in participants, we are always reluctant to tear down the fragile unity of the self that is being expressed. That is the kind of risk it is perhaps fair to ask of yourself, but not of others, relative strangers.[99]

In other words, community arts today tends to self-censor out of fear that underprivileged collaborators will not be able to understand more disruptive modes of artistic production.

Aesthetic quality, which had been deliberately left off the agenda of the Association of Community Artists (founded in 1972), forms the most fraught core of this debate. It is important to remember that the community arts movement rejected this question as synonymous with cultural hierarchy because at the time (the '70s and '80s) the idea of funding culture by and for the marginalised (the working classes, ethnic minorities, women, LGBT, etc.) was automatically dismissed by the establishment as risible and necessarily void of quality. On the other hand, advocating process over product did nothing to rethink the problem of devising alternative criteria by which to reframe evaluation. By avoiding questions of artistic criteria, the community arts movement unwittingly perpetuated the impression that it was full of good intentions and compassion, but ultimately not talented enough to be of broader interest. One of the key problems here – which has many parallels with socially engaged art today – is the fact that community arts has no secondary audience: it has no discursive framing nor an elaborated culture of reception to facilitate comparison and analysis with similar projects, because community art is not produced with such a critical audience in mind. Comparison and evaluation create hierarchy, which is inimical to the principle of equality underlying the community arts project. This prioritisation of individual expression over critical self-examination is, ironically, one of the main reasons for community arts' ghettoisation by the 1980s: a lack of public critical discourse ensured that the stakes were kept low, rendering community art harmless and unthreatening to social and cultural stability.

In the late 1960s, community arts was highly oppositional, since funding for culture was in the hands of the upper classes, who evaluated aesthetic quality on the basis of established culture. Today, when the majority of people in the West have the means to be a producer of their own images and to upload them to a global audience via Flickr, Facebook, and so on, such a dehierarchising agenda arguably has less urgency – even while the bases of these networks are unquestionably commercial, and access to technology is also a class issue. A levelling of access to cultural production nevertheless calls into question the difference between a work of art and social networking. Contemporary art has arguably become a mass-cultural practice, but art requires a spectator: who today is possibly able to view the immeasurable amount of mass contemporary art that exists online? Perhaps, as Boris Groys notes, there is no more society of the spectacle, only a 'spectacle without spectators'.[100] Yet at the same time as virtual communities proliferated in the 1990s, the lure of face-to-face interactions seemed to grow stronger amongst professional artists.[101] Long-term, process-based projects with specific constituencies – of the kind initiated by community arts – return with renewed vigour in this decade under the frame of site specificity. This third iteration of the 'social turn' forms the focus of the following chapter and final section of this book.

7

Former West:
Art as Project in the Early 1990s

In the preceding chapters I have mapped out the history of significant attempts to rethink the role of the artist and the work of art in relationship to society in various forms of participatory art from Europe, Russia and South America. Significantly, these have clustered around two moments of revolutionary upheaval: 1917 (in which artistic production was brought into line with Bolshevik collectivism), and 1968 (in which artistic production lent its weight to a critique of authority, oppression and alienation). The third moment, I would like to posit, is 1989.[1] As might be anticipated, this has a less direct relation to artistic production than the previous two flashpoints, which were characterised respectively by top-down restructuring in the wake of revolution and by a momentum of more or less co-ordinated challenges to authority that were gradually internalised as institutional reform. By contrast, 1989 marks the fall of really existing socialism, a collapse that in the early 1990s was initially celebrated as the end of a repressive regime and then gradually, by the end of the decade, mourned as the loss of a collective political horizon. In Western Europe, this melancholy was given impetus by the dismantling of the welfare state (whose preservation had hitherto provided an important balance to the state provisions of the Eastern bloc) and numerous other neoliberal reforms, particularly in education. In Eastern Europe, the introduction of free market capitalism in the first half of the 1990s was accompanied by an initial optimism that rapidly gave way to disillusionment when faced with the reality of privatisation and 'primitive accumulation'; freedom from the regime had been delivered in only the form of expanded consumer freedom. Because of the slow burn characterising these changes, the impact of 1989 on artistic production is less rapid and less straightforward than the leftist triumph of 1917 and its heroic last moment of resistance in 1968.

What I would like to track in this chapter is the way in which a certain impulse of leftist thinking visibly migrated into Western European artistic production after the collapse of 'grand narrative' politics in 1989. One of the main ways this became manifest was in the rise of a particular term to describe art in the 1990s: the 'project'. Although the term 'project' was used by conceptual artists in the late 1960s (most notably by the Amsterdam-based gallery Art and Project), it tends to denote a *proposal* for a work of art. A project in the sense I am identifying as crucial to art after 1989 aspires to replace the work of art as a finite object with an open-ended, post-studio, research-based, social process, extending over time and mutable in form.[2] Since the 1990s, the project has become an umbrella term for many types of art: collective practice, self-organised activist groups, transdisciplinary research, participatory and socially engaged art, and experimental curating. By focusing on the last two of these tendencies, it is hoped that the trajectory mapped in this chapter will provide a counternarrative to the mainstream commercial and institutional history of art since 1990, which has tended to celebrate identity politics, the apotheosis of video installation, large-scale cibachrome photographs, design-as-art, relational aesthetics, conceptual painting, and spectacular new forms of installation art.[3] My key point, however, is less to define a new tendency than to note that the word chosen to describe these open-ended artistic activities arrives at a moment when there is a conspicuous lack of what we could call a *social* project – a collective political horizon or goal. The fraught relationship between the artistic project and a political project is the central thrust of this chapter.

When surveying art since 1989, it quickly becomes apparent that the interest in participation and social engagement that we now consider to be a characteristic tendency of the last twenty years was in fact rather slow to emerge. The early years of the 1990s are best characterised, perhaps unsurprisingly, as a continuation of the 1980s, unaffected by the newly opened border to the East or the non-Western purview of Jean-Hubert Martin's 'Magiciens de la Terre' (1989), billed as the 'world's first global art show'. Documenta 9 (1992), for example, included only a handful of non-Western artists (in deference to the precedent of 'Magiciens'), but was still an exhibition of European and North American sculpture and painting, focused on the twin centres of New York and Cologne. By contemporary standards its curatorial rhetoric seems irremediably dated, evoking the romantic spirit of the individual producer.[4] Between Documenta 9 and Documenta 10 (1997) lies an aesthetic and intellectual chasm: Catherine David's interdisciplinary approach to the latter exhibition included an 830-page catalogue pointing to a renewed interest in art's social and political orientation. Supplementing art historical essays with texts by philosophers, urbanists and anthropologists, David posited political philosophy and sociology as the new transdisciplinary frameworks for contemporary art.[5] At the same time, it is telling that Documenta 10 as an exhibition did not reflect many of the collective, activist and documentary practices that had already begun to emerge in Europe (and whose promotion would be the task of Documenta 11).

In tracing the re-emergence of a social turn in Europe, 1993 is a key transitional year. Until that point, artist collectives had been a predominantly North American phenomenon, and activist in orientation, as a result of the AIDS crisis and ensuing 'culture wars' over NEA funding. In 1993 we begin to see the formation of Northern European collectives such as Superflex (1993), N55 (1994) and Park Fiction (1994). It is telling that this collectively driven work derives from site-specific practice rather than from theatre and performance, as has tended to be the case in previous chapters. This year, 1993, also marks the consolidation of a new type of site-specific exhibition that would become an important reference point for the emerging globalised contemporary art biennial: exhibitions that directly addressed site as a *socially* constituted phenomenon, rather than as a formal or phenomenological entity. This is in contrast to previous types of site-specific curating, such as 'Sculpture Projects Münster' (1987) and 'Places with a Past: New Site-Specific Art at Charleston's Spoleto Festival' (1991), both of which used site as an evocative formal backdrop for work imbued with historical resonance. To examine this shift I will look at three exhibitions that mark a transition from site-specificity as a matter of tailored formal arrangement to the project of embedding the artist in the social field.[6]

I. 'Project Unité', 'Sonsbeek 93' and 'Culture in Action'

In Europe, two exhibitions paved the way for the shift described above: Kasper König's outdoor sculpture show 'Sculpture Projects Münster' (1987), and Jan Hoet's 'Chambres d'Amis' (1986), an experimental exhibition in which (mainly male and European) artists were invited to create installations in over fifty private homes in Ghent. Although viewing the works in 'Chambres d'Amis' inevitably involved liaising with the owners of each residence, this was not understood to be the exhibition's primary goal.[7] Any social benefits were collateral rather than intentional: 'Chambres d'Amis' was, Hoet notes, an opportunity 'for a fertile aesthetic dialogue between different cultures', and led to 'warm and cordial contacts, not only between artists and hosts, but also between occupiers and visitors'.[8] Most of the works comprised formal and atmospheric reconfigurations of domestic space, rather than dealing with class or identity; the one exception to this was the Belgian artist Jef Geys, who placed French revolutionary slogans on the doors of six lower-income households.[9]

The artist Christian Philipp Müller saw 'Chambres d'Amis' while working with König on the 1987 edition of Münster. Three years later, Müller was invited by the French curator Yves Aupetitallot to have a solo exhibition in Saint Etienne, and while preparing the show decided to visit a housing estate by Le Corbusier in the nearby town of Firminy. Modelled on the Unité d'Habitation in Marseille, the estate in Firminy was in a considerable state of disrepair. Located at the top of a steep hill on the outskirts of the city (in the traditionally dominant position of the aristocracy), the complex was isolated from the city centre and populated by single parents, students, immigrants and old age pensioners. The kindergarten on the roof was fabricated entirely in concrete and therefore unpopular, while Le Corbusier's plans to have a floor of the Unité dedicated to shops was never realised. Since 1983, half of the building had been empty and boarded up, leaving entire 'streets' of apartments empty and uninhabited, separated from the rest of the building by plastic sheeting. Müller suggested to Aupetitallot that it might be possible to hold an exhibition in these apartments. Each one could be taken over by an artist as the site for an installation, on the model of 'Chambres d'Amis', but now using the uninhabited spaces of this aesthetically and ideologically loaded modernist dinosaur.

The exhibition took four years to be realised; in order to pave the way for the project, three newsletters were designed by Müller and circulated from November 1992 onwards. In the final exhibition, forty European and US artists, architects and designers were invited to work *in situ*; they assumed the role of inhabitants, producing work for twenty-nine empty apartments within what one critic called a 'living monument to an unfulfilled utopian pragmatics, a grand, if flawed, integration of art, architecture, design, national culture, economics, politics, and the social'.[10] This insistence led to some difficult experiences for the artists: Mark Dion, for example, recalls being left alone in the apartment over a weekend, unable to speak French, and feeling desperate.[11] A similar feeling afflicted Renée

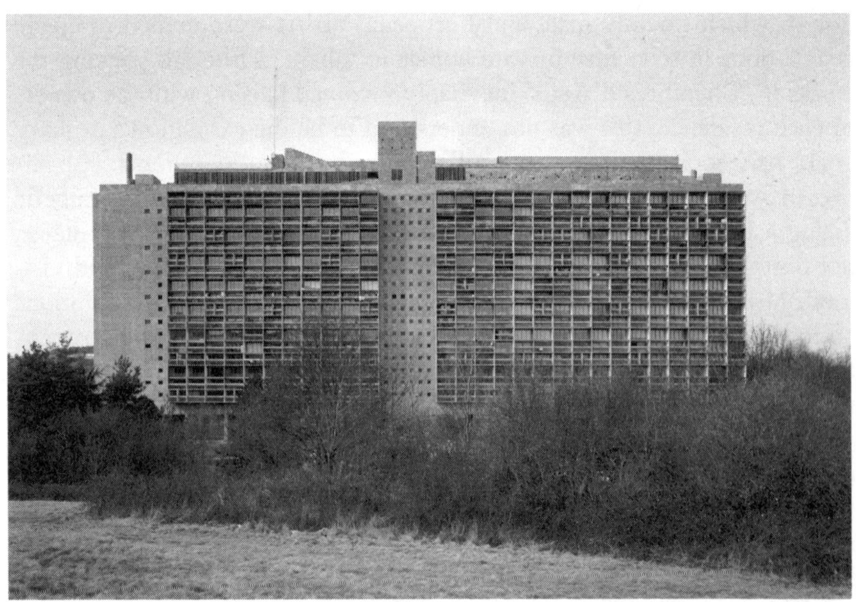

Le Corbusier, Unité d'Habitation, Firminy, begun 1965

Green, whose proposal directly tackled the problem of being invited to work site-responsively: she wore a jacket bearing the word 'immigration', slept in a tent in the apartment, and kept a diary of her time in the building, which she compared to 'the big hotel that Jack Nicholson is supposed to be the caretaker of in *The Shining*'.[12] Aupetitallot hoped to engage some of the working-class Algerian immigrant residents in discussion with the artists; he saw the site as a way to deal with art's relationship to society, with the building as a perfect frame for this question.[13]

In the event, however, most of the artists chose to use the apartment spaces as self-contained galleries for their work, many of which inevitably addressed the building and its architecture. Mark Dion and the French collaborative duo Art Orienté Objet's installation *Scenic Drive 1993* dealt with two aspects of Le Corbusier's architecture – its relationship to nature as vista, and its present-day condition as half inhabited and half ruined.[14] Müller's *Individual Comfort* dealt with the poor acoustics in each apartment, which had turned the utopia of collective living into the nightmare of being permanently aware of one's neighbours; he hired a sound-proofing company to prepare a report on the building's acoustic sound insulation, had the pages framed in gold, and hung them on the walls of a 'bourgeois' interior furnished with soft beige carpets and curtains.

Some artists managed to engage directly with the building's inhabitants. The US duo Clegg & Guttmann devised a *Firminy Music Library*, in which residents made tape compilations from their music collections, and stored them in a cabinet that formed a model of the Corbusier building, each tape placed in a slot that corresponded to the location of the donor's apartment.

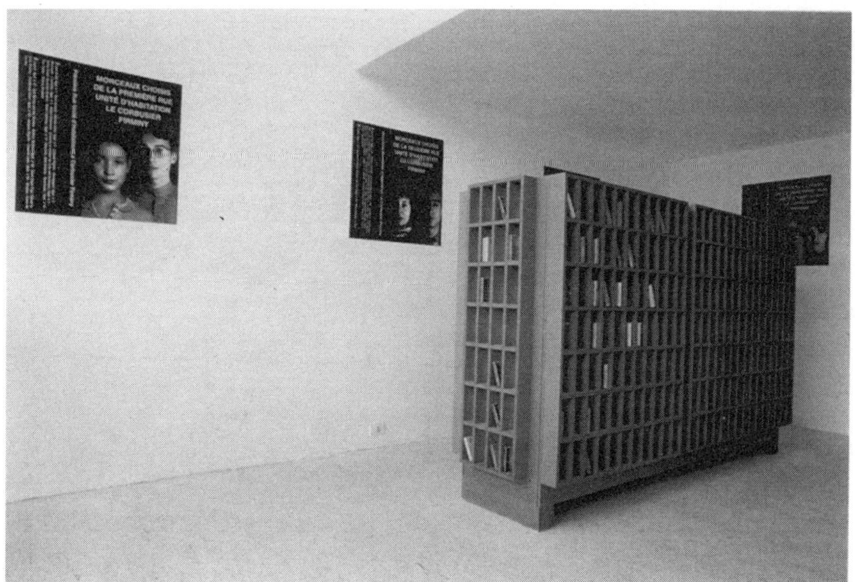

Clegg & Guttmann, *Firminy Music Library*, 1993

Martha Rosler's *How Do We Know What Home Looks Like?* was more socio-logical in spirit, comprising video interviews with residents and statistical information concerning the inhabitants. Milan-based collective Premiata Ditta's *Relationship Maps* attempted to visualise data derived from question-naires handed out to the Unité's residents, while the German artist Regina Möller worked with some of the children in the building to create dolls' houses, an allusion to Le Corbusier's concept of the apartment as a playful pedagogical space. Heimo Zobernig converted one of the apartments into a café, reportedly the most popular installation in the whole show.[15]

A smaller group of artists, seemingly at a loss as to what to do in the building, reflected on the process of making site-specific work. Renée Green's *Apartment Inhabited by the Artist Prior to the Opening* pondered the problems of being a nomadic artist: viewers could see traces of her daily living activity and attempts to perform the role of an artist in her notes and sketches of the landscape. A. Arefin presented an installation of files show-ing the correspondence between each of the artists and Yves Aupetitallot, while Stephan Dillemuth, invited to participate in both 'Project Unité' and 'Sonsbeek 93', produced documentaries about both shows, screening the Firminy video at Sonsbeek and vice versa.

As this range of works indicate, 'Project Unité' is clearly transitional but contains a number of projects that shift European exhibition-making into a more socially conscious framework. Firstly, its location in a partially inhabited building whose architecture contained the aspiration to func-tional and communal living. In this instance, the use of the word 'project' rather than 'exhibition' in the title seems to imply that the totality of the

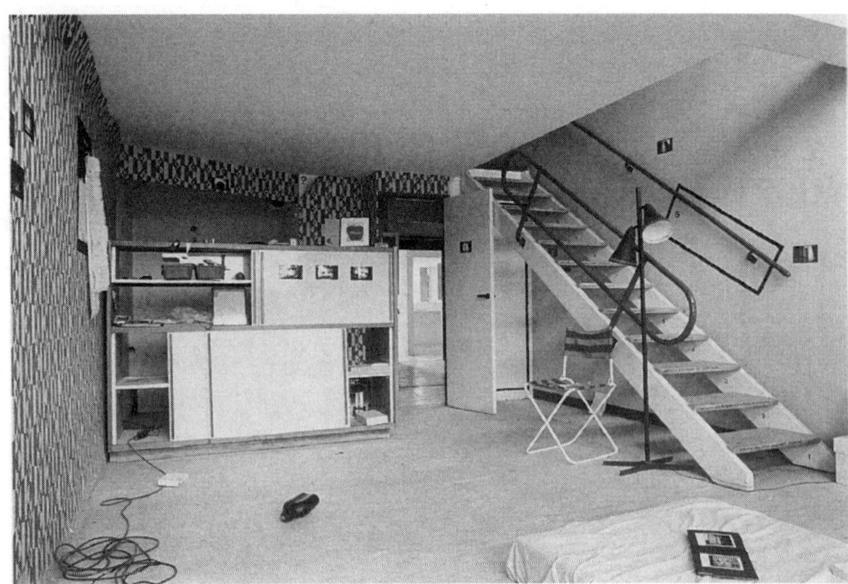

Renée Green, *Apartment Inhabited by the Artist Prior to the Opening*, 1993

situation (building, residents, artist residencies, installations) was more important than a final exhibition of 'works'. It carries connotations (which would accelerate in the 1990s) of art overlapping and engaging with the social sphere, rather than being at one remove from it – more akin to an architectural project, a particularly apt point of reference for Firminy. Secondly, art was put into direct confrontation with an 'authentic' everyday audience. This encounter, however, was accompanied by manifold anxieties about the artists' authenticity of response.[16] The confrontation between artists and locals made the question of patronage and intervention particularly acute. Renée Green recalled that the opening was awkward: artists and residents were all invited to a party on the top floor of the building, but 'there was a palpable tension in the air. The artists stayed in groups with other artists and art world infrastructural personnel, the tenants stayed in groups with their friends and neighbours. No speech was made. What could have been said?' A fight broke out as an inebriated male tenant began punching in all directions.[17] This tension became one of the central arguments in Hal Foster's influential essay 'The Artist as Ethnographer', in which he argued that inviting artists to work site-specifically, particularly in areas with lower-income residents, shifted the discursive frame from class to cultural alterity, from an economic discrepancy to questions of cultural identity.[18] Alluding to Walter Benjamin's essay 'The Author as Producer' – in which Benjamin criticised an artistic attitude of benevolent 'patronage' towards the working class by merely representing the latter in art and literature – Foster argues that contemporary artists of the kind exhibiting at Firminy operated on a similar basis of 'sociological condescension'.[19] In the light of Benjamin's article, which famously advocates collaborative authorship and the development of an 'apparatus' that allows as many people to collaborate as possible, it seems striking that Foster nevertheless dismisses as 'facilitated self-representation' those artists who tried to produce a participatory apparatus (such as Clegg & Guttmann).

Foster's argument highlights the widening gap between North American criteria for social engagement and European approaches to this problem in the 1990s. It is telling, for example, that 'Project Unité' included French artists who would later be associated with relational aesthetics (Dominique Gonzalez-Foerster and Philippe Parreno) who produced works that have only an oblique engagement with context; rather than addressing the environment with a theoretical or critical framework, they created a fictional, literary, imaginative correlate within the space of the exhibition.[20] The German/US artists, by contrast, have a more pragmatic and critical approach (exemplified in Rosler's sociological documentary, or Müller's investigation into the building's acoustics). This separation between the French 'relationality' and German/North American 'criticality' becomes more marked as the 1990s progress; 'Project Unité' is one of the last moments when this generation of artists appear alongside each other. The 'relational' Europeans would come to perceive the critical mode as didactic, while the North Americans would denigrate the relational work as uncritically spectacular. Although there is a grain of truth in both characterisations, these positions can be ascribed to different intellectual and pedagogic formations in the 1980s: the French artists were reared on post-structuralist authors (Lyotard, Deleuze and especially Baudrillard) for whom there is no 'outside' position. The reception of critical theory in the US was largely centred on psychoanalysis and the strong critical judgements of the Frankfurt School, along with critical ethnography, identity politics and post-colonialism, which gave rise to the idea of clearly oppositional modes of artistic 'criticality'. The resulting difference is between forms that operate through fiction and opacity, and those that are expressed unambiguously (through interviews, information, statistics, and so on).

We can move more swiftly through the other two exhibitions: one month after the opening of 'Project Unité', 'Sonsbeek 93' opened in Sonsbeek Park in the Dutch town of Arnhem. Unlike Firminy, which took place in a city without a tradition of public art, Arnhem had intermittently hosted an outdoor sculpture festival since 1949. For the 1993 edition, its North American curator Valerie Smith produced a diaristic catalogue that usefully allows us to trace the process of commissioning site-specific art at this moment, and the curatorial expectations surrounding it. In this extraordinarily frank publication, Smith reproduces her correspondence with the artists, including failed and rejected proposals, and allows us to see her criteria for inclusion and exclusion.[21] She proposes to make an exhibition of work about 'context-oriented issues' and 'the individual's relation to the social environment': 'The art for "Sonsbeek 93" should be site-specific or situational work', she wrote. 'The work must create meaning from and for the place in which it exists.'[22] As she goes about negotiating with artists in preparation for the show, she admits to her disappointment when they arrive in Arnhem with a preconceived idea about what they want to do (e.g. Marc Quinn) or when they avoid a site visit altogether (e.g. Alighiero e Boetti).[23] Her assumption is that artists will spend at least twenty-four hours in Arnhem and develop a response to the city, which will give them a clear idea for a project – by today's standards, a very brief time indeed. What emerges from Smith's candid publication of correspondence is not just a case study in site-specific curating, but the clear impression that the curator is no longer a mediator between artist and public (in the museum model), but someone with a clear desire to co-produce a socially relevant art for multiple audiences, and who views the exhibition itself as a total argument.[24]

Although most of the work in 'Sonsbeek 93' was sculptural, there were two projects key to the history I am tracing. Firstly, Mark Dion's intervention in Bronbeek, a museum attached to the royal home for retired veterans, whose collection comprised objects that Dutch soldiers and sailors had brought back from their overseas missions (stuffed animals, plant specimens, ethnographic objects, and so on). His contribution addressed the display system of the museum but also a situation of conflict there: the retired veterans disliked the museum's curator, whose job it was to decide which of their objects would enter the collection after they passed away. Dion's project proceeded from a lithograph showing the museum's original nineteenth-century display cabinets (destroyed after the institution had been revamped in the 1960s); he had two of these refabricated, filling one with the objects that appeared in the lithograph, and the other with mementos belonging to the veterans, specifically those objects which would not make it into the collection upon their deaths, but which were of great personal significance: a cookbook from a prisoner of war camp; a carved figurine from a man who had to leave behind the love of his life in Indonesia; and a silver steam-engine, built by one of the veterans as his wife was dying of cancer.[25] Secondly, Irene and Christine Hohenbüchler's residency in Arnhem prison, working with inmates to produce a series of paintings, installed in little huts outside the prison, plus an installation in the main hall of the panopticon, using the artists' signature materials of wool and fabric. The residency built upon their previous collaborations with adults with learning disabilities and led to

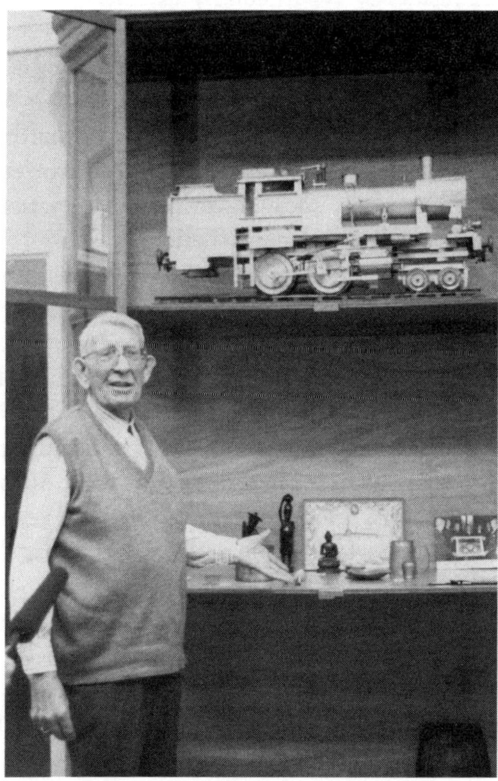

Mark Dion, *Project for the Royal Home for the Retirees*, 1993

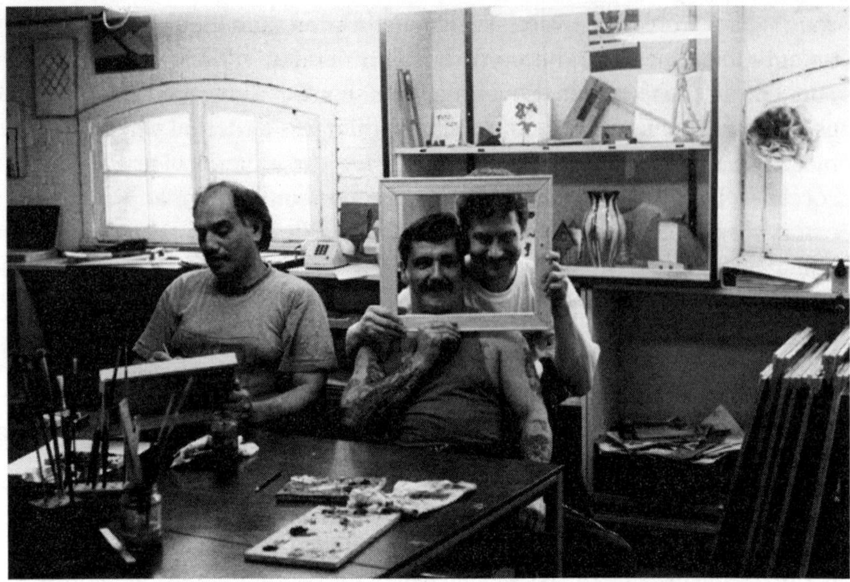

Irene and Christine Hohenbüchler, untitled project for 'Sonsbeek 93'

subsequent projects in two psychiatric clinics in Germany, but the sisters recall the Sonsbeek residency as particularly stressful.

Given the current vogue for referring to this kind of work as 'social' and 'political', it seems surprising that Smith was reluctant to label her show as such.[26] It is striking that Yves Aupetitallot expresses the same sentiments when interviewed by Dillemuth about 'Project Unité': 'the starting point of this project was and is', he says, 'the relation between art and society, but society in a very large sense, it's not only social art or public art'.[27] Later, Aupetitallot explains that, for him, the social denotes 'national responsibility' rather than 'specific social groups', and he alludes to the Le Corbusier building as cultural patrimony. That both curators are reluctant to call their shows 'social', despite this being an important aspect of their curatorial agendas, indicates the degree of conservatism that was then dominant in the art world (no better image of which was the press's hostile response to the 1993 Whitney Biennial, which opened in March that year and embraced a critical identity politics); it also points to the lack of vocabulary for describing this work. Prior to the institutionalisation of participatory art in the wake of relational aesthetics there was simply no adequate language for dealing with works of art in the social sphere that were not reducible to activism or community art.[28]

If Smith and Aupetitallot show a reluctance to name their exhibitions as shows of 'social art', then the community-based work being formulated in the US at this time — which was about to be framed by the artist Suzanne Lacy as 'new genre public art' — showed no shortage of faith in such a mission. There, an artistic project dovetailed with a social conscience, if not exactly an explicitly leftist political project. Lacy was one of eight artists and collectives who participated in an ambitious exhibition of socially engaged art, 'Culture in Action', curated by Mary Jane Jacob in Summer 1993. The eight projects comprising this show stand as the most extreme instance of 'the social turn' in exhibition form that year.

Intended as a critique of Sculpture Chicago, a biennial that had taken place throughout the 1980s, 'Culture in Action' built on Chicago's eminent public art tradition as one of the first cities to install a large-scale work in public following the introduction of the NEA's Art in Public Places programme in 1967 (when Picasso's *Untitled [Head of a Woman]* was installed in Daley Plaza). In contrast to this 'plop art' model, 'Culture in Action' deliberately moved commissions away from the central downtown area and into marginalised, predominantly low-income neighbourhoods. It resulted in eight projects from a wide cross-section of artists who worked with local community groups over a number of months and even years. Only one of the projects could be said to have resulted in a conventionally 'sculptural' object, Suzanne Lacy's *Full Circle*: a temporary sculpture of boulders (with bronze plaques) that formed a monument to women in Chicago, both compensation for and commentary on the fact that no women had ever been honoured in the city's public monuments. But although the work resembles a sculptural intervention in the manner of Beuys's *7,000 Oaks* (1982), it would be wrong to read it solely in visual terms. The process of nominating and selecting 100 women to be honoured on the boulders was done by an advisory group of fifteen women, and culminated in a *Full Circle* dinner on 30 September 1993 – a meal for fourteen eminent women leaders from around the world. The work is typical of Lacy's output in its symbolism, ritualistic finale and relatively strong visual identity – even if the process remains invisible in the final object.

Of the seven other projects, I will focus only on that of Mark Dion, since he participated in all three exhibitions that form the focus of this chapter. In Chicago, Dion worked with a team of fifteen high-school students drawn from two schools (one private and one public) on a project that anticipates the present decade's fascination with education, discussed in Chapter 9. Dion's project had three phases: firstly, a rainforest study programme; secondly, a field trip to Belize (where the artist had worked on a Tropical Education Center in 1989–90); and thirdly, the creation of the Chicago Urban Ecology Action Group, based in an experimental field station set up in the Lincoln Park district of the city. Located in a former clubhouse, the field station was intended to operate as 'an art installation, a workshop, and an ecology information center in operation all summer long'.[29] Each week was themed around topics – such as Darwin, Ecology, or Classification – and featured guest speakers, cooking and tours, while also serving as a hub for the group's community gardening and lagoon cleaning projects. Dion recalls that the response to this 'eco drop-in centre and clubhouse' was disappointing: although the group was on site throughout the summer,

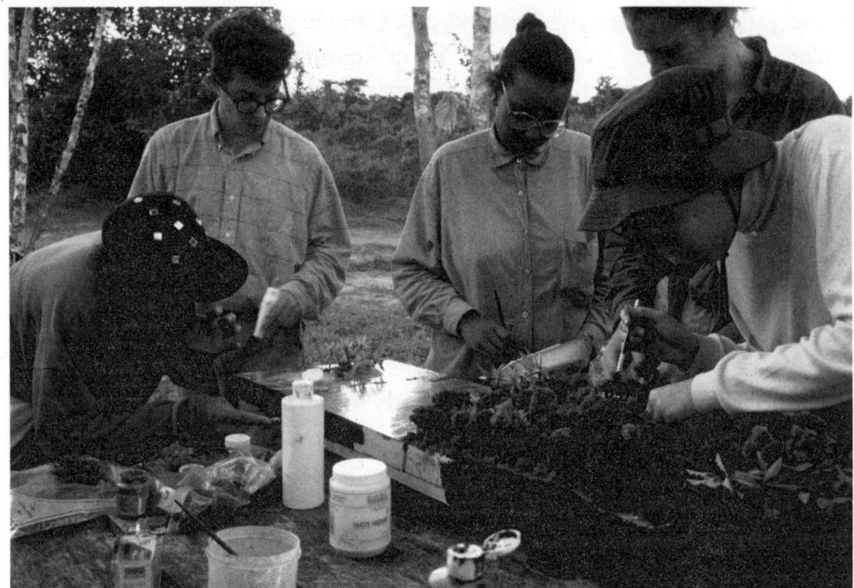

Mark Dion, *Chicago Urban Ecology Action Group*, 1993. The Chicago Tropical Ecology Study Group in the Cockscombe Basin Wildlife Sanctuary, Belize.

hardly any visitors showed up beyond the bus tours on Saturdays, and even then people didn't know how to engage with a participatory, process-based project that encouraged first-hand involvement.[30] Today, he says, viewers have learnt how to look at this type of work, but in 1993, 'the art world did not salute this flag'.[31]

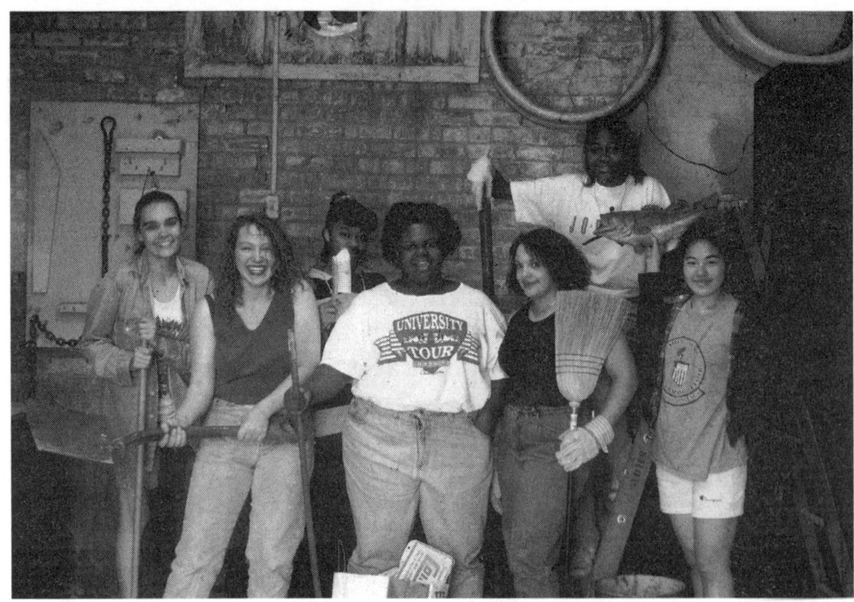

Mark Dion, *Chicago Urban Ecology Action Group*, 1993. Members of the Chicago Urban Ecology Action Group in the clubhouse.

As Dion indicates, this change of approach to exhibition-making – embedding artists in the social field, with the request that they work with specific constituencies – not only changed the artists' relationship to the work of art (which became a set of more or less finely tuned social relationships, rather than a portable or even visible object), it also changed the viewer's relationship to seeing art. Johanne Lamoureux has noted how site-specific exhibitions turn the viewer into a flâneur or tourist: 'the traditional exhibition, complete with its clashes and joys in the placing of works, yields to the journey. *As the map substitutes for the picture, the city replaces the museum.*'[32] With 'Culture in Action', even the city ceded and dissolved into social constituencies. As a consequence, the demands placed upon the viewer were even tougher, to the point where spectatorship became an almost impossible position. Christian Philipp Müller recalls the anti-climactic nature of the official bus tour: hours of traffic had to be negotiated in order to see the eight projects, but there was barely anything to view at each site. The artists Grennan and Sperandio, who had collaborated with unionised members of a confectionary plant to design and produce their own candy bar called *We Got It!*, recall that their stop 'took in a display in a supermarket retailing the chocolate, with a meet and greet and free gift'.[33] Müller's memory of this was even more fleeting: being driven at high speed past a billboard advertising *We Got It!* with Mary Jane Jacob exclaiming 'There it is! There it is! . . . Oh, you missed it.'[34]

The emergence of the term 'project' to describe the new social orientation of art emerges with full force at this juncture. 'Project Unité' self-evidently references this shift by referring to its entire enterprise as a 'project', with all the connotations of an architectural project that organises social relations. In the catalogue for 'Sonsbeek 93', Valerie Smith states that she would like to include 'collaborative *projects*, which would directly question the idea of a single artistic identity and celebrate collective creativity': 'In "Sonsbeek 93" artists are penetrating institutions. They take on another role, like . . . working in a prison, making a radio narrative, making a work where you have to eat a meal in a restaurant.'[35] Although Mary Jane Jacob doesn't define the term 'project', it is her systematic word of choice for the eight practices she presented in 'Culture in Action': all are embedded in real social systems and involve participation with lower class or marginalised communities. On a formal level they are uncertain in their beginnings and endings, and impossible to represent visually through photographic documentation. In terms of a social goal, the projects in 'Culture in Action' are also somewhat contradictory: on the one hand, they express an activist desire to be interacting directly with new audiences and accomplishing concrete goals; on the other, they do this through an embrace of open-endedness, in which the artist is reconfigured as a facilitator of others' creativity. The inadequacy of the traditional catalogue format to convey this conflicting agenda is painfully apparent: the photographs in *Culture in Action* are largely unhelpful illustrations accompanying a series of conventional monographic essays and a general theoretical overview; a busy layout with awkwardly cropped photographs, frequently overlaid with text, tries to compensate for the images' inability to convey the complexity of each project. The two European exhibitions are more adventurous in attempting to translate the new attitude into publishing formats. As previously noted, the catalogue of 'Sonsbeek 93' took the form of a diaristic journal in which we follow the curator's attempt to communicate her desire for a contextually sensitive art to a more or less willing selection of artists. Yet this catalogue is also confusing, as the reader has no way of differentiating between proposals, semi-realised projects, and those that became finished works. In the case of Firminy, this research-based approach was to take the form of five books, of which only three were produced: the first comprises the architectural history of the Unité d'Habitation at Firminy, together with sociological information about its inhabitants (age, class, occupation, etc.). The second presents the project proposals, in greater or lesser degrees of comprehensibility; some are shown as drawings, some as essays, while some artists don't contribute anything at all. The third volume shows the final realised projects and installation shots.[36]

Further differences can be noted between the European iterations of this trend and the North American. Compared to the European shows, 'Culture in Action' was fully theorised, grounded, critical, pragmatic and consistent – but the professionalism of this structure also attracted criticism, even from the artists ('If "Culture in Action" often felt and looked like a charity fundraiser, that's because it articulated that queasy, self-contradictory relationship between patronage and cause that such events always do').[37] The European shows were less rigorously analysed, more evocative, and explored the social in the sense of a collaborative working process and cultural patrimony, rather than targeting specific (and disenfranchised) communities. The 'social' therefore holds myriad connotations at this moment: dialogue, collaboration, process, diversified audiences, democratic participation – with the spectre of socialism as a political analogue for all of this hovering uncertainly in the background. The question of how to gauge the success of these projects continues to be vexed. At the time, they were almost unanimously perceived to be failures (as one reviewer of 'Sonsbeek 93' noted: '[this] is primarily an exhibition by and for the artists themselves. The public, unfortunately, is left stranded on Platform 4B, secure only in the knowledge that they are missing something').[38] Yet the task these exhibitions began to undertake was an important one: to reconceive the audience as plural, a combination of participants and viewers from many levels of society.[39]

II. Performative Exhibitions

Similar experiments with spectatorship were taking in place in France at this time (and to a lesser extent in Germany), but with an emphasis on 'sociability' rather than social responsibility. A younger generation of artists including Pierre Huyghe, Philippe Parreno and Dominique Gonzales-Foerster turned to the exhibition as a creative medium. The formal experiments introduced by these artists included prolonging the period before an exhibition opened and after it closed, including works that may be off-site or absent from the actual exhibition space, changing the appearance of the exhibition through the duration of the show, and interfering with the exhibition's communicational apparatus (audio-guides, information labels, tours, and so on). Another strategy was to read other presentation formats through the lens of the exhibition: a magazine (Maurizio Cattelan's *Permanent Food*, 1995–), a night of performance (Parreno and Hans-Ulrich Obrist's 'Il Tempo del Postino', 2007–) or a farm in Thailand (Rirkrit Tiravanija's *The Land*, 1999–) were all conceived as types of display. The actual importation of other formats *into* the exhibition – music, magazines, cooking, journalism, advertising, television, new technologies, and particularly cinema – substituted for sytems of representation and illustration.[40] Nicolas Bourriaud went so far as to claim that 'it is the *socius* . . . that is the true exhibition site for artists of the current generation' – a socius understood, however, less in terms of society's users and inhabitants, than as the distributive channels through which information and products flow.[41]

For this generation of artists, the desire to experiment with exhibitions derived primarily from a frustration with the conventions of exhibition-making as inherited from the 1980s, based around the presentation of objects for consumption on the market.[42] As early as 1991, the curator Eric Troncy dismissed the extent to which 'an exhibition is nothing more than a social show, a convention', and he later lamented how the 1980s had reduced the exhibition to a 'mere showroom'.[43] In particular he objected to thematic group shows weighed down by a theme and resulting in an illustrative outcome. Rather than conceiving of the exhibition as an a posteriori format in which to exhibit already existing works, Troncy preferred to think the exhibition as 'an *a priori* artists' project – an experiment whose outcome was altogether uncertain . . . throughout the different phases of its successive materialisations'.[44] At stake in this shift – from a group show organised around a theme, to the creation of a project that unfolds in time – was a position of authorial renunciation: to 'delegate to the artists the collective responsibility for the exhibition in its entirety'.[45] Troncy thus positioned himself as a collaborator or facilitator working alongside the artist (a position not unlike that of the community artist working to facilitate lay creativity). This desire for open-endedness formed part of a generational value-system that rejected prescriptive meanings *tout court*; for Troncy, Bourriaud and their collaborators, open-endedness stood against the closed meanings of critical art in the '60s and '70s.[46]

A glance at Eric Troncy's 'No Man's Time' (1991) evidences this recon-figuration of interest in the exhibition as an open-ended project with an emphasis on collaboration and showing work in process. The twenty-two artists invited to 'No Man's Time' at the Villa Arson in Nice spent a month in residence to participate in a brainstorming session prior to the exhibition, which showed projects created or performed specifically for the venue. The catalogue contains the curator's diary of these weeks (the 'black box') emphasising the conviviality of this method: beer, barbecues, the coming and going of different artists, and transcripts of their conversations. One of the key ideas to emerge was that of the exhibition as a film, with various works taking the form of actors – some with starring roles, others as extras. Several pieces actually comprised performances, including Pierre Joseph's 'walk-ons' – a leper and a medieval warrior roaming the exhibition space – and Philippe Parreno's *No More Reality* (a demonstration by children, in which they held banners bearing this slogan).[47] The cinematic reference was pursued in Parreno's billboard, installed outside the exhibition venue, emblazoned with the slogan 'Welcome to Twin Peaks', in reference to David Lynch's popular TV series. Inside, a labyrinth with variously sized doors was positioned at the entrance to the space, with a view to mildly disorienting the spectator. Theory was less important than popular culture – as manifested in the 'playlist' section at the back of the

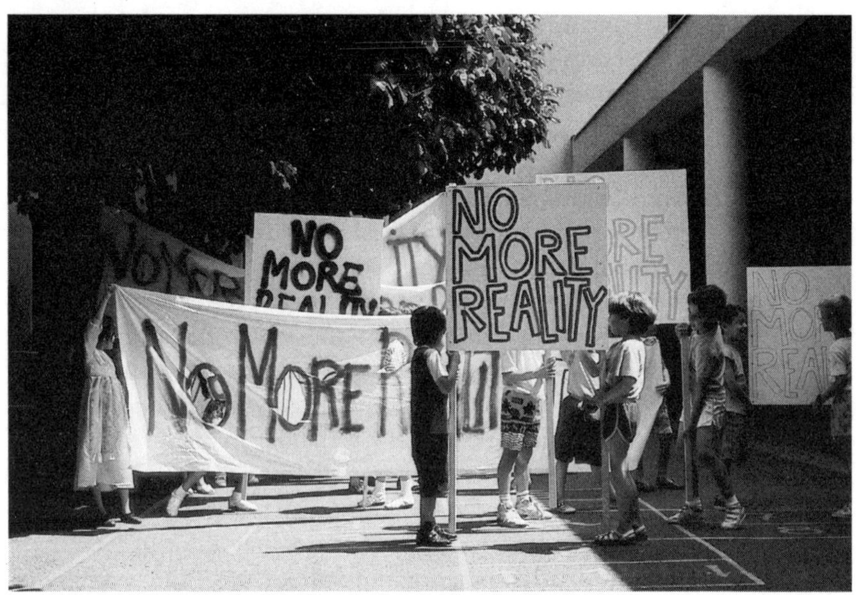

Philippe Parreno, *No More Reality*, 1991

'No Man's Time' catalogue, in which each artist nominated their top five songs and works of art. For a general audience, such lists offered a way to know the artists through their preferences, but they also reinforce the impression that Troncy's exhibitions were organised by selecting personalities rather than works; as Tiravanija summarised: 'The artist is the work. Invite them and they will make/or not make'.[48]

'No Man's Time', like many of Troncy's exhibitions, was less a thesis on society or pop culture than an assertion of the common cultural interests of that particular constellation of artists. Asserting that 'we went out of our way to avoid installing anything definitive', since 'even the title of our show places it in interval territory', Troncy's self-reflexive elusiveness epitomised his peers' preference for opacity and narrative over didacticism.[49] Yet, it hardly undertook the job of mediating this position to an outside audience, which Troncy readily acknowledged when he noted that 'while the protagonists may be enthralled by their subject matter, it may prove boring for some of the public'.[50] The viewer was subject to an experience of incompletion – of being put in the position, Troncy wrote, of piecing together the show like 'fragments which enable the reconstruction of a crime'.[51] In the case of 'No Man's Time', the 'crime' was an invisible month of social interactions before the exhibition opened to the public, and to which the latter had only partial access through the oblique and diaristic narratives of the catalogue.

It has often been remarked that 'relational' exhibitions from this period have the appearance of a non-individualised totality rather than being the work of many individuals – although in retrospect particular works stand out as distinctly authored, and floor plans indicate quite clearly defined individual areas of display. One of the most notable contributors to this body of exhibitions, although not included in 'No Man's Time', was Rirkrit Tiravanija, whose installations and events have done more than any other artist to propel convivial and open-ended participation into the artistic and institutional mainstream. Many of his works in the early 1990s were contributions to the prolonged period of collective gestation leading to the opening of a show. In 'Backstage' (1993), curated by Barbara Steiner and Stephan Schmidt-Wulffen at the Hamburger Kunstverein, thirty-one artists were encouraged to interact with the newly opened space, including the exhibition halls, cellar, storage area, restrooms and the director's office, in order to scrutinise the role of the institution. Tiravanija's contribution, *untitled 1993 (flädlesuppe)*, comprised a table and two benches, with industrial metal shelving (near the delivery entrance) supporting basic cooking equipment. It was operational only in the weeks leading up to the show, rather than during the exhibition itself. One of the paradoxes of Tiravanija's practice is that in intensifying convivial relations for a small group of people (in this case, the exhibiting artists), it produces greater exclusivity vis-à-vis the general public.

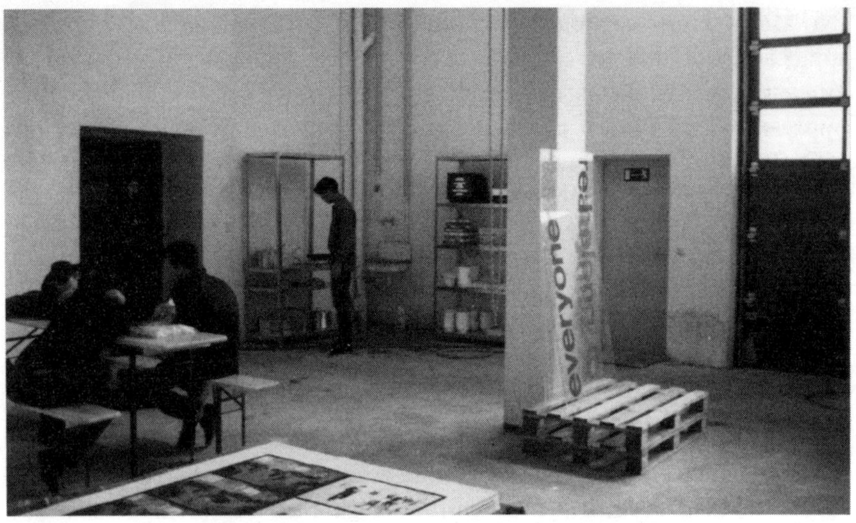

Rirkrit Tiravanija, *untitled 1993 (flädlesuppe)*, 1993

Troncy has repeatedly stressed that his curatorial experimentation derived from the artists' own interests in open-endedness.[52] The success of this approach nevertheless relies on a group of artists who are loosely sympathetic to each other's work, who are already in dialogue with each other, and among whom communication is relatively clear. When this model of exhibition-making is imposed by a curator on a group of artists who were not already in conversation, and for whom a reflection on the exhibition as medium was not a direct problematic in their work, the results immediately become more fraught. The exhibition 'Interpol' (1996, Färg-fabriken, Stockholm), a curatorial collaboration between the Russian curator Viktor Misiano and Swedish curator Jan Åman, provides an important final case study in considering the plight of spectatorship in performative exhibitions, as well as highlighting the differences between Western artists and those from the newly emergent former East. Like many of Eric Troncy's exhibitions, the entire structure of 'Interpol' consciously attempted to be 'performative', in other words, to be made on site by the artists in collaboration with each other: the curators aspired to 'abandon the rules of the old game and create a process that would set its own rules'.[53] Diplomatically, the project was an exercise in cultural politics: the aim was to form 'a new, collaborative and democratic model for the realisation of the Russian-Western project at the international and Moscow scenes'.[54] To achieve this, Åman and Misiano chose artists from Sweden and Russia respectively, who could in turn select one or more co-authors from any region.[55] However, the playfulness of this exhibition structure quickly hit rocky ground: the different ideological contexts from which the participants were drawn led to outright disagreements and eventually to a complete breakdown of communication.

The artists were asked to meet in both Stockholm (1994) and Moscow (1995) over the three-year planning process to formulate the exhibition as a collective. Ostensibly, then, we have a continuation of the 'social' understood as conviviality that can be seen in Troncy's shows of this period. However, the geopolitical stakes were higher in the case of 'Interpol', since Misiano notes that both Sweden and Russia were experiencing the 'end of socialism' in different ways: for Northern Europe, in the dismantling of the welfare state, and for Russia, in the transition to deregulated neoliberal capitalism. This was further reflected in ideological and artistic differences between the two regions: state protectionism guaranteed a good livelihood and prestige for Swedish artists, while in Russia the arts were marginalised and without institutional support. Indeed, Misiano argued that being an artist in Russia was a result of 'moral self-identification' rather than 'common sense', since there was no possible career to be made from this decision.[56]

The curators hoped to fill the hangar-like space of Färgfabriken with a total installation, but cultural rifts formed early on: Misiano reports that the Russian artists had clearly articulated ideas that they wanted to discuss, while the Swedes were dismissive of the idea of discussion. The Europeans resented the Russians for shirking responsibility for their projects, while the latter felt that they received no help or support from Stockholm. Many of the artists began to request to work alone, collaborations shifted and dissolved and a few participants (such as Lotta Antonsson) quit before the exhibition was finalised. Increasingly, East/West prejudices set in, so that when it came to the time of installation, dialogue had all but broken down into hardened stereotypes. On the night before the opening, Dmitri Gutov executed a performance entitled *The Last Supper*, in which both curators and all the artists participated in a dinner; Gutov urged them to discuss the artistic co-operation leading up to the show and videotaped the proceedings.[57] During the meal, the Russian artist Alexander Brener stated that the project was a failure, and expressed scepticism that a participatory structure could itself be the content of the show, with no further guidance or position from the curators.[58] This open-endedness had of course, worked successfully in Troncy's shows, since the artists – already in dialogue – had risen to the occasion. But when there were ideological differences (particularly over the centrality or otherwise of dialogue in making art), it led to conflicts between the participants, and a disconnected, incoherent exhibition.

Mirroring 'Interpol''s participatory structure, several of the artists' contributions sought to involve the audience directly. Vadim Fishkin proposed a work in which each of the participating artists would have a mobile phone, on which visitors to the exhibition could reach them at any point.[59] Carl Michael von Hausswolff and two collaborators organised a 'sleep in', comprising a row of mattresses on which the audience was invited to sleep alongside the artists for the first few nights of the

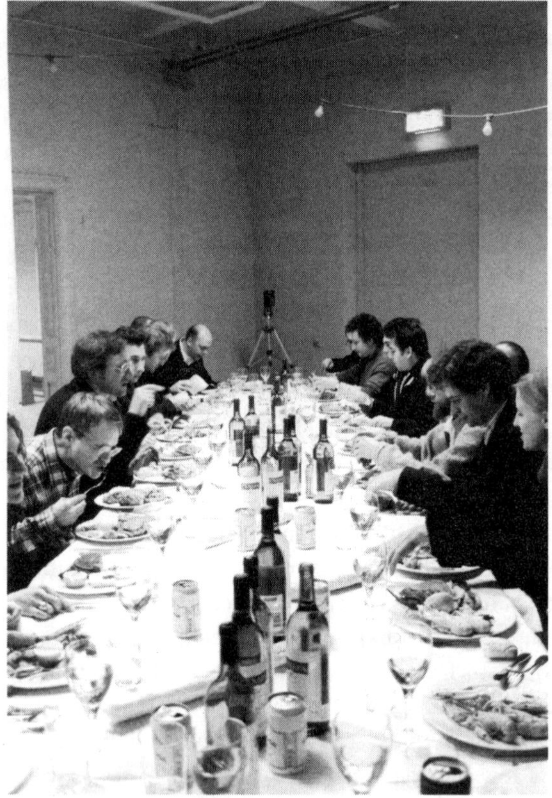

Dmitri Gutov, *The Last Supper*, 1996

exhibition. As with Troncy's shows, there were special performances during the private view; however, during the opening, relations between the artists grew openly antagonistic. Dominating the centre of the exhibition hall was a large installation by Chinese artist Wenda Gu, who had collected hair from Russia and Sweden and used it to create a large, tunnel-like structure; in the middle of this was suspended a rocket, on loan from the Swedish army. According to Gu, the installation was meant to symbolize the collaboration between East and West. Brener, however, objected to the installation's dominant position (and perhaps also to its heavy-handed symbolism). After his ninety-minute drum performance *The Language of Emotion*, Brener began to destroy Wenda Gu's installation by tearing down the tunnel of hair – arguing that it received far more floor space than any other work, and symbolised the failure of the exhibition project as a whole. After this, Oleg Kulik, who was naked and chained to a kennel, executing one of his well-known dog performances, also became increasingly hostile. Soft nibbles turned into bites and assaults. Trying to push Kulik back inside his kennel, Jan Åman kicked the artist in the face, which provoked the artist to become yet more violent; the police were called in and Kulik was arrested, charged and later released with a fine.

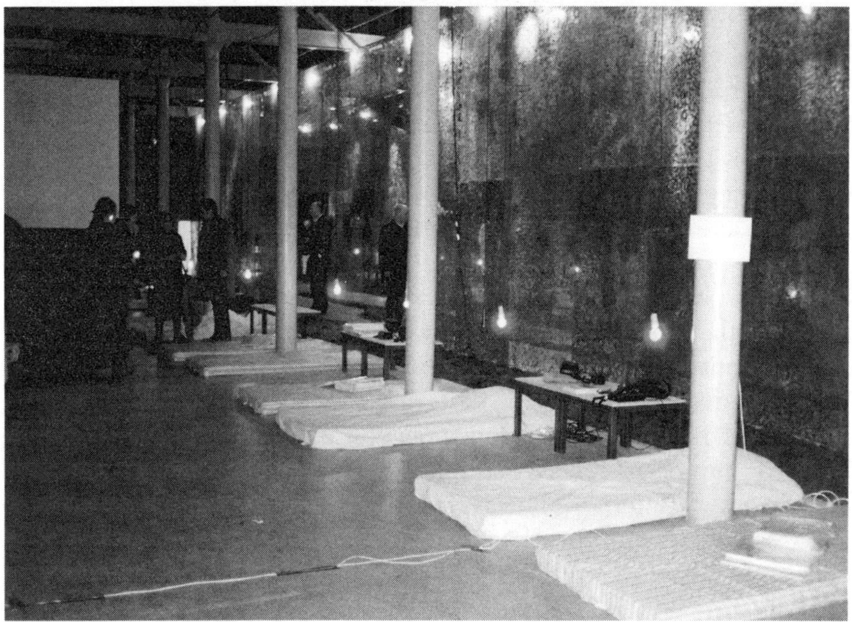

Carl Michael von Hausswolff, Andrew M. McKenzie and Ulf Bilting, *Exchange of Mental, Physical and Un-detected Substances of Known and Un-known Matter During a Period of Four Nights*, 1996

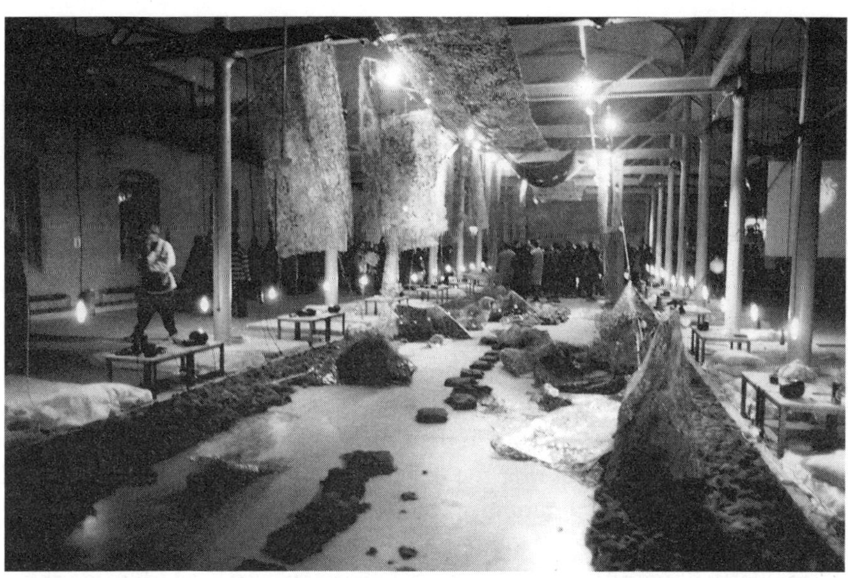

Installation view of Wenda Gu's *United Nations – Sweden and Russia Monument*, 1996, after being destroyed by Alexander Brener

The extensive press coverage that resulted from this debacle led to the Western artists writing an 'Open Letter to the Art World' accusing the Russians of being 'against art and democracy' and Misiano of 'using theory to legitimise a new form of totalitarian ideology'.[60] (It is telling that 'Interpol''s Western participants understood the performative exhibition structure to be too determining, while for Troncy's collaborators in France it connoted non-prescriptive open-endedness.) The conflict surrounding this open letter has been well recounted in a book documenting the exhibition and its aftermath, edited by the Slovenian collective IRWIN. *Rashomon* style, it offers four conflicting accounts. From the perspective of post-'89 cultural politics, the most revealing aspect of the show is the degree to which it reinforces Cold War stereotypes about the 'capitalist' or 'careerist' Western artists and the 'collaborative' or 'collectivist' Eastern artists. Misiano admits that 'Interpol' failed because of his 'romantic desire to export the specifically Eastern European collectivist experience into a Western European framework'.[61] 'Interpol', however, forced a collaboration between two groups of artists with completely different understandings of their role in society. In Misiano's words:

> In art they [the Russians] are first and foremost concerned with the intellectual quest, with the solution of global ontological and existential problems. With regard to the *weltanschauung* aspect of their work they are very much concerned with principle, but are more flexible in matters of material embodiment. Swedish artists, for their part, acquire their identity through social and institutional mechanisms. Art for them represents an autonomous realm, a language of one's own. That's why the material side of an artwork, its representative function is inseparable from the sense of the work . . . Finally, for Russian artists, art is the experience of living. For Swedish artists, it is the positioning of oneself within the boundaries of the art world system.[62]

However romanticised this reading, there is nevertheless a substrata of truth in Misiano's diagnosis, especially when he demonstrates the Russian and European approaches to art through the opposed examples of Brener and Cattelan. Brener destroyed someone else's work, while Cattelan gave the budget for his contribution to the show to the French magazine *Purple Prose*: 'in other words, during the exhibition, the East constituted around the understanding of communication as destruction and protest and the West – as the circulation of money'.[63]

Intellectually and artistically, 'Interpol' seems to have been an unequivocal failure, but as an exhibition case study it offers a vivid document of intercultural friction underlying iterations of open-endedness in the immediate post-Cold War period, and reveals much about the self-perceived role of

artists at this time. The Europeans embrace indeterminacy and participation in so far as it contributes to individual careers (the next project,
another exhibition), while the Russians viewed art as an existential act,
of sabotage if need be. 'Interpol', together with 'No Man's Time', also
indicate the degree to which, during the early 1990s, the exhibition itself
becomes conceptualised as an open-ended, process-based, convivial
'project' without a definable goal beyond collaboration as a good in
itself. But however worthwhile the motivations for this performative
turn – the rejection of a highly polished exhibition-showroom conceived
a posteriori – the net effect for the viewer was less certain. If fortunate
enough to be invited to the opening night, the audience might gain
access to a glimpse of this collaborative process, but in all other cases the
exhibition would be experienced as only the fragment of a larger, ongoing interaction.

III. The Projective City

If my suggestion is correct, and the 'project' is the indicator of a renewed
social awareness of artists in the 1990s, then this shift is yet to be fully theorised by art historians and critics.[64] The clearest articulation of the 'project'
as a way of working is to be found in sociology, put forward by Christian
Boltanski and Eve Chiapello in *The New Spirit of Capitalism* (1999).[65] They
argue that the current 'spirit of capitalism' emerged in the 1970s and '80s in
response to two critiques that came to a head in 1968 (but which have
remained constant for more than centuries): the artistic critique (a demand
for more autonomy, independence and creative fulfilment at work) and the
social critique (a demand for more parity, transparency and equality). I will
return to this distinction in the conclusion of this book; for the moment it
will suffice to draw attention to their characterisation of the current phase
of capitalism as the dominance of networks and projects, a 'connexionist'
world in which fluidity and mobility are the most esteemed values. Although
Boltanski and Chiapello draw their conclusions from a survey of management literature from the past thirty years, many points in their analysis
sound like a description of the globalised contemporary art world, and
even more specifically that of the post-studio, site-responsive artist and the
roving global curator. They describe today's working life as a succession
of 'projects' based on successful connections with others, giving rise to a
universe of value that they call 'the projective city': what is valued and
gives status in this world is the ability to be adaptable, flexible and intellectually mobile.[66] As such, a career today consists 'not in filling "vacancies"
but in engaging in a multitude of often very heterogeneous projects':

> is not today's artist, even today's intellectual or researcher, likewise a
> network creature in search of producers, the realisation of whose projects

demands costly, heterogeneous and complex arrangements, an ability to arrive at an understanding with distant, multiple actors who hold very different positions . . . and whom he must interest, persuade, win over?[67]

It is telling that in the projective city, a successful project is not one that has intrinsic value, but one that allows the worker to integrate him/herself into a new project afterwards; in other words, a good project is one that is generative of further projects through the connections he/she has established. The parallels with artistic practice are highly suggestive. Although the project is introduced as a term in the 1990s to describe a more embedded and socially/politically aware mode of artistic practice, it is equally a survival strategy for creative individuals under the uncertain labour conditions of neoliberalism.[68] What is intended (in art) as a radical overhaul of the portable work of art and its lack of social agency is *at the same time* an internalisation of the '60s logic of post-studio service-based art that, by the 1990s, comes to prioritise personal qualities of interaction rather than the production of objects: personality traits (such as adaptability, nimbleness, creativity and risk) replace the production of visually resolved 'works' or ideas. When faced with a slew of site-responsive projects in exhibitions, biennials and 'project spaces', it is tempting to speculate that the most successful artists are those who can integrate, collaborate, be flexible, work with different audiences, *and* respond to the exhibition's thematic framework.

Today it is a familiar argument to say that flexibility and indeterminacy of labour are a direct consequence of the withdrawal of manual skills in industry (and in art), and both result in long-term projects more akin to services than commodities (visual objects).[69] When these new process-based experiments are put into conjunction with old formats of display like the exhibition, there is necessarily a conflict between these models. Often, for example, there is barely any object to look at, and the role of the audience is severely limited, if not foreclosed altogether. As such, experimental exhibitions like 'Culture in Action', while striving to democratise the production and reception of art, are also in a certain sense profoundly *unequal* (albeit in a completely different sense), since they privilege those who do not need to be mobile: those who can participate in the project are those who can spend the most time on site. Participation and spectatorship seem to be mutually exclusive terms, mirrored in the incompatibility of the project and the exhibition.

The connection between project-based art and neoliberalism is just one side of the story, however. In the post-'89 context, there is also the question of artists' own political allegiances and the extent to which these impact upon their production. For the US/Germans, project work seems to mark the desire *for* a pre-existing political position to which the artists and audience could subscribe, but for relational artists, it seems to denote an *aversion* to such a position, since this led to didactic criticality in past art. Both approaches, however, result in a formal indeterminacy in which duration and process are privileged over formal resolution, be this staged in relationship to the artists' own community or to lower-income/marginalised social constituencies.

The reason why it is *exhibitions* (rather than individual works) that frame this discussion of art's renewed interest in the social in the early 1990s becomes clearer in this light. It is striking that the most forceful statements of this period are by curators rather than artists: in all of the examples I have discussed, the curatorial framework is tighter and stronger than the projects by individual artists, which are open-ended, unframed, and moreover made in response to a curatorial proposition. It is also striking that artists embrace the exhibition as a medium at this time ('Sonsbeek 93', for example, even included an entire exhibition, *The Uncanny*, curated by Mike Kelley); they argue that an exhibition is a signifying 'series' (Parreno) or a 'chain' (Huyghe) and that the spaces between the objects are as important as the objects themselves.[70] In paying attention to relationships, rather to individual objects, it is the conceptualisation of the ensemble that seems to gain strength while the individual works recede.[71]

Recent writing on the exhibition has tended to celebrate it as a place of assembly – as a forum that exhibits *us* as viewers as much as the objects, and which thereby compels us to reflect on our own position and perspective.[72] Yet all of the exhibitions discussed in this chapter place the idea of the exhibition as a unified assembly under pressure, since they multiply and fragment its publics. Their open-endedness – whether on the curatorial level of abdicating decisions about content to the artists, or on the artistic level of creating an open space for participants – is frequently experienced by the viewing public as a loss, since the process that forms the central meaning of this work is rarely made visible and explicit.

The parallels with community arts here are manifold. Although the logical conclusion of participatory art is to foreclose a secondary audience (everyone is a producer; the audience no longer exists), for these actions to be meaningful, for the stakes to be high, there need to be ways of communicating these activities to those who succeed the participants. Subsequent experiments in the 2000s have given rise to more vivid ways of conveying such projects to secondary audiences. The implications of this reconciliation between dematerialised social process and the object (together with its inevitable circulation on the market) is one of the themes of the next chapter, which addresses contemporary art performance.

8

Delegated Performance: Outsourcing Authenticity

During the post-'89 period outlined in the previous chapter, which saw a surge of artistic and curatorial interest in undertaking projects with socially marginalised constituencies, with a concomitant reinvention of the exhibition as a site of production rather than display, a further manifestation of the social turn in contemporary art was emerging through a new genre of performance. Its hallmark is the hiring of non-professional performers, rather than these events being undertaken by the artists themselves (as was the case in the majority of body art works of the 1960s to 1980s: think of Marina Abramovic, Chris Burden, Gina Pane or Vito Acconci). If this tradition valorised live presence and immediacy via the artist's own body, in the last decade this presence is no longer attached to the single performer but instead to the *collective* body of a social group.[1] Although this trend takes a number of forms, some of which I will describe below, all of this work – in contrast to the projects explored in the previous chapter – maintains a comfortable relationship to the gallery, taking it either as the frame for a performance or as a space of exhibition for the photographic and video artefact that results from this. I will refer to this tendency as 'delegated performance': the act of hiring non-professionals or specialists in other fields to undertake the job of being present and performing at a particular time and a particular place on behalf of the artist, and following his/her instructions. This strategy differs from a theatrical and cinematic tradition of employing people to act on the director's behalf in the following crucial respect: the artists I discuss below tend to hire people to perform their own socio-economic category, be this on the basis of gender, class, ethnicity, age, disability, or (more rarely) a profession.

This chapter marks a break with previous chapters in that I have seen or experienced most of the works discussed; the tone is less historical since the material is newer and a critical point is at stake. Much of this work has not been addressed or analysed in depth by art historians or critics, so my position forms a response not so much to existent writing but to the reactions that this work repeatedly elicits – both from the general public and specialist art world – at conferences, panel discussions and symposia. One of the aims of this chapter is to argue against these dominant responses for a more nuanced way to address delegated performance as an *artistic* practice engaging with the ethics and aesthetics of contemporary labour, and not simply as a micro-model of reification. I will be begin by outlining three different manifestations of this tendency, and the different performance traditions they draw upon: body art, Judson Dance and Fluxus, and docu-drama.[2]

I. A Provisional Typology

My first type of delegated performance comprises actions outsourced to non-professionals who are asked to perform an aspect of their identities, often in the gallery or exhibition. This tendency, which we might call 'live installation', can be seen in the early work of Paweł Althamer (working with homeless men in *Observator*, 1992, and with lady invigilators for the Zachęta exhibition 'Germinations', 1994), or Elmgreen & Dragset hiring, variously, gay men to lounge around in the gallery listening to headphones (*Try*, 1997) or unemployed men and women to be gallery invigilators (*Reg[u]arding the Guards*, 2005). It is telling that this work developed primarily in Europe: its light and playful tone marks a decisive break with the more earnest forms of identitarian politics that were so crucial to US art of the 1980s.

Consider, for example, one of the earliest examples of this tendency by Maurizio Cattelan. In 1991 the Italian artist assembled a football club of

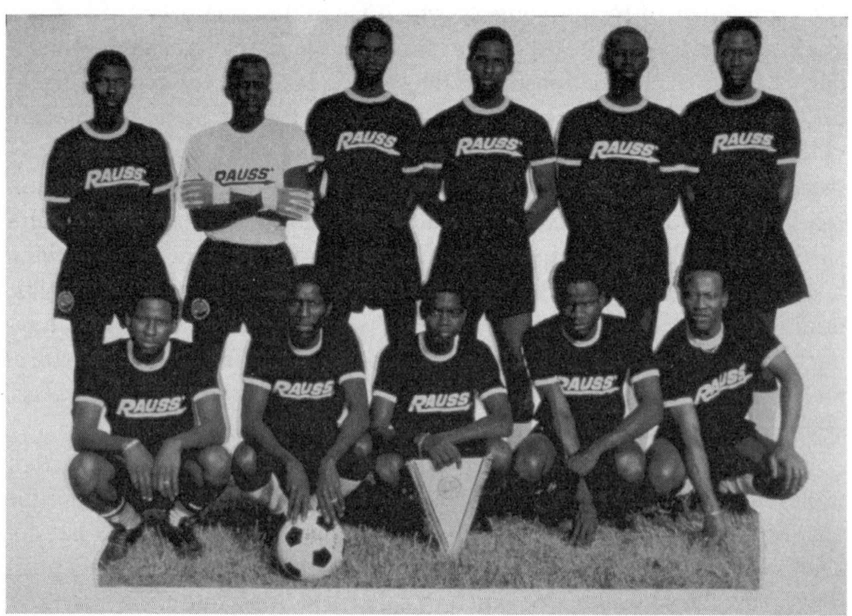

Maurizio Cattelan, *Southern Suppliers FC*, 1991

North African immigrants, who were deployed to play local football matches in Italy (all of which they lost). Their shirts were emblazoned with the name of a fictional sponsor Rauss: the German word for 'get out', as in the phrase *Ausländer raus*, or 'foreigners out'. The title of the project, *Southern Suppliers FC*, alludes to immigrant labour ('suppliers' from the south), but also to the trend, then hotly debated in the Italian press, of hiring foreign footballers to play in Italian teams. Cattelan's gesture draws a contrast between two types of foreign labour at different ends of the economic spectrum – star footballers are rarely perceived in the same terms as working-class immigrants – but without any discernable Marxist rhetoric. Indeed, through this work, Cattelan fulfils the male dream of owning a football club, and apparently insults the players by dressing them in shirts emblazoned Rauss. At the same time, he nevertheless produces a confusing image: the word Rauss, when combined with the startling photograph of an all-black Italian football team, has an ambiguous, provocative potency, especially when it circulates in the media, since it seems to blurt out the unspoken EU fear of being deluged by immigrants from outside 'fortress Europe'. *Southern Suppliers FC* is a social sculpture as cynical performance, inserted into the real-time social system of a football league.[3] Francesco Bonami therefore seems to ascribe a misplaced worthiness to the project when he claims that Cattelan aimed 'for a democratic new way to play the artist, whilst remaining central to the work as the coach and manager of the teams'.[4] At a push, the collaborative process of *Southern Suppliers FC* could be said to share out the performance limelight, but it is highly directorial and far from straightforward in its political message.

Cattelan turned to sport as a popular point of reference, but music is a more frequent focus of collaboration. Swedish artist Annika Eriksson's *Copenhagen Postmen's Orchestra* (1996) and British artist Jeremy Deller's *Acid Brass* (1997) both invited workers' bands to perform recent pop music in their own idiom. The Copenhagen Postmen's Orchestra played a song by the British trip-hop group Portishead, while the Williams Fairey Brass Band (historically connected to an aircraft factory in Manchester) interpreted a selection of acid house tracks. Eriksson's event resulted in a five-minute video, while Deller's has become numerous live performances, a CD, and a diagram elaborately connecting these two forms of regional working-class music. Beyond the aesthetic frisson of mixing together two types of popular music, part of the appeal of both projects lies in the fact that the artists employ real bands. These are not actors hired to play electronic music on brass instruments, but 'genuine' working-class collaborators who have agreed to participate in an artistic experiment – a rather formal one in the case of Eriksson (the camera remains static throughout the video), more research-led in the case of Deller.[5] The musicians perform their public personae (determined by their employment and strongly linked to class) and come to exemplify a collectively shared passion (in this case, performing music) – a recurrent theme in both artists' work. These follow the trend for light and humorous ways in which delegated performance in Europe in the '90s is used to signify class, race, age, or gender. These bodies are a metonymic shorthand for politicised identity, but the fact that it is not the artist's own body being staged means that this politics can be pursued with a cool irony, wit and distance.

A rupture with this mood arrived in 1999, with the performances of Spanish artist Santiago Sierra. Prior to 1999, Sierra's work comprised a forceful combination of minimalism and urban intervention; over the course of that year his work shifted from installations produced by low-paid workers to displays of the workers themselves, foregrounding the economic transactions on which the installations depend. There is a clear path of development from *24 Blocks of Concrete Constantly Moved During a Day's Work by Paid Workers* (Los Angeles, July), in which the workers are not seen but their presence and payment is made known to us, to *People Paid to Remain inside Cardboard Boxes* (G&T Building, Guatemala City, August), in which the low-paid workers are concealed within cardboard boxes, a metaphor for their social invisibility. The first piece in which the participants were rendered visible is *450 Paid People* (Museo Rufino Tamayo, Mexico City, October), which led to a work that continues to be inflammatory: *250cm Line Tattooed on 6 Paid People* (Espacio Aglutinador, Havana, December). Many of these early performances involve finding people who were willing to undertake banal or humiliating tasks for the minimum wage. Sierra's works are stripped of the light humour that

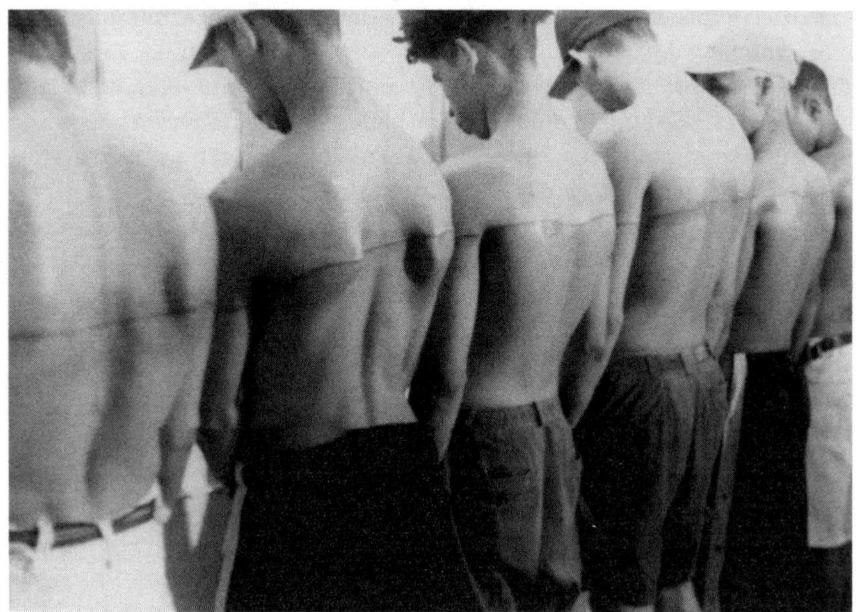

Santiago Sierra, *250cm Line Tattooed on 6 Paid People*, 1999

accompanies many of the projects mentioned above, since they frequently take place in countries already at the disadvantaged end of globalisation, most notably in Central and South America. Consequently, he has been heavily criticised for merely repeating the inequities of capitalism, and more specifically of globalisation, in which rich countries 'outsource' or 'offshore' labour to low-paid workers in developing countries. Yet Sierra always draws attention to the *economic* systems through which his works are realised, and the way these impact upon the work's reception. In his work, performance is outsourced via recruitment agencies and a financial transaction takes place that leaves the artist at arm's length from the performer; this distance is evident in the viewer's phenomenological encounter with the work, which is disturbingly cold and alienated. Unlike many artists, Sierra is at pains to make the details of each payment part of the work's description, turning the economic context into one of his primary materials.[6]

In its emphasis on the phenomenological immediacy of the live body and on specific socio-economic identities, we could argue that this type of delegated performance owes most to the body art tradition of the late 1960s and early 1970s. At the same time, it differs from this precursor in important ways. Artists in the 1970s used their *own* bodies as the medium and material of the work, often with a corresponding emphasis on physical and psychological transgression. Today's delegated performance still places a high value upon immediacy, but if it has any transgressive character, this tends to derive from the perception that artists are exhibiting and exploiting other subjects.[7] As a result, this type of performance, in which the artist uses other people as the material of his or her work, tends to occasion heated debate about the ethics of representation. Duration, meanwhile, is reconfigured from a spiritual question of individual stamina and endurance to the economic matter of having sufficient resources to pay for someone else's ongoing presence.

A second strand of delegated performance, which began to be introduced in the later 1990s, concerns the use of professionals from other spheres of expertise: think of Allora and Calzadilla hiring opera singers (*Sediments, Sentiments [Figures of Speech]*, 2007) or pianists (*Stop, Repair, Prepare*, 2008), of Tania Bruguera hiring mounted policemen to demonstrate crowd-control techniques (in *Tatlin's Whisper 5*, 2008), or of Tino Sehgal hiring university professors and students for his numerous speech-based situations (*This Objective of That Object*, 2004; *This Progress*, 2006).[8] These performers tend to be specialists in fields other than that of art or performance, and since they tend to be recruited on the basis of their professional (elective) identity, rather than for being representatives of a particular class or race, there is far less controversy and ambivalence around this type of work. Critical attention tends to focus on the conceptual frame (which more often than not is instruction-based) and on the specific abilities of the performer or interpreter in question, whose skills are incorporated into the performance as a ready-made. The work has an instruction-based character which – along with the fact that many of the performers in these works are Caucasian and middle-class – has facilitated the repeatability of this type of work, and enhanced its collectability by museums.

The best-known example of this tendency is unarguably Tino Sehgal, who is adamant that his practice not be referred to as 'performance art' but as 'situations', and that his performers be referred to as 'interpreters'.[9] While his insistence is somewhat pedantic, it nevertheless draws our attention to the scored nature of Sehgal's work, and to its relationship with dance: as every critic of his output has observed, the artist was trained in choreography and economics before turning to visual art. *This Objective of That Object*, for example, places the viewer within a highly controlled experience: as you enter the gallery, five performers with their backs turned to you urge you to join in a discussion on subjectivity and objectivity. The performers tend to be philosophy students, but their semi-scripted dialogue comes over as somewhat depersonalised and rote, and any contribution you make to the debate feels self-conscious and hollow, since it is impossible to alter the work's structure, only to assume your role within it. (If you remain silent, the performers wilt onto the floor until a new visitor enters the gallery.) Although Sehgal makes a point of renouncing photographic reproduction, his works seem actively to tear apart any equation between liveness and authenticity; indeed, the very fact that his work runs continually in the space for the duration of an exhibition, performed by any number of interpreters, erodes any residual attachment to the idea of an original or ideal performance.

A less well-known – and less gallery-based – approach that deploys similar methods can be found in the conceptual performances of Spanish artist Dora García. Several of her early performances explicitly allude to avatars and surveillance (such as *Proxy/Coma*, 2001) but her most compelling projects blur into the outside world and can potentially last for years, as in *The Messenger* (2002). In this work, a performer (the 'messenger') must deliver a message in a foreign language that he/she does not understand – but to do so must search for someone who can identify and understand that language.[10] The performer is entrusted with the task, and it is important to note that García – like Sehgal – is a meticulous recruiter: *The Beggar's Opera* (2007) required one performer to play a charming beggar in the streets of Münster, while *The Romeos* (2005), involved hiring handsome young men to establish seemingly spontaneous conversation with visitors to the Frieze Art Fair.[11] This form of 'invisible theatre' operates less to raise consciousness (as in the Augusto Boal model) than to insinuate a moment of doubt and suspicion in the viewer's habitual experiences of city life.[12] García often strikes a careful balance between an

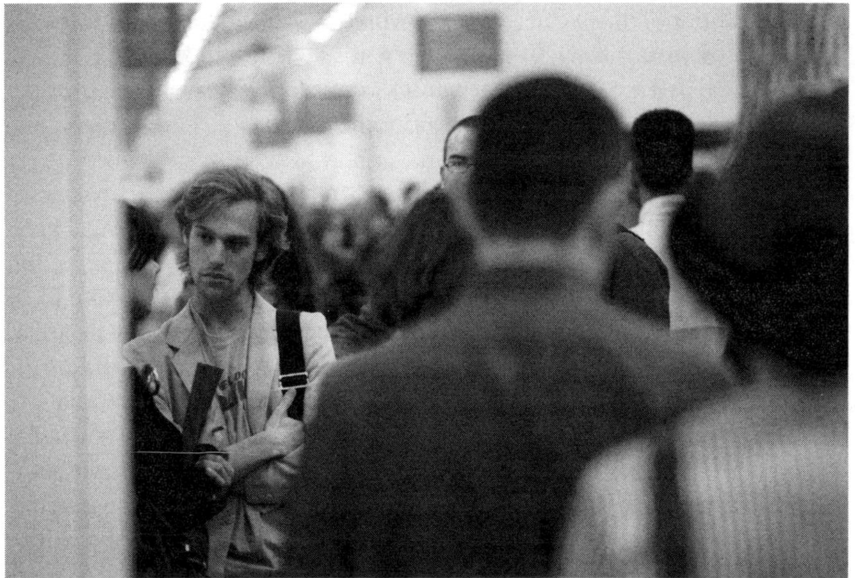

Dora García, *The Romeos*, 2008

open-ended score and the performer's interpretation of her instructions. If Sehgal's works are self-reflexive, cerebral, and encourage the subjective contribution of the audience, then García's are less visibly participatory and seem to reinforce doubt and unease.

Sehgal and García exemplify a type of performance that emphasises simple instructions, which are carried out in a manner that allows for individual variation and a quotidian aesthetic. As such, they evoke several precursors from the 1960s and '70s. Boal's 'invisible theatre' seems an immediate point of reference, but neither artists would subscribe to his political agenda; another would be the task-based participatory instructions of Fluxus.[13] Judson Dance, with its emphasis on everyday gestures, clothes and movements as the basis for choreographic invention, is perhaps the closest precedent, especially Steve Paxton's walking pieces from the mid 1960s. One of them, *Satisfyin' Lover* (1967), was first performed with forty-two dancers, and comprises three movements only: walking, standing and sitting.[14] Paxton's score is structured into six parts, in each of which the performers walk a certain number of steps and stand for a certain number of counts before exiting, at roughly thirty-second intervals. He describes the pace of walking as 'an easy walk, but not slow. Performance manner is serene and collected'; the costumes are 'casual'.[15] As Yvonne Rainer observes, 'it was as though you had never seen ordinary people walk across a space. It was highly revelatory.'[16] Judson Dance finds its direct lineage in contemporary choreography such as Jérôme Bel's *The Show Must Go On* (2001), which makes use of everyday movements to literalise the lyrics of pop songs. Several of these strands come together in

Martin Creed's *Work no.850* (2008), in which professional sprinters ran the eighty-six metres of the Duveen Gallery at Tate Britain, at fifteen-second intervals; the artist compared the pauses between these sprints to the rests in a piece of music, reinforcing the connection between choreography and daily life.[17]

A third strand of delegated performance comprises situations constructed for video and film; key examples might include Gillian Wearing, Artur Żmijewski and Phil Collins. Recorded images are crucial here since this type frequently captures situations that are too difficult or sensitive to be repeated. (Here it should be reiterated that my interest is not in artists working in a documentary tradition, but on works where the artist *devises* the entire situation being filmed, and where the participants are asked to perform themselves.) Depending on the mode of filming, these situations can trouble the border between live and mediated to the point where audiences are unsure of the degree to which an event has been staged or scripted. Because the artist assumes a strong editorial role, and because the work's success often relies on the watchability of the performers, this kind of work also tends to attract ethical criticism both from over-solicitous leftists and from the liberal and right-wing media.

They Shoot Horses (2004) by the British artist Phil Collins is a striking example of this tendency. Collins auditioned and paid nine teenagers in Ramallah to undertake an eight-hour disco-dancing marathon in front of a garish pink wall to an unrelentingly cheesy compilation of pop hits from the past four decades. The resulting videos are shown as a two-channel installation, in which the performers are projected to more or less the same size as the viewers, creating an equivalence between them. Although we don't hear the teenagers talk, their dancing speaks volumes: as the gruelling day continues, their performances shift from individual posturing to collective effort (increasingly daft moves by way of generating mutual entertainment). At several panel discussions about this work, I have heard members of the audience raise concerns about the artist's 'exploitation' of his performers – for example, by not listing their names in the credits.[18] Yet the point of Collins' project is not to be an exemplary instance of artistic collaboration, but to universalise his participants by addressing multiple genres of artistic and popular experience: the portrait, endurance-based body art, reality television (and its precursor in depression-era dance marathons, to which his title alludes).[19] It is also a deliberately perverse approach to site-specificity: the Occupied Territories are never shown explicitly but are ever-present as a frame or *hors cadre*. This knowledge colours our reception of the banal pop lyrics, which seem to comment on the kids' double endurance of the dance marathon and the political crisis in which they are mired. In subjecting the teenagers to an onslaught of Western pop, Collins plays an ambiguous role: both ally and taskmaster, he depicts them as generic globalised teenagers; the more usual media representation of

Palestinians is that of victim or fundamentalist (hence Collins' use of the 'usual suspects' backdrop, akin to a police line-up).

Artur Żmijewski's *Them* (2007) offers a more troubling narrative, less concerned with portraiture than with the role of images in reinforcing ideological antagonism. The artist set up a series of painting workshops for four different groups in Warsaw: ladies from the Catholic Church, Young Socialists, Young Jews and Polish Nationalists. Each group produced a symbolic depiction of its values, which were printed onto T-shirts worn by each member of the group in subsequent workshops. Żmijewski then encouraged each group to respond to each others' paintings, altering and amending the images as they saw fit. The first gestures were gentle – such as cutting open the door of a church, to make the building more open – but became more violent, culminating in an explosive *impasse*: painting over an image entirely, setting fire to it, and even assaulting the other participants by cutting their T-shirts or taping over their mouths. As in many of Żmijewski's videos, the artist adopts an ambiguous role and it is never clear to what degree his participants are acting of their own volition, or being gently manipulated to fulfil the requirements of his pre-planned narrative. The action unfolds with apparently minimal direction from the artist, who nevertheless establishes the structure of the participants' encounters, records the escalating conflict between them and edits this into a narrative. Following the first screening of this work in Warsaw, many of the participants were angry at this pessimistic representation of the workshops as ending in an irresolvable antagonism.[20] However, artists like Żmijewski are less interested in making a faithful documentary of this situation than in constructing a narrative, grounded in reality, that conveys a larger set of points about social conflict. *Them* offers a poignant meditation on

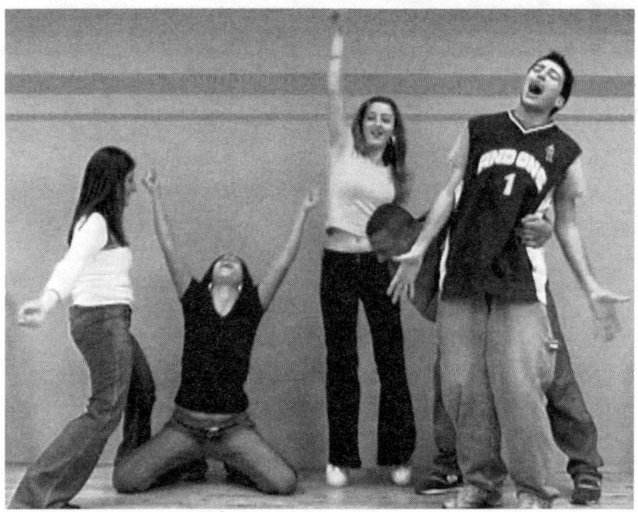

Phil Collins, video still of *They Shoot Horses*, 2004

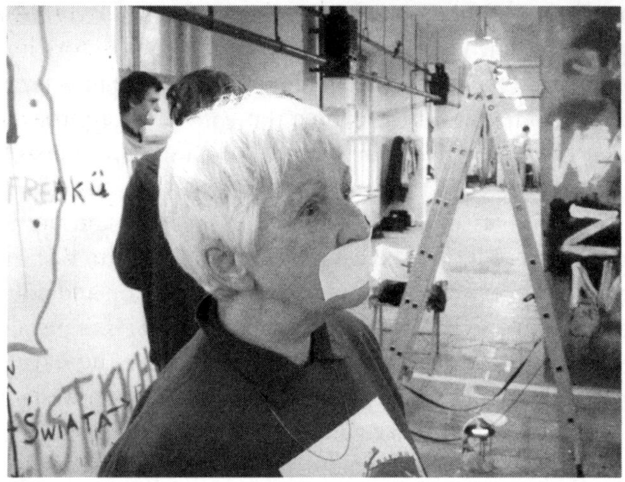

Artur Żmijewski, *Them*, 2007, video still

collective identification, the role of images in forging these identifications, as well as a harsh parable about social antagonisms and the facility with which ideological differences become hardened into irresolvably blocked patterns of communication.

The genealogy for this type of performance work is complex. On the one hand it bears a strong relationship to the contemporaneous emergence of reality television, a genre that evolved from the demise of documentary TV and the success of US tabloid TV in the 1990s.[21] Like reality television, it also has roots in a longer tradition of observational documentary, mock-documentary and performative documentary that emerged in the 1960s

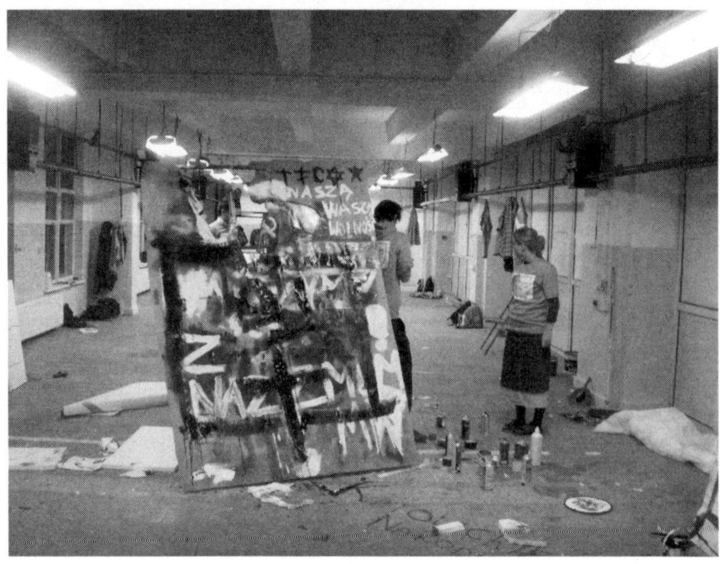

Artur Żmijewski, *Them*, 2007, video still

and '70s.[22] Although Italian Neorealist cinema, particularly the later films of Roberto Rossellini, incorporated non-professional actors in secondary roles in order to stretch the prevailing boundaries of what was then considered realism, the singularity of contemporary artists' approaches is more comparable to idiosyncratic film auteurs such as Peter Watkins (b.1935). Watkins's early work used non-professional actors, handheld cameras and tight framing as a way to address contentious social and political issues, such as the consequences of nuclear attack in his 1966 film *The War Game*.[23] He is an apt point of reference for contemporary artists, and not just for his subject matter and use of amateur performers: firstly, his films exceed the conventional length of mainstream cinema and can be extremely long (eight hours in the case of *La Commune*, 2001), and secondly, he frequently configures the camera as an agent or performer within the narrative, even when the story is set in a period prior to the invention of film; the conceit of *La Commune*, for example, is that the protagonists are being interviewed for a television report on the events of 1871 as they are taking place.

We can see from this rapid overview that what I am calling delegated performance in all its contemporary iterations (from live installation to constructed situations) brings clear pressures to bear on the conventions of body art as they have been handed down to us from the 1960s. Contemporary performance art does not necessarily privilege the live moment or the artist's own body, but instead engages in numerous strategies of mediation that include delegation and repetition; at the same time, it continues to have an investment in immediacy via the presentation of authentic non-professional performers who represent specific social groups. If body art in the '60s and '70s was produced quickly and inexpensively (since the artist's own body was the cheapest form of material), delegated performance today, by contrast, tends to be a luxury game.[24] It is telling that it takes place primarily in the West, and that art fairs and biennials were among the earliest sites for its popular consumption. Jack Bankowsky has coined the term 'art fair art' to designate a mode of performance in which the spectacular and economic context of the art fair is integral to the work's meaning, and against which the artist's gestures provide a mildly amusing point of friction.[25] Many of his examples are delegated performances, with the Frieze Art Fair as a significant incubator for this type of work: consider Elmgreen & Dragset's doubling of the booth of their Berlin gallery Klosterfelde, complete with identical works of art and a lookalike dealer (2005); Gianni Motti's *Pre-emptive Act* (2007), a policeman meditating in a yoga position; or numerous performances staged by Cattelan's Wrong Gallery, such as Paola Pivi's *100 Chinese* (1998–2005), 100 identically dressed Chinese people standing in the gallery's booth. Whereas once performance art sought to break with the art market by dematerialising the work of art into ephemeral events, today dematerialisation and rumour have become one of the most effective forms of hype.[26] Performance excites media attention,

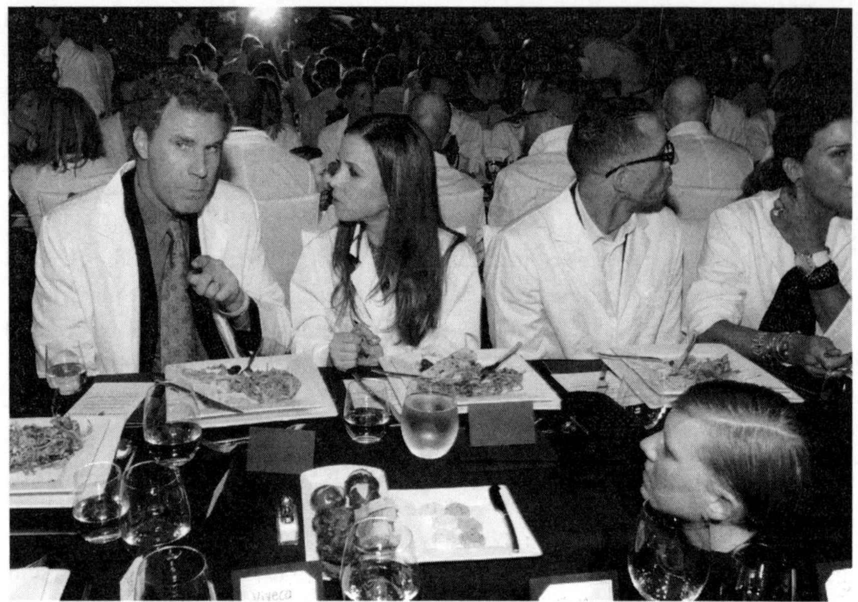

Marina Abramovic, untitled performance for Los Angeles MoCA, annual gala, 2011

which in turn heightens the symbolic capital of the event – as seen in numerous covers of *The Guardian*'s annual supplement to accompany the Frieze Art Fair, but also the recent controversy around Marina Abramovic's 'human table decorations' for the LA MoCA gala (November 2011): eighty-five performers were paid \$150 to kneel on a rotating 'lazy susan' beneath the tables, with their heads protruding above, staring into the eyes of diners who had paid upwards of \$2,500 for a ticket.[27] Yvonne Rainer wrote to LA MoCA, denouncing this 'exploitative' and 'grotesque spectacle' as reminiscent of Pasolini's *Salo* (1975). Yet the problem with Abramovic's table decorations is that they don't become more than table decorations. What is shocking is the performance's banality and paucity of ideas, and the miserable fact that a museum such as LA MoCA requires this kind of media stunt dressed up as performance art to raise money. My point is that not all examples of delegated performance should be tarnished with the label of 'art fair art' or 'gala art': the better examples offer more pointed, layered and troubling experiences, both for the performers and viewers, which problematise any straightforward Marxist criticism of these performances as reification.

II. Performance as Labour and Pleasure

As I have indicated, the repeatability of delegated performance – both as a live event or as a video loop – is central to the economics of performance since 1990, enabling it to be bought and sold by institutions and individuals, performed and reperformed in many venues.[28] It is not coincidental that this tendency has developed hand in hand with managerial changes in the economy at large, providing an economic genealogy for this work that parallels the art historical one outlined above. 'Outsourcing' labour became a business buzzword in the early 1990s: the wholesale divesting of important but non-core activities to other companies, from customer service call-centres to financial analysis and research. With the growth of globalisation, 'offshore outsourcing' became a term that refers – with not altogether positive connotations – to the use of hired labour and 'virtual companies' in developing countries, taking advantage of the huge differences in wages internationally. For those sceptical of globalisation, outsourcing is little more than a legal loophole that allows national and multi-national companies to absolve themselves of the legal responsibility for unregulated and exploitative labour conditions. It is strange and striking that most UK guides to outsourcing emphasise the importance of *trust*: companies give responsibility for some aspect of their production to another company, with all the risks and benefits that this shared responsibility entails. In the light of the present discussion, it is telling that all of these textbooks agree that the primary aim of outsourcing is to 'improve performance' (understood here as profit). But there are also important differences: if the aim of outsourcing in business is to *decrease* risk, artists frequently deploy it as a means to *increase* unpredictability – even if this means that a work might risk failing altogether.[29]

Noting the simultaneous rise of outsourcing in both economics and in art in the 1990s is not to suggest that the latter exists in complicity with the former, even though it seems telling that a boom in delegated performance coincided with the art market bubble of the 2000s, and with the consolidation of a service industry that increasingly relies upon the marketing of certain qualities in human beings.[30] Both performance and business now place a premium on recruitment, and in many cases, the work of finding suitable performers is delegated to the curator, who now finds him- or herself becoming a human resources manager (negotiating qualifications, shifts and contracts). Although unique qualities are sought in each performer, these are – paradoxically – also infinitely replaceable: since contemporary performance increasingly tends to be on display for the duration of an exhibition, shift-work becomes necessary. There is less emphasis on the frisson of a single performance, even while the impact of the live remains: performance enters 'gallery time' as a constant presence, eight hours a day for the duration of an exhibition, rather than being assigned to a few intense hours (as is customary with 'theatre time'). Presence today is arguably less a matter of anti-spectacular immediacy (as was the case during the 1960s) than evidence of precarious labour, but artists are more likely to sustain this economy than to challenge it.

If I seem to be overstressing these economic changes, it's because they provide not just the contextual backdrop for contemporary art but also affect our reception of it. Financial transactions have become increasingly essential to the realisation of delegated performance, as anyone who has organised an exhibition of this work can corroborate: contractual waged labour for performers is the largest outgoing expense in such shows, which operate with an inverse economy to that of installing more conventional art. (As Tino Sehgal points out, the longer a steel sculpture by Richard Serra is on display, the cheaper the cost of its installation becomes, whereas Sehgal's own works accrue more costs for the institution the longer they are exhibited.[31]) But despite the centrality of economics to delegated performance, and the impact it has upon our understanding of duration, it is rare for artists to make an explicit point about financial transactions; more usually, such arrangements tend to be tacit. Unlike theatre, dance and film, where there are long-established codes for experiencing a performer's relationship to labour, contemporary art has until recently been comparatively artisanal, based on the romantic persona of the singular (and largely unpaid) artist-performer. It is only in the last twenty years that performance art has become 'industrialised', and this shift – from festival to museum space, mobilising large numbers of performers, unionised modes of remuneration, and ever larger audiences – means that contemporary art increasingly exists in a sphere of collaboration akin to theatre and dance, even while it retains art's valorisation of individual authorship. (There is no serious market, for example, for signed photographs of theatrical productions.)

One of the most successful exhibition projects of recent years has addressed this intersection of performance and the economy head on: the itinerant three-day exhibition 'La Monnaie Vivante' (The Living Currency) by the French curator Pierre Bal-Blanc. The first iteration of this continually changing performance experiment began in Paris in 2006; subsequent versions have been held in Leuven (2007), London (2008), Warsaw and Berlin (2010).[32] Most of the works exhibited are delegated performances, drawn from a diverse range of generations (from the 1960s to today) and geographical locations (from Eastern and Western Europe to North and South America) that match the purview of this book. 'La Monnaie Vivante' places visual art performance into direct conversation with contemporary choreographers interested in the 'degree zero' of dance, such as Compagnie les Gens d'Uterpan (Annie Vigier and Franck Apertet) and Prinz Gholam. Curatorially, 'La Monnaie Vivante' is distinctive in presenting performances as overlapping in a single space and time (a combination of exhibition and festival); this format forges an intense and continually shifting proximity between the different performances, as well as between performers and viewers, who occupy the same space as the works and move among them. At Tate Modern in 2008, for example, performances of varying duration took place on the Turbine Hall bridge,

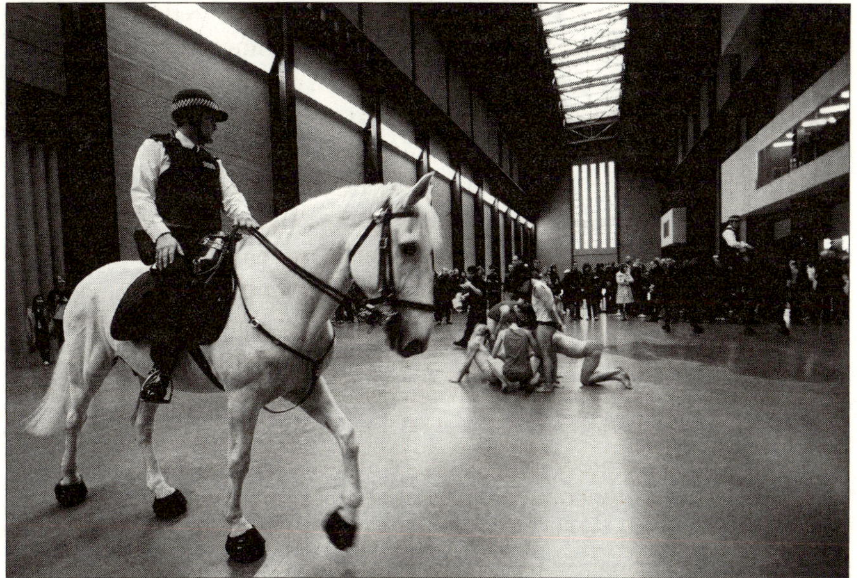

'La Monnaie Vivante', Tate Modern, 2008. Tania Bruguera, *Tatlin's Whisper #5*, 2008 (foreground); Compagnie les Gens d'Uterpan, *X-Event 2*, 2007 (background).

ranging from a six-hour live installation by Sanja Iveković (*Delivering Facts, Producing Tears*, 1998–2007) to fleeting instruction pieces by Lawrence Weiner (shooting a rifle at a wall, emptying a cup of sea water onto the floor). This led to some sublime juxtapositions, such as Santiago Sierra's *Eight People Facing A Wall* (2002) as the backdrop to Tania Bruguera's *Tatlin's Whisper #5* (2008, two mounted policemen demonstrating crowd-control techniques on the audience), which in turn circled around six dancers holding poses, and salivating onto the floor, choreographed by Annie Vigier and Franck Apertet.

The title of Bal-Blanc's exhibition is taken from Pierre Klossowski's enigmatic and near impenetrable book of the same name, published in 1970, in which he argues for a troubling mutual imbrication of the economy and pleasure (*jouissance*), rather than perceiving them to be separate domains. The 'living currency' of his title is the human body. Building on his analyses of Fourier and Sade (most notably in 'Le Philosophe scélérat', 1967), Klossowski's text is organised around the premise that industrial mechanisation introduces new forms of perversion and pleasure.[33] Klossowski defines perversion as the separation that occurs as soon as the human is aware of a distinction between reproductive instincts and pleasure ('voluptuous emotion'): this first perversion distinguishes the human from the mechanical, the functional from the non-functional, but it is subsequently appropriated and contained by institutions as a way to organise the processes of production towards specific and highly policed ends.[34] As such, industry engages in a perverse act (reducing human actions to a functional tool, fixated on doing only one thing) while at the same time expelling as perverse everything that overruns and exceeds this functional gesture. Klossowski argues that art (which comes under his category of '*simulacre*') is thought to die in this domain of excess because it is not functional, but in fact art should also be seen as a tool, since it is compensatory and creates new experiences ('*l'usage, c'est-à-dire, la jouissance*').[35] Klossowski pressures the dialectic of use and non-use, the functional and the non-functional, to argue that industrial processes and art are *both* libidinal *and* rational, since the drives ignore such externally imposed distinctions. Humans are 'living currency', and money is the mediator between libidinal pleasure and the industrial/institutional world of normative imposition.

Using this to interpret performance art, Bal-Blanc argues that the whole impulse to produce 'open form' in the 1970s is an inversion or reversal of the industrial system, which is itself a form of perversion.[36] Artists today are therefore redefining transgression by making a dual appeal to the reification of the body on the one hand, and to the embodiment of the object on the other, two poles that he sums up in the evocative oxymorons 'living/object' and 'inanimate/body'. It is no coincidence that delegated performance makes up the majority of works exhibited in 'La Monnaie Vivante', but Bal-Blanc places these paid bodies alongside the performance of conceptual art instructions (such as those of Lawrence Weiner) and more obviously participatory works (such as Lygia Clark's *Caminhando*, 1963, or

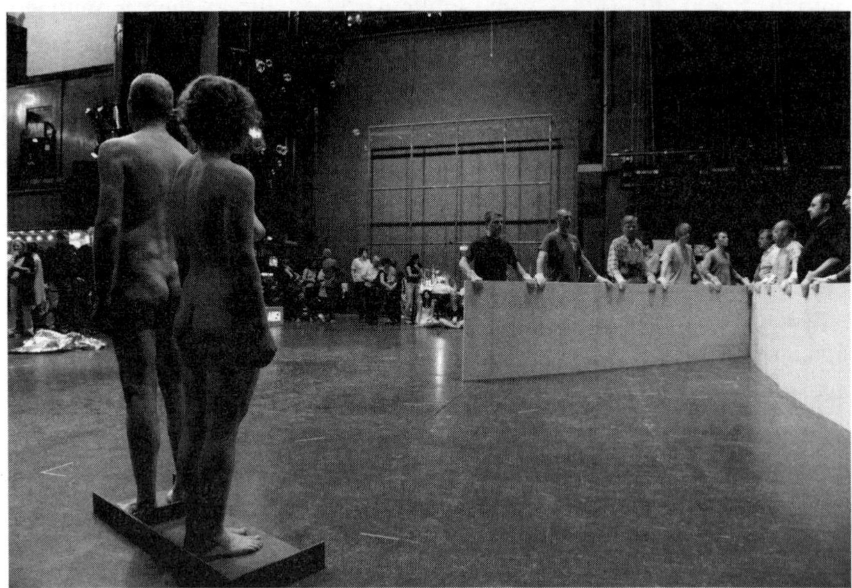

'La Monnaie Vivante', 6th Berlin Biennale for Contemporary Art, 2010. Franz Erhard Walther, *Standing Piece in Three Sections*, 1975 (foreground); Santiago Sierra, *111 Constructions Made with 10 Modules and 10 Workers*, 2004 (background).

Franz Erhard Walther's steel *Standing Pieces* of the 1970s). These works blur the difference between many types of participatory art, as is reinforced in the photographic documentation of 'La Monnaie Vivante', in which more recent types of so-called 'exploitative' art are placed next to earlier work, reminding us that the dancers of, say, Simone Forti's *Huddle* (1961) are also being paid for their bodily labour. This juxtaposition of generations and types of work (participatory, conceptual, theatrical, choreographic) is also staked as an engagement with *interpassivity* (rather than interactivity), because this is the dominant mode installed by mass media and an information society. Bal-Blanc argues that all the works he exhibits show the way in which individual drives are subordinated to economic and social relations, and how these rules are parsed in the entertainment industry's laws of transmission and reception ('interpassivity reveals what interactivity conceals, an admission of dependence on the user; interactivity, by contrast, gives the impression that the subject masters his language').[37] In other words, interpassivity is the secret language of the market, which degrades bodies into objects, *and it is also the language that artists use to reflect on this degradation.*

It is not unimportant that Bal-Blanc's development of this project was rooted in his own experience performing for two and a half months in Felix Gonzalez-Torres's *Untitled (Go-Go Dancing Platform)*, 1991. In this work, a scantily clad male wears headphones and dances upon a light-bulb-studded minimalist podium for at least five minutes a day for the duration of the exhibition in which it appears.[38] Bal-Blanc's feeling of depressed subjection after a month of performing this work raised a number of questions for him that were only answered when he later encountered the performances of Santiago Sierra.[39] Like many of the artists in 'La Monnaie Vivante', Sierra seems to use perversity as a meditation on the degree to which social and

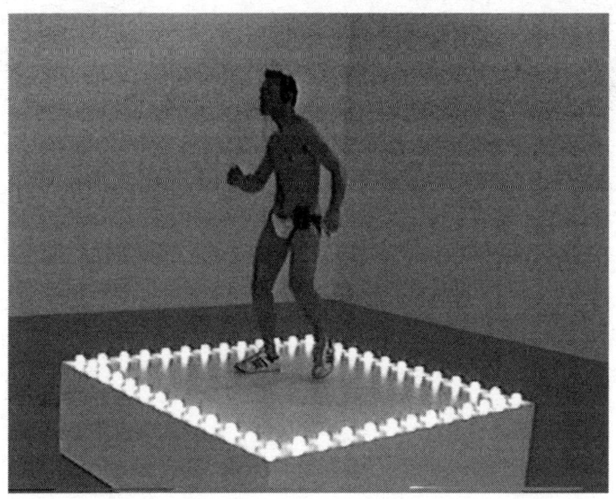

Pierre Bal-Blanc, video still of *Working Contract*, 1992

economic institutions assure the triumph of perversion. For Bal-Blanc, the difference between works of art and capitalism is that artists appropriate perverted power *for themselves*, in order to produce reoriented and multiple roles (as opposed to the singular roles of industrialisation). As such, they propose new forms of transgression, and prompt a '*secousse*' (jolt) in the viewer. As Bal-Blanc suggests, in delegated performance two types of perversion confront each other face to face: the perversity exercised by institutions and presented as a norm, and that employed by artists which by contrast appears as an anomaly.

III. Perversion and Authenticity

Klossowski arguably provides a bridge in French theory between Bataille and Lacan and a subsequent generation of thinkers including Lyotard, Baudrillard and Foucault, who take from him respectively the ideas of libidinal economy, the simulacrum, and institutional discourse. For Klossowski, Sade's sexual perversions work against all normative values and structures, both rational and moral, but it is hard to ascertain Klossowski's relationship to the system he describes.[40] His interest in the human body as 'living currency' seems to be a meditation on how subjects may come to pervert and thereby enjoy their own alienation at work, but his invocation of industrialised labour also seems rather dated. *La monnaie vivante* was published in 1970, at the moment of transition between what Boltanski and Chiapello identify as the second and third spirits of capitalism: from an industrialised model of labour, organised by management, in which the worker feels exploited and unrealised, to a connexionist, project-based model, structured by networks, in which the worker is arguably even more exploited but feels greater fulfilment and autonomy. To the extent that the third spirit of capitalism is marked by elaborate forms of self-exploitation (rather than a monodirectional, hierarchical flow), Klossowski's understanding of the way we find perverse pleasure in labour is arguably even more relevant.

Following Klossowski's logic, it is as if the delegated performance artist puts him/herself in a Sadean position, exploiting because he/she knows from experience that this exploitation and self-display can itself be a form of pleasure.[41] From this perspective, it is only doing half the job to point out that delegated performance 'reifies' its participants. From a Sadean point of view, this reading doesn't establish the occult pleasure of the participant in exploiting his subordination in these works of art, nor does it account for the evident pleasure of viewers in watching him/her. This interlacing of *voyeur* and *voyant* is core to Pierre Zucca's quaintly perturbing photographic vignettes accompanying the first edition of Klossowski's publication (in which two men and a woman engage in sado-masochistic acts), and is essential for rethinking the stakes of delegated performance for both the audience's visual pleasure and that of the participant. (The most brutal image of this reciprocal pleasure recently is Sierra's two-channel video *Los Penetrados* [2010], showing a multiple and near-industrialised array of anal penetration between couples of different races and genders.)

Klossowski's writings therefore invite us to move beyond the impasse of certain intellectual positions inherited from the 1960s: on the one hand, arguments that society is all-determining as a set of institutional and disciplinary constraints (Frankfurt School, structuralism), and on the other hand, arguments for the perpetual vitality and agency of the subject which continually subverts and undermines these restrictions (post-structuralism, Deleuze and Guattari). Rather than collapsing these positions, Klossowski requires us to take on board a more complex network of libidinal drives that require perpetual restaging and renegotiation. This tension between structure and agency, particular and universal, spontaneous and scripted, *voyeur* and *voyant*, is key to the aesthetic effect and social import of the best examples of delegated performance.

Although the artist delegates power to the performer (entrusting them with agency while also affirming hierarchy), delegation is not just a one-way, downward gesture. In turn, the performers also delegate something to the artist: a guarantee of authenticity, through their proximity to everyday social reality, conventionally denied to the artist who deals merely in representations. By relocating sovereign and self-constituting authenticity *away* from the singular artist (who is naked, masturbates, is shot in the arm, etc.) and *onto* the collective presence of the performers who metonymically signify an irrefutable socio-political issue (homelessness, race, immigration, disability, etc.), the artist outsources authenticity and relies on his performers to supply this more vividly, without the disruptive filter of celebrity. At the same time, the realism invoked by this work is clearly not a return to modernist authenticity of the kind dismantled by Adorno and post-structuralism. By setting up a situation that unfolds with a greater or lesser degree of unpredictability, artists give rise to a highly directed form of authenticity: singular authorship is put into question by delegating control of the work to the performers; they confer upon the project a guarantee of realism, but do this through a highly authored situation whose precise outcome cannot be foreseen. In wresting a work of art from this event, the artist both relinquishes and reclaims power: he or she agrees to temporarily lose control over the situation before returning to select, define and circulate its representation.[42] Authenticity is invoked, but then questioned and reformulated, by the indexical presence of a particular social group, who are both individuated *and* metonymic, live *and* mediated, determined *and* autonomous.

At the same time, the phenomenological experience of confronting these performers always testifies to the extent to which people relentlessly exceed the categories under which they have been recruited. Using amateurs is essential in this regard, for it ensures that delegated performance will never assume the seamless character of professional acting, and keeps open a space of risk and ambiguity. That this amateurism nevertheless provokes a sense of moral outrage betrays the extent to which institutional perversion has been internalised as fully normal, while that of the artists comes across as unacceptable. The logic is one of fetishistic disavowal: I know that society is all-exploiting, but all the same, I want artists to be an exception to this rule. When artists make the patterns of institutional subordination that we undergo every day both visible and available for experiential pleasure, the result is a moral queasiness; and yet the possibility of this also being a source of *jouissance* and a 'tool' is precisely the point of Klossowski's disturbing analysis. What becomes thinkable if the pleasure of reification in these works of art is precisely analogous to the pleasure we all take in our own self-exploitation?

IV. Performance in Context

It should be clear by now that I am trying to argue for a more complicated understanding of delegated performance than that offered by a Marxist framework of reification or a contemporary critical discourse rooted in positivist pragmatics and injunctions to social amelioration (as discussed in Chapter 1), all of which reduce these works to standard-issue questions of political correctness. The perverse pleasures underlying these artistic gestures offer an alternative form of knowledge about capitalism's commodification of the individual, especially when both participants and viewers appear to enjoy the transgression of subordination to a work of art. If one is not to fall into the trap of merely condemning these works as reiterations of capitalist exploitation, it becomes essential to view art not as part of a seamless continuum with contemporary labour, but as offering a specific space of experience where those norms are suspended and put to pleasure in perverse ways (to return to Sade, a space not unlike that of BDSM sex). Rather than judging art as a model of social organisation that can be evaluated according to pre-established moral criteria, it is more productive to view the conceptualisation of these performances as properly *artistic decisions*. This is not to say that artists are uninterested in ethics, only to point out that ethics is the ground zero of any collaborative art. To judge a work on the basis of its preparatory phase is to neglect the singular approach of each artist, how this produces specific aesthetic consequences, and the larger questions that he/she might be struggling to articulate.[43]

And what might these larger questions be? Artists choose to use people as a material for many reasons: to challenge traditional artistic criteria by reconfiguring everyday actions as performance; to give visibility to certain social constituencies and render them more complex, immediate and physically present; to introduce aesthetic effects of chance and risk; to problematise the binaries of live and mediated, spontaneous and staged, authentic and contrived; to examine the construction of collective identity and the extent to which people always exceed these categories. In the most compelling examples of this work, a series of paradoxical operations is put into play that impedes any simplistic accusation that the subjects of delegated performance are reified (decontextualised, and laden with other attributes). To judge these performances on a scale with supposed 'exploitation' at the bottom and full 'agency' at the top is to miss the point entirely. The difference, rather, is between 'art fair art' and the better examples of this work that reify *precisely in order to discuss reification*, or which exploit precisely *to thematise exploitation itself*. In this light, the risk of superficiality that occasionally accompanies the reductive branding or packaging of social identities in a work of art ('the unemployed', 'the blind', 'children', 'brass band players', etc.) should always be set against the dominant modes of mediatic representation against which these works so frequently intend to do battle.[44] This, for me, is the dividing line between the facile gestures of so much gala and art fair art and those more troubling works that do not simply take advantage of contemporary labour conditions but foreground our relationship to them through the presentation of conventionally under-exposed constituencies. It is true that at its worst, delegated performance produces quirkily staged reality designed *for* the media, rather than paradoxically mediated presence. But at its best, delegated performance produces disruptive events that testify to a shared reality between viewers and performers, and which defy not only agreed ways of thinking about pleasure, labour and ethics, but also the intellectual frameworks we have inherited to understand these ideas today.

9

Pedagogic Projects: 'How do you bring a classroom to life as if it were a work of art?'

This chapter of this book has been the most difficult to write, because pedagogic art projects touch most closely my own professional field of activity: teaching and research. When artistic practice claims to be pedagogic, it immediately creates conflicting criteria in my mind: art is given to be seen by others, while education has no image. Viewers are not students, and students are not viewers, although their respective relationships to the artist and teacher have a certain dynamic overlap. The history of participatory art nevertheless incites us to think of these categories more elastically. For many decades, artists have attempted to forge a closer connection between art and life, referring to their interventions into social processes as art; most recently this includes educational experiments. As I have indicated throughout this book, such categorical expansions place considerable pressure on spectatorship as conventionally understood. Indeed, in its strictest sense, participation forecloses the traditional idea of spectatorship and suggests a new understanding of art without audiences, one in which everyone is a producer. At the same time, the existence of an audience is ineliminable, since it is impossible for everyone in the world to participate in every project.

The 2000s saw a marked rise of pedagogic projects undertaken by contemporary artists and curators. The cancellation of Manifesta 6 (2006), an attempt to re-organise the itinerant European biennial as an art school in Nicosia, was the moment when this trend began to accelerate. There was a conspicuous surge of interest in examining the relationship between art and pedagogy, dually motivated by artistic concerns (a desire to augment the intellectual content of relational conviviality) and developments in higher education (the rise of academic capitalism, discussed below).[1] Since then, both artists and curators have become increasingly engaged in projects that appropriate the tropes of education as both a method and a form: lectures, seminars, libraries, reading-rooms, publications, workshops and even full-blown schools.[2] This has paralleled the growth of museum education departments, whose activities are no longer restricted to classes and workshops to enhance the viewer's understanding of a particular exhibition or collection, but can now include research networks with universities, symposia reflecting upon their practice, and interdisciplinary conferences whose scope extends far beyond the enhancement of a museum's exhibition programme.[3] In museums and art schools throughout Europe (and increasingly the US), conferences have been held to re-examine the politics and potentialities of art education, while numerous art magazines have produced special issues examining the intersection of art, education and performance.[4] The most recent developments have been institutional and corporate variants on the self-organised model, such as the Serpentine Gallery's off-site education base in London (*The Centre for Possible Studies*, 2009 onwards), Bruno Latour's interdisciplinary *School of Political Arts* at Université Sciences-Po (Paris, 2010 onwards), but also Nike's collaboration with Cooper Hewitt to produce art and design workshops for teenagers (*Make Something*, New York, 2010). It should be stressed, however, that pedagogic projects are still marginal in relation to the ongoing business of the art market, even though they are increasingly influential in the European public sector.[5]

The first thing that seems important to note in this efflorescence of artistic interest in education is its indication of a changing relationship between art and the academy. If in the past, academia was perceived as a dry and elitist institution (an association that persists in the use of 'academic' as a derogatory adjective), today education is figured as art's potential ally in an age of ever-decreasing public space, rampant privatisation and instrumentalised bureaucracy. At the same time, as Irit Rogoff notes, there is a certain slippage between terms like 'education', 'self-organised pedagogies', 'research' and 'knowledge production', so that the radical strands of the intersection between art and pedagogy blur easily with the neoliberal impetus to render education a product or tool in the 'knowledge economy'.[6] So how can we tell the difference between 'pedagogical aesthetics' and more generative intersections of art and education?[7] The current literature on art and pedagogy (of which Irit Rogoff's contribution is frequently cited) tends not to deal with specific modes of this intersection and the differences between art and education as discourses. For Rogoff, both art and education revolve around Foucault's notion of 'parrhesia' or 'free, blatant public speech': an educational turn in art and curating, she argues, might be 'the moment when we attend to the production and articulation of truths – not truth as correct, as provable, as fact, but truth as that which collects around it subjectivities that are neither gathered nor reflected by other utterances'. Rogoff's theory has been influential, but has the drawback of being rather general: no specific examples are given or analysed. The artist Luis Camnitzer is more to the point when he surveys the history of Latin American conceptual art, and notes that art and alternative pedagogy shared a project in resisting abuses of power by the state in the 1960s.

In the southern hemisphere, educational upheavals were premised on increasing access to education and equipping people with new creative tools; in the US and Europe, by contrast, the oppressed were equated with students, leading to changes only in the content of education, premised on freeing individuality with the assumption that democracy would follow.[8]

The history that Camnitzer outlines is formative for the one I am tracing, since the moment of institutional critique in art arrived at the same time as education's own self-examination, most notably in Paulo Freire's *Pedagogy of the Oppressed* (1968), which I will return to below. These ruptures resulted in similar moves away from authoritarian models of transferring knowledge and towards the goal of empowerment through collective (class) awareness. Camnitzer – along with Joseph Beuys, Lygia Clark, Jef Geys and Tim Rollins (to name just a handful of figures) – is one of the most important precursors for contemporary artists working at the interface of art and pedagogy. For all of these artists, education was – or continues to be – a central concern in their work.

It is Joseph Beuys, however, who remains the best-known point of reference for contemporary artists' engagement with experimental pedagogy; in 1969 he claimed that 'to be a teacher is my greatest work of art'.[9] Ten years after he began working in the sculpture department of the Düsseldorf Kunstakademie, Beuys protested against admission restrictions and in August 1971 accepted 142 students onto his course.[10] This attempt to synchronise a professional position with his credo that 'everyone is an artist' (or at least, an art student) led to his expulsion from the Kunstakademie just over a year later, and to the formation, in 1973, of his own institution, the Free International University for Creativity and Interdisciplinary Research (still operational in the mid 1990s). Dedicated to realising the capacity of each person to be a creative being, this free, non-competitive, open academy offered an interdisciplinary curriculum in which culture, sociology and economics were integrated as the foundations of an all-encompassing creative programme. The Free International University sought to implement Beuys's belief that economics should not be restricted to a question of money but should include alternative forms of capital, such as people's creativity.[11] Prior to founding the FIU, Beuys's performances had, from 1971 onwards, already turned away from symbolic, quasi-shamanic actions towards a pedagogic format – most notably lectures and seminars on social and political structures. In February 1972, for example, he held two lecture-actions on consecutive days at Tate and the Whitechapel Art Gallery, the former lasting a marathon six and a half hours. During that Summer, he set up the *Bureau for Direct Democracy* at Documenta 5 (1972) and engaged in debate with the casual public about electoral reform. As the '70s progressed, the blackboards bearing traces of these performance-discussions became installations, occupying the space for the remainder of the exhibition as a trace of social and intellectual exchange.[12]

From a contemporary perspective, one of Beuys's most salient later projects is *100 Days of the Free International University*, organised for Documenta 6 (1977). Thirteen interdisciplinary workshops, open to the public, featured trade unionists, lawyers, economists, politicians, journalists, community workers, educationalists and sociologists speaking alongside actors, musicians and young artists.[13] In moving beyond the humanities to embrace the social sciences, Beuys prefigures an important strand of recent curatorial and artistic activity.[14] However, there are important differences between Beuys and artists working today: Beuys's commitment to free education was for the most part dependent on his own charismatic leadership, rendering unclear the line between education and one-man performance; today's artists, by contrast, are less likely to present themselves as the central pedagogic figure. They outsource the work of lecturing and teaching to specialists in the field – in line with the broader tendency in recent performance art to delegate performance to other people (as discussed in the previous chapter). Very little attention has been paid in Anglophone art history to Beuys's activities of the 1970s, despite the fact that they form the most central precursor of contemporary socially engaged art, intersecting artistic goals with social, political and pedagogic ambitions. Only Jan Verwoert provides a nuanced reading of Beuys's persona as a teacher in the 1970s (and it is telling that his parents were both students of the artist). He argues that Beuys's output should be characterised as a hyper-intensity of pedagogic and political commitment – an excess that both reinforced and undermined his institutional position. Beuys was both 'too progressive and too provocative': rejecting a

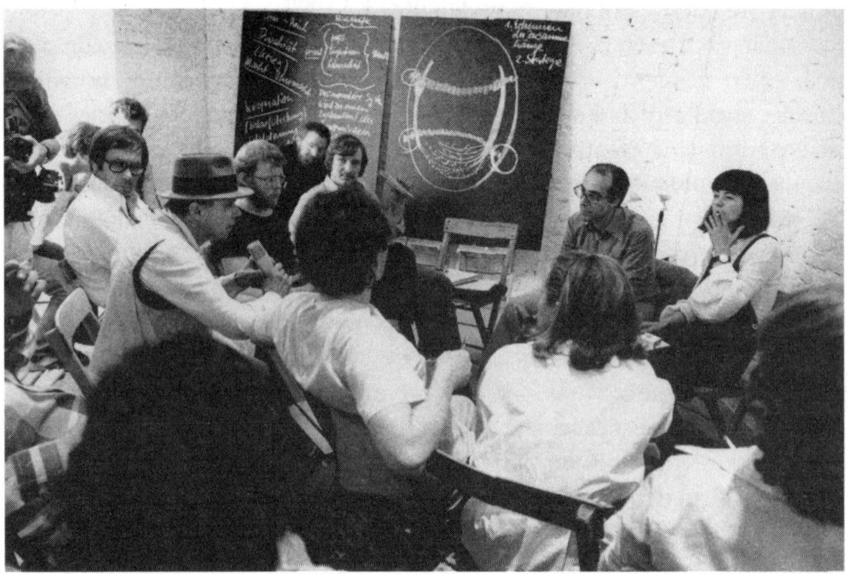

Joseph Beuys, Free International University seminar, 1977

curriculum, offering day-long critiques of student work, but also physically attacking the student's art if a point needed to be made.[15] During an official matriculation ceremony at the Kunstakademie, for example, he greeted the new students by carrying an axe and uttering inarticulate barking sounds into a microphone for ten minutes (*ÖÖ-Programm*, 1967). For Verwoert, the humour and excess of this gesture does not easily fit into his critics' narratives of mystical creativity, and seems to open up a parodic, more subversive aspect to Beuys's work as an artist and professor.

Furthermore, Verwoert also argues that Beuys's practice of speaking publicly 'should be treated not as a metadiscourse *on* his art but as an artistic medium sui generis'.[16] As seen in the reception of APG's activities (see Chapter 6), in the 1970s it was not yet possible to conceptualise public discussion as an artistic activity.[17] Beuys himself seemed to reinforce this impression that discussion was not a didactic medium, but a more immediate, quasi-spiritual mode of communication: 'I want to get to the origin of the matter, to the thought behind it . . . In the simplest terms, I am trying to reaffirm the concept of art and creativity in the face of Marxist doctrine.'[18] Today, we can recognise not just speech, but also teaching as an artistic medium. If Beuys drew a conceptual line between his output as a sculptor and his discursive/pedagogic work, many contemporary artists see no fundamental distinction between these categories. Programming events, seminars and discussions (and the alternative institutions that might result from these) can all be regarded as artistic outcomes in exactly the same way as the production of discrete objects, performances and projects. At the same time, pedagogic art raises a persistent set of epistemological problems for the art historian and critic: What does it mean to do education (and programming) *as art*? How do we judge these experiences? What kind of efficacy do they seek? Do we need to experience them first hand in order to comment on them?

Such questions can also be asked of most long-term art projects with activist or therapeutic goals, but the ambiguous status of pedagogic projects seems even more pressing for those of us already engaged in institutional education. I began writing this chapter when working at Warwick University, where the question of criteria of judgement in relation to academic activities had become crushingly remote from the motivations that first led me into this profession.[19] When I encountered artists speaking of education in creative and liberatory terms, it seemed perplexing, if not wilfully misguided: for me, the university was one of the most bureaucratic and stiflingly uncreative environments I had ever encountered. At the same time, I was sympathetic towards the disciplinary reorientation I was witnessing: artists seemed to be moving a 'relational' practice (in which open-ended conviviality was sufficient evidence of social engagement) towards discursive situations with high-level intellectual content. As an outsider, however, I was often dissatisfied with the visual and conceptual rewards of these projects. When I found projects I liked and respected, I had no idea how to communicate them to others: their dominant goal seemed to be the production of a dynamic experience for participants, rather than the production of complex artistic forms. The spectatorial implications of art becoming education are therefore a recurrent theme in the following case studies I have chosen to focus on: Tania Bruguera, Paul Chan, Paweł Althamer and Thomas Hirschhorn. Each presents a different approach to this problem of spectatorship in relation to the pedagogic task, and show the advances that have taken place in both project-based work and its documentation since 'Culture in Action' (1993, discussed in Chapter 7). I have necessarily presented these projects in a more narrative, subjective voice than my examples in previous chapters.

I. Useful Art

The first, and perhaps longest running, pedagogic project of the 2000s was *Cátedra Arte de Conducta* (2002–9): an art school conceived as a work of art by Cuban artist Tania Bruguera (b.1968). Based at her home in Havana Vieja and run with the help of two staff, it was dedicated to providing a training in political and contextual art for art students in Cuba. Bruguera established *Arte de Conducta* (or 'behaviour art') at the end of 2002, after returning to her country from participating in Documenta 11 with a sense of dissatisfaction at the limitations of creating artistic experiences for viewers. Instead she wished to make a concrete contribution to the art scene in Cuba, partly in response to its lack of institutional facilities and exhibition infrastructure, and partly in response to ongoing state restrictions on Cuban citizens' travel and access to information. A third factor was the recent and rapid consumption of Cuban art by US tourists in the wake of the 2000 Havana Biennial, in which young artists had found their work bought up wholesale and rapidly integrated into a Western market over which they had no control.[20] One of the aims of Bruguera's project was therefore to train a new generation of artists to deal self-reflexively with this situation, mindful of a global market while producing art that addressed their local context.

Strictly speaking, *Arte de Conducta* is best understood as a two-year course rather than as an art school proper: it was a semi-autonomous module under the auspices of the Instituto Superior de Arte (ISA) in Havana. Students didn't get credits for attending it, but the institutional affiliation was necessary in order for Bruguera to secure visas for visiting lecturers. In the early years, many of these visitors were funded by Bruguera herself, through a teaching position at the University of Chicago (2004–9).[21] *Conducta* or 'behaviour' is Bruguera's alternative to the Western term 'performance art', but it also evokes the Escuela de Conducta, a school for juvenile delinquents where Bruguera used to teach art. *Arte de Conducta,* however, was not concerned with enforcing disciplinary norms but with the opposite: its focus was art that engages with reality, particularly at the interface of usefulness and illegality – since ethics and the law are, for Bruguera, domains that need continually to be tested. One of the archetypal works produced at the school (and the first one I was exposed to in a crit) is *El Escandalo de lo Real* (2007) by Susana Delahante. When the student showed me the photograph of this work I had no idea what I was looking at; she explained that it was an image showing herself being impregnated, via a speculum, with the semen of a recently deceased man.[22] A less visceral example would be Celia and Yunior's *Registro de Población* (2004), in which the artists took advantage of the legal loophole by which it is possible to repeatedly apply for identity cards: accumulated sequentially, the dated cards evoke a work by On Kawara, while also undermining the authenticated uniqueness we associate with proofs of identity.

One of the first questions that tends to be raised in relation to pedagogic art projects concerns the composition of the student body. In the case of *Arte de Conducta*, this was both rigid and very fluid. Bruguera took on eight students each year, plus an art historian, who was expected to make art (like the other students) as well as producing a continual report of the project over that year, thereby guaranteeing that *Arte de Conducta* formed a historical account of itself from within. Beyond this official intake, the workshops were also open to everyone interested: previous students, their partners, and the general public (mainly professional artists and critics). This openness is an important difference between *Arte de Conducta* and other artist's schools, such as the Kuitca programme in Buenos Aires.[23] As such, the structure of Bruguera's school is both official and informal:

> The symbolic structure is the one where I'm reproducing the recognizable elements of an educational program, one that I install but do not respect. For example to enter the project one has to go through a selection process in front of an international jury who chooses the 'best' candidates. But once the workshops start I let in anybody who wants to attend even if they didn't make it through the selection committee.[24]

Some aspects of the course are more or less conventional: teaching, for example, is structured around one-week workshops that always include a public talk and crits of the students' work. Invited artists assign the students a specific project: Dan Perjovschi asked the students to make a newspaper, while Artur Żmijewski assigned the task of making a 'non-literal adaptation' of a communist propaganda film from Poland. Most of the visiting artists are engaged in performance in some way, and many are from former socialist countries, in order to help the Cuban students understand the transition their own society will inevitably be going through. There have also been curators and theorists (including myself), who together with the artists amount to an imported exhibition culture: bringing images and ideas to the island that do not otherwise circulate there due to severe restrictions on internet usage. Bruguera has also invited a lawyer and a journalist (to advise students on the legal and press implications of undertaking performance in the public sphere), as well as historians, sociologists and mathematicians. Teachers were encouraged to regard *Arte de Conducta* as a 'mobile school' and to use the whole city as a base for operations; during my time there, the Kosovan artist Sislej Xhafa asked students to make actions in a hotel (which Cubans are forbidden from entering), outside the Museum of the Revolution, and at a barber's shop. Each workshop ends with a Friday night fiesta at Bruguera's home. The aim is to produce a space of free speech in opposition to dominant authority (not unlike Freire's aims in Brazil) and to train students not just to make art but to experience and formulate a civil society.

If the question of representation is an ongoing theme in most art classes, the question of how to communicate this school-as-art to an external audience is an ongoing problem. It is telling that Bruguera did not attempt to do this for the first five years of the project. When invited to participate in the 2008 Gwangju Biennial, however, Bruguera decided to show *Arte de Conducta*; rather than exhibiting documentation, she made the decision to show a representative sample of the students' work, albeit in a rather conventional and unsatisfying installation. A more dynamic solution was found to mark the end of the school during the 2009 Havana Biennial. Entitled *Estado de Excepción*, it comprised nine group shows over as many days, open to the public between 5 and 9 p.m., de-installed every night and

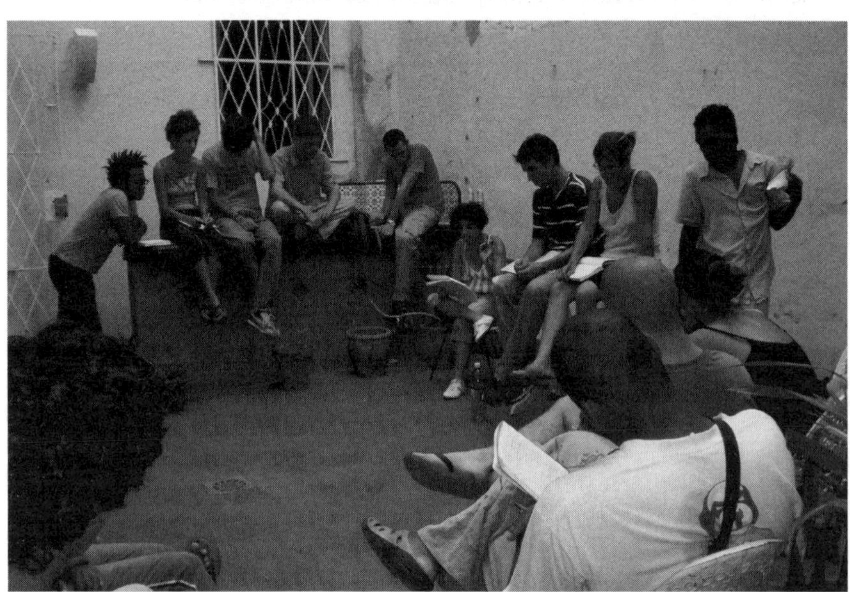

Tania Bruguera, *Cátedra Arte de Conducta*, 2002–9. Workshop with Elvia Rosa Castro.

re-installed every morning, thereby aiming to capture the urgency and intensity of the school as a whole. Each day was organised around themes such as 'Jurisdiction', 'Useful Art', and 'Trafficking Information', and presented a selection of work from the school alongside work by visiting lecturers (often sent as instructions), including Thomas Hirschhorn and Elmgreen & Dragset. Each night the space looked completely different, while the students' short, sharp interventions often outstripped everything else in the biennial in terms of their subversive wit and direct engagement with the Cuban situation. Many works dealt with issues of censorship, internet restrictions and social taboos; Alejandro Ulloa, for example, simply placed the most expensive piece of computer equipment in Cuba on a plinth – an anonymous grey cable for connecting a data projector.

The question remains, however, as to why *Arte de Conducta* needs to be called a work of art, rather than simply an educational project that Bruguera undertook in her home city. One possible answer invokes her authorial identity as an artist. The school, like many of the student projects it produced, can be described as a variation on what Bruguera has designated as 'useful art' (*arte util*) – in other words, art that is both symbolic *and* useful, refuting the traditional Western assumption that art is useless or without function. This concept allows us to view *Arte de Conducta* as inscribed within an ongoing practice that straddles the domains of art and social utility. Presenting *Arte de Conducta* at the Havana biennial was 'useful' in that it allowed Bruguera to expose to an international audience a younger generation who would never otherwise be chosen by the Biennial committee. During the same Havana Biennial, Bruguera presented *Tatlin's Whisper #6*, a controversial performance in which the Cuban public were offered one minute of free speech on a podium inside the Centro Wilfredo Lam.[25] While both of these projects could fall under the category of 'doing good' (as in the recent proliferation of NGO-style art projects), Bruguera defines useful art more broadly as a performative gesture that affects social reality, be this civil liberties or cultural politics, and which is not necessarily tied to morality or legality (as seen for example, in Susana Delahante's *El Escandalo do Real*, or in Bruguera's own *Tatlin's Whisper #6*).

Bruguera's practice, aiming to impact on both art and reality, requires that we grow accustomed to making double judgements, and to considering the impact of her actions in both domains. In the case of *Arte de Conducta*, it's necessary to apply the criteria of experimental education *and* of artistic project. From the former perspective, the conceptual framework devised for the school testifies to a rethinking of both art-school education and the genres being taught. For example, she refers not only to *conducta* or 'behaviour' instead of performance, and to 'guests' and 'members' rather than teachers and students, but membership of the school is both controlled (by applications and a jury) and open to all. Her own home is the school's headquarters and library, and she has an informal relationship with the students (who frequently stay overnight at her house, even in her bed, when she is away). As an artwork, the dynamic time-based solution that she eventually found for the project – a rapidly changing exhibition of the students' works alongside those of previous teachers – was exhilaratingly intense, sociable and artistically rewarding, widely agreed to be one of the best contributions to an otherwise ideologically leaden Havana Biennial.

However, one drawback of making these divisions between art and education, and their attendant disciplinary criteria, is the assumption that the way we judge respective disciplines is fixed (rather than mutable); it risks foreclosing the emergence of new criteria from their intersection. Although Bruguera views the project as a work of art, she does not address what might be artistic in *Arte de Conducta*. Her criterion is the production of a new generation of socially and politically engaged artists in Cuba, but also the exposure of visiting lecturers to new ways of thinking about teaching in context. Both of these goals are long-term and unrepresentable. Rhetorically, Bruguera always privileges the social over the artistic, but I would argue that her entire shaping of *Arte de Conducta* is reliant on an artistic imagination (an ability to deal with form, experience and meaning). Rather than perceiving art as something separate (and subordinate) to a 'real social process', art is in fact integral to her conception of each project. Equally, her artistic imagination was manifest in the method she devised to display this project to the viewers of the Havana Biennial. Both art and education can have long-term goals, and they can be equally demateralised, but imagination and daring are crucial to both.

II. A Project in Three Parts

If Bruguera attempts to merge art and education, then the US artist Paul Chan (b.1973) keeps them at one remove. Best known for highly aestheticised animated video installations, such as *The 7 Lights* (2005–7), and for his works on paper, Chan is an eloquent artist who has frequently defended an Adornian understanding of art as a language that cannot be subject to instrumentalised rationality, and whose political potency lies in this very exceptionalism. This is important to bear in mind when considering his *Waiting for Godot in New Orleans* (2007), a project premised on a clear division between process and outcome. As with many works in the public sphere, some preamble is needed to set the scene. Chan always recounts the story in the same way: in October 2006 he visited New Orleans to install one of his works and give a talk at Tulane University. There he first saw the impact of Hurricane Katrina, which one year earlier had ravaged the poorest areas of the city and left certain districts, such as the Lower Ninth Ward, in a state of apocalyptic devastation. Entire houses were washed away, leaving only the ghostly remainder of concrete steps leading to what was once a home. Chan recalls how, standing in this landscape, he had an uncanny sense of déjà-vu: 'it had the feel of every production of Godot I'd ever seen'.[26] Shortly afterwards, he made a drawing of this landscape as a stage set which, with the assistance of New York-based commissioning agency Creative Time, was realised during November 2007 as five performances of Beckett's *Waiting for Godot* staged by the Classical Theatre of Harlem.[27] The choice of Beckett's bleak high modernist play seemed painfully appropriate to New Orleans, since the central political scandal of the US government's response to the aftermath of Hurricane Katrina had been one of chronic delay.

Chan is at pains to state, however, that *Waiting for Godot in New Orleans* did not solely comprise the theatrical production:

> [T]o imagine that the play was the thing is to miss the thing. We didn't simply want to stage a site-specific performance of Godot. We wanted to create, in the process of staging the play, an image of art as a form of reason. What I mean is that we wanted to use the idea of doing the play as the departure point for inaugurating a series of causes and effects that would bind the artists, the people in New Orleans, and the city together in a relationship that would make each responsible for the other. The project, in other words, was an experiment in using art to organize a new image of life in the city two years after the storm.[28]

To reflect this, the production's subtitle was 'A tragicomedy in two acts, a project in three parts'. The former self-evidently refers to Beckett's play, while the latter alludes to a 'DIY residency' comprising eight months of workshops and teaching; to the open-air performances in the Lower Ninth Ward and Gentilly areas of New Orleans; and to a 'shadow fund' in which money was raised and left behind for local organisations engaged in rebuilding the city.[29] In effect, however, despite the clarity of Chan's tripartite conceptualisation, in which the three elements are theoretically equal, the main focus of critical attention to date has always focused on the play.[30] In reading this project through the lens of art and education I therefore want to cut against the grain of *Godot*'s reception to date and take seriously the artist's claim that all three aspects of the project were equally weighted.

Given the almost fail-proof combination of a canonical modernist play, a well-established theatre company, a hauntingly bleak location, and the backdrop of a natural disaster and unquestionable political injustice, one may well wonder why the artist went to such lengths to pave the way for this production in the form of eight months' residency and teaching. The artist has explained this situation in terms that are part ethical (not imposing one's vision on a population, responding to its needs) and part strategic (generating a body of supporters to realise his vision and protect it). According to Chan's narrative, he met with great opposition and resistance in New Orleans; the suggestion to work with schools and produce a shadow fund came out of his conversations with residents, who were sick of being a backdrop to catastrophe tourism. They didn't want art, but concrete help. Chan moved to the city in August 2007 and began teaching for free at New Orleans University (which needed a contemporary art history class, since their teacher had perished in Katrina) and at Xavier University (which needed studio classes on how to do a resumé and portfolios). This teaching helped him to build up a base of volunteers and to spread news of the project by word of mouth. At the same time, he sought to establish relationships with key activists and organisers through potluck dinners (Chan refers to this as 'the political work of disarming'). The Classical Theatre of Harlem, meanwhile, also relocated to New Orleans, and began rehearsing in an abandoned Catholic school, where they held workshops for community theatre groups if requested.

It is significant that Chan's educational work was not an interrogation into the uses of education in and of itself, but the means to an end: using the skills he had in order to integrate himself into the city, build up alliances, and realise his vision. Competencies were maximised: unlike Bruguera outsourcing teaching to others, Chan used his own expertise. His weekly art history seminars were themed around artists he admired (plus 'Theodor Adorno on the occasion of his birthday'), while the studio classes – 'Directed Reading, or Art Practicum' – offered a guide to the art world: how to write artists' statements, get funding, compose press releases, and so on.[31] The play's production and theatre workshops, meanwhile, were handed over to the Classical Theatre of Harlem, for whom residencies and workshops are already a regular part of their practice. In other words, skills were carefully parcelled out to maximise efficacy. The strength of this approach could be said to reside in precisely such a clear division between the domains of education, art and performance: Chan reminds us that his organisational techniques are learnt from activism, and describes the project as a 'campaign'. On the other hand, this division between organisation, fundraising and final production maintains a clear separation between the managerial and creative aspects of the project in a way that could be seen as artistically conservative; Bruguera, for instance, would insist on viewing all parts of such a process as art. It is telling that on Chan's website we can find the syllabi for his courses, but no images of the classes. Likewise, no official footage of the performance exists, only a bootleg video. The visual images that do circulate around the project always revolve around the carefully wrought production: Chan's initial drawing (available as a free download), production stills, and photographs of the signage advertising *Godot* – unforgettable shots of a desolate New Orleans landscape punctuated by a white sign with black text, bearing Beckett's opening stage directions: 'A country road. A tree. Evening.'

Chan has recently sold the *Godot* archive to MoMA, where it has been displayed as three walls of papers pasted onto blown-up photographs of the

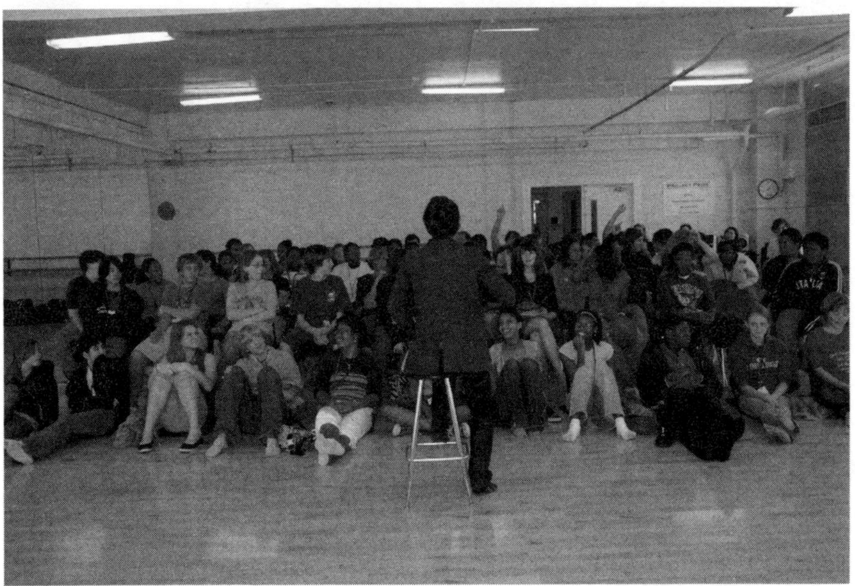

Paul Chan, *Waiting for Godot in New Orleans*, 2007. The artist teaching at Lusher High School.

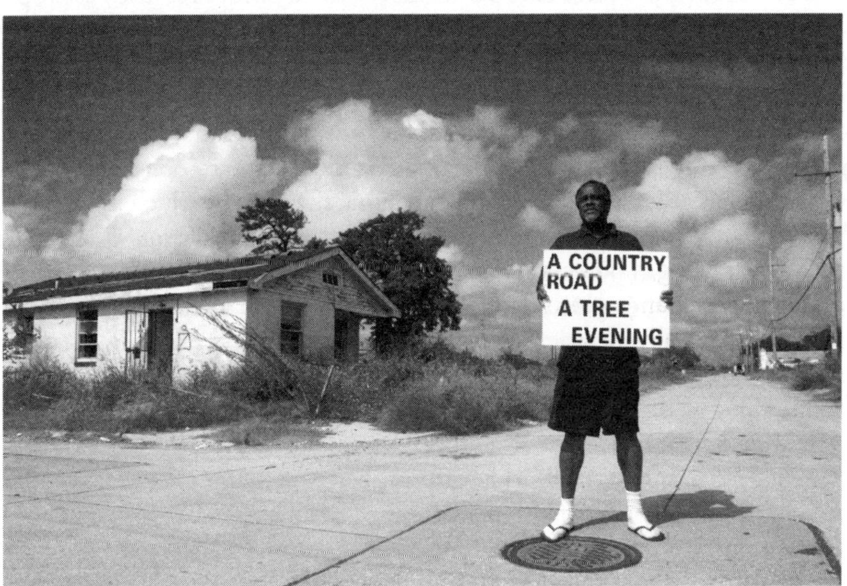

Paul Chan, *Waiting for Godot in New Orleans*, 2007. Robert Green and production signage.

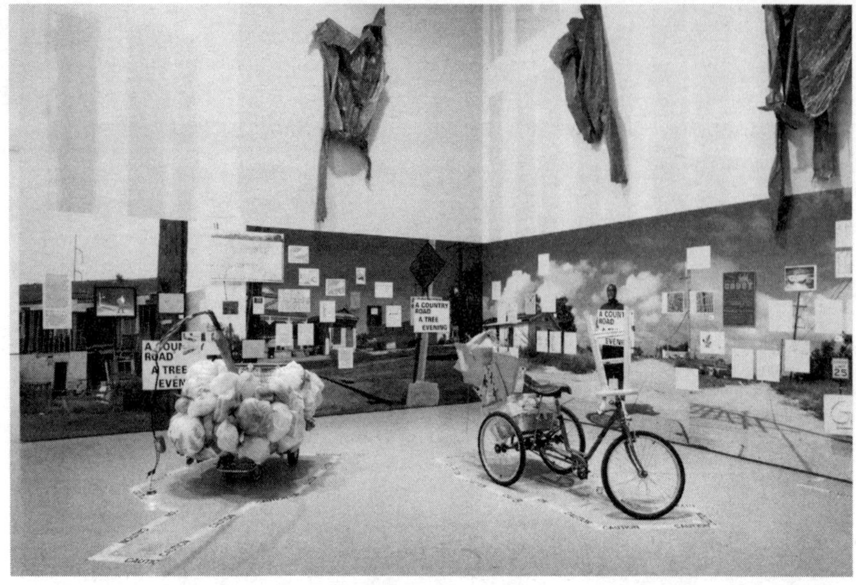

Paul Chan, *Waiting for Godot in New Orleans Archive*, 2010, installation view at MoMA

Lower Ninth Ward (working notes, maps, the seminar syllabi, Susan Sontag's essay on her production of *Waiting for Godot in Sarajevo*), radical pamphlets framed behind glass, three blue plastic sheets, three 'sculptures' used as props in the performances, and a small plasma screen showing the 'bootleg video' (which makes its unofficial status questionable). Unlike Jeremy Deller's archive of *The Battle of Orgreave* (discussed in Chapter 1), the selection of objects in Chan's display is geared towards representing the theatrical production rather than to the social and political events occasioning this work. He has also edited a book documenting the project, which is comprehensive but classical in format, including a careful selection of images charting the work's process, press clippings about Katrina, reprinted essays (Sontag once more, plus Alain Badiou and Terry Eagleton), the school syllabi, and Chan's interviews with key participants. The overall impression is one of order, rather than the chaotic polyvocality and dissent that mark the publications of, say, Thomas Hirschhorn.

Listening to Chan speak about the process of realising *Godot*, one realises that the best documentation of this project is neither the archive nor the book, but the performative medium of the lecture accompanied by a powerpoint: live, narrative and time-based. To my knowledge, Chan has given this talk three times in New York City; I have heard it twice and both times the audience were gripped. The story he tells is a meditation on art, politics and community-building – in short, everything that is glossed over in the archival presentation at MoMA. Even though *Waiting for Godot in New Orleans* was not participatory in any conventional sense,

Chan identifies two types of social and political work that took place in relation to realising the project: before the event (which was 'painfully conventional – like any politics') and during the event ('which makes possible a place where these things [i.e. politics] don't matter any more').[32] In other words, Chan sustains simultaneously two different registers of the political: as instrumentalised diplomacy, and as the suspension of this instrumentalisation in the autonomy of the work of art. This Adornian inclination towards art as a sanctuary where means-ends rationality is set aside makes Chan an unusual figure among artists today: rather than using art to bring about social change, he uses activist strategies to realise a work of art. The more common tendency for socially engaged artists is to adopt a paradoxical position in which art as a category is both rejected and reclaimed: they object to their project being called art because it is also a real social process, while at the same time claiming that this whole process is art.

III. Common Tasks

Chan's articulate understanding of the dual nature of art's politics could not be further from the intuitive operations of Polish artist Paweł Althamer (b.1967), who also works across sculpture (invariably a form of self-portraiture) and collaborative projects, but who views all parts of this process as an artistic adventure. His longest-running collaboration is with the Nowolipie Group, an organisation in Warsaw for adults with mental or physical disabilities, to whom he has been teaching a Friday night ceramics class since the early 1990s. Although these began in a conventional pedagogic mode – each week he sets the group an assignment; when I visited, they were building castles – increasingly, the class leads Althamer: the experience of teaching provides a rich source of ideas for him, for whom the educational process cuts two ways ('They teach me to be more mad').[33] For example, one of the group, Rafal Kalinowski, always builds clay biplanes regardless of the week's set theme. In 2008 Althamer arranged for the group to wear matching overalls and take a trip on a biplane, which became the subject of a short film by Althamer's frequent collaborator, Artur Żmijewski (*Winged*, 2008). This long-term collaboration recently led to a series of works called *Common Task* (2009), a 'science fiction film in real time', in which Althamer took the Nowolipie Group and his neighbours in the Bródno district of Warsaw (residents of a socialist-era housing estate), all dressed in gold jumpsuits, to visit the Atomium in Brussels. Subsequent voyages, with a smaller team of travellers, were then made to Niemeyer's architecture in Brasília, and to the Dogon people in Mali.[34]

Since 2000, Althamer's work has moved in an increasingly unexhibitable direction, a shift that has coincided with an extension of his interest in education. In 2005 he was commissioned by a German institution to make a work celebrating the centenary of Albert Einstein. Rather than producing a portable sculpture, Althamer developed *Einstein Class*, a six-month project to teach physics to a group of seven juvenile delinquents in Warsaw, most of whom had been expelled from school. The tutor he selected for this task was a maverick science teacher who had recently lost his job due to his unconventional teaching style. The male pupils, who all came from the run-down Praga district of Warsaw, were taught playful science experiments in a number of locations: in the teacher's garden, in a field, on a beach and in Althamer's studio (also in Praga). The boys then demonstrated these experiments to their neighbours. The whole project was documented on video by the Polish filmmaker Krzysztof Visconti (*Einstein Class*, 2006), who interspersed it with interviews with Althamer, the children and their parents. As documentation, the video is unremarkable, and bears no relation to the chaotic intensity of the project; it seems at pains to normalise Althamer's initiative and prove its positive effect upon the students. The dynamic of *Einstein Class* was, in my experience, far more vivid and demanding. One evening I accompanied Althamer to the science teacher's house, where he wanted to show the first edit of the documentary to the boys. When we arrived, full-scale mayhem was underway: the boys were playing gabba music at full blast, surfing the internet, smoking, throwing fruit around, fighting and threatening to push each other into the garden pond. In the middle of this frenzy stood an oasis of calm: the science teacher and Althamer, utterly oblivious to the chaos around them. Only a handful of the boys watched the video (which depicted nothing of this bedlam); the rest were more interested in trying to steal my mobile phone or surf the net. As the evening progressed, it became clear that Althamer had placed two groups of outsiders together – the

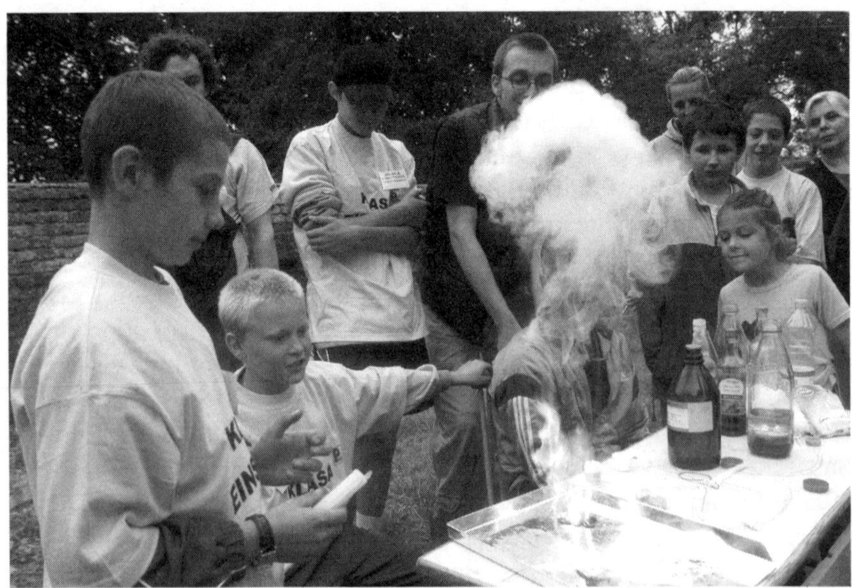

Paweł Althamer, *Einstein Class*, 2005

kids and the science teacher – and this social relationship operated as a belated corrective to his own experience of feeling disengaged at school. *Einstein Class*, like many of Althamer's works, is typical of his identification with marginal subjects, and his use of them to realise a situation through which he can retro-actively rehabilitate his own past.

In exhibition, Althamer has attempted to deal with the problem of documentation performatively: when the Einstein exhibition opened in Berlin, the teacher and kids all travelled to Germany for the opening as a continuation of their education.[35] When the film was screened in London in 2006, Althamer insisted that the Polish boys be invited to the opening, and their local equivalents hired to supply a dubbed translation for the film. As in many of Althamer's projects, altruism is inseparable from institutional inconvenience and upheaval (which the London exhibition made explicit in its title, 'What Have I Done to Deserve This?').[36] Althamer's subsequent projects with students, such as *Au Centre Pompidou* (2006), attempted to visualise an educational process through a collectively produced puppet show. And yet, for both this project and *Einstein Class*, one feels as if the visual outcome was forced, produced as a result of institutional pressure for visibility. At their best, the eccentricity of Althamer's ideas are self-sufficient and need no visual documentation.

Althamer's own academic formation is worth attending to, since it underlies many of his more vivid projects. Althamer was part of the so-called Kowalski Studio at the Warsaw Academy of Fine Arts, along with many of today's leading generation of Polish artists, including Artur Żmijewski and Katarzyna Kozyra. Professor Grzegorz Kowalski rejected the traditional model of 'master' to 'apprentice' in favour of 'visual games' – open-ended tasks that also functioned as a form of collective analysis, both critical and therapeutic. Under the working title 'Common Space – Private Space', Kowalski foregrounded the work of art as an effect of complex non-verbal communication performed by artists in interaction with each other, neutralising individualism.[37] Kowalski derived this technique from the architectural theory of his teacher, Oskar Hansen, who in 1959 had proposed 'open form', in which a structure can be added to, encouraging participation and a more vital relationship with reality, in contrast to 'closed form', to which it is impossible to incorporate additions.[38] One of the basic tenets of open form is that 'no artistic expression is complete until it has been appropriated by its users or beholders', whereas closed form reduces subjectivity to a passive element within a larger hierarchical structure.[39] As the curator Łukasz Ronduda has argued, when Hansen's idea of open form is translated into art, it brings about a 'death of the author', opening the way towards 'experimentation and highly complex (trans-individual) collective projects'.[40] Kowalski adopted Hansen's ideas as a pedagogic principle, but differs from his teacher's austere rationalism in encouraging a more subjective, poetic and quasi-Surrealist approach.

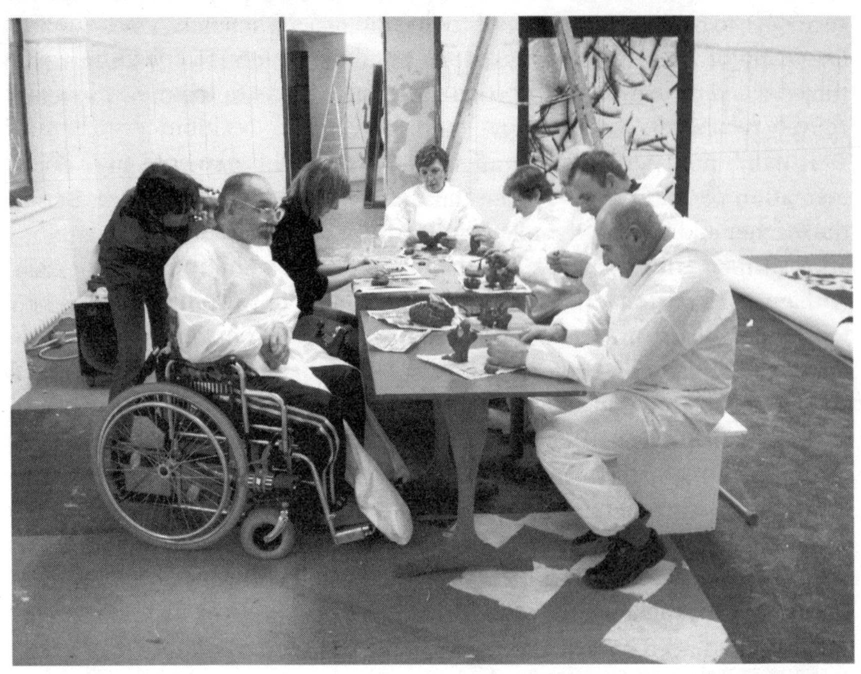

Paweł Althamer and Artur Żmijewski, *[S]election.pl*, 2005. The Nowolipie Group at work in the gallery.

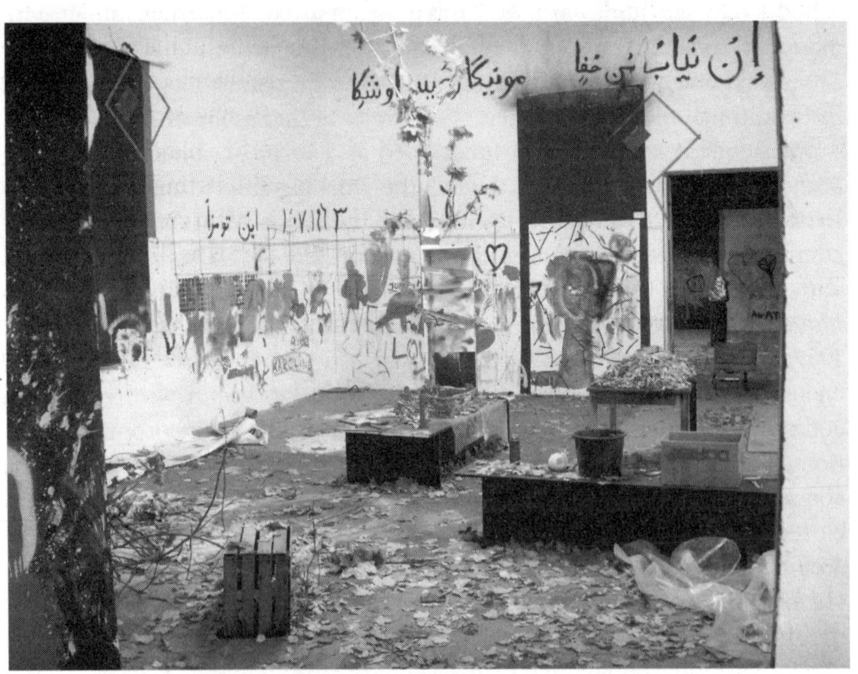

Paweł Althamer and Artur Żmijewski, *[S]election.pl*, 2005

In 2005, Żmijewski and Althamer revisited Kowalski's pedagogic method in a project called *Wybory.pl* ([S]election.pl). When CCA Ujazdowski Castle offered the two artists solo shows, they decided to collaborate on a process-based exhibition with their former colleagues from the Kowalski Studio. Constantly mutating and entirely chaotic, the exhibition was spread through several galleries of the CCA but defiantly broke both educational and exhibition conventions by subjecting individual contributions to one rule: anyone could adapt or amend or improve or destroy anyone else's work. Unlike 'Interpol' and the other performative exhibitions discussed in Chapter 7, *[S]election.pl* was open to the public during this process, who could observe the changes taking place as they happened. Żmijewski produced a fifty-minute video of the experience, showing its various phases over several weeks: from the artists making works, and gradually altering each other's pieces, to Althamer introducing other people into the process, such as children, the Nowolipie Group, and (most controversially) some prostitutes. A revealing sequence occurs when Althamer takes his daughter Veronika around the museum in a shopping trolley, encouraging her to interact with the objects, until he is brought to a cursory halt by a gallery invigilator. In this juxtaposition of the girl's tactile curiosity and museum prohibition, the viewer sees yet another indictment of the museum as mausoleum, but this time staged as a confrontation between a child's enthusiasm and the deadening interdictions of the institution. Żmijewski's careful editing of this incident allows the relationship of artist/teacher and viewer/student to come into particularly sharp focus. Throughout the video we see two divergent impulses at work. On the one hand, Althamer's urge to bring diverse constituencies into the museum and his Beuysian request that they see themselves as contemporary artists.[41] On the other hand, Żmijewski's interest in antagonism and destruction, continually setting fire to other people's politely crafted objects as if to assert that artistic creation can only occur *ex nihilo*, by erasing such conventional forms. It is as if Althamer and Żmijewski want to honour their former teacher by rewriting his pedagogic methods more trenchantly, encouraging their colleagues *and* the museum's employees to reflect more acutely on the meaning of art and why it comes to be exhibited.

As an exhibition, *[S]election.pl* was critically panned as incomprehensible, and even Kowalski sought to distance himself from what was being done in his honour.[42] Like *Einstein Class*, *[S]election.pl* suggests that experimental art-as-pedagogy doesn't necessarily lead to a cohesive and completed work of art or exhibition at the time of its making. Moreover, it is telling that the best documentation of *[S]election.pl* is time-based, like Chan's lectures, or Bruguera's *Estado de Excepción*. Through Żmijewski's video, we understand that while the show can be seen in the tradition of institutional critique (*qua* an analysis of institutional functions and conventions), it is also a series of vignettes documenting an education – for the children who painted on the floor, for the artists' former colleagues who watched their efforts cruelly incinerated, and for the museum itself, as seen in Żmijewski's curt exchange with one of the lady invigilators. Yet at the same time it also suggests that education is a closed process of social exchange, undertaken with mutual commitment, over a long duration, rather the performance of acts to be observed by others. It takes an artist with an eye for painfully telling detail to give a compelling structure and narrative to such a formless and invisible exchange.[43]

IV. What Functions, Produces

My final example is the Paris-based sculptor Thomas Hirschhorn (b.1957), who at regular intervals in the last decade has organised large-scale social projects in the form of a 'monument', often dedicated to a philosopher and produced in collaboration with residents who live near the site of its making, usually on the outskirts of a city. Since 2004, a pedagogic component has become increasingly important to these works. *Musée Précaire Albinet* (2004), located in the Aubervilliers district of north-east Paris near Hirschhorn's studio, involved the collaboration and training of local residents to install seven weekly exhibitions of works loaned from the Pompidou Centre collection (Beuys, Warhol, Duchamp, Malevich, Léger, Mondrian and Dalí). These were supported by a weekly timetable of events: an *atelier pour enfants* on Wednesdays, a writing workshop for adults on Thursdays, a general debate on Fridays, and a discussion with an art historian or critic on Saturdays. This timetable continued with a dinner, made by a family or group (using funds from the project) on Sundays; the de-installation and installation of work on Mondays; and the *vernissage* and party on Tuesdays.

As can be imagined, the primary audience for the *Musée Précaire Albinet* was the local and regularly returning inhabitants, rather than a general public of art enthusiasts. In 2009 Hirschhorn addressed the problem of this division in a large-scale project located in a suburb of Amsterdam called the Bijlmer. Its title, *The Bijlmer-Spinoza Festival*, was deliberately misleading: the project was not so much a festival as a large installation environment for hosting a programme of daily lectures and workshops. The construction was topped with an oversized sculpture of a book (Spinoza's *Ethics*), decorated with bunting, and framed by the residential tower blocks, a running track and an elevated railway line. A noticeboard and pile of free newspapers were positioned by the nearest path to entice passers-by, along with a car covered in brightly coloured votive objects for Spinoza. Entering the structure, one passed an unlicensed bar. The rest of the installation took its layout from the aerial view of an open book: the 'pages' were walls, and the spaces in between were rooms with different functions: a library of books by and about Spinoza, a newspaper office, an archival display about the history of Bijlmer (including footage of the plane crash that decimated one of the buildings in 1992), an internet room (hogged by children), and a workspace for the 'Ambassador', an art historian in residence. Some of these components gently parodied conventional methods of didactic display, such as a plinth showing enlarged photographs of 'book covers of important books from Spinoza's lifetime', and an empty vitrine bearing the sign 'Here was exhibited from the 2nd to the 10th May a copy of the "Tractatus Theologico-Politicus" of B.de Spinoza.'

However didactic these library/archive areas, they were less notable in this context than the planned schedule of workshops and lectures. Every day the same timetable was followed: 'Child's Play' at 4.30 p.m., a workshop in which local children learnt to re-enact classic works of body art from the 1970s (culminating in a performance on Saturdays); at 5.30 p.m. a lecture by philosopher Marcus Steinweg; and at 7 p.m. a play written by Steinweg, directed by Hirschhorn, and performed by local residents. On the first day I attended, adults drank, talked and smoked marijuana at the bar while the children (aged between six and twelve) were absorbed in the 'Child's Play' workshop, repeatedly shouting the word 'Abramovic' and doing lots of screaming.[44] After the workshop, the children hung around and played on various pieces of gym equipment while Steinweg gave his daily lecture – a largely improvised philosophical ramble delivered in English, and without notes, to an audience of around ten people seated on plastic chairs. The topic was 'Does Autonomy Exist?' None of us were taking notes, but this seemed fine since Steinweg didn't really deliver an argument so much as a stream of philosophical consciousness. The most enjoyable aspect of the lecture was the montage effect produced by the kids on running machines and general activity around the bar while Steinweg earnestly burbled on. The unfurling of these juxtapositions was more poignant and meaningful than the supposedly academic content of the lecture.

After precisely half an hour, Steinweg stopped talking and people drifted towards the bar. During this interlude, Hirschhorn set up the scenery for the 7 p.m. play by moving the gym equipment to the front of the stage – along with microphones, speakers and a human-sized box slathered in brown tape – and surrounded the whole ensemble with a wonky yellow 'brick wall' on a sheet of fabric. What proceeded is hard to describe as a play. Even though it was all in Dutch, I could still tell that there was no characterisation, no plot and no narrative. There were seven performers – although this varied from night to night, depending on how many decided to turn up. All of them read from a hand-held script, and took turns to speak their lines falteringly while engaged in various physical tasks: working on the treadmill, boxing a punchbag, weightlifting an oversized cardboard copy of the *Ethics*, or retreating to the tall box to announce the edict that banished Spinoza from Amsterdam in 1656. I won't dwell on the

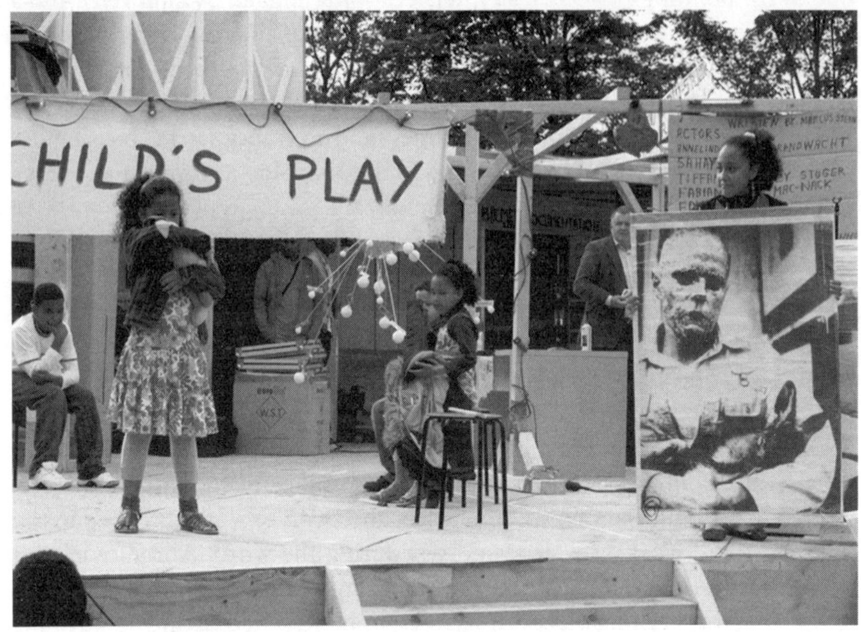

Thomas Hirschhorn, *The Bijlmer-Spinoza Festival*, 2009, 'Child's Play' workshops

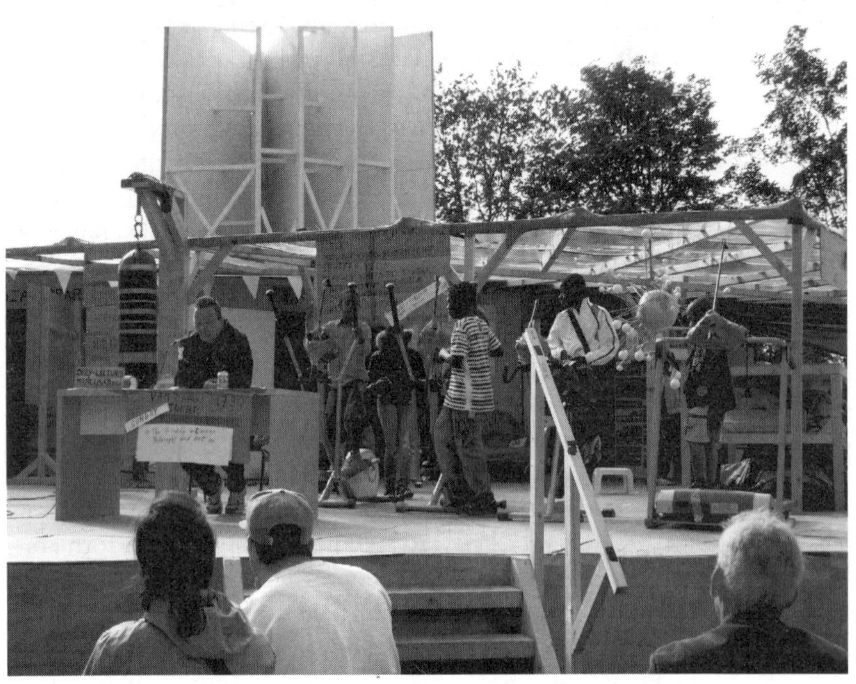

Thomas Hirschhorn, *The Bijlmer-Spinoza Festival*, 2009, Marcus Steinweg lecturing

play, only note my amused frustration at its impenetrability (to me, but also to the performers I spoke to).[45] Looking at the audience, I could not understand why such a mixed bag of people kept coming to hear these obscure lectures and watch these opaque – almost gruelling – performances. However, going through the whole experience again the following day, I realised that this random collective presence was the point. Rain was drizzling so there was less peripheral action; listening to Steinweg and watching the audience I understood the function of the lecture not to be one of information transfer, but of a shared experience in which many different sectors of society were brought together. You didn't need to follow the content, just give yourself over to a quiet meditative space (not unlike being in an open air, non-denominational church) and use this as a time for pondering whatever came to mind.

During the play, the drizzle became torrential rain. For the first time during *The Bijlmer-Spinoza Festival*, the performance had to stop and be relocated inside, in a cramped space under the plastic sheeting. The bedraggled audience surrounded the cast, while rain thrashed onto the plastic roof, occasionally leaking torrents, and rendering the performers' voices near inaudible. The finale of this insanely abstract quasi-Dadaist play was a sequence in which two of the speakers alternated the lines 'Wat functioneert, dat produceert' (what functions, produces) for two minutes (which felt more like ten); this now became an incantation in the face of the most unsympathetic and least functioning of environments. It was both bathetically funny and extremely poignant. Everyone was there for no reason other than the desire to see and do the same thing: to share a play initiated by an artist, whose singular energy propelled a self-selecting, entirely disparate bunch of people to show up every night and perform or watch an abstract play that nobody fully understood. The core of *The Bijlmer-Spinoza Festival* seemed to be this juxtaposition of social types around a series of mediating objects that were never quite what they seemed. The philosopher's lectures were not arguments to be understood or disputed, but were performances of philosophy; they were the spoken equivalent of the piles of photocopied Steinweg essays that form a sculptural presence in other Hirschhorn installations (for example, *U-Lounge*, 2003). The meaning of the theatre production also lay in the fact of its dogged performance, relentlessly taking place every day, regardless of the weather or number of performers who showed up. Like the lectures, it is pointless to analyse the specific content of this shambling spectacle; more important is to pay attention to its ongoing existence, willed into being by the artist, who managed to motivate people into performing something strange enough to continually captivate an audience. Similarly, the newspaper must be produced each day, regardless of the availability of news, or images, or relevant stories. At no point in *The*

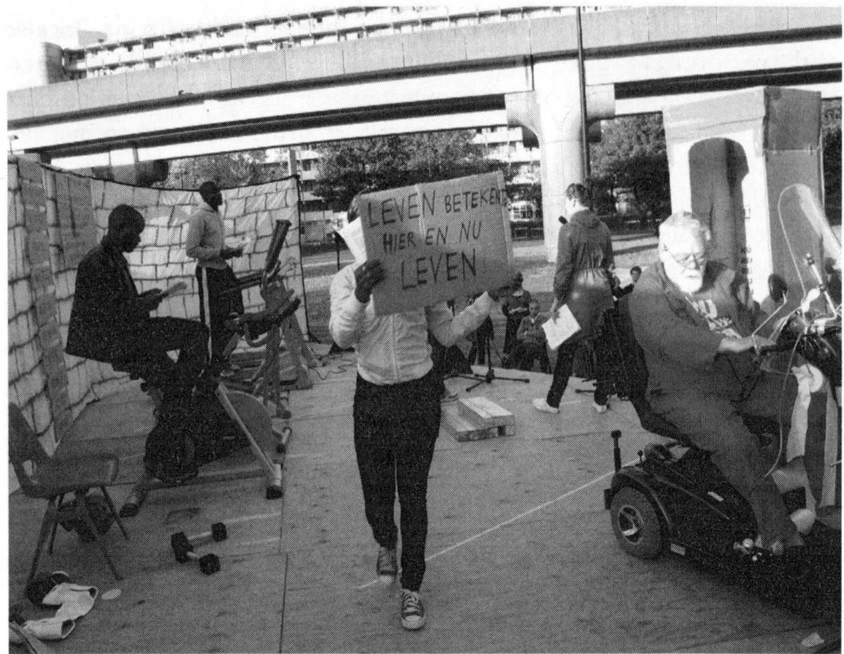

Thomas Hirschhorn, *The Bijlmer-Spinoza Festival*, 2009, The Spinoza Play

Bijlmer-Spinoza Festival was the ostensible content given to us to be analysed in a straightforward manner. The project was more akin to a machine, whose meaning lay in everyone's continual production and collective presence, and only secondarily in the content of what was being produced; it was not unlike endurance-based performance art – which is why the 'Child's Play' workshops seemed so apt an inclusion.

Hirschhorn frequently asserts that he is not interested in 'participation' or 'community art' or 'relational aesthetics' as labels for his work, preferring the phrase 'Presence and Production' to describe his approach to public space:

> I want to work out an alternative to this lazy, lousy 'democratic' and demagogic term 'Participation'. I am not for 'Participative-art', it's so stupid because every old painting makes you more 'participating' than today's 'Participative-art', because first of all real participation is the participation of thinking! Participation is only another word for 'Consumption'![46]

Hirschhorn's conjunction of art, theatre and education in *The Bijlmer-Spinoza Festival* was so memorable because it avoided the pitfalls of so much participatory art, in which there is no space for critical reflection, nor for a spectatorial position. Several audiences were addressed simultaneously and equally: both visitors to the 'Straat van Sculpturen' exhibition into which the project was integrated, and local residents who ran and used the site. Like Chan in his account of *Godot*, Hirschhorn gives an impressively polished lecture about the project, articulating its four phases (preparation, set up, exhibition, dismantling) and sixteen 'beams' of activity, but this structural overview fails to convey the unpredictable social mix that was magnetised by his idiosyncratic celebration of Spinoza. In the past, Hirschhorn has produced documentation of his 'monuments' in the form of a book gathering together all the correspondence, images, press coverage and audience feedback into one overwhelmingly dense publication that serves as a textual analogue for the event's social and organisational complexity. Unlike Chan's clearly structured rationale, however, there is an overt contradiction between Hirschhorn's words and his methods: he makes claims for art as a powerful, autonomous, almost transcendent force of non-alienation, but through projects that spill into the complexity of social antagonisms and deluge us with extra-artistic questions. Underlining this is a montage principle of co-existing incompatibilities: if Hirschhorn's gallery-based installations juxtapose horrific images of violence with high culture and philosophy (e.g. *Concretion-Re*, 2007), and (at their best) throb with social pessimism and anger, his public projects juxtapose different social classes, races and ages with a fearless defence of art and philosophy, and pulsate with eccentric optimism. It has become fashionable for contemporary artists to adopt the role of programming lectures and seminars, often as a substitute for research; in Hirschhorn's case, these events stand *in toto* as a form of artistic research and social experimentation. *The Bijlmer-Spinoza Festival* brought together a series of supposedly incompatible montage elements to prompt unforeseen collective and durational encounters; these experiences can in part be submitted to artistic criteria we have inherited from performance art, even while they also demand that we stretch these criteria in new directions.

V. Education, in Theory

Hirschhorn is a tricky character to end this chapter on, since he unabashedly maintains that art is the central motivation of his work, and that he is more interested in viewers than in students.[47] His contemporaries have tended to engage with this question by combining the production of students and viewers in different ways: Bruguera's *Arte de Conducta*, and Anton Vidokle's *unitednationsplaza* (2007–8) and *Night School* (2008–9) all unite an application procedure and an openness to all comers.[48] But in all of these contemporary examples, the artist operates from a position of amateur enthusiast rather than informed expert, and delegates the work of lecturing to others. It is as if the artist wants to be a student once more, but does this by setting up their own school from which to learn, combining the student/teacher position. The most celebrated theoretical model for this is Jacques Rancière's *The Ignorant Schoolmaster* (1987), in which he examines the case of maverick nineteenth-century teacher Joseph Jacotot, who is French, but finds himself teaching a class that speaks exclusively Flemish.[49] They have no language in common, rendering impossible a straightforward transmission of knowledge; Jacotot resolves this by reading a bilingual book with the class, painstakingly comparing the French and Flemish texts. What interests Rancière is not the successful outcome of this task (the students learning to speak French, or their understanding of the content of the book) but Jacotot's presumption of an *equality of intelligence* between himself and his students. The point, for Rancière, is not to prove that all intelligence is equal, but to see what can be achieved under that supposition. For Rancière, equality is a method or working principle, rather than a goal: equality is continually verified by being put into practice. *The Ignorant Schoolmaster* was written against the backdrop of educational changes taking place in France during the 1980s, but it is also, like much of Rancière's writing, a rejection of his own former teacher, Louis Althusser, who understood education to be a transmission of knowledge to subjects who do not have this knowledge.[50]

Rancière's book has been frequently cited in recent discussions of art and pedagogy – albeit more for its catchy title and case-study of Jacotot than for its theorisation of equality – but it is striking that his polemic makes no reference to the emergence of critical pedagogy in the late 1960s, which attempted to empower subjects through very similar means.[51] One of the foundational texts of critical pedagogy, Paulo Freire's *Pedagogy of the Oppressed* (1968), calls into question the 'banking' model of education, by which teachers deposit information into pupils to produce manageable subjects under a paternalistic social apparatus – a technique that reinforces oppression rather than granting the students consciousness of their position as historical subjects capable of producing change. Freire in Latin America, like Henry Giroux in the US, proposes the teacher as a co-producer of knowledge, facilitating the student's empowerment through collective and non-authoritarian collaboration. Unlike Rancière, it is significant that Freire maintains that hierarchy can never be entirely erased: 'Dialogue does not exist in a political vacuum. It is not a "free space" where you say what you want. Dialogue takes place inside some programme and content. These conditioning factors create tension in achieving goals that we set for dialogic education.' In other words, critical pedagogy retains authority, but not authoritarianism: 'Dialogue means a permanent tension between authority and liberty. But, in this tension, authority continues to be because it has authority vis-à-vis permitting student freedoms which emerge, which grow and mature precisely because authority and freedom learn self-discipline.'[52] Freire's framework applies equally to the history of participatory art I have been tracing through this book: a single artist (teacher) allows the viewer (student) freedom within a newly self-disciplined form of authority. Tellingly, the best examples provide 'programme and content' (Spinoza, for example, or Beckett), rather than a utopian space of undirected, open collaboration.

Critical pedagogy can therefore be seen as a rupture in the history of education that is contemporaneous with upheavals in art's own history circa 1968: its insistence on the breakdown of teacher/pupil hierarchy and participation as a route to empowerment finds its direct correlate in the breakdown of medium-specificity and a heightened attention to the viewer's role and presence in art. Continuing this analogue, we could even say that education has its own historic avant-garde in the experimental school Summerhill, founded by A. S. Neill in 1921, near Dresden, and relocated to the UK two years later. Neill maintained that in starting the school he had left education and taken up child psychology (indeed, he later pursued his own analysis with Wilhelm Reich). The first pupils were initially problem children who had been expelled from other institutions, rather like Althamer's *Einstein Class*; Neill reportedly dealt with them by subverting his authority – encouraging the vandals to smash more windows, and so on.[53] Summerhill continues to operate on the basis of self-organised anarchy, with voluntary attendance at classes, no punishment for swearing, and rules established in collaboration with the pupils at a weekly meeting. As A. S. Neill writes:

> You cannot make children learn music or anything else without to some degree converting them into will-less adults. You fashion them into accepters of the *status quo* – a good thing for a society that needs obedient sitters at dreary desks, standers in shops, mechanical catchers of the 8.30 suburban train – a society, in short, that is carried on the shabby shoulders of the scared little man – the scared-to-death conformist . . . Summerhill is a self-governing school, democratic in form. Everything connected with social, or group, life, including punishment for social offences, is settled by vote at the Saturday night General School Meetings.[54]

Summerhill continues to be a focus of controversy in the UK due to its regular battles with OFSTED (the Office for Standards in Education, Children's Services and Skills), most recently in 2007, yet its reputation for anarchy is misplaced: as in Freire (and in the best examples of participatory art), its organisation dialectically sustains a tension between freedom and structure, control and agency. But if both critical pedagogy and participatory art effectively produce a form of institutional critique within their respective disciplines in the 1960s, what does it mean for these two modes to converge so frequently today, as they do in projects of the past decade?

V. Academic Capitalism

Anton Vidokle, the artist-curator of *unitednationsplaza* and *Night School*, recently observed that

> Schools are one of the few places left where experimentation is to some degree encouraged, where emphasis is supposedly on process and learning rather than product. Schools are also multidisciplinary institutions by nature, where discourse, practice and presentation can co-exist without privileging one over the other.[55]

From a position internal to the academy, however, this emphasis on free experimentation can seem somewhat idealised. Professional academia in the UK, and increasingly in Europe, has since the 1980s become increasingly subject to the continual withdrawal of government subsidies, leading higher education to operate within a business framework.[56] Entrepreneurial research activities, encouraging partnerships with industry, increased student participation at lower national cost, and incentivising the recruitment of high-fee-paying overseas students all led to the encroachment of the profit motive into the university and to what has been called 'academic capitalism'.[57] As such, the ethos of education has shifted accordingly. In *The University in Ruins* (1996), Bill Readings argues that the university was once 'linked to the destiny of the nation-state by virtue of its role as producer, protector and inculcator of an idea of national culture'.[58] Under economic globalisation this situation has changed: the university's function is no longer tied to the self-reproduction of the nation-state. Instead, the key currency of today's university, Readings argues, is no longer culture or moral values but the de-referentialised concept of 'excellence': it doesn't matter *what* is being taught or researched, only that it is being done 'excellently'. Recently this situation has changed once more. Since the financial crash of 2008, the benchmark is no longer excellence, but market success: if the content attracts students, and therefore income, it is justified.[59]

Academic capitalism leads to changes in the roles of both students and teachers, and affects both the aesthetic and ethos of an educational experience. Today the administrator rather than the professor is the central figure of the university.[60] Learning outcomes, assessment criteria, quality assurance, surveys, reports, and a comprehensive paper trail (to combat potentially litigious students) are all more important than experimental content and delivery. Assessment must fit standardised procedures that allow credit points to be comparable across all subjects in the university – and with the introduction of the Bologna Process (1999), to be equivalent across Europe.[61] In the UK, the introduction of tuition fees in the early 1990s and the replacement of student grants by loans has rapidly turned students into consumers. Education is increasingly a financial investment, rather than a creative space of freedom and discovery; a career move, rather than a place of epistemological inquiry for its own sake. Ostensibly in the name of protecting students' rights, laborious measures of control have been introduced that submit students and teachers to an exhaustive training in bureaucracy: all students in UK universities today (including art students) have to fill in compulsory 'Personal Development Plans' to address their career development – a mechanism to ensure that emerging artists and scholars always keep an eye on developing 'transferable skills' for a future in the 'knowledge economy'. In other words, the contemporary university seems increasingly to train subjects for life under global capitalism, initiating students into a lifetime of debt, while coercing staff into ever more burdensome forms of administrative accountability and disciplinary monitoring. More than ever, education is a core 'ideological state apparatus' through which lives are shaped and managed to dance in step with the dominant tune.

It's clear that a *curatorial* interest in education is a conscious reaction to these trends. In 2006, the Van Abbe Museum in Eindhoven, the Museum van Hedendaagse Kunst in Antwerp, and the Hamburg Kunstverein collaborated on a conference and exhibition project called *A.C.A.D.E.M.Y* that explicitly positioned itself as a response to these ideological shifts, and specifically against the Bologna Process.[62] For the curators of *A.C.A.D.E.M.Y*, the autonomy of the university and the museum are equally under threat, and yet both institutions offer the greatest potential for rethinking how we generate knowledge – and indeed, for understanding what type of autonomy and freedom we want to defend.[63] It is harder to argue that contemporary *artists* are engaging with these changes directly, even while these ideological shifts form the most compelling backdrop for the recent surge of interest in education as the site of political change. While Group Material were explicitly influenced by Paulo Freire, the formative pedagogic models for the artists discussed here seem at first glance largely idiosyncratic: their own teachers (in the case of Althamer), or Joseph Beuys (in the case of Bruguera and Hirschhorn). And yet, as Mark Dion notes, there is a general sense among artists who teach in art schools that 'education as a countercultural experience is endangered': not simply through the strict timetabling of classes (because the use of every room is costed), but through compulsory training in 'faculty sensitivity', designed to eliminate fraternising and all risk of improper conduct between students and teachers.[64]

The hyper-bureaucratisation of education in the Western hemisphere does not, of course, account for artists turning to education in non-Western contexts, where their projects tend to be a compensation for more acute institutional shortcomings. This difference is evident in two contemporary library projects by artists: *Martha Rosler Library* (2006), a collection of books that this US artist has amassed since the late 1960s,

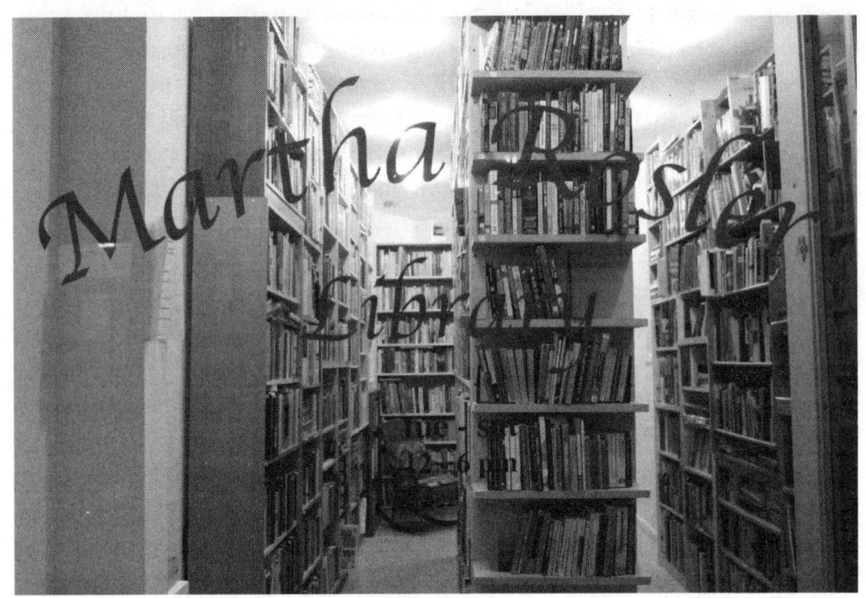

Martha Rosler Library, New York, 2006

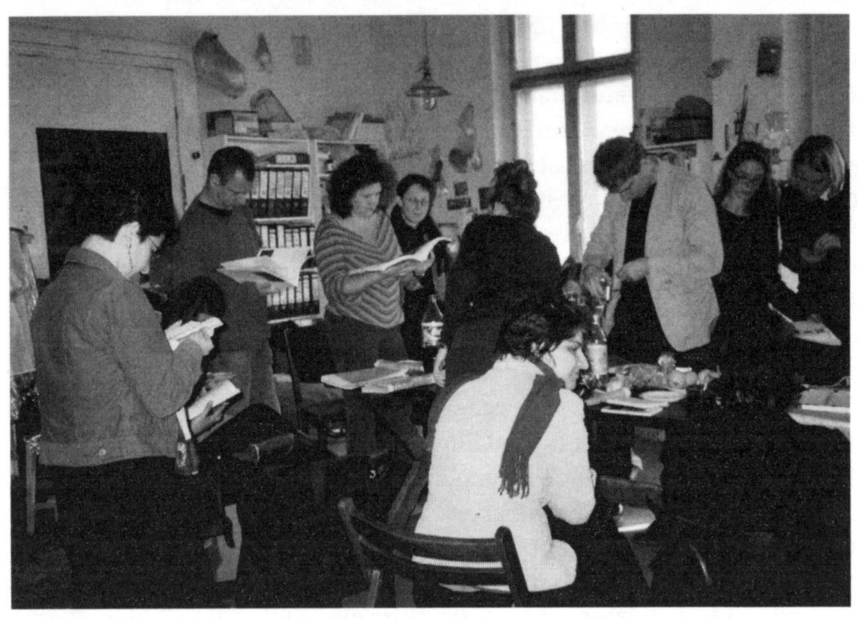

Lia Perjovschi, *Centre for Art Analysis*, 1990

and Lia Perjovschi's *Contemporary Art Archive*, or *Centre for Art Analysis* (1990–) in Bucharest, an idiosyncratic collection of photocopied articles and publications accumulated since the fall of Ceaușescu's dictatorship, and housed in her studio. If Rosler's library has an interdisciplinary outlook and a double function (it's both a reading room, and overcomes her problem of no storage space in New York), then Perjovschi's room provides a resource on contemporary art that doesn't exist anywhere else in Bucharest; she particularly welcomes students from the Academy (located in the neighbourhood of her studio), where conceptual and performance practices are still not taught. In the midst of New York's cultural over-availability, there is a risk that Rosler's library ends up as a portrait of the artist, a sculpture that gains in meaning if you already know her work.[65] For Perjovschi, by contrast, the act of assembling this information is at the same time a continuation of her practice, as seen in her drawings that map ideas and references autodidactically culled from Eastern and Western European sources, and a collective resource for young artists in Bucharest. The point here is not to argue that Rosler or Perjovschi offers the better project, since the contexts are barely compa-rable. The point is that pedagogic projects respond to the different urgencies of their moment, even while both offer a reflection on discipli-narity, functionality, and the role of research within art.

VI. Aesthetic Education

It would be an oversight to conclude this chapter without considering art itself as a form of education, regardless of its form or medium. Friedrich Schiller's twenty-eight *Letters on the Aesthetic Education of Man* were published in 1795, partly in response to what Schiller perceived as the barbarisms of the French Revolution. The struggle of the French people for human rights and political freedom had led, in his eyes, not to a reign of freedom and humanity, but to violence and terror. A problem of political education became for Schiller the problem of human progress in general; caught between a 'state of nature' (physical drives) and a 'state of reason' (cool rationality), man could, he argued, find a path to moral betterment through aesthetic education. In making this argument, Schiller took issue with Kant's *Critique of Judgment* (1790), in particular with his theory of disinterested beauty removed from bodily urges and in turn submitted to the rigours of Kant's transcendental method. For Schiller, Kant's approach belied the profound connection between art and individual drives: to educate the viewer, he argued, art had to keep a connection with the bodily chaos it claimed to conquer, not remain at one remove from it. If Kant had proposed a separation of the faculties, each articulated differently accord-ing to its realm (the moral, the rational, or the aesthetic), Schiller emphasised a binary opposition (the physical and the intellectual) and turned it into stages towards a goal: from the physical, through the aesthetic, to the moral.[66] In Schiller's *Letters*, Kant's 'free play of imagination and understanding' became the fusion of contradictory life impulses into a form of play that has its own seriousness. For Schiller, the aesthetic is fundamentally tied to education, that is, to the moral improvement of the unrefined individual.

The extent to which Schiller's *Letters* outline an ideal scenario, or are intended as a concrete pedagogic programme, remains unclear. Although the *Letters* were produced for a Danish prince, and acknowledge that social reform is the prerequisite of aesthetic education, Schiller's ideas nevertheless found practical application in their influence upon his colleague, Wilhelm von Humboldt, who integrated his notion of *Bildung* into Prussian reforms of the higher education system in 1809. The same problem of *actual* or *ideal education*, a *universal audience* or *specific students*, faces all pedagogically oriented art projects today. Very few of these projects manage to overcome the gap between a 'first audience' of student-participants and a 'second audience' of subsequent viewers. Perhaps this is because, ultimately, education has no spectators.[67] The most effective education is a closed social process: as Roland Barthes observes, 'the famous "teaching relation" is not the relation of teacher to taught, but the relation of those taught to each other'.[68] Institutional pedagogy never needs to take on board the question of its communicability to those beyond the classroom (and if it does, it only takes the form of wholly inadequate evaluative questionnaires). Yet this task is essential to projects in the artistic realm if they are to fulfil the ambitions of an aesthetic education. For all that Barthes emphasises the invisible libidinal dynamic of the seminar, he also manages to convey this to us in his mastery of language. It seems telling that when the most artistically successful instances of pedagogy-as-art today manage to communicate an educational experience to a secondary audience, it is through modes that are time-based or performative: through video (Żmijewski), the exhibition (Bruguera), the lecture (Chan) or the publication (Hirschhorn). The secondary audience is ineliminable, but also essential, since it keeps open the possibility that *everyone* can learn something from these projects: it allows specific instances to become generalisable, establishing a relationship between particular and universal that is far more generative than the model of exemplary ethical gesture.

To conclude, however, we ought to question how closely we want to remain within the terms of Schiller's project. In rejecting Kant's assertion of art's autonomy, Schiller effectively instrumentalises the aesthetic: he fuses the two opposing poles of physical sensuousness and intellectual reason in order to achieve a morality that reaches beyond the individual. In so doing, the aesthetic state is merely a path to moral education, rather than an end in itself.[69] The quote that forms the title of this chapter cues us to another framework, one that operates from a less authoritarian relationship to morality. Near the end of his last book *Chaosmosis* (1993), Félix Guattari asks: 'how do you bring a classroom to life as if it were a work of art?' For Guattari, art is an endlessly renewable source of vitalist energy and creation, a constant force of mutation and subversion.[70] He lays out a tripartite schema of art's development, arguing that we are on the brink of a new paradigm in which art is no longer beholden to Capital. In this new state of affairs, which he names the 'ethico-aesthetic paradigm', art should claim 'a key position of transversality with respect to other Universes of value', bringing about mutant forms of subjectivity and rehumanising disciplinary institutions.[71] Transversality, for Guattari, denotes a 'militant, social, undisciplined creativity'; it is a line rather than a point, a bridge or a movement, motored by group Eros.[72] By way of illustration, one cannot help thinking of the experimental institution with which Guattari was himself involved – the psychiatric clinic at La Borde, best known for its radically dehierarchised blurring of work identities. Established by Jean Oury in the Département de Loir-et-Cher in 1953, the clinic began to employ Guattari in 1955. There, he organised patient-staff parity commissions, creative workshops, self-management (after 1968), and most famously, the *grille* (or grid) with rotating tasks and roles: doctors, nurses, caretakers, service workers and patients exchanged roles in a project of 'disalienation'.[73] Influenced by Jacques Lacan, existential Marxism and structural linguistics, La Borde aimed to produce new types of singular (rather than normalised, serialised) subjectivity. Nicolas Philibert's documentary about the clinic's annual play, involving all patients and staff, *La Moindre des Choses* (Every Little Thing, 1996), poignantly conveys this dehierarchisation: we are often unsure if the person shown mopping the floor, answering the phone, or counting out medication is a patient or a nurse. La Borde, like Summerhill, seems to be the kind of organisational and experiential comparison we need to bring to bear on contemporary art projects that seek to create a rapprochement between art and the social field.

Significantly, however, Guattari is insistent that the ethico-aesthetic paradigm involves overthrowing current forms of art as much as current forms of social life.[74] It does not denote an aestheticisation of the social or a complete dissolution of disciplinary boundaries. Rather, the war is to be waged on two fronts: as a critique of art, and as a critique of the institutions into which it permeates, because art blurring entirely into life risks 'the perennial possibility of eclipse'.[75] To protect against this threat of art's self-extinction, Guattari suggests that each work of art must have a 'double finality': '[Firstly] to insert itself into a social network which will either appropriate or reject it, and [secondly] to celebrate, once again, the Universe of art as such, precisely because it is always in danger of collapsing.'[76] Guattari's language of a double finality speaks to the double ontology of cross-disciplinary projects we are so frequently presented with today, preeminently among them art-as-pedagogy. Like all long-term participatory projects, this art must tread the fine line of a dual horizon – faced towards the social field but also towards art itself, addressing both its immediate participants and subsequent audiences. It needs to be successful within both art *and* the social field, but ideally also testing and revising the criteria we apply to both domains. Without this double finality, such projects risk becoming 'edu-tainment' or 'pedagogical aesthetics'. These latter will never be as compelling as Summerhill and La Borde – examples that establish their own institutional frameworks and operate in ways that continue to trouble the parameters of existing social structures. If artists ignore the double finality, viewers may rightly wonder whether Guattari's question should in fact be reversed: how do we bring a work of art to life as though it were a classroom? Pedagogic art projects therefore foreground and crystallise one of the most central problems of all artistic practice in the social field: they require us to examine our assumptions about both fields of operation, and to ponder the productive overlaps and incompatibilities that might arise from their experimental conjunction, with the consequence of perpetually reinventing both. For secondary viewers like ourselves, perhaps the most educational aspect of these projects is their insistence that we learn to think both fields together and devise adequate new languages and criteria for communicating these transversal practices.

Conclusion

The dominant narrative that emerges from the examples surveyed in this book is one of negation: activation of the audience in participatory art is positioned against its mythic counterpart, passive spectatorial consumption. Participation thus forms part of a larger narrative that traverses modernity: 'art must be directed against contemplation, against spectatorship, against the passivity of the masses paralyzed by the spectacle of modern life'.[1] This desire to activate the audience in participatory art is at the same time a drive to emancipate it from a state of alienation induced by the dominant ideological order – be this consumer capitalism, totalitarian socialism, or military dictatorship. Beginning from this premise, participatory art aims to restore and realise a communal, collective space of shared social engagement. But this is achieved in different ways: either through constructivist gestures of social impact, which refute the injustice of the world by proposing an alternative, or through a nihilist redoubling of alienation, which negates the world's injustice and illogicality on its own terms. In both instances, the work seeks to forge a collective, co-authoring, participatory social body – but one does this affirmatively (through utopian realisation), the other indirectly (through the negation of negation).

One of the questions that is continually posed to me after lectures on this subject is the following: surely it is better for one art project to improve one person's life than for it not to take place at all? The history of participatory art charted in this book allows us to gain critical distance on this question, and to see it as the latest instantiation of the art vs real life debate that so typifies the twentieth century. This tension – along with that between equality and quality, participation and spectatorship – indicate that social and artistic judgements do not easily merge; indeed, they seem to demand different criteria. This impasse surfaces in every printed debate and panel discussion on participatory and socially engaged art. For one sector of artists, curators and critics, a good project appeases a superegoic injunction to ameliorate society; if social agencies have failed, then art is obliged to step in. In this schema, judgements are based on a humanist ethics, often inspired by Christianity. What counts is to offer ameliorative solutions, however short-term, rather than the exposure of contradictory social truths. For another sector of artists, curators and critics, judgements are based on a sensible response to the artist's work, both in and beyond its original context. In this schema, ethics are nugatory, because art is understood continually to throw established systems of value into question, including questions of morality; devising new languages with which to represent and question social contradiction is more important. The social discourse accuses the artistic discourse of amorality and inefficacy, because it is insufficient merely to reveal, reduplicate, or reflect upon the world; what matters is social change. The artistic discourse accuses the social discourse of remaining stubbornly attached to existing categories, and focusing on micropolitical gestures at the expense of sensuous immediacy as a potential locus of disalienation. Either social conscience dominates, or the rights of the individual to question social conscience. Art's relationship to the social is either underpinned by morality or it is underpinned by freedom.[2]

This binary is echoed in Boltanski and Chiapello's perceptive distinction between artistic and social critiques of capitalism. The artistic critique, rooted in nineteenth-century bohemianism, draws upon two sources of indignation towards capitalism: on the one hand, disenchantment and inauthenticity, and on the other, oppression. The artistic critique, they explain, 'foregrounds the loss of meaning and, in particular, the loss of the sense of what is beautiful and valuable, which derives from standardisation and generalised commodification, affecting not only everyday objects but also artworks . . . and human beings'. Against this state of affairs, the artistic critique advocates 'the freedom of artists, their rejection of any contamination of aesthetics by ethics, their refusal of any form of subjection in time and space and, in its extreme form, any kind of work'.[3] The social critique, by contrast, draws on different sources of indignation towards capitalism: the egoism of private interests, and the growing poverty of the working classes in a society of unprecedented wealth. This social critique necessarily rejects the moral neutrality, individualism and egotism of artists. The artistic and the social critique are not directly compatible, Boltanski and Chiapello warn us, and exist in continual tension with one another.[4]

The clash between artistic and social critiques recurs most visibly at certain historical moments, as the case studies in this book have indicated. The appearance of participatory art is symptomatic of this clash, and tends to occur at moments of political transition and upheaval: in the years leading to Italian Fascism, in the aftermath of the 1917 Revolution, in the widespread social dissent that led to 1968, and in its aftermath in the 1970s. At each historical moment participatory art takes a different form, because it seeks to negate different artistic and socio-political objects. In our own times, its resurgence accompanies the consequences of the collapse of really existing communism, the apparent absence of a viable left alternative, the emergence of the contemporary 'post-political' consensus, and the near total marketisation of art and education.[5] But the paradox of this situation is that participation in the West now has more to do with the populist agendas of neoliberal governments. Even though participatory artists invariably stand against neoliberal capitalism, the values they impute to their work are understood formally (in terms of opposing individualism and the commodity object), without recognising that so many other aspects of this art practice dovetail even more perfectly with neoliberalism's recent forms (networks, mobility, project work, affective labour).

As this ground has shifted over the course of the twentieth century, so the identity of participants has been reimagined at each historical moment: from a crowd (1910s), to the masses (1920s), to the people (late 1960s/ 1970s), to the excluded (1980s), to community (1990s), to today's volunteers whose participation is continuous with a culture of reality television and social networking. From the audience's perspective, we can chart this as a shift from an audience that demands a role (expressed as hostility towards avant-garde artists who keep control of the proscenium), to an audience that enjoys its subordination to strange experiences devised for them by an artist, to an audience that is encouraged to be a co-producer of the work (and who, occasionally, can even get paid for this involvement). This could be seen as an heroic narrative of the increased activation and agency of the audience, but we might also see it as a story of our ever-increasing voluntary subordination to the artists' will, and of the commodification of human bodies in a service economy (since voluntary participation is also unpaid labour). Arguably this is a story that runs in parallel with the rocky fate of democracy itself, a term to which participation has always been wedded: from a demand for acknowledgement, to representation, to the consensual consumption of one's own image – be this in a work of art, Facebook, Flickr, or reality TV. Consider the media profile accorded to Antony Gormley's *One and Other* (2009), a project to allow members of the public to continuously occupy the empty 'Fourth Plinth' of Trafalgar Square, one hour at a time for 100 days. Gormley received 34,520 applications for 2,400 places, and the activities of the plinth's occupants were continually streamed online.[6] Although the artist referred to *One and Other* as 'an open space of possibility for many to test their sense of self and how they might communicate this to a wider world', the project was described by *The Guardian*, not unfairly, as 'Twitter Art'.[7] In a world where everyone can air their views to everyone we are faced not with mass empowerment but with an endless stream of egos levelled to banality. Far from being oppositional to spectacle, participation has now entirely merged with it.

This new proximity between spectacle and participation underlines the necessity of sustaining a tension between artistic and social critiques. The most striking projects that constitute the history of participatory art unseat

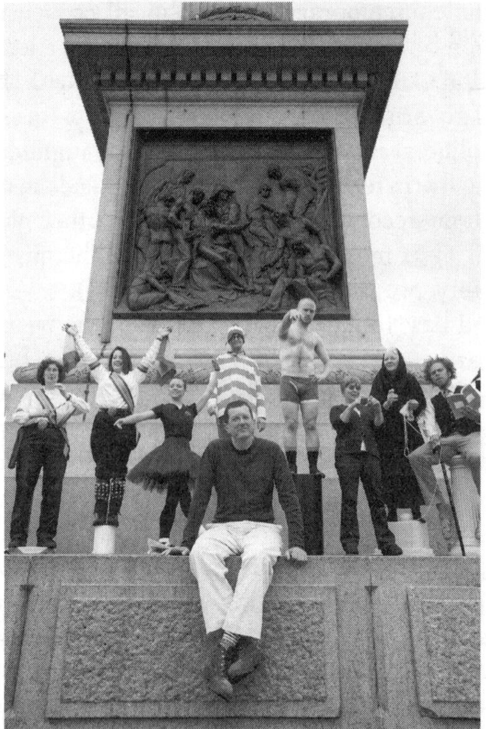

Antony Gormley and participants in *One and Other*, 2009

all of the polarities on which this discourse is founded (individual/collective, author/spectator, active/passive, real life/art) but not with the goal of collapsing them. In so doing, they hold the artistic and social critiques in tension. Guattari's paradigm of transversality offers one such way of thinking through these artistic operations: he leaves art as a category in its place, but insists upon its constant flight into and across other disciplines, putting both art and the social into question, even while simultaneously reaffirming art as a universe of value. Rancière offers another: the aesthetic regime is constitutively contradictory, shuttling between autonomy and heteronomy ('the aesthetic experience is effective inasmuch as it is the experience of that *and*').[8] He argues that in art, theatre and education alike, there needs to be a mediating object that stands between the idea of the artist and the feeling and interpretation of the spectator: 'This spectacle is a third term, to which the other two can refer, but which prevents any kind of "equal" or "undistorted" transmission. It is a mediation between them, and that mediation of a third term is crucial in the process of intellectual emancipation. [...] The same thing that links them must also separate them.'[9] In different ways, these philosophers offer alternative frameworks for thinking the artistic and the social simultaneously; for both, art and the social are not to be reconciled, but sustained in continual tension.

I. The Ladder and the Container

These theoretical models drawn from continental philosophy do not reduce art to a question of ethically good or bad examples, nor do they forge a straightforward equation between forms of democracy in art and forms of democracy in society. Most of the contemporary discourse on participatory art implies an evaluative schema akin to that laid out in the classic diagram 'The Ladder of Participation', published in an architectural journal in 1969 to accompany an article about forms of citizen involvement.[10] The ladder has eight rungs. The bottom two indicate the least participatory forms of citizen engagement: the non-participation of mere presence in 'manipulation' and 'therapy'. The next three rungs are degrees of tokenism – 'informing', 'consultation' and 'placation' – which gradually increase the attention paid by power to the everyday voice. At the top of the ladder we find 'partnership', 'delegated power', and the ultimate goal, 'citizen control'. The diagram provides a useful set of distinctions for thinking about the claims to participation made by those in power, and is frequently cited by architects and planners. It is tempting to make an equation (and many have done so) between the value of a work of art and the degree of participation it involves, turning the Ladder of Participation into a gauge for measuring the efficacy of artistic practice.[11] But while the ladder provides us with helpful and nuanced differences between forms of civic participation, it falls short of corresponding to the complexity of artistic gestures. The most challenging works of art do not follow this schema, because models of democracy in art do not have an intrinsic relationship to models of democracy in society. The equation is misleading and does not recognise art's ability to generate other, more paradoxical criteria. The works I have discussed in the preceding chapters do not offer anything like citizen control. The artist relies upon the participants' creative exploitation of the situation that he/she offers – just as participants require the artists' cue and direction. The relationship between artist/participant is a continual play of mutual tension, recognition and dependency – more akin to the BDSM model mentioned in Chapter 8, or even the collectively negotiated dynamic of stand-up comedy – rather than a ladder of progressively more virtuous political forms.

One final case study illustrates this view of art as both grounded in and suspending reality: *Please Love Austria* (2000) devised and largely performed by the German film-maker and artist Christoph Schlingensief (1960–2010). Commissioned to produce a work for the Weiner Festwochen, Schlingensief chose to respond directly to the recent electoral success of the far-right nationalist party led by Jörg Haider (Freiheitliche Partei Österreichs, or FPÖ). The FPÖ's campaign had included overtly xenophobic slogans and the word *überfremdung* (domination by foreign influences), once employed by the Nazis, to describe a country overrun with foreigners. Schlingensief

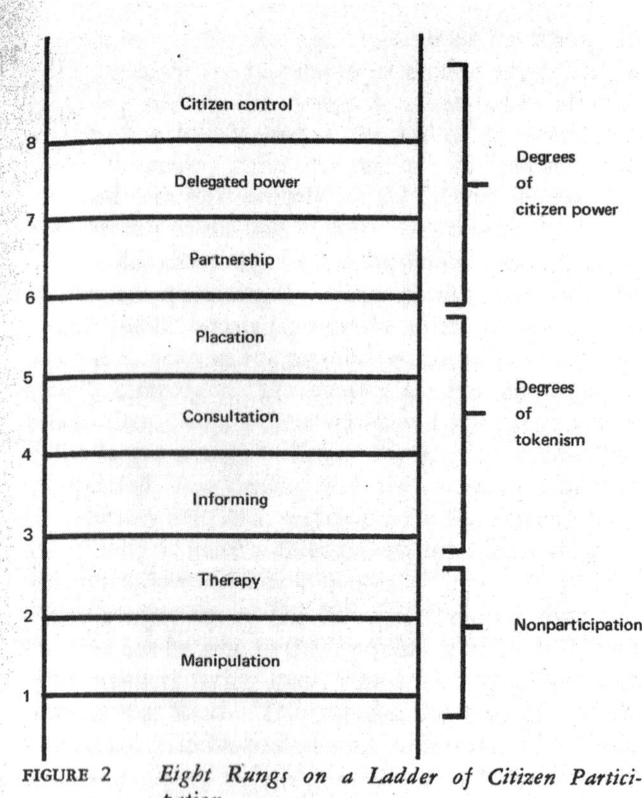

FIGURE 2   *Eight Rungs on a Ladder of Citizen Participation*

Anonymous, 'The Ladder of Participation', from the *Journal of the American Institute of Planners*, 1969

erected a shipping container outside the Opera House in the centre of Vienna, topped with a large banner bearing the phrase *Ausländer Raus* (Foreigners Out). Inside the container, *Big Brother*-style living accommodation was installed for a group of asylum-seekers, relocated from a detention centre outside the city. Their activities were broadcast through the internet television station webfreetv.com, and via this station viewers could vote daily for the ejection of their least favourite refugee. At 8 p.m. each day, for six days, the two most unpopular inhabitants were sent back to the deportation centre. The winner was purportedly offered a cash prize and the prospect – depending on the availability of volunteers – of Austrian citizenship through marriage. The event is documented by the Austrian filmmaker Paul Poet in an evocative and compelling ninety-minute film *Ausländer Raus! Schlingensief's Container* (2002).

Please Love Austria is typical Schlingensief in its desire to antagonise the public and stage provocation. His early film work frequently alluded to contemporary taboos: mixing Nazism, obscenities, disabilities and assorted sexual perversions in films such as *German Chainsaw Massacre* (1990) and *Terror 2000* (1992), once described as 'filth for intellectuals'.[12]

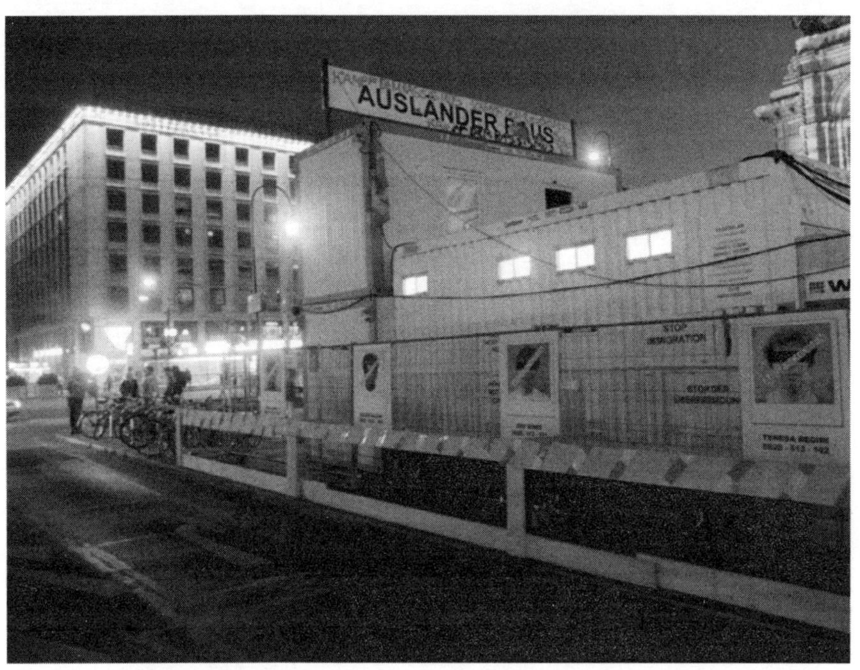

Christoph Schlingensief, *Please Love Austria*, 2000. View of the container.

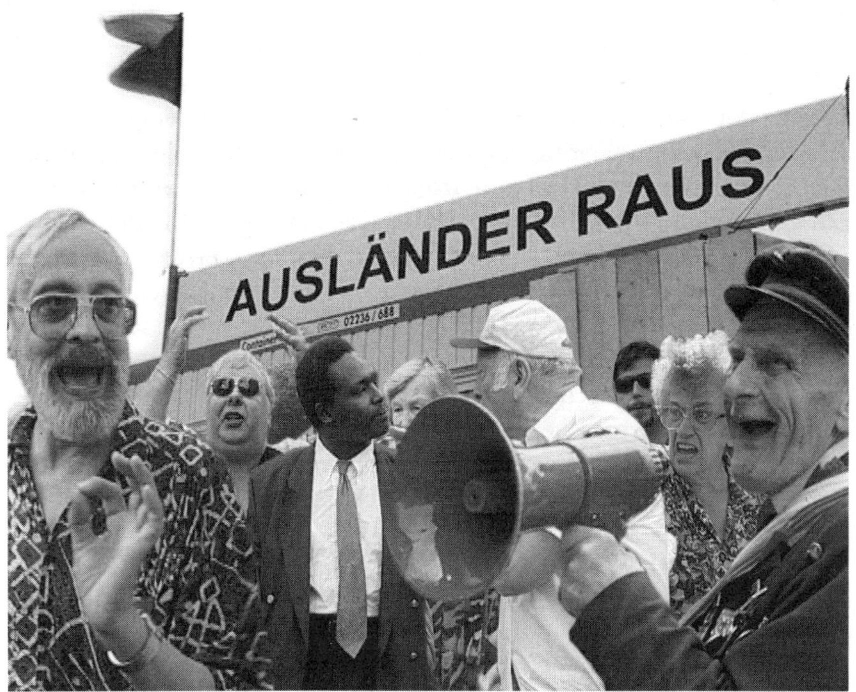

Christoph Schlingensief, *Please Love Austria*, 2001

In the late 1990s Schlingensief began making interventions into public space, including the formation of a political party, *Chance 2000* (1998–2000), targeted at the unemployed, disabled and other recipients of welfare, with the slogan 'Vote For Yourself'. *Chance 2000* did not hesitate to use the image of Schlingensief's long-term collaborators, many of whom have mental and/or physical handicaps. *Please Love Austria*, Schlingensief's refugee participants were barely visible, disguised in assorted wigs, hats and sunglasses.[13] In the square, the public had only a limited view of the immigrants through peep-holes; the bulk of the performance was undertaken by Schlingensief himself, installed on the container's roof near the 'Foreigners Out!' banner. Speaking through a megaphone, he incited the FPÖ to come and remove the banner (which they didn't), encouraged tourists to take photographs, invited the public to air their views, and made contradictory claims ('This is a performance! This is the absolute truth!') while parroting the most racist opinions and insults back to the crowd. As the various participants were evicted, Schlingensief provided a running commentary to the mob below: 'It is a black man! Once again Austria has evicted a darkie!'

Although in retrospect – and particularly in Poet's film – it is evident that the work is a critique of xenophobia and its institutions, in Vienna the event (and Schlingensief's charismatic role as circus-master) was ambiguous enough to receive approval and condemnation from all sides of the political spectrum. An elderly right-wing gentleman covered in medals gleefully found it to be in sympathy with his own ideas, while others claimed that by staging such a shameful spectacle Schlingensief himself was a dirty foreigner who ought to be deported. Left-wing student activists attempted to sabotage the container and 'liberate' the refugees, while assorted left-wing celebrities showed up to support the project, including Daniel Cohn-Bendit (a key figure from May '68), and the Laureate author Elfriede Jelinek (who wrote and performed a puppet play with the asylum-seekers). In addition, large numbers of the public watched the programme on webfreetv.com and voted for the eviction of particular refugees. The container prompted arguments and discussion – in the square surrounding it, in the print media, and on national television. The vehemence of response is palpable throughout the film, no more so than when Poet's camera pans back from a heated argument to reveal the entire square full of agitated people in intense debate. One elderly woman was so infuriated by the project that she could only spit at Schlingensief the insult 'You . . . artist!'

A frequently heard criticism of this work is that it did not change anyone's opinion: the right-wing pensioner is still right-wing, the lefty protestors are still lefty, and so on. But this instrumentalised approach to critical judgement misunderstands the artistic force of Schlingensief's intervention. The point is not about 'conversion', for this reduces the work of art to a question of propaganda. Rather, Schlingensief's project draws attention to the contradictions of political discourse in Austria at that moment. The shocking fact is that Schlingensief's container caused more public agitation and distress than the presence of a *real* deportation centre a few miles outside Vienna. The disturbing lesson of *Please Love Austria* is that an *artistic* representation of detention has more power to attract dissensus than an *actual* institution of detention.[14] In fact, Schlingensief's model of 'undemocratic' behaviour corresponds precisely to 'democracy' as practised in reality. This contradiction is the core of Schlingensief's artistic efficacy – and it is the reason why political conversion is not the primary goal of art, why artistic representations continue to have a potency that can be harnessed to disruptive ends, and why *Please Love Austria* is not (and should never be seen as) morally exemplary. Participatory art is not an automatic formula for political art, but one strategy (among many) that can be deployed in particular contexts to specific ends.

II. The End of Participation

In his essay 'The Uses of Democracy' (1992), Jacques Rancière notes that participation in what we normally refer to as democratic regimes is usually reduced to a question of filling up the spaces left empty by power. Genuine participation, he argues, is something different: the invention of an 'unpredictable subject' who momentarily occupies the street, the factory, or the museum – rather than a fixed space of allocated participation whose counter-power is dependent on the dominant order.[15] Setting aside the problematic idea of 'genuine' participation (which takes us back to modernist oppositions between authentic and false culture), such a statement clearly pertains to *Please Love Austria*, and to many of the case studies in this book. It is telling that the better examples of participatory art in recent years, some of which are addressed in Chapters 8 and 9, have constituted a critique of participatory art, rather than upholding an unproblematised equation between artistic and political inclusion.

The fact that the Ladder of Participation culminates in 'citizen control' is worth recalling here. At a certain point, art has to hand over to other institutions if social change is to be achieved: it is not enough to keep producing activist *art*. The historic avant-garde was always positioned in relation to an existent party politics (primarily communist) which removed the pressure of art ever being required to effectuate change in and of itself. Later, the post-war avant-gardes claimed open-endedness as a radical refusal of organised politics – be this inter-war totalitarianism or the dogma of a party line. There was the potential to discover the highest artistic intensity in the everyday and the banal, which would serve a larger project of equality and anti-elitism. Since the 1990s, participatory art has often asserted a connection between user-generated content and democracy, but the frequent predictability of its results seem to be the consequence of lacking *both* a social *and* an artistic target; in other words, participatory art today stands without a relation to an existing political project (only to a loosely defined anti-capitalism) and presents itself as oppositional to visual art by trying to side-step the question of visuality. As a consequence, these artists have internalised a huge amount of pressure to bear the burden of devising new models of social and political organisation – a task that they are not always best equipped to undertake. That the 'political' and 'critical' have become shibboleths of advanced art signals a lack of faith *both* in the intrinsic value of art as a de-alienating human endeavour (since art today is so intertwined with market systems globally) *and* in democratic political processes (in whose name so many injustices and barbarities are conducted).[16] Rather than addressing this by collapsing art and ethics together, the task today is to produce a viable international alignment of leftist political movements and a reassertion of art's inventive forms of negation as valuable in their own right.[17] We need to recognise art as a form of experimental activity overlapping with the world, whose negativity may lend support towards a political project (without bearing the sole responsibility for devising and implementing it), and – more radically – we need to support the progressive transformation of existing institutions through the transversal encroachment of ideas whose boldness is related to (and at times greater than) that of artistic imagination.[18]

In using people as a medium, participatory art has always had a double ontological status: it is both an event in the world, and at one remove from it. As such, it has the capacity to communicate on two levels – to participants and to spectators – the paradoxes that are repressed in everyday discourse, and to elicit perverse, disturbing and pleasurable experiences that enlarge our capacity to imagine the world and our relations anew. But to reach the second level requires a mediating third term – an object, image, story, film, even a spectacle – that permits this experience to have a purchase on the public imaginary. Participatory art is not a privileged political medium, nor a ready-made solution to a society of the spectacle, but is as uncertain and precarious as democracy itself; neither are legitimated in advance but need continually to be performed and tested in every specific context.

Acknowledgements

This book took a long time to write. My chosen subject matter seemed to demand a completely different methodology to ones I had previously used, and I too frequently relied on friends and colleagues for feedback. All my thinking experiments were undertaken in public, inflicted on dozens of audiences who patiently listened to my rambling before offering advice or, more frequently, attacking me for daring to criticise or defend the art under discussion. I am indebted to all those audiences who gave me constructive feedback, but even more to my long-suffering students at the Royal College of Art, CUNY Graduate Center, Hunter College and Cátedra Arte de Conducta, who were the most stimulating interlocutors I could hope for. You are too many to name individually, but I'm so grateful to you all for your incisive questions, comments, ideas, references and help with translations.

I owe abundant thanks to all the artists, curators and art historians I've talked to in the last six years, raiding their brains and archives: Allora and Calzadilla, Paweł Althamer, Doug Ashford, Uthit Atamana, Carlos Basualdo, Jérôme Bel, Ed Berman, the team at The Blackie (Bill Harpe, Neil Johnson, Sally Morris), Stuart Brisley, Tania Bruguera, Luis Camnitzer, Graciela Carnevale, Paul Chan, Phil Collins, Mark Cousins, Teddy Cruz, Ekaterina Degot, Jeremy Deller, Stephan Dillemuth, Mark Dion, Elmgreen and Dragset, Charles Esche, Alex Farquharson, Briony Fer, Tom Finkelpearl, Milija Gluhovic, Romy Golan, Dominique Gonzalez-Foerster, Simon Grennan, Boris Groys, Daniel Grún, Nicolás Guagnini, Vit Havránek, Jens Haaning, Jeanne van Heeswijk, Thomas Hirschhorn, Christine and Irene Hohenbüchler, Pierre Huyghe, IRWIN (especially Miran Mohar and Borut Vogelnik), Margaret Iversen, Alfredo Jaar, Roberto Jacoby, Lu Jie, Yelena Kalinsky, Mira Keratova, Barbora Klimová, Alison Knowles, Surasi Kusolwong, Pablo Lafuente, Lars Bang Larsen, Pablo León de la Barra, Kamin Lerdchaiprasert, David Levine, Ana Longoni, Sven Lütticken, Francesco Manacorda, Aleksandra Mir, Viktor Misiano, Christian Philipp Müller, Joanna Mytkowska, Victoria Noorthoon, Linda Norden, Oda Projesi, Roman Ondák, Boris Ondreicka, Tomas Pospiszyl, Andrzej Przywara, Maria Pask, Dan and Lia Perjovschi,

Oda Projesi, Janelle Reinelt, Pedro Reyes, Nicholas Ridout, David Riff, Tim Rollins, Joe Scanlan, Christoph Schlingensief, Carolee Schneemann, Tino Sehgal, Valerie Smith, Barbara Steveni, Superflex, Sally Tallant, Temporary Services, Per Gunnar Tverbakk, Mierle Laderman Ukeles, Bob Whitman, Artur Żmijewski.

Thanks also to Jenny Tobias at MoMA Library, graduate students who helped me with translations (Arnaud Gerspacher, Anya Pantuyeva, Liz Donato) and photo research (Tina Kukielski), and especially to those artists who allowed me to reproduce images of their work without a fee. For invaluable editorial advice I am indebted to Tim Clark, Lindsay Caplan, TJ Demos and the wonderful Nikki Columbus.

The research for this book was kick-started by an Early Career Fellowship from the Leverhulme Trust (2004–6), which enabled me to take two years to think and travel without the pressure of delivering immediate returns. This is a rare model of funding in the UK and was foundational to this research. It was supplemented by residencies at tranzit (Prague, 2009) and El Centro de Investigaciones Artísticas (Buenos Aires, 2009), and by travel and research funds generously made available to me as faculty of CUNY Graduate Center. Under the auspices of *Former West* (2008–10) I was involved in the organisation of three conferences that informed this research: 1968–1989: Political Upheaval and Artistic Change (Muzeum Sztuki Nowoczesnej, Warsaw, July 2008); Where the West Ends (Muzeum Sztuki Nowoczesnej, Warsaw, March 2010); and Art and The Social: Exhibitions of Contemporary Art in the 1990s (Tate Britain, London, April 2010). The last two are available online at formerwest.org.

Finally, huge thanks to my wonderful family for putting up with, and encouraging, my idiosyncracies and obsessions. This book is dedicated to Joyce and Claude.

Notes

Introduction

1 Jeremy Deller: 'Francis Bacon was socially engaged, Warhol was socially engaged, if you're a good artist you're socially engaged, whether you're painting or making sculptures.' (Interview with the author, 12 April 2005.)

2 For example, Bourriaud argues that relational art takes as its theoretical horizon 'the realm of human interactions and its social context, rather than the assertion of an independent and *private* symbolic space'. (Bourriaud, *Relational Aesthetics*, Dijon: Presses du Réel, 2002, p. 14.) But when we look at the artists he supports independently of his arguments, we find that they are less interested in intersubjective relations and social context than in spectatorship as more generally embedded within systems of display, temporality, fiction, design and the 'scenario'. The present book takes up from my critique of *Relational Aesthetics* published in *October*, 110, Fall 2004, pp. 51–79.

3 See for example the MFA programmes in Art and Social Practice at Portland State University and California College of the Arts; in Public Practice at Otis College of Art and Design, and in Contextual Practice at Carnegie Mellon University, Pittsburgh. The Leonore Annenberg Prize for Art and Social Change (New York) was inaugurated in 2009, while the International Prize for Participatory Art (promoted by the Region Emilia-Romagna, Italy) was inaugurated in 2011.

4 Claire Bishop, 'The Social Turn: Collaboration and Its Discontents', *Artforum*, February 2006, pp. 178–83.

5 It should be stressed that this tripartite ideological structure is less applicable to two of the regions covered in this book. In Argentina, 1968 was associated more with resistance to military oppression (the Onganía dictatorship) than with leftist revolution, although artists knew of the upheavals in France and made reference to them in their work. As Nicolás Guagnini notes: 'If anything, the dates of a South American chronology

could oscillate between the AI5 in Brazil in 1964 and Pinochet's exit in 1986; the social experience that leads to '68 in South America is that of repression. All the later work in the subcontinent (Grupo CADA, Proyecto Venus, Eloísa Cartoñera, Cildo Meireles' interventions) aims to reconstruct the social ties destroyed by the dictatorships, Kissinger's policies, the Condor Plan, etc.' (Guagnini, email to the author, 8 October 2010.) In former Czechoslovakia, 1968 connotes the Soviet invasion and the beginning of so-called 'normalisation'; in former Yugoslavia, by contrast, 1968 was synonymous with student calls for a more authentic form of communism. The formation of the Soviet Bloc in 1947 would therefore be a more significant date for this region than 1968.

6 André Breton, 'Artificial Hells, Inauguration of the "1921 Dada Season" ', *October*, 105, Summer 2003, p. 139.

7 Field trips were undertaken to Rirkrit Tiravanija and Kamin Lerdchaiprasert's *The Land* (Chiang Mai) and to Lu Jie's *Long March Project* (Beijing) but these projects sat uncomfortably within my narrative, despite the fact that the instigators of both projects were trained in the West.

8 Key texts would include the discussion around New Genre Public Art in the early 1990s (Mary Jane Jacob, Suzanne Lacy, Michael Brenson), texts on art and activism (Nina Felshin, Grant Kester, Gregory Sholette), and theoretical approaches to public art and site specificity (Rosalyn Deutsche, Miwon Kwon). Of these authors, I feel most indebted to Rosalyn Deutsche.

9 An in-house conversation with the curatorial and education staff at the Walker Art Center in Minneapolis brought up many instances when the artist(s) went away to work on other exhibitions, leaving the education department to keep their community project going. (Discussion at the Walker Art Center, 31 October 2008.)

10 See for example Jeremy Till, Peter Blundell Jones and Doina Petrescu (eds.), *Architecture and Participation*, London: Spon, 2005.

11 Art's discursive shift towards the social sciences is reflected in a number of exhibition 'readers' since the late 1990s, which reject the conventional catalogue format (with its art historical essays, glossy photographs, and descriptions of the works exhibited). The key moments in this regard are Group Material's *Democracy* (Seattle: Bay Press, 1990), Martha Rosler's *If You Lived Here* (Seattle: Bay Press, 1991) and Peter Weibel's catalogue for the Austrian pavilion at the Venice Biennale, 1993.

12 The seminar is in fact the ideal forum for this research: the continual dynamic of debate and analysis in the classroom allows the material to remain alive and contested far more than in a book.

13 See for example: WHW (eds.), *Collective Creativity*, Kassel: Fridericianum, 2005; Blake Stimson and Gregory Sholette (eds.), *Collectivism After Modernism: The Art of Social Imagination After 1945*, Minneapolis:

University of Minnesota Press, 2007; Johanna Billing, Maria Lind and Lars Nilsson (eds.), *Taking the Matter into Common Hands: On Contemporary Art and Collaborative Practices*, London: Black Dog Publishing, 2007; Charles Esche and Will Bradley (eds.), *Art and Social Change: A Critical Reader*, London: Afterall and MIT Press, 2007.

Chapter One   The Social Turn

1 See for example the questionnaire in which artist-collectives are requested to cite their influences, in WHW, *Collective Creativity*, Kassel: Fridericianum/Frankfurt: Revolver, 2005, pp. 344–6.

2 Grant Kester, *Conversation Pieces: Community and Communication in Modern Art*, Berkeley: University of California Press, 2004, p. 29.

3 Jeanne van Heeswijk, 'Fleeting Images of Community', available at www.jeanneworks.net.

4 Blake Stimson and Gregory Sholette (eds.), *Collectivism After Modernism: The Art of Social Imagination After 1945*, Minneapolis: University of Minnesota Press, 2007, p. 12. They go on to quote El Lissitzky, who in 1920 wrote that 'The private property aspect of creativity must be destroyed; all are creators and there is no reason of any sort for this division into artists and nonartists.'

5 Nicolas Bourriaud, *Relational Aesthetics*, Dijon: Presses du Réel, 2002, p. 85, p. 113. Elsewhere: 'art is the place that produces a specific sociability' because 'it *tightens the space of relations*, unlike TV' (p. 18).

6 Jacques Rancière, 'Aesthetic Separation, Aesthetic Community: Scenes from the Aesthetic Regime of Art', *Art and Research: A Journal of Ideas, Contexts and Methods*, 2:1, Summer 2008, p. 7.

7 See David Harvey, *A Brief History of Neoliberalism*, Oxford: Oxford University Press, 2005.

8 Paolo Virno, interviewed in Alexei Penzin, 'The Soviets of the Multitude: On Collectivity and Collective Work', *Manifesta Journal*, 8, 2009–10, p. 56.

9 Kester, *Conversation Pieces*, p. 112.

10 See Andrew Brighton, 'Consumed by the Political: The Ruination of the Arts Council', *Critical Quarterly*, 48:1, 2006, p. 4, and Mark Wallinger and Mary Warnock (eds.), *Art for All? Their Policies and Our Culture*, London: Peer, 2000.

11 For an incisive critique of social inclusion policies from a feminist perspective see Ruth Levitas, *The Inclusive Society? Social Exclusion and New Labour*, Basingstoke: Macmillan, 1998.

12 The dominant tone of Labour's social inclusion policy, as Ruth Levitas has pointed out, is strongly imbued with what she calls 'MUD' (the moral underclass discourse, which focuses on the behaviour of the poor rather than the structure of society) and 'SID' (social integration discourse,

which replaces welfare with the goal of work) rather than 'RED' (a redistributionist discourse primarily concerned with reducing poverty and inequality). (Levitas, *The Inclusive Society?*, Chapter 1.)

13 François Matarasso, *Use or Ornament? The Social Impact of Participation in the Arts*, Comedia, London, 1997.

14 Paola Merli, 'Evaluating the Social Impact of Participation in Arts Activities', *International Journal of Cultural Policy*, 8:1, 2002, pp. 107–18.

15 Ulrich Beck, *Risk Society: Towards A New Modernity*, cited in Zygmunt Bauman, *The Individualized Society*, Cambridge: Polity Press, 2001, p. 106.

16 David Cameron, 'Big Society Speech', 19 July 2010, available at www.number10.gov.uk.

17 Ministry of Economic Affairs and Ministry of Education, Culture and Science, *Our Creative Potential*, Amsterdam, 2005, p. 3.

18 Ibid., p. 8.

19 'Gemeente Amsterdam, Amsterdam Topstad: Metropool, Economische Zaken Amsterdam' (14 July 2006), cited in Merijn Oudenampsen, 'Back to the Future of the Creative City', *Variant*, 31, Spring 2008, p. 17. The reference, of course, is to Richard Florida's gentrification handbook, *Cities and the Creative Class* (London: Routledge, 2005).

20 See Peter Hewitt, *Beyond Boundaries: The Arts After The Events of 2011*, speech given at the National Portrait Gallery, 12 March 2002, p. 13. Hewitt was speaking as Chief Executive of Arts Council England, the government funding agency for the arts.

21 The creative industries are those that 'have their origin in individual creativity, skill and talent and which have a potential for wealth and job creation through the generation and exploitation of intellectual property'; they include music, publishing, films, games, advertising, fashion, design, TV and radio, all of which have obvious commercial potential. See DCMS, *Creative Industries: Mapping Document 1*, London, 2001, p. 4.

22 DCMS, *Culture and Creativity: The Next Ten Years*, London 2001. A Green Paper is a government report that forms the first stage in changing UK law.

23 Angela McRobbie, '"Everyone is Creative": Artists as Pioneers of the New Economy?', available at www.k3000.ch/becreative.

24 McRobbie, '"Everyone is Creative" '.

25 Andrew Ross, *No-Collar: The Humane Workplace and its Hidden Costs*, New York: Basic Books, 2003, p. 258. The result, Ross argues, is greater freedom for workers (and a sense of fulfilment), but the trade-off is less social justice and protection.

26 The distinction between creativity (as the capacity of many) and art (as the skill of a few) goes back to the Russian avant-garde: *isstkustva* (art) was the term rejected by Proletkult theorists in favour of *tvorchestvo* (creativity).

27 Charles Esche, 'Superhighrise: Community, Technology, Self-Organisation', available at www.superflex.net.

28 I say schizophrenically, since Benjamin advocates new technology and mass audiences, while Debord scathingly critiques a society of mass consumption.

29 Reinaldo Laddaga, 'From Forcing to Gathering: On Liisa Robert's "What's the Time in Vyborg?" ', unpublished manuscript, p. 1.

30 Projects sharing similar values to contemporary art can be found the world over, from a travelling cinema in a lorry that tours the Outer Hebrides (*The Screen Machine*), to the 'ethical capitalism' of the microfinance movement in India, to *Slim Peace* (a network of Arab-Israeli self-help weight-loss groups for women in Israel).

31 Oda Projesi in Claire Bishop, 'What We Made Together', *Untitled*, 33, Spring 2005, p. 22.

32 Ibid.

33 Maria Lind, 'Actualisation of Space', in Claire Doherty (ed.), *Contemporary Art: From Studio to Situation*, London: Black Dog, 2004, pp. 109–21.

34 For a detailed discussion of *Bataille Monument*, see Thomas Hirschhorn's article in *Resistancia/Resistance*, Third International Symposium on Contemporary Art Theory (SITAC), Mexico City, 2004, pp. 224–44, and my 'Antagonism and Relational Aesthetics', *October*, 110, Fall 2004, pp. 51–79.

35 Lind, 'Actualisation of Space', this and all subsequent quotes from pp. 114–15.

36 Suzanne Lacy, 'Introduction', in Lacy (ed.), *Mapping the Terrain: New Genre Public Art*, Seattle: Bay Press, 1995. Of all the essays in this collection, Suzi Gablik's 'Connective Aesthetics: Art After Individualism' offers the most far-reaching denunciation of modernism as solipsistic: 'With its focus on radical individualism and its mandate of keeping art separate from life, modern aesthetics circumscribed the role of the audience to that of a detached spectator-observer. Such art can never build community. For this we need interactive and dialogic practices that draw others into the process . . .' (Gablik, in Lacy, *Mapping the Terrain*, p. 86.)

37 Lucy Lippard, 'Entering the Bigger Picture', in Lippard, *The Lure of the Local: Senses of Place in a Multicentered Society*, New York: New Press, 1997, pp. 286–90. See especially her eight-point 'ethic of place', pp. 286–7.

38 Kester, *Conversation Pieces*, p. 151.

39 Erik Hagoort, *Good Intentions: Judging the Art of Encounter*, Amsterdam: Netherlands Foundation for Visual Arts, Design and Architecture, 2005, pp. 54–5.

40 See for example: 'The standards Superflex have adopted for evaluating their work completely transcend the rewards to which most artists aspire. Since most of their contemporaries, given the choice between fighting world poverty and getting a positive review in a magazine, would most likely choose the latter, perhaps Superflex's most meaningful contribution to date has been to demonstrate to the international art community

that our responsibility as world citizens does not leave off where our careers begin.' (Dan Cameron, 'Into Africa', *Afterall*, pilot issue, 1998–9, p. 65.)

41 Walter Benjamin, 'The Author as Producer', in Benjamin, *Understanding Brecht*, London: Verso, 1998, p. 98.

42 Kester, *Conversation Pieces*, p. 12.

43 Ibid., p. 24.

44 Ibid., p. 150.

45 Peter Dews, 'Uncategorical Imperatives: Adorno, Badiou and the Ethical Turn', *Radical Philosophy*, 111, January–February 2002, p. 33.

46 See Alain Badiou, *Ethics: An Essay on the Understanding of Evil*, London: Verso, 2001; Slavoj Žižek, 'Multiculturalism, or, the Cultural Logic of Multinational Capitalism', *New Left Review*, September–October 1997, and 'Against Human Rights', *New Left Review*, July–August 2005; Jacques Rancière, *Hatred of Democracy*, London: Verso, 2006.

47 See Gillian Rose, 'Social Utopianism – Architectural Illusion', in *The Broken Middle*, Oxford: Blackwell, 1992, p. 306.

48 Art has a 'relatively autonomous position, which provides a sanctuary where new things can emerge', writes Jeanne van Heeswijk ('Fleeting Images of Community', available at www.jeanneworks.net); 'the world of culture is *the only space left* for me to do what I can do, there's nothing else', says the Chilean artist Alfredo Jaar (interview with the author, 9 May 2005). A recent discussion with five socially engaged artists at Tania Bruguera's Immigrant Movement International (New York, 23 April 2011) foregrounded the artists' lack of accountability: community activists and organisers persistently questioned the artists about the need to take their gestures to the next level by pressing for policy change.

49 Jacques Rancière, 'The Aesthetic Revolution and its Outcomes: Emplotments of Autonomy and Heteronomy', *New Left Review*, March–April 2002, p. 137, and *The Politics of Aesthetics*, London: Continuum, 2004.

50 For Rancière, dissensus is the core of politics: 'a dispute over what is given and about the frame within which we sense something is given'. Consensus, by contrast, is understood to foreclose the field of debate and reduce politics to the authoritarian actions of the 'police'. See Jacques Rancière, *Dissensus: On Politics and Aesthetics*, London: Continuum, 2010, p. 69.

51 Jacques Rancière, 'The Emancipated Spectator', *Artforum*, March 2007, pp. 271–80.

52 Jacques Rancière, *Malaise dans l'esthétique*, Paris: Editions Galilée, 2004, p. 145, my translation.

53 Ibid., p. 159, my translation.

54 Rancière, 'The Politics of Aesthetics', available at http://theater.kein. org.

55 Rancière, *Malaise dans l'esthétique*, p. 66, my translation.

56 'Suitable political art would ensure, at one and the same time, the production of a double effect: the readability of a political signification and a sensible or perceptual shock caused, conversely, by the uncanny, by that which resists signification. In fact, this ideal effect is always the object of a negotiation between opposites, between the readability of the message that threatens to destroy the sensible form of art and the radical uncanniness that threatens to destroy all political meaning.' (Rancière, *The Politics of Aesthetics*, p. 63.)

57 Rancière, *Malaise dans l'esthétique*, p. 67, my translation.

58 See David Callaghan, 'Still Signaling Through the Flames: The Living Theater's Use of Audience Participation in the 1990s', in Susan Kattwinkel (ed.), *Audience Participation: Essays on Inclusion in Performance*, Connecticut: Praeger, 2003.

59 Mike Figgis, director of *Leaving Las Vegas* (1995) and *Timecode* (2000), is a veteran of the community theatre group The People Show. His film *The Battle of Orgreave* is distributed by Artangel and Channel 4. Deller's book *The English Civil War Part II: Personal Accounts of the 1984–85 Miners' Strike*, was published by Artangel, London, in 2002, while the Orgreave archive was acquired by Tate in 2004.

60 'I was surprised people said it was a healing experience. That wasn't really why I did it. I wanted to remind people that something had happened there – not the locals, because they knew exactly what had happened. If anything, it was about digging up a hastily buried corpse and giving it a proper post-mortem.' (Deller, cited in John Slyce, 'Jeremy Deller: Fables of the Reconstruction', *Flash Art International*, January–February 2003, p. 76.)

61 '. . . there is no such thing as society. There are individual men and women, and there are families.' (Margaret Thatcher, *Woman's Own* magazine, 31 October 1987.) In this notorious soundbite, Thatcher was referring to her project of dissolving social solidarity in favour of individualism, personal responsibility, private property and family values.

62 Alex Farquharson, 'Jeremy Deller, The Battle of Orgreave', *Frieze*, 61, September 2001. The event also replicated a surreal incident from 1984 when an ice-cream van called *Rock On Tommy* continued to sell ice-cream even while surrounded by police. See Howard Giles, 'The Battle of Orgreave from a Tactical Point of View', in Deller (ed.), *The English Civil War Part II*, p. 30.

63 David Gilbert, 'Review of Jeremy Deller, *The English Civil War Part II: Personal Accounts of the 1984–5 Miners' Strike*', *Oral History*, 33:1, Spring 2005, p. 105.

64 Deller, introduction to *The English Civil War Part II*, p. 7.

65 'We will require a professional attitude and a willingness to stick to an agreed script. You will need to conform to a dress code and to look the part. . . . You will also be asked to sign a standard contract, which will

serve as proof of identity for access to the site and for payment.' ('Orgreave Re-enactment June 16/17 2001: Notes to Participants', reprinted in ibid., p. 154, and included in *The Battle of Orgreave Archive [An Injury to One is an Injury to All]*, 2004.) Performers were paid £80 per day in cash for their participation in the event.

66 Paweł Althamer, '1000 Words', *Artforum*, May 2006, pp. 268–9.

67 Deller, cited in Slyce, 'Jeremy Deller: Fables of the Reconstruction', p. 76.

68 Deller, cited in Dave Beech, 'The Uses of Authority', *Untitled*, 25, 2000, p. 10.

69 Deller, cited in ibid, p. 11.

70 Deller, cited in Slyce, 'Jeremy Deller: Fables of the Reconstruction', p. 76.

71 See for example Laurie Rojas, 'Jeremy Deller's Battle with History and Art', available at www.chicagoartcriticism.com

72 Alice Correia, 'Interpreting Jeremy Deller's *The Battle of Orgreave*', *Visual Culture in Britain*, 7:2, 2006, p. 101. This view is shared by David Gilbert: 'other voices from the strike remain silent – those miners that returned to work in Yorkshire are shadowy figures to be demonised or pitied . . .'. (Gilbert, 'Review of Jeremy Deller, *The English Civil War Part II*', p. 105.)

73 Dave Beech, '"The Reign of the Workers and Peasants Will Never End": Politics and Politicisation, Art and the Politics of Political Art', *Third Text*, 16:4, 2002, p. 387.

74 Tom Morton, 'Mining for Gold', *Frieze*, 72, January–February 2003, p. 73.

75 Neil Cummings and Marysia Lewandowska, 'A Shadow of Marx', in Amelia Jones (ed.), *A Companion to Contemporary Art Since 1945*, Oxford: Blackwell, 2006, p. 405.

76 '*The Battle of Orgreave* is a political work without a doubt . . . It's about the state and the power of the state. And also, the lengths the state will go to in order to see its aims seen through.' (Deller, cited in Beech, 'The Uses of Authority', p. 10.)

77 As one reviewer noted, Deller's event and book shows that 'there are stronger commonalities between the language of 1926 [the General Strike] and 1984, than between 1984 and today. It is some measure of the defeat suffered by organised labour in the 1980s that the very language used to express its struggles now sounds strange and anachronistic, even in a society just as marked by inequalities of wealth and power.' (Gilbert, 'Review of Jeremy Deller, *The English Civil War Part II*', p. 105.)

78 The Sealed Knot's webpage specifies that it is 'NOT politically motivated and has no political affiliation or ambitions whatsoever', available at www.thesealedknot.org.uk.

79 'This kind of work is open to such accusations that are often knee-jerk when any interaction with the general public is involved, and its subtext is that the general public is not intelligent enough to understand the context of or ideas behind the work. The fact that not only do they understand the process but they enjoy it and then "make" the work almost makes the critics' role redundant. People aren't stupid. I think any miner who has been effectively at war with the government for a year can handle himself working with an artist.' (Deller, cited in Slyce, 'Jeremy Deller: Fables of the Reconstruction', p. 77.)

80 A precedent for this multiple ontology would be Robert Smithson's *Spiral Jetty* (1970–72), which exists as an earthwork, an essay and a film.

81 'It is simply no longer possible to disconnect the intention of an artist's work, even when the content is deeply social or an institutional critique, from the marketplace in which even hedge fund investors now partake.' (Gregory Sholette, 'Response to Questionnaire', *October*, 123, Winter 2008, p. 138.)

82 See for example Philip Auslander, *Liveness: Performance in a Mediatized Culture*, London: Routledge, 1999; Peggy Phelan, *Unmarked: The Politics of Performance*, London: Routledge, 1993.

83 Rancière, 'The Emancipated Spectator', p. 277. 'The less the dramaturge knows what the spectators must do as a collective, the more he knows that they *must* become a collective, turn their mere agglomeration into the community that they virtually are' (p. 278).

84 See Jacques Rancière, interview with François Ewald, 'Qu'est-ce que la classe ouvrière?', in *Magazine Littéraire*, 175, July–August 1981, cited in Kristin Ross's introduction to Rancière's *The Ignorant Schoolmaster*, Stanford, CA: Stanford University Press, 1991, p. xviii.

85 Jacques Rancière, *The Philosopher and His Poor*, Durham, NC and London: Duke University Press, 2003, p. 188.

86 Ibid., p. 189.

87 Jacques Lacan, *The Ethics of Psychoanalysis, 1959–1960*, London: Routledge, 1992, p. 80.

88 Rancière, 'The Aesthetic Revolution and its Outcomes', p. 150.

Chapter Two   Artificial Hells

1 The centrality of Futurism to histories of performance art has been put forward most classically in RoseLee Goldberg's *Performance Art: From Futurism to the Present*, New York: Harry N. Abrams, 1988. Goldberg reads Futurism through the lens of visual art, while this chapter will argue for its indebtedness to theatrical models.

2 An exception to this general rule would be the performances of Oskar Kokoschka, such as his shadow play *The Speckled Egg* (1907), and the

plays *Sphinx and Strawman* (1909) and *Murderer Hope of Women* (1909). Kokoschka's plays were composed of theatrical images and focused on the aural quality of words rather than on conventional acting techniques.

3 Performance historian Günter Berghaus points to Marinetti's ten-year experience reciting Symbolist and anarchist poetry in various French and Italian theatres, 'causing altercations and agitated audience reactions', and notes this influence on Futurist recitation. See Berghaus, *Avant-garde Performance: Live Events and Electronic Technologies*, Basingstoke: Palgrave Macmillan, 2005, p. 32.

4 Filippo Tommaso Marinetti, 'Prime battaglie futuriste', *Teoria e invenzione futurista*, Milan: Mondadori, 1968, p. 201; translation in Milton Cohen, *Movement, Manifesto, Melée: The Modernist Group 1910–1914*, Lanham, Maryland: Lexington Books, 2004, p. 136.

5 Filippo Tommaso Marinetti, 'Futurist Manifesto', *Le Figaro*, 20 February 1909, reprinted in R. W. Flint (ed.), *Marinetti: Selected Writings*, New York: Farrar, Straus and Giroux, 1971, pp. 39–44.

6 Christine Poggi, 'Folla/Follia: Futurism and the Crowd', *Critical Inquiry*, 28:3, Spring 2002, pp. 744–5.

7 Filippo Tommaso Marinetti, Emilio Settimelli, Bruno Corra, 'The Futurist Synthetic Theatre', in *Marinetti: Selected Writings*, p. 123. Passéist is the conventional English translation of *passatista*, an old-fashioned, conservative person.

8 See Marinetti, 'The Variety Theatre' (1913), in *Marinetti: Selected Writings*, pp. 116–22.

9 Futurist Painters (Balla, Boccioni, Carrà, Russola, Severini), 'Exhibitors to the Public' (1912), *Exhibition of Works of the Italian Futurist Painters*, London: Sackville Gallery, 1912, pp. 2–15, cited in Christina Taylor, *Futurism: Politics, Painting and Performance*, Michigan: Ann Arbor, UMI Research Press, 1974 (second edition 1979), p. 20.

10 Marinetti, 'The Variety Theatre', p. 118.

11 Ibid., pp. 33–4. These ideas were translated into Russian Futurist theatre following an Italian tour there in 1913–14: at a Cubo-Futurist recital in Moscow in October 1913, the poet Aleksei Kruchenykh spilled hot tea on the front row of the audience and demanded to be booed off stage.

12 Marinetti apparently replied, 'If I deserve a bullet of lead, you deserve a bullet of shit!' Reported in Berghaus, *Avant-garde Performance*, p. 37.

13 As Christine Poggi argues, Futurist texts have a strong gender subtext, aiming to infuse a 'feminised' audience with a 'masculine' will to power. In Futurist writing as well as in painting, the crowd is frequently figured as feminine in its 'malleability, its incapacity to reason, its susceptibility to flattery and hysteria, and its secret desire to be seduced and dominated'. (Poggi, 'Folla/Follia: Futurism and the Crowd', p. 712.)

14 Michael Kirby, *Futurist Performance*, New York: E. P. Dutton and Co., 1971, p. 27.

15 Wassily Kandinsky, 'Franz Marc', cited in Cohen, *Movement, Manifesto, Melée*, p. 137.

16 Albert Gleizes, cited in Cohen, *Movement, Manifesto, Melée*, pp. 137–8. Gleizes goes on to note the constituency present at the opening day was not just artists and critics: 'socialites, genuine art-lovers and picture-dealers jostle one another, along with the dairyman and the concierge who have been given an invitation by the artist who is a customer of theirs or lives in the block'. It is worth bearing in mind these accounts when considering the quietly respectful crowds at contemporary art exhibitions today, and the way in which vociferous debates about art are now confined to panel discussions, seminars and symposia at a safe remove from the work itself.

17 Other events seemed to target a middle- and upper-class audience, such as Marinetti's lectures at opera houses (which included attacks on the *passéist* values of this art form), including La Fenice in Venice (7 May 1911) and La Scala in Milan (2 March 1911).

18 Marinetti, Settimelli, Corra, 'The Futurist Synthetic Theatre', p. 128.

19 Compare this sentiment to Breton's observation (discussed below) that 'a successful man, or simply one who is no longer attacked, is a dead man'. (André Breton, 'Artificial Hells, Inauguration of the "1921 Dada Season" ', *October*, 105, Summer 2003, p. 141.)

20 Manifesto 1912, 'Exhibitors to the Public', cited in Taylor, *Futurism: Politics, Painting and Performance*, p. 21.

21 Boris Groys, in Claire Bishop and Boris Groys, 'Bring the Noise', *Tate Etc*, Summer 2009, p. 33.

22 Francesco Cangiullo, *Le serate futuriste*, Pozzuoli: Tirena, 1930, pp. 160–1, translation by Berghaus in *Avant-garde Performance*, p. 36.

23 For the script of this work, and many others, see Michael Kirby, *Futurist Performance*, New York: PAJ Publications, 1986, pp. 290–1.

24 Enrico Prampolini, 'Futurist Scenography' (1915), in Taylor, *Futurism: Politics, Painting and Performance*, pp. 57–60.

25 As Boris Groys provocatively notes, only destruction is truly participatory, something in which everyone can equally participate: 'it is clear that there is an intimate relationship between destruction and participative art. When a Futurist action destroys art in this traditional form, it also invites all the spectators to participate in this act of destruction, because it does not require any specific artistic skills. In this sense fascism is more democratic than communism, of course. It is the only thing we can all participate in.' (Groys, in Bishop and Groys, 'Bring the Noise', p. 38.)

26 '[Mankind's] alienation has reached such a degree that it can experience its own destruction as an aesthetic pleasure of the first order.' (Walter

Benjamin, 'The Work of Art in the Age of Mechanical Reproduction', in *Illuminations*, New York: Schocken, 1969, p. 235.)

27 Leon Trotsky, *Literature and Revolution*, London: RedWords, 1991, p. 160.

28 Ibid., p. 163.

29 Theatre's accessibility also meant that it flourished in rural communities: 'The lack of means, the almost complete lack of ideologically acceptable films, the high cost of borrowing, and a number of other things have made films available only in the cities . . .' (V. Stanev, 'Cinema in the Countryside', in William Rosenberg [ed.], *Bolshevik Visions: First Phase of the Cultural Revolution in Soviet Russia*, Part 2, Ann Arbor: University of Michigan Press, 1990, p. 113.)

30 Zenovia A. Sochor, *Revolution and Culture: The Bogdanov–Lenin Controversy*, Ithaca: Cornell University Press, 1988, p. 134.

31 Aleksandr Bogdanov, 'The Proletarian and Art' (1918), in John Bowlt (ed.), *Russian Art of the Avant-garde: Theory and Criticism 1902–34*, New York: Viking Press, 1976, p. 177.

32 Lenin, cited in Max Eastman, *Artists in Uniform: A Study of Literature and Bureaucratism*, New York: Alfred A. Knopf, 1934, p. 244. Sochor characterises the main difference between Bogdanov and Lenin as concerning their position on utopia: for Bogdanov it was to be kept alive and realised, while for Lenin it was to be pigeonholed and deferred. See Sochor, *Revolution and Culture*, p. 233.

33 Lenin, 'On Proletarian Culture' (1920), in V. I. Lenin, *On Literature and Art*, Moscow: Progress Publishers, 1967, p. 155.

34 Bogdanov, 'The Paths of Proletarian Creation' (1920), in Bowlt (ed.), *Russian Art of the Avant-garde*, pp. 181–2.

35 Ibid., p. 181.

36 Ibid., pp. 178–82.

37 Alexei Gan, 'Constructivism', in Camilla Gray, *The Great Experiment: Russian Art 1863–1922*, London: Thames and Hudson, 1962, p. 286.

38 Bogdanov, 'The Paths of Proletarian Creation', p. 180.

39 Bogdanov, cited in Sochor, *Revolution and Culture*, p. 148.

40 Trotsky, *Literature and Revolution*, p. 168.

41 Ibid., p. 432. Citing the Marxist adage that art is a hammer with which to shape society, rather than a mirror that passively holds up a reflection to it, Trotsky argued that society needs *both* the hammer and the mirror — since what is the use of a hammer unless you can accurately see what you are shaping?

42 Comrade N. I. Goncharko (Proletkult delegate for the city of Saratov), cited in Kerzhentsev, 'The Proletarian Theatre', report and discussion at the First All-Russian Conference of the Proletkult, 17 September 1918, in Rosenberg (ed.), *Bolshevik Visions*, p. 131.

43 See Huntly Carter, *The New Theatre and Cinema of Soviet Russia*, London: Chapman and Dodd, 1924, Chapter 6. Approximately 120,000 people saw

Mystery-Bouffe in just over five months. Trotsky, however, expressed reservations about Mayakovsky's success when leaving 'his individualist orbit' and attempting 'to enter the orbit of the Revolution'. (Trotsky, *Literature and Revolution*, pp. 187–8.)

44 Platon Mikhailovich Kerzhentsev, *Tvorcheskii Theatr*, 1923, cited in Robert Leach, *Revolutionary Theatre*, London: Routledge, 1994, p. 23.

45 Carter, *The New Theatre and Cinema of Soviet Russia*, p. 89.

46 Kerzhentsev, *Tvorcheskii Theatr*, p. 38, cited by Katerina Clark, *Petersburg: Crucible of Revolution*, Cambridge, MA: Harvard University Press, 1995, p. 125.

47 Viktor Shklovsky, cited in Lynn Mally, *Culture of the Future: The Proletkult Movement in Revolutionary Russia*, Berkeley: University of California Press, 1990, p. 245.

48 Carter, *The New Theatre and Cinema of Soviet Russia*, p. 103.

49 Robert Leach gives the example of workers producing the play *Don't Go* on the basis of analysing the social relations depicted in a painting in their club room. See Leach, *Revolutionary Theatre*, p. 39.

50 Clark, *Petersburg*, p. 110.

51 Lunacharsky, cited in Sheila Fitzpatrick, *The Commissariat of Enlightenment: Soviet Organization of Education and the Arts under Lunacharsky, October 1917–1921*, Cambridge: Cambridge University Press, 1970, pp. 146–7.

52 Kerzhentsev, 'The Proletarian Theatre', in Rosenberg (ed.), *Bolshevik Visions*, p. 129. One solution was to adapt existing plays, such as Verhaeren's *Zor*, by reducing the role of the hero and increasing the role of the masses.

53 Evgeny Zamyatin, 'The Modern Russian Theatre' (1931), in E. and C. R. Proffer (eds.), *The Ardis Anthology of Russian Futurism*, Ann Arbor, Michigan: Ardis, 1980, p. 204.

54 Ibid., p. 205.

55 For a more detailed contextual account, see Mel Gordon, 'Eisenstein's Later Work at the Proletkult', *TDR*, 22:3, September 1978, pp. 111–12.

56 Jay Leyda, *Kino: A History of the Russian and Soviet Film*, London: Allen and Unwin, 1960, cited in *Transform the World! Poetry Must be Made by All!*, Stockholm: Moderna Museet, 1969, p. 43.

57 See John W. Casson, 'Living Newspaper: Theatre and Therapy', *TDR*, 44:2, Summer 2000, pp. 108–9.

58 See René Fülöp-Miller, *The Mind and Face of Bolshevism: An Examination of Cultural Life in Soviet Russia*, London and New York: Putnam's Sons, 1965 (first published 1927), Chapter 7.

59 Gray, *The Great Experiment*, pp. 217–18. Gray's source was a participant in the event, the Constructivist architect Berthold Lubetkin (p. 309, note 7).

60 Platon Mikhailovich Kerzhentsev, *Das Schöpferische Theater*, Hamburg,

1922. Romain Rolland, *Le Théâtre du Peuple*, Paris: Cahiers de la Quinzaine, 1903, preface, n.p.

61 Kerzhentsev, *The Creative Theatre*, 1918, cited in Leach, *Revolutionary Theatre*, p. 24.

62 A. I. Piotrovsky, cited in Richard Stites, *Revolutionary Dreams: Utopian Vision and Experimental Life in the Russian Revolution*, Oxford: Oxford University Press, 1989, p. 94.

63 Fülöp-Miller, *The Mind and Face of Bolshevism*, p. 146.

64 James von Geldern, 'Putting the Masses in Mass Culture: Bolshevik Festivals, 1918–1920', *Journal of Popular Culture*, 31:4, 1998, p. 137.

65 Ibid., p. 138.

66 František Deák, 'Russian Mass Spectacles', *TDR*, 19:2, June 1975.

67 Nikolai Evreinov, interview in *Life of Art*, 30 September 1920, in Vladimir Tolstoy et al., *Street Art of the Revolution: Festivals and Celebrations in Russia 1918–33*, London: Thames and Hudson, 1990, p. 137.

68 Stites, *Revolutionary Dreams*, p. 96. Clark notes that presentations of mass spectacles in the West reached their peak during or just after a period of war, when it was possible to mobilise such large numbers of people and equipment. In Russia, this peak year was 1920, when the Civil War was winding down and the troops were less engaged at the front but yet to be demobilised. See Clark, *Petersburg*, p. 133.

69 Deák, 'Russian Mass Spectacles', p. 20. This search for authentic participants was also adopted by Eisenstein when casting his 1927 film *October: Ten Days That Shook the World*.

70 Susan Buck-Morss, *Dreamworld and Catastrophe: The Passing of Mass Utopia in East and West*, Cambridge, MA: MIT Press, 2002, p. 144.

71 Evreinov, *Teatr dlya sebya*, vol. 1, pp. 69–83, cited in Clark, *Petersburg*, p. 106.

72 Stites, *Revolutionary Dreams*, p. 97.

73 Fülöp-Miller, *The Mind and Face of Bolshevism*, Chapter 7, 'Theatricalised Life'.

74 Emma Goldman, *My Disillusionment in Russia*, London: William Heinemann, 1923.

75 Fülöp-Miller, *The Mind and Face of Bolshevism*, p. 151.

76 Ibid., p. 151. In other words, mass spectacles were both too artistic and too political, which amounted to the same thing.

77 Kerzhentsev, cited in Richard Stourac and Kathleen McCreery, *Theatre as a Weapon: Workers' Theatre in the Soviet Union, Germany and Britain, 1917–1934*, London and New York: Routledge and Kegan Paul, 1986, pp. 13–14.

78 Carter, *The New Theatre and Cinema of Soviet Russia*, p. 109.

79 Goldman, *My Disillusionment in Russia*, p. 75.

80 Ibid., p. 78.

81 See Mona Ozouf, *Festivals and the French Revolution*, Cambridge, MA: Harvard University Press, 1988.

82 Kerzhentsev, cited in Leach, *Revolutionary Theatre*, p. 24.

83 See Amy Nelson, *Music for the Revolution: Musicians and Power in Early Soviet Russia*, University Park, PA: Pennsylvania State University Press, 2004, Chapter 7. 'Without the visual image of the conductor's interpretative directions, performers and audiences alike experienced the music more directly, focusing more completely on the auditory element of musical performance' (p. 193).

84 Stites, *Revolutionary Dreams*, p. 136. Persimfans was dissolved by Stalin in 1932.

85 See Fülöp-Miller, *The Mind and Face of Bolshevism*, p. 179.

86 Ibid., p. 182.

87 Ibid., p. 184.

88 Exceptions would be T. J. Demos, 'Dada's Event: Paris, 1921', in Beth Hinderliter et al. (eds.), *Communities of Sense: Rethinking Aesthetics and Politics*, Durham, NC: Duke University Press, 2009, and Matthew Witkowsky, 'Dada Breton', *October*, 105, Summer 2003, pp. 125–36.

89 Louis Aragon, *Projet d'histoire litteraire contemporaine*, Paris: Marc Dachy 1994, p. 103, my translation.

90 Ibid., my translation.

91 André Breton, 'Entretiens Radiophoniques, IV' (1952), in *Oeuvres Complètes*, Vol. 3, Editions Gallimard, 1999, p. 462, my translation.

92 André Breton, cited in Hans Richter, *Dada: Art and Anti-Art*, London: Thames and Hudson, 1965, p. 174.

93 See Victoria Nes Kirby, 'Georges Ribemont-Dessaignes', *TDR*, 16:1, March 1972, p. 106.

94 Richter, *Dada*, p. 174. Thanks to Germán García for this reference.

95 Ibid., p. 176.

96 Richter, *Dada*, p. 183.

97 Georges Hugnet, *L'aventure Dada, 1916–1922*, Editions Seghers, 1971 (first published 1957), p. 97, my translation. He noted that the excursion did not aim to find the tomb of Julien and Marguerite de Ravalet (a brother and sister sent to the block for their incestuous love), which would have been an obvious point of attraction for Breton.

98 Aragon records that the group took their inspiration for the strategy of the *Grande Saison Dada* from the menace and terror of the French Revolution, which they felt to be a good comparison with their intellectual state. Aragon, *Projet d'histoire litteraire contemporaine*, pp. 103–4.

99 Richter, *Dada*, p. 184.

100 Breton, 'Artificial Hells', p. 141.

101 For the event at Théâtre de l'Oeuvre on 27 March 1920, Tzara claimed that even after 1,200 people were turned away, there were three spectators to every seat. See Tristan Tzara, 'Some Memoirs of Dadaism', in *Vanity Fair*, July 1922, p. 91 (published in French as

'Quelques Souvenirs', in Tzara, *Oeuvres Complètes*, Vol. 1, Paris: Flammarion, 1975, p. 596). This is comparable to the large numbers who attended the Futurist *serata* at Teatro Verdi in Florence on 12 December 1913: *Lacerba* reports 5,000 people in the audience, while the *Corriere della sera* reports 7,000. See Berghaus, *Avant-garde Performance*, p. 34.

102 See Michel Sanouillet, *Dada à Paris*, Paris: Jean-Jacques Pauvert, 1965, pp. 246–7, and Georges Ribemont-Dessaignes, *Déjà Jadis, ou du mouvement Dada à l'espace abstrait*, Paris: Julliard, 1958, p. 94, my translation.

103 See Breton, 'Artificial Hells', p. 140.

104 Sanouillet, *Dada à Paris*, p. 248. The audience's enthusiasm for Dada is indicated by the title of a contemporary review: 'The Disciples of "Dada" at the Eglise Saint Julien-le-Pauvre', *Comoedia*, 15 April 1921.

105 Breton, 'Artificial Hells', pp. 140–1.

106 Richter, *Dada*, p. 183. Here he is citing Ribemont-Dessaignes.

107 Tzara, 'Some Memoirs of Dadaism', p.91.

108 Breton, cited in Ribemont-Dessaignes, *Déjà Jadis*, p. 86, my translation.

109 Breton, 'Artificial Hells', p. 138.

110 Ibid., p. 139.

111 Ibid., p. 140, emphasis added.

112 Picabia, cited in Hugnet, *L'aventure Dada*, p. 98, my translation.

113 Press release transcribed in Sanouillet, *Dada à Paris*, p. 244, my translation.

114 Breton, 'Entretiens Radiophoniques', p. 469.

115 The flier reads: 'Twelve spectators will constitute the jury. We would be grateful to everyone who would like to take part to register in advance at Au Sans Pareil, 37 Avenue Kléber, before 11 May 1921' (my translation).

116 *Acte d'accusation du Procès Barrès*, May 1921, reprinted in Hugnet, *L'aventure Dada*, p. 235, my translation. A full transcription is published in *Littérature*, August 1921.

117 Breton, 'Artificial Hells', p. 140; Aragon, *Projet d'histoire litteraire contemporaine*, p. 104, my translation.

118 Tzara, 'Procès Barrès', in *Oeuvres Complètes*, Vol. 1, p. 576.

119 See Hugnet, *L'aventure Dada*, p. 102.

120 Ribemont-Dessaignes, *Déjà Jadis*, p. 97, translation in Richter, *Dada*, p. 186.

121 Richter, *Dada*, p. 186.

122 Lunacharsky, 'Revolution and Art', in Bowlt (ed.), *Russian Art of the Avant-garde*, p. 192. He goes on to reference this dream as the one 'the French Revolution dreamed of' (p. 193).

123 This negation becomes apparent when we compare Paris Dada to the more overtly partisan forms of Berlin Dada, with their denunciations of

the Great War, the Weimar Republic, nationalism and the rising power of Hitler.

124 George L. Mosse, *The Nationalization of the Masses: Political Symbolism and Mass Movement in Germany from the Napoleonic Wars Through the Third Reich*, New York: Howard Fertig, 1975, p. 205. See also Hans-Ulrich Thamer, 'The Orchestration of the National Community: The Nuremberg Party Rallies of the NSDAP', in Günter Berghaus (ed.), *Fascism and Theatre: Comparative Studies on the Aesthetics and Politics of Performance in Europe, 1925–45*, Oxford: Berghahn, 1996, pp. 172–90.

Chapter 3 *Je participe, tu participes, il participe . . .*

1 Opposing itself to functionalism, unitary urbanism advocated giving oneself over to the city – to idleness and the pleasures found in aimless drifting and heightened sensitivity to ambiance. See Unsigned, 'Unitary Urbanism at the End of the 1950s', in Elisabeth Sussman (ed.), *On the Passage of a Few People Through a Rather Brief Moment in Time: The Situationist International, 1957–1972*, Cambridge, MA: MIT Press, 1989, p. 143.

2 Guy Debord, 'Theory of the Dérive', *Internationale Situationniste*, 2, 1958, translated in Ken Knabb (ed.), *Situationist International Anthology*, Berkeley: Bureau of Public Secrets, 1981, p. 53.

3 See Guy Debord, 'Two Accounts of the Dérive', in Libero Andreotti and Xavier Costa (eds.), *Theory of the Dérive and Other Situationist Writings on the City*, Barcelona: MACBA, 1996, pp. 28–32.

4 This seemed to offer a psychogeographic hub for the pair, opening as it did onto two streets and two canals, evoking the type of illustrations found in children's books where many geographical features are packed into a single image; they note that Claude Lorrain often uses this device in his paintings.

5 More recent developments in art, many of which are influenced by the SI (including research-led collaborative projects investigating gentrification, urban space and provisional architecture), make the Situationist *dérive* appear somewhat unfocused and arbitrary; in turn, the Situationists' approach seems historically and materially specific when compared to the Surrealists' nocturnal strolls. See the entry on 'Psychogeography' in *Imus Nocte et consumimur Igni: The Situationist International (1957–72)*, Basel: Museum Tinguely, 2007, n.p.

6 Abdelhafid Khatib, 'Attempt at a Psychogeographical Description of Les Halles', *Internationale Situationniste*, 2, 1958; English translation in Andreotti and Costa (eds.), *Theory of the Dérive*, pp. 72–6.

7 Guy Debord, 'Guy Debord's report to the Seventh SI Conference in Paris', in *The Real Split in the International: Theses on the Situationist International and Its Time, 1972*, London: Pluto, 2003, p. 139.

8 Participation for the SI is not to be understood in the sense that Lebel and GRAV use this term, that is, to describe an artistic strategy. Rather, the SI's interest in participation denotes full participation in society; see the unsigned 'Manifeste' dated 17 May 1960, *Internationale Situationniste*, 4, 1960, p. 37.

9 See for example Greil Marcus, *Lipstick Traces: A Secret History of the Twentieth Century*, Cambridge, MA: Harvard University Press, 1989, and Sadie Plant, *The Most Radical Gesture: The Situationist International in a Postmodern Age*, London and New York: Routledge, 1992. A rare comparative study is Jon Erikson's 'The Spectacle of the Anti-spectacle: Happenings and the Situationist International', *Discourse*, 14:2, Spring 1992, pp. 36–58. Catherine Millet's *Contemporary Art in France* (Paris: Flammarion, 2006), is more typical in including only one reference to Debord and the SI in her nearly 400-page survey.

10 'On the Passage of a Few People Through a Rather Brief Moment in Time: The Situationist International, 1957–1972' toured from the Centre Pompidou to the London ICA and culminated at the ICA, Boston 1989–90.

11 Rod Kedward, *La Vie en Bleu: France and the French Since 1900*, London: Allen Lane/Penguin, 2005, p. 404. 'A man is alienated when his only relationship to the social direction of his society is the one the ruling class accords him . . . cancelling out social conflict by creating dependent participation.' (Alain Touraine, *The Post-Industrial Society*, London: Wildwood House, 1974, p. 9.)

12 See for example the SI: 'While participation becomes more impossible, the second-rate inventors of modern art demand the participation of everyone.' Unsigned, 'The Avant-Garde of Presence', *Internationale Situationniste*, 8, 1963, p. 315, my translation.

13 Michel Ragon, 'Vers une démocratisation de l'art', in *Vingt-cinq ans d'art vivant*, Paris: Casterman, 1969, pp. 355–73.

14 Frank Popper, *Art – Action, Participation*, New York: New York University Press, 1975, p. 12.

15 Ibid., p. 280.

16 Jean-Jacques Lebel, having grown up in close proximity to the Surrealist group (and been eventually excluded from it), deliberately avoided this approach, while Guy Debord continued to use Breton's 'papal' model of leadership for the SI.

17 The institutional recuperation of Dada began to take place at the end of the 1950s, given momentum by Robert Motherwell's anthology *The Dada Painters and Poets* (1951); the Stedelijk Museum, Amsterdam, held the large exhibition 'Dada' in 1959; in the same year, 'L'Aventure Dada' was organised by Georges Hugnet at Galerie de l'Institut, Paris, and followed by a Dada retrospective in 1966 at the Musée Nationale d'art Moderne. We could also cite the Nouveaux Réalisme exhibition

'40° au-dessous de Dada' (40 degrees below Dada) at Galerie J, Paris, in 1961.

18 Cited in Sarah Wilson, 'Paris in the 1960s: Towards the Barricades of the Latin Quarter', in *Paris: Capital of the Arts, 1900–1968*, London: Royal Academy of Art, 2002, p. 330.

19 Greil Marcus is typically strident on this point, siding with Debord and Wolman to describe Isou as 'unoriginal, academic and precious . . . Lettrisme was a screaming oxymoron, systematised dada'. (Marcus, *Lipstick Traces*, p. 256.)

20 Unsigned, 'Amère victoire du surréalisme', *Internationale Situationniste*, 1, 1957, p. 3, my translation.

21 Unsigned, 'Le bruit et la fureur', *Internationale Situationniste*, 1, 1957, p. 5, my translation.

22 Bernstein, cited in Marcus, *Lipstick Traces*, p. 181.

23 Lefebvre was expelled from the French Communist Party in 1958 and pursued a less orthodox form of analysis, combining Marxism with sociology, literary analysis, philosophy and poetry. In his *Critique de la vie quotidienne* (1947), a key text for the SI, Lefebvre called for an art to transform everyday life, attacking Surrealism for its recourse to the 'marvellous'. Debord, Bernstein and Vaneigem held long working sessions with Henri Lefebvre in 1960 and 1961 in Strasbourg and Nanterre, but relations between them became tense. In 1967 Lefebvre mocked their hopes for the people rising up to a successful revolt before proceeding 'to the eternal Festival and the creation of situations'. (Lefebvre, cited in Plant, *The Most Radical Gesture*, p. 96.)

24 Guy Debord, 'The Situationists and New Forms of Action in Politics or Art' (1963), in Sussman (ed.), *On the Passage of a Few People Through a Rather Brief Moment in Time*, p. 151.

25 'It is even a notable fact that of the 28 members of the SI whom we have had to exclude so far, 23 were among those situationists who had an individually characterised artistic practice, and even an increasingly profitable success from this.' (The SI [J. V. Martin, Jan Strijbosch, Raoul Vaneigem, René Viénet], 'Response to a Questionnaire from the Center for Socio-Experimental Art', *Internationale Situationniste*, 9, 1964, p. 43, my translation.)

26 Peter Wollen, 'The Situationist International', *New Left Review*, 1: 174, March–April 1989, p. 94.

27 T. J. Clark and Donald Nicholson-Smith, 'Why Art Can't Kill the Situationist International', *October*, 79, Winter 1997, pp. 15–31. The authors adopt a hectoring tone to dismiss Wollen, but usefully point out that the SI was directed as much at the orthodox left and Stalinism as it was at consumerist spectacle.

28 Tom McDonough, 'Rereading Debord, Rereading the Situationists', *October*, 79, Winter 1997, p. 7.

29 Debord's denunciation not just of contemporary art but also of art criticism as a mode of spectacular consumption is a wake up call to the critic; however, it is a reproof that could only be issued by a wealthy intellectual dandy able to survive on parental handouts (even if this privileged distance was formative for his critical acuity). See Andrew Hussey, *The Game of War: The Life and Death of Guy Debord*, London: Jonathan Cape, 2001, p. 131, p.144. Hussey notes that Michèle Bernstein, by contrast, earned a living by writing advertising copy, along with horoscopes for horses, which were published in racing magazines.

30 'The artist relinquishes the lived intensity of the creative moment in exchange for the durability of what he creates, so that his name may live on in the funeral glory of the museum. And his desire to produce a durable work is the very thing that prevents him from living imperishable instants of real life.' (Raoul Vaneigem, *The Revolution of Everyday Life*, London: Aldgate Press, 2003 [first published in French 1967], p. 113.)

31 Debord, 'The Situationists and New Forms of Action in Politics or Art', p. 148.

32 Ibid., p. 150.

33 The SI organised an exhibition 'to salute and extend this first attack against the ruling organisation of social space' in Denmark, reissuing the *Danger! Official Secret* tract alongside a theoretical text, 'The Situationists and New Forms of Action in Politics or Art'. See *Internationale Situationniste*, 9, 1964.

34 See Marcus, *Lipstick Traces*, pp. 422–45.

35 These are reproduced in *Internationale Situationniste*, 9, 1964, p. 21 and p. 36. Another example, also from *I.S.* 9, alludes to current affairs, namely the marriage of Princess Anne-Marie of Denmark to King Constantine II of Greece. Lewis Morley's celebrated photograph of Christine Keeler is captioned with the following: 'As the SI says, it's a far far better thing to be a whore like me than the wife of a fascist like Constantine.'

36 Chtcheglov describes the *dérive* as being akin to psychoanalysis: 'Just abandon yourself to the flow of words, the analyst says . . . The *dérive* is really a technique, indeed almost a therapy. In any case, it can have a therapeutic effect.' (Chtcheglov, *Ecrits Retrouvés*, reprinted in *Imus Nocte et consumimur Igni*, n.p.)

37 Unsigned, 'Definitions', in *Internationale Situationniste*, 1, 1958, p. 13.

38 Guy Debord, 'Report on the Construction of Situations' (1957), translated in Knabb (ed.), *Situationist International Anthology*, p. 18.

39 Lefebvre, *La Somme et le Reste* (1960), cited as the epigraph to the unsigned article 'The Theory of Moments and the Construction of Situations', *Internationale Situationniste*, 4, 1960, pp. 10–11.

40 Guy Debord, 'Theses on Cultural Revolution', *Internationale Situationniste*, 1, p. 21.

41 Here we can note the SI's debt to J. Huizinga's *Homo Ludens* (1944), with

its emphasis on play as a free and meaningful activity carried out for its own sake.

42 Unsigned, 'Preliminary Problems in Constructing a Situation', *Internationale Situationniste*, 1, 1958, pp. 11–12, translated in Knabb (ed.), *Situationist International Anthology*, p. 44.

43 Ibid.

44 For a full account of the installation and the reasons for its cancellation, see the unsigned report 'Die Welt als Labyrinth', *Internationale Situationniste*, 4, pp. 5–7.

45 Unsigned, 'L'avant-garde de la Presence', *Internationale Situationniste*, 8, 1963, p. 16. The article was a response to a recent essay by Lucien Goldmann on the 'avant-garde of absence' (nihilist work by Beckett, Ionesco, Duras, etc.) published in *Médiations* 4. Umberto Eco theorised these new forms in *The Open Work* (1962), translated into French in 1965.

46 The signatories of the first manifesto of the group (1960) were Hugo Demarco, François Morellet, Moyano, Servanes, Francisco Sobrino, Joël Stein and Jean-Pierre Yvaral.

47 GRAV, 'Propositions générales du GRAV', 25 October 1961, signed by Rossi, Le Parc, Morellet, Sobrino, Stein and Yvaral, reproduced in Luciano Caramel (ed.), *Groupe de recherche d'art visuel 1960–1968*, Milan: Electa, 1975, p. 25, my translation.

48 'Manifeste du GRAV', in *Abstract Art*, Vol. 2 of *Art Since Mid-Century: The New Internationalism*, Greenwich, CT: NY Graphic Society, 1971, p. 296.

49 Stein, in *Douze ans d'art contemporain en France*, p. 386.

50 A critic in *Studio International* observed that: 'the initial impression may be one of pleasant triviality. . . . the dominant works are "gags", which the visitor is invited to manipulate and play with: distorting spectacles and mirrors, ping-pong balls, a board with lights which spell out a mildly blue poem. Sophisticated toys? Toys perhaps, but not very sophisticated. Many hardly rise above the level of pooh-sticks.' (Cyril Barrett, 'Mystification and the Groupe de Recherche', *Studio International*, 172: 880, August 1966, pp. 93.)

51 See 'L'instabilità: Il labyrinto groupe recherche d'art visuel', in Caramel (ed.), *Groupe de recherche d'art visuel 1960–1968*, p. 32, my translation. The group also produced a second, smaller *Labyrinth* for the exhibition 'Nouvelle Tendence' at the Musée des Arts Décoratifs, Paris (1964), and a third in New York, at 992 Madison Avenue, in 1965.

52 GRAV, 'Assez des mystifications', in Caramel (ed.), *Groupe de recherche d'art visuel 1960–1968*, p. 36, my translation and emphasis. An English variation of this manifesto can be found in the same publication under the title 'Stop Art!' (1965), p. 41.

53 Richard Schechner, 'Happenings', *Tulane Drama Review*, 10:2, Winter 1965, pp. 230–1.

54 'Manifeste du GRAV', *Abstract Art*, p. 296, my emphasis.

55 It is important to be attuned to the difference between *individualism*, demonised in the discursive criteria of today's socially engaged art, and Debord's critique of *isolation* in *The Society of the Spectacle*.

56 A questionnaire was also handed out to the public, which included questions like: 'Modern art – such as it is found in the galleries, salons and museums – is it interesting, indifferent, necessary, incomprehensible, intelligent or gratuitous?', and 'In your opinion, what sort of initiative has this been: one that could be described as publicity-seeking, cultural, experimental, artistic, sociological, political, or in no way at all?' (Reported in Popper, *Art – Action, Participation*, p. 26.)

57 GRAV, 'Une journée dans la rue', in Caramel (ed.), *Groupe de recherche d'art visuel 1960–1968*, p. 44, my translation.

58 Ibid., my translation.

59 Unsigned, 'L'avant-garde de la Presence', pp. 16–17.

60 Unsigned, 'L'avant-garde de la Presence', p. 19, my translation. GRAV's commitment to formal experimentation, with the metaphor of political connotations deployed as a supplementary justification (rather than motivating *raison d'être*), has much in common with Bourriaud's defence of relational aesthetics.

61 Stein, in *Douze ans d'art contemporain*, p. 386. By 1975, Le Parc also recognised these failings, but in artistic rather than Marxist terms. When asked for his main criticisms of GRAV between 1960 and 1968, he replied: 'not enough shared work, not enough confrontation, not enough imagination, and [not enough] effort to produce collective activities, not enough daring; too little risk, too much fear of the ridiculous, too much respect for conventions, too much slowness; the fact of being always late in relation to events.' (Le Parc, in Caramel [ed.], *Groupe de recherche d'art visuel 1960–1968*, p. 131, my translation.)

62 Unsigned, 'L'avant-garde de la Presence', p. 20, my translation.

63 The 'chose' (thing) was made by Tinguely and was ritually carried up the Grand Canal in a gondola before being thrown into the lagoon off San Giorgio, with white flowers. For a longer description see Gunnar Kvaran, 'Lebel/Rebel', in *Jean-Jacques Lebel: Bilder, Skulpturen, Installationen*, Vienna: Museum Moderner Kunst Stiftung Ludwig Wien, 1998, pp. 54–5; and Jean-Jacques Lebel and Androula Michaël (eds.), *Happenings de Jean-Jacques Lebel, ou l'insoumission radicale*, Paris: Editions Hanzan, 2009, pp. 36–41.

64 Jean-Jacques Lebel, 'Flashback', in Lebel and Michaël (eds), *Happenings de Jean-Jacques Lebel*, pp. 7–8.

65 Jean-Jacques Lebel, 'On the Necessity of Violation', *Tulane Drama Review*, 13:1, Autumn 1968, p. 103.

66 This was not true, however, of work by Claes Oldenburg, Red Grooms, Bob Whitman and others, which is more accurately referred to as artist's

theatre. In this context, Kaprow's interest in participation was the exception rather than the rule. See Allan Kaprow, *Assemblage, Environments and Happenings*, New York: Harry N. Abrams, 1966.

67 *Household*, for example, was commissioned by Cornell University and presented on 3 May 1964. Kaprow's score tells us that 'There were no spectators at this event, which was to be performed regardless of weather. Participants attended a preliminary meeting on May 2, where the Happening was discussed and parts were distributed.' (Full script in Allan Kaprow, *Some Recent Happenings*, New York: A Great Bear Pamphlet, 1966, n.p.)

68 This technique was also deployed by The Living Theatre, and is discussed in Lebel's book-length interview with Julian Beck and Judith Malina, *Entretiens avec Le Living Theatre*, Paris: Editions Pierre Belfond, 1969.

69 Günter Berghaus, 'Happenings in Europe in the '60s: Trends, Events, and Leading Figures', *TDR*, 37:4, Winter 1993, pp. 161–2.

70 Lebel, 'On the Necessity of Violation', p. 98.

71 Poster for *Pour conjurer l'esprit de catastrophe* (first version, 1962), in Lebel and Michaël (eds), *Happenings de Jean-Jacques Lebel*, p. 48, my translation.

72 Lebel, interview with Arnaud Labelle-Rojoux, in Lebel and Labelle-Rojoux, *Poesie Directe: Happenings/Interventions*, Paris: Opus International Edition, 1994, p. 70, my translation.

73 In summer 1964 The Living Theatre went into voluntary exile in Europe after the government seized their Fourteenth Street theatre because Julian Beck and Judith Malina had failed to pay federal excise and payroll taxes.

74 Lebel gives the example of a Happening in which Taylor Meade brought a lover, with his camel, to the performance. The camel went on stage and wouldn't come down for two days. 'So this is the thing, it changed all our plans. We really allowed things to happen. It was the contrary of rigidity. Everything was free flowing.' (Lebel, interview with the author, Paris, 22 July 2010.)

75 Gualtiero Jacopetti and Paolo Cavara's *Malamondo* (1964) is a film that Lebel has publicly denounced as a conscious misrepresentation of his Happening to produce a scandalous object of consumption. Footage of other events is edited into this pseudo-documentary, including stock shots of Dachau concentration camp, nudist skiing, a gay rights festival in Montparnasse, and a 'night orgy' in a cemetery. See Lebel, 'Flashback', pp. 12–13.

76 It is worth bearing in mind that Lebel was also a close associate of Allen Ginsberg and William Burroughs, who lived in Paris 1959–66 and whose work Lebel translated into French.

77 Lebel, interview with the author, Paris, 22 July 2010.

78 Lebel, interview with the author, Paris, 22 July 2010. Lebel was close friends with Deleuze and Guattari, whom he had met in 1955 and 1965

respectively, and became a model for their idea of the artist. See Kristine Stiles, 'Jean-Jacques Lebel's Phoenix and Ash', in *Jean-Jacques Lebel: Works from 1960–1965*, London: Mayor Gallery, 2003, pp. 3–15.

79 Lebel, interview with the author, Paris, 22 July 2010; see also Lebel, *Le Happening*, Paris: Les Lettres Nouvelles-Denoel, 1966, p. 22, note 1.

80 *Déchirex* was the culmination of a week of events in the Second Festival of Free Expression, 17–25 May 1965. It included nudity, live sex, spaghetti, a motorbike, and the destruction of a Citroën car. *Déchirex* attracted considerable press coverage, both in France and internationally (including *Time* magazine), after the cultural organiser at the American Center was fired and the new director announced that Happenings would no longer be held at the venue. Fifty minutes of the fifty-five-minute film documentation of *Déchirex* were censored.

81 This account is based on the one found in Lebel and Michaël (eds.), *Happenings de Jean-Jacques Lebel*, pp. 176–86. Alyce Mahon also reports that the audience were offered sugar cubes laced with LSD. See Mahon, 'Outrage aux Bonnes Moeurs: Jean-Jacques Lebel and the Marquis de Sade', in *Jean-Jacques Lebel: Bilder, Skulpturen, Installationen*, p. 106.

82 Alyce Mahon argues that 'the obscenity of this act was profound'. One of the reasons that Cynthia had wanted to perform in the Happening was that she was not allowed to exhibit herself even in Pigalle. Ironically, the event was halted by a brothel owner, Madame Martini, who called the police to complain about an 'outrage aux bonnes moeurs'. See Mahon, 'Outrage aux Bonnes Moeurs', p. 107.

83 Reported in Lebel and Michaël (eds.), *Happenings de Jean-Jacques Lebel*, p. 185. It is important to note that Lebel's father was the first biographer of Duchamp, and that Jean-Jacques grew up in New York surrounded by the Surrealist group in exile from Paris. He went to school with André Breton's daughter Aube, was friends with Ernst, Duchamp and Benjamin Péret, and at the age of twenty-two exhibited in the Surrealist group's late exhibition 'Eros' at the Galerie Daniel Cordier, Paris (1959).

84 Susan Sontag, 'Happenings: An Art of Radical Juxtaposition', in *Against Interpretation*, London: Vintage Books, 2001, p. 265.

85 See note 27 in Chapter 4.

86 Jean-Paul Sartre in *Le Nouvel Observateur*, 18 January 1967. Quoted in Lebel and Michaël (eds.), *Happenings de Jean-Jacques Lebel*, p. 147, note 32.

87 Carolee Schneemann, in Nelcya Delanoë, *Le Raspail Vert: L'American Center à Paris 1934–1994*, Paris: Seghers, 1994, p. 122, my translation. Schneemann notes that Man Ray, Max Ernst and Eugène Ionesco were in the audience.

88 For a description and analysis of the work, see Allan Kaprow, 'A Happening in Paris', in Jean-Jacques Lebel et. al, *New Writers IV: Plays and Happenings*, London: Calder and Boyars, 1967, pp. 92–100.

89 Lebel, interview with the author, Paris, 22 July 2010. Debord and Lebel had met as early as 1952 (both having relatives who lived in Cannes) and Lebel was sympathetic to all SI activities, even though Debord did not attend any of his events: 'He relied – can you believe this – he relied on newspapers! How warped can your perception be? Actually I met him on Boulevard Saint Germain one day in the '60s and I said, "What are you writing about? You never came to see one of my Happenings nor anybody else's Happenings" and I realised that he and his friends were talking through newspapers. How can you do that? He laughed and said "Who cares". He was being dogmatic. So it doesn't matter. He was being dismissive, but I just took it as a joke.'

90 'The Happening is the materialisation of a collective dream and the vehicle of an intercommunication.' (Lebel, *Le Happening*, p. 36.)

91 Lebel, 'On the Necessity of Violation', p. 103.

92 Lebel, in Lebel and Michaël (eds.), *Happenings de Jean-Jacques Lebel*, p. 184, my translation. See also Kaprow: in 1958 he argued that 'objects of every sort are materials for the new art: paint, chairs, food, electric and neon lights, smoke, water, old socks, a dog, movies, a thousand other things'. By 1966, he also regarded 'people' to be materials of the work, with a consequent elimination of the audience; the viewer's role thus moved from a formal element in the work (providing colour and movement) to one of completing the work as a 'co-creator'. (Kaprow, 'The Legacy of Jackson Pollock', p. 9.)

93 Vaneigem, *The Revolution of Everyday Life*, p. 114.

94 Unsigned, 'L'avant-garde de la presence', p. 17, my translation.

95 Jean-Paul Sartre, in *Le Nouvel Observateur*, 18 January 1967, quoted in *Jean-Jacques Lebel: Retour d'Exil, Peintures, dessins, collages 1954–1988*, Paris: Galerie 1900/2000, 1988, p. 76.

96 'We were not the only ones – I am not saying May '68 happened because of us – I am saying that we were a little movement of all those little tiny movements that concurred towards that aim.' (Lebel, interview with the author, Paris, 22 July 2010.)

97 Jean-Jacques Lebel, 'Notes on Political Street Theatre, Paris: 1968, 1969', *TDR*, 13:4, Summer 1969, p. 112–13.

98 Constant, interview in *Imus Nocte et consumimur Igni*, p. 100.

99 Guy Debord and Gianfranco Sanguinetti, 'Theses on the SI and its Time', *The Real Split in the International*, p. 11.

100 Guy Debord, 'Notes to Serve Towards the History of the SI from 1969–1971', in *The Real Split in the International*, pp. 93–4.

101 In an interview with the group in 1970, GRAV ascribe various reasons to their disbanding: the tension between individual and collective efforts, economic inequalities between members, differences of responsibility, opinion, and the will to work as a team. See Caramel (ed.), *Groupe de recherche d'art visuel 1960–1968*, pp. 130–6. Stein also noted that 'Once my

proposition . . . for members of the group to get rid of all "individual" signatures was rejected, it was inevitable that the group should disappear once individual success appeared.' (Stein, *Douze ans d'art contemporain*, p. 386.)

102 In a late article called 'The Latest Exclusions', Debord noted that the group had recently 'refused some fifty or sixty requests for admission – which has spared us an equal number of exclusions.' (Debord, in *Internationale Situationniste*, 12, 1969, translated in Knabb [ed.], *Situationist International Anthology*, p. 377.)

Chapter 4   *Social Sadism Made Explicit*

1 Boal was one of several influences on Argentinian theatre in the 1970s, the others being Fernando Arrabal and Alejandro Jodorowsky's Teatro Pánico, and Tadeusz Kantor's Theatre of Death.

2 For example, Roberto Jacoby was trained in sociology, Raúl Escari in philosophy, and Eduardo Costa in literature and art history.

3 The 'Dirty War' of 1976–83 was the darkest time in Argentina's history. The junta, led by General Videla, began a campaign to 'purify' the country by imprisoning, torturing and executing leftists, trade unionists and Peronists. Babies of the 'disappeared' were reallocated to military families. Education, media and the arts were brought under the control of the armed forces in every public institution. The works of Freud, Jung, Marx, Darwin and many others were all banned from universities. Videla famously stated that 'In order to achieve peace in Argentina all the necessary people will die.'

4 Masotta referenced Lacan's work in an article for the journal *Centro* in 1959. In 1974 he founded the Escuela Freudiana de Buenos Aires, modelled after Lacan's École Freudienne de Paris. Masotta has only a marginal presence in Andrea Giunta's *Avant-Garde, Internationalism and Politics: Argentine Art in the Sixties*, Durham, NC: Duke University Press, 2007, and in Luis Camnitzer's *Conceptualism in Latin American Art: Didactics of Liberation*, Austin: University of Texas Press, 2007. He does not feature at all in Waldo Rasmussen's *Latin American Artists of the Twentieth Century*, New York: MoMA, 1992.

5 Lucy Lippard visited Argentina in 1968, but does not credit Masotta for the term 'dematerialisation' which became the focus of her 1973 publication *Six Years: The Dematerialization of the Art Object 1966–1972*, New York: Praeger, 1973.

6 The ITDT was founded in 1958 as a cultural centre dedicated to avant-garde art, theatre and music, in memory of the Italian-Argentine engineer Torcuato Di Tella. See John King, *El Di Tella y el desarrollo cultural argentino en la década del sesanta*, Buenos Aires: Ediciones de Arte Gaglianone, 1985. For texts by Masotta, see *El 'Pop' Art*, Buenos Aires:

Editorial Columba, 1967, and *Happening*, Buenos Aires: Editorial Jorge Álvarez, 1967, extracts of which are translated in Inés Katzenstein (ed.), *Listen, Here, Now! Argentine Art of the 1960s: Writings of the Avant-Garde*, New York: MoMA, 2004, hereafter referred to as *LHN*.

7 This synthetic aspect of his work is not given enough credit in Philip Derbyshire's 'Who Was Oscar Masotta?', *Radical Philosophy*, November–December 2009, pp. 11–23. Derbyshire condescendingly dismisses Masotta as 'the bearer of the European message' (p. 12).

8 Of these, Barthes and Saussure had particular impact, especially Barthes' *Mythologies* (1957), which was central to the group's critical demystification of the Happenings. (Roberto Jacoby, interview with the author, Buenos Aires, 5 December 2009.)

9 Kaprow declared Buenos Aires to be a 'city of happenistas', although he never actually visited Argentina. Lebel visited and made work in Buenos Aires (*Venceremos*) and Montevideo (*Hommage à Lautréamont*) in April 1967, but his work was already well known to Argentinian artists who had lived in Paris, such as Marta Minujín who performed in his *Tableaux-Happenings* (1964). See Ana Longoni and Mariano Mestman, *Avant-Garde and Politics in Argentine '68: The Itinerary Towards Tucumán Arde* (unpublished English translation of *Del Di Tella a 'Tucumán arde'. Vanguardia artística y política en el 68 argentino*, Buenos Aires: El Cielo por Asalto Ediciones, 2000), p. 52. The present chapter is indebted to this groundbreaking study; many thanks to Ana Longoni for making the unpublished English translation of her book available to me.

10 See Roberto Jacoby and Eduardo Costa, 'Creation of the First Work', in *LHN*, pp. 225–9.

11 Minujín first went to New York in 1965, where she met Warhol, who she claims had already heard of her following the scandal of her *Suceso Plástico* in Uruguay (discussed below), reported in the *New York Times*. *The Long Shot* was an environmental installation into which Minujín added the live component of rabbits and flies, enclosed in transparent cages; the work is described in detail by Masotta in 'Three Argentinians in New York' (1966), in *LHN*, pp. 185–90.

12 The aim of the event was already to play with the different temporalities of mediated information, gathering together 'several Happenings that had already happened into one Happening', to tell the story of Happenings' 'historical progression'. Masotta confessed that he was more excited by the *information* about events than by the events themselves. (Masotta, cited in Longoni and Mestman, 'After Pop, We Dematerialise: Oscar Masotta, Happenings, and Media Art at the Beginnings of Conceptualism', in *LHN*, p. 162.)

13 Roberto Jacoby, 'Against the Happening', in *LHN*, p. 230.

14 Masotta, 'I Committed a Happening', *LHN*, p. 200.

15 Ibid., p. 191.

16 'The military junta under General Onganía has rapidly established an almost total dictatorship; all parties have been disbanded; Parliament and the regional assemblies have been abolished and the traditionally autonomous universities have been brought under firm state control; the new regime has proclaimed itself the "representative of all the people," and President Onganía now exercises all legislative and executive powers, with complete discretion over whether or not to select a Constituent Assembly to advise him on drafting laws.' (Robert Looker, '*Coup* in Argentina', *The Notebook, International Socialism*, No. 27, Winter 1966–67, pp. 5–6.)

17 Masotta, 'I Committed a Happening', p. 196. These, he imagined, would be 'seated motionless in a motley array, on a platform'.

18 'I told them that they should dress as poor people, but they shouldn't use make-up. They didn't all obey me completely; the only way not to totally be objects, totally passive, I thought, was for them to do something related to the profession of an actor.' (Ibid., p. 200.)

19 Ibid., p. 199.

20 Ibid., p. 200.

21 Ibid.

22 It also anticipates the idea of humans as 'living currency' in Pierre Klossowski's *La monnaie vivante* (1972), discussed in Chapter 8.

23 Lacan sums up this demand with the question, 'have you acted in conformity with your desire?' See Jacques Lacan, *The Ethics of Psychoanalysis, 1959–60*, London: Routledge, 1992, p. 311. It is important to stress that for Lacan, acting in conformity with one's desire is not hedonism or libertarianism, but a painful encounter with the truth of one's own being: 'even for him who goes to the end of his desire, all is not a bed of roses' (p. 323).

24 Ibid., p. 314. It is worth noting that Masotta would not have had access to Seminar 7, although he had known about Lacan since 1959 via debates in *Les Temps modernes*; his ethical framework was more Sartrean than Lacanian. Thanks to German García for this point.

25 Masotta had also seen a Happening by Lebel in Paris in April that year (possibly *Déchirex*) and noted that 'practically – and sexually – everything happened: a naked woman masturbating, an act of coitus in the middle of the space' ('I Committed a Happening', p. 201). Masotta immediately took a stance against Lebel: 'our Happenings had to fulfill only one condition: they must not be very French, that is, very sexual' (p. 197). He also explained the title as referring to a change in his *own* image: 'from a critic or an essayist or a university researcher, I would become a Happening-maker' (p. 197).

26 Ibid., p. 195.

27 Sontag writes: 'Perhaps the most striking feature of the Happening is its treatment (this is the only word for it) of the audience. The event seems

designed to tease and abuse the audience. . . . There is no attempt to cater to the audience's desire to see everything. In fact this is often deliberately frustrated, by performing some of the events in semi-darkness or by having events go on in different rooms simultaneously. . . . This abusive involvement of the audience seems to provide, in default of anything else, the dramatic spine of the Happening.' (Susan Sontag, 'Happenings: An Art of Radical Juxtaposition' [1962], in *Against Interpretation*, London: Vintage, 2001, pp. 265, 267.) Masotta quotes part of this passage in his essay 'Three Argentines in New York' (1966), *LHN*, pp. 185–90. My conversations with US artists from this period (Schneemann, Bob Whitman, Julie Martin, Alison Knowles, interviewed in February 2010) counter Sontag's view: all of them confirmed that US Happenings (or better, 'artists' theatre') were far from aggressive, and characterised by a sympathetic spirit, with a focused and concentrated audience.

28 Oscar Masotta, *Sexo y traicion en Roberto Arlt (Sex and Betrayal in Roberto Arlt)*, Buenos Aires: Editorial Jorge Álvarez, 1965.

29 The account given here is taken from the document 'Suceso Plástico' in the Marta Minujín archive, and an interview with Marta Minujín in Buenos Aires, 7 December 2009. Before the adoption of Happenings as a descriptor, Minujín referred to her work as *sucesos*, or events, a word that carries the connotation of something evolving successively in time. Her definition evokes the value system of Happenings: 'It is the development of an idea through live situations that use contrast, dissociation, and a speed almost without everyday time, to provoke a type of shock, removing the spectator from his inertia and transforming everything into a collective situation. . . . It is not a spectacle because there's no distance between the viewer and the action, the spectator participates, takes part in the *suceso*.' (M.L.T., 'Marta Minujín: sus "Sucesco" y la Creciente Desaparición de las Galerías y Marchands', *El Pais*, Montevideo, 19 July 1965, in Minujín archive, Buenos Aires, my translation.)

30 All of these participants seem to have been secured on the morning of the event, by Minujín roving the streets (with three buses) to see what kind of participants she could find.

31 The event was a scandal in Uruguay and led to a trial, resulting in Minujín being banned from that country for twenty years. Although the cause of scandal was the treatment of a chicken by one of the participants (who tore it apart and began using its blood to paint), a greater shock for Uruguayans was the overt waste of food resources in an impoverished neighbourhood. (Conversation with Luis Camnitzer, New York, 23 March 2010.)

32 *The Ghost Message* is closer to the media art experiments of Jacoby and Costa and clearly evolved in dialogue with them. On 16 and 17 July 1966, Masotta put up a poster bearing the neutral statement, 'This poster will be broadcast on Television Channel 11 on July 20'. On July 20, two

advertisements were broadcast on Channel 11, using an announcer to say that 'This medium announces the appearance of a poster the text of which we are now projecting.' The text of the posters then appeared on screen, albeit in a different font.

33 The 'missed encounter' is a key theme of Lacan's eleventh Seminar, *The Four Fundamental Concepts of Psychoanalysis, 1964–5* (London: Vintage, 1998). However, the Lacanian missed encounter should be understood as a missed encounter with the 'real', understood as traumatic and inaccessible to consciousness. The excessive presence of the real can only be signified negatively, as absence.

34 Discontinuity is a recurrent theme in Argentine conceptualism of the 1960s: see Masotta's essay 'Los medios de informacíon de masas y la categoría de "discontinuo" en la estética contemporánea' ('The Mass Information Media and the Category of "Discontinuity" in the Contemporary Aesthetic'), in Masotta, *Revolución en el arte* (Buenos Aires: Edición Edhasa, 2004), which takes its lead from Barthes' essay 'Literature and Discontinuity' (1962). See also Andrea Giunta, 'An Aesthetic of Discontinuity', in *Oscar Bony: El Mago, Obras 1965–2001*, Buenos Aires: MALBA, 2007, pp. 269–74; and Daniel Quiles, *Between Code and Message: Argentine Conceptual Art 1966–1976*, PhD Dissertation, Graduate Center, City University of New York, 2010.

35 Masotta, 'After Pop, We Dematerialise' (1967), in *LHN*, p. 213.

36 The annual exhibition 'Experiencias' replaced the Premio Di Tella in 1967, 1968 and 1969. I have chosen not to translate 'Experiencias' since in Spanish this connotes both experience and experiment.

37 Email to the author from Roberto Jacoby, 17 January 2006.

38 Invited to restage this work for the 7th Havana Biennial in 2000, Bony proposed *La Familia Cubana*: an authentic Cuban family who would be present for the duration of the exhibition, and able to talk to visitors. He eventually withdrew from the exhibition after the Cuban government insisted that it would select the family to be on display.

39 In recent restagings of this work, the mother has required payment as well as the father.

40 Jorge Romero Brest, 'Experiencias 68', in *LHN*, p. 130.

41 Horacio Verbitsky, *Arte y Politica*, cited in *Instituto Di Tella Experiencias 68*, p. 78.

42 Lind: 'I thought it would be fun to see human beings in this context instead of objects.' (Cited in a letter to the author from Cecilia Widenheim, Curator at Moderna Museet, 23 January 2006.)

43 The work was restaged by the Wrong Gallery for Frieze Art Fair in 2006.

44 De Dominicis, quoted in Adrian Searle, 'How Much for the Invisible Sculpture?', *Guardian*, 12 October 2006.

45 The press reacted to the piece with predictable outcry, but the scandalised headlines ('*Un povero minorato "esposato" alla biennale d'arte di Veneʒia*',

'*Un mongoloide "esposto" alla biennale de Venezia*', '*La mostra degli orrori*') reveal more about the small-minded discomfort of the press than offering a serious consideration of De Dominicis' metaphysical proposition.

46 Bony, cited in *Instituto Di Tella Experiencias 68*, p. 79, my translation. Camnitzer notes that for Bony, *The Worker's Family* was 'in lieu of the work of art and not the art itself'. (Camnitzer, *Conceptualism in Latin American Art*, p. 178 and p. 296, note 17.)

47 *Revista Análisis*, cited in *Instituto Di Tella Experiencias 68*, p. 76, my translation.

48 Bony interviewed in *La Maga* magazine, Buenos Aires, 16 June 1993; p. 11, cited in Longoni and Mestman, *Avant-Garde and Politics in Argentine '68*, p. 80.

49 After May '68 Bony ceased to make art and became a rock photographer, shooting album covers for bands such as La Joven Guardia, Arco Iris, Manal and Los Gatos. During this decade Jacoby was also involved in rock music, writing lyrics for the band Virus and as artistic director of their live stage shows. In 1975 Bony returned to painting after this self-proclaimed 'artistic suicide'.

50 Minujín's archive contains numerous letters of feedback from the participants, in response to a questionnaire sent out by the artist. They describe their experiences, and most are rapturously enthusiastic: going to a mock birthday party, a cocktail lounge, a reception for Mott the Hoople, a hair-cutting salon. Each 'adventure' was accompanied by a photographer. (Marta Minujín archive, Buenos Aires.)

51 The Braque Prize (inaugurated in 1964) was organised by the French Embassy, who in 1968 added an extra page of regulations to the call for applications, in which it was stated that the organisers held the right 'to make all necessary changes' to the works proposed. In other words, they reserved the right to censor works of art.

52 Graciela Carnevale, interview with the author, Rosario, 8 December 2009. It should be stressed that the whole international scene was influential on the Grupo de Artistas de Vanguardia, and not just European theory: the Vietnam War, the Cuban Revolution, Che Guevara, and El Movimiento de Sacerdotes para el Tercer Mundo (the movement of priests for the third world).

53 Longoni and Mestman, *Avant-Garde and Politics in Argentine '68*, p. 109, p. 113.

54 Puzzolo's event lasted from 28 May to 8 June 1968. See Juan Pablo Renzi's account in *LHN*, pp. 303–4.

55 Longoni and Mestman, *Avant-Garde and Politics in Argentine '68*, p. 110. Bonina's event lasted from 1–13 July 1968.

56 Ibid., p. 111. The work is one of many closed gallery works of this period, including Robert Barry's *During the Exhibition the Gallery Will be Closed* (1969).

57 Ibid.

58 Emilio Ghilioni and Rodolfo Elizalde, 'Proposal for the Ciclo de Arte Experimental, September 23–28 1968', in ibid., pp. 112–13.

59 Carnevale, in *LHN*, p. 299.

60 Carnevale, interview with the author, Rosario, 8 December 2009.

61 In the event, the majority of press coverage came from arts publications, since the media were too wary of running such an overtly anti-propagandist story in the mainstream news. Attempts to connect the project to militant research and political intervention tended to come from abroad, such as 'Les Fils de Marx et Mondrian: Dossier Argentine', *Robho*, 5–6, 1971, pp. 16–22.

62 'I can tell you for certain that there was no relationship between my husband [Augusto Boal] and Masotta nor between Boal and contemporary artists. My husband's theatre was very clearly engaged with the revolutionary left and pursued by the dictatorships of that period in Latin America, and all his research was directed towards helping the oppressed and the militants who were fighting against the dictatorships, of which he had himself also been a victim when he was kidnapped, imprisoned and tortured, after which we had to exile ourselves. It's for this reason that his priority goal was to help the left . . .' (Cecilia Boal, email to the author, 19 October 2010.) At the same time, however, Cecilia Boal – a psychoanalyst – participated in study groups with Masotta.

63 See, for example, Image Theatre, Newspaper Theatre, Photo-Romance, Myth Theatre, etc., discussed in Augusto Boal, *Theatre of the Oppressed*, London: Pluto Press, 2000, pp. 120–55. This emphasis on empowerment was directly indebted to Paulo Freire, whose Christian Socialism embraced a non-orthodox form of Liberation Theology. I will return to Freire in Chapter 9.

64 Ibid., p. 141.

65 Augusto Boal, *Hamlet and the Baker's Son: My Life in Theatre and Politics*, London and New York: Routledge, 2001, p. 304.

66 Ibid.

67 For the full account of this intervention, see Boal, *Theatre of the Oppressed*, pp. 144–7. A different version is given in his *Hamlet and the Baker's Son*, emphasising the humanitarian law.

68 Boal, *Theatre of the Oppressed*, p. 147. Boal notes that this works against the very premises of an artist's desire to work in public: 'Consternation: The reason we do theatre is to be seen, isn't it?' (Boal, *Hamlet and the Baker's Son*, p. 304).

69 The US-backed Onganía dictatorship had forbidden mini-skirts for women and long hair for men, operated a policy of clampdown on perceived opponents in the universities, and cracked down on labour unrest (in 1969). By the mid 1970s the repression was even more extreme, with secret detention centres where 20–30,000 kidnapped people were

taken, most of whom were in their teens and twenties; 54 percent were from the working class (to paralyse working-class reaction to the regime), 30 percent were women, of whom 3 percent were pregnant. The Catholic Church was complicit in this regime of terror, and objecting priests were also 'disappeared'. See Jo Fisher, *Mothers of the Disappeared*, Boston: South End Press, 1989.

70 Boal, *Hamlet and the Baker's Son*, p. 194. Boal recalls that in north-east Brazil, 'we did a play that ends with our telling people to fight for their freedom, to give their blood. After, someone came up to us and said, "OK, if you think like that, come with us and let's fight the government." We had to answer that our rifles were false. "Yes", he answered, "your rifles are false but you are true – you come, we have enough real rifles for everyone." Then we had to say, "We are true, but we are truly artists and not truly peasants." We were ashamed to have to say that. From that point on, and never again, have I incited audiences to do things that I would not do myself. So the seed of forum was to not give solutions, to not incite people. Let them express their own solutions.' (Boal, cited in Michael Taussig and Richard Schechner, 'Boal in Brazil, France, the USA: An Interview with Augusto Boal', in Mady Schutzman and Jan Cohen-Cruz [eds.], *Playing Boal: Theatre, Therapy, Activism*, London and New York: Routledge, 1994, p. 24.)

71 Boal, cited in ibid., p. 29.

72 Augusto Boal, *Games for Actors and Non-Actors*, London and New York: Routledge, 1992, p. 19.

73 Ibid., p. 19.

74 Boal, cited in Taussig and Schechner, 'Boal in Brazil, France, the USA', p. 27. For Boal, Brechtian epic theatre still places too much emphasis on understanding (*dianoia*) rather than on the possibility of change.

75 Boal, *Theatre of the Oppressed*, p. 142.

76 See Boal, *Games for Actors and Non-Actors*, Chapter 1. This is also in line with the general shift from Marxism to identity politics across numerous disciplines in the 1980s.

77 Boal, *Hamlet and the Baker's Son*, p. 324.

78 Mady Schutzman, 'Brechtian Shamanism: The Political Therapy of Augusto Boal', in Schutzman and Cohen-Cruz (eds.), *Playing Boal: Theatre, Therapy, Activism*, pp. 138–9.

79 See Taussig and Schechner, 'Boal in Brazil, France, the USA', p. 21.

80 Catherine Wood, 'From Invisible Theatre to Thai Soup', *Untitled*, 32, Summer 2004, p. 45. See also Carrie Lambert-Beatty, 'Make-Believe: Parafiction and Plausibility', *October*, 129, Summer 2009, p. 54: describing what she calls 'parafictional' art projects (fictions that are experienced as fact, but which leave the audience unsettled as to whether this is actually the case), she argues that such works deal less with the disappearance of reality into simulacrum than with the 'pragmatics of trust' (p. 54).

81 Some of the texts we think of as fundamental to Western art theory since the 1960s were already known and received in South America. The work of Merleau-Ponty was introduced to the Brazilian context in the late 1940s by art critic Mario Pedrosa, a good fifteen years before it was harnessed by artists and critics in New York to explain the effect of viewing minimalist sculpture. I have already mentioned Barthes and Lacan; the latter was received in Argentina a decade before Lacanian theory impacted upon Marxist-feminist critiques of vision in Europe in the 1970s. Moreover, the reception of Lacan in Argentina permeated many aspects of culture and was not confined to academia, as continues to be the case in Europe and North America.

82 Longoni and Mestman, *Avant-Garde and Politics in Argentine '68*, p. 122.

83 Ferrari, cited in ibid., p. 122.

84 Renzi, cited in ibid., p. 129.

85 In the final paragraphs of *The Society of Spectacle*, Guy Debord asserts that 'a critique capable of surpassing the spectacle must *know how to bide its time*' (Debord, *The Society of the Spectacle*, New York: Zone Books, 1994, p. 154). Messianic Marxism proposes that the contradictions of capitalism will in time become apparent and lead to its collapse; all we can do is wait.

86 Jacoby, for example, returned to the sociological research he had abandoned in 1965; Carnevale turned to teaching.

Chapter 5   *The Social Under Socialism*

1 'The spectacle exists in a concentrated or a diffuse form depending on the necessities of the particular stage of misery which it denies and supports. In both cases, the spectacle is nothing more than an image of happy unification surrounded by desolation and fear at the tranquil center of misery.... Wherever the concentrated spectacle rules, so does the police.' (Guy Debord, *The Society of the Spectacle*, New York: Zone Books, 1994, sections 63 and 64.)

2 Membership of the Union of Soviet Artists (founded 1957) was essential for all artists working in the Soviet bloc, and was a means to bring artistic practice under strict ideological supervision. Artists expelled from the Union could not exhibit their work in galleries nor make money from their creative activities.

3 IRWIN (ed.), *East Art Map*, Cambridge, MA: MIT Press, 2007. In the case of this chapter, Czech artists had more contact with Germany (via Jindřich Chalupecký), while Slovakian artists were more in touch with developments in France (via Pierre Restany).

4 Of course, memories of class difference were not entirely erased. In 'The Power of the Powerless', Václav Havel speaks of his social awkwardness

at having to work in a brewery in the mid 1970s (Havel, *Open Letters*, London: Faber and Faber, 1991, pp. 173–4). The artist Vladimír Boudník (1924–68) worked in a print factory and declared, a good decade before Joseph Beuys did, that everyone was artist. He viewed his art as having an educative mission: he produced work in the streets (late 1940s–50s), finding images in peeling paint and stains on walls, occasionally adding to them, and framing them (for example with paper), before encouraging passers-by to converse with him about their meaning. In 1960 he stated that he had realised c.120 artistic actions between 1949–53, at which often over a hundred people were present – although there are no independent accounts to corroborate this claim. See *Vladimír Boudník*, Prague: Gallery, 2004. Milan Knížák was aware of Boudník's work, and some of his early actions make reference to everyday workers (see Milan Knížák, *Actions For Which at Least Some Documentation Remains, 1962–1995*, Prague: Gallery, 2000, p. 73).

5 The socialist calendar in Slovakia, for example, included organised mass parades for Victorious February (25 February), International Women's Day (8 March), International Workers' Day (1 May), Liberation Day (9 May) and International Children's Day (1 June), as well as Nationalisation (28 October) and the Great October Socialist Revolution (7 November).

6 Jindřich Chalupecký, 'The Intellectual Under Socialism', in Tomáš Pospiszyl and Laura Hoptman (eds.), *Primary Documents: A Sourcebook for Eastern and Central European Art Since the 1950s*, New York: MoMA, 2002, p. 31. Tomáš Pospiszyl has been an invaluable interlocutor in the preparation of this chapter and I am indebted to his generosity.

7 Ibid., p. 33.

8 Pierre Restany describes the 1965–66 season in Paris as dominated by the Czech presence, particularly at the 4th Paris Biennial and in group exhibitions at Galerie Lambert and the gallery Peintres du Monde. Jiří Kolář showed at Galerie Riquelme, while the climax was a large exhibition of Czech Cubism at the Musée national d'art moderne. See Pierre Restany, *Ailleurs: Alex Mlynárčik*, Paris: Galerie Lara Vincy and Bratislava: Galerie Nationale Slovaque, 1994, pp. 23–4. In return, Restany organised shows of Yves Klein and Martial Raysse at the National Gallery of Prague in 1968 and 1970 respectively.

9 Václav Havel's description of being under house arrest in 1979 gives a depressingly clear picture of what this dogged police presence involved. See Havel, 'Reports on My House Arrest', *Open Letters*, pp. 215–29.

10 Czech audiences in general were underwhelmed by Fluxus, which was introduced in a tour by Eric Andersen, Addi Kopcke and Tomas Schmit in April 1966. 'It strikes us as absurd to present happenings in Czechoslovakia in which some kind of disorder is artificially created, something stops working or a mess is made. It seems ridiculous to us, for whom this

is an everyday reality.' (Bohumila Grögerová, cited in Pavlina Morganova, 'Fluxus in the Czech Period Press', in *Fluxus East: Fluxus Networks in Central Eastern Europe*, Berlin: Kunstlerhaus Bethanien GmbH, 2007, p. 181.)

11 Milan Knížák, 'The Principles of Action Art According to Milan Knížák' (1965), in Knížák, *Actions For Which at Least Some Documentation Remains*, p. 7. He continues: 'Vostell exhorts: *reality is more interesting than fiction*, even as he makes engines and cars collide whilst the participants observe calmly and with interest, knowing that nobody will be hurt and that this is not an accident, but the staging of an accident. Vostell also describes the poor reactions of participants, such as those who began to sing an unpopular song in the bus during one of his happenings in Wuppertal. However, there is no such thing as a poor reaction on the part of participants, only a poor happening' (p. 8).

12 Knížák, cited in Morganova, 'Fluxus in the Czech Period Press', p. 183, emphasis added. He continues: 'Thank god for the so-called Iron Curtain. Little art and its little creators suffered, of course, on this account. One couldn't see through the "curtain". But this perfect isolation meant that we did not degenerate as swiftly or as tragically as the rest of Europe.' The third issue of Aktual's samizdat journal had the title *Ntuna cinnost*: necessary activity.

13 The work was produced in collaboration with Vít Mach, Soňa Švecová and Jan Trtílek. A full description of the work, titled *A Demonstration for All the Senses*, is included in Kaprow's anthology *Assemblage, Environments & Happenings*, New York: Harry N. Abrams, 1966, p. 305. See also Knížák, *Actions For Which at Least Some Documentation Remains*, pp. 42–3.

14 Surrealism remained a strong force in the 1960s in Prague in the circle around Karel Teige, although Knížák paid more attention to Fluxus.

15 On the rare occasions when Knížák makes reference to current political events, it is in the context of reading articles from the daily press through a loudspeaker – as in *Ritus* (1964). However, this happens simultaneously with another person reading conventional love poetry, while a third barks orders at the participants ('Hurry up! Faster! Barbarians! Faster!'). See Knížák, *Actions For Which at Least Some Documentation Remains*, pp. 54–5.

16 Ibid., p. 61. Tomáš Pospiszyl has argued that the circulation of public letters has a long tradition in Czech art history; see Pospiszyl, *Srovnávací Studie*, Prague: Agite/Fra, 2005. Vladimír Boudník wrote hundreds of letters each year (produced as prints) and sent them to significant figures and organisations such as embassies, the United Nations, the Pope, etc. In the 1960s Knížák and Boudník were aware of each others' work and had something of a mutual rivalry.

17 'In the beginning the former method [i.e. enforced participation] was

employed to disorient the participant; what followed was a natural development of the latter method [i.e. spontaneous reaction].' Knížák saw evidence of the latter when an ordinary working girl participating in one of his actions declared: "I have completely torn my one and only skirt up to the waist, and destroyed my stockings completely, *but I do not regret it one bit!*" (Knížák, *Actions For Which at Least Some Documentation Remains*, pp. 7–8.)

18 Ibid., p. 7.

19 Knížák is one of the few artists of this period to keep a track record of audience response to some of his works, although this is invariably a catalogue of reactions without analysis. See also his documentation of *People Who Were Given Paper Planes on October 3, 1965*, in Knížák, *Invollstandige Dokumentation/Some Documentary 1961–1979*, Berlin: Edition Ars Viva, 1980, pp. 100–2.

20 Milan Knížák and Jan Maria Mach, 'An Event for the Post Office, the Police, and the Occupants of no.26 Vaclavkova Street, Prague 6, and for all Their Neighbours, Relatives and Friends', in Pospiszyl and Hoptman (eds.), *Primary Documents*, p. 121.

21 Milan Knížák, 'A-Community 1963–1971', in *Fluxus East*, p. 80.

22 Knížák, *Actions For Which at Least Some Documentation Remains*, p. 158. Knížák claims that this work was first produced in 1966 in Prague but there is no documentary evidence to support this.

23 *Difficult Ceremony* is closer to recent iterations of this theme, such as Carsten Höller's *The Baudouin/Boudewijn Experiment* (2000). See Claire Bishop (ed.), *Participation*, London: Whitechapel and Cambridge, MA: MIT Press, 2006, pp. 144–5.

24 *Action for My Mind* comprises a long series of questions, beginning: 'Do I exist? Who am I? What am I like? Am I good? How many hands do I have? Am I the Buddha? What do I want? Do I believe in God? Do I believe in anything? In someone? Could I kill? Have I killed?', and so on.

25 A full transcript, plus two accounts by participants, can be found in Geoffrey Hendricks (ed.), *Critical Mass: Happenings, Fluxus, Performance, Intermedia and Rutgers University, 1958–1972*, Rutgers, New Brunswick: Rutgers University Press, 2003, pp. 113–15.

26 Pierre Restany, 'De Varsovie, Žilina, Prague, avec Amour', *Domus*, 518, January 1972, p. 56.

27 Milan Knížák, *Travel Book*, English translation by Paul Wilson in Claire Bishop and Marta Dzeiwańska (eds.), *1968–1989: Political Upheaval and Artistic Change*, Warsaw: Museum of Modern Art, 2010, p. 216. First published in Czech as Milan Knížák, *Cestopisy*, Prague: Post, 1990.

28 Ibid., p. 214.

29 'I was also at the New School for an evening put together by Ron Gross from the work of Dick Higgins, Jackson McLow and Larry Friedfeld.

Dick is already a classic at thirty. At times I find it a little embarrasing. . . . why for God's sake does the avant-garde become academic so quickly, so rapidly? In the Museum of Modern Art I saw a fantastic Pollock and a Mathies and it seemed to me less academic than when Dick Higgins, on a darkened stage, shouts beautifully and savagely . . . and then the lights came up and people clapped! And I don't even think he forgot to bow: performer Dick.' (Ibid., pp. 214–15.)

30 As Tomáš Pospiszyl notes: 'The audience for photo documentation of Czech performers from the 1970s is not a group of anonymous watchers. This is not only because we often know them by names and that they know very well that they are taking part in an art action. They know that the photographs will be seen by a large secondary audience and maybe by the police, who can decode them as a disturbance of the peace. They take that risk. Just the fact that they are present and photographed means they become part of the event. They are not people from the street as in Knížák's happenings. Even if they remain passive during the whole event, they are participants, accomplices.' See Pospiszyl, 'Look Who's Watching: Photographic Documentation of Happenings and Performances in Czechoslovakia', in Bishop and Dziewańska (eds.), *1968–1989: Political Upheaval and Artistic Change*, p. 85. The Czech sections of this chapter are indebted to Pospiszyl's nuanced reading of this period.

31 The article also notes that Knížák was unable to participate in this work 'for political reasons'. See Knížák, *Actions For Which at Least Some Documentation Remains*, p. 202.

32 See Knížák, *Invollstandige Dokumentation/Some Documentary 1961–1979*, p. 80.

33 Pospiszyl, 'Look Who's Watching', p. 82.

34 In focusing this discussion on Mlynárčik and his large-scale participatory works, I will be omitting reference to his production of assemblages and photomontages, and his work with the experimental architecture group VAL (*Voies et Aspects du Lendemain*), 1968–74, a research team producing visionary proposals along the lines of Archigram in the UK. Like Knížák's experiments with music, these parallel activities show the extent to which these artists are not solely interested in participatory art actions.

35 In the 1990s, Mlynárčik's name – along with that of Ján Budaj and the philosopher Egon Bondy – appeared on a list of people who had collaborated with the Státna Bezpečnost or secret service. However, it remains debatable to what extent Mlynárčik actually did inform on fellow artists or was expected simply to report on his numerous travels abroad; this may simply have been a concession he was willing to make in order to be afforded more artistic freedom and travel. Knížák, by contrast, was Chancellor of the Prague Academy of Fine Arts (1990–97) and director

general of the National Gallery in Prague (1999–2009), and is viewed today as a right-wing, nationalist figure of the establishment.

36 For an examination of parallels between the 1960s and 1990s generations of Slovak art see Mária Hlavajová (ed.), *60–90. 4th Annual Exhibition of SCCA Slovakia*, Bratislava: Soros Center, 1997. Koller is paired with Roman Ondák, Stano Filko with Boris Ondreička, and Jana Želibska with Elena Pätoprstá. At first glance, Koller's work seems to be participatory, but as the Slovak critic Tomáš Štraus points out, Koller's works are 'pseudo-performances', better described as 'photo-action' or 'photo-documentation', since they primarily aim at the viewer through *photography,* rather than through participants' first-hand experience. (Štraus, 'Three Model Situations of Contemporary Art Actions', in *Works and Words*, Amsterdam: De Appel, 1979, p. 72.)

37 Restany notes that graffiti was important for showing the 'active participation of the viewer'. (Restany, *Ailleurs*, p. 24.) He also notes the importance of American neo-Dada and John Cage's 'Theory of Inclusion', although these are never mentioned by Mlynárčik.

38 The best-known examples here are not necessarily the most interesting (e.g. Manzoni's *Scultura vivente*, 1961); more poetic and poignant is Alberto Greco's *Vivo-Dito* series (1962–65), in which the artist drew (and signed) empty chalk circles in the streets that were fleetingly occupied by passers-by (discussed briefly in Chapter 4).

39 Andrea Batorova has argued that these dates were not selected for political reasons, merely as a suitable time frame: 'They selected a "natural" time frame for their projects, one that existed in reality; within this, real people in their real surroundings and real time could participate in the project.' (Andrea Bátorová, 'Alternative Trends in Slovakia', in *Fluxus East*, p. 172.)

40 By choosing two official state events as frame and documentation, *Happsoc I* lends weight to Boris Groys's delightfully controversial thesis that Socialist Realism (and communist society at large) is a 'total work of art', a continuation of the historic avant-garde's project to fuse art and life. See Groys, *The Total Art of Stalinism*, Princeton: Princeton University Press, 1992.

41 Alex and Elena Mlynáričk, 'Memorandum' (1971), in Restany, *Ailleurs*, p. 256, my emphasis. They are citing the *Happsoc* manifesto, a variant translation of which can be found in Pospiszyl and Hoptman (eds.), *Primary Documents*, p. 87. Like Knížák, Slovak artists rejected the Happenings for their theatricality, particularly the eroticised spectacles of Jean-Jacques Lebel.

42 Raoul-Jean Moulin, 1969, cited in Restany, *Ailleurs*, p. 252.

43 Restany, *Ailleurs*, p. 22. Over a decade later, Jindřich Chalupecký wrote that 'the title [*Happsoc*] can mislead: in reality *Happsoc* has very little in common with Happenings; it is closer to conceptual art which subsequently appeared'. (Cited in Jana Gerzova, 'The Myths and Reality of

the Conceptual Art in Slovakia', in *Conceptual Art at the Turn of the Millennium*, p. 26.)

44 Filko, Mlynárčik and Kostrová, 'Manifest Happsoc', in Pospiszyl and Hoptman (eds.), *Primary Documents*, p. 87.

45 Instructions for the action included going to the station for ten minutes at 6 p.m. on 27 December, lighting a candle on 30 December, and so on. Rather than seizing the city as a ready-made, it requested a small-scale simultaneity of events from its participants. The schema is not unlike the small collective actions required of participants (sometimes an entire village) by the young Czech artist Katerina Šedá.

46 Restany describes Mlynárčik's move to the land as a question of spiritual survival under normalisation. (Restany, *Ailleurs*, p. 53.) US Land Art's engagement with open, uninhabited spaces is exactly synchronous with Eastern European art's move to the landscape, but motivated by quite different reasons (a desire to circumnavigate the commercial art world, to engage with the sublime expanses of the US landscape, and so on).

47 These 'hommages' to assorted artists could be compared to the efforts made by Argentinian artists to recreate various Happenings from North America during the mid 1960s. But if the Slovakian artists operate on the basis of playful hommage to their international colleagues (which was not censored), the Argentinians are more analytical; performance re-enactments (discussed in Chapter 4) became a way to analyse, criticise and surpass the works of their better-known contemporaries from the hegemonic centre.

48 Chalupecký notes that the event 'cost a small fortune. Mlynárčik didn't have, as is usual elsewhere, anyone to fund him. He had to be a sponsor to himself. He realized a lot of decorative projects for architecture, paintings, sculptures, glass works and metal works and he dedicated all earnings to his manifestations, interpretations, games and celebrations.' (Chalupecký, *Na hranicích umění*, pp. 118–19, translation by Tomáš Pospiszyl.) It was possible for artists to earn good money in the 1960s and 1970s, particularly if they sold works overseas (Mlynárčik was unusual in having gallery representation in Paris). All artists were required to have a job, of which the highest paid was to produce monumental commissions for new architectural projects (Filko); other professions include teaching art (Koller), designing film posters (Knížák), and working in the zoo (Peter Bartoš) or museums (Kovanda, Štembera, Miler).

49 See Henry Périer, *Pierre Restany: L'Alchemiste de l'art*, Paris: Editions Cercle d'Art, 1998, p. 335: 'Then he handed out the presents; twenty works of art that Mlynárčik had requested from his artist friends around the world. Thus it was that an electrician and his wife who would have hoped for useful presents hailing from the West actually found them-selves with a collection of César, Nikos, Niki de Saint-Phalle, Bertini, Hains . . . objects that were curious to their eyes, and which they didn't

suspect of having any value' (my translation). Mlynárčik had used this technique in *Edgar Degas' Memorial*, asking Restany to secure works of art from Nouveaux Réalistes as donations to the festival, which were then auctioned off to provide cash prizes for the horse-racing competition.

50 Mlynárčik, cited in Restany, *Ailleurs*, p. 123.

51 As reported by Restany, 'De Varsovie, Žilina, Prague, avec Amour', p. 56.

52 With the advent of communism, 'individual property rights were decimated. Still, when compared to the situation in the mid-1940s, in some ways the economic situation for ordinary persons improved. The rural regions of Slovakia, in particular, benefited. In order to supplement their incomes, farmers, who lost their lands to collectivisation and were forced to work in industry, actually experienced a rise in income. In other ways the standard of living in rural areas went up. Government-subsidised modernisation programmes brought electricity to villages and the number of schools also increased. Health facilities grew, and medical care became more readily available.' (June Granatir Alexander, 'Slovakia', in Richard C. Frucht, *Eastern Europe: An Introduction to the People, Lands and Culture*, Santa Barbara: ABC-Clio, 2005, p. 300.)

53 This is in contrast to, for example, Yugoslav students during this period who were arguing for a better and more just type of communism. The Slovak critic Tomáš Štraus notes that the only excursion Mlynárčik makes into the realm of politics was during May '68 in Paris, when he wrote the Manifesto *Ferme pour cause d'inutilité: 18 Mai 1968 – Paris, Musée National d'Art Moderne*. (Štraus, 'Three Model Situations of Contemporary Art Actions', p. 72.)

54 Alex Mlynárčik interviewed by Ján Budaj, in Budaj's samizdat publication *3SD*, 1981, n.p.; 2nd edition 1988; reprinted in *Umenie Akce/Action Art 1965–1989*, Bratislava: National Gallery, 2001, pp. 276–7, translation by Mira Keratova. The full interview is translated in Bishop and Dziewańska (eds.), *1968–1989: Political Upheaval and Artistic Change*, pp. 221–32.

55 Tatiana Ivanova, cited by Alex and Elena Mlynárčik, 'Memorandum' (1971), in Restany, *Ailleurs*, p. 256.

56 The participants in Želibská's *Betrothal of Spring* (1970), held in the Small Carpathians, were decorated in ribbons (similar to those worn by guests at wedding celebrations) while musicians performed spring-themed music under the trees. A plane passed overhead and dropped more white ribbons, which were bound around the trees by participants – effectively unifying the guests and nature in one coherently embellished environment. The aim of the festival was to pay homage to the transition from Spring to Summer, viewed as analogous to the moment when a girl becomes a woman, designed to generate intense emotive experiences. Much of Želibská's work concerns questions of gender and eroticism.

57 'The main themes of official competitions and exhibitions were revolutionary traditions, the October Revolution, the History of the Communist
Party of Czechoslovakia, the Slovak National Uprising and the Liberation of Czechoslovakia by the Soviet Army.' (English summary of *Slovak
Visual Art 1970–1985*, Bratislava: SNG, 2002, p. 236.)

58 Jaroslav Anděl, 'The Present Czechoslovakian Situation', in *Works and
Words*, p. 69. Anděl also draws attention to the different uses of photography in Prague and Bratislava: in Prague, artists using photography did
not receive a traditional academic art education, and used photography as
documentation, influenced by Happenings and Action Art. In Slovakia,
they had a more formal art training and used photography as graphics,
more influenced by Nouveau Réalisme and Pop (p. 70).

59 See for example *Suspension*, 1974 (the artist hanging in an attic room, his
ears plugged with beeswax and his eyes covered with opaque black mask-
ing tape); *Climbing Mount Kotel*, 1974 (climbing a mountain in bad
weather); *There and Back, Prague, 24 May 1976* (sending a letter to
strangers requesting that they assault the person described in the letter,
which was himself). In a recent interview, Mlčoch recalls that Chris
Burden came to Czechoslovakia in the early 1970s, along with Terry Fox,
Marina Abramovic and Ulay, and Tom Marioni, who were influential.
See 'The Shift From the Personal to the Social: A Conversation Between
the Ládví Group and Jan Mlčoch', *Notebook for art, theory and related
zones*, 1–2, Prague: Academy of Fine Arts, 2007, p. 102.

60 Mlčoch's *View of the Valley* (1976) is no less quietly galling: fifteen people
were invited to come to a meeting on the outskirts of Prague, the location
marked by a black metal rod. Prior to the meeting, the artist was wrapped
in white material and buried by the black rod; after 45 minutes he was dug
out, by which point some of those invited had left.

61 Mlčoch text, reprinted in Ludvík Hlaváček, 'Vzpomínka na akčni umění
70.let, rozhovor s Janem Mlčochem', *Výtvarné Umění: The Magazine for
Contemporary Art* (Prague), 3, 1991, p. 74.

62 Mlčoch text, reprinted in ibid., p.76.

63 Kovanda, interview with Hans-Ulrich Obrist, in Vit Havránek (ed.), *Jiří
Kovanda: Actions and Installations 1976–2005*, Prague: tranzit and JRP
Ringier, 2006, p. 108. It should be stressed that the invisibility of Kovanda's actions have very little in common with that of Augusto Boal's,
discussed in Chapter 4, beyond a desire to escape detection by police
informers. Kovanda's documentations are not scores to be repeated, but
documents of a single encounter.

64 See Pospiszyl, 'Look Who's Watching', in Bishop and Dziewańska (eds.),
1968–1989: Political Upheaval and Artistic Change.

65 See Ilya Kabakov, 'On the Subject of "The Void" ', in Kabakov, *Das
Leben der Fliegen*, Kölnischer Kunstverein/Edition Cantz, 1992, pp. 234–5.
'This structure is basically not a social one . . . Except for acquaintances

almost no interaction or interrelations exist between the inhabitants of one burrow and the inhabitants of another. There is less sociableness here than between animals who live in the forest . . .' Thanks to Vit Havránek for this reference.

66 Georg Schöllhammer, in Havránek (ed.), *Jiří Kovanda*, p. 111. He continues: 'Kovanda's question is, "Can you imagine – and not in an everyday sense – what it means to step away from this society, to reject it, to reject its language, and to think of yourself as the Other, as an autonomous subject?"'

67 'For me it was something more personal than society's alienation, or people's alienation from that society. I always felt it was more of a personal matter for each individual and not a social matter. . . . The personal aspect always predominated over the social.' (Kovanda, interview with Hans-Ulrich Obrist, in ibid., p. 107.) In this light, comparisons to US body artists seem less apt than references to a younger generation of Eastern European artists, specifically Paweł Althamer's *Real Time Movie* (2000) or Roman Ondák's *Good Feelings in Good Times* (2003); see Havránek, 'Jiří Kovanda: The Faint Breeze of the Everyday', *Flash Art*, November–December 2007, p. 81.

68 Kovanda, interview with Hans-Ulrich Obrist, in Havránek (ed.), *Jiří Kovanda*, p. 108.

69 Mlčoch, quoted in Hlaváček, 'Vzpomínka na akčni umění 70.let, rozhovor s Janem Mlčochem', p. 77.

70 *Lunch II* (1979) took place in the Main Square of Bratislava.

71 See Budaj, interview with Jan Richter for Czech Radio, 24 May 2007, transcribed at www.radio.cz.

72 The experimental theatre director L'ubomir Durček produced brief choreographed actions in public space: formal disruptions such as *Barrier* (1979), in which a group of people held hands across a busy street.

73 Andrei Erofeev, 'Nonofficial Art: Soviet Artists of the 1960s' (1995), in Pospiszyl and Hoptman (eds.), *Primary Documents*, p. 42. See also William J. Tompson, *Khrushchev: A Political Life*, Basingstoke: Macmillan, 1995, Chapter 10.

74 Groys, interview with the author, New York, 28 January 2010.

75 'The communal apartment is a place where the social dimension occurs in its most horrifying, most obtrusive, and most radical form, where the individual is laid bare to the gaze of others. Furthermore, this gaze belongs to largely hostile strangers who consistently exploit their advantages of observation in order to gain advantage in the power struggle within the communal apartment' (Boris Groys, 'The Theatre of Authorship', in Toni Stoos [ed.], *Ilya Kabakov: Installations 1983–2000, Catalogue Raisonné, vol.1*, Kunstmuseum Bern: Richter Verlag, 2003, p. 40).

76 In 2005 there were six members, according to an interview with Monastyrsky in *Flash Art*, October 2005 (p. 114). The initial group were Nikita

Alekseev, Georgii Kizevalter, Andrei Monastyrsky and Nikolai Panitkov, later joined by Igor Makarevich, Elena Elagina and Sergei Romashko. The group continue to produce around eight performances a year, although the character of this work has changed considerably since 1989: the actions are more complex, with more references to Eastern mysticism, and frequently make use of documentation (especially tape recordings) from earlier actions.

77 Regarding the literary aspects of Moscow Conceptualism, Kabakov has noted the central role of the Russian literary tradition of the nineteenth century: 'Literature took upon itself all moral, philosophical, pedagogical, and enlightening functions, concentrating them all in itself and not simultaneously in the plastic arts, which did happen in the West.' (Kabakov, 'On the Subject of the Local Language', in Kabakov, *Das Leben Der Fliegen*, p. 237.)

78 It should be noted that CAG also designed actions for individuals or pairs; for example *For N Panitkov (Three Darknesses)*, 1980; *For G Kizevalter (Slogan-1980)*, 1980; *The Encounter*, 1981; *For N Alekseev*, 1981. It was rarer for actions to take place in private apartments (*Playback*, 1981) or in the city streets (*Exit*, 1983; *The Group*, 1983).

79 Monastyrsky refers to this as a psychological state of 'pre-expectation', created through the form of the invitation, and through the spatio-temporal peculiarities of the journey to the site of the event. See Monastyrsky, 'Preface to the First Volume of Trips to the Countryside', in Boris Groys (ed.), *Total Enlightenment: Conceptual Art in Moscow 1960–1990*, Frankfurt: Schirn Kunsthalle / Hatje Cantz, 2008, p. 335.

80 'And yet, if the experience so far was that of pure expectation, this experience now transforms upon the appearance of the object of perception on the real field. *It is interrupted*, and there begins a process of strenuous looking, accompanied by the desire to understand what this object means. In our view, this new stage of perception constitutes a pause. While it is a necessary stage in the process of perception, it is by no means the event for the sake of which all of this was arranged.' (Ibid., p. 336.)

81 Ibid., p. 333.

82 Andrei Monastyrsky, 'Seven Photographs', translated by Yelena Kalinsky, available at http://conceptualism.letov.ru.

83 Ibid.

84 Ibid.

85 Ilya Kabakov, 'Ten Appearances', in Kollektivnye deistviya, *Poezdki za gorod*, Moskva: Ad marginem, 1998, pp. 151–2, translated by Anya Pantuyeva.

86 Andrey Monastyrsky, 'Ten Appearances' (1981), reprinted in Bishop (ed.), *Participation*, p. 129.

87 This is corroborated by Kabakov's account: 'I had some space of freedom and I had to make up my mind what to do then. But actually, I had no doubt or speculation about what to do – to leave, etc. – not at all. What I

wanted to do immediately was to share this joy I experienced with the others, and also thank those people who made it happen for me.' (Kabakov, 'Ten Appearances', p. 153.)

88 Viktor Tupitsyn: 'The same happens in combat: while you're in the thick of it, everyone is so busy with the "physical stuff" that all kinds of hermeneutic activities are foreclosed. Later, though, this void is going to be filled with interpretations, whose excessiveness will compensate for the lack of interpretation at the site of Action.' Monastyrsky: 'Exactly! . . . Quite a number of texts about our Actions were composed by both spectators and organisers, who were equally fond of writing down what had really happened – first Kabakov, followed by Leiderman, and then by Bakshtein and others. They were impelled to do so in order to compensate for the impossibility of commenting on and interpreting the Actions as they occurred.' (Tupitsyn and Monastyrsky, unpublished interview, 1997, archive of Exit Art, New York.)

89 English translations of the works and photo-documentation can be found at http://conceptualism.letov.ru.

90 Groys, 'Communist Conceptual Art', in Groys (ed.), *Total Enlightenment*, p. 33.

91 Boris Groys, in Claire Bishop and Boris Groys, 'Bring the Noise', *Tate Etc*, Summer 2009, p. 38.

92 Groys again: 'When looking at a painting, normal Soviet viewers quite automatically, without ever having heard of Art and Language, saw this painting inherently replaced by its possible ideological-political-philosophical commentary, and they took only this commentary into account when assessing the painting in question – as Soviet, half-Soviet, non-Soviet, anti-Soviet, and so on.' (Groys, 'Communist Conceptual Art', p. 31.)

93 Tupitsyn and Monastyrsky, unpublished interview, 1997, archive of Exit Art, New York.

94 The snowy fields have variously been compared to Malevich's *White Paintings* and the white pages of Kabakov's albums. It is worth noting that Francisco Infante had also deployed the field as a site for photo-conceptualist works in the late 1960s, such as *Dedication* (1969), a Malevich-style composition made of coloured papers on white snow.

95 Sergei Sitar, 'Four Slogans of "Collective Actions" ', *Third Text*, 17:4, 2003, p. 364.

96 Tupitsyn and Monastyrsky, unpublished interview, 1997, archive of Exit Art, New York.

97 Cited in 'Serebrianyi Dvorets', a conversation between Ilya Kabakov and Victor Tupitsyn, *Khudozhestvennyi Zhurnal no.42*, Moscow, 2002, pp. 10–14, cited in Viktor Tupitsyn, *The Museological Unconscious: Communal (Post-)Modernism in Russia*, Cambridge, MA: MIT Press, 2009, p. 70.

98 Kabakov again: 'This [action] actualised one of the most pleasant and practically unknown sides of the socius, the socius that is so painful in our time. Here the social is not antagonistic to you, but instead good-willed, reliable, and extremely welcoming. This feeling is so unusual, so not experienced before, that it not only recovers you, but also becomes an amazing gift compared to everyday reality.' (Kabakov, 'Ten Appearances', p. 154, translated by Anya Pantuyeva.)

99 One sign of the intensity of this attitude can be found in an interview with Joseph Beuys undertaken by two Russians, V. Bakchahyan and A. Ur, in the samizdat magazine *A-Ya* at the time of his Guggenheim retrospective. Their questions make explicit their wariness of art having anything to do with social change, since the work of the avant-garde post-1917 was so flagrantly co-opted by political officials: 'Our Russian experience shows that to flirt with politics is dangerous for an artist. . . . Aren't you afraid that the artist who's inside you is being conquered by the politician?' (V. Backchahyan and A. Ur, 'Joseph Beuys: Art and Politics', *A-Ya*, 2, 1980, pp. 54–5.)

100 An exception to this, and an important point of contrast, would be the student movement in former Yugoslavia, who in 1968 demanded a more authentic and equal form of communism. Student Cultural Centres housed the galleries where experimental art of this period was first shown.

Chapter 6   Incidental People

1 O+I stands for Organisation and Imagination, and is an independent international artist consultancy and research body.

2 A conference at Tate Britain in 2005 sought to emphasise the relevance of APG for contemporary artists, including Carey Young, Platform, and Böhm and Lang. See *Art and Social Intervention: The Incidental Person*, Tate Britain, 23 March 2005, available at www.tate.org.uk. More recently, Douglas Gordon has compared his method in making *Zidane: A 21st Century Portrait* (2006, with Philippe Parreno) as 'part of an extended practice of a 1960s idea of the Artist Placement Group. We placed ourselves with the help of many people, but keeping the idea of the Artist Placement Group, we didn't construct an event, but included ourselves in it.' (Gordon, in Hans-Ulrich Obrist, *The Conversation Series: Philippe Parreno*, Köln: Walther König, 2008, p. 116.)

3 Latham remained on the margins of main tendencies in the 1960s, but participated in the exhibitions 'New Realists' (Sidney Janis Gallery, New York, 1962) and 'Information' (MoMA, New York, 1970).

4 Founder members were Steveni and Latham, plus Jeffrey Shaw and Barry Flanagan; they were joined soon after by Stuart Brisley, David Hall and Ian MacDonald Munro.

5 Initial board members included the artist William Coldstream, Frank

Lawson, Julie Lawson (then secretary to Roland Penrose), Michael Compton (curator at Tate), and the Swiss collector Bernard Bertinger as chairman. (Interview with Barbara Steveni by Melanie Roberts, 22 June 1998, National Sound Archive, British Library, Tape 8.)

6 Letter from G. F. R. Barclay (departmental head at the Civil Service) to other government departments asking if they were interested in working with APG. January 1973; John Walker papers, Tate Archive: 9913/1/4, p. 5.

7 Evans recounts that he became involved in APG 'by the back door', since the British Steel Corporation decided to act on Steveni's invitation by establishing a one-year fellowship for an artist, to run alongside other fellowships for industry, engineering, and so on. The fellowship was sought by open call, thereby avoiding the intermediary negotiations of APG. (Evans, interview with the author, New York, 22 September 2009.)

8 Latham viewed artists as pre-eminently suitable personnel within companies because they already operate on a longer time-base than other groups in society, are skilled in handling conceptually unfamiliar material, and are noted for their independence and their creativity.

9 Stuart Brisley, interview with the author, London, 7 August 2009. Steveni, who confesses to not taking no for an answer, places the overall ratio a little higher, with around one in ten letters receiving some kind of response.

10 The festival '9 Evenings: Theatre and Engineering', the exhibition 'Some More Beginnings' and the Pepsi Pavilion at Expo '70 are the most prominent milestones of EAT's achievements. Highlights of the Art and Technology programme included James Turrell and Robert Irwin experimenting with sensory deprivation chambers and ganzfeld spaces, the latter being formative for the development of Turrell's installation work in the 1970s and 1980s.

11 The open brief is one in which there is no expectation that the artist will produce results.

12 Latham, cited in John Walker, 'APG: The Individual and the Organisation, A Decade of Conceptual Engineering', *Studio International*, 191:980, March–April 1976, p. 162.

13 Brisley maintains that he painted the factory equipment according to the workers' suggestions less as a work of art than as a device for stirring up the idea that they were able to influence their surroundings. (Naveen Khan, 'Artists on the Shop Floor', *Arts Guardian*, 2 August 1971.) He also recalls that the noticeboard scheme was swiftly co-opted by the management who took control of the noticeboards to disseminate information to employees. (Brisley, interview with the author, London, 7 August 2009.) See also Brisley, interview by Melanie Roberts, September/October 1996, National Sound Archive, British Library.

14 Brisley, interview with Peter Byrom (1975), cited in Katherine Dodd, *Artists Placement Group 1966–1976*, MA thesis, Courtauld Institute of Art, 1992, p. 24.

15 Brisley, cited in Robert Hewison, *Too Much: Art and Society in the Sixties, 1960–1975*, New York: Oxford University Press, 1987, p. 234.

16 Dodd reports that 'Inno70' was a name coined by Latham as 'a kind of complementary otherness to the international exhibition called Expo'. (Dodd, *Artists Placement Group 1966–1976*, p. 17.)

17 Dodd reports an apocryphal story that on seeing these 'For Sale' posters, a visiting American tycoon expressed interest in buying the Hayward Gallery. (Ibid., p. 57.)

18 The show possibly included Brisley's chair sculpture from Hille: Steveni maintains that this was installed on one of the sculpture courts at the Hayward; Brisley says that it was not, and that he cannot recall anything of his on display in 'Inno70'. (Steveni, email to the author, 20 August 2010; Brisley, email to the author, 20 August 2010.)

19 The initial proposal had been to have a live sound feed of numerous steel mills played into the Hayward, but the proposal was rejected by British Steel Corporation for fear that exhibition viewers would be able to overhear the workers' bad language. (Garth Evans, interview with the author, New York, 22 September 2009.)

20 Latham: 'This was one of the bones of contention – the public was not part of the act and they were often very annoyed that they weren't . . . they were given a noticeboard where they could put up their comments.' (Dodd, *Artists Placement Group 1966–1976*, p. 58.)

21 These varied in tone – some were serious, some humorous, such as the collage showing the Hayward Gallery's distinctive brutalist roof as the container for a mound of giant potatoes.

22 APG's use of the magazine as a catalogue is comparable to Seth Siegelaub's use of the magazine as an exhibition space in the July/August 1970 issue of *Studio International*. During this period, *Studio International* was particularly pioneering in terms of its willingness to experiment with exhibition formats and engage in socio-political debate around art.

23 Caroline Tisdall, 'Profit Without Honour', *Guardian*, December 1971, undated press cutting, APG archive, Tate.

24 Guy Brett, 'How Professional?', *The Times*, undated press cutting, APG archive, Tate.

25 Nigel Gosling, *Observer*, undated press cutting, APG archive, Tate.

26 Benjamin H. D. Buchloh, 'Conceptual Art 1962–1969: From the Aesthetics of Administration to the Critique of Institutions', *October* 55, 1990, pp. 105–43.

27 Gustav Metzger, 'A Critical Look at Artist Placement Group', *Studio International*, 183:940, January 1972, p. 4.

28 Ibid., p. 4.

29 See, for example, the audience response to Steveni's APG presentation in *Art and Economics II*, Apex Art, New York, February 2010.

30 Peter Fuller, 'Subversion and APG', *Art and Artists* magazine, December 1971, p. 20. Leslie Julius, managing director at Hille, later remarked that one 'cannot expect industry and commerce to put out money for art, if the artists themselves are going to attack everything that industry and commerce stand for . . . I am very resentful that all my intentions, which I think are good intentions, should be undermined by the artist on a political basis. . . . if a man wants to overthrow the capitalist system I don't see why, as a capitalist, I should provide him with the money to do it.' (Interview with Peter Byrom [1975], in Dodd, *Artists Placement Group 1966–1976*, p. 25.)

31 In Fuller's eyes, Latham failed to realise 'that anyone paid almost double the wages of the workers, practising an abstruse bourgeois ideology, and having constant access to the boardroom and its facilities will automatically be aligned with the management, even if he did get some degree of acceptance from the men'. (Fuller, 'Subversion and APG', p. 22.)

32 For Brisley, artists were being asked to serve the needs of those who control power and who create the circumstances for the production and acquisition of profit. See Stuart Brisley, 'No it is Not On', *Studio International*, 183:942, March 1972, pp. 95–6 (his title puns on Latham's term 'noit', discussed below).

33 Fuller, 'Subversion and APG', p. 22.

34 Ibid.

35 Latham, cited in John Walker, *John Latham: The Incidental Person – His Art and Ideas*, London: Middlesex University Press, 1995, p. 100.

36 For a clear explanation of the 'Delta unit', see Walker, 'APG: The Individual and the Organisation', pp. 162–4. For a crushing dismissal of it (and its role in APG's 'Report and Offer for Sale'), see Metzger, 'A Critical Look at Artist Placement Group', p. 4.

37 Although APG was directly engaged with contemporary society and industry, the objective of the group's focus lay in the future, not with the immediate present. This is why, John Walker explains, attacks on the Hayward show were premature: it would not be possible to judge the efficacy of APG's activities 'until at least 1986'. (Walker, 'APG: The Individual and the Organisation', p. 162.)

38 Latham, cited by Brisley, in 'No it is Not On', p. 96.

39 O+I Foundation, leaflet, undated, but after 1989; 9913/1/4, p. 8, in John Walker papers, Tate Archive. 'What IPs [Incidental Persons] would bring to industry were longer-term perspectives, imagination, creativity, visual skills, non-commercial values and inclusiveness. Their value to industry could be compared to that of inventors and research scientists.'

(Walker, *John Latham: The Incidental Person*, p. 100.) In a letter to Walker, Steveni argued that most artists had been happy to go along with being called an Incidental Person instead of an artist, noting that 'in particular, Beuys at Documenta 6 when APG gave an exposé of the work, proclaimed "Incidental Person Yes, Artist No" '. (Letter, 18 July 1994, from Barbara Steveni to John Walker; 9913/1/4, p. 9, in John Walker papers, Tate Archive.)

40 Breakwell: 'they thought it would be interesting for me to look at the abnormal society, the closed world of Broadmoor, as a diarist. So there's an obvious connection there. Whereas I don't know what I would possibly have found of interest in British Steel, for instance. This was about illness, mental states, people, and they are central to my works. I'm not interested so much in materials.' (Breakwell, interviewed by Victoria Worsley, December 2004/January 2005, National Sound Archive, British Library, Tape 16910, side A.)

41 Ian Breakwell, 'From the Inside: A Personal History of Work on Placement with the Department of Health and Related Work 1976–1980', *Art Monthly*, 40, October 1980, p. 4. Because of the restriction of the Official Secrets Act, Breakwell tended to present this project only in APG events and symposia, rather than in exhibitions. These discussions include the Stadtische Kunstmuseum Bonn ('Kunst alz Soziale Strategie', 1977), the Royal College of Art ('Incidental Person Approach to Government', 27 October 1977), and Documenta 6 (1977).

42 Mick Kemp, architect, cited in 'Ian Breakwell Feasibility Study phase 1 and 2', 1976, Tate Archive.

43 Ian Breakwell, 'APG Report', cited in Dodd, *Artists Placement Group 1966–1976*, p. 69.

44 Dodd, *Artists Placement Group 1966–1976*, p. 47.

45 The Reminiscence Aids Project was a 'nostalgia jukebox' for the elderly and senile, devised by Mick Kemp, in collaboration with two other APG artists, David Toop and Hugh Davies (both artists and musicians). See Breakwell, 'From the Inside', pp. 2–6, and the Department of Health and Society Security's 'Report of Research Findings and Recommendations for Future Development of Reminiscence Aids', 1980.

46 Initially the Russian constructivist architect Bertolt Lubetkin had provided plans for the town, but he resigned in 1950; a few years later the abstract painter Victor Pasmore was brought onto the project as a consultant; between 1963 and 1970 Pasmore produced an elegant modernist pavilion that had, by the later 1970s, been abandoned by the council and was something of a tip.

47 Brisley recalls that his father had been a strong union worker for the railways, and was involved in the National Strike of 1926; he had instilled in Brisley 'the notion of miners as the avant-garde of the working class'. (Brisley, interview with the author, London, 7 August 2009.)

48 See Brisley, in *Artist Project Peterlee Report*, undated pamphlet (after 1976), Newcastle upon Tyne: The Copy Shop, n.p. Scanned pdf downloadable at www.stuartbrisley.com.

49 Another point of reference is the History from Below movement of the 1960s. (Brisley, interview with the author, London, 7 August 2009.)

50 Questions such as 'Why can't we paint our front doors the colour we want? Why can't we have allotments? Why are the new Jaguar plant not employing people over 35?' (Ibid.)

51 Ibid.

52 Brisley argues that 'for work to be satisfactory, there needs to be an aesthetic component', in relation to both the work of art and labour itself. (Ibid.)

53 Graham Stevens, 'How the Arts Council Destroys Art Movements', *AND: Journal of Art and Art Education*, 27, 1992, p. 2.

54 Robin Campbell, letter of 11 January 1971 to APG. See also the letter from Professor Christopher Cornford to Barbara Steveni, giving the Arts Council advisory panel's eight reasons for no longer supporting the APG. These included the following objections: 'APG does not produce any results, tangible or otherwise, that are worth mentioning.' 'Its language is incomprehensible and mystificatory.' 'It is highly compromised by dubious relationships with industry, capital, and other ancillary agencies.' 'The whole enterprise is, in any case, chimerical and quixotic, because either it will liberate the workers and dish capitalism, or, if it doesn't then it is a cosmetic operation. It is not the business of the Arts Council to support "social engineering".' Both cited in Dodd, *Artists Placement Group 1966–1976*, pp. 55–6.

55 As Breakwell notes, the Arts Council 'dumbed down' the idea of placements and turned them into residencies, thereby breaking two basic principles: first, the Arts Council paid for the artist, rather than the host organisation (who then had less commitment to the project); and second, the artist was no longer expected to get involved in the host organisation, but advised to stay separate from it. (Breakwell, interviewed by Victoria Worsley, December 2004/January 2005, National Sound Archive, British Library, Tape 16910, side B.)

56 In a preparatory document for the exhibition, APG cites Robert Kelly in *Business Horizons* (June 1968): 'If business wants to read its future, it had better look not just at business but at the whole culture of our time, including the arts – painting, music, theatre, literature – and philosophy and religion. It is in these activities that tomorrow's markets, business legislation and new business structures are most clearly prefigured.' The last sentence is cited three times within the document. Art and Economics 1970 (Inno 70), working document, undated, early 1969?; uncatalogued APG archive at Tate.

57 See for example APG's Industrial Negative Symposium (Mermaid Theatre, London, 1968), at Kunsthalle Düsseldorf (1971) and discussion panels at the Hayward Gallery (1971) and Documenta 6 (1977), the latter as part of Beuys's *100 Days of the Free International University*. Marcel Broodthaers can be seen in some photographs their discussions (presumably in Düsseldorf).

58 Breakwell, 'From the Inside', p. 6.

59 Steveni, interview with the author, London, 7 August 2009.

60 Walker, 'APG: The Individual and the Organisation', p. 162.

61 These points have been synthesised from a number of texts on community art, including: Su Braden, *Artists and People*, London and New York: Routledge and Kegan Paul, 1978; Malcolm Dickson (ed.), *Art with People*, Sunderland: AN Publications, 1995; Owen Kelly, *Community, Art and the State: Storming the Citadels*, London: Comedia, 1984; Charles Landry, *What a Way to Run a Railroad: An Analysis of Radical Failure*, London: Comedia, 1985.

62 This is in sharp contrast to the literature on community theatre. See for example, Baz Kershaw, *The Politics of Performance: Radical Theatre as Cultural Intervention*, London: Routledge, 1992; James Harding and Cindy Rosenthal (eds.), *Restaging the Sixties: Radical Theaters and Their Legacies*, Ann Arbor: University of Michigan Press, 2007; John Frick (ed.), *Theatre at the Margins: The Political, The Popular, The Personal, The Profane*, Tuscaloosa: University of Alabama Press, 2000.

63 I shall be leaning heavily on both Kelly and Landry in what follows, as well as on interviews with various key figures involved in the UK community arts movement and its funding: Ed Berman, Chris Cooper, Bill Harpe, Bill McAlistair, Sally Morris, David Powell and Alan Tompkins.

64 Educational projects are not discussed in the art press, even if these projects are by the same artists who exhibit in the gallery.

65 I am dating the emergence of the community arts movement to the late 1960s, but the Baldry Report (produced by the Arts Council Great Britain in 1974) offers a timeline beginning in 1962 with the Traverse Bookshop in Edinburgh, which expanded its activities to include a coffee bar and a performance area to present small-scale experimental theatre and mixed-media productions. See *Community Arts: The Report of the Community Arts Working Party, June 1974*, London: Arts Council of Great Britain, 1974, p. 36.

66 It would be fair to say that the majority of community arts projects were organised by the educated middle classes rejecting their parents' lifestyles and value systems.

67 As Sally Morgan has argued: 'Philosophically [the British community arts movement] existed somewhere between Joseph Beuys's proposition that art and life had no edges, the Situationist position of Guy Debord,

which saw creative action as "a temporary field of activity favourable to . . . desires", and Paulo Freire's notion of cultural action as political action.' (Sally J. Morgan, 'Beautiful Impurity: British Contextualism as *Processual* Postmodern Practice', in *Journal of Visual Art Practice*, 2:3, 2003, p. 140.)

68 *Community Arts: The Report of the Community Arts Working Party, June 1974*, p. 8, emphases added.

69 Ibid., p. 24.

70 In the interests of transparency, I should note that I was referred to The Blackie by Barbara Steveni, and arrived at Inter-Action through The Blackie's Bill Harpe introducing me to David Powell, an art consultant and former Inter-Action team member. Other organisations could have been my focus (such as The Welfare State community theatre group, also founded in 1968), but The Blackie and Inter-Action provided the most fruitful contrast. The Blackie has extensively archived all ephemera, correspondence and printed matter since its inception, while Inter-Action has just a handful of leaflets detailing its activities. I have tried to provide equal space to both, despite the proportionally disparate materials available.

71 Anon, 'Moving in on the Fund-Raising Game', *7-Up*, 1976, p. 24. *7-Up* is The Blackie's in-house newspaper celebrating seven years of their activities.

72 *7-Up* proudly lists its in-house sound equipment as: four tape-recorders, two turntables, a twelve-channel mixer and a four-channel mixer, a synthesiser, numerous amplifiers and loudspeakers, twelve microphones and three headphones; five Sony video recorders, three monitors, a vision-mixer and two tripods with dollies. (Ibid., p. 4, p. 20.)

73 'Participation in deciding how to spend money is undertaken by everyone attending staff meetings. Participation in raising money is more theory than reality. Only three members of staff have done any major fund-raising. Participation in signing cheques (taking the final responsibility) is limited to Bill and Wendy Harpe with second signatures from Mr Leslie Jones (solicitor)....' (Anonymous, 'Plastic Bags on the Move . . . It's how the accounts are kept in check', ibid., p. 24.)

74 Anonymous, 'Anyone Expecting to be 100% Creative in their Working Life is also Expecting to be a Parasite', ibid., p. 17.

75 This building was erected despite huge problems reconciling Price's idealism with practical requirements, resulting in several lawsuits. (Ed Berman, interview with the author, London, 8 January 2010.) It is important to mention the influence of Joan Littlewood in this regard, who had conceived and developed the Fun Palace with Price, and who was an influential point of contact between Inter-Action and the professional theatre world.

76 Berman claims that McKinsey and KPMG helped Inter-Action to set up 1,200 new community groups in the 1970s. He states that he is interested

in the interaction between many things, and as such does not rule out business: 'the starting point is to take any field and make its principles available and useful to people who feel outside it, or who are poor. . . . I want to see people getting their hands on things that improve their lives.' (Berman, interview with the author, London, 8 January 2010.) From the beginning, Inter-Action had worked with a mixed economy: Equity (the UK trade union for professional actors), public funding, individual donors and liberal trusts.

77 The three actors were John Perry (Edward Lear), Phil Ryder (William Shakespeare) and Gary Brooking (Captain Cook), members of the Inter-Action co-operative. Shakespeare and Lear visited Los Angeles in November 1979.

78 David Powell, telephone interview with the author, 13 May 2010.

79 Anonymous, 'Sticking Together', in *7-Up*, first edition, 1976, p. 3. When I visited, the most recent creative task had been to make a picture of a bird from woodworking materials.

80 Bill Harpe, *All in the Games* (DVD, 10 mins), undated.

81 Bill Harpe, *Games for the New Years: A DIY Guide to Games for the 21st Century*, Liverpool: The Blackie/Great Georges Community Cultural Project, 2001. See also Chris Arnot, 'Playmates', *Guardian*, Society supplement, 7 November 2001, p. 6.

82 Berman, interview with the author, London, 8 January 2010. Some of Berman's games are catalogued in Clive Barker's *Theatre Games: A New Approach to Drama Training*, London: Eyre Methuen, 1977. Barker was a trustee of Inter-Action and taught the first generation of Dogg's Troupe actors.

83 Berman maintains that he follows the Swiss psychologist Jean Piaget, believing that creativity is one of the brain's genetically inherited structures. David Powell, a former member of the Inter-Action co-operative, describes the aims of Berman's games method as twofold: 'to balance the individual's capacity to play a role in a group effort' with 'ways to invent things anew collectively'. (Powell, telephone interview with the author, 13 May 2010.) It is timely to recall that team-building via games is now a staple component of corporate culture, even if these take place annually rather than weekly, and rarely involve the invention of new games.

84 One of The Blackie's long-standing team members, Sally Morris, reflects that if anything the performances were depressing, based on researched statistics and 'holding a mirror up to nature'. (Sally Morris, interview with the author, Liverpool, 5 August 2009.)

85 In a document analysing *Sanctuary*, The Blackie team observe that 'Large scale or abstract change . . . was best achieved by unofficial action, and even then by group activity rather than individual action.' (Anonymous, 'Sanctuary Report' [1969], n.p., The Blackie Archive.) However, the report also notes that the discussion following the performance was

limited, and tended to revolve around whether *Sanctuary* was good theatre or not. A point that participants repeatedly brought up was the high degree of participation expected of them, and that they had not behaved as they would do in real life. At the same time, the tenants of the middle- and upper-class housing had been far more apathetic than Box Street, all of which seemed to correspond to their behaviour in reality. The report concludes: 'those who claimed that they were not aware of the role they were to play were during the show undergoing an inward struggle about whether to participate or not, which reflected the dilemma they live with in real life'.

86 Bill Harpe, 'Notes: Towards a Common Language – exhibition – Walker Art Gallery', October 1973, The Blackie Archive.

87 Starting in 1965, for example, Medalla is regularly reviewed or featured in art magazines, which tend to position him as a kinetic artist.

88 Guy Brett refers to this work as a 'game', and draws a connection between Medalla's use of colour and materials and that of Brazilian artists Lygia Clark and Hélio Oiticica, whom he had showed (alongside Medalla) at Signals Gallery. See Guy Brett, *Exploding Galaxies: The Art of David Medalla*, London: Kala Press, 1995, Chapter 6, 'Any Number of People'.

89 Ed Berman left Inter-Action in 1984, but others continued with the project, today known as InterChange and based in Hampstead Town Hall.

90 Ed Berman, interview with the author, London, 8 January 2010. In 1981–82, Berman was invited by Michael Heseltine (Secretary of State for the Environment in Thatcher's cabinet) to be special advisor on inner city problems and the voluntary sector. Berman also courted the Royal Family: Princess Anne opened the Inter-Action Centre (designed by Cedric Price) in 1977, while Prince Charles presented a BBC TV programme on Inter-Action in 1979.

91 An exception to this is London, where from 1981 onwards the left-wing Greater London Council (GLC) funded a wide range of alternative popular arts across poorer boroughs of the city, in deliberate opposition to central government. Prior to this, cultural funding had been dedicated only to a handful of high cultural institutions (National Theatre, Royal Ballet, etc.). One of the main instigators of GLC community arts policy was Alan Tompkins, an Open University faculty member influenced by Stuart Hall and E. P. Thompson. Tompkins recalls with pleasure his experiences of sitting on various funding panels and allocating money to gay and lesbian theatre groups, marching bands for teenage girls in Peckham, and other forms of identitarian and/or popular culture. (Tompkins, interview with the author, London, 4 August 2009.)

92 Landry, *What a Way to Run a Railroad*, Chapter IV, pp. 38–48.

93 Kelly, *Community, Art and the State*, p. 1.

94 Ibid., pp. 30–1.

95 Martha Rosler points to a similar situation in the US when she notes that 'art institutions and art-makers adapt their offerings to the tastes of grant-givers (that is, to the current ideological demands of the system)'. See Martha Rosler, 'Theses on Defunding' (1980), in Rosler, *Decoys and Disruptions: Selected Writings 1975–2001*, Cambridge, MA: MIT Press, 2004, p. 330.

96 Here I am paraphrasing Kelly, *Community, Art and the State*, p. 17.

97 *Community Arts: The Report of the Community Arts Working Party, June 1974*, p. 7.

98 In the US, the equivalent would be various temporary installations produced at the Burning Man festival in Nevada, from 1986 onwards.

99 Sean Cubitt, 'Public/Media/Arts', in Dickson (ed.), *Art with People*, p. 100.

100 The argument that social networking is a form of mass conceptual art is put forward by Boris Groys in 'Comrades of Time', *e-flux journal*, 11, December 2009, available at www.e-flux.com.

101 New communications technology haunts the pages of Bourriaud's *Relational Aesthetics*: 'we feel meagre and helpless when faced with the electronic media, theme parks, user-friendly places, and the spread of compatible forms of sociability, like the laboratory rat doomed to an inexorable itinerary in its cage . . . The general mechanisation of social functions gradually reduces the relational space.' (Nicolas Bourriaud, *Relational Aesthetics*, Dijon: Presses du Réel, 2002, p. 8, p. 17.)

Chapter 7   Former West

1 This chapter was written as a contribution to Former West, a European research project whose title inverts the familiar shorthand 'former East' as a label for those countries that underwent the transition from communism from 1989 to 1991. The project investigates the impact of the fall of communism on the production and reception of art in Europe since 1989, arguing that this upheaval also affected the political and cultural imaginary of Western Europe. See www.formerwest.org.

2 Further definitions of the 'project' (compared to the work of art), amassed during a workshop at Arte de Conducta, Havana (2007), include presentness, possibility, openness to change and contamination, a space of production, unlimited time and space, and a dialogue with the social to reach audiences beyond art.

3 *Art Since 1900*, for example, identifies the following three themes as key to the 1990s: identity politics, women artists and the body; large-scale video projection (Viola); large-scale figurative photography (Gursky, Wall). Only the last section (on 2003) makes reference to experimental curating via a discussion of 'Utopia Station' and to the emergent theme of 'precarity' in the work of Thomas Hirschhorn. See Hal Foster et al., *Art Since 1900: Modernism, Anti-modernism, Postmodernism*, London: Thames and Hudson, 2004.

4 In his introduction, Jan Hoet argued that 'Artists do not investigate the aesthetics of things: they revel in the hidden beauty, the essence, the ecstasy.' Hoet, 'An Introduction', *Documenta IX*, Stuttgart: Edition Cantz, 1992, vol. 1, p. 17.

5 For a good discussion of transdisciplinarity in 1990s exhibition catalogues, see Liz Donato, 'The Disciplinary Shift in Contemporary Art Exhibition Practices, 1990s–Today', available at www.formerwest.org

6 In making this distinction I am indebted to Miwon Kwon's history of site-specificity, *One Place After Another: Site-Specific Art and Locational Identity*, Cambridge, MA: MIT Press, 2002. Kwon's focus, however, is North American rather than European, and revolves around questions of judgement centered on the model of community proposed by site-specific art in the 1980s and 1990s, rather than on the subject of curating and spectatorship. In the US, a central frame of reference for site-specific curating was the trial and removal of Richard Serra's *Tilted Arc* from Federal Plaza in 1989.

7 Rather, Hoet frames the exhibition in poetic terms: it indicates a transformation of the museum into 'a metaphor of that quiet (today more than ever), forgotten place, an almost inaccessible place, a mythical place: the place of Mystery'. (Jan Hoet, '"Chambres d'Amis": A Museum Ventures Out', in *Chambres d'Amis*, Ghent: Museum van Hedendaagse Kunst, 1986, p. 350.) Pragmatically, the ambition was to produce more support for the Museum van Hedendaagse Kunst in Ghent, of which Hoet was director, by increasing the city's interest in contemporary art.

8 Ibid., p. 345–6.

9 In the catalogue, Geys's contribution is illustrated with installation shots of the artist standing next to the doors, while the six hosts are represented by a short paragraph written by each of them, detailing their employment, income and views (if any) of his project.

10 Joshua Decter, 'Back to Babel: Project Unité', *Artforum*, November 1993, p. 92.

11 Mark Dion, interview with the author, New York, 25 November 2009.

12 Renée Green, 'Scenes from a Group Show: "Project Unité" ', in Alex Coles (ed.), *Site-Specificity: The Ethnographic Turn*, London: Black Dog, 2000, p. 121.

13 Aupetitallot, in Stephan Dillemuth, *Project Unité*, DVD, 1993.

14 The installation accelerated the ruination, creating a dystopian image of the building as if left abandoned, surrounding a Le Corbusier bench with walls covered in bird shit and piles of dead insects on the floor, in deliberate contrast to the cleanliness of the architect's imagined scheme.

15 'It can be said with confidence that, of all the exhibits, Zobernig's space was the most visited and for the longest periods of time – or at least it was until marauding bands of (presumably atypical) drunken Unité residents

had looted it.' (James Roberts, 'Down With the People', *Frieze*, 12, September–October 1993.)

16 Renée Green, for example, felt that it was impossible to produce something meaningful in this environment; to do something socially ambitious that would affect the residents, she claimed, she would have to learn to speak French and live there for five years. (Green interviewed in Dillemuth, *Project Unité*, DVD.)

17 Green, 'Scenes from a Group Show', pp. 133–4.

18 Hal Foster, 'The Artist as Ethnographer', in *The Return of the Real*, Cambridge, MA: MIT Press, 1996, p. 173.

19 Ibid., p. 196.

20 Philippe Parreno's *The Night of the Heroes* comprised a fiction film on video, co-authored with Bourriaud, using the apartment as the setting for a story about a crazy man and a young girl who lived next door; the installation featured a gothic church window and poetic texts written on cardboard. The installation *Suzanne et le Pacifique*, a collaboration between Dominique Gonzalez-Foerster and Anne Frémy, took the form of a colourful environment partly based on a book by Jean Giraudoux about a female Robinson Crusoe; the rooms also included references to different temporary architectures and non-European uses of modernist architecture.

21 Smith's harshest letter of rejection is for a young Maurizio Cattelan, who proposed to organise a fake skinhead rally in Arnhem: 'I don't think you have thoroughly thought out what you are proposing . . . If fear is really the only emotion you want to evoke and this is the only way you can do it then we cannot work together' (Valerie Smith, in *Sonsbeek 93*, Ghent: Snoeck Ducaju and Zoon, 1993, p. 35).

22 Smith in *Sonsbeek 93*, p. 8.

23 See *Sonsbeek 93*, p. 19 (Quinn), p. 17 (Boetti).

24 At one point Smith responds curtly to the artist Ann Hamilton, who is on the verge of withdrawing from the show: 'Getting your letter was a kind of slap in the face after all this time. I am going through my own creative process in making this exhibition and it has been very hard and difficult . . .' (Ibid., p. 112.) We can compare this degree of curatorial control to that of Mary Jane Jacob in 'Culture in Action': although she invited artists with a track record of social engagement, her selection was also highly directed, as Kwon has demonstrated with respect to Renée Green's eventual de-selection from the show. See Kwon, *One Place After Another*, pp. 140–1.

25 A booklet explaining the objects accompanied the display, while Dutch television made a programme showing the veterans installing the cabinets and discussing their chosen objects. (Mark Dion, interview with the author, New York, 21 August 2010.)

26 'It's too bad that so-called social art or political art has a bad rep . . . For me it's not the result, it's not the goal, it's the way the artists approach

their work, it's the methodology that's most interesting, the process. And I think most of the art world can't deal with that here because they're so locked into this formalism.' (Smith, interviewed by Stephan Dillemuth in *Sonsbeek 93*, DVD, 1993.)

27 Aupetitallot, interviewed in Dillemuth, *Project Unité*, DVD.

28 By way of contrast, it is conspicuous that in 'Kontext Kunst' (1993), Peter Weibel did not hesitate to argue *for* the social, although he understood this to operate on the level of theme and process rather than as a diversification of art's audience; the artists in his show, he writes, are part of a longer tradition of artists 'who intend to create reality through art and not only its representation', placing 'the psychic and social constitution of society and its institutions into the centre'. (Peter Weibel, 'Vorwort', *Kontext Kunst*, Köln: DuMont, 1994, p. xiii, my translation.)

29 Mary Jane Jacob, *Culture in Action*, Seattle: Bay Press, 1995, p. 111. According to Joe Scanlan, the cleaned-up clubhouse 'had the eerie charm of a 1950s high school chemistry lab'. (Scanlan, 'Culture in Action', *Frieze*, 13, November–December 1993.)

30 Mark Dion, interview with the author, New York, 25 November 2009.

31 Dion also noted that Sonsbeek, which in his view was a much tighter and more adventurous show than Firminy, was also criticised because people had to work at finding and seeing the work; it was no longer a consumable array of sculptural objects in the park.

32 Johanne Lamoureux, 'The Museum Flat', in Bruce Ferguson, Reesa Greenberg, Sandy Nairne (eds.), *Thinking about Exhibitions*, London: Routledge, 1996, p. 129.

33 'As to what visitors from out of town saw beyond the tours, the conference, the launch event, the media and the publishing, I would have said very little. Perhaps because it was simply impossible to do so, "Culture in Action" didn't attempt to frame disparate people, activities and parts of the city as though they were displays in an exhibition, and I think for some visitors expecting exhibition/biennial protocol, this was challenging, baffling, unfulfilling or inadequate.' (Simon Grennan, email to the author, 7 April 2010.)

34 See Christian Philipp Müller, 'Art and the Social: Exhibitions of Contemporary Art in the 1990s', conference at Tate Britain, 30 April 2010, available at www.formerwest.org.

35 Valerie Smith, 'Proposal Sonsbeek 93', *Sonsbeek 93*, p. 9, my emphasis; Mark Kremer, 'Change is Possible: Interview with Valerie Smith', *Kunst & Museumjournaal*, 4:6, 1993, p. 9.

36 Neither publishing scheme was brought to closure: the last two volumes of *Project Unité* were not realised, nor the second volume of *Sonsbeek 93*, in which the final projects would be documented.

37 Simon Grennan, email to the author, 7 April 2010. As several reviewers of 'Culture in Action' noted, there was a continual tension between the

exhibition rhetoric (namely, its claims to concrete achievements) and the often modest and elusive ambitions of the artists. See Joe Scanlan's review in *Frieze*, 13, November–December 1993.

38 Michael Gibbs, 'Sonsbeek 93', *Art Monthly*, Jul/Aug 1993, p.25.

39 Lynne Cooke noted that 'the two principal audiences' for 'Culture in Action' had quite different experiences: 'the professional art world spectators, who were bussed from site to site, quickly became conscious of their status as voyeurs . . . By contrast, those who by reason of their residence in a certain part of the city became associated with and/or participated in a project at a local level rarely seem to have visited those projects located elsewhere. These two audiences . . . proved almost mutually exclusive.' (Lynne Cooke, 'Arnhem and Chicago: Outdoor Exhibitions of Contemporary Art', *The Burlington Magazine*, 135, November 1993, pp. 786–7.)

40 See for example Nicolas Bourriaud, *Relational Aesthetics*, Dijon: Presses du Réel, 2002, p. 73; Peter Weibel, 'Vorwort', *Kontext Kunst*, p. 13. This is the opposite of Smith at Sonsbeek hoping to send artists *out* into the community.

41 Nicolas Bourriaud, *Postproduction*, New York: Lukas and Sternberg, 2002, p. 65.

42 Conversation with Pierre Huyghe, 2 December 2009; conversation with Dominique Gonzalez-Foerster, 7 April 2010.

43 Eric Troncy, 'No Man's Time', *Flash Art*, July–September, 2008, p. 169; Troncy, 'Discourse on Method', in *Surface de Réparations*, Dijon: FRAC Bourgogne, 1994, p. 52.

44 Troncy, 'Discourse on Method', p. 52.

45 Ibid., p. 52. Troncy aligns his work with the precedent of 'À Pierre et Marie' (p. 53), an exhibition *en travaux* held in an abandoned church in Paris between January 1983 and October 1984. Devised by a team of five artists and curators (including Daniel Buren and Jean-Hubert Martin), the exhibition involved over sixty-nine artists participating in a project whose organising principle was the game of consequences: each artist could renew and modify their contribution throughout the duration of the show.

46 See for example Nicolas Bourriaud: 'social utopias and revolutionary hopes have given way to everyday micro-utopias and imitative strategies, any stance that is "directly" critical of society is futile . . .' (Bourriaud, *Relational Aesthetics*, p. 31.) In his essay on 'No Man's Time' in *Flash Art*, Troncy is at pains to differentiate his approach from 1970s models of critical art: the works were not based on resistance to the museum system, he claimed, and were barely concerned with the site or space.

47 Other performances included Karen Kilimnik's *Madonna and Backdraft* ('a scene from a concert with music by Madonna and a boy dancer') and Dominique Gonzalez-Foerster's *Son esprit vert fit autor d'elle un monde vert*, 'a portrait in three stages of a woman at large wearing a green dress'. (Troncy, 'No Man's Time', p. 168.)

48 Rirkrit Tiravanija, in *Surface de Réparations*, p. 91.

49 Troncy, 'No Man's Time', p. 168. The poster was advertised as 'August–July 1988', i.e. three years earlier, prior to the fall of the Berlin Wall and the Gulf War. In the Guggenheim catalogue entry on this exhibition, Michael Archer explicitly connects 'No Man's Time' to Fukuyama's eulogy to liberalism, 'The End of History?', *The National Interest*, 16, Summer 1989, pp. 3–18.

50 Troncy, 'No Man's Time', p. 169.

51 Ibid, p. 169.

52 'The exhibition setting is not merely a whim on the part of the curator but simply an attempt to correspond the model of the show with that of the works.' (Ibid., p. 169.)

53 Jan Åman, 'One of Four Introductions', in Eda Čufer and Victor Misiano (eds.), *Interpol: The Art Exhibition Which Divided East and West*, Ljubljana: IRWIN/Moscow Art Magazine, 2000, p. 6. Misiano was living in Paris in 1992 and met many of the protagonists of the French scene. However, he claims that 'Interpol' was less a response to European experiments than the 'conclusion to a series of performative curatorial exercises I was doing in Moscow and abroad from 1992. . . . But crucial for me was my participation in the "Molteplici Culture" project organized by Carolyn Christov-Bakargiev in Rome in 1992 . . . The generational difference in curatorial approaches was revealed there visibly.' (Misiano, email to the author, 25 September 2009.)

54 Viktor Misiano, 'Introduction', *Interpol: A Global Network from Stockholm and Moscow*, Stockholm: Färgfabriken and Aggerborgs, 1996, n.p.

55 Misiano chose five Russian artists (Alexander Brener, Vadim Fishkin, Dmitri Gutov, Yuri Leiderman and Anatoly Osmolovsky), who in turn selected three more: Maurizio Cattelan (Italy), IRWIN (Slovenia) and Wenda Gu (China, based in Paris). Åman chose six Swedish artists (Johannes Albers, Bigert & Bergström, Ernst Billgren, Carl Michael von Hausswolff, Birgitta Muhr, Ella Tideman), who in turn invited Matthias Wegner from Cologne, Oleg Kulik from Moscow and Ionna Theocaropoulou from Greece.

56 Misiano, 'Interpol – An Apology of Defeat', in Čufer and Misiano (eds.), *Interpol*, p. 45.

57 The videotape of the meal/discussion was then intended to be shown on a loop during the remainder of the exhibition, next to the remains of the meal on the dining table – but even this plan failed, as the food and detritus were promptly cleaned away by the gallery staff.

58 Alexander Brener, 'Ticket that Exploded', in Čufer and Misiano (eds.), *Interpol*, p. 10.

59 Fishkin's piece only worked for a few hours during the opening.

60 'An Open Letter to the Art World', in Čufer and Misiano (eds.), *Interpol*, p. 22.

61 Misiano, email to the author, 13 August 2010. The legacy of 'Apt-Art' and

close artistic collaboration (discussed in Chapter 5) continued to be a hallmark of Russian art during and after the transition in 1991, key moments of which included IRWIN's discursive installation *NSK Embassy Moscow* (1992) and Misiano's Visual Anthropology Workshop with the philosopher Valery Podoroga, held at the Centre for Contemporary Art, Moscow, 1994–95.

62 Misiano, 'Interpol – An Apology of Defeat', in Čufer and Misiano (eds), *Interpol*, p. 47.

63 Ibid., *Interpol*, p. 56.

64 The only exception is Boris Groys, who – without actually defining the project – argues that all artistic projects (by which he seems to mean proposals) are visions of an alternative future, and thus the more successful the more they maintain the gap between present and future. See Groys, 'The Loneliness of the Project', in *Going Public*, Berlin: Sternberg Press/e-flux, 2010, pp. 70–83.

65 Christian Boltanski and Eve Chiapello, *The New Spirit of Capitalism*, London: Verso, 2005. The 'spirit of capitalism' is the ideological justification for engaging with capitalism internalised by each age. The first spirit of capitalism, characterised by the bourgeois family entrepreneur from the end of the nineteenth century, relies on themes of utility, general well-being and progress; the second refers to the organisation, headed by a directorial class (1930s–1960s), propelled by a spirit of social justice (security, pensions, guaranteed careers).

66 In Chapter 2, they compare the projective city to a number of other value systems, all of which co-exist (rather than succeeding each other chronologically), including the reputational city, the inspirational city, the domestic city and the commercial city. See Boltanski and Chiapello, *The New Spirit of Capitalism*, p. 112.

67 Ibid., p. 312.

68 Boltanski and Chiapello are critical of this trend, since the valuation of flexibility privileges those without ties (familial, health or otherwise) and exploits those who lack such social and geographical mobility.

69 This shift was already identified by Andrea Fraser in 1997. See her 'What's Intangible, Transitory, Mediating, Participatory, and Rendered in the Public Sphere?', *October*, 80, Spring 1997, pp. 111–16: 'Whether the shift to service provision . . . represents the failure of the critique of the political economy of art, or the realisation of at least some of its goals, would remain open to question' (p. 116).

70 Parreno, in Hans-Ulrich Obrist, *The Conversation Series: Philippe Parreno*, Köln: Verlag der Buchhandlung Walther König, 2009, p. 1; Huyghe, conversation with the author, 2 December 2009.

71 This was corroborated by the exhibition catalogue for 'theanyspacewhatever' (New York: Guggenheim Museum, 2008), which offered essays not only on the individual artists in the show (Parreno, Huyghe, Gillick,

Gonzalez-Foerster, etc.) but also on the key exhibitions in which they appeared, elevating the latter to the status of works of art.

72 See, for example, Boris Groys: 'Art today is thus social and political on a purely formal level, because it reflects on the space of the assembly, on the formation of community, and does so independently of whether an individual artist has a specific political message in mind or not.' (Groys, *Art Power*, Cambridge, MA: MIT Press, 2008, p. 182.)

Chapter 8   Delegated Performance

1 Of course there are exceptions, such as Cildo Meireles hiring five 'bodyguards' to watch over his flammable sculpture *Fiat Lux* for 24 hours (1979), or Sophie Calle hiring a detective to follow her (*Detective*, 1980). The difference between these and more recent examples is one of degree: the extent to which the presence and identity of the hired labourer is a central component of the work of art.

2 I will not be addressing re-enacted performances in this chapter, althought they often cover similar territory (see for example the recent retrospectives of Marina Abramovic at MoMA and Tania Bruguera at the Neuberger Museum of Art, both 2010, or the European tour of Allan Kaprow's 'Art as Life', initiated by Haus der Kunst, Munich, 2006). Re-enactment, like delegated performance, has accelerated with the institutionalisation of performance art and facilitates its collectibility. For a good summary of re-enactment see the catalogue *Life, Once More*, Rotterdam: Witte de With, 2005.

3 Cattelan's other works of the 1990s also revolve around a displacement of the artist's identity: *Super Noi* (1992), for example, comprises fifty drawings of the artist based on descriptions given by his friends and acquaintances and drawn by police composite portrait sketchers. Here the acts of both description and production are delegated to a kind of artist whose skills are not typically valued on the contemporary art market.

4 Francesco Bonami, in *Maurizio Cattelan*, London: Phaidon, revised edition, 2003, p. 58.

5 Significantly, Deller's collaboration has now become part of the Fairey Band's repertoire and features on their website. See www.faireyband.com.

6 In each of Sierra's publications, works are documented in black-and-white photographs, the artwork title, a brief caption that explains where and when the performance took place, and information about how much the participants were paid. Sierra's more recent work is more sensationalist and does not foreground the question of remuneration.

7 A frequent point of reference is the 'ethnological spectacles' shown at the World's Fairs in the late nineteenth and early twentieth century, such as

the *village nègre* at the 1878 and 1889 Paris World's Fair. Such events propagandised the imperial mission of France and were formative in generating enthusiasm for 'primitive' art. See Burton Benedict, 'International Exhibitions and National Identity', *Anthropology Today*, 7:3, June 1991, pp. 5–9. Benedict notes that 'the whole of the Exposition Coloniale in 1931 was a theatrical performance' (p. 7).

8 Here we could also consider the Berlin-based performance group Rimini Protokoll and their use of 'experts in everyday life' as the basis for performances such as *Soko São Paulo* (2007, using Brazilian policemen), *Airport Kids* (2008, using children who have lived in three or more countries) or *Deadline* (2003, which included a crematorium employee, a forensic doctor, a stonemason and a florist).

9 By using this term, Sehgal does not intend any reference to the constructed situations of the Situationist International.

10 See www.doragarcia.net for a log of each iteration of *The Messenger* as it happens.

11 Visitors were made aware of the performances thanks to a large poster displayed in the fair, although the casual observer would never know the outcome of these encounters. The piece was based on the memoirs of a former East German spy who had used attractive young male agents to seduce lonely female secretaries in Bonn as a means to access confidential information.

12 García has acknowledged the influence of Augusto Boal, but rejects his assumption that art should be politically useful. (Email to the author, 22 December 2010.)

13 Consider Alison Knowles' *Make a Salad* (1962) or *Shoes of Your Choice* (1963), in which the artist respectively makes a large salad for the audience to consume, or invites people to hold up their footwear and tell the audience about it.

14 *Satisfyin' Lover* has also been performed with as few as thirty and as many as eight-four people. Forty-two was the number of friends that the choreographer had during a residency in Salt Lake City. (Steve Paxton, email to author, 21 June 2010.) For a full score and instructions to performers, see Sally Banes, *Terpsichore in Sneakers: Post-Modern Dance*, Middletown, CT: Wesleyan University, 1987, pp. 71–4.

15 Steve Paxton, 'Satisfyin' Lover' (1967), in Banes, *Terpsichore in Sneakers*, p. 74. See also Sally Banes, *Democracy's Body: Judson Dance Theater 1962–1964*, Durham, NC: Duke University Press, 1993, p. 137; Jill Johnston, 'Paxton's People', *Village Voice*, 4 April 1968, reprinted in Jill Johnston, *Marmalade Me*, New York: Dutton, 1971, p. 137.

16 Rainer, cited in Chrissie Iles, 'Life Class', *Frieze*, 100, June-August 2006.

17 Creed, cited in Charlotte Higgins, 'Martin Creed's New Piece for Tate Britain: A Show That Will Run and Run', *Guardian*, 1 July 2008. Creed's *Ballet (Work no.1020)* (2009) involves five dancers restricted to

using the five core classical ballet positions, each of which are ascribed a musical note.

18 For example, at 'Art in Politically Charged Places' (Photographers' Gallery, London, 13 December 2004) and 'Public Time: A Symposium' (Modern Art Oxford, 25 May 2006).

19 Collins' title refers to Sidney Pollack's film *They Shoot Horses, Don't They?* (1969), which follows a handful of characters competing in a dancing marathon held during the Great Depression. The film foreshadows a contemporary culture of reality television, in which the participants' quest for fame and financial success seamlessly dovetails with commercial exploitation.

20 See the transcript of this discussion in Claire Bishop and Silvia Tramontana (eds.), *Double Agent*, London: ICA, 2009, pp. 99–106. Żmijewski is clear about his authorial role: 'You can say I decide where the plot is to begin – and life takes it from there. Only this means a loss of control, or only partial control over the course of events. Therefore the answer is that things always get out of control – I do not know what the film is going to look like, I do not work with actors that imitate reality. I have no script. My protagonists are unpredictable and their behaviour is beyond my control. […] it is a voyage into the unknown. There is no plan – no script – I do not know where the trip ends.' (Żmijewski, in 'Terror of the Normal: Sebastian Cichocki interviews Artur Żmijewski', *Tauber Bach*, Leipzig: Galerie für Zeitgenössische Kunst, 2003, p. 112.)

21 Annette Hill, *Reality TV: Audiences and Popular Factual Television*, London: Routledge, 2005, p. 17. Hill notes that 'reflexivity, performance, and the boundaries between fact and fiction are all hallmarks of reality programming' (p. 20).

22 For a discussion of these categories, see Jane Roscoe and Craig Hight, *Faking It: Mock-Documentary and the Subversion of Factuality*, Manchester: Manchester University Press, 2001. Observational documentary emerged from 1960s 'direct cinema' (US) and cinema verité (France) and from 'fly on the wall' television (UK) in the 1970s. See Hill, *Reality TV*, p. 20.

23 Watkins describes the process of recruiting participants, which has more in common with visual art than traditional film casting, in 'The War Game', in Alan Rosenthal, *The New Documentary in Action: A Casebook in Film Making*, Berkeley: University of California Press, 1971, pp. 151–63: 'You have to get to know the character, and you have to pull him into the communal thing of making films. . . . what holds them might possibly be my personality, but it certainly has to do with what you have impressed on them as the meaning of the subject' (p. 159).

24 Performance was 'a democratic mode, where young artists who did not have access to art galleries or enough money to produce studio art for exhibition could show their work quickly to other artists in the

community.' (Dan Graham, 'Performance: End of the 60s', in *Two-Way Mirror Power*, Cambridge, MA: MIT Press, 1999, p. 143.)

25 Jack Bankowsky, 'Tent Community', *Artforum*, October 2005, pp. 228–32.

26 As Philip Auslander has argued, 'Despite the claim . . . that performance's evanescence allows it to escape commodification, it is performance's very evanescence that gives it value in terms of cultural prestige.' Auslander, *Liveness: Performance in a Mediatized Culture*, London and New York: Routledge, 1999, p. 58. He continues: 'Even within our hyper-mediatized culture, far more symbolic capital is attached to live events than to mediatized ones.'

27 See 'Yvonne Rainer Blasts Marina Abramović and MOCA LA', *The Performance Club*, http://theperformanceclub.org/2011/11/yvonne-rainer-douglas-crimp-and-taisha-paggett-blast-marina-abramovic-and-moca-la/.

28 Tate appointed a performance curator in 2002, while MoMA created a Department of Media (as a breakaway from Film) in 2006, which changed its name to the Department of Media and Performance Art in 2009. The Pompidou Centre has never had a curator of performance, nor considered it as a possible department, since it has always come under the administration of Contemporary Art. (Bernard Blistène, email to the author, 17 August 2010.)

29 For the exhibition 'Double Agent' (ICA London, 2008), Mark Sladen and I attempted to commission a new work from Phil Collins. His proposal, *Ghost Rider*, involved hiring a ghost writer to write a feature on ghost writers, which would appear in *The Guardian* newspaper, signed by Phil Collins. The resulting article was considered unsuitable by Collins in both its tone and content, since the ghost writer had decided to try to mimic the artist's language and vocabulary, and the feature did not go to press.

30 Boltanski and Chiapello have referred to the extraction of profit from the intangible uniqueness of a given place, person or service as the 'commodification of the authentic'. (Christian Boltanski and Eve Chiapello, *The New Spirit of Capitalism*, London: Verso, 2007, p. 444.) For a promotional take on the issue, see James Gilmore and B. Joseph Pine II, *Authenticity: What Consumers Really Want*, Boston, MA: Harvard Business School, 2007.

31 Tino Sehgal, in discussion at the ICA, London, 19 November 2004.

32 Each version also experimented with a different venue: a mirrored dance studio (Paris); a theatre (Leuven, Warsaw, Berlin); a gallery (Tate Modern's Turbine Hall).

33 Klossowski refers to Sade's *Nouvelle Justine*: d'Esterval can only sleep with someone if they also agree to be paid. Valuing one partner (to the exclusion of thousands of others) is marked by financial evaluation. See Pierre Klossowski, *La monnaie vivante*, Paris: Editions Joëlle Losfeld, 1994, p. 62.

34 In other words, since the advent of industrialisation, 'voluptuous emotion' is no longer tied to the auratic artisanal object, but attaches itself to the superficial, mass-produced commodity, which allows desire to be externalised and exchanged, but always through the institutional norms of the economy.

35 Klossowski, *La monnaie vivante*, p. 12.

36 Pierre Bal-Blanc, in Elisabeth Lebovici, 'The Death of the Audience: A Conversation with Pierre Bal-Blanc', *e-flux journal*, 13, February 2010, available at www.e-flux.com.

37 Pierre Bal-Blanc, 'Notes de mise en scène: La Monnaie Vivante', p. 5 (my translation); pdf available at www.cacbretigny.com.

38 First shown in Gonzalez-Torres' exhibition 'Every Week There is Something Different' (2 May to 1 June 1991, Andrea Rosen Gallery, New York), *Untitled (Go-Go Dancing Platform)* was subsequently installed at the Hamburger Kunstverein where Bal-Blanc took on the role of go-go dancer.

39 Of all the people I have spoken to who have appeared in delegated performances, it is striking that Bal-Blanc is the only one who didn't enjoy his time performing. The more usual reaction is one of enjoyment in the face of a new experience. As Joe Scanlan notes, participants' enjoyment can extend so far as to lack a critical engagement with the works that they appear in, resulting in a kind of Stockholm syndrome whereby they are grateful to their artistic captors, and unable to admit the paucity of returns on their labour invested in the work of art. See Joe Scanlan, response to Don Byrd, letters page, *Artforum*, September 2010, pp. 54, 56.

40 Klossowski's second edition of *Sade Mon Prochain* (*Sade My Neighbour*, 1947) revises his earlier reading of Sade in line with his post-Catholic outlook. In the later revision, he views Sade's sexual perversions as universally oppositional, rather than being a secret affirmation of God. See Ian James, *Pierre Klossowski: The Persistence of a Name*, Oxford: Legenda/European Humanities Research Centre, 2000.

41 'It would never occur to the sadist to find pleasure in other people's pain if he had not himself first undergone the masochistic experience of a link between pain and pleasure.' (Gilles Deleuze, *Masochism: Coldness and Cruelty*, New York: Zone Books, 1989, p. 43.)

42 In general, much more attention needs to be paid to the modes in which this representation is figured – be this huge cibachrome prints in the case of Vanessa Beecroft, or short documentary videos in the case of Żmijewski – rather than dismissing artists equally out of hand for exploitation.

43 For example, a distinction can be made between those artists whose work addresses ethics as an explicit theme (e.g., Żmijewski's *80064*, 2004), and those who use ethical discomfort as a technique to express and foreground questions of labour (such as Sierra) or control (Bruguera).

44 As Phil Collins's *Return of the Real* (2006–7) makes so abundantly clear, reality television depends upon the merciless shoehorning of participants to fit stereotypical characters in clichéd narratives whose predictability is designed to attract high viewing figures.

Chapter 9   Pedagogic Projects

1 In 2007 I was commissioned to write an article about this trend, focusing on an outdoor work by Maria Pask, *Beautiful City*, at Sculpture Projects Münster. Claire Bishop, 'The New Masters of the Liberal Arts: Artists Rewrite the Rules of Pedagogy', *Modern Painters*, September 2007, pp. 86–9.

2 A cross-section of recent projects could include: *Cybermohalla* by Sarai. net in New Delhi (2001–); the School of Missing Studies (2002–); Nils Norman's *Exploding School* (integrated into the Royal Danish Academy of Art, 2007–) and *University of Trash* (Sculpture Center, New York, 2009); Vik Muniz's art school for children from the Rio favelas (*Centro Espacial Vik Muniz*, 2006–); Anton Vidokle's *unitednationsplaza*, Berlin (2007–8) and *Night School*, New York (2008–9); The Bruce High Quality Foundation University (New York, 2009–); and 16 Beaver's weekly readings and discussions (1999).

3 Museum education departments are, however, a notable exclusion from the recent critical discourse around contemporary art and pedagogy. Andrea Phillips is typical in arguing that the creative and affectual claims of pedagogic art differ from the educational work of museum educators. See Andrea Phillips, 'Educational Aesthetics', in Paul O'Neill and Mick Wilson (eds.), *Curating and the Educational Turn*, Amsterdam: De Appel/ Open Editions, 2010, p. 93.

4 An incomplete list of events would include Tate Modern's conference Rethinking Arts Education for the 21st Century (July 2005); Portikus's conference Academy Remix (November 2005); the joint exhibition/ publication project between the Van Abbe Museum in Eindhoven and MuHKA in Antwerp called *Academy: Learning from Art/Learning from the Museum* (Autumn 2006); SUMMIT: Academy as Potentiality, a two-day workshop in Berlin (May 2007); Transpedagogy: Contemporary Art and the Vehicles of Education (MoMA, New York, 2009); Questioning the Academy, Cooper Union, New York (Autumn 2009); Radical Education, Moderna Galerija Ljubljana (Autumn 2009); Extra-Curricular: Between Art & Pedagogy (University of Toronto, Spring 2010); Schooling and De-Schooling (Hayward Gallery, May 2010) and Beyond the Academy: Research as Exhibition (Tate Britain, May 2010). To these we could add *Frieze* magazine's special issue on art schools (September 2006); the September 2007 issue of *Modern Painters*; the March 2007 issue of *Maska* titled 'Art in the Grip of Education'; and numerous articles in

e-flux journal, especially the special issue no. 14 (March 2010) edited by Irit Rogoff and focusing on the Bologna Process. See also the publication *Art Schools*, edited by Steven H. Madoff (Cambridge, MA: MIT Press, 2009), and O'Neill and Wilson (eds.), *Curating and the Educational Turn*, and Brad Buckley and John Conomos (eds.), *Rethinking the Contemporary Art School* (Halifax: Nova Scotia College of Art and Design, 2010). The third of Documenta 12's leitmotifs, 'What is to be done?', focused on education, the eponymous title of the last of its three Readers.

5 A fuller examination of this tendency would need to take into account curatorial trends such as 'new institutionalism' and state pressure on museum education departments to involve marginalised demographics euphemistically referred to as 'new audiences', but the present chapter will leave these issues to one side in order to focus on artist-initiated projects.

6 Irit Rogoff, 'Turning', *e-flux journal*, 0, November 2008, available at www.e-flux.com.

7 For Rogoff, 'pedagogical aesthetics' refers to the way in which 'a table in the middle of the room, a set of empty bookshelves, a growing archive of assembled bits and pieces, a classroom or lecture scenario, or the promise of a conversation have taken away the burden to rethink and dislodge daily those dominant burdens ourselves'. (Ibid.)

8 Luis Camnitzer, 'The Input of Pedagogy', in *Conceptualism in Latin American Art: Didactics of Liberation*, Austin: University of Texas Press, 2007, pp. 109–15.

9 Beuys, interviewed by Willoughby Sharp, *Artforum*, November 1969, reprinted in Lucy Lippard, *Six Years: The Dematerialization of the Art Object 1966–72*, Berkeley: University of California Press, 1997, p. 121.

10 Beuys also organised an occupation of the Kunstakademie Düsseldorf offices in October 1971, with sixteen students who had been refused admission. After three days they were allowed to stay, but Beuys was dismissed in October 1972, days after he had finished the end of Documenta 5, where he had spent three months discussing direct democracy with visitors to the exhibition.

11 In this regard, it is important to stress Beuys's debt to Rudolf Steiner, whose holistic educational goals the artist saw as fully compatible with 'Marxist, Catholic, Evangelist, liberal, anthroposophical, and ecological concepts of the alternative'. See Joseph Beuys, 'Appeal for the Alternative', originally published in the *Frankfurter Rundschau*, 23 December 1978, reprinted in Lucrezia De Domizio, *The Felt Hat: Joseph Beuys, A Life Told*, Milan: Charta, 1997, p. 180.

12 *Directional Forces*, for example, is the name both of Beuys' discussion at the London ICA in 1974, and of the blackboard installation it became a year later at the Rene Block Gallery, New York.

13 The first workshop at Documenta 6, for example, concerned the future of small countries and their attempts to find alternatives to the hegemony of power in economically dominant countries. Caroline Tisdall notes that of the artists taking part elsewhere in Documenta, only three participated in Beuys's FIU programming: Nam June Paik, John Latham and Arnulf Rainer. See Tisdall, *Joseph Beuys*, New York: Solomon Guggenheim Museum, 1979, p. 260.

14 See for example the revival of the FIU's format as a series of interdisciplinary lectures organised by Catherine David in Documenta 10 (*100 Days–100 Guests*), and by Okwui Enwezor in the form of four conference 'platforms' preceding Documenta 11, 2002.

15 Jan Verwoert, 'Class Action', *Frieze*, September 2006, pp. 150–5.

16 Jan Verwoert, 'The Boss: On the Unresolved Question of Authority in Joseph Beuys' Oeuvre and Public Image', *e-flux journal*, 1, December 2008, available at www.e-flux.com.

17 The nearest thing to dialogue as art was the tightly structured, dematerialised but certificated 'discussions' of Ian Wilson from 1976 onwards, and to a lesser extent, Tom Marioni's free beer salons (1970–).

18 Beuys, interviewed by Willoughby Sharp, in Lippard, *Six Years*, pp. 121–2.

19 The Research Assessment Exercise (RAE) and Quality Assurance Audit (QAA) are the two central, and most burdensome, systems of evaluation for UK universities.

20 As Bruguera notes, 'Some artists in Cuba began to imagine what was wanted from them, from their art. Pleasing the foreigners involved another kind of process of social engagement as well as another kind of censorship.' (Tania Bruguera, interview with Tom Finkelpearl, in Finkelpearl (ed.), *Art as Social Cooperation*, forthcoming.)

21 Cuba's dual economy means that Bruguera could exploit the gap between *moneda nacional*, Cuban Convertibles (CUC) and US dollars. An official teaching job (at University of Chicago) therefore subsidised the experimental teaching as art (in Havana).

22 I was of course staggered. Delahante had miscarried, but there had been extensive discussion at the school as to whether or not the insemination had actually taken place. The documentation of this work exists as hospital records, inaccessible even to the artist.

23 The Kuitca programme is an independent studio programme set up by the Argentinian painter Guillermo Kuitca in 1991, to compensate for the lack of MFA courses in Buenos Aires.

24 Bruguera, interview with Tom Finkelpearl.

25 For a review of this see Claire Bishop, 'Speech Disorder', *Artforum*, Summer 2009, pp. 121–2; plus the letter by Coco Fusco and my reply, *Artforum*, October 2009, pp. 38 and 40. Other works in the *Tatlin's Whisper* series include a molotov cocktail making workshop at a Galería Juana

de Aizpuru in Madrid (*Tatlin's Whisper #3*, 2006) and asking mounted policemen to deploy their range of crowd control techniques on visitors to Tate Modern (*Tatlin's Whisper #5*, 2008).

26 Paul Chan, *Night School*, Public Seminar 7, New Museum, New York, 11 September 2008. All further quotes by Chan are from this lecture unless otherwise stated.

27 The Classical Theatre of Harlem had already staged a production of *Godot* in 2006 in response to Hurricane Katrina, with a flooded stage and the action taking place on the roof. Wendell Pierce, the main actor in this production, who also performed for Chan, is originally from New Orleans.

28 Paul Chan, 'Next Day, Same Place: After Godot in New Orleans', *TDR*, Winter 2008, p. 3.

29 The aim had been to equal the production costs of the play, but in fact this fell short as costs ballooned. Eventually $53,000 was raised for a selection of community organisations in the neighbourhoods in which the artist worked.

30 See for example Tim Griffin, 'Waiting for Godot', *Artforum*, December 2007.

31 Syllabi for both this and the Xavier University course are available online at Chan's website: www.nationalphilistine.com.

32 Chan, in conversation with the author, 22 September 2008.

33 Althamer, in Claire Bishop and Silvia Tramontana (eds.), *Double Agent*, London: Institute of Contemporary Arts, 2009, p.10.

34 See Claire Bishop, 'Something for Everyone', *Artforum*, February 2011, pp. 175–81.

35 This expedient approach is frequently adopted by Althamer. When he received the Vincent Prize in 2004, Althamer took his teenage son Bruno and friends to hang out in the exhibition space, ostensibly done to shift their horizons of the world by experiencing another country, while giving them a holiday he couldn't himself afford. The work is known as *Bad Kids*, 2004.

36 'What Have I Done to Deserve This?', Cubitt Gallery, London, 2006.

37 'Each of the participants had at his/her disposal "a space of their own" . . . where they could build elements of their own visual language, and the "common space" open to everyone, where they could conduct simultaneous dialogues with the other participants. All without using words.' (Grzegorz Kowalski, in Maryla Sitkowska [ed.], *Grzegorz Kowalski: Prace Dawne I Nowe*, Bydgoszcz: Muzeum Okręgowe w Bydgoszczy im. Leona Wyczółkowskiego w Bydgoszczy, 2002, p. 266.)

38 See Oskar Hansen, *Towards Open Form*, Warsaw: Foksal Gallery Foundation, 2004, p. 121.

39 Łukasz Ronduda, 'Games, Actions and Interactions: Film and the Tradition of Oskar Hansen's Open Form', in Łukasz Ronduda and Florian

Zeyfang (eds.), *1, 2, 3… Avant-Gardes: Film/Art between Experiment and Archive*, Warsaw and Berlin: CCA Uzajdowski Castle and Sternberg Press, 2007, p. 91. Aside from being an influential teacher in his own right, Hansen constructed one of Poland's largest social housing projects and undertook numerous 'humanisation studies' with a view to improving existing urban environments built on the principle of 'closed form'.

40 Ibid., p. 92.

41 'I would like to invite you to take part in a game that we are organising with our artist friends', says Althamer to a group of children. 'You are artists and we would also like to invite you. You are, aren't you?' Bemused, they chorus back, 'Yes' (Artur Żmijewski, *[S]election.pl*, DVD, 2006).

42 Kowalski, invited by CCA to have a show in parallel to *[S]election.pl*, preferred to represent his teaching practice through more conventional photographic documentation of his workshops, which were installed in a separate gallery.

43 The strength of Żmijewski's *[S]election.pl* (which is clearly the precursor for his solo project *Them* [2007], discussed in Chapter 8) shows up the weak conventionality of Krzysztof Visconti's *Einstein Class*, 2006.

44 The 'Child's Play' workshops were devised by curator Guillaume Désanges, but led by a local teacher, Muriel Monsels. Désanges had previously used this format of re-enactment in a workshop for eight-year-olds in Iasi, Romania.

45 To one Surinamese performer in her twenties, I asked: 'What do you think of us, sitting there listening to this play that we don't understand?' She replied: 'I'm thinking, what do they think of us, performing this play *we* don't understand!'

46 Hirschhorn, email to the author, 7 March 2009.

47 '"The students are secondary?" – Yes, absolutely, the students are secondary! The students are secondary – but not the audience – not the non-exclusive audience! . . . So this is the first distinction: "non-exclusive audience" vs "students" and following this, I do not take the non-exclusive audience for students! (my mission is to work always for the non-exclusive audience). . . . To do a lecture, a workshop or a seminar in my projects is not a gesture of education or a pedagogic-attitude, to me it's a gift – an aggressive gift. It's a Form. And it's the assertion that Art – because it's Art – can transform each human being.' (Hirschhorn, email to the author, 7 March 2009.)

48 Vidokle describes *Night School* as 'an informal, free university type series of seminars, conferences, lectures, film screenings and occasional performances with a focus on contemporary art, that continues for one year'. Lectures were open to the public, while at the same time a core group of twenty-five students had extra seminars with the visiting speaker. Anton Vidokle, 'Night School opening remarks, January 2008', available at www.newmuseum.org.

49 Jacques Rancière, *The Ignorant Schoolmaster*, Stanford, CA: Stanford University Press, 1991. For a good critique of Rancière's essay see Kristin Ross, 'Rancière and the Practice of Equality', *Social Text*, 29, 1991, pp. 57–71.

50 In 1964, for example, Althusser wrote that 'The function of teaching is to transmit a determinate knowledge to subjects who do not possess this knowledge. The teaching situation thus rests on the absolute condition of *an inequality between a knowledge and a nonknowledge.*' See Louis Althusser, 'Problèmes Etudiants', *La Nouvelle Critique*, 152, January 1964, quoted in Kristin Ross, 'Translator's Introduction', in Rancière, *The Ignorant Schoolmaster*, p. xvi. Althusser would also argue that this model is essential for students to understand their class position.

51 Based in Marxism and Christian liberation theory, critical pedagogy regards education as a participatory, collective practice for social justice. The key theorists include Paulo Freire, Henry Giroux and Ivan Illich.

52 Freire, in Paulo Freire and Ira Shor, *A Pedagogy for Liberation: Dialogues on Transforming Education*, London: Macmillan, 1987, p. 102.

53 See Christopher Turner, 'Free-for-all', *Cabinet*, 39, Fall 2010, pp. 63–6.

54 A. S. Neill, *Summerhill: A Radical Approach to Child Rearing*, republished in William Ayers, *On the Side of the Child: Summerhill Revisited*, New York: Teachers College Press, Columbia University, 2003, pp. 79 and 90.

55 Anton Vidokle, 'Night School opening remarks, January 2008', available at www.newmuseum.org.

56 This is due to the gradual withdrawal of state funding at the same time as an increased involvement of the state in the regulation and governance of universities. See Henry Miller, *The Management of Change in Universities: Universities, State and Economy in Australia, Canada and the United Kingdom*, Buckingham: Open University Press, 1995. For a chilling account of how UK academia came to be controlled by business models imported from the US, see Simon Head, 'The Grim Threat to British Universities', *New York Review of Books*, 13 January 2011.

57 Sheila Slaughter and Larry L. Leslie, *Academic Capitalism: Politics, Policies and the Entrepreneurial University*, Baltimore and London: Johns Hopkins University Press, 1997, pp. 8–9.

58 Bill Readings, *The University in Ruins*, Cambridge, MA: Harvard University Press, 1996, p. 3.

59 See Claire Bishop, 'Con-Demmed to the Bleakest of Futures', *e-flux journal*, 22, available at www.e-flux.com.

60 See Readings, *The University in Ruins*, p. 3. We could compare this shift to that of the contemporary museum director, who today is more likely to be an administrator and fundraiser than an art historian.

61 See Dietrich Lemkel, 'Mourning Bologna', *e-flux journal*, 14, March 2010, available at www.e-flux.com. BBC News reported that the Bologna Accord will lead to 'a bigger postgraduate market, with tens of thousands

of new higher-level courses. The report for the business school group says these will include 12,000 new business courses' (http://news.bbc. co.uk, 21 January 2005). The Bologna Accord also changes the ethos of education itself. Degrees will be short-term with clear and comparable outcomes, instead of a more individual system tailored to the needs of each subject.

62 See Irit Rogoff, 'Academy as Potentiality', in *A.C.A.D.E.M.Y*, Frankfurt: Revolver, 2006, pp. 13–20.

63 Two key words for the *A.C.A.D.E.M.Y.* project, and for Rogoff's writing on the 'educational turn' in curatorial practice, are 'potentiality' and 'actualisation'. She defines potentiality as a possibility not limited to an ability, and a possibility of failure. Actualisation refers to the potential for liberation in objects, situations, actors and spaces. (Rogoff, 'Turning'.) Rogoff's prioritisation of openness as an inherent value parallels that of many contemporary artists.

64 Mark Dion, conversation with the author, 25 November 2009. This is one reason why Dion (with J. Morgan Puett) has set up Mildred's Lane, a summer residency programme for art students on a farm in Pennsylvania. See www.mildredslane.com.

65 *Martha Rosler Library* toured from New York to Liverpool, Edinburgh, Paris, Frankfurt, Berlin and Antwerp (in other words, to European venues that could afford to cover the transportation costs).

66 'Man in his physical state merely suffers the dominion of nature; he emancipates himself from this dominion in the aesthetic state, and he acquires mastery over it in the moral.' (Friedrich Schiller, 'Twenty-Fourth Letter', in Walter Hinderer and Daniel Dahlstrom [eds.], *The German Library vol.17: Essays*, New York: Continuum, 1998, p. 156.)

67 One is reminded of the Brazilian artist Lygia Clark, who insisted upon this privacy in relation to her experiments at La Sorbonne in the early 1970s. Yve-Alain Bois recalls that when a curator asked to come along to her classes there she erupted in anger: 'It was impossible to "attend" one of these "courses", to retreat from it as a spectator. Anyone not wishing to take part in the great collective body fabricated there, each time according to a different rite, was sent packing.' (Clark, cited in Bois, 'Nostalgia of the Body', *October*, 69, Summer 1994, p. 88.)

68 Roland Barthes, 'To the Seminar', in *The Rustle of Language*, Berkeley: University of California Press, 1996, p. 333. He begins the article with a poignant observation: 'Our gathering is small, to safeguard not its intimacy but its complexity: it is necessary that the crude geometry of big public lectures give way to a subtle topology of corporeal relations, of which knowledge is only the *pre-text*' (p. 332).

69 Unlike the beautiful, which for Kant remains autonomous, 'purposiveness without a purpose', in distinct contrast to practical reason and morality.

70 'Patently, art does not have the monopoly on creation, but it takes its capacity to invent mutant coordinates to extremes: it engenders unprecedented, unforeseen and unthinkable qualities of being.' (Félix Guattari, *Chaosmosis: An Ethico-aesthetic Paradigm*, Bloomington and Indianapolis: Indiana University Press, 1995, p. 106.)

71 The first paradigm described by Guattari is the 'proto-aesthetic paradigm' of primitive society, in which life and art are integrated under a transcendent principle. The second moment is the capitalist 'assemblage', in which the components of life are separated and divided but held together under master signifiers such as Truth, the Good, Law, the Beautiful, Capital and so on (see ibid., p. 104). It is informative to compare this tripartite schema with that proposed by Peter Bürger in *Theory of the Avant-garde* (1974) and that of Rancière in *The Politics of Aesthetics* (2000).

72 Gary Genosko, 'The Life and Work of Félix Guattari: From Transversality to Ecosophy', in Félix Guattari, *The Three Ecologies*, London and New York: Continuum, 2000, pp. 151 and 155. Transversality has recently been deployed as a central term in Gerard Raunig's *Art and Revolution: Transversal Activism in the Long Twentieth Century*, Los Angeles: Semiotext(e), 2007. However, Raunig uses this term strictly in the sense of acentric lines of flight that elude fixed points and co-ordinates, without any attachment to art as a privileged category. He argues that the first wave of transversal activist groups appeared in the 1980s, such as ACT UP (1987), Women's Action Coalition (1991–97) and Wohlfahrtsausschüsse (1992–93) (pp. 205–6).

73 See Julian Bourg, *From Revolution to Ethics: May 1968 and Contemporary French Thought*, Montreal and Kingston: McGill-Queen's University Press, 2007, Chapter 10, 'Institutional Psychotherapy and the La Borde Psychiatric Clinic'. See also Guattari, 'La Borde: A Clinic Unlike Any Other', in *Chaosophy*, New York: Semiotexte, 1995, pp. 187-208.

74 Guattari, *Chaosmosis*, p. 131. It is thus not unlike the first model (the proto-aesthetic paradigm) in which art is fused with social praxis, the key difference being that the ethico-aesthetic paradigm is not organised around the totemic aura of myth.

75 Ibid., p. 130.

76 Ibid., p. 131.

Conclusion

1 Boris Groys, 'Comrades of Time', *e-flux journal*, 11, December 2009, available at www.e-flux.com.

2 Tony Bennett phrases the same problem differently: art history as a bourgeois, idealist discipline is in permanent conflict with Marxism as an anti-bourgeois, materialist revolution in existing disciplines. There is no

possibility of reconciling the two. See Tony Bennett, *Formalism and Marxism*, London: Methuen, 1979, pp. 80–5.

3 Luc Boltanski and Eve Chiapello, *The New Spirit of Capitalism*, London: Verso, 2005, pp. 37–8.

4 The implication of Boltanski and Chiapello's book is that in the third spirit of capitalism the artistic critique has held sway, resulting in an unsupervised capitalism that lacks the 'invisible hand' of constraint that would guarantee protection, security and rights for workers.

5 For a clear summary of 'post-politics' see Jodi Dean, *Democracy and Other Neoliberal Fantasies: Communicative Capitalism and Left Politics*, Durham, NC: Duke University Press, 2009, p. 13. She presents two positions: 'post-politics as an ideal of consensus, inclusion, and administration that must be rejected' (Chantal Mouffe, Jacques Rancière) and 'post-politics as a description of the contemporary exclusion or foreclosure of the political' (Slavoj Žižek).

6 The difference between Gormley's webstreaming and that of Christoph Schlingensief (discussed below) is that the latter is a conscious parody of reality television's banality, while the former uncritically replicates it. A press shot of Gormley with the participants in his work evokes the image of Simon Cowell with his protegés in *American Idol*.

7 Antony Gormley, www.oneandother.co.uk. Charlotte Higgins, 'The Birth of Twitter Art', *Guardian*, 8 July 2009, available at www.guardian. co.uk.

8 Jacques Rancière, 'The Aesthetic Revolution and Its Outcomes: Emplotments of Autonomy and Heteronomy', *New Left Review*, 14, March–April 2002, p. 133.

9 Jacques Rancière, 'The Emancipated Spectator', *Artforum*, March 2007, p. 278.

10 Sherry Arnstein, 'A Ladder of Citizen Participation', *Journal of the American Institute of Planners*, 35:4, July 1969, pp. 216–24. The diagram has recently been the subject of some historical reassessment among architects and planners, reflecting the renewed interest in participation in this sector.

11 See for example Dave Beech's distinction between participation and collaboration. For Beech, participants are subject to the parameters of the artist's project, while collaboration involves co-authorship and decisions over key structural features of the work; 'collaborators have rights that are withheld from participants.' (Beech, 'Include Me Out', *Art Monthly*, April 2008, p. 3.) Although I would agree with his definitions, I would not translate them into a binding set of value judgements to be applied to works of art.

12 Herbert Achternbusch, cited in Marion Löhndorf, 'Christoph Schlingensief', *Kunstforum*, 142, October 1998, pp. 94–101, available at www. schlingensief.com

13 During their evictions, the asylum-seekers covered their faces with a

newspaper, inverting the celebratory, attention-seeking exits of contestants from the *Big Brother* house. Rather than viewing this absence of identity as an assault on their subjectivity, we could see this as an artistic device to allow the asylum-seekers to be catalysts for discussion around immigration in general (rather than individual case studies for emotive journalism).

14 Silvija Jestrović has explained this preference for the performance of asylum rather than its reality by way of reference to Debord's *Society of the Spectacle*, specifically the epigraph by Feuerbach with which it opens: 'But certainly for the present age, which prefers the sign to the thing signified, the copy to the original, representation to reality, the appearance to essence . . . illusion only is sacred, truth profane.' (Jestrović, 'Performing Like an Asylum Seeker: Paradoxes of Hyper-Authenticity in Schlingensief's Please Love Austria', in Claire Bishop and Silvia Tramontana [eds.], *Double Agent*, London: ICA, 2009, p. 61.)

15 Rancière argues that participation in democracy is a 'mongrel' idea deriving from the conflation of two ideas: 'the reformist idea of necessary mediations between the centre and the periphery, and the revolutionary idea of the permanent involvement of citizen-subjects in every domain'. (Jacques Rancière, 'The Uses of Democracy', in Rancière, *On the Shores of Politics*, London: Verso, 2007, p. 60.)

16 The Slovenian collective IRWIN have recently suggested that 'critical' and 'political' art is as necessary to neoliberalism as socialist realism was to the Soviet regime.

17 A positive example of new developments is the new left organisation Krytyka Polityczna in Poland, a publishing house that produces a magazine, organises events, and maintains a regular, forceful presence in the media (via its charismatic young leader Sławomir Sierakowski). The artists that have affiliated themselves with this project are as varied as Artur Żmijewski and the painter Wilhelm Sasnal.

18 Latin America has been pre-eminent in instituting such solutions. See for example the 'sub art' initiatives introduced by Antanas Mockus when mayor of Bogotá (1995-7, 2001-3), discussed in María Cristina Caballero, 'Academic Turns City into a Social Experiment', *Harvard University Gazette*, 11 March 2004, available at www.news.harvard.edu.

Illustration Credits

Cover	Tania Bruguera, *Tatlin's Whisper #5*, 2008. Medium: Decontextualization of an action, Behavior Art. Materials: Mounted police, crowd control techniques, audience. Installation view during 'Living Currency', Tate Modern, 2008. Courtesy the artist.
Frontispiece	Thomas Hirschhorn, *Spectre of Evaluation*, 2010, ink on paper. Courtesy the artist and Gladstone Gallery.

Chapter 1

p. 17 (top)	Superflex, *Tenantspin* (2000–) view of Coronation Court, Liverpool. Courtesy Superflex.
p. 17 (bottom)	Superflex, *Tenantspin* (2000–), Kath operating film equipment. Courtesy the artists.
p. 20	Oda Projesi, *FAIL # BETTER* project by Lina Faller, Thomas Stussi, Marcel Mieth and Marian Burchardt, 2004. Two-week workshop about building structures in the city, using woodsticks, in the Oda Projesi courtyard. Courtesy the artists.
p. 22	Thomas Hirschhorn, *Bataille Monument*, Kassel, 2002. Installation view showing library. Photo: Werner Maschmann. Courtesy the artist and Barbara Gladstone Gallery.
p. 24 (top)	Rachel Whiteread, *House*, Bow, London, 1993. Photo: John Davies. Courtesy the artist and Artangel.
p. 24 (bottom)	Loraine Leeson, *West Meets East*, Tower Hamlets, London, 1992. Courtesy the artist.
p. 31	Jeremy Deller, *The Battle of Orgreave*, 2001. Photo: Martin Jenkinson. Courtesy the artist, Artangel and Channel 4.
p. 34	Jeremy Deller, *The Battle of Orgreave Archive (An Injury to One is an Injury to All)*, 2004. Installation view. Courtesy the artist and Tate.

Chapter 2

p. 42	Gerardo Dottori, *Futurist Serata in Perugia*, 1914. Ink on paper. Courtesy Archivi Dottori, Perugia.

Chapter 3

p. 76   Atelier Populaire, *Je participe, tu participes, il participe…*, 1968. Poster screenprint on paper. Courtesy International Institute of Social History, Amsterdam.

p. 85   Guy Debord, *Psychogeographical Guide to Paris*, 1957. Courtesy Bibliothèque Kandinsky.

p. 90   Groupe Recherche d'Art Visuel, *A Day in the Street*, Paris, 1966. View showing participants in Montparnasse. Courtesy the artists and DACS.

p. 92   Groupe Recherche d'Art Visuel, itinerary for *A Day in the Street*, Paris, 1966. Courtesy the artists.

p. 96   Jean-Jacques Lebel, *Pour conjurer l'espirit de catastrophe*, 1962. Courtesy A.D.G.A.P., Jean-Jacques Lebel Archive, Paris.

p. 97 (left)   Jean-Jacques Lebel, *120 minutes dédiées au Divin marquis*, 1965. Shirley Goldfarb descending from the balcony. Courtesy A.D.G.A.P., Jean-Jacques Lebel Archive, Paris.

p. 97 (right)   Jean-Jacques Lebel, *120 minutes dédiées au Divin marquis*, 1965. The spanked rendition of 'La Marseillaise'. Courtesy A.D.G.A.P., Jean-Jacques Lebel Archive, Paris.

p. 98   Jean-Jacques Lebel, *120 minutes dédiées au Divin marquis*, 1965. Cynthia washing herself. Courtesy A.D.G.A.P., Jean-Jacques Lebel Archive, Paris.

Chapter 4

p. 107   El Grupo de los Artes de los Medios Masivos, *Total Participation*, 1966. Courtesy Roberto Jacoby.

p. 110   Oscar Masotta, *To Induce the Spirit of the Image*, Buenos Aires, 1966. View of participants. Courtesy Susana Lijtmaer.

p. 112   Marta Minujín, *Suceso Plástico*, Montevideo, 1965. Installation shot. Courtesy the artist.

p. 114   Oscar Bony, *La familia obrera* (The Worker's Family), 1968, and audience during 'Experiencias 68', Instituto Torcuato Di Tella, Buenos Aires. Courtesy Oscar Bony Archive.

p. 115   Pi Lind, *Living Sculptures*, Stockholm, 1968. Courtesy the artist and Moderna Museet, Stockholm.

p. 120   Grupo de Artistas de Vanguardia, *Cycle of Experimental Art*, Rosario, 1968: action by Graciela Carnevale. Image: Carlos Militello. Courtesy Graciela Carnevale.

Chapter 5

p. 133   Milan Knížák, *A Demonstration for All the Senses*, Prague, 1964. Courtesy the artist.

p. 134   Milan Knížák, *A Demonstration for All the Senses*, Prague, 1964. Courtesy the artist.

p. 184 (top) The Blackie, *Sanctuary*, participatory performance at Quarry Bank High School, Liverpool, 1969. View showing middle-class housing 'Riverdale' with occupant. Courtesy Bill and Wendy Harpe.

p. 184 (bottom) The Blackie, *Sanctuary*, participatory performance at Quarry Bank High School, Liverpool, 1969. View showing the housing department. Courtesy Bill and Wendy Harpe.

p 186 The Blackie, 'Towards A Common Language', installation view of participatory exhibition at the Walker Art Gallery, Liverpool, 1973. Courtesy Bill and Wendy Harpe.

p. 187 David Medalla, *A Stitch in Time*, Gallery House, London, 1972. Photo: John Dugger. Courtesy the artist.

p. 186 Inter-Action, main hall of the Cedric Price building in Kentish Town, London, undated. Courtesy David Powell.

Chapter 7

p. 196 Le Corbusier, Unité d'Habitation, Firminy, begun 1965. Photo: Olivier Martin-Gambier. Courtesy the photographer, Fondation Le Corbusier and A.D.G.A.P.

p. 197 Clegg & Guttmann, *Firminy Music Library*, 1993, installation view at 'Project Unité'. Courtesy the artists.

p. 198 Renée Green, *Apartment Inhabited by the Artist Prior to the Opening*, 1993, installation view at 'Project Unité'. Courtesy the artist.

p. 201 Mark Dion, *Project for the Royal Home for the Retirees*, 1993, 'Sonsbeek 93', Arnhem. Installation view showing one of the retirees and Dion's reconstructed display cabinet. Photo: Mark Dion. Courtesy the artist and Tanya Bonakdar Gallery.

p. 202 Irene and Christine Hohenbüchler, untitled project for 'Sonsbeek 93'. View of workshops in which the artists collaborated with prisoners in the penitentiary institute De Berg, Arnhem. Courtesy the artists.

p. 204 (top) Mark Dion, *Chicago Urban Ecology Action Group*, 1993. View of the Chicago Tropical Ecology Study Group in the Cockscombe Basin Wildlife Sanctuary, Belize, 1993. Photo: Jessica Rath. Courtesy the artist and Tanya Bonakdar Gallery.

p. 204 (bottom) Mark Dion, *Chicago Urban Ecology Action Group*, 1993. Some members of the Chicago Urban Ecology Action Group in the clubhouse. Photo: Mark Dion. Courtesy the artist and Tanya Bonakdar Gallery.

p. 208 Philippe Parreno, *No More Reality*, 1991, in 'No Man's Time', 1991. Courtesy the artist.

p. 210 Rirkrit Tiravanija, *untitled 1993 (flädlesuppe)*, in 'Backstage: Topologie zeitgenössischer Kunst', Kunstverein in Hamburg,

1993. Courtesy the artist, Gavin Brown's Enterprise and Kunstverein in Hamburg.

p. 212   Dmitri Gutov, *The Last Supper*, project for 'Interpol', Färgfabriken, Stockholm, 1996. Courtesy the artist.

p. 213 (top)   Carl Michael von Hausswolff, Andrew M. McKenzie and Ulf Bilting, *Exchange of Mental, Physical and Un-detected Substances of Known and Un-known Matter During a Period of Four Nights*, installation view at 'Interpol', Färgfabriken, Stockholm, 1996. Courtesy the artists.

p. 213 (bottom)   Installation view of Wenda Gu's *United Nations – Sweden and Russia Monument*, 1996, in 'Interpol', after being destroyed by Alexander Brener, Färgfabriken, Stockholm. Courtesy Viktor Misiano/IRWIN.

Chapter 8

p. 220   Maurizio Cattelan, *Southern Suppliers FC*, 1991. Courtesy the artist and Marian Goodman Gallery.

p. 222   Santiago Sierra, *250cm Line Tattooed on 6 Paid People*, Havana, 1999. Courtesy the artist, Team Gallery and Galeria Helga de Alvear.

p. 225   Dora García, *The Romeos*, Frieze Art Fair, 2008. Courtesy the artist.

p. 227   Phil Collins, video stills of *They Shoot Horses*, 2004. Synchronised two channel colour video projection with sound, 420 min. Courtesy the artist.

p. 228 (top)   Artur Żmijewski, video still of *Them*, 2007. Courtesy the artist and Foksal Gallery Foundation.

p. 228 (bottom)   Artur Żmijewski, video still of *Them*, 2007. Courtesy the artist and Foksal Gallery Foundation

p. 230   Marina Abramovic, untitled performance for the Los Angeles Museum of Contemporary Arts Gala, November 2011. Photo by Frazer Harrison/Getty Images for MOCA.

p. 233   Installation view of 'La Monnaie Vivante', Tate Modern, London. Tania Bruguera, *Tatlin's Whisper #5*, 2008 (foreground); Annie Vigier and Franck Apertet, Compagnie les Gens d'Uterpan, *X-Event 2*, 2007 (background). Photo: Sheila Burnett. Courtesy the artists.

p. 234   Installation view of 'La Monnaie Vivante', 6th Berlin Biennale for Contemporary Art. Franz Erhard Walther, *Standing Piece in Three Sections*, 1975 (foreground); Santiago Sierra, *111 Constructions Made with 10 Modules and 10 Workers*, 2004 (background). Photo: Uwe Walter and Christian Sievers. Courtesy the artists, Berlin Biennale for Contemporary Art 2010, and Galerie Jocelyn Wolff.

p. 235   Pierre Bal-Blanc, video still of *Contrat de travail* (Working Contract), 1992. Bal-Blanc is performing Felix Gonzalez-Torres, *Untitled (Go-Go Dancing Platform)*, 1991, in an exhibition at Hamburg Kunstverein. Courtesy the artist.

Chapter 9

p. 244   Joseph Beuys, Free International University seminar at Documenta 6, Kassel, 1977. Courtesy ARS.

p. 248   Tania Bruguera, *Cátedra Arte de Conducta*, Havana, 2002-9. Workshop with Elvia Rosa Castro. Courtesy Studio Bruguera.

p. 253 (top)   Paul Chan, *Waiting for Godot in New Orleans*, 2007. The artist teaching at Lusher High School. Courtesy the artist.

p. 253 (bottom)   Paul Chan, *Waiting for Godot in New Orleans*, 2007. Robert Green and production signage. Courtesy the artist.

p. 254   Paul Chan, *Waiting for Godot in New Orleans Archive*, installation view during the exhibition 'Contemporary Art from the Collection', MoMA, 30 June 2010-19 September 2011. Photo: Digital image @ the Museum of Contemporary Art/licensed by SCALA/Art Resource, NY. Courtesy the artist.

p. 256   Paweł Althamer, *Einstein Class*, 2005. Courtesy the artist and Foksal Gallery Foundation.

p. 258 (top)   Paweł Althamer and Artur Żmijewski, installation view of *[S]election.pl*, 2005, CCA Uzajdowski Castle, Warsaw. View of the galleries with Nowolipie Group. Courtesy the artists and Foksal Gallery Foundation.

p. 258 (bottom)   Paweł Althamer and Artur Żmijewski, installation view of *[S]election.pl*, 2005, CCA Uzajdowski Castle, Warsaw. View of the galleries. Courtesy the artists and Foksal Gallery Foundation.

p. 262 (top)   Thomas Hirschhorn, *The Bijlmer-Spinoza Festival*, Bijlmer, Amsterdam, 2009. Daily Lecture by Marcus Steinweg. Photo: Jan-Reinier van der Vliet/Straat van Sculpturen. Courtesy the artist and Barbara Gladstone Gallery.

p. 262 (bottom)   Thomas Hirschhorn, *The Bijlmer-Spinoza Festival*, 2009. View of the 'Child's Play' workshops. Courtesy the artist and Barbara Gladstone.

p. 264   Thomas Hirschhorn, *The Bijlmer-Spinoza Festival*, 2009. View of the 'Spinoza Play'. Courtesy the artist and Barbara Gladstone.

p. 270 (top)   *Martha Rosler Library*, New York, 2006. Courtesy Martha Rosler and e-flux.

p. 270 (bottom)   Lia Perjovschi, *Centre for Art Analysis*, Bucharest, 1990–. View with curators from Austria, Germany and Romania, 2005. Courtesy the artist.

Chapter 10

 p. 278 Antony Gormley and participants in *One and Other*, Trafalgar Square, London, 2009. Photo: Peter Macdiarmid.

 p. 281 (top) Christoph Schlingensief, *Please Love Austria*, Vienna, 2000. View of the container. Photo: David Baltzer. Courtesy the Estate of Christoph Schlingensief.

 p. 281 (bottom) Christoph Schlingensief, *Please Love Austria*, montage, undated. Courtesy the Estate of Christoph Schlingensief.

Index